CONTEMPORARY CRIMINOLOGY

CONTEMPORARY CRIMINOLOGY

LEONARD D. SAVITZ
TEMPLE UNIVERSITY

NORMAN JOHNSTON
BEAVER COLLEGE

175 YEARS OF PUBLISHING
1807 1982

JOHN WILEY & SONS

New York   Chichester   Brisbane   Toronto   Singapore

Library of Congress Cataloging in Publication Data:

Main entry under title:

Contemporary Criminology.

Includes index.
1. Crime and criminals—United States—Addresses,
essays, lectures.   I. Savitz, Leonard D.   II. Johnston,
Norman Bruce, 1921–

HV6789.A7	364'.973	81–15975
ISBN 0–471–08336–4		AACR2

Printed in the United States of America

10 9 8 7 6 5 4 3 2 1

PREFACE

The basic purpose of *Contemporary Criminology* is to provide the student of criminology access to most of the more significant current research and literature in the field. No book of readings can be so broad-based that every teacher and every student finds an abundance of materials fitting his or her own range of interests. On the other hand, a book such as this, attempting to survey the entire field, cannot represent only one point of view or a single version of what is important. In this book and in its companion volume, *Legal Process and Corrections,* we present a range of viewpoints and ideological beliefs that includes both empirical studies and more descriptive selections. The present volume then should be of value to students in a variety of courses in criminology and juvenile delinquency, either as the basic text or as supplemental reading.

We have spent almost two years reviewing an enormous amount of materials, including the usual American and foreign journals as well as governmental and agency reports, books, and relatively inaccessible papers prepared for meetings and private research organizations. In several instances, experts on certain topics have written papers especially for this book, either updating their own earlier work or surveying their fields of expertise anew.

The great majority of items reviewed could not be included due to space limitations. This is particularly true for historical materials. In other instances, excellent studies were excluded simply because they were dated, or were too narrow in scope, or were exotically descriptive but not broadly applicable. Some gaps in the areas covered reflect our inability to find appropriate research.

It is our experience that most classroom teachers use both readers and textbooks as tools, picking and choosing certain portions to buttress and to supplement their classroom lectures and discussions. Although we provide brief section introductions, individual selections are presented without extensive comment and lengthy introductory essays are not included. We believe that it is the selections themselves that are of value and that individual instructors will wish to place such articles in the context of their own courses and frames of reference.

Criminal statistics have always had an important place in the speculations of criminologists and are at the very center of the controversies concerning the proper strategies for treatment of criminals and the reduction of crime. We therefore devote the introductory section to a consideration of the issues that deal with the measurement of crime. Although practitioners, researchers, and theorists will continue to rely on police-based statistics, dissatisfaction with these data has led to the development of new forms of data acquisition such as surveys of victims and self-reporting surveys. The frequent use and misuse of crime statistics make it imperative that students of criminology understand how such figures are generated, what they mean, and how they should be used.

Section II, Theories of Crime, deals with several currently relevant or widely discussed theoretical explanations of crime. Although the period of so-called "grand theories" in criminology seems now past, one cannot ignore the more significant theoretical statements concerning the causes of crime in our society. Within obvious space limitations, we can do little more than include several examples of the more prominent current theoretical perspectives, particularly Marxist economic theories.

The search for the causes of crime has become increasingly complex and sophisticated. The latter sections of the book mirror the range of that complexity. Persons who classify themselves as "criminologists" are most frequently sociologists. Nevertheless, psychologists, biologists, political scientists, and others have made very significant contributions to an understanding of crime. Over a period of time the field of criminology follows unpredictable fashions and trends in explanations of crime, with first one discipline and then another in the ascendancy. Given the serious, unresolved issues in the study of crime and delinquency, we feel that a multidisciplinary approach in this book is more than justified.

Practitioners from different disciplines such as biology and sociology explain crime from different points of view. Researchers studying newer kinds of crime such as, for example, computer-based offenses or large-scale racketeering enterprises, have found it necessary to develop research techniques quite different from those used in studying more conventional offenses such as burglary or theft. Consequently, we have grouped empirical and descriptive studies from biology and psychology, and sociology. These are followed by sections devoted to special categories of crimes that are sufficiently unlike conventional crimes that we feel they merit separate consideration.

In the past ten years the general public, legislators, the legal profession, and researchers have become increasingly aware of the impact of organized criminal syndicates on communities and the nation. Researchers have begun to study groups rarely portrayed in earlier criminology texts, such as persons who make life careers out of crimes of bank robbery, confidence games, or pickpocketing. Section V contains realistic descriptions and analyses of some of these skilled and lucrative professional crimes, and of criminal networks, which the media conveniently call "crime families."

Certain other types of crimes are so different from ordinary or street crimes that they deserve special consideration. We have grouped two of these categories of special offenses—sexual and drug-related crimes—in the next section, sorting out from an enormous and growing literature several items that, it is hoped, will shed more light than heat in these volatile areas.

The final section deals with crimes sometimes referred to as "white collar crimes," committed largely by middle- or upper-class individuals or by business corporations.

We express our gratitude and respect to the authors and researchers whose work has made this book possible and especially to those who have contributed papers. We are indebted to the following reviewers for their thoughtful and helpful comments: Jacqueline Boles, Georgia State University; Donald Gibbons, Portland State University; Eleanor Miller, University of Wisconsin-Milwaukee, Hugh Whitt, University of Nebraska-Lincoln. Finally, we also express our appreciation to our own students who were exposed to many of these and other selections before the book was put together and whose reactions have guided our final selection.

Leonard D. Savitz
Norman Johnston

Philadelphia, 1982

CONTENTS

CONTEMPORARY CRIMINOLOGY

SECTION I

MEASURING CRIME

Two major sources of criminological statistics are widely used today to estimate the extent and changes of crime in modern society. Official police statistics usually involve criminal events that are detected, reported to the police, confirmed by the responding police, and that then become part of the official tabulations commonly described as "Crimes Known to the Police." In recent years we have seen the rise of federally-funded national victimization surveys. These use sample survey techniques to secure information from a large population of randomly selected households about criminal victimizations, which are previous offenses perpetrated against specified family members.

The selections in this first section are critical evaluations of these techniques of measuring crime. The selection by Savitz focuses on official statistics: it is a broad critique of official law enforcement data on crime, primarily of the *Uniform Crime Reports* prepared annually by the FBI. The seven "major" offenses that constitute the so-called Index of Crimes are examined in detail, and a comprehensive statement is made of the value of police statistics generally and the manner in which diachronic changes in official crime rates may be explicated. His conclusion is that, with all of its limitations, the *UCR* is still useful and remains probably the best and most valuable source of regularly produced information on crime in America.

The article by Fishman explores how crime waves are often constructs of the mass media, involving news judgment of media organizations, a particular orientation or dynamic regarding "crime waves," and reporters' reliance and dependence on police accounts of crime.

In a careful critique of crime victimization surveys, Levine describes all of the major sources of error that can artificially and incorrectly inflate victimization crime rates. Subject biases (false reporting, memory errors, mistaken interpretation of events, and erroneous classification of actions that might be crimes), interviewer biases, and coding errors are all considered in the last selection in this section.

1

OFFICIAL STATISTICS

LEONARD D. SAVITZ

INTRODUCTION

Criminal statistics are the regular and systematic collection and publication of a body of statistical data dealing with a specific aspect of the criminal justice system. Typically a social agency in some manner involved in the criminal justice system produces these statistical reports.

Criminal statistics are developed and disseminated to present reasonably accurate information on the incidence and prevalence of specified types of criminality and about likely or proven offenders. The data are useful as an admittedly crude measure of the amount or the "seriousness" of crime within legal jurisdictions or within a cluster of jurisdictions having common geographic or demographic characteristics. Such statistics are most useful in offering comparison among jurisdictions and for revealing diachronic changes in official crime rates within a single jurisdiction.

The primary purpose of the gathering and dissemination of statistics, as Wilkins (68) states, is for its *utility*. Statistics are a way of classifying events (crimes) that maximizes the power of the information for purposes of social action.

Crime acts are legally prohibited to adults and are punishable in judicial proceedings.

Source: Paper written especially for this volume.

These events are defined within a criminal code. For a crime to exist, five features theoretically should be present:

1. The act, almost always, must consist of a conscious, voluntary, external harm. (Intention is not the deed.)
2. The harmful effect of the act must be legally prohibited at the time it is undertaken. (Ex post facto laws are prohibited under several sections of the Constitution.)
3. The perpetrator of the act must be construed as having *mens rea* (criminal intent or guilty mind) at the time of the crime. If the person committing the act is insane, or it is a nonculpable accident, or the action is below the age of culpability, or the act was due to unavoidable coercion, the perpetration is deemed to be lacking in *mens rea*, and the event itself, arguably, is not a crime.
4. The voluntary misconduct by the actor must lead to the legally punishable harm; that is, there must be a *causal relationship* between one's behavior and the crime for which he is ultimately charged.
5. There must exist a legally prescribed punishment.

Criminal is a more difficult concept to deal with. It is possible to argue that a criminal is a person who commits a crime whether or not anyone ever becomes aware of the crime. Or a criminal might be defined as an adult who commits an act that he or she knows to be a crime. Most usually, criminal is a label applied to the person who is officially arrested for a criminal offense. The individual here may consecutively be an arrestee, an accused, and perhaps in time, a defendant. The bulk of criminological research defines as criminals persons who are *thought* to be a criminal by a victim/complainant/third party who then solicits police intrusion into the matter (the most usual manner by which police enter into criminal events). The police respond to the request. If they agree that a crime has in fact taken place (the crime is "founded") and if a suspect may be arrested because it appears that a prima facie case can be made against this culpable (blameworthy) individual an arrest will occur. The arrest usually represents then a judgment by some civilian(s) that a crime has occurred and a confirmation of this judgment by a police officer with the subsequent legal apprehension of the "likely" perpetrator.

It is important to emphasize that most arrested persons are *not subsequently convicted*. Evidence is available that about one in five arrests results in conviction in a court of law. Legally, the strongest case could be made that "criminals" are simply adults who are convicted in a court of law. They represent, admittedly, a very small fraction of all perpetrators of crimes and a distinct minority of all arrestees.

Crimes and criminals (variously defined) become *official* statistics when the event and the perpetrator become known to the police. As stated above, the most usual sequence involves some citizen who informs the police that a crime has been committed. The police are dispatched to the scene, arrive, and confirm the occurrence of a crime. If possible they will also apprehend a likely offender. There are also crimes that become part of official records because police directly see a crime occurring (an "on-view" offense). These, however, represent a minority of all of the crimes that make up official statistics.

UNIFORM CRIME REPORTS—CRIME IN THE UNITED STATES

Without question the most important and valuable source of official criminal statistics in the United States is the *Uniform Crime Reports (UCR). This is an annual publication of the Federal Bureau of Investigation of the reports it receives monthly and annually from the majority of police departments in the United States. The Bureau selects certain data submitted to it; these data are collated and presented to the public.*

The primary focus of the UCR is on "Crimes Known to the Police," which are those crimes that came to the official attention and that, on police investigation, are "founded" or accepted by the police.

For various reasons, the *UCR* concentrates, almost to the exclusion of all other offenses, on seven crimes. These are known now as "Index Crimes" and were chosen, the FBI argues, because they are crimes most likely to be reported to the police and because they occur with "sufficient frequency" to provide an adequate basis for comparisons. These, then, are defined as "serious crimes" by virtue of their nature and/or their volume.

The seven Index Crimes, as defined by the *Uniform Crime Reporting Handbook* (57), are as follows:

1. *Murder and Nonnegligent Manslaughter*. These are killings of live human beings that are *not*: accidental death, assaults to murder, attempted murder, nor excusable or justifiable homicide. (Killing persons by gross negligence, traffic deaths, etc., are subsumed under Manslaughter by Negligence, which is *not* an Index Crime.)

2. *Forcible Rape*. Included here are rape by force and all attempts to commit forcible rape. The so-called statutory rapes and other sex offenses are excluded. (Note that if several males rape one female, this is counted as a single rape, with several punishable offenders.)

3. *Robbery.* This is the taking or attempt to take something of value from the care, custody, or control of a person, by use of force, threat of force, or by putting the victim into fear.
4. *Aggravated Assault.* The category includes an unlawful attack by a person upon another for the purpose of inflicting severe or aggravated bodily harm. It usually involves the use of a weapon or means likely to produce death or great bodily harm.
5. *Burglary (Breaking or Entering).* This crime is the unlawful entry into a structure to commit or attempt to commit a felony or theft. The types of structure entered could be dwelling houses, garages, churches, schools, trailers, barns, vessels, public buildings, offices, apartments, stables, and ships. (Shoplifting and theft from cars are not classed as burglary.) These offenses are: *Forcible Entry* (use of any kind of force to unlawfully enter a structure to commit a felony or theft, including use of tools, breaking of windows, forcing doors, or cutting screens) and *Unlawful Entry* (no force used, but the unit is entered through an unlocked door or window. If the area entered is one of "open access," the theft is technically larceny, not burglary.
6. *Larceny-Theft.* Involved here is the unlawful taking, carrying, leading, or riding away of property that is the possession of others. Excluded are car thefts, robbery, burglary, embezzlement, fraud, larceny by check, and check fraud. The amount of property taken is irrelevant. (The nine types of larceny range from pocket-picking, through theft of bicycles, to theft from coin-operated devices.)
7. *Motor Vehicle Theft.* This is the theft or attempted theft of a motor vehicle.

These offenses, the basic Index Crimes, include, it may be recalled, five crimes (rape, robbery, forcible entry, theft, and auto theft) for which *attempts* are lumped together with *completed* offenses.

In recent years, the *UCR* has presented data on Index Crimes (known to the police) in tabular form with some exposition as regards national totals. They display both actual reported totals and their own "estimated" totals (The *UCR*, curiously, extrapolates or inflates figures reported to it by various police departments to derive an estimate of ALL Index Crimes committed in the United States, even those occurring in areas where the police do not report to the FBI. This technique will be dealt with below.)

The *Uniform Crime Reports* typically presents estimated yearly totals, percentage change in rates from previous to current year, percentage change over the last five years, for each of the seven Index Crimes. Furthermore, for each of the seven crimes, data are presented by degree of urbanization of reporting areas (Standard Metropolitan Statistical Area [SMSA]/Other Cities/Rural), by region of the country (Northeast/North Central/South/West), by individual states, and by SMSA/Other City/and Rural groupings within each state. Information is also presented by several measures of population density. Comparisons are made of cities of over 250,000 with those cities of under 250,000; cities of over 250,000 are subdivided into 250,000 to 500,000, 500,000 to 1,000,000, and over 1,000,000 and compared with one another; most demographic comparisons are of areas demographically divided into populations of: over 250,000, 100,000 to 250,000, 50,000 to 100,000, 25,000 to 50,000, 10,000 to 25,000, under 10,000, "suburban," and "rural."

The FBI also secures a much smaller body of information on 22 other "non-Index" crimes. These data are not used to construct rates for these offenses but are used primarily as they relate to arrests and dispositions for these "lesser" crimes. The offenses are: other assaults, arson, forgery and counterfeiting, fraud, embezzlement, stolen property, vandalism, weapons, prostitution and commercial vice, sex offenses (including adultery, fornication, incest, and intercourse with insane, epileptic, or venereal diseased person), gambling, offenses against family and children (desertion, nonsupport, neglect, and abuse), driving while intoxicated, liquor laws (illegal manufacture and sales), disorderly conduct (disturbing peace, disorderly conduct, illegal prize fights), vagrancy, miscellaneous (including abduction, abortion, blackmail, bribery, and "suspicion"), curfew and loitering law violations (for juveniles), runaway (for juveniles), and narcotic drug laws.

It is instructive at this point to examine a few tables from the recent *FBI Uniform Crime Report—Crime in the United States, 1978.*

Table 1 reveals a total of 11,141,334 reported Index Crimes or a rate of 5109.3 per 100,000 inhabitants in the United States. The SMSA rate is highest (over 5800) whereas for smaller urban areas (other cities) the rate was considerably less (under 4500). The crime index rate was lower (under 2000) for rural areas. The property crime rate was about 10 times that for violent crimes (4622.4 to 486.9). Of its seven Index Crimes, the highest rates were for larceny-theft and burglary while murder represented only .002 of all Index Crimes.

Table 2 shows the number of total arrests for 1977 and 1978, by the variable of sex. Arrests for all Index and non-Index offenses are shown. Percentage change from the previous (1977) to the instant year (1978) are revealed as are the percentages of arrests for both males and females, who are under the age 18.

The limitations, or cautions regarding this uncritical use of these data, will be described in the next section, and more still extensively in the final section.

GENERAL LIMITATIONS OF POLICE-BASED STATISTICS

Several serious problems are generally associated with any source of police-derived crime statistics. These limitations are discussed in some detail, not because they finally vitiate the use of official criminal statistics, but because they indicate cautions to their unqualified use.

The relationship between crimes known to the police and the sum total universe of all crimes committed in the "universe" is unknown. Clearly crimes known to the police represent a *percentage* of all events that could have been classified as crimes. There exists a widespread, and probably false, belief that the ratio of crimes known to the police to the totality of all committed crime, while unknown, is stable and constant, so that changes in the crimes known to the police perfectly reflect similar rates of change in the universe of all crime committed.

In fact, many factors could, and likely do, operate to alter official crime rates significantly over time, in addition to the increase possible as a result of more crime actually being committed.

DEMOGRAPHIC CHANGES
Alterations in the age structure, sex ratio, and degree of urbanization in a jurisdiction probably influence the amount of crime committed and the amount reported to the police (17).

CHANGES IN POLICE PRACTICES
An increase in the number of police might well result in greater detection of previously undetected crimes, and a greater capability of police reaction to previously not-responded-to crimes. Also, enhanced efficiency, training, professionalism, or sophistication of the police may also result in an increase in the number of crimes that come to official attention and the accuracy with which these actions are recorded as offenses (7, 18, 25). Better law enforcement record-keeping practices and capabilities are also likely to produce more accurate crime statistics. Sagi and Wellford (44) found that the increased percentage of civilian employees within a police department from 1958 to 1964 was associated with increases in reported crime rates. Also, technological advances may impact on police work and increase law enforcement efficiency, for example, quicker police response time to the scene of a crime. Research has shown that quicker police response

TABLE 1 Index of Crime, United States, 1978

Area	Population	Crime index total	Violent crime	Property crime	Murder and non-negligent manslaughter	Forcible rape	Robbery	Aggravated assault	Burglary	Larceny-theft	Motor vehicle theft
United States total	218,059,000	11,141,334	1,061,826	10,079,508	19,555	67,131	417,038	558,102	3,104,496	5,983,401	991,611
Rate per 100,000 inhabitants		5,109.3	486.9	6,622.4	9.0	30.8	191.3	255.9	1,423.7	2,743.,9	454.7
Standard Metropolitan Statistical Area	159,388,199										
Area actually reporting	99.0%	9,282,753	925,984	8,356,769	15,683	58,168	395,892	456,241	2,573,406	4,900,044	883,319
Estimated total	100.0%	9,356,438	930,629	8,425,809	15,740	58,468	397,219	459,202	2,592,698	4,942,712	890,399
Rate per 100,000 inhabitants		5,870.2	583.9	5,286.3	9.9	36.7	249.2	288.1	1,626.7	3,101.1	558.6
Other cities	25,890,583										
Area actually reporting	96.3%	1,085,750	71,060	1,014,690	1,299	3,901	12,490	53,370	256,604	699,591	58,495
Estimated total	100.0%	1,129,850	73,882	1,055,968	1,347	4,059	12,963	55,513	267,110	728,152	60,706
Rate per 100,000 inhabitants		4,363,9	285.4	4,078.6	5.2	15.7	50.1	214.4	1,031.7	2,812.4	234.5
Rural	32,786,218										
Area actually reporting	93.8%	627,488	54,255	573,233	2,303	4,332	6,394	41,227	233,778	300,828	38,627
Estimated total	100.0%	655,046	57,315	597,731	2,468	4,604	6,856	43,387	244,688	312,537	40,506
Rate per 100,000 inhabitants		1,997.9	178.4	1,823.1	7.5	14.0	20.9	132.3	746.3	953.3	123.5

Source. FBI Uniform Crime Report—Crime in the United States, 1978.

TABLE 2 Total Arrest Trends, Sex, 1977–1978
[10,319 agencies; 1978 estimated population 179,569,000]

Offense charged	Males						Females					
	Total			Under 18			Total			Under 18		
	1977	1978	Percent change	1977	1978	Percent change	1977	1978	Percent change	1977	1978	Percent change
Prostitution and commercialized vice	19,366	21,967	+ 13.4	895	891	− .4	45,755	46,812	+ 2.3	1,987	2,031	+ 2.2
Sex offenses (except forcible rape and prostitution)	48,039	47,825	− .4	9,195	8,953	− 2.6	4,664	4,116	−11.7	1,053	897	−14.8
Drug abuse violations	430,585	426,682	− .9	101,000	101,855	+ .8	69,410	69,347	− .1	20,086	20,774	+ 3.4
Gambling	39,426	37,566	− 4.7	1,756	1,547	−11.9	3,976	3,782	− 4.9	99	74	−25.3
Offenses against family and children	46,211	45,127	− 2.3	1,887	1,711	− 9.3	5,216	5,169	− .9	1,131	953	−15.7
Driving under the influence	930,421	993,468	+ 6.8	20,986	22,789	+ 8.6	84,583	92,076	+ 8.9	2,115	2,432	+15.0
Liquor laws	261,068	272,604	+ 4.4	90,724	89,991	− .8	45,521	47,291	+ 3.9	25,069	25,392	+ 1.3
Drunkenness	1,008,105	919,200	− 8.8	39,706	33,949	−14.5	80,551	74,897	− 7.0	6,336	5,381	−15.1
Disorderly conduct	485,983	518,816	+ 6.8	90,655	93,452	+ 3.1	98,273	99,505	+ 1.3	21,180	19,582	− 7.5
Vagrancy	20,125	17,954	−10.8	4,237	3,849	− 9.2	6,149	7,092	+15.3	1,002	808	−19.4
All other offenses (except traffic)	987,070	1,023,489	+ 3.7	208,913	201,172	− 3.7	197,337	198,449	+ .6	59,655	55,600	− 6.8
Suspicion (not included in totals)	19,012	15,717	−17.3	4,963	4,327	−12.8	3,161	2,358	−25.4	905	756	−16.5
Curfew and loitering law violations	64,176	57,048	−11.1	64,176	57,048	−11.1	17,743	15,687	−11.6	17,743	15,687	−11.6
Runaways	74,370	66,515	−10.6	74,370	66,515	−10.6	101,192	89,984	−11.1	101,192	89,984	−11.1

Source. FBI Uniform Crime Report—Crime in the United States, 1978.

TABLE 2 Total Arrest Trends, Sex, 1977–1978 (Continued)
[10,319 agencies; 1978 estimated population 179,569,000]

Offense charged	Males						Females					
	Total			Under 18			Total			Under 18		
	1977	1978	Percent change	1977	1978	Percent change	1977	1978	Percent change	1977	1978	Percent change
TOTAL	6,657,275	6,755,387	+ 1.5	1,530,909	1,507,287	− 1.5	1,296,122	1,318,348	+ 1.7	428,924	410,628	− 4.3
Murder and nonnegligent manslaughter	12,558	12,736	+ 1.4	1,321	1,197	− 9.4	2,240	2,234	− .3	135	149	+ 10.4
Forcible rape	22,087	22,608	+ 2.4	3,618	3,526	− 2.5	231	186	− 19.5	84	58	− 31.0
Robbery	88,123	88,928	+ .9	27,294	27,272	− .1	7,184	6,911	− 3.8	2,144	1,985	− 7.4
Aggravated assault	161,795	172,849	+ 6.8	25,669	26,452	+ 3.1	23,557	25,033	+ 6.3	4,550	4,618	+ 1.5
Burglary	376,233	376,982	+ .2	198,758	199,105	+ .2	24,465	24,977	+ 2.1	12,766	13,070	+ 2.4
Larceny-theft	626,194	636,550	+ 1.7	287,981	285,416	− .9	291,513	299,371	+ 2.7	113,338	112,794	− .5
Motor vehicle theft	103,413	107,690	+ 4.1	56,423	56,121	− .5	9,502	10,430	+ 9.8	5,796	6,331	+ 9.2
Violent crime[1]	284,563	297,121	+ 4.4	57,902	58,447	+ .9	33,212	34,364	+ 3.5	6,913	6,810	− 1.5
Property crime[2]	1,105,840	1,121,222	+ 1.4	543,162	540,642	− .5	325,480	334,778	+ 2.9	131,900	132,195	+ .2
Crime Index total	1,390,403	1,418,343	+ 2.0	601,064	599,089	− .3	358,692	369,142	+ 2.9	138,813	139,005	+ .1
Other assaults	318,511	332,081	+ 4.3	56,144	56,607	+ .8	51,210	53,266	+ 4.0	14,540	14,359	− 1.2
Arson	13,231	13,400	+ 1.3	6,853	6,866	+ .2	1,637	1,786	+ 9.1	695	719	+ 3.5
Forgery and counterfeiting	42,753	42,682	− .2	5,435	5,734	+ 5.5	17,813	18,626	+ 4.6	2,192	2,520	+ 15.0
Fraud	113,120	122,039	+ 7.9	3,962	3,941	− .5	69,717	83,087	+ 19.2	1,551	1,681	+ 8.4
Embezzlement	4,698	4,951	+ 5.4	576	574	− .3	1,365	1,693	+ 24.0	159	207	+ 30.2
Stolen property; buying, receiving, possessing	80,577	79,367	− 1.5	27,887	27,762	− .4	9,949	10,276	+ 3.3	2,707	2,819	+ 4.1
Vandalism	166,698	178,336	+ 7.0	101,924	104,265	+ 2.3	15,368	16,287	+ 6.0	8,351	8,533	+ 2.2
Weapons; carrying, possessing, etc.	112,339	115,927	+ 3.2	18,564	18,727	+ .9	10,001	9,978	− .2	1,268	1,190	− 6.2

Source. FBI *Uniform Crime Report—Crime in the United States, 1978.*
[1] Violent crimes are offenses of murder, forcible rape, robbery, and aggravated assault.
[2] Property crimes are offenses of burglary, larceny-theft, and motor vehicle theft.

time is associated with greater chances of police noting, founding, arresting, and clearing of the crimes that come to their attention (32).

Administration changes in police policy results in police attention and resources being focused on specific crimes instead of on others, and probably alters reported incidences of both the newly important and the less important crimes. Similarly, a prosecutor's arbitrary decisions on the marginal crimes he or she will or will not "paper" or prosecute impacts on police practices and on the crimes the police will note, found, and clear by arrests.

Additionally, Black (9) argues that there are distinctive police "styles," classified as Reactive (where much crime is known to the police, but police produce low rates of clearances by arrest) and Proactive (which would result in higher arrest rates, compared with the Reactive style).

It has been shown (38) that variations in police "founding" practices have considerable effect on crime rates. National statistics reveals that unfounding rates range from 3 to 18% for different crimes (the lowest being for larceny and the highest being for rape). Not only does founding vary by offense, but there also seems to be enormous jurisdictional variations. The differential founding practices considerably influence the statistics reported by the police.

Furthermore, the accuracy of the original police classification of a crime is said to vary with officers' legal competence, their desire to make a "good pinch," and their estimates of subsequent plea bargaining practices in their jurisdiction (3).

Evidence has been adduced showing a large number of errors in police classification of *UCR* offenses (21). Beyond this, police have been *accused* of bias (13) and dishonesty (38) in their data collection practices. In fact, however, little systematic evidence has ever been produced to substantiate these claims. Some commentators argue the police are unhappy with their own statistics, and tend to be cynical about their validity and use (23). Seidman and Couzens (46) conclude that the police decision to

react to the event as a crime is often correlated with such *extra*legal factors as:

1. The desire of the complainant.
2. Relational distance separating parties in the crime.
3. Deference shown toward the police.
4. The status of the complainant.

CHANGES IN PUBLIC "ACCEPTANCE" OF CRIME

Alterations in the public's willingness to have hired functionaries (police) intrude into certain crimes. Certain events, although legally crimes, are thought to be, in some populations, "private matters," to be disposed of without calling in the police. In time this view may change; then previous constraints against informing the police are eliminated, and official rates for these crimes soar. With the rising demand of the poor and minorities for greater police protection *and intervention*, many events that were previously not reported have become public, official concerns. Also relevant is that increasing American involvement with insurance has led to a greater need for reporting crimes to the police to collect insurance compensation (18).

Center and Smith (12) describe the need for developing "tolerance quotients" and "threshold values" of the particular community, which could measure how bad specified crimes must be, before the victim or observer have the police intrude. [Ennis (12) asked a large number of crime victims why they had not reported the crime (and their victimization) to the police; the most usual reasons given were that the police would be indifferent or ineffective.]

CHANGES IN THE LEGAL CODE

When a legislative body criminalizes previously legal behavior, or decriminalizes current crimes, or alters the classification of a crime (from a misdemeanor to a felony or the reverse), this necessarily results in a change in the official statistics of these events.

CHANGES IN LOCAL DATA NEEDS

When a community decides that there is some peculiar and pressing need for certain forms of criminal information, the result is the focusing of attention and law enforcement resources on these new priorities and interests (25).

LIMITATIONS OF THE UNIFORM CRIME REPORTS

There are additionally a number of methodological problems peculiar to the *Uniform Crime Reports*.

1. No federal cases are included, and these involve an appreciable number of crimes.
2. Reports are submitted voluntarily by most police departments, and the data vary enormously in completeness and accuracy; the FBI states in its report that it does not guarantee accuracy or completeness of data. They do, however, arithmetically check all reports and examine them for "reasonableness."
3. Not all police departments submit reports to the FBI, and one cannot assume that nonresponding departments have the same crime experiences as reporting departments.
4. Not satisfied with the data received from responding police departments, the FBI inflates or increases police-reported figures to gain an estimate of *total crime*. This arbitrary (and extremely doubtful) practice may be of little consequence when a state has reported the criminality for 99 percent of its population, with the FBI adding 1 percent to this figure. But with lower reporting states, the practice of amplification adds enormously to the reported data. Thus, Mississippi (in 1978) had a total population of 2,405,000. The police servicing 97.3 percent of all "Standard Metropolitan Statistical Areas" reported to the FBI who increased the total by 2.7 percent; 88.5 percent of "Other Cities" reported so their reported figures were inflated by 11.5 per-

cent. Police in only 47.4 percent of all Mississippi "rural" areas (almost one half of the population of the state) reported so that the actual reported index rate (of 4770) was estimated to be more than double (10,066).

5. The *UCR* openly acknowledges the grave problems of comparability of rates across jurisdictions because of the many differences in population, socioeconomic factors, and police characteristics.
6. Arrest does not equal crime solution. Neither are persons arrested criminals simply by reason of their arrest. About 20 percent of all arrested persons subsequently plead or are found guilty in a court of law.
7. Unfortunately, much data sent to the FBI by local police departments are not used in the *UCR*; some of this information is important in explicating crime rates, such as the percentage of arrests that are unfounded. Furthermore, some commentators believe that much of the unused data may be particularly valuable in ascertaining basic causes of areal crime variations (25, 38).

PROBLEMS OF CRIME CLASSIFICATION

8. There is only one crime classification given for each criminal event, even if multiple offenses have occurred during the crime. If a crime involves murder, rape, and drug use, it will be classified simply by the most important or serious crime—murder, and hence there would be no listing of the lesser crimes of rape and Narcotic Drug Law violation (3, 17, 25).
9. The number of offenses listed varies by type of crime committed (40); thus, for violent crimes the number of offenses equals the number of persons injured. If someone enters a bar and assaults six patrons, this could be counted as six assaults. For property crimes, however, each operation is a single offense. The same person who enters a bar and robs six persons would have

this criminal action listed, for *UCR* purposes, as one robbery.

10. The arbitrariness of concentration on those seven Index Crimes has been attacked (39). Most of the crimes committed and most of the crimes brought to the attention of the police do not fall under the seven Index Crimes. Furthermore, the largest portion of a Total Index Crime Rate is made up of the two least serious crimes: larceny and auto theft. It may be recalled that the seven crimes were chosen because they were defined as serious and/or had a high reported volume. But if these were the sole criteria, why, then, are Narcotic Drug Law violations not included (12)?

11. Considerable dissatisfaction has been expressed with the inclusion of auto theft among the Index Crimes. More than 80 percent of all stolen cars are recovered, and the high reportability of this offense is attributable to insurance requirements and the fact that even without insurance, legal control over the car impels the owner to report any loss.

12. In recent years, larceny of any amount is an Index Crime. The theft of an item worth $0.05 is equal in weight to a murder in the constructed Total Crime Index Rate.

13. All Index Crimes are unweighted in the Total Index Crime Rates used in the *UCR*. This produces a false picture of the extent and any change in serious crimes. It has been noted that most of the crimes that produce bodily injury (e.g., simple assault) are classified as non-Index Crimes (17).

14. As mentioned before, completed and non-completed (attempted) acts are lumped equally, for five of the seven Index Crimes.

15. The FBI, by arbitrarily defining seven offenses to be major crimes have made police, almost of necessity, concentrate their attention and effort on these offenses, with lesser attention being paid to other, non-Index Crimes.

16. Robbery is classified as a personal crime, and is one of four Index Crimes used in the construction of "Personal Crime Index Rates." Yet, the President's Commission on Violence and other governmental agencies seem to agree that robbery could properly be classified as either a personal or a property crime.

17. Relatively few victimless crimes and white-collar crimes are included in the *UCR*.

18. Strong disagreements exist between *UCR* and state definitions of specified crimes (12). Under California's Criminal Code shoplifting is a form of burglary; however, the *UCR* requires that burglary must contain the element of unlawful entry. Thus, in California, the reporting officer must first classify shoplifting by state specifications and then someone must later reclassify the same act by *UCR* handbook requirements.

19. The *UCR* Handbook describes several offenses in ambiguous manners, particularly the narcotic offenses (25, 33).

20. Little if any justification exists for the inclusion of "suspicion," very minor juvenile "status" delinquencies such as curfew violations, loitering, and runaway in the *UCR*'s arrest data.

PROBLEMS RELATING TO THE CONSTRUCTION OF CRIME RATES

21. The *UCR* concentrates not on the total *numbers* of reported offenses, but on the *rate* of those offenses, per 100,000 inhabitants. The use of the total population in constructing crime rates is absurd in that not all adults are equally open to the risk of certain crimes (11, 17, 40). Thus all women should constitute the denominator for any rape rate; women over a certain age for purse-snatching; the number of dwelling and commercial units for burglary; and the number of cars for auto theft. Boggs (11) has argued that one should use "environmental opportunities" to determine true risk groups. For aggravated assault and criminal homicide, she suggests the use of pairs of person; for auto

theft, the amount of space given over to parking (as a measure of untended parked cars); and for highway robbery, the number of square feet of street (as a crude index of the number of people on public streets).

22. The use of different-size population bases to construct rates of crime causes differential social perceptions of the seriousness of crime (40). Thus a robbery rate of 200 per 100,000 persons is viewed as more serious than an identical rate of 20 per 10,000 persons, while a robbery rate of only 2 per 1000 seems almost no real problem at all in the view of some people.

*

In the face of these problems, which are associated with any source of official police statistics, and with the Uniform Crime Reports in particular, one might well ask if these statistics can be used for *any* serious purpose. The considered answer must be clearly in the affirmative. With all of their limitations, the *Uniform Crime Reports* remains probably the most valuable source of criminal statistics currently available. Even serious critics of the *UCR* agree that it is the most adequate general measure available of change in the incidence of criminal behavior (17). Comparing the *UCR* and the National Crime Survey (Law Enforcement Assistance Administration's national panel survey of criminal victimization), Maltz (32) found that greatest accuracy was achieved by the use of both rather than the use of either. Hindelang (24) compared homicide data from the *UCR* with homicide data developed by the Center for Health Statistics. He also compared a range of *UCR* data with information developed in Ennis' study of *Criminal Victimization in the United States* in 1967 (20). He determined that the *UCR* and the Center's homicide data both depicted essentially similar patterns over time. He concluded that the *UCR* produced "robust estimates" of relative incidence of police known index offenses; and surprisingly, he found that the unweighted *UCR* statistics produce patterns very similar to those produced when the crimes were weighted.

REFERENCES

1. Beattie, R. H. (1967). "A system of integrated criminal statistics." *Criminologica* **5**(2):12–19.

2. Beattie, R. H. (1960). "Criminal statistics in the United States—1960." *Journal of Criminal Law, Criminology, and Police Science* **51**:49–65.

3. Beattie, R. H. (1950). *Manual of Criminal Statistics.* New York: American Prison Association.

4. Beattie, R. H (1955). "Problems of criminal statistics in the United States." *Journal of Criminal Law, Criminology, and Police Science* **46**:178–186.

5. Beattie, R. H. (1959). "Sources of Statistics on Crime and Correction." *Journal, American Statistical Association* **54** (September):582–592.

6. Biderman, A. D. (1967). "Surveys of Population Samples for Estimating Crime Incidence." *Annals of the American Society of Political and Social Sciences,* **374**:16–35.

7. Biderman, A. D. (1966). "Social Indicators and Goals." In R. A. Bauer (ed.), *Social Indicators.* Cambridge, Mass.:M.I.T. Press. Pp. 111–129.

8. Biderman, A. D., and A. J. Reiss (1967). "On Exploring the Dark Figure of Crime," *Annals of the American Society of Political and Social Sciences,* **374**:1–15.

9. Black, D. J. (1970). "The Production of Crime Rates." *American Sociological Review* **35**:733–748.

10. Bloch, P. B., and C. Ulberg (1974). *Auditing Clearance Rates.* Washington, D.C.: Police Foundation (December).

11. Boggs, S. L. (1965). "Urban Crime Patterns." *American Sociological Review* **30**:899–908.

12. Center, L. J., and T. G. Smith (1973). "Criminal Statistics—Can They Be Trusted?" *The American Criminal Law Review* **11**:1045–1086.

13. Chambliss, W., and R. H. Nagasawa (1969). "On the Validity of Official Statistics." *Journal of Research on Crime and Delinquency* **6**:71–77.

14. Chilton R. J. (1968). "Persistent Problems of Crime Statistics." In S. Dinitz and W. C. Reckless (eds.), *Critical Issues in the Study of Crime.* Boston: Little Brown. Pp. 89–95.

15. Chilton, R. J., and A. Spielberger (1972). "Increases in Crime: The Utility of Alternative Measures." *Journal of Criminal Law, Criminology, and Police Science* **63**:68–74.

16. Cressey, D. (1951). "Criminological Research and the Definition of Crime." *American Journal of Sociology* 56:546–552.

17. Cressey, D. (1957). "The State of Criminal Statistics." *NPPA Journal* 3 (July):230–241.

18. Doleschal, E. (n.d.). *Criminal Statistics.* Crime and Delinquency Topics. National Institute of Mental Health, Center for Studies of Crime and Delinquency. DHEW Publication No. 72–9094.

19. Engleman, H. O., and K. Throckmorton (1967). "Interaction Frequency and Crime Rates." *Wisconsin Sociologist*, 5:33–36.

20. Ennis, P. (1967). *Criminal Victimization in the United States: A Report of a National Survey.* Field Survey II. President's Commission on Law Enforcement and Administration of Justice. Washington, D.C.: U.S. Government Printing Office.

21. Ferracuti, R., R. Hernandez, and M. E. Wolfgang (1962). "A Study of Police Errors in Crime Classification." *Journal of Criminal Law, Criminology, and Police Science,* 53:113–119.

22. Frankel, E. (1947). "Statistics of Crime." In V. C. Branham, and S. B. Kutash (eds.), *Encyclopedia of Criminology* New York: Philosophical Library. Pp. 478–489.

23. Griffin, J. L. (1950). "New Perspectives in Police Statistics." *Journal of Criminal Law, Criminology, and Police Science* 46:879–881.

24. Griffin, J. L. (1960). "Current Problems in Police Statistics." *Proceedings of the Social Statistics Section, American Statistics Association,* Pp. 18–20.

25. Hindelang, M. (1974). "The Uniform Crime Reports Revisited." *Journal of Criminal Justice* 2:1–17.

26. Isaacs, N. E. (1961). "The Crime of Present Day Crime Reporting." *Journal of Criminal Law, Criminology, and Police Science* 52:405–410.

27. Kitsuse, J., and A. V. Cicourel (1963). "A Note on the Uses of Official Statistics." *Social Problems* 11 (Fall):131–139.

28. Law Enforcement Assistance Administration (1974). *Crime in the Nation's Five Largest Cities.* Washington, D.C.: U.S. Government Printing Office.

29. Law Enforcement Assistance Administration (1974). National Criminal Justice Information and Statistics Service, *Crime and Victims. A Report on the Dayton-San Jose Pilot Survey of Victimization.* Washington, D.C.: U.S. Government Printing Office.

30. Lejins, P. P. (1960). "Measurement of Juvenile Delinquency." *Proceedings of the Social Statistics Section, American Statistics Association.* Pp. 47–49.

31. Lejins, P. P. (1966). "Uniform Crime Reports." *Michigan Law Review* 64 (April):1011–1030.

32. Maltz, M. D. (1975). "Crime Statistics: A Mathematical Perspective." *Journal of Criminal Justice* 3:177–194.

33. Mandel, J. (1969). "Problems of Official Statistics with Official Drug Statistics." *Stanford Law Review* 21 (May):991–1040.

34. McClintock, F. H. "Criminological and Penological Aspects of the Dark Figure of Crime and Criminality." *Sixth European Conference of Directors of Criminological Research Institutes* (Council of Europe).

35. Morris, A. (1965). "What are the Sources of Knowledge About Crime in the United States?" *Correctional Research Bulletin,* No. 15 (November) pp. 6–13.

36. Normandeau, A., and Schwartz, R. (1971). "A Crime Classification of American Metropolitan Areas." *Criminology* 9:228–247.

37. Park, R. B. (1975). "Sources of Limitations of Data in Criminal Justice Research." In J. A. Gardiner and M. A. Mulkey (eds.), *Crime and Criminal Justice.* Lexington, Mass.: D. C. Health and Co. Pp. 31–42.

38. Pittman, D. J., and W. F. Handy (1962). "Uniform Crime Reporting: Suggested Improvements." *Sociology and Social Research* 46 (January):135–143.

39. Price, J. E. (1966). "Testing the Accuracy of Crime Statistics." *Social Problems,* 14 (Fall):214–221.

40. Reiss, A. J. (1967). "Measurement of the Nature and Amount of Crime." *Studies in Crime and Law Enforcement in Metropolitan Areas, Volume I.* Washington, D.C.: U.S. Government Printing Office. Pp. 1–183.

41. Reiss, A. J. (1972). *Methodological Studies in Crime Classification.* Report Prepared for the National Institute of Law Enforcement and Criminal Justice (June).

42. Robison, S. (1936). *Can Delinquency Be Measured?* New York: Columbia University Press.

43. Robison, S. (1966). "A Critical View of the *Uniform Crime Reports.*" *Michigan Law Review* 64 (April):1031–1054.

44. Sagi, P., and C. F. Wellford (1968). "Age Composition and Patterns of Change in Criminal Statis-

tics." *Journal of Criminal Law, Criminology, and Police Science* **59**:29–35.

45. Schulman, H. M. (1966). "The Measurement of Crime in the United States." *Journal of Criminal Law, Criminology, and Police Science* **57**:483–492.

46. Seidman, D., and M. Couzens (1974). "Getting the Crime Rate Down. Political Pressure and Crime Reporting." *Law and Society Review* **8**:457–493.

47. Sellin, T. (1954). "Problems of Criminal Statistics." *Correction* **19**:3–9.

48. Sellin, T. (1932). "Problems of National Crime Statistics." *Proceedings, American Prison Association* **62**:300–314.

49. Sellin, T. (1951). "The Significance of Records of Crime." *Law Quarterly Review* **67**:496–504.

50. Sellin, T., and M. E. Wolfgang (1964). *The Measurement of Delinquency.* New York: John Wiley & Sons.

51. Skogan, W. G. (1975). "Measurement Problems in Official and Survey Crime Rates." *Journal of Criminal Justice* **3**:17–32.

52. Sutherland, E. H., and C. C. Van Vechten (1934). "The Reliability of Criminal Statistics." *Journal of Criminal Law, Criminology, and Police Science* **25**:10–20.

53. Turner, S. H. (1965). "Some Methods for Estimating Uncleared Juvenile Offenses." *Journal of Criminal Law, Criminology, and Police Science* **56**:54–58.

54. United States District Court, Administrative Office (1972). *Federal Offenders in the United States District Courts—1970.* Washington, D.C.: Government Printing Office.

55. United States Department of Justice, Federal Bureau of Investigation, *Review of the Report of the Consultation Committee on Uniform Crime Reporting. Special Issue of Uniform Crime Reports, 1958.*

56. United States Department of Justice, Federal Bureau of Investigation (1959). *Ten Years of Uniform Crime Reporting, 1930–1939.* Washington, D.C.: U.S. Government Printing Office.

57. United States Department of Justice, Federal Bureau of Investigation (1974). *Uniform Crime Reporting Handbook.* Washington, D.C.: U.S. Government Printing Office.

58. United States Department of Justice, Federal Bureau of Investigation (1979). *Uniform Crime Reports—1978. Crime in the United States.* Washington, D.C.: U.S. Government Printing Office.

59. United States Department of Justice, Law Enforcement Assistance Administration, National Criminal Justice Information and Statistics Service. *Criminal Victimization Survey in the Nation's Five Largest Cities. National Panel Survey of Chicago, Detroit, Los Angeles, New York and Philadelphia.* Washington, D.C.: U.S. Government Printing Office, 1975.

60. United States Department of Justice, Law Enforcement Assistance Administration, National Crime Justice Information and Statistics Service, *Prisoners in State and Federal Institutions on December 31, 1971, 1972, 1973. NPS. National Prisoner Statistics Bulletin.* No. SD-NPS-PSF-1 (May 1975).

61. United States Department of Justice, Law Enforcement Assistance Administration, National Institute of Law Enforcement and Criminal Justice, Statistics Division, *San Jose Methods Test of Known Crime Victims.* Statistics Technical Report No. 1. Washington, D.C. (June 1972).

62. United States, President's Commission on Law Enforcement and the Administration of Justice, "Crime Statistics," in Task Force Report: *Crime and Its Impact: An Assessment.* Washington, D.C.: U.S. Government Printing Office, 1967.

63. Ward, P. (1970). "Careers in Crime: The F.B.I. Story." *Journal of Research in Crime and Delinquency* **7**:207–218.

64. Walker, N. (1971). *Crimes, Courts and Figures: An Introduction to Criminal Statistics.* Baltimore: Penguin Books.

65. Wellford, C. F. (1975). "Age Composition and the Increase in Recorded Crime." *Criminology* **11**:61–70.

66. Wheeler, S. (1967). "Criminal Statistics: A Reformulation of the Problem." *Journal of Criminal Law, Criminology, and Police Science,* **58**:317–324.

67. Wilkins, L. T. (1963). "The Measurement of Crime." *Journal of Criminal Law, Criminology, and Police Science* **53**:321–341.

68. Wilkins, L. T. (1965). "New Thinking in Criminal Statistics." *Journal of Criminal Law, Criminology, and Police Science* **56**:227–284.

69. Wingersky, M. F. (1954). "Some Aspects of Criminal Statistics and a Statistical Methodology in Areas of Criminal Law and Procedure." *De Paul Law Review* **3** (Spring):199–220.

70. Wolfgang, M. E. (1963). "Uniform Crime Reports: A Critical Appraisal." *University of Pennsylvania Law Review* **111**:708–738.

2

CRIME WAVES AS IDEOLOGY

MARK FISHMAN

When we speak of a crime wave, we are talking about a kind of social awareness of crime, crime brought to public consciousness. It is something to be remarked upon at the corner grocery store, complained about in a community meeting, and denounced at the mayor's press conference. One cannot be mugged by a crime wave, but one can be scared. And one can put more police on the streets and enact new laws on the basis of fear. Crime waves may be "things of the mind," but they have real consequences.

Crime waves are prime candidates for ideology. This study analyzes a specific crime wave that occurred in New York City in late 1976. This case both illustrates and informs my analysis that the crime waves which periodically appear in the press are constructs of the mass media and contribute to an ideological conception of crime in America.[1]

My use of the term ideology follows Dorothy Smith (1972). All knowledge is knowledge from some point of view, resulting from the use of procedures for knowing a part of the world. Ideological accounts arise from "procedures which people use as a means *not to know*" (1972:3, emphasis mine). Routine news gathering and editing involve "procedures not to know." The business of news is embedded in a configuration of institutions. These include a community of news organizations from which journalists derive a sense of "what's news now," and governmental agencies upon which journalists depend for their raw materials. Through their interactions and reliance on official sources, news organizations both invoke and reproduce prevailing conceptions of "serious crime."

CRIMES AGAINST THE ELDERLY

In late 1976, New York City experienced a major crime wave. The city's three daily newspapers and five local television stations reported a surge of violence against elderly people. The crime wave lasted approximately seven weeks, eventually receiving national television and newspaper coverage.

Source: "Crime Waves as Ideology," *Social Problems* (June 1978), **25**: 531–543. Reprinted by permission.

[1] This paper focuses on the generation of crime waves, not their effects. Thus, I infer that media crime waves contribute to existing images and fears of crime in society. To substantiate this inference would require a study of crime wave effects with a different method from that used here. There is, however, research indicating that people's fears and images of crime derive, in large part, from the news media. See, for example, Davis (1952:330) and Biderman, et al. (1967:128).

* This is a revised version of a paper presented at the 1977 Annual Meeting of the Society for the Study of Social Problems. I wish to acknowledge Ronald Vandor and Davis Lester, whose many hours of research assistance made this paper possible, Pamela Fishman, who helped clarify much of my thinking about crime news, and Malcolm Spector and Gaye Tuchman for their helpful comments on an earlier draft.

One consequence of this was the public definition of a new type of crime.[2] "Crimes against the elderly" became a typical crime with typical victims, offenders, and circumstances. Reported muggers, murderers, and rapists of the elderly were usually black or hispanic youths with long juvenile records. They came from ghetto neighborhoods near enclaves of elderly whites who, for various reasons (usually poverty), had not fled the inner city. Using this scenario, journalists reported incident after brutal incident throughout November and December 1976.

The outcry against these crimes was immediate. The Mayor of New York City, who was preparing to run for re-election, criticized the juvenile justice system and the criminal courts. The New York City Police Department gave its Senior Citizens Robbery Unit (S.C.R.U.) manpower to extend plain-clothes operations. Camera crews from local news stations filmed S.C.R.U. officers dressed as old people and arresting muggers. Local police precincts held community meetings to advise the elderly how to protect themselves. New York State legislators introduced bills to make juvenile records available to a judge at the time of sentencing, to deny sixteen to nineteen year olds juvenile status if they victimized an old person, and to mandate prison sentences for crimes of violence against the aged. These proposals were

passed in both the State Senate and Assembly, but were eventually vetoed by the Governor on August 19, 1977—nine months after the crime wave had ended.

A May 1977 Harris poll suggested the crime wave also had a nation-wide effect on people's fear of crime. Moreover, it had an effect on the crime categories which the Harris organization used in its surveys; this poll included a new type of crime, crimes against elderly, not previously present in Harris polls. Harris found that sixty percent of his respondents felt that assaults against elderly people in their home areas had been going up, and that fifty percent of those age fifty or older said they were more uneasy on the streets than they had been one year ago.[3]

It is doubtful that there really was a crime wave or any unusual surge of violence against elderly people. No one really knows, least of all the journalists who reported the crime wave. The police statistics from the N.Y.P.D. do not show a crime wave.[4] In fact, for one type of crime, homicide, the police showed a nineteen percent *drop* over the previous year's rate of elderly people murdered. This is significant because the news media began their reporting with coverage of several gruesome murders. (Twenty-eight percent of the stories reported by the three media organizations I surveyed were stories about homicides. In contrast, the police reported that homicides made up less than one percent of crimes against the elderly in 1976.)

For other types of crime with elderly victims, police statistics showed an increase over the previous year. Crime victimization, however, rose for all age categories in 1976. In some cases, the increases were greater for elderly victims, in others less. Robbery was up ten percent in the general population, nineteen percent for the elderly. Grand larceny was up

---

[2] While the New York City crime wave represents the first widely publicized formulation of "crimes against the elderly," the issue was not first defined by the New York media. Fredric DuBow (personal communication) has pointed out that the law enforcement establishment had formulated crimes against the elderly as a new type of crime at least two years prior to the crime wave: Since 1974 it was an important funding theme of L.E.A.A.; in 1975 it was the subject of a major conference; and in February 1976 *Police Chief* devoted a special issue to it.

These earlier law enforcement formulations probably led to the creation of the New York Police Department's Senior Citizens Robbery Unit (S.C.R.U.) well before the city's crime wave. As we shall see, S.C.R.U. played a crucial role in directing media attention to crimes against the elderly in the first stages of the crime wave. Thus, it seems that early "professional formulations" led to the establishment of a specialized agency which, in turn, enabled the media publicly to formulate a category for crimes against elderly.

[3] Reported in the *New York Post*, May 9, 1977.
[4] Thus far I have been unable to obtain a complete, month-by-month set of 1976 N.Y.P.D. crime rates. Therefore, for all but the homicide rate, the figures described below are tentative, based on partial rates for 1976.

twenty-nine percent for the general population, twenty-five percent for the elderly. In short, police statistics substantiate only that there was a continuing increase in victimization of the elderly (as well as of the general population), not that old people were singled out, as never before. Moreover, the homicide rate contradicts the media presentation of a crime wave.

This paper, however, is not a study in the disparity between police statistics and crime news. Prior studies of crime news and crime waves (Davis, 1952; Roshier, 1973) as well as anecdotal reports (Steffens, 1931:285–291), have shown the irony of crime waves: although the public is alarmed and politicians respond to media reports of a dramatic increase in crime, such "waves" have no basis in police statistics. This study goes beyond sociological irony to examine *how and why news organizations construct crime waves*. Crime waves are taken to be waves of coverage of some topic in crime. Crime waves as *media waves* may or may not be related to something happening "on the streets" or in the police crime rates. Studying crime waves means studying processes in the mass media.

METHOD

I collected two kinds of data. First, two student researchers and I conducted participant observation from November 1976 to April 1977 on a New York City local television station, WAVE (a pseudonym). One student was a full-time WAVE journalist who worked as a news writer, program producer, and assignment editor. We focused on how the assignment editor assembled the daily news program by deciding what major stories would be covered for the day and assigning reporters and camera crews to these stories. In addition, we conducted interviews with journalists from WAVE and the New York *Daily News*.

Second, we kept a record of all news relating to crimes against the elderly reported from September 1976 through February 1977 in two

newspapers, the New York *Daily News* and the *New York Post*, and on WAVE, which aired a one hour newscast in the evening. This enabled us to "locate" the New York crime wave, to determine when it began and ended, and to determine the kind of coverage crimes against the elderly received before, during, and after the crime wave period.

THE CRIME WAVE: A VIEW FROM THE OUTSIDE

Over the six-month period of observation the *News*, the *Post*, and WAVE presented eighty-nine stories of crimes against the elderly. Fifty-six stories or sixty-three percent occurred during the crime wave period. The weekly frequencies of news stories from all three media are shown in Figure 1. This graph clearly indicates a wave of media reporting that began in the last week of October and trailed off by the second week of December. It shows a sharp, swift rise in coverage for the first two weeks, then a slow, uneven decline for the remaining five weeks.

Examining the individual patterns of coverage for each news organization reveals that prior to the crime wave each organization was reporting approximately one story of crime against the elderly every other week. After the wave, coverage in all three media was sporadic, but heavier than coverage during the prewave period, indicating that the media appear to have been sensitized to the topic.

The three individual crime waves in the *News*, the *Post*, and WAVE show that the marked increase in coverage did not coincide in all three media. The *News* had a sudden increase in the third week of October; WAVE and the *Post* did not increase their coverage until the fourth week of October. Further, in this fourth week the two "latecomers" began their increase *simultaneously*. Prior to their increased coverage, the *Post* and WAVE did not parallel each other. It was only after the *News* began reporting a wave that the others developed a synchronous pattern. This trend sug-

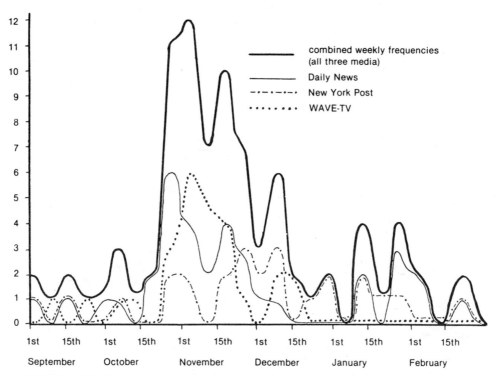

FIGURE 1.   Week-by-week frequencies of stories on crime against the elderly appearing in the *Daily News, New York Post,* and WAVE-TV.

gests that the other media simultaneously responded to the *Daily News'* portrayal of a wave of violence against the elderly.

All three media show different crime wave profiles. WAVE steeply increased coverage to a single peak, then had an equally steep decline (seventeen days rising and sixteen days falling). In contrast, the *Daily News* and the *Post* show bimodal curves. In the *News* there was a swift initial rise (ten days), from which coverage subsided slowly, then it turned upward to a second peak (lower than the first), and finally declined.

The unevenness of the *Daily News's* wave was echoed in the *Post.* The *Post* participated less actively in the crime wave than did the *News* or WAVE. We might even say that the *Post* did not show a crime wave, except that the period of its heaviest coverage coincided with the crime wave period in the other media. Moreover, the *Post's* pre- and post-wave patterns were similar to the other media, and during the crime wave it showed a bimodal wave which paralleled that of the *Daily News.* Thus, the *Post's* wave seems to have been a weak reflection of the *Daily News's* curve.

How can we explain these bimodal patterns? The likely reason why the *News* and *Post* reduced their coverage after the first peaks involves a major news event coinciding with this drop; the 1976 Presidential Election of November 2. The elections seem to have crowded out crimes against the elderly from the newspapers, but not from local TV news, since stations like WAVE were not trying to compete with network coverage of the Presidential race. Thus, during the slow news period after the elections, the *News* and *Post* seemed to have "rediscovered" the crime wave, which was still present in local TV news.

In other words, it seems the *News'* and the *Post's* second peak was a response to the continuing crime wave in the television media (assuming other TV stations behaved like WAVE). Just as the initial appearance of the crime wave in the *Daily News* seems to have spurred increased coverage by the *Post* and WAVE, so the continuing coverage of the crime wave on television seems to have "re-awakened" interest in the topic by the *Daily News* and the *Post*. Thus, *the behavior of each news organization during the crime wave seems to have been in response to the other media.*

SEEING THEMES IN CRIME: A VIEW FROM THE INSIDE

How do individual crimes come to be seen as a crime wave? The answer is found in the methods by which news is organized. News workers make crime waves by seeing "themes" in the news. Crime waves are little more than the continued and heavy coverage of numerous occurrences which journalists report as a single topic (for example, "crimes against the elderly").

News themes are various: "everything Jimmy Carter did today," "the taxi cab strike," "Vietnam," "the disintegrating American family," or "labor disputes." A news theme is unifying concept. It presents a specific news event, or a number of such events, in terms of some broader concept. For example, the mugging of an eighty-two-year-old Bronx woman can be reported as "the latest instance of the continuing trend in crimes against the elderly." A news theme allows journalists to cast an incident as an *instance* of something.

The Glasgow Media Group (1976:355) provides an interesting example of thematized news events from one British television newscast:

> The week had its share of unrest. Trouble in Glasgow with striking dustmen and ambulance controllers, short time in the car industry, no Sunday Mirror or Sunday People today and a fair amount of general trouble in Fleet Street and a continuing rumble over the matter of two builders pickets jailed for conspiracy.

As the authors point out, disparate incidents are reported together under the single theme of "unrest." Calling these things "unrest" imposes order on the events reported. Audience members are meant to see the events as unified, as instances of a single theme.

Themes give news shows and newspapers a presentational order. Items are presented in groups organized around a theme. Some themes are related to others, making it possible for groups of news stories to be placed near each other. For instance, during the crime wave against the elderly, the first ten minutes of a sixty-minute news program at WAVE was organized around interrelated themes:

1. Police apprehend three youngsters who allegedly mugged an elderly Queens couple.
2. Police and senior citizens meet at a Queens precinct to discuss fighting crimes against the elderly.
3. A feature report on the Senior Citizens Robbery Unit.
4. Police seize guns and drugs intended for warring gangs in the Bronx.
5. Two members of a youth gang are arrested for robbing someone at knife point.
6. R.O.T.C. cadet charged in the stabbing death of another cadet.
7. New York State audit finds the city police have been mishandling $9.1 million of federal funds.
8. New York City and the police union are still working on a new contract, at the same time that some layed-off firemen and subway cops will be rehired.

First, there are small groups of stories, each containing a theme that the stories in the group share in common (the first three stories are about "crimes against the elderly" and the next three about "youth crime"). Second, groups of stories are placed next to other groups, since the different themes of each group share common features (the group of crimes against the elderly and the group of youth crimes both can be seen to be about youthful perpetrators and police responses to them).

Journalists do not create themes merely to show an audience the appearance of order. News themes are very useful in newswork itself. In particular, editors selecting and organizing the day's stories need themes.[5] Every day, news editors face a glut of "raw materials" (wire service reports, press releases, police crime dispatches) out of which they must fashion relatively few news stories. This task involves a selection process which operates somewhat differently in television and newspaper newsrooms. The essentials of the process are the same: individual news items are identified and sorted according to possible themes.

The chances that any event or incident will be reported increase once it has been associated with a current theme in the news. Crime incidents are rarely reported unless news workers see them related to a past or emerging trend in criminality or law enforcement. A brief description of how the assignment editor at WAVE developed the first segment of the news show just cited illustrates this point. The assignment editor determined the top stories for the day when he noticed that several previously unrelated stories were all part of the same current newsworthy theme; crimes against the elderly. And the discovery of this theme was no coincidence; that day's program was in the midst of the crime wave period.

The assignment editor did not begin his day knowing that crime news, and, in particular, that crimes against the elderly, would receive top billing in the evening's news show. When he started work at 8:45 AM he already knew of two stories that he would most likely cover:[6] One was a feature report on the Senior Citizen's Robbery Unit fighting crimes against the elderly. This feature, which eventually ran as the third story in the evening newscast, had been taped days before; it was part of a continuing series on S.C.R.U. the station had been airing for the past few weeks. The second story was a feature report on a "food fair" that afternoon in Manhattan. The editor planned to send a reporter and camera crew to cover it, but also wanted to line up, as he put it, "some better stories" for the day.

Ten minutes after he arrived in the newsroom the assignment editor began scanning his news sources for lead stories. He sifted through reams of wire service news that had collected overnight under the wire machines; he scanned the police dispatches of the previous night's and that morning's crime incidents (about ten or twelve) received through a teletype called "the police wire." He also looked to other news media for story ideas: he read the *Daily News* and *New York Times* and he listened to an all-news radio station.

In the *Daily News* he found a small story about rehiring firemen and Transit Authority police who had been laid off. He thought this would be a good story because "this indicates things may be turning around in the city." This incident became newsworthy when the assignment editor could see it as part of a current newsworthy theme (New York's fiscal crisis).

Still, the assignment editor despaired that he had "no real news," that this was a "slow news day." However, around ten AM two things happened. First, when scanning the police crime dispatches, the assignment editor found

---

[5] The editor's use of news themes is part of the more general tendency of newsworkers to code and categorize news events in order to "routinize their unexpectedness." See Tuchman, 1973.

[6] The assignment editor started with these two stories because his superior in the newsroom had suggested that they be covered.

that in the 113th precinct in Queens an elderly couple had been mugged, and that one perpetrator was wounded by police. As he was clipping this dispatch, he heard over the all-news radio that the 112th precinct in Queens, very close to where the mugging occurred, was holding a crime prevention meeting with senior citizens. He now knew what his lead stories for the day would be, and he knew what he had to do to line them up:

1. He would send a reporter out to the 113th precinct to find, and get on film, whatever he could about the mugging (interviews with police, perhaps with some witnesses or with the victims themselves; and, if he was lucky, film of any suspects that were apprehended).
2. Then the reporter could go over to the nearby 112th precinct to film the police meeting with senior citizens.
3. These two reports would be followed by the pre-taped feature on S.C.R.U.
4. The story on rehiring firemen and Transit police, as well as a few other brief wire service reports relevant to crime which might come in during the rest of the day, would all follow the above three lead stories in some as yet undetermined order. The story on the "food fair" would be placed further back in the show.

Each story, seen independently, might not have merited attention. But seen together, all of them were made newsworthy by the perception of a common theme. The editor's "discovery" of the theme of crime against the elderly made the day's news come together. He knew how to assign a schedule to his reporter and camera crew; and he knew pretty much what the day's news was going to be.

The selection of news on the basis of themes is one component in the ideological production of crime news. It constitutes a "procedure not to know." This procedure requires that an incident be stripped of the actual context of its occurrence so that it may be relocated in a new, symbolic context: the news theme. Because

newsworthiness is based on themes, the attention devoted to an event may exceed its importance, relevance, or timeliness were these qualities determined with reference to some theory of society. In place of any such theoretical understanding of the phenomena they report, newsworkers make incidents meaningful only as *instances of themes*—themes which are generated within the news production process. Thus, something becomes a "serious type of crime" on the basis of what is going on inside newsrooms, not outside them.

FROM CRIME THEMES TO CRIME WAVES

Crime themes are potential crime waves. A news organization cannot make a crime wave without the collaboration of other media reporting the same crime theme. Crime waves emerge out of an interaction among news organizations.

THE INDEFINITE OVERLAPPING CHARACTER OF NEWS JUDGMENTS

All newsworkers depend on other media organizations for their sense of "what's news today," For example, the WAVE assignment editor began his day by reading the morning papers, the *Daily News* and *The New York Times*, and by listening to an all-news radio station. He later read the *New York Post* and watched when other TV stations aired their news. This editor told me that he did not mind using "anything, any source of news. I'm not proud. I'll steal any source of news."

In reality, stories were not stolen wholesale; rather, the other news media provided an important pool of ideas for story assignments. The noon and evening TV news shows rarely were used for the purpose because, by the time these shows were aired, most of the editor's news was set. The news on other stations mainly confirmed the assignment editor's news judgments, since his planned 10 PM news was, with few exceptions, identical to what his competitors were broadcasting. It seems his competitors were doing just what he was doing:

reading the *Times* and the *News*, listening to the all-news radio, and taking stories from the same news sources (wire services, police news dispatches, and press releases).[7]

News judgments continuously overlap in space and time. Editors of afternoon and evening media look for, and are oriented by, the news in the morning media. Editors of the morning media derive their sense of news from afternoon and evening media. Since these media may be in different regions and different cites, news judgments spread throughout an indefinite expanse of territory. The wire services and a few nationally-read newspapers, *The New York Times* and *Washington Post*, increase the diffusion of news judgments throughout the U.S.

Moreover, this overlap provides a continuity of news judgments. A specific incident or theme presented in the morning will be covered in the evening, perhaps with fresh incidents, more details, a new development or a "local angle" on the story. The process may repeat itself the next day, reproducing the theme of the previous evening.

THE CRIME WAVE DYNAMIC

When journalists notice each other reporting the same crime theme, it becomes entrenched in a community of media organizations. Reporters and editors will know that "this kind of crime is news." To use Sack's (1972:333) term, journalists have established a "consistency rule": *every crime incident that can be seen as an instance of the theme, will be seen and reported as such.* The rule is used to identify the newsworthiness of certain crimes. Reporters and editors will know, for example, that a certain incident is "another one of those crimes against the elderly" and not just an incident that can be categorized in a variety of ways.

Each use of the consistency rule reestablishes the rule. Any use of the principle invites

[7] While my example of overlapping news judgments is drawn from a local television station, the same phenomenon occurs both on newspapers and national network news (Epstein, 1973:150).

readers or viewers of the news, including other journalists, to use the same principle. In order to recognize a crime incident as an instance of a theme, readers or viewers must use the same consistency rule which was used to produce that news.

Journalists who have not yet seen a particular crime theme learn to see it simply by watching their competition. They are able, using the consistency rule, to report the same crime theme their competition taught them to see. At this point, when a crime theme is beginning to spread through more and more media organizations, the "reality" of the theme is confirmed for the media organizations who first reported it. They now see others using the theme. Moreover, as the theme persists, news organizations already using the theme will not hesitate to report new instances, because they confirm a past news judgment that "this thing really is a type of crime happening now." Thus, each use of the theme confirms and justifies its prior uses.

If it continues long enough, the process constitutes a crime wave dynamic. All crime waves begin as simple themes but by means of this dynamic can swell into waves. Crime themes constantly appear in the media and few reach the proportions of full-scale crime waves. After all, it only takes one editor with a little imagination to introduce a new theme into the news. Why is it that few crime themes go beyond a few days of coverage by one or two news organizations?

Clearly, something more than the crime wave dynamic is necessary for a theme to grow into a wave: *There must be a continuous supply of crime incidents that can be seen as instances of a theme.* Journalists may be primed to report a wave of crime incidents, but they also must know of enough incidents to report the wave. (During the period of my research, New York City journalists had been frustrated in reporting an expected "mafia war." This theme never persisted long for lack of enough incidents. Thus, "mafia war" was a hungry crime theme, starved of enough incidents to make it the crime wave it could have become.) The supply of incidents is crucial in determining the growth of crime waves. What are journalists' sources of crime news?

Perpetrators of crime could be a source, but news workers rarely learn of crimes directly from offenders. The primary source is law enforcement agencies.[8] In the newsroom of WAVE, journalists first learned of crime incidents through three sources:[9] the "police wire," the police radio, and other news organizations (wire service reports, the all-news radio station, and the *Daily News)*. The first two of these were direct links to the city police. Crime news is really police news. Thus, *the media's supply of crime incidents is a function of the crime reporting practices of law enforcement agencies*. This reliance on law enforcement agencies constitutes another component of the ideological production of crime news. News workers will not know that the police do not routinely detect or transmit to them. What journalists do know of crime is formulated for them by law enforcement agencies.

THE POOL OF POTENTIAL CRIME WAVES

The police supply news organizations with an assortment of crime incidents every day. For media organizations in towns and small cities this assortment often consists of *all* crimes known to the police in a twenty-four-hour period. But in large urban areas there are far too many crimes known to the police for any reporter to know them all. Therefore, urban journalists depend on the police to provide a "summary" of these incidents.

In New York City, the daily summary is known as the "police wire." All the city's major media have a teletype that receives crime dis-

patches from the N.Y.P.D.'s Office of Public Information. In one day, this police wire types out anywhere from twelve to twenty-five messages. The crime items appearing over the police wire constitute a "crime wave pool": a collection of crime incidents known to the media and having the potential of being seen as certain crime themes. Crime themes steadily supplied with instances over the police wire can become crime waves.

While journalists may invent crime themes (I suspect the police suggest and encourage many of them), a crime wave needs enough incidents on the police wire to support it. The police have power both to veto and promote the media's construction of crime waves. The collection of crime incidents the police provide to news organizations may systematically preclude certain themes from becoming waves (the enabling power).

For three ten-day periods from mid-February to the end of March 1977, a copy of all crime dispatches of the police wire was kept. Over this thirty-day period, 468 individual dispatches (averaging 15.6 per day) were received. Of these, I ignored ninety-seven (21%) which the police and journalists did not consider crime items. (They were mostly traffc advisories and non-suspicious fires.)

The remaining 371 crime dispatches reveal that the police wire provides journalists with a heavy and steady diet of "street crimes." Two thirds (246 items or 66.3%) of the crime items consisted of: a) robberies and burglaries (eighty-five items or twenty-three percent of all crime items), b) unspecified shootings and stabbings (156 items or forty-two percent) and c) a sprinkling of other assaults (five items or one percent—mostly rapes).

The remaining one-third of the police wire consisted of a variety of incidents: thirteen bombings; nine police suspended or arrested; six demonstrations requiring police action; five hostage situations; four raids for gambling, pornography, and drugs; three people run over by subway trains; one arson; and one hit-and-run. In addition, this third contained in-

---

[8] The only exception that comes to mind is the coverage of mafia news by specialized reporters on large New York publications: *The New York Times*, the New York *Daily News*, the *New York Post*, the *Wall Streeet Journal*, and *Newsday*.

[9] There was an occasional fourth source: phone calls from the police.

cidents which, I assume, the police considered "strange" and consequently of interest to the media (for example, a bus stolen, the theft of a large amount of poisons, a man threatening to set himself on fire, a person crushed by an elevator, and the discovery of a disembodied head.)

The first thing worth noting about the police wire is that it does *not* contain: incidents of price-fixing, consumer fraud, sub-standard housing, unhealthy food, environmental pollution, political bribery and corruption, and the like. None appear in this pool of crime incidents from which crime waves arise, yet all of these may occur enough to constitute a crime wave if the media were to have routine access to knowledge of their occurrence.

One reason why these do not appear over the police wire is that agencies other than the city police enforce the laws governing these kinds of crime. Because police manpower is devoted to street crimes, it is street crime reports that the police wire carries. If journalists are to report other kinds of crime, they must draw on other sources (usually the wire services and other media organizations) which provide instances of such crime only sporadically.

Moreover, in the police wire one is unable to find a number of very common crimes which local police *do* know about, but consider "uninteresting" and, thus, not worth transmitting to the media.[10] These included what journalists told me were "too common" to be news: everything from bicycle theft, liquor store stick-ups and rapes, to wife beating, child molesting and other "family matters" not resulting in homicide or hospitalization.

It is likely that a large number of the street crimes reported over the police wire were, in fact, family disputes, crimes against women, and racial conflict. But it was difficult to tell this from the information in the crime dispatches. This is particularly true of the large number of shootings and stabbings, which reporters tended to ignore.

Any descriptive features in a crime dispatch provide important clues to newsworkers looking for themes in crimes. From reading the police wire, I was struck by the lack of detail. Victims, if they were identified at all, and if they were persons not businesses, were identified by sex and age. When more was told, they were described as: (1) "elderly" (for homicides and robberies), (2) policemen (for any assaults), or (3) banks (for robberies). Perpetrators (and in the police wire these were always persons, not businesses) were usually identified by sex and a specific age. When more was said, it was almost always in connection with a "youth gang" or the offender's youth. Victim-offender relationships were rarely mentioned. It was quite difficult to identify cases where the victim and offender knew each other. Thus the police wire gives one the impression most crimes occur between strangers. Finally, the location of a crime was usually provided in terms of a specific address or intersection. But a *type* of location was mentioned only when it could be said the incident occurred in a public or semi-public place, for example, a street, a subway, a schoolyard, or an apartment hallway.

Thus, the kinds of crime items and the descriptions of them in the police wire support only special sorts of crime themes that journalists may report. Crime in public places, crimes between strangers, and crime specific to age are themes that the police wire can and does provide numerous instances of. "Crimes against the elderly" is one theme that has already blossomed into a crime wave with the help of the police wire. But other themes such as "youth gang crime," "subway crime," and "school yard crime," have an excellent chance of becoming new crime waves.

Apparently, the police who transmit crime dispatches to the media select incidents that they think will interest journalists. This crite-

---

[10]There were some exceptions. A handful of common crimes did appear over the police wire (e.g., four rapes in a thirty day observation period). The journalist I observed could not explain why these were there, and they ignored them.

rion of selectivity has two consequences, both keeping the present image of "serious crime" from changing in the news. First, when the police perceive that the media are interested in a certain type of crime (for example, crimes against the elderly), they include instances of it in the police wire whenever they can. Thus, the police bolster emerging crime waves as long as those waves pertain to crimes the police routinely detect (that is, street crime). Second, the police decide what the media are interested in on the basis of what the media have reported before.

The police-supplied incidents that make up the media's crime wave pool all support prevailing notions of "serious crime." The crime wave pool leads the media to reproduce a common image that "real crime" is crime on the streets, crime occurring between strangers, crime which brutalizes the weak and defenseless, and crime perpetrated by vicious youths. Such crimes exist, but this imagery becomes *the only reality of crime* which people will take seriously because it is the only reality impressed upon them in the media. And it is the only reality news workers are able to report continuously as themes in crime, and, periodically, as full-scale crime waves.

THE ROLE OF AUTHORITIES

I have described the crime wave pool as if it were only composed of crime incidents. This description is only partially true. During the initial phase of crime waves, media organizations mostly report crime incidents as instances of their theme-becoming-a-wave. But as soon as a crime theme looks like it is catching on and becoming a wave, journalists have another kind of news to report: the response of politicians, police, and other officials.

The first signs of New York's crime wave against the elderly appeared in the last week of October 1976, when the city's media began reporting incidents of crime against old people. There was widespread coverage of three inci-

dents: the murder of two aged sisters in their Bronx apartment, the rape-murder of an eighty-five-year-old Manhattan woman, and the release on fifty dollars bail of a youth who beat an elderly person. After this third incident, the first official response appeared: Mayor Beame called a news conference and, with the Police Commissioner at his side, he vowed to make the city safe for old people by beefing up the police's Senior Citizens Robbery Unit and by working for reforms in the criminal justice system. From this point on, "crimes against the elderly" became a favorite topic for political rhetoric and proposed reforms.

Starting from the very first week of the crime wave, the media could report both crimes against the elderly *and* stories of what the authorities were saying and doing about it. The entire wave was bolstered throughout its seven week course by coverage of official statements, possible reforms of the criminal justice system, legislative debate and action, the formation of new police programs, and community conferences on the problem. These kinds of stories made up thirty-five percent of the crime-wave-related news published during the period.

Officials and authorities were willing to assume from the outset that the crime wave represented something real or, at least, they were unwilling to express any doubts in public, Thus, by making public statements and taking official action on the basis of this assumption, authorities made the wave look even more real. And they guaranteed that the wave would go on for some time. As official responses to "the problem" trailed off in mid-December, so did the number of crime incidents known to the media from the police wire and other police sources. The wave finally died.

It is clear that officials with a stake in "doing something" about crime, have power over crime waves. Whether or not they· inspire crime waves, they can attempt to redirect the focus of coverage of a crime wave already being reported. Nowhere is this clearer than in the first four weeks of *Daily News* coverage of the wave of crimes against the elderly. *News* headlines during the first week emphasized "the problem," citing instance after instance. But in the next three weeks the stories (starting with the Mayor's first press conference) shifted focus to "what is being done about the problem."

Politicians and police use their news-making power to channel the coverage of social problems into a definite direction (Molotch and Lester, 1974): news of the problem becomes news of how the system is working to remedy the situation. Authorities may also use their newsmaking powers to stop certain crime themes from becoming crime waves. There is tentative data indicating that another crime theme, "crimes on the subways," was stopped from becoming a full-scale crime wave by the New York City Transit Authority.

In the third week of February 1977, the *Daily News*, the *New York Post*, and WAVE all suddenly increased their coverage of murders and muggings in subways. In the middle of that week the Police Chief of the Transit Authority told a *Daily News* reporter there was no crime wave and, soon thereafter, three senior Transit officials called a news conference to assert that the subways were safer than the city streets. From that point on, coverage of subway crime steadily decreased to its pre-wave level.

If an unwanted crime wave should arise, officials can use their newsmaking powers to deny the wave's existence or to redirect crime coverage into a "safe" direction. There is some evidence, however, that crimes against the elderly was not an "unwanted crime wave"—at least for some officials in the New York City Police Department.

The *Daily News* reporter who wrote the feature articles which turned out to be the beginning of the crime wave, told me that he received "considerable help" from the Senior Citizens Robbery Unit, whose job it was to catch muggers and murderers of the elderly (and the same unit that the Mayor expanded early in the crime wave). On October 7, the reporter first wrote a story on two crimes with

elderly victims that appeared over the police wire on the same day. This story was published October 8, two weeks before the wave. At that time, a *Daily News* editor thought it would be a good idea for the reporter to do a series of feature stories on "this kind of crime." (Such features had shown up periodically in other media organizations before.)

While he was first researching these feature stories, the reporter was in frequent contact with S.C.R.U. This police unit let him know they felt beleaguered, under-staffed, and that they were fighting a battle that deserved more attention. (According to the reporter, "They proselytized a lot.") After he had written his feature stories, police from S.C.R.U. began calling him whenever they knew of a mugging or murder of an elderly person. This enabled the reporter to follow up his series with reports of specific crime incidents. Finally, it was S.C.R.U. which first told the reporter about the youth who was let out on fifty dollars bail after beating an elderly person. All major media in New York quickly picked up this story after the *News* reported it. At that point, the crime wave had begun.

I do not want to assert that from this brief history of one crime wave all waves are inspired by the police or politicians. It is not that simple. The crime wave against the elderly in New York seems to have resulted from a mixture of happenstance and police assistance. The history of this crime wave, however, does show that officials can and do use their positions to nurture fledgling crime themes first identified by journalists. Equally, they may use their positions to deny the reality of crime waves.

SUMMARY AND CONCLUSIONS

Crime waves begin as crime themes that journalists perceive in the process of organizing and selecting news to be presented to a public. Because journalists depend on one another for their sense of "what news," a crime theme can spread throughout a community of news organizations. As each news organization sees the theme presented by other organizations, they learn to use the theme and present it in their news.

But for this crime wave dynamic to occur, journalists must be able to associate a crime theme with a continuous supply of incidents that can be seen as instances of the theme. Media organizations know of crime almost exclusively through law enforcement agencies. The media's major sources of supply for crime incidents in New York City is the N.Y.P.D.'s police wire. Crime dispatches over this wire are largely reports of street crimes: robberies, burglaries, shootings, stabbings, and other assaults. These constitute a pool of potential crime waves, excluding the possibility of certain themes. Non-street crime themes, if they were to receive massive publicity as crime waves, might challenge prevailing notions of "serious crime" in this society.

Moreover, once crime themes receive heavy coverage in the media, authorities can use their power to make news in an attempt to augment, modify, or deny a burgeoning crime wave. Thus, official sources not only control the supply of raw materials upon which crime news is based, but also the growth of crime waves.

While this study has dealt with the generation of crime waves, the news-making processes it reveals have broad implications. News plays a crucial role in formulating public issues and events, and in directing their subsequent course. Just as the interplay between local politics and local media organizations brought about New York City's crime wave, so the interplay between national elites and national media organizations may well have given rise to a number of social issues now widely accepted as fixtures in the recent American political scene.

Consider Watergate. As a few investigative reporters persisted in digging up news about the illegal activities of the Nixon administration, national elites competed among one another to halt, support, or redefine the growing Watergate news theme. Eventually, special prosecutors and Congressional committees were formed; that is, a bureaucratic apparatus was set up which began to feed the media with fresh instances of the Watergate theme. Once Nixon was deposed, this apparatus was dismantled, and so was the Watergate "news wave."

Watergate, the Bert Lance affair, the "death" of political activism of the 1960's, and many other accepted political "realities" may have been produced by the same ideological machinery that underlies crime waves.

REFERENCES

Biderman, Albert, Louise Johnson, Jennie McIntyre, and Adrianne Weir (1967). "Report on a Pilot Study in the District of Columbia on Victimization and Attitudes Toward Law Enforcement." Washington, D.C.: U.S. Government Printing Office.

Davis F. James (1952). "Crime News in Colorado Newspapers." *American Journal of Sociology* **57**:325–30.

Epstein, Edward Jay (1973). *News From Nowhere.* New York: Random House.

Glasgow Media Group (1976). "Bad News." *Theory and Society* **3**:339–63.

Molotch, Harvey and Marilyn Lester. (1974). "News as Purposive Behavior: the Strategic Use of Routine Events, Accidents, and Scandals." *American Sociological Review* **39**:101–12.

Roshier, Bob. (1973). "The Selection of Crime News in the Press." Pp. 28–39 in S. Cohen and J. Young (eds.). *The Manufacture of News.* Beverly Hills: Sage.

Sacks, Harvey (1972). "On the Analyzability of Stories by Children." Pp. 325–45 in J. Gumperz and D. Hymes (eds.). *Direction in Sociolinguistics.* New York: Holt, Rinehart and Winston.

Smith, Dorothy, (1972). "The Ideological Practice of Sociology." Unpublished paper, Department of Sociology, University of British Columbia.

Steffens, Lincoln (1931). *The Autobiography of Lincoln Steffens.* New York: Harcourt Brace.

Tuchman, Gaye (1973). "Making News by Doing Work: Routinizing the Unexpected." *American Journal of Sociology* **79**:110–31.

3

CRIMINAL VICTIMIZATION SURVEYS

JAMES P. LEVINE

The criminal victimization survey is being used increasingly as an alternative or supplement to reported crime data in assessing the seriousness of crime in various localities (U.S. Department of Justice, 1975) and in evaluating the effectiveness of particular crime prevention programs and policies (Kelling et al., 1974). Although this procedure for measuring crime is rather costly, it has several properties which have made it quite attractive to those engaged in criminal justice research. The most obvious advantage of this method is that it detects the apparently substantial number of crimes that are not reported to the police—what has been called "the dark figure of crime" (Biderman and Reiss, 1967). Indeed, national and city crime rates projected from survey data are roughly twice as high as those based on reported crimes which are summarized annually by the FBI in the Uniform Crime Reports (U.S. Department of Justice, 1974a).

Not only do reported crime rates omit many crimes actually committed, but since the degree of underreporting can fluctuate both geographically and temporally, it is hazardous to make comparisons between areas or to discern

Source: "The Potential for Crime Overreporting in Criminal Victimization Surveys," *Criminology* (November 1976), 14:307–330. Reprinted by permission of the American Society of Criminology and of the Publisher, Sage Publications, Inc.

trends within areas on the basis of police reports (Kamisar, 1972). Many factors may cause this variation: the efficiency of police in discovering crime (Greenwood and Wadycki, 1973), the sophistication of police crime-reporting procedures, political and administrative pressure put on police officers to distort the true amount of crime by failing to record some crimes and misclassifying others (Seidman and Couzens, 1974; Milakovich and Weis, 1975), the amount of public confidence in the police, the varying legal definitions of crimes in different jurisdictions, and the extent to which victims of crime are insured and therefore specifically motivated to report crimes. Although Skogan's (1974) comparison of reported crime data and survey data in the large cities shows a moderate correspondence between the two measures, the study reaffirms that the magnitudes of crime yielded by both methods vary considerably.

Because survey research is constrained by a commonly accepted set of methodological rules and considerable administrative supervision (in the more sophisticated studies), it seems less likely that the amount of errors that do occur will change much from one survey to another. The reliability of properly conducted criminal victimization surveys is fairly high, so they are useful instruments with which to compare the crime rates of various communities and to assess the utility of alternative crime prevention programs.

UNDUE FAITH IN VICTIMIZATION SURVEYS

As valuable as crime surveys are, they present certain validity problems which proponents have tended to overlook. Just as unjustified faith is often placed in questionable economic indicators like the gross national product (Morgenstern, 1963) and the consumer price index (Samuelson, 1974), the victimization surveys have emerged as a kind of talisman—foolproof way of telling the *actual* amount of crime that is committed.

Although surveys of a socially complex phenomenon like crime are plagued by sampling difficulties and the intrusion of "response errors" arising out of the artificiality of the interview situation, the accuracy of results is rarely challenged. The language of research reports is infrequently qualified, and the findings have been uncritically accepted by both professionals dealing with law enforcement and the lay public.

Thus, a Law Enforcement Assistant Administration study reports on the basis of about 10,000 personal interviews that "250,000 incidents of rape, assault, robbery, burglary, or larceny *occurred* in San Jose during 1970; 140,000 *occurred* in Dayton" (italics added; U.S. Department of Justice, 1974b). Likewise, an earlier study conducted under the auspices of the President's Commission on Law Enforcement and the Administration of Justice was said to "show that the *actual amount* of crime in the United States is several times that reported in the Uniform Crime Reports" (italics added; President's Commission . . ., 1967:21).

Even less cautious are the words of two legal scholars who state that "these [victimization] studies *unanimously agree* that *the actual rate* [of crime] *is* several times greater than that shown in the *Uniform Crime Reports*" (italics added; Center and Smith, 1973: 1045). Ironically, this comment is included in an analysis of the value

of the Uniform Crime reports entitled "Criminal Statistics—Can They Be Trusted?" The question is a good one, but it must be directed at the new methods of crime measurement as well as the old.

The so-called unreported crime uncovered in the surveys may well include many "crimes" that never took place at all, and the "gap" between reported and unreported crime may be more aptly interpreted as the difference between two fallible measurement techniques rather than a showing of a massive failure of victims to notify police. Whereas Thompson (1971: 457), in characterizing survey findings, asserts "that there is at least twice as much crime than is ever reported to police," it is equally logical to reach the opposite conclusion that only half as much crime ever occurs as is reported to interviewers. In reality, neither of these statements is probably correct: while police reports no doubt suffer from crime underreporting, surveys may be flawed by crime overreporting which leads to inflated crime rates.

Methodological evaluations of victimization surveys have emphasized factors that lead to omission of crimes, such as sampling biases (e.g., leaving out commuters in city surveys), "memory fading" (the inability of victims to recall crimes), and communications barriers between respondents and interviewers that inhibit free expression about personal matters such as crime. For example, "known victims" (i.e., those in police files) have been interviewed to ascertain what percentage revealed the crimes that have apparently been committed against them (U.S. Department of Justice, 1972).

There has been less attention paid to the reverse problem of overreporting—the inclusion in survey results of non-criminal events that have been misrepresented as crimes.[1] There

---

[1] Thus, a recent 270-page report of the Law Enforcement Assistance Administration analyzing surveys of the "National Crime Panel" conducted in 13 cities treats the problem of response error in a total of two sentences (U.S., Department of Justice, 1975: 257).

are three central participants in surveys whose actions may distort results—the respondents themselves, the interviewers, and the coders of the data. How each of them may contribute to excessively high crime figures will now be discussed.

FALSE REPORTING BY RESPONDENTS

Response invalidity is a persistent problem in survey research. Not only do respondents often conceal real opinions and attitudes, but they frequently give incorrect information when asked for seemingly innocuous factual information. Indeed, two social psychologists who

are authorities on interviewing reach the following sobering conclusion (Cannel and Kahn, 1968: 548):

> We believe that the generalization to be made with the greatest confidence is that significant problems of invalidity and unreliability are common in interview data, even for apparently simple questions asked under conditions of obvious legitimacy.

Numerous studies have shown high levels of error when attempts are made to verify survey responses by the use of behavioral indicators. Table I is a compilation of research findings demonstrating significant deviation

TABLE I   Invalid Factual Information Given by Respondents in Various Social Surveys

Study	Factual item	Verification source	Sample size	Percent of respondents giving incorrect information
Hyman (1944)	Whether grocers put up government posters they receive	Visual observation of premises	221	42
Parry & Crossley (1950)	Whether Denver residents voted in all six recent elections	Official voting records	Unclear	46[a]
Goddard, Broder, Wenar (1961)	When children of clinic users were vaccinated	Clinic records	20	80
Lansing, Ginsburg, Braaten (1961:64)	Amount of money in savings account	Bank records	109	47[b]
Lansing, Ginsburg, Braaten (1961:97)	Whether debtors had outstanding cash loan	Creditors' records	94	61
David (1962)	Amount of money given to welfare recipients	Official records	46	63[c]
Udry & Morris (1967)	Whether women had sexual intercourse on previous day	Urine analysis (check for semen)	15	20
Tittle & Hill (1967)	Whether students voted in student elections	Actual voting records	301	9
Hagburg (1968)	Number of class sessions attended by adult students	Instructors' attendance records	227	64.
Weiss (1968)	Whether children of welfare mothers had failed grades	School records	680	37

[a] For each election, incorrect responses ranged from 14 percent to 29 percent.

[b] Answers were considered incorrect if respondents failed to mention an existing account or failed to state the correct amount in the account within $1,000 of the true balance.

[c] Answers were considered incorrect if respondents failed to admit receiving welfare or there was more than a 10 percent discrepancy between the amount given and the amount reported.

between facts articulated by respondents and independent measures of the same phenomena. The wide range of topics concerning which incorrect responses were given raises questions about the authenticity of crimes described to interviewers. If people are not trustworthy in talking about their voting behavior, financial position, business practices, sex lives, and the academic progress of their children, then surely we should not take for granted their reporting of crime.

There are specific attributes of the victimization survey which render reports of crime particularly suspect. Not only may respondents purposely fabricate incidents, but they may unintentionally provide false information by wrongfully interpreting misfortunes that befall them as crimes, by misunderstanding the legal definition of crimes, or by forgetting exactly when crimes occurred. Each of these processes may artificially inflate crime data and it is therefore important that they be understood.

MISTAKEN INTERPRETATION OF INCIDENTS AS CRIMES

Epistemologists have gone to great lengths to explain that all human observations entail the making of inferences. Hanson (1958: 7) expresses this idea glibly, but accurately: "There is more to see than meets the eyeball." The shapes, sounds, colors, and textures we perceive are interpreted according to our theories and intuitions about how the world functions.

The subjectivity of perceptions surely affects whether certain harms that are experienced are conceived of as criminal in nature or are thought to result from less malevolent forces, like bad luck or personal negligence. Of course some events, like armed bank robberies, leave little room for varying hypotheses—they are clearly crimes. On the other hand, many occurrences are more mysterious in nature, requiring the victim to use his own judgment to figure out what happened. Many incidents which are honestly thought of as crimes by

respondents may well have been misconstrued because the victim either lacks sufficient information to understand the situation correctly or jumps to improper conclusions in assessing the evidence available to him.

Examples of this type of error abound. A broken house window may be thought of as evidence of an attempted burglary when the damage was really caused by a baseball thrown by children playing in the street. The wallet presumed to have been stolen by a pickpocket may have been accidentally left on a store counter. A woman may perceive sexual advances as an attempted rape when in fact the man involved had every intention of stopping if the woman seriously objected. Respondents may report all of these matters as crimes when something quite different has really transpired.

There are various reasons why people might make such mistakes. A generalized fear of crime may lead some to paranoid interpretations of unsettling experiences. If criminals are thought to be lurking everywhere, it is only natural to blame them when something goes awry.

Even relatively calm people are capable of serious misperceptions when they are in distress. The accuracy of observations is diminished under conditions of high emotion (Cannel and Kahn, 1968: 543), so it is quite possible that someone who is upset about a loss or injury or who feels uncomfortable in an alien environment may have his perceptions impaired. This blurring of perception was most tragically demonstrated during the Detroit riots in 1967 when police and national guardsmen wound up shooting each other because the panic which seized them lessened their ability to discriminate law-breakers from law-enforcers; "snipers" often turned out to be colleagues (National Advisory Commission on Civil Disorders, 1968: 97–104). This was an extreme situation, but even in less dire circumstances people who are searching for an explanation of otherwise inexplicable events may well distort, embellish, or completely imagine facets to convince themselves and others that they have been victims of crimes.

INCORRECT CLASSIFICATION OF INCIDENTS AS CRIMES

It is virtually impossible to construct survey instruments that communicate the same specific meaning of questions to each and every respondent. Asking the seemingly simple question, "Which magazines have you read in the past seven days?" can evoke a variety of ideas because the verb "read" can be understood to mean glanced at, skimmed, thoroughly perused, or studied in detail. Likewise, an Englishman asked how often he has tea might think of the beverage, or a late afternoon snack, or the main evening meal, or an elegant Sunday repast. No amount of care and qualification in question-wording can totally eliminate the ambiguities of human speech.

Consequently, questions asked in crime surveys may elicit quite different recollections from different people. Because of misunderstanding, respondents may volunteer incidents that fall *outside* the category of events intended to be covered by the questions. Even when complex legal definitions of crimes are painstakingly translated into laymen's language, there remains ample room for confusion. This is demonstrated by studies showing that even the slightest changes in the wording or ordering of questions on victimization can affect the nature of responses (Reiss, 1967: 148–149).

For example, one question used on the Census Bureau interview schedule asks: "Did anyone beat you up, attack you, or hit you with something such as a rock or a bottle?" This attempt to determine whether the respondent has been assaulted may bring forth many noncriminal events because "attack" can be broadly construed to mean being chased, cursed, nudged, jostled, bumped, or impeded. Those who are hypersensitive to victimization might relate all kinds of encounters which fail to satisfy the legal requirements of assault.

Moreover, certain responses that are given presume a knowledge of legal nuances which may be lacking. One of the Census Bureau crime incident questions asks: "How did the person(s) attack you?" and one of the choices is "raped" or "tried to rape." To accept the alleged victim's designation of her experience as a rape ignored the fact that this crime is fraught with complexities—requiring the presence of several elements (force or the threat of it, penetration, and so on) and permitting a host of legal defenses (consent, mistake, and the like). Many women who think and say that they are raped are wrong because they have a mistaken understanding of the law. In many cases they may have been offended, insulted, mistreated, or abused; but legally they have not been raped and it is erroneous to include their misfortunes when measuring crime.

The extent of popular misconceptions about what constitutes a crime is indicated by Ennis's (1967: 90–93) study in which trained evaluators scrutinized the reports of 3296 cases of alleged criminal victimization mentioned by respondents in a national survey. Over one-third (34.9%) of all the events initially recorded as crimes were disqualified because the facts averred by respondents were insufficient to meet the criteria defining a criminal act. This is a problem which continuously confronts and frustrates police who are frequently asked by distraught people to intervene in disputes or disorders where no infraction of criminal law has occurred and police action is inappropriate. Laymen who are untutored in law are simply not competent to make conclusive judgments about whether they have been criminally victimized.

Respondent ignorance about the law may result in bona fide crimes being classified as more serious than they really are. Thus, the definition of aggravated assault used in the Law Enforcement Administration surveys requires that victims be injured from a weapon or "seriously" injured from a weaponless attacker (U.S. Department of Justice, 1974b: 74).

A person who discovers some ugly bruises the day after being hit may truly think he was quite badly hurt and therefore describe his injury as serious, but the damage inflicted upon him may have been insufficient for labeling the assault as aggravated.

All of this reflects an even more profound taxonomy problem. What is called criminal behavior is partially the result of social norms defining deviant behavior, and in practice communities regularly modify the criminal law "on the books" tolerating certain kinds of conduct which are technically illegal (Wheeler, 1967). Victimization surveys, on the other hand, are designed to produce a recitation of a broad spectrum of crime-related life experiences many of which were not originally very disturbing to those affected and therefore of questionable relevance to crime statistics.

Thus, while almost any nonaccidental, unprovoked shove is an assault, there are innumerable such infractions which are shrugged off as minor annoyances by those who are victimized (such as the aggressiveness of rush-hour subway riders competing for empty seats). Likewise, if neighborhood children abscond with odd change left on a table after an afternoon of play, most people sustaining the loss would hesitate to identify their actions as larceny. Many of these kinds of matters may be recounted as crimes in response to the thorough cross-examination of interviewers even though they were conceived of as minor irritations when they first happened.

In fact, the most common reason given by respondents for not reporting crimes to police is that they were not very important or the damage done was negligible (U.S. Department of Justice, 1974a: 5). More than half of the unreported crimes detected in the San Jose and Dayton surveys involved larcenies of less than $50.00 (U.S. Department of Justice, 1974b: 24). What this implies is that many trivial grievances which stay out of police records because people are not very upset are elevated to criminal status by the aggressive probing and searching of interviewers.

As Lejins (1966: 1018) correctly notes, regarding such minor incidents as crimes runs contrary to a fundamental juridical precept— *de minimus non curat lex* (i.e., the law does not concern itself with trifles). The legal system itself routinely countenances many criminal acts that are deemed insignificant: citizens refuse to sign complaints, police fail to intervene, prosecutors dismiss charges, and juries acquit defendants whose guilt seems undeniable. If the commission of many offenses does not warrant judicial interest and disapproval, it is questionable whether these acts deserve to be counted as crimes at all. Since survey findings seem to include many of these trivial occurrences, the results are highly skewed and give an unrealistically grim portrayal of the crime problem.

MEMORY FAILURES ABOUT WHEN CRIMES OCCURRED

It is commonplace for people who have experienced some dreadful event to say that it seems like "just yesterday" when it happened. Traumatic crimes are no doubt imprinted in victims' minds and there may well be a convergence of the *immediate* recollection of what took place and the *past* occurrence of the incident. This may result in a tendency to erroneously remember the crime as having taken place more recently than was actually the case. The potential for this kind of mistake is small if respondents were asked whether they were victimized in the last 24 hours or even the past week, but in order to keep the numbers in the sample of respondents down to an economically feasible size, most surveys use a time period of 12 months, which seems too long to expect reliable recall about the date when a crime transpired.

Memory fallibility about the timing of events is indicated by a study in which husbands and wives were separately asked when they moved into the local community and considerable disparity emerged in their answers even though they were reporting the same event (Asher, 1974: 476). More direct evidence of the forward telescoping of earlier crimes into a more recent time frame was adduced in a Washington, D.C. study in which it was estimated that 17% of crimes recalled by respondents actually took place before the six-month cutoff point (Skogan, 1975: 27).

An additional test of this phenomenon is provided by the Dayton-San Jose crime surveys conducted in January and February 1971. The number of incidents identified as having occurred in the first half of 1970 was much lower than the number alleged to have taken place in the last half of the year (U.S. Department of Justice, 1974b: 37). Some of this difference may be explained by the failure of victims to remember crimes in the first six months ("memory fading"), but no doubt some of the crimes placed by respondents in the last six months actually occurred earlier.

These temporal errors can significantly increase the crime rates based on survey data. Surely some crimes that took place prior to the time period under consideration are inaccurately moved ahead by respondents and therefore improperly recorded. For the few months immediately preceding the time period of the survey, the number of such mistakes may be quite high. Indeed, Biderman (1970: 2) points out that those interviewed may unconsciously shift earlier crimes into the time period under study to avoid the uneasy experience of giving a long series of negative answers to questions about victimization (which are thought to be disturbing to the interviewer).

Since there is no very feasible way of detecting these errors, many are wrongly included in the calculation of annual crime rates. Official crime data, in contrast, is not subject to this kind of error because most reports to police are made very soon after crimes actually happen.

LYING

It is obvious that some victims may intentionally conceal crimes when interrogated by interviews for the same reasons that they sometimes do not file reports with police (embarrassment, fear of repercussions, and the like). What is less clear is the opposite possibility—deliberate fabrication of crimes that never occurred or lying about the gravity of genuine crimes. Just as the self-serving lies and evasions of businessmen often make a mockery of economic data based on information garnered from them (Morgenstern, 1963: 17–28), the respondents in victimization surveys may have good reasons for concocting false stories about crime.

The very characteristics of the survey method which enable it to uncover some crimes that victims do not report to the police can operate to encourage falsification of crimes. Guarantees of anonymity and the unofficial nature of responses may encourage some victims to talk who would otherwise remain silent, but by the same token these factors provide conditions of impunity for those who dishonestly manufacture or exaggerate incidents. Whereas falsely reporting a crime to police or knowingly giving false information about crimes is a criminal offense in most jurisdictions that can result in imprisonment, no such consequences face those who lie to interviewers.

Various motivations might inspire such lying. A number of respondents may pervert the truth in an attempt to justify false insurance claims or illegitimate income tax deductions. Some may overstate the seriousness of the crime in order to gain the sympathy of the interviewer. Others may think of themselves as performing a social service by dramatizing the crime problem, perhaps feeling that it is unjust that lucky people like themselves who have managed to escape crime were selected for the survey while so many less fortunate acquaintances who *were* victimized were left out.

Role expectations may prompt falsification. Respondents may feel obligated to give the interviewer what they think he is seeking—a showing of as much crime as possible. Such sentiments are likely to be accentuated among those included in the National Crime Panel, a national probability sample being reinterviewed by the Law Enforcement Assistance Administration every six months about victimization. Panel members may think that they are failing to do the job for which they were chosen if they regularly fail to report any crime. This kind of "panel conditioning" affects many long-term surveys in which respondents who are periodically reinterviewed wind up reporting things as they think they should rather than as they are (Moser and Kalton, 1972: 142).

Thus, there is good reason to doubt the authenticity of many allegations of victimization made in surveys. It has been estimated that as many as one-third of the complaints made to the police are "unfounded," i.e., without sufficient basis in fact or law to constitute crime (Cameron, 1972: 317; Center and Smith, 1973: 1078). In the less revealing context of the survey, we would a fortiori expect an even greater number of wrongful reports. Response error in crime surveys is a formidable problem.

INTERVIEWER BIASES

Interviewers are another source of errors in surveys. It is well documented that survey responses are affected by the characteristics of the interviewers and the nature of their interactions with respondents (Kish, 1962; Phillips and Clancy, 1972; Cosper, 1972; Williams, 1968). The demeanor of the interviewer, his rapport with respondents, the way he phrases questions, and the manner in which he clarifies ambiguities are all potentially biasing factors. The fact that the identical survey instrument is used by all interviewers in no way precludes them from wittingly or unwittingly cuing respondents to answer in an particular way.

Moreover, there is always the possibility that the interviewer will blatantly tamper with the findings by recording answers incorrectly or making up the answers to questions they do not ask. This has been aptly referred to as "the cheater problem in polling" (Crespi, 1945).

These problems could be discounted if it could be assumed that biases in one direction caused by some interviewers were simply cancelled out by the opposite kind of bias introduced by other interviewers. If an equal amount of overreporting and underreporting is encouraged by interviewers, the net result would not grossly distort reality. However, it is more plausible that interviewer bias in victimization surveys is unevenly balanced in its impact and systematically tends to engender abnormally high levels of crime reporting.

The major reason is interviewer self-interest. As Roth (1966) has so trenchantly argued, paid employees who engage in social research are, like many other workers, most concerned with keeping their jobs, avoiding work that is unpleasant, and giving the boss what he wants. Interviewers who must engage in the same repetitive task on a daily basis and who presumably receive relatively little intrinsic job satisfaction are unlikely to be intensely committed to the canons of scientific objectivity. On the contrary, they may act in a fashion designed to please their superiors by producing results in keeping with what they think is most advantageous to the organization for which they are working.

Prodding respondents to mention crimes or distorting their responses to registering crimes can accomplish two self-serving purposes. It reduces the tedium of a steady stream of negative answers which makes the interview session itself rather dull, and it promotes results that are consonant with the ultimate purpose of the study. Since the development of victimization surveys has been predicated on the assumption that a vast number of crimes go unreported, it is essential to find evidence of such crimes in order to justify continuance of this costly method of crime accounting. If official crime data were nearly equivalent to that reported in surveys, there would be little sense in expending substantial funds merely to replicate statistics already gathered by police in the course of their normal duties.

In a practical sense, thousands of jobs are dependent on a showing of more crime than has been previously reported. The National Crime Panel of the Law Enforcement Assistance Administration is composed of literally tens of thousands of respondents and therefore creates a huge number of interviewing jobs. Discovery of high crime rates well above those based on police data confirms the importance of these interviews, while contrary findings may raise doubts about the wisdom of continuing such endeavors and the organizations which carry them out. From academicians who direct and analyze crime surveys to the rank-in-file workers in the "field," all those benefiting from such projects have a stake in the framing of favorable results. While rigor and impartiality compose one set of norms governing any polling organization, "the more crime, the better" is likely to become a countervailing institutional ethos.

Consequently, it is not surprising that interviewers who were required in a 1967 National Opinion Research Center survey to judge the accuracy of respondents statements on the basis of intangible factors such as facial expression and speech hesitancy found very few of the crime anecdotes told to them to be questionable. The fact that interviewers had reservations about the authenticity or exactitude of fewer than one-half of 1% of the crimes reported (Biderman, 1967: 36) suggests that the presumed interest of those in charge to boost the amount of crime detected is well appreciated by those responsible for collecting the data.

Even if interviewers are scrupulously dedicated to the professional norm of neutrality, they are still bound to be subconsciously affected by the "expectation bias" that to a greater or lesser extent affects all kinds of behavioral research. Some of the most rigorously controlled experiments on both humans and animals in which the discretion of the researcher would seem to be insignificant have been shown to be influenced by a priori predictions about results (Rosenthal, 1966). Since the post hoc nature of surveys makes them an intrinsically sloppier method of data collection, the opportunity for interviewer expectations to distort outcomes would seem to be even

greater, and several studies have indeed demonstrated the intrusion of this kind of error (Smith and Hyman, 1950; Wyatt and Campbell, 1950).

A striking manifestation of this phenomenon occurred in the 1948 preelection polling done by the American Institute of Public Opinion which indicated a Dewey landslide in the Presidential race. In a subsequent post mortem to determine where the survey went wrong, some interviewers revelaed that they anticipated a Dewey sweep and therefore created an informal "quota" system for themselves according to which they would try to bring in a relatively high proportion of pro-Dewey answers each day. When they failed to meet their daily target, they felt as if somehow they were doing their job in an unsatisfactory manner (Hyman, 1954: 35–36).

The high amount of unrecorded crime commonly acknowledged and discovered in previous surveys is surely well known to interviewers. They may inadvertently strive to meet these levels by subtly ferreting out crimes from respondents who otherwise would have given negative answers. In all good conscience, interviewers may encourage more crime reporting than is warranted in order to produce outcomes consistent with past research and current hypotheses.

CODING UNRELIABILITY

Surveys evoke descriptions of harmful incidents experienced by respondents which must be assessed as to possible criminality and classified into various crime categories. It has been shown that even relatively simple coding tasks are characterized by low levels of intercoder reliability and therefore high degrees of measurement error (Crittenden and Hill, 1971). Where complex judgments are required, as is the case in coding victimization data, scientifically desired objectivity ought not be presumed. Because coders must make decisions solely on the basis of the unclear, incomplete accounts of respondents as filtered secondhand by interviewers, they inevitably play a role in determining the amount and kinds of crime ultimately extracted from interviews.

The unreliable quality of the coding process was demonstrated by one study in which the judgments of National Opinion Research Center coders was compared with that of detectives and lawyers who used the same interview data to decide whether respondents were criminally victimized. A great deal of dissensus emerged, with NORC coders disagreeing with the lawyers in 36% of the cases and with the police in 35% of the cases (Ennis, 1967:93).

This variation means that the crime designations made by coders are subject to the same biases that contaminate the interview stage of data collection. Like interviewers, coders also stand to gain if higher crime levels are found. Since there are many marginal cases of criminality that are reported and few precise coding guidelines, many "crimes" that emanate from the surveys may be artifacts of the coding process rather than legally recognizable criminal events.

MEASURING RESPONSE ERROR

Although response error is a thorny problem in the victimization survey, the overreporting biases discussed above are mainly conjectural. It is necessary to undertake research which confirms or rejects these hypotheses about the nature of errors so that crime rates based on survey results can be adjusted accordingly.

To measure response error, a sample of alleged victimizations could be thoroughly investigated for corroborating evidence about what happened, just as insurance companies try to verify claims made by policy holders who contend they were robbed or burglarized. Specifically, some respondents could be questioned in much greater detail than is ordinarily done in an attempt to expose incongruities or suspicious lapses of information. Also, relatives and associates of those claiming to have been victimized could be contacted to obtain validating information. While many minor

crimes are not discussed much by victims, it would seem normal for news of serious offenses to be communicated within the victim's circle of acquaintances, unless it is an embarrassing crime like rape where a great indignity was suffered.

Various checks can be made on interviewers to assess and control the quality of their work. Simply analyzing the variation in crime reporting among respondents questioned by different interviewers will determine whether individual propensities of interviewers are affecting outcomes, but it will not show whether there are biases common to all interviewers. Utilizing persons outside the polling organization to conduct some of the interviews and comparing the data which they amass with that produced by employees of the organization might bring forth evidence of systematic bias introduced by the entire regular interviewing contingent. Another monitoring technique is to use outsiders to revisit some respondents and repeat the interview to determine whether the same tale of crime is forthcoming.

The subjectivity of coders should also be evaluated. To detect variation in coders' inclinations, not only can different individuals be assigned to code some of the same interviews, but the aggregate results emerging from various coders can be compared. To check for nonrandom skewing of the data in the same direction by all employed coders, a subsample of completed questionnaires could be independently coded by personnel unaffiliated with victimization surveys who would seemingly have less incentive to prejudice outcomes.

CONCLUSION

Users of victimization surveys have been careless in reporting results without due regard for the many methodological weaknesses of survey research. It is not the occasional faux pas that is the problem but a range of distortions generated by all those involved in surveys which cumulatively may produce overblown crime rates out of proportion to the real level of crime.

In an area of research as fraught with measurement difficulties as the enumeration of crimes, it behooves us to use multiple indicators in an effort to get a best estimate of the "true" amount of crime. As Chilton and Spielberger (1972: 74) remark, "any single measure of crime will have serious disadvantages if it is used alone." In light of the underreporting of crime in official records and the apparent overcounting of surveys, a prudent course may be to average crime rates based on the two data sets to derive a reasonable approximation of the actual incidence of crime. Only an omniscient deity would be capable of providing an exact tabulation of crime, and in lieu of such an authoritative accounting it is probably most sensible to develop a crime index based on various admittedly faulty measures rather than to pretend that any single source of data provides a perfect image of reality.

Certainly skepticism is in order concerning the central finding of victimization surveys that massive amounts of crime go unreported to police. Uncritical acceptance of these dubious results has many untoward consequences which ought to be avoided. Not only is an already unnerved public likely to be further distraught about physical security, but unwise government policies may be adopted in response to these findings which purport to show so many more crimes than were previously thought to exist. In particular, additional funds may be allocated to law enforcement agencies to fight crime which might be spent better elsewhere, and civil liberties may be sacrificed on the basis of an exaggerated view of the crime peril. Finally, the growth of knowledge in the field of criminology will be retarded if unsound data is used to learn about the characteristics of victims, perpetrators, and crimes.

REFERENCES

Asher, H. (1974). "Some Consequences of Measurement Error in Survey Data." *Amer. J. of Pol. Sci.*, **18** (May): 469–485.

Biderman, A., (1970). Time Distortions of Victimization Data and Mnenomic Effects. Washington, D.C.: Bureau of Social Research.

—— (1967). "Surveys of Population Samples for Estimating Crime Incidence." *Annals of the Amer. Academy of Pol. and Social Sci.* **374** (November): 16–33.

—— and A. Reiss (1967). "On Exploring the 'Dark Figure' of Crime." *Annals of the Amer. Academy of Pol. and Social Sci.* **374** (November): 1–15.

Cameron, N (1972). "Lies, Damned Lies, and Statistics." *Victoria University of Wellington Law Rev.* 6 (August): 310–321.

Cannell, C, and R. Kahn (1968). "Interviewing," in G. Lindzey and E. Aronson (eds.) *The Handbook of Social Psychology, II.* Reading, Mass.: Addison-Wesley.

Center, L., and T. Smith (1973). "Criminal Statistics—Can They Be Trusted?" *Amer. Criminal Law Rev.* **11** (Summer): 1045–1086.

Chilton, R., and A. Spielberger (1972). "Increases in Crime: the Utility of Alternative Measures." *J. of Criminal Law, Criminology, and Police Sci.* **63** (March): 68–74.

Cosper, R. (1972). "Interviewing Effects in a Survey of Drinking Practices." *Soc. Q.* **13** (Spring): 228–236.

Crespi, L (1945). "The Cheater Problem in Polling." *Public Opinion Q.* **9** (Winter): 432–445.

Crittenden, K., and R. Hill (1971). "Coding Reliability and Validity of Interview Data." *Amer. Soc. Rev.* **36** (December): 1073–1080.

David, M. (1962). "The validity of income reported by a sample of families who received welfare assistance during 1959." *J. of the Amer. Statistical Association* **57** (March): 680–685.

Ennis, P. (1967). Criminal Victimization in the United States: A Report of a National Survey. Chicago: National Opinion Research Center.

Goddard, K., G. Broder, and C. Wenar (1961). "Reliability of Pediatric Histories: a Preliminary Study." *Pediatrics* **28** (December): 1011–1018.

Greenwood, M., and W. Wadycki (1973). "Crime Rates and Public Expenditures for Police Protection: Their Interaction." *Rev. of Social Economy* **31** (October): 138–151.

Hagburg, E. (1968). "Validity of Questionnaire Data: Reported and Observed Attendance in an Adult Education Program." *Public Opinion Q.* **32** (Fall): 453–455.

Hanson, N. R. (1958) *Patterns of Discovery*. England: Cambridge Univ. Press.

Hyman, H. (1954). *Interviewing in Social Research*. Chicago: Univ. of Chicago Press.

—— (1944). "Do they tell the truth?" *Public Opinion Q.* **8** (Winter): 557–559.

Kamisar, Y. (1972). "How to Use Abuse—and Fight Back with—Crime Statistics." *Oklahoma Law Rev.* **25** (May): 239–258.

Kelling, G., T., Pate, D. Dieckmann, and C. Brown (1974). *The Kansas City Preventative Patrol Experiment: A Summary Report*. Washington, D.C.: Police Foundation.

Kish, L. (1962). "Studies of Interviewer Variance on Attitudinal Variables." *J. of Amer. Statistical Association* **57** (March): 92–115.

Lansing, J., G. Ginsburg, and K. Braaten (1961). An Investigation of Response Error. Urbana: University of Illinois Bureau of Economic and Business Research.

Lejins, P. (1966). "Uniform Crime Reports." *Michigan Law Rev.* **64** (April: 1011–1030.

Milakovich, M., and K. Weis (1975). "Politics and Measures of Success in the War on Crime." *Crime and Delinquency* **21** (January): 1–10.

Morgenstern, O. (1963). *On the Accuracy of Economic Observations*. Princeton, N.J.: Princeton Univ. Press.

Moser, C. A., and G. Kalton (1972). *Survey Methods in Social Investigation*. New York: Basic Books.

National Advisory Commission on Civil Disorders (1968) Report. New York: Basic Books.

Parry, H., and H. Crossley (1950). "Validity of Responses to Survey Questions." *Public Opinion Q.* **14** (Spring): 61–80.

Phillips, D., and K. Clancy (1972). " 'Modeling Effects' in Survey Research." *Public Opinion Q.* **34** (Summer): 246–253.

President's Commission on Law Enforcement and Administration of Justice (1967). *The Challenge of Crime in a Free Society*. Washington, D.C.: Government Printing Office.

Reiss, A. (1967). "Measurement of the Nature and Amount of Crime," in President's Commission on Law Enforcement and Administration of Justice, *Studies in Crime and Law Enforcement in Major Metropolitan Areas: Field Surveys III*, Volume I. Washington, D.C.: Government Printing Office.

Rosenthal, R. (1966). *Experimenter Effects in Behavioral Research*. New York: Appleton-Century-Crofts.

Roth, J. (1966). "Hired Hand Research." *Amer. Sociologist* **1** (August): 190–196.

Samuelson, R. (1974). "Riding the Monthly Escalator: the Consumer Price Index." *New York Times Magazine* (December 8); 34–35.

Seidman, D., and M. Couzens (1974). "Getting the Crime Rate Down: Political Pressure and Crime Reporting." *Law and Society Rev.* **8** (Spring): 457–494.

Skogan, W. (1975). "Measurement Problems in Official and Survey Crime Rates." *J. of Criminal Justice* **3** (Spring): 17–31.

—— (1974). "The Validity of Official Crime Statistics: an Empirical Investigation." *Social Sci. Q.* **55** (June): 25–38.

Smith, H., and H. Hyman (1950). "The Biasing Effect of Interviewer Expectations on Survey Results." *Public Opinion Q.* **14** (Fall): 491–506.

Thompson, C. (1971). "Computerization of Criminal Law: Phase One—Criminal Statistics." *Indiana Legal Forum* **4** (Spring): 446–470.

Tittle, C., and R. Hill (1967). "The Accuracy of Self-Reported Data and Prediction of Political Activity." *Public Opinion Q.* **31** (Spring): 103–106.

Udry, J., and N. Morris (1967). "A Method for Validation of Reported Sexual Data." *J. of Marriage and Family Living* **29** (August): 442–446.

U.S. Department of Justice (1975). *Criminal Victimization Surveys in Thirteen American Cities*. Washington, D.C.: Law Enforcement Assistance Administration.

—— (1974a). *Crime in the Nation's Five Largest Cities*. Washington, D.C.: Law Enforcement Assistance Administration.

—— (1974b). *Crimes and Victims: A Report on the Dayton-San Jose Pilot Survey of Victimization*. Washington, D.C.: Law Enforcement Assistance Administration.

—— (1972). *San Jose Methods Test of Known Crime Victims*. Washington, D.C.: National Institute of Law Enforcement and Criminal Justice, Statistics Division.

Weiss, C. (1968). "Validity of Welfare Mothers' Interview Responses." *Public Opinion Q.* **32** (Winter): 622–633.

Wheeler, S. (1967). "Criminal Statistics: A Reformulation of the Problem." *J. of Criminal Law, Criminology, and Police Sci.* **58** (September) 317–324.

Williams, J. A. (1968). "Interviewer Role Performance: a Further Note on Bias in the Information Interview." *Public Opinion Q.* **32** (Summer): 287–294.

Wyatt, D., and D. Campbell (1950). "A Study of Interviewer Bias as Related to Interviewers' Expectations and Own Opinions." *Int'l J. of Opinion and Attitude Research* **4**: 77–83.

SECTION II

THEORIES OF CRIME

In this section we examine several relevant and still widely discussed theoretical explanations of delinquent and criminal behavior. Robert K. Merton's article on "Social Structure and Anomie" is a sociological classic. In it he describes the disproportionate relationship between two basic elements of the social structure: culturally approved goals and institutionalized means to these goals. In one mode of adjustment, innovation, lower-class boys are said to subject conventional means to success while, at the same time, accepting and desiring conventional economic goals and rewards; delinquency becomes a solution to otherwise insoluble problems.

This section concludes with three selections that represent controversial and opposing contemporary currents of thought in criminology. Unquestionably the most influential criminological model in recent years has been that of "radical criminology," offering, as it does, a neo-socialist-Marxist ideology of crime causation. One of the most preeminent and prolific proponents of this view is Richard Quinney who, in a selection from his *Class, State and Crime*, deals with the political economy of any specialist system which, he holds, is characterized by dominance and repression. Likewise, Jeffrey Reiman, in a subsequent selection, suggests that the criminal law (and by implication, establishment criminology) focuses on the individual—diverting attention from the evils of our capitalistic society and coming down hard on the poor but not the rich and powerful. Quite the opposite view is offered by van den Haag, who attacks, with some force, liberal sentiments that seem to favor the criminal instead of the victim or society. This view is less a systematic explanation of crime than an onslaught on the radical perspective.

4

SOCIAL STRUCTURE AND ANOMIE

ROBERT K. MERTON

There persists a notable tendency in sociological theory to attribute the malfunctioning of social structure primarily to those of man's imperious biological drives which are not adequately restrained by social control. In this view, the social order is solely a device for "impulse management" and the "social processing" of tensions. These impulses which break through social control, be it noted, are held to be biologically derived. Nonconformity is assumed to be rooted in original nature.[1] Conformity is by implication the result of an utilitarian calculus or unreasoned conditioning. This point of view, whatever its other deficiencies, clearly begs one question. It provides no basis for determining the nonbiological conditions which induce deviations from prescribed patterns of conduct. In this paper, it will be suggested that certain phases of social structure generate the circumstances in which infringement of social codes constitute a "normal" response.[2]

Source: "Social Structure and Anomie," *American Sociological Review* (October 1938), 3:672–682. Reprinted with permission.

[1] *E.g.*, Ernest Jones, *Social Aspects of Psychoanalysis*, 28, London, 1924. If the Freudian notion is a variety of the "original sin" dogma, then the interpretation advanced in this selection may be called the doctrine of "socially derived sin."

[2] "Normal" in the sense of a culturally oriented, if not approved, response. The statement does not deny the relevance of biological and personality differences which may be significantly involved in the *incidence* of deviate conduct. Our focus of interest is the social and cultural matrix; hence we abstract from other factors. It is in this sense, I take it, that James S. Plant speaks of the "normal reaction of normal people to abnormal conditions." See his *Personality and the Cultural Pattern*, 248, New York, 1937.

The conceptual scheme to be outlined is designed to provide a coherent, systematic approach to the study of socio-cultural sources of deviate behavior. Our primary aim lies in discovering how some social structures *exert a definite pressure* upon certain persons in the society to engage in nonconformist rather than conformist conduct. The many ramifications of the scheme cannot all be discussed; the problems mentioned outnumber those explicitly treated.

Among the elements of social and cultural structure, two are important for our purposes. These are analytically separable although they merge imperceptibly in concrete situations. The first consists of culturally defined goals, purposes, and interests. It comprises a frame of aspirational reference. These goals are more or less integrated and involve varying degrees of prestige and sentiment. They constitute a basic, but not the exclusive, component of what Linton aptly has called "designs for group living." Some of these cultural aspirations are related to the original drives of man, but they are not determined by them. The second phase of the social structure defines, regulates, and controls the acceptable modes of achieving these goals. Every social group invariably couples its scale of desired ends with moral or institutional regulation of permissible and required procedures for attaining these ends. These regulatory norms and moral imperatives do not necessarily coincide with technical or efficiency norms. Many procedures which form the standpoint of *particular individuals* would be most efficient in securing desired values, e.g., illicit oil-stock schemes, theft, fraud, are rules out of the institutional area of permitted conduct. The choice of expedients is limited by the institutional norms.

To say that these two elements, culture goals and institutional norms, operate jointly is not to say that the ranges of alternative behaviors and aims bear some constant relation to one another. The emphasis upon certain goals may vary independently of the degree of emphasis upon institutional means. There may develop a disproportionate, at times, a virtually exclusive, stress upon the value of specific goals, involving relatively slight concern with the institutionally appropriate modes of attaining these goals. The limiting case in this direction is reached when the range of alternative procedures is limited only by the technical rather than institutional considerations. Any and all devices which promise attainment of the all important goal would be permitted in this hypothetical polar case.[3] This constitutes one type

of cultural malintegration. A second polar type is found in groups where activities originally conceived as instrumental are transmuted into ends in themselves. The original purposes are forgotten and ritualistic adherence to institutionally prescribed conduct becomes virtually obsessive.[4] Stability is largely ensured while change is flouted. The range of alternative behaviors is severely limited. There develops a tradition-bound, sacred society characterized by neophobia. The occupational psychosis of the bureaucrat may be cited as a case in point. Finally, there are the intermediate types of groups where a balance between culture goals and institutional means is maintained. These are the significantly integrated and relatively stable, though changing, groups.

An effective equilibrium between the two phases of the social structure is maintained as long as satisfactions accrue to individuals who conform to both constraints, viz., satisfactions from the achievement of the goals and satisfactions emerging directly from the institutionally canalized modes of striving to attain these ends. Success, in such equilibrated cases, is twofold. Success is reckoned in terms of the product and in terms of the process, in terms of the outcome and in terms of activities. Continuing satisfactions must derive from sheer *participation* in a competitive order as well as from eclipsing one's competitors if the order itself is to be sustained. The occasional sacrifices involved in institutionalized conduct must be compensated by socialized rewards. The distribution of statuses and roles through competition must be so organized that positive incentives for conformity to roles and adherence to status obligations are provided *for every position* within the distributive order. Aberrant conduct, therefore, may be viewed as a symp-

---

[3] Contemporary American culture has been said to tend in this direction. See André Siegfried, *America Comes of Age,* 26–37, New York, 1927. The alleged extreme (?) emphasis on the goals of monetary success and material prosperity leads to dominant concern with technological and social instruments designed to produce the desired result, inasmuch as institutional controls become of secondary importance. In such a situation, innovation flourishes as the *range of means* employed is broadened. In a sense, then, there occurs the paradoxical emergence of "materialists" from an "idealistic" orientation. Cf. Durkheim's analysis of the cultural conditions which predispose toward crime and innovation, both of which are aimed toward efficiency, not moral norms. Durkheim was one of the first to see that "contrairement aux idées courantes le criminel n' apparait plus comme un être radicalement insociable, comme une sorte d'élément parasitaire, de corps étranger et inassimilable, introduit au sein de la société; c'est un agent régulier de la view sociale." See *Les Régles de la Méthode Sociologique,* 86–89, Paris, 1927.

[4] Such ritualism may be associated with a mythology which rationalizes these actions so that they appear to retain their status as means, but the dominant pressure is in the direction of strict ritualistic conformity, irrespective of such rationalizations. In this sense, ritual has proceeded farthest when such rationalizations are not even called forth.

ton of dissociation between culturally defined aspirations and socially structured means.

Of the types of groups which result from the independent variation of the two phases of the social structure, we shall be primarily concerned with the first, namely, that involving a disproportionate accent on goals. This statement must be recast in a proper perspective. In no group is there an absence of regulatory codes governing conduct, yet groups do vary in the degree to which these folkways, mores, and institutional controls are effectively integrated with the more diffuse goals which are part of the culture matrix. Emotional convictions may cluster about the complex of socially acclaimed ends, meanwhile shifting their support from the culturally defined implementation of these ends. As we shall see, certain aspects of the social structure may generate countermores and antisocial behavior precisely because of differential emphases on goals and regulations. In the extreme case, the latter may be so vitiated by the goal-emphasis that the range of behavior is limited only by considerations of technical expediency. The sole significant question then becomes, which available means is most efficient in netting the socially approved value?[5] The technically most feasible procedure, whether legitimate or not, is preferred to the institutionally prescribed conduct. As this process continues, the integration of the society becomes tenuous and anomie ensues.

Thus, in competitive athletics, when the aim of victory is shorn of its institutional trappings and success in contest becomes construed as "winning the game" rather than "winning through circumscribed modes of activity," a premium is implicitly set upon the use of illegitimate but technically efficient means. The star of the opposing football team is surreptitiously slugged; the wrestler furtively incapacitates his opponent through ingenious but illicit techniques; university alumni covertly subsidize "students" whose talents are largely confined to the athletic field. The emphasis on the goal has so attenuated the satisfactions deriving from sheer participation in the competitive activity that these satisfactions are virtually confined to a successful outcome. Through the same process, tension generated by the desire to win in a poker game is relieved by successfully dealing oneself four aces, or when the cult of success has become completely dominant, by sagaciously shuffling the cards in a game of solitaire. The faint twinge of uneasiness in the last instance and the surreptitious nature of public delicts indicate clearly that the institutional rules of the game *are known* to those who evade them, but that the emotional supports of these rules are largely vitiated by cultural exaggeration of the success-goal.[6] They are microcosmic images of the social macrocosm.

Of course, this process is not restricted to the realm of sport. The process whereby exaltion of the end generates a *literal demoralization*, i.e., a deinstitutionalization, of the means is one which characterizes many[7] groups in which the two phases of the social structure

---

[5] In this connection, one may see the relevance of Elton Mayo's paraphrase of the title of Tawney's well known book. "Actually the problem *is not that of the sickness of an acquisitive society; it is that of the acquisitiveness of a sick society.*" *Human Problems of an Industrial Civilization*, 153, New York, 1933. Mayo deals with the process through which wealth comes to be a symbol of social achievement. He sees this as arising from a state of anomie. We are considering the unintegrated monetary-success goals as an element in producing anomie. A complete analysis would involve both phases of this system of interdependent variables.

[6] It is unlikely that interiorized norms are completely eliminated. Whatever residuum persists will induce personality tensions and conflict. The process involves a certain degree of ambivalence. A manifest rejection of the institutional norms is coupled with some latent retention of their emotional correlates. "Guilt feelings," "sense of sin," "pangs of conscience" are obvious manifestations of this unrelieved tension; symbolic adherence to the nominally repudiated values or rationalizations constitute a more subtle variety of tensional release.

[7] Many," and not all, unintegrated groups, for the reason already mentioned. In groups where the primary emphasis shifts to institutional means, i.e., when the range of alternatives is very limited, the outcome is a type of ritualism rather than anomie.

are not highly integrated. The extreme emphasis upon the accumulation of wealth as a symbol of success[8] in our own society militates against the completely effective control of institutionally regulated modes of acquiring a fortune.[9] Fraud, corruption, vice, crime, in short, the entire catalogue of proscribed behavior, becomes increasingly common when the emphasis on the *culturally induced* success-goal becomes divorced from a coordinated institutional emphasis. This observation is of crucial theoretical importance in examining the doctrine that antisocial behavior most frequently derives from biological drives breaking through the restraints imposed by society. The difference is one between a strictly utilitarian interpretation which conceives man's ends as random and an analysis which finds these ends deriving from the basic values of the culture.[10]

Our analysis can scarcely stop at this juncture. We must turn to other aspects of the social structure if we are to deal with the social genesis of the varying rates and types of deviate behavior characteristic of different societies. Thus far, we have sketched three ideal types of social orders constituted by distinctive patterns of relations between culture ends and means. Turning from these types of *culture patterning*, we find five logically possible, alternative modes of adjustment or adaptation *by individuals* within the culture-bearing society or group.[11] These are schematically presented in the following table, where $(+)$ signifies "acceptance," $(-)$ signifies "elimination" and $(\pm)$ signifies "rejection and substitution of new goals and standards."

		Culture goals	Institutionalized means
I.	Conformity	$+$	$+$
II.	Innovation	$+$	$-$
III.	Ritualism	$-$	$+$
VI.	Retreatism	$-$	$-$
V.	Rebellion[12]	$\pm$	$\pm$

Our discussion of the relation between these alternative responses and other phases of the social structure must be prefaced by the observation that persons may shift from one alternative to another as they engage in different social activities. These categories refer to role adjustments in specific situations, not to personality *in toto*. To treat the development of this process in various spheres of conduct would introduce a complexity unmanageable within the confines of this paper. For this reason, we shall be concerned primarily with economic activity in the broad sense, "the production, exchange, distribution and consumption of goods and services" in our competitive society, wherein wealth has taken on a highly symbolic cast. Our task is to search out some of the factors which exert pressure upon in-

---

[8] Money has several peculiarities which render it particularly apt to become a symbol of prestige divorced from institutional controls. As Simmel emphasized, money is highly abstract and impersonal. However acquired, through fraud or institutionally, it can be used to purchase the same goods and services. The anonymity of metropolitan culture, in conjunction with this peculiarity of money, permits wealth, the sources of which may be unknown to the community in which the plutocrat lives, to serve as a symbol of status.

[9] The emphasis upon wealth as a success-symbol is possibly reflected in the use of the term "fortune" to refer to a stock of accumulated wealth. This meaning becomes common in the late sixteenth century (Spencer and Shakespeare). A similar usage of the Latin *fortuna* comes into prominence during the first century B.C. Both these periods were marked by the rise to prestige and power of the "bourgeoisie."

[10] See Kingsley Davis, "Mental Hygiene and the Class Structure," *Psychiatry*, 1928, I esp. 62–63; Talcott Parsons, *The Structure of Social Action*, 59–60, New York, 1937.

[11] This is a level intermediate between the two planes distinguished by Edward Sapir; namely, culture patterns and personal habit systems. See his "Contribution of Psychiatry to an Understanding of Behavior in Society," *Amer. J. Social.*, 1937, 42:862-70.

[12] This fifth alternative is on a plane clearly different from that of the others. It represents a *transitional* response which seeks to *institutionalize* new procedures oriented toward revamped cultural goals shared by the members of the society. It thus involves efforts to *change* the existing structure rather than to perform accommodative actions *within* this structure, and introduces additional problems with which we are not at the moment concerned.

dividuals to engage in certain of these logically possible alternative responses. This choice, as we shall see, is far from random.

In every society, Adaptation I (conformity to both culture goals and means) is the most common and widely diffused. Were this not so, the stability and continuity of the society could not be maintained. The mesh of expectancies which constitutes every social order is sustained by the modal behavior of its members falling within the first category. Conventional role behavior oriented toward the basic values of the group is the rule rather than the exception. It is this fact alone which permits us to speak of a human aggregate as comprising a group or society.

Conversely, Adaptation IV (rejection of goals and means) is the least common. Persons who "adjust" (or maladjust) in this fashion are, strictly speaking, *in* the society but not *of* it. Sociologically, these constitute the true "aliens." Not sharing the common frame of orientation, they can be included within the societal population merely in a functional sense. In this category are *some* of the activities of psychotics, psychoneurotics, chronic autists, pariahs, outcasts, vagrants, vagabonds, tramps, chronic drunkards and drug addicts.[13] These have relinquished, in certain spheres of activity, the culturally defined goals, involving complete aim-inhibition in the polar case, and their adjustments are not in accord with institutional norms. This is not to say that in some cases the source of their behavioral adjustments is not in part the very social structure which they have in effect repudiated nor that their very existence within a social area does not constitute a problem for the socialized population.

[13] Obviously, this is an elliptical statement. These individuals may maintain some orientation to the values of their particular differentiated groupings within the larger society or, in part, of the conventional society itself. Insofar as they do so, their conduct cannot be classified in the "passive rejection" category (IV). Nels Anderson's description of the behavior and attitudes of the bum, for example, can readily be recast in terms of our analytical scheme. See *The Hobo*, 93–98, *et passim*, Chicago, 1923.

This mode of "adjustment" occurs, as far as structural sources are concerned, when both the culture goals and institutionalized procedures have been assimilated thoroughly by the individual and imbued with affect and high positive value, but where those institutionalized procedures which promise a measure of successful attainment of the goals are not available to the individual. In such instances, there results a twofold mental conflict insofar as the moral obligation for adopting institutional means conflict with the pressure to resort to illegitimate means (which may attain the goal) and inasmuch as the individual is shut off from means which are both legitimate *and* effective. The competitive order is maintained, but the frustrated and handicapped individual who cannot cope with this order drops out. Defeatism, quietism and resignation are manifested in escape mechanisms which ultimately lead the individual to "escape" from the requirements of the society. It is an expedient which arises from continued failure to attain the goal by legitimate measures and from an inability to adopt the illegitimate route because of internalized prohibitions and institutionalized compulsives, *during which process the supreme value of the success-goal has as yet not been renounced.* The conflict is resolved by eliminating *both* precipitating elements, the goals and means. The escape is complete, the conflict is eliminated and the individual is socialized.

Be it noted that where frustration derives from the inaccessibility of effective institutional means for attaining economic or any other type of highly valued "success," that Adaptations II, III and V (innovation, ritualism and rebellion) are also possible. The result will be determined by the particular personality, and thus, the *particular* cultural background, involved. Inadequate socialization will result in the innovation response whereby the conflict and frustration are eliminated by relinquishing the institutional means and retaining the success-aspiration; an extreme assimilation of institutional demands will lead to ritualism wherein the goal is dropped as beyond one's reach but conformity to the mores persists; and rebellion occurs when emancipation from the reigning standards, due to frustration or to marginalist perspectives, leads to the attempt to introduce a "new social order."

Our major concern is with the illegitimacy adjustment. This involves the use of conventionally proscribed but frequently effective means of attaining at least the simulacrum of culturally defined success,—wealth, power, and the like. As we have seen, this adjustment occurs when the individual has assimilated the cultural emphasis on success without equally internalizing the morally prescribed norms governing means for its attainment. The question arises, Which phases of our social structure predispose toward this mode of adjustment? We may examine a concrete instance, effectively analyzed by Lohman,[14] which provides a clue to the answer. Lohman has shown that specialized areas of vice in the near north side of Chicago constitute a "normal" response to a situation where the cultural emphasis upon pecuniary success has been absorbed, but where there is little access to conventional and legitimate means for attaining such success. The conventional occupational opportunities of persons in this area are almost completely limited to manual labor. Given our cultural stigmatization of manual labor, and its correlate, the prestige of white collar work, it is clear that the result is a stain toward innovational practices. The limitation of opportunity to unskilled labor and the resultant low income can not compete *in terms of conventional standards of achievement* with the high income from organized vice.

For our purposes, this situation involves two important features. First, such antisocial behavior is in a sense "called forth" by certain conventional values of the culture *and* by the class structure involving differential access to the approved opportunities for legitimate, prestige-bearing pursuit of the culture goals.

---

[14] Joseph D. Lohman, "The Participant Observer in Community Studies," *Amer. Sociol. Rev.*, 1937, **2**:890–98.

The lack of high integration between the means-and-end elements of the cultural pattern and the particular class structure combine to favor a heightened frequency of antisocial conduct in such groups. The second consideration is of equal significance. Recourse to the first of the alternative responses, legitimate effort, is limited by the fact that actual advance toward desired success-symbols through conventional channels is, despite our persisting open-class ideology,[15] relatively rare and difficult for those handicapped by little formal education and few economic resources. The dominant pressure of group standards of success is, therefore, on the gradual attenuation of legitimate, but by and large ineffective, strivings and the increasing use of illegitimate, but more or less effective, expedients of vice and crime. The cultural demands made on persons in this situation are incompatible. On the one hand, they are asked to orient their conduct toward the prospect of accumulating wealth and on the other, they are largely denied effective opportunities to do so institutionally. The consequences of such structural inconsistency are psychopathological personality, and/or antisocial conduct, and/or revolutionary activities. The equilibrium between culturally designated means and ends becomes highly unstable with the progressive emphasis on attaining the prestige-laden ends by any means whatsoever. Within this context, Capone represents the triumph of amoral intelligence over morally prescribed "failure," when the channels of vertical mobility are closed or nar-

---

[15] The shifting historical role of this ideology is a profitable subject for exploration. The "office-boy-to-president" stereotype was once in approximate accord with the facts. Such vertical mobility was probably more common then than now, when the class structure is more rigid. (See the following note.) The ideology largely persists, however, possibly because it still performs a useful function for maintaining the *status quo*. For insofar as it is accepted by the "masses," it constitutes a useful sop for those who might rebel against the entire structure, were this consoling hope removed. This ideology now serves to lessen the probability of Adaptation V. In short, the role of this notion has changed from that of an approximately valid empirical theorem to that of an ideology, in Mannheim's sense.

rowed[16] *in a society which places a high premium on economic affluence and social ascent for all its members.*[17]

This last qualification is of primary importance. It suggests that other phases of the social structure besides the extreme emphasis on pecuniary success, must be considered if we are to understand the social sources of antisocial behavior. A high frequency of deviate behavior is not generated simply by "lack of opportunity" or by this exaggerated pecuniary emphasis. A comparatively rigidified class structure, a feudalistic or caste order, may limit such opportunities far beyond the point which obtains in our society today. It is only when a system of cultural values extols, virtually above all else, certain *common* symbols of success *for the population at large* while its social structure rigorously restricts or completely eliminates access to approved modes of acquiring these symbols *for a considerable part of the same population,* that antisocial behavior ensues on a considerable scale. In other words, our egalitarian ideology denies by implication the existence of noncompeting groups and individuals in the pursuit of pecuniary success. The same body of success-symbols is held to be desirable for all. These goals are held to *transcend class lines,* not to be bounded by them, yet the actual social organization is such that there exist class differentials in the accessibility of these *common* success-symbols. Frustration and thwarted aspiration lead to the search for avenues of escape from a culturally induced intolerable situation; or unrelieved ambition may eventuate in illicit attempts to acquire the dominant values.[18] The American stress on pecuniary success and ambitiousness for all thus invites exaggerated anxieties, hostilities, neuroses and antisocial behavior.

This theoretical analysis may go far toward explaining the varying correlations between crime and poverty.[19] Poverty is not an isolated variable. It is one of a complex and interdependent social and cultural variables. When viewed in such a context, it represents quite different states of affairs Poverty as such, and consequent limitation of opportunity, are not sufficient to induce a conspicuously high rate of criminal behavior. Even the often mentioned

[16] There is a growing body of evidence, though none of it is clearly conclusive, to the effect that our class structure is becoming rigidified and that vertical mobility is declining. Taussig and Joslyn found that American business leaders are being *increasingly* recruited from the upper ranks of our society. The Lynds have also found a "diminished chance to get ahead" for the working classes in Middletown. Manifestly, these objective changes are not alone significant; the individual's subjective evaluation of the situation is a major determinant of the response. The extent to which this change in opportunity for social mobility has been recognized by the least advantaged classes is still conjectural, although the Lynds present some suggestive materials. The writer suggests that a case in point is the increasing frequency of cartoons which observe in a tragicomic vein that "my old man says everybody can't be President. He says if ya can get three days a week steady on W.P.A. work ya ain't doin' so bad either." See F. W. Taussig and C. S. Joslyn, *American Business Leaders,* New York, 1932; R. S. and H. M. Lynd, *Middletown in Transition,* 67 ff., Chap. 12, New York, 1937.

[17] The role of the Negro in this respect is of considerable theoretical interest. Certain elements of the Negro population have assimilated the dominant caste's values of pecuniary success and social advancement, but they also recognize that social ascent is at present restricted to their own caste almost exclusively. The pressure upon the Negro which would otherwise derive from the structural inconsistencies we have noticed are hence not identical with those upon lower class whites. See Kingsley Davis, *op. cit.,* **63**; John Dollard, *Caste and Class in a Southern Town,* 66 ff., New Haven, 1936; Donald Young, *American Minority Peoples,* 581, New York, 1932.

[18] The psychical coordinates of these processes have been partly established by the experimental evidence concerning *Anspruchsniveaus* and levels of performance. See Kurt Lewin, *Vorsatz, Wille und Bedurfnis,* Berlin, 1926; N. F. Hoppe, "Erfolg und Misserfolg," *Psychol. Forschung,* 1930, **14**:1–63; Jerome D. Frank, "Individual Differences in Certain Aspects of the Level of Aspiration," *Amer. J. Psychol.,* 1935, **47**:119–28.

[19] Standard criminology texts summarize the data in this field. Our scheme of analysis may serve to resolve some of the theoretical contradictions which P. A. Sorokin indicates. For example, "not everywhere nor always do the poor show a greater proportion of crime . . . many poorer countries have had less crime than the richer countries . . . The [economic] improvement in the second half of the nineteenth century, and the beginning of the twentieth, has not been followed by a decrease of crime." See his *Contemporary Sociological Theories,* 560–61, New York, 1928. The crucial point is, however, that poverty has varying social significance in different social structures, as we shall see. Hence, one would not expect a linear correlation between crime and poverty.

"poverty in the midst of plenty" will not necessarily lead to this result. Only insofar as poverty and associated disadvantages in competition for the culture values approved for *all* members of the society is linked with the assimilation of a cultural emphasis on momentary accumulation as a symbol of success is antisocial conduct a "normal" outcome. Thus, poverty is less highly correlated with crime in southeastern Europe than in the United States. The possibilities of vertical mobility in these European areas would seem to be fewer than in this country, so that neither poverty *per se* nor its association with limited opportunity is sufficient to account for the varying correlations. It is only when the full configuration is considered, poverty, limited opportunity and a commonly shared system of success symbols, that we can explain the higher association between poverty and crime in our society than in others where rigidified class structure is coupled with *differential class symbols of achievement*.

In societies such as our own, then, the pressure of prestige-bearing success tends to eliminate the effective social constraint over means employed to this end. "The-end-justifies-the-means" doctrine becomes a guiding tenet for action when the cultural structure unduly exalts the end and the social organization unduly limits possible recourse to approved means. Otherwise put, this notion and associated behavior reflect a lack of cultural coordination. In international relations, the effects of this lack of integration are notoriously apparent. An emphasis upon national power is not readily coordinated with an inept organization of legitimate, i.e., internationally defined and accepted, means for attaining this goal. The result is a tendency toward the abrogation of international law, treaties becomes scraps of paper, "undeclared warfare" serves as a technical evasion, the bombing of civilian populations is rationalized,[20] just as the same societal situation induces the same sway of illegitimacy among individuals.

The social order we have described necessarily produces this "strain toward dissolution." The pressure of such an order is upon outdoing one's competitors. The choice of means within the ambit of institutional control will persist as long as the sentiments supporting a competitive system, i.e., deriving from the possibility of outranking competitors and hence enjoying the favorable response of others, are distributed throughout the entire system of activities and are not confined merely to the final result. A stable social structure demands a balanced distribution of affect among its various segments. When there occurs a shift of emphasis from the satisfactions deriving from competition itself to almost exclusive concern with successful competition, the resultant stress leads to the breakdown of the regulatory structure.[21] With the resulting attenuation of the institutional imperatives, there occurs an approximation of the situation erroneously held by utilitarians to be typical of society generally wherein calculations of advantage and fear of punishment are the sole regulating agencies. In such situations, as Hobbes observed, force and fraud come to constitute the sole virtues in view of their relative efficiency in attaining goals,—which were for him, of course, not culturally derived.

It should be apparent that the foregoing discussion is not pitched on a moralistic plane. Whatever the sentiments of the writer or reader concerning the ethical desirability of coordinating the means-and-goals phases of the social structure, one must agree that lack of such coordination leads to anomie. Insofar as one of the most general functions of social organizations is to provide a basis for calculability and regularity of behavior, it is increas-

---

[20] See M. W. Royse, *Aerial Bombardment and the International Regulation of War*, New York, 1928.

[21] Since our primary concern is with the sociocultural aspects of this problem, the psychological correlates have been only implicitly considered. See Karen Horney, *The Neurotic Personality of Our Time*, New York, 1937, for a psychological discussion of this process.

ingly limited in effectiveness as these elements of the structure become dissociated. At the extreme, predictability virtually disappears and what may be properly termed cultural chaos or anomie intervenes.

This statement, being brief, is also incomplete. It has not included an exhaustive treatment of the various structural elements which predispose toward one rather than another of the alternative responses open to individuals; it has neglected, but not denied the relevance of, the factors determining the specific incidence of these responses; it has not enumerated the various concrete responses which are constituted by combinations of specific values of the analytical variables; it has omitted, or includes only by implication, any consideration of the social functions performed by illicit responses; it has not tested the full explanatory power of the analytical scheme by examining a large number of group variations in the frequency of deviate and conformist behavior; it has not adequately dealt with rebellious conduct which seeks to refashion the social framework radically; it has not examined the relevance of cultural conflict for an analysis of culture-goal and institutional-means malintegration. It is suggested that these and related problems may be profitably analyzed by this scheme.

5

CAPITALISM AND CRIMINAL JUSTICE

RICHARD QUINNEY

DEVELOPMENT OF CAPITALIST ECONOMY

Crime is a manifestation of the material conditions of society. The failure of conventional criminology is to ignore, by design, the material conditions of capitalism. Since the phenomena of crime are products of the substructure—are themselves part of the superstructure—any explanation of crime in terms of other elements of the superstructure is no explanation at all. Our need is to develop a general materialist framework for understanding crime, beginning with the underlying historical processes of social existence.

*

Any investigation of the meaning (and changing meanings) of crime in America, requires a delineation of the periods of economic development in the United States. A few attempts at such delineation already exist, but for other than the study of crime. For example, Douglas Dowd in his book *The Twisted Dream* notes briefly three different periods of American development, with particular reference to the role of the state in American economic life:

(1) American mercantilism, up to Jackson's Presidency; (2) laissez-faire capitalism, coming to a climax in the decades after the Civil War; and (3) maturing industrial capitalism, up to the present.[1] Similarly, in another treatment, William A. Williams in his book *The Contours of American History* arranges American history according to the following periods: (1) the age of mercantilism, 1740–1828; (2) the age of laissez nous faire, 1819–96; and (3) the age of corporate capitalism, 1882 to the present.[2] To this scheme, others add that American capitalism is now in the stage of either "monopoly capital" or "finance capital."[3]

It is debatable, nevertheless, in our study of crime in the United States, whether America was capitalist from the beginning, with capitalism merely imported from the Old to the New World. Or whether, as James O'Connor has recently argued, capitalist development

---

[1] Douglas F. Dowd, *The Twisted Dream: Capitalist Development in the United States Since 1776* (Cambridge, Mass.: Winthrop, 1974), pp. 42–48.

[2] William Appleman Williams, *The Contours of American History* (New York: World, 1961).

[3] Paul A. Baran and Paul M. Sweezy, *Monopoly Capital: An Essay on the American Economic and Social Order* (New York: Monthly Review Press, 1966). Robert Fitch and Mary Oppenheimer, "Who Rules the Corporations," *Socialist Revolution*, no. 4 (July-August 1970): 73–107; no. 5 (September-October 1970): 61–114; no. 6 (November-December 1970):33–94.

Source: *Class, State and Crime: On the Theory and Practice of Criminal Justice*, first edition. New York: Longman, Inc., copyright © 1977, Longman Inc. Reprinted with permission [of Longman, Inc.]

has occurred in only fairly recent times.[4] For the first hundred years of nationhood the United States resisted large-scale capitalist production. Independent commodity production predominated; farmers, artisans, small manufacturers and other petty producers were the mainstay of the economy. Only as northern capitalists acquired land from the farmers (thus appropriating their labor power) and as immigrant labor power was imported from Europe did capitalism finally emerge in the United States. American capitalism emerged when capitalists won the battle as to who was to control labor power. Surplus labor was now in the hands of a capitalist ruling class. Workers could be exploited.

For certain, we are today in a stage of late, advanced capitalism in the United States. The current meaning of crime in America can be understood only in relation to the character of capitalism in the present era. Similarly, the meanings of crime at various times in the past have to be understood according to the particular stage of development. Only in the investigation of crime in the development of capitalism do we truly understand the meaning of crime. Concrete research will provide us with knowledge about the role of crime in the development of capitalism.

DOMINATION AND REPRESSION

The capitalist system must be continuously reproduced. This is accomplished in a variety of ways, ranging from the establishment of ideological hegemony to the further exploitation of labor, from the creation of public policy to the coercive repression of the population. Most explicitly, the *state* secures the capitalist order. Through various schemes and mechanisms, then, the capitalist class is able to dominate. And in the course of this domination, crimes are carried out. These crimes, committed by the capitalist class, the state, and the agents of the capitalist class and state, are the crimes of domination.

*

The coercive force of the state, embodied in law and legal repression, is the traditional means of maintaining the social and economic order. Contrary to conventional wisdom, law instead of representing community custom is an instrument of the state that serves the interests of the developing capitalist ruling class. Law emerged with the rise of capitalism, as Stanley Diamond writes: "Law arises in the breach of a prior customary order and increases in force with the conflicts that divide political societies internally and among themselves. Law *and* order is the historical illusion; law *versus* order is the historical reality."[5] Law and legal repression are, and continue to serve as, the means of enforcing the interests of the dominant class in the capitalist state.

Through the legal system, then, the state forcefully protects its interests and those of the capitalist ruling class. Crime control becomes the coercive means of checking threats to the existing social and economic order, threats that result from a system of oppression and exploitation. As a means of controlling the behavior of the exploited population, crime control is accomplished by a variety of methods, strategies, and institutions.[6] The state, especially through its legislative bodies, establishes official policies of crime control. The administrative branch of the state establishes and enforces crime-control policies, usually setting the design for the whole nation. Specific agencies of law enforcement, such as the Federal Bureau of Investigation and the recent Law Enforcement Assistance Administration, determine the nature of crime control. And the state is able through its Department of Justice

---

[4] James O'Connor, "The Twisted Dream," *Monthly Review* **26** (March 1975): 46–53.

[5] Stanley Diamond, "The Rule of Law Versus the Order of Custom," *Social Research* **38** (Spring 1971): 71.

[6] See Richard Quinney, *Critique of Legal Order: Crime Control in Capitalist Society* (Boston: Little, Brown, 1974), pp. 95–135.

officially to repress the "dangerous" and "subversive" elements of the population. Altogether, these state institutions attempt to rationalize the legal system of employing the advanced methods of science and technology. And whenever any changes are to be attempted to reduce the incidence of crime, rehabilitation of the individual or reform within the existing institutions is suggested.[7] Drastically to alter the society and the crime-control establishment would be to alter beyond recognition the capitalist system.

*

Although the capitalist state creates and manages the institutions of control (employing physical force *and* manipulation of consciousness), the basic contradictions of the capitalist order are such that this control is not absolute and, in the long run, is subject to defeat. Because of the contradictions of capitalism, the capitalist state is more weak than strong.[8] Eventually the capitalist state loses its legitimacy, no longer being able to perpetuate the ideology that capital accumulation for capitalists (at the expense of workers) is good for the nation or for human interests. The ability of the capitalist economic order to exist according to its own interests is eventually weakened.[9] The problem becomes especially acute in periods of economic crisis, periods that are unavoidable under capitalism.

In the course of reproducing the capitalist system crimes are committed. It is a contradiction of capitalism that some of its laws must be violated in order to secure the existing system.[10] The contradictions of capitalism produce their own sources of crime. Not only are these contradictions heightened during times of crisis, making for increased crimes of domination, but the nature of these crimes changes with the further development of capitalism.

The crimes of domination most characteristic of capitalist domination are those that occur in the course of state control. These are the *crimes of control.* They include the felonies and misdemeanors that law-enforcement agents, especially the police, carry out in the name of the law, usually against persons accused of other violations. Violence and brutality have become a recognized part of police work. In addition to these crimes of control, there are the crimes of more subtle nature in which agents of the law violate the civil liberties of citizens, as in the various forms of surveillance, the use of provocateurs, and the illegal denial of due process.

Then there are the *crimes of government,* committed by the elected and appointed officials of the capitalist state. The Watergate crimes, carried out to perpetuate a particular governmental administration, are the most publicized instances of these crimes. There are also those offenses committed by the government against persons and groups who would seemingly threaten national security. Included here are the crimes of warfare and the political assassination of foreign and domestic leaders.

Crimes of domination also consist of those crimes that occur in the capitalist class for the purpose of securing the existing economic order. These *crimes of economic domination* include the crimes committed by corporations, ranging from price fixing to pollution of the environment in order to protect and further capital accumulation. Also included are the economic crimes of individual businessmen and professionals. In addition, the crimes of the capitalist class and the capitalist state are joined in or-

[7] Alexander Liazos, "Class Oppression: The Functions of Juvenile Justice," *Insurgent Sociologist 5* (Fall 1974): 2–24.

[8] Wolfe, "New Directions in the Marxist Theory of Politics." p. 155.

[9] See Stanley Aronowitz, "Law, Breakdown of Order, and Revolution," in *Law Against the People: Essay to Demystify Law, Order and the Courts,* ed. Robert Lefcourt (New York: Random House, 1971), pp. 150–82; and John H. Schaar, "Legitimacy in the Modern State," in *Power and Community: Dissenting Essays in Political Science,* ed. Philip Green and Sanford Levinson (New York: Random House, 1979), pp. 276–327.

[10] See Richard Quinney, *Criminology: Analysis and Critique of Crime in America* (Boston: Little, Brown, 1975), pp. 131–61.

ganized crime. The more conventional criminal operations of organized crime are linked to the state in the present stage of capitalist development. The operations of organized crime and the criminal operations of the state are united in the attempt to assure the survival of the capitalist system.

Finally, many *social injuries* are committed by the capitalist class and the capitalist state that are not usually defined as criminal in the legal codes of the state.[11] These systematic actions, involving the denial of basic human rights (resulting in sexism, racism, and economic exploitation) are an integral part of capitalism and are important to its survival.

Underlying all the capitalist crimes is the appropriation of the surplus value created by labor. The working class has the right to possess the whole of this value. The worker creates a value several times greater than the labor power purchased by the capitalist. The excess value created by the worker over and above the value of labor power is the surplus value which is appropriated by the capitalist. Surplus value, as exploitation, is essential to capitalism, being the source of accumulation of capital and expansion of production.

Domination and repression are a basic part of class struggle in the development of capitalism. The capitalist class and state protect and promote the capitalist order by controlling those who do not own the means of production. The labor supply and the conditions for labor must be secured. Crime control and the crimes of domination are thus necessary features and the natural products of capitalist political economy.

*

For the unemployed, as well as for those who are always uncertain about their employ-ment, the life condition has its personal and social consequences. Basic human needs are thwarted when the life-giving activity of work is lost or curtailed. This form of alienation gives rise to a multiplicity of psycho-social maladjustments and psychic disorders.[12] In addition, unemployment means the loss of personal and family income. Choices, opportunities, and even life maintenance are jeopardized. For many people, the appropriate reaction consists not only of mental disturbance but also of outright acts of personal and social destruction.

Although the statistical evidence can never show conclusively the relation between unemployment and crime, largely because such statistics are politically constructed in the beginning to obscure the failings of a capitalist economy, there is sufficient observation to recognize the obvious fact that unemployment produces criminality. Crimes of economic gain increase whenever the jobless seek ways to maintain themselves and their families. Crimes of violence rise when the problems of life are further exacerbated by the loss of life-supporting activity. Anger and frustration at a world that punishes rather than supports produce their own forms of destruction. Permanent unemployment—and the acceptance of that condition—can result in a form of life where criminality is an appropriate and consistent response.

Hence, crime under capitalism has become a response to the material conditions of life.[13] Nearly all crimes among the working class in capitalist society are actually a means of *survival*, an attempt to exist in a society where survival is not assured by other, collective means. Crime is inevitable under capitalist conditions.

Yet, understanding crime as a reaction to capitalist conditions, whether as acts of frus-

[11] Tony Platt, "Prospects for a Radical Criminology in the United States," *Crime and Social Justice* 1 (Spring-Summer, 1974): 2–10; Herman and Julia Schwendinger, "Defenders of Order or Guardians of Human Rights?" *Issues in Criminology* 5 (Summer 1970): 123–57.

[12] K. William Kapp, "Socio-Economic Effects of Law and High Employment," *Annals of the American Academy of Political and Social Science* 418 (March 1975): 60–71.
[13] David M. Gordon, "Capitalism, Class, and Crime in America," *Crime and Delinquency* 19 (April 1973): 163–86.

tration or means of survival, is only one side of the picture. The other side involves the problematics of the *consciousness* of criminality in capitalist society.[14] The history of the working class is in large part one of rebellion against the conditions of capitalist production, as well as against the conditions of life resulting from work under capitalism. Class struggle involves, after all, a continuous war between two dialectically opposed interests: capital accumulation for the benefit of a nonworking minority class that owns and controls the means of production and, on the other hand, control and ownership of production by those who actually labor. Since the capitalist state regulates this struggle, the institutions and laws of the social order are intended to assure the victory of the capitalist class over the working class. Yet the working class constantly struggles against the capitalist class, as shown in the long history of labor battles against the conditions of capitalist production.[15] The resistance continues as long as there is need for class struggle, that is, as long as capitalism exists.

With the instruments of force and coercion on the side of the capitalist class, much of the activity in the working-class struggle is defined as criminal. Indeed, according to the legal codes, whether in simply acting to relieve the injustices of capitalism or in taking action against the existence of class oppression, actions against the interest of the state are crimes. With an emerging consciousness that the state represses those who attempt to tip the scales in favor of the working class, working-class people engage in actions against the state and the capitalist class. This is crime that is politically conscious.

[14] Taylor, Walton, and Young, *New Criminology*, pp. 220–21.

[15] Sidney Lens, *The Labor Wars: From the Molly Maguires to the Sitdowns* (New York: Doubleday, 1973); Jeremy Brecher, *Strike!* (Greenwich, Conn.: Fawcett, 1972); Samuel Yellin, *American Labor Struggles* (New York: S. A. Russell, 1936); Richard O. Boyer and Herbert M. Morais, *Labor's Untold Story* (New York: Cameron Associates, 1955).

Crimes of accommodation and resistance thus range from unconscious reactions to exploitation, to conscious acts of survival within the capitalist system, to politically conscious acts of rebellion. These criminal actions, moreover, not only cover the range of meaning but actually evolve or progress from *unconscious reaction to political rebellion*. Finally, the crimes may eventually reach the ultimate state of conscious political action—*revolt*. In revolt, criminal actions are not only against the system but are also an attempt to overthrow it.

*

THE MEANING OF CRIME

A Marxist understanding of crime, as developed here, begins with an analysis of the political economy of capitalism. The class struggle endemic to capitalism is characterized by a dialectic between domination and accommodation. Those who own and control the means of production, the capitalist class, attempt to secure the existing order through various forms of domination, especially crime control by the capitalist state. Those who do not own and control the means of production, especially the working class, accommodate and resist in various ways to capitalist domination.

Crime is related to this process. Crime control and criminality (consisting of the crimes of domination and the crimes of accommodation) are understood in terms of the conditions resulting from the capitalist appropriation of labor. Variations in the nature and amount of crime occur in the course of developing capitalism. Each stage in the development of capitalism is characterized by a particular pattern of crime. The meaning and changing meanings of crime are found in the development of capitalism.

What can be expected in the further development of capitalism? The contradictions and related crises of capitalist political economy are now a permanent feature of advanced capitalism. Further economic development along capitalist lines will solve none of the internal contradictions of the capitalist mode of production.[16] The capitalist state must, therefore, increasingly utilize its resources—its various control and repressive mechanisms—to maintain the capitalist order. The dialectic between oppression by the capitalist class and the daily struggle of survival by the oppressed will continue—and at an increasing pace.

The only lasting solution to the crisis of capitalism is, of course, socialism. Under late, advanced capitalism, socialism will be achieved only in the struggle of all people who are oppressed by the capitalist mode of production, namely, the workers and all elements of the surplus population. An alliance of the oppressed must take place.[17] Given the objective conditions of a crisis in advanced capitalism, and the conditions for an alliance of the oppressed, a mass socialist movement can be formed, cutting across all divisions within the working class.

The objective of Marxist analysis is to lead to further questioning of the capitalist system, leading to an improved understanding of the consequences of capitalist development. The *ultimate meaning* of crime in the development of capitalism is the need for a socialist society. And as the preceding discussion indicates, in moving toward the socialist alternative, our study of crime is necessarily based on an economic analysis of capitalist society. Crime is essentially a product of the contradictions of capitalism. Crime is sometimes a force in social development: when it becomes part of the class struggle, increasing political consciousness. But our real attention must continue to be on the capitalist system itself. Our understanding is furthered as we investigate the nature, sources, and consequences of the development of capitalism. As we engage in this work, the

development of socialism becomes more evident.

*

CRIME AND CONSCIOUSNESS

Is crime more than a by-product of capitalism? If more than a by-product, when and how does crime become a *force* in the class struggle? The question is crucial to a Marxist analysis of crime; the answer determines whether (or better, in what instances) criminality is to be considered as an active part in structuring social life and in the dynamics of social change. It is thus the consciousness of criminal behavior that becomes important in our investigation. For it is consciousness that gives behavior a rational purpose in human history.

For the working class there are several possibilities for breaking through the conditions of capitalism: "One possibility involves conscious, organized efforts aimed at the goal of eliminating capitalist society itself as the historical manifestation of the class contradiction. The other possibility involves crude, unconscious reactions against the social position of working class people in the form of evading bourgeois laws through criminal acts."[18] Actions thus range from unconscious reactions to exploitation, to conscious acts of survival, to politically conscious acts of rebellion.

The problem regarding criminality, therefore, becomes that of the consciousness of the working class. The problem is stated precisely as follows:

> This means that the questions must be pursued as to how to determine the concrete causes of behavior which in the social setting of the proletariat lead either to conscious class struggle on the one hand, or to conforming behavior or delinquent behavior on the other. In pursuing this

[16] Ernest Mandel, "The Industrial Cycle in Late Capitalism," *New Left Review* **90** (March-April 1975): 3–25.

[17] O'Connor, *Fiscal Crisis of the State*, pp. 221–56.

[18] Falco Werkentin, Michael Hofferbert, and Michael Baurmann, "Criminology as Police Science or: 'How Old Is the New Criminology?' " *Crime and Social Justice* **2** (Fall-Winter 1974): 27.

question, it would be necessary to characterize the general conditions which under capitalist conditions contribute to the evolution of proletarian class consciousness and organized political praxis, and which contain as well, in their contradiction, the delusion of individuals and the hindering of the development of class struggle. Besides these general conditions, it would be necessary to characterize the specific circumstances which lead to the development of criminal behavior patterns within the proletariat. This implies that the intellectual interests of such an analysis must be measured against a critical understanding of science which is fundamentally oriented toward the principal necessity of the overthrow of capitalist ruling apparatus.[19]

In theoretically considering the problematics of consciousness of criminality we assist in the transformation of unconscious criminality into conscious political activity. The development of class consciousness and struggle is the goal of a Marxist analysis of crime.

*

The revolutionary character of the working class, in relation to urban crime, was noted by Engels in his study of the conditions of the working class in mid-nineteenth-century England.[20] Engels saw in crime, at this stage in the capitalist development of England, all of its contradictory nature. Generally, criminality represents a response to the oppression of the working class. Engels describes much of this behavior as being committed by an underclass of the surplus population that includes people who have lost all hope of ever returning to work, vagabonds, beggers, paupers, and prostitutes. Yet from this mass of suffering Engels sees a kind of person emerging who, provoked by intense distress, revolts openly against society.

Throughout Engels' discussion there is the recognition that criminality is a primitive form

of insurrection, a response to deprivation and oppression. Criminality in itself is not a satisfactory form of politics. As Steven Marcus notes in his study of Engels' writing on crime:

"Crime is a primitive form of insurrection, driven by need and deprivations, an incomplete but not altogether mistaken response to a bad situation, and coming into active existence only by overcoming the resistance of inherited values and internalized sanctions. . . . Nevertheless, an inescapable part of the meaning of crime is its essential failure. It is insufficiently rational and excessively, or too purely, symbolic and symptomatic. Most of all, in it the criminal remains socially untransformed: he is still an isolated individual pursuing activities in an underground and alternate marketplace; if he is successful, he is a small-time entrepreneur; at best, he is the member or leader of a gang. In no instance is he capable of organizing a movement to withstand the institutional forces that are arrayed against him. He lives in a parallel and parasitic world whose horizon is bounded and obscured by the larger society upon which it depends.[21]

This is crime, as Engels recognized, in its early phase of development, before becoming a political force.

The initial failure of crime is contradicted by the fact that for some people criminality is the beginning of a conscious rebellion against capitalist conditions. In the larger context, as Engels realized, criminality is transitional, an action against brutalizing conditions, a possible stage in the development of political consciousness.[22] *If* criminally defined behavior becomes a conscious activity in the organization of workers, including the organization of those who are unemployed (in the surplus population), then crime attains a political and revolutionary character. In conscious response to social and economic oppression, action that is defined by the state as criminal could become a part of the revolutionary process.

[19] Ibid.
[20] Frederick Engels, *The Condition of the Working Class in England in 1844*, trans. Florence Kelley Wischnewetzky (New York: J. W. Lovell, 1887).

[21] Steven Marcus, *Engels, Manchester, and the Working Class* (New York: Random House, 1974), pp. 223–24.
[22] Ibid., pp. 224–26.

6

A RADICAL PERSPECTIVE ON CRIME

JEFFREY H. REIMAN

THE IMPLICIT IDEOLOGY OF CRIMINAL JUSTICE

Every criminal justice system conveys a subtle, yet powerful message in support of established institutions. It does this for two interconnected reasons.

First, because it concentrates on *individual* wrongdoers. This means that *it diverts our attention away from our institutions, away from consideration of whether our institutions themselves are wrong or unjust or indeed "criminal."*

Second, because the criminal law is put forth as the *minimum neutral ground rules* for any social living. We are taught that no society can exist without rules against theft and violence, and thus the criminal law is put forth as politically neutral, as the minimum requirements for *any* society, as the minimum obligations that any individual owes his fellows to make social life of any decent sort possible. Thus, it not only diverts our attention away from the possible injustice of our social institutions, but *the criminal law bestows upon those institutions the mantle of its own neutrality.* Since the criminal law protects the established institutions (e.g., the prevailing economic arrangements are pro-

tected by laws against theft, etc.), attacks on those established institutions become equivalent to violations of the minimum requirements for any social life at all. In effect, *the criminal law enshrines the established institutions as equivalent to the minimum requirements for* **any** *decent social existence—and it brands the individual who attacks those institutions as one who has declared war on* **all** *organized society and who must therefore be met with the weapons of war.*

This is the powerful magic of criminal justice. By virtue of its focus on *individual* criminals, it diverts us from the evils of the *social* order. By virtue of its presumed neutrality, it transforms the established social (and economic) order from being merely *one* form of society open to critical comparison with others into *the* conditions of *any* social order and thus immune from criticism. Let us look more closely at this process.

What is the effect of focusing on individual guilt? Not only does this divert our attention from the possible evils in our institutions, but it puts forth half the problem of justice as if it were the *whole* problem. To focus on individual guilt is to ask whether or not the individual citizen has fulfilled his obligations to his fellow citizens. *It is to look away from the issue of whether his fellow citizens have fulfilled their obligations to him.*

Source: The Rich Get Richer and the Poor Get Prison: Ideology, Class, and Criminal Justice. New York: John Wiley & Sons, Copyright © 1979. Pp. 143–156. Reprinted by permission.

To look only at individual responsibility is to look away from social responsibility. To look only at individual criminality is to close one's eyes to social injustice and to close one's ears to the question of whether our social institutions have exploited or violated the individual. *Justice is a two-way street—but criminal justice is a one-way street.*

Individuals owe obligations to their fellow citizens because their fellow citizens owe obligations to them. Criminal justice focuses on the first and looks away from the second. *Thus, by focusing on individual responsibility for crime, the criminal justice system literally acquits the existing social order of any charge of injustice!*

This is an extremely important bit of ideological alchemy. It stems from the fact the same act can be criminal or not, unjust or just, depending on the conditions in which it takes place. Killing someone is ordinarily a crime. But if it is in self-defense or to stop a deadly crime, it is not. Taking property by force is usually a crime. But if the taking is just retrieving what has been stolen, then no crime has been committed. Acts of violence are ordinarily crimes. But if the violence is provoked by the threat of violence or by oppressive onditions, then, like the Boston Tea Party, what might ordinarily be called criminal is celebrated as just. This means that when we call an act a crime *we are also making an implicit judgment about the conditions in response to which it takes place.* When we call an act a crime, we are saying that the conditions in which it occurs are not themselves criminal or deadly or oppressive or so unjust as to make an extreme response reasonable or justified, that is, to make such a response noncriminal.

This means that when the system holds an individual responsible for a crime, *it is implicitly conveying the message that the social conditions in which the crime occurred are not responsible for the crime,* that they are not so unjust as to make a violent response to them excusable. The criminal justice system conveys as much by what it does not do as by what it does. By holding the individual responsible, *it literally acquits the society of criminality or injustice.*

Judges are prone to hold that an individual's responsibility for a violent crime is diminished if it was provoked by something that might lead a "reasonable man" to respond violently and that criminal responsibility is eliminated if the act was in response to conditions so intolerable that any "reasonable man" would have been likely to respond in the same way. In this vein, the law acquits those who kill or injure in self-defense and treats lightly those who commit a crime when confronted with extreme provocation. The law treats leniently the man who kills his wife's lover and the woman who kills her brutal husband, even when neither has acted directly in self-defense. By this logic, when we hold an individual completely responsible for a crime, we are saying that the conditions in which it occurred are such that a "reasonable man" should find them tolerable. In other words, by focusing on individual responsibility for crimes, *the criminal justice system broadcasts the message that the social order itself is reasonable and not intolerably unjust.*

Thus the criminal justice system serves to focus moral condemnation on individuals and to deflect it away from the social order that may have either violated the individual's rights or dignity or literally pushed him or her to the brink of crime. This not only serves to carry the message that our social institutions are not in need of fundamental questioning, but it further suggests that the justice of our institutions is obvious, not to be doubted. Indeed, since it is deviations from these institutions that are crimes, the established institutions become the implicit standard of justice from which criminal deviations are measured.

This leads to the second way in which a criminal justice system always conveys an implicit ideology. It arises from the presumption that the criminal law is nothing but the politically neutral minimum requirements of any decent social life. What is the consequence of this?

Obviously, as already suggested, this presumption transforms the prevailing social order into justice incarnate and all violations of the prevailing order into injustice incarnate. This process is so obvious that it may be easily missed.

Consider, for example, the law against theft. It does indeed seem to be one of the minimum requirements of social living. As long as there is scarcity, any society—capitalist or socialist—will need rules preventing individuals from taking what does not belong to them. But the law against theft is more: it is a law against stealing what individuals *presently* own. *Such a law has the effect of making present property relations a part of the criminal law.*

Since stealing is a violation of law, this means that present property relations become the implicit standard of justice against which criminal deviations are measured. Since criminal law is thought of as the minimum requirements of any social life, this means that present property relations become equivalent to the minimum requirements of *any* social life. And the criminal who would alter the present property relations becomes nothing less than someone who is declaring war on all organized society. The question of whether this "war" is provoked by the injustice or brutality of the society is swept aside. Indeed, this suggests yet another way in which the criminal justice system conveys an ideological message in support of the established society.

Not only does the criminal justice system acquit the social order of any charge of injustice, it specifically cloaks the society's own crime-producing tendencies. I have already observed that by blaming the individual for a crime, the society is acquitted of the charge of injustice. I would like to go further now and argue that by blaming the individual for a crime, the society is acquitted of the charge of complicity in that crime! This is a point worth developing, since many observers have maintained that modern competitive societies such as our own have structural features that tend to generate crime. Thus, holding the individual

responsible for his or her crime serves the function of taking the rest of society off the hook for their role in sustaining and benefiting from social arrangements that produce crime. Let us take a brief detour to look more closely at this process.

Cloward and Ohlin argue in their book *Delinquency and Opportunity*[1] that much crime is the result of the discrepancy between social goals and the legitimate opportunities available for achieving them. Simply put, in our society everyone is encouraged to be a success, but the avenues to success are open only to some. The conventional wisdom of our free enterprise democracy is that anyone can be a success if he or she has the talent and the ambition. Thus, if one is not a success, it is because of their own shortcomings: laziness or lack of ability or both. On the other hand, opportunities to achieve success are not equally open to all. Access to the best schools and the best jobs is effectively closed to all but a few of the poor and begins to open wider only as one goes up the economic ladder. The result is that many are called but few are chosen. And many who have taken the bait and accepted the belief in the importance of success and the belief that achieving success is a result of individual ability must cope with the feelings of frustration and failure that result when they find the avenues to success closed. Cloward and Ohlin argue that one method of coping with these stresses is to develop alternative avenues to success. Crime is such an alternative avenue. Crime is a means by which people who believe in the American dream pursue it when they find the traditional routes barred. Indeed, it is plain to see that the goals pursued by most criminals are as American as apple pie. I suspect that one of the reasons that American moviegoers enjoy gangster films—movies in which gangsters such as Al Capone,

[1] Richard A. Cloward and Lloyd E. Ohlin, *Delinquency and Opportunity: A Theory of Delinquent Gangs* (New York: The Free Press, 1960), esp. pp. 77–107.

Bonnie and Clyde, or Butch Cassidy and the Sundance Kid are the heroes, as distinct from police and detective films whose heroes are defenders of the law—is that even where they deplore the hero's methods, they identify with his or her notion of success, since it is theirs as well, and respect the courage and cunning displayed in achieving that success.

It is important to note that the discrepancy between success goals and legitimate opportunities in America is not an aberration. It is a structural feature of modern competitive industrialized society, a feature from which many benefits flow. Cloward and Ohlin write that

> . . . a crucial problem in the industrial world . . . is to locate and train the most talented persons in every generation, irrespective of the vicissitudes of birth, to occupy technical work roles. . . . Since we cannot know in advance who can best fulfill the requirements of the various occupational roles, the matter is presumably settled through the process of competition. But how can men throughout the social order be motivated to participate in this competition? . . .
>
> One of the ways in which the industrial society attempts to solve this problem is by defining success-goals as potentially accessible to all, regardless of race, creed, or socioeconomic position.[2]

But since these universal goals are urged to encourage a competition to weed out the best, there are necessarily fewer openings than seekers. And since those who achieve success are in a particularly good position to exploit their success to make access for their own children easier, the competition is rigged to work in favor of the middle and upper classes. As a result, "many lower-class persons . . . are the victims of a contradiction between the goals toward which they have been led to orient themselves and socially structured means of striving for these goals."[3]

> [The poor] experience desperation born of the certainty that their position in the economic

structure is relatively fixed and immutable—a desperation made all the more poignant by their exposure to a cultural ideology in which failure to orient oneself upward is regarded as a moral defect and failure to become mobile as proof of it.[4]

The outcome is predictable. "Under these conditions, there is an acute pressure to depart from institutional norms and to adopt illegitimate alternatives."[5]

In brief, this means that the very way in which our society is structured to draw out the talents and energies that go into producing our high standard of living has a costly side effect: it produces crime. But by holding individuals responsible for this crime, those who enjoy that high standard of living can have their cake and eat it. They can reap the benefits of the competition for success and escape the responsibility of paying for the costs of that competition. By holding the poor crook legally and morally guilty, the rest of society not only passes the costs of competition on to the poor, but they effectively deny that they (the affluent) are the beneficiaries of an economic system that exacts such a high toll in frustration and suffering.

Willem Bonger, the Dutch Marxist criminologist, maintained that competitive capitalism produces egotistic motives and undermines compassion for the misfortunes of others and thus makes human beings literally *more capable of crime*—more capable of preying on their fellows without moral inhibition or remorse—than earlier cultures that emphasized cooperation rather than competition.[6] Here again, the criminal justice system relieves those who benefit from the American economic system of the

---

[2] Ibid., p. 81.
[3] Ibid., p. 105.

[4] Ibid., p. 107.
[5] Ibid., p. 105.
[6] Willem Bonger, *Criminality and Economic Conditions*, abridged and with an introduction by Austin T. Turk (Bloomington, Indiana: Indiana University Press, 1969), pp. 7–12, 40–47. Willem Adriaan Bonger was born in Holland in 1876 and died by his own hand in 1940 rather than submit to the Nazis. His *Criminalité et conditions économiques* first appeared in 1905. It was translated into English and published in the United States in 1916. Ibid., pp. 3–4.

costs of that system. By holding criminals morally and individually responsible for their crimes, we can forget that the motives that lead to crime—the drive for success at any cost, linked with the beliefs that success means outdoing others and that violence is an acceptable way of achieving one's goals—are the same motives that powered the drive across the American continent and that continue to fuel the engine of America's prosperity.

David Gordon, a contemporary political economist, maintains "that nearly all crimes in capitalist societies represent perfectly *rational* responses to the structure of institutions upon which capitalist societies are based."[7] That is, like Bonger, Gordon believes that capitalism tends to provoke crime in all economic strata. This is so because most crime is motivated by a desire for property or money and is an understandable way of coping with the pressures of inequality, competition, and insecurity, all of which are essential ingredients of capitalism. Capitalism depends, Gordon writes,

> . . . on basically competitive forms of social and economic interaction and upon substantial inequalities in the allocation of social resources. Without inequalities, it would be much more difficult to induce workers to work in alienating environments. Without competition and a competitive ideology, workers might not be inclined to struggle to improve their relative income and status in society by working harder. Finally, although rights of property are protected, capitalist societies do not guarantee economic security to most of their individual members. Individuals must fend for themselves, finding the best available opportunities to provide for themselves and their families . . . Driven by the fear of economic insecurity and by a competitive desire to gain some of the goods unequally distributed throughout the society, many individuals will eventually become "criminals."[8]

To the extent that a society makes crime a reasonable alternative for a large number of its members from all classes, that society is itself not very reasonably or humanely organized and bears some degree of responsibility for the crime it encourages. Since the criminal law is put forth as the minimum requirements that can be expected of any "reasonable man," its enforcement amounts to a denial of the real nature of the social order to which Gordon and the others point. Here again, by blaming the individual criminal, the criminal justice system serves implicitly but dramatically to acquit the society of its criminality.

THE BONUS OF BIAS

We turn now to consideration of the additional ideological bonus that is derived from the criminal justice system's bias against the poor. This bonus is a product of the association of crime and poverty in the popular mind. This association, the merging of the "criminal classes" and the "lower classes" into the "dangerous classes," was not invented in America. The word "villain" is derived from the Latin *villanus*, which means a farm servant. And the term "villein" was used in feudal England to refer to a serf who farmed the land of a great lord and who was literally owned by that lord.[9] In this respect, our present criminal justice system is heir to a long and hallowed tradition.

The value of this association was already seen when we explored the "average citizen's" concept of the Typical Criminal and the Typical Crime. It is quite obvious that throughout the great mass of middle America, far more fear and hostility is directed toward the predatory acts of the poor than the rich. Compare the fate of politicians in recent history who call for tax reform, income redistribution, prosecution of corporate crime, and any sort of regulation of business that would make it better serve American social goals with that of politicians who erect their platform on a call for "law and order," more police, less limits on police

---

[7] David M. Gordon, "Capitalism, Class and Crime in America," *Crime and Delinquency* (April 1972) p. 174.
[8] Ibid., p. 174.

[9] William and Mary Morris, *Dictionary of Word and Phrase Origins*, II (New York: Harper and Row, 1967), p. 282.

power, and stiffer prison sentences for crimi-nals—and consider this in light of what we have already seen about the real dangers posed by corporate crime and business-as-usual.

In view of all that has been said already, it seems clear that Americans have been system-atically deceived as to what are the greatest dangers to their lives, limbs and possessions. The very persistence with which the system functions to apprehend and punish poor crooks and ignore or slap on the wrist equally or more dangerous individuals is testimony to the stick-ing power of this deception. That Americans continue to tolerate the gentle treatment meted out to white-collar criminals, corporate price fixers, industrial polluters, and political-influ-ence peddlers, while voting in droves to lock up more poor people faster and longer, indi-cates the degree to which they harbor illusions as to who most threatens them. It is perhaps also part of the explanation for the continued dismal failure of class-based politics in Amer-ica. American workers rarely seem able to for-get their differences and unite to defend their shared interests against the rich whose wealth they produce. Ethnic divisions serve this div-isive function well, but undoubtedly the vivid portrayal of the poor—and, of course, the blacks—as hovering birds of prey waiting for the opportunity to snatch away the workers' meager gains serves also to deflect opposition away from the upper classes. A politician who promises to keep their communities free of blacks and their prisons full of them can get their votes even if the major portion of his or her policies amount to continuation of favored treatment of the rich at their expense. Surely this is a minor miracle of mind control.

The most important "bonus" derived from the identification of crime and poverty is that it paints the picture that the threat to decent middle Americans comes from those below them on the economic ladder, not those above. For this to happen the system must not only identify crime and poverty, but *it must also fail to reduce crime so that it remains a real threat.* By doing this, it deflects the fear and discontent

of middle Americans, and their possible op-position, away from the wealthy. The two pol-iticians who most clearly gave voice to the dis-content of middle Americans in the post-World War II period were George Wallace and Spiro Agnew. Is it any accident that their politics was extremely conservative and their anger re-served for the poor (the welfare chiselers) and the criminal (the targets of law and order)?

There are other bonuses as well. For in-stance, if the criminal justice system functions to send out a message that bestows legitimacy on present property relations, the dramatic im-pact is mightily enhanced if the violator of the present arrangements is propertyless. In other words, the crimes of the well-to-do "redistrib-ute" property among the haves. In that sense, they do not pose a symbolic challenge to the larger system in which some have much and many have little or nothing. If the criminal threat can be portrayed as coming from the poor, then the punishment of the poor criminal becomes a morality play in which the sanctity and legitimacy of the system in which some have plenty and others have little or nothing is dramatically affirmed. It matters little who the poor criminals really rip off. What counts is that middle Americans come to fear that those poor criminals are out to steal what they own.

There is yet another and, I believe, still more important bonus for the powerful in America, produced by the identification of crime and poverty. It might be thought that the identi-fication of crime and poverty would produce sympathy for the criminals. My suspicion is that is produces or at least reinforces the re-verse: *hostility toward the poor.*

Indeed, there is little evidence that Ameri-cans are very sympathetic to criminals or poor people. I have already pointed to the fact that very few Americans believe poverty to be a cause of crime. Other surveys find that most Americans believe that police should be tougher than they are now in dealing with crime (83 percent of those questioned in a 1972 survey); that courts do not deal harshly enough with criminals (75 percent of those questioned in a 1969 survey); that a majority of Americans would like to see the death penalty for convicted murderers (57 percent of those questioned in November 1972); and that most would be more likely to vote for a candidate who advocated tougher sentences for lawbreakers (83 percent of those questioned in a 1972 survey).[10] Indeed, the experience of Watergate seems to suggest that sympathy for criminals begins to flower only when we approach the higher reaches of the ladder of wealth and power. For some poor ghetto youth who robs a liquor store, five years in the slammer is our idea of tempering justice with mercy. When a handful of public officials try to walk off with the U.S. Constitution, a few months in a minimum security prison will suffice. If the public official is high enough, resignation from office and public disgrace tempered with a $60,000-a-year pension is punishment enough.

My view is that since the criminal justice system—in fact and fiction—deals with *individual legal* and *moral guilt,* the association of crime with poverty does not mitigate the image of individual moral responsibility for crime, the image that crime is the result of an individual's poor character. My suspicion is that it does the reverse: it generates the association of poverty and individual moral failing and thus *the belief that poverty itself is a sign of poor or weak character.* The clearest evidence that Americans hold this belief is to be found in the fact that attempts to aid the poor are regarded as acts of charity rather than as acts of justice. Our welfare system has all the demeaning attributes of an institution designed to give handouts to the undeserving and none of the dignity of an institution designed to make good on our responsibilities to our fellow human beings. If we acknowledged the degree to which our economic and social institutions themselves breed poverty, we would have to recognize our own responsibilities toward the poor. If we

can convince ourselves that the poor are poor because of their own short-comings, particularly moral shortcomings like incontinence and indolence, then we need acknowledge no such responsibility to the poor. Indeed, we can go further and pat ourselves on the back for our generosity and handing out the little that we do, and of course, we can make our recipients go through all the indignities that mark them as the undeserving objects of our benevolence. By and large, this has been the way in which Americans have dealt with their poor.[11] It is a way that enables us to avoid asking the question of why the richest nation in the world continues to produce massive poverty. It is my view that this conception of the poor is subtly conveyed by the way our criminal justice system functions.

Obviously, no ideological message could be more supportive of the present social and economic order than this, It suggests that poverty is a sign of individual failing, not a symptom of social or economic injustice. It tells us loud and clear that massive poverty in the midst of abundance is not a sign pointing toward the need for fundamental changes in our social and economic institutions. It suggests that the poor are poor because they deserve to be poor, or at least because they lack the strength of character to overcome poverty. When the poor are seen to be poor in character, then economic poverty coincides with moral poverty and the economic order coincides with the moral order—as if a divine hand guided its workings, capitalism leads to everyone getting what they morally deserve!

If this association takes root, then when the poor individual is found guilty of a crime, the criminal justice system acquits the society of its responsibility not only for crime *but for poverty as well.*

---

[10] *Sourcebook,* pp. 203, 204, 223, 207; see also p. 177.

[11] Historical documentation of this can be found in David J. Rothman, *The Discovery of the Asylum: Social Order and Disorder in the New Republic* (Boston: Little, Brown, 1971); and in Frances Fox Piven and Richard A. Cloward, *Regulating the Poor: The Functions of Public Welfare* (New York: Pantheon, 1971), which carries the analysis up to the present.

With this, the ideological message of criminal justice is complete. The poor rather than the rich are seen as the enemies of the mass of decent middle Americans. Our social and economic institutions are held to be responsible for neither crime nor poverty and thus are in need of no fundamental questioning or reform. The poor are poor because they are poor of character. The economic order and the moral order are one. And to the extent that this message sinks in, the wealthy can rest easily—even if they cannot sleep the sleep of the just.

Thus, we can understand why the criminal justice system creates the image of crime as the work of the poor and fails to stem it so that the threat of crime remains real and credible. The result is ideological alchemy of the highest order. The poor are seen as the real threat to decent society. The ultimate sanctions of criminal justice dramatically sanctify the present social and economic order, and *the poverty of criminals makes poverty itself an individual moral crime!*

Such are the ideological fruits of a losing war against crime whose distorted image is reflected in the criminal justice carnival mirror and widely broadcast to reach the minds and imaginations of America.

7

NO EXCUSE FOR CRIME

ERNEST VAN DEN HAAG

Environment is the root of all evil—and nothing else! A favourite phrase. And the direct consequence of it is that if society is organized on normal lines, all crimes will vanish at once, for there will be nothing to protest against, and all men will become, righteous in the twinkling of an eye.[1]

Except in narrowly specifiable conditions, the law does not see offenders as victims of conditions beyond their control. But criminologists often do.[2] Paul Bator describes views shared by many:

> . . .that the criminal law's notion of just condemnation is a cruel hypocrisy visited by a smug

society on the psychologically and economically crippled; that its premise of a morally autonomous will with at least some measure of choice whether to comply with the values expressed in a penal code is unscientific and outmoded; that its reliance on punishment as an educational and deterrent agent is misplaced, particularly in the case of the very members of society most likely to engage in criminal conduct; and that its failure to provide for individualized and humane rehabilitation of offenders is inhuman and wasteful.[3]

GHETTOES AND "POLITICAL PRISONERS"

Most criminologists are not quite so explicit. But some are. Consider two. S. I. Shuman, Professor of Law and Psychiatry at Wayne State University goes farther than Bator. Shuman maintains that "if the ghetto victim does what for many such persons is inevitable and is then incarcerated . . . he is in a real sense a political prisoner," because he is punished for "the inevitable consequences of a certain socio-political status."[4] If these consequences

Source: "No Excuse for Crime," *Annals, American Academy of Political and Social Sciences* (January 1966) **423**:133–141. Reprinted by permission.

[1] Fedor Dostoevski, *Crime and Punishment* (1866). Dostoevski's novel is directed against this notion, which he puts in the mouth of one of Raskolnikov's friends. The notion itself is still around. Thus, Alex Thio in *The American Sociologist*, vol. 9, no. 1 (February 1974), p. 48: ". . . laws benefit the powerful, for it is much easier and less costly for them to punish the powerless criminals than to eradicate the cause of the crimes by changing the basic structure of society . . . laws, by virtue of enabling the powerful to perpetuate the social-structural causes of murder, rape, arson and burglary, ensure the perpetuation of those crimes."

[2] To legally excuse an offense, it must be shown that external conditions were such that a reasonable person, acting with normal diligence could not have avoided his act—unless it is shown that the offender lacked the mental competence to know what he was doing or that what he was doing was wrong.

[3] Paul Bator, "Finality in Criminal Law and Federal *Habeas Corpus* for State Prisoners," *Harvard Law Review* **76** (1963).

[4] S. I. Shuman, *Wayne Law Review*, March 1973, pp. 853–4. Professor Shuman's argument is more intelligent than most, but otherwise prototypical.

were indeed "inevitable," the punishment would be unjust, as Professor Shuman argues. Why, however, would the (unjustly) punished offender become a "political prisoner," as Professor Shuman also claims?

All punishments are imposed, or sanctioned, by the political order which the law articulates. Are all convicts, then, political prisoners? or all those unjustly punished? or all convicts who come from disadvantaged groups? If such a definition were adopted, every convict, all disadvantaged convicts, or everyone unjustly punished would be a political prisoner. "Political prisoner" would become a synonym for "convicted," for "disadvantaged," or for "unjustly punished."

If we want to distinguish between political and other prisoners, a "political prisoner" must be defined as someone imprisoned because he tried to change the political system. The aim of his crime determines whether or not the criminal is political; the offender who intended personal enrichment cannot become a political criminal independently of his actual intent, simply because a penalty is imposed for "the inevitable consequences of a socio-political status," which led him to enrich himself illegally. If any unlawful attempt to improve one's personal situation within the existing order "because of the inevitable consequences of a certain socio-political status" is a political crime, then all crimes committed by severely deprived persons are political. But is the ghetto dweller who becomes a pimp, heroin dealer, or mugger a political criminal just as the one who becomes a violent revolutionary? Ordinarily, an offender who did not address the political order is not regarded as a political criminal, whether he is a victim of politics or not, whereas an offender whose crime did address the political order is a political criminal, even if he is not a victim of politics. This usage permits a meaningful distinction, which Professor Shuman obliterates by making "political" refer to presumptive causes rather than to overt intentions.

INEVITABLE CRIMES?

Professor Shuman goes on to claim that

> . . .arguing that inevitability is too strong a connection between crime and poverty or ghetto existence because not all such persons commit crimes, is rather like arguing that epilepsy or heart attack ought not to excuse because not all epileptics or persons with weak hearts are involved in a chain of events which results in injury.

He adds that "those poverty or ghetto victims who do not commit crimes are extraordinary."

Surely "extraordinary" is wrong here as a statistical generalization: most poor people do not commit crimes;[5] those who do are extraordinary, not those who don't. Perhaps Professor Shuman means that it takes more resistance within than it does outside the "ghetto" not to commit crimes, which is quite likely. But "inevitability"? Here, the analogy with epilepsy or heart diseases is unpersuasive. Such conditions serve as legal excuses only because they produce seizures beyond the control of the person affected. These seizures are legal excuses only when they are the cause of the crime or injury or of the failure to control it. Otherwise a "weak heart" or an epileptic condition is not an excuse. Thus, poverty could not be an excuse, unless it can be shown to produce seizures beyond their control which cause the poor to commit crimes.

Poverty does not produce such seizures. Nor would poverty deprive the victim, if he were to experience a seizure (of criminality?), of control in the way an epileptic seizure does the epileptic. Poverty affects motivation and increases temptation, as does sexual frustration or, sometimes, marriage—hardly an uncontrollable seizure. To have little or no money

---

[5] Perhaps they do—if questionnaires rather than conviction records are followed. (The reliability of questionnaire data is as questionable as that of police records.) It seems likely that about three times as many crimes are committed as are recorded. If so, the statement "most poor people do not commit crimes" remains correct.

NO EXCUSE FOR CRIME

makes it tempting to steal; the poverty-stricken person is more tempted than the rich. But a poor person is not shorn of his ability to control temptation. Indeed it is to him that the legal threat is addressed. He is able to respond to it unless he suffers from a specific individual defect or disease which makes him incompetent.

There is a generous and strong moral bias in Shuman's arguments, although he does not seem fully aware of it. The bias was already noted by Friedrich Nietzche when he wrote in *Beyond Good and Evil*: "[writers] are in the habit of taking the side of criminals." States in un-disguised moral terms, the argument goes: the poor are entitled to rob or rape because of the injustice they suffer—poverty. The moral nature of the argument is concealed by an erroneous factual claim: poor offenders can't help committing crimes and, therefore, should not be held responsible.

The nonfactual, moral nature or bias of the argument is easily revealed if "power" is substituted for "poverty." Suppose one were to credit fully Lord Acton's famous saying: "Power tends to corrupt and absolute power corrupts absolutely." Those who hold power, then, could be held responsible for criminal acts only to some degree, since they live in conditions which tend to corrupt them. Those who hold "absolute power" cannot be held responsible for criminal acts at all. They would be "power victims," as ghetto dwellers are "ghetto victims." Their rapes would be political acts, and they would be political prisoners when punished for them. Power would become a legal excuse. "Absolute power" would be an absolute excuse.

This does not appear to be what Shuman advocates. Yet he urges that poverty (or slums) should be an excuse since—like power—it leads to crime. Shuman wants to excuse the poor and not the wealthy and powerful, not because, as he suggests, poverty is causally more related to crime than wealth; rather, he sees deprivation as morally unjust and painful, and power and wealth as morally undeserved

and pleasant, wherefore he wants to excuse the poor and punish the wealthy.[6] He is morally prejudiced against those corrupted by undeserved wealth—whom he gives no sign of excusing—and in favor of those corrupted by unjust deprivation.

The generosity of his prejudice leads Shuman to overlook a logical error in his argument. In some sense, everybody is what he is, and does what he does, as a result of his genetic inheritance and the influence of his environment—poverty or wealth or power—that interacted with his genetic inheritance and produced him and his conduct. This is no more the case for the poor than for the rich, for criminals than for noncriminals. However, there is no reason to believe that, except in individual cases (which require specific demonstration), genetics, or the environment, so compel actions that the actor must be excused because he could not be expected to control them.

Unless none of us is responsible for what he does, it would have to be shown why criminals, or why poor criminals, are less able to control their conduct and therefore less responsible than others. This cannot be shown by saying that they are a product of the conditions they live in. We all are. Nor can non-responsibility be claimed by showing that their living conditions are more criminogenic than others. Greater temptation does not excuse from responsibility or make punishment unjust. The law, in attempting to mete out equal punishment, does not assume equal temptation.

When it is used to excuse crime in the way advocated by Shuman, moral indignation about squalor, however well justified, may have the paradoxical effect of contributing to high crime rates. Crime becomes less odious if moral dis-

[6] What are the psychological reasons (the scientific or causal as distinguished from the moral ones they rationalize) for excusing the slum-dwelling robber (who wishes to support his habit, or girl friend) and not the embezzler (who wishes to take his girl friend to Acapulco)? Wherein is the embezzler's ambition, greed, wish for prestige, sexual desire less strong, less excusable, or less predetermined by his character and experience than the slum dweller's?

approval of poverty, slums, or ghettoes becomes intense, pervasive, and exculpatory enough to suggest to the "underprivileged" that they are entitled to take revenge through crime and, when they do, to be spared punishment. Those inclined to offenses will perceive the reduced certainty and severity of punishment in such a moral climate as a failure of society to defend its social order. Offenders, not unreasonably, will attribute this failure to doubts about the justification of the social order and to guilt feelings about those deprived by it, who are believed to be "driven to crime" and, when caught, to be unjustly punished "political prisoners."

In my opinion, Shuman is wrong, but Richard Quinney[7] is embarrassing. After explaining "critical philosophy" (the Frankfurt pseudonym of Marxism) at remarkable length by means of pronouncements such as, "a critical philosophy is radically critical," and "Marx held that only under the appropriate conditions can human possibilities be realized," Quinney concludes that "criminal law is an instrument . . . to maintain and perpetuate the existing social and economic order," as though revealing something interesting, or linked to the capitalist order. Yet the criminal law always defends the existing order and those who hold power in it by penalizing those who violate it; and the legal order never can do less than articulate the "social and economic order" capitalist or socialist. How could it be otherwise? If, within a given social order, some people lawfully are richer or more powerful than others, the criminal law must *inter alia* defend their advantages.

Further, in any social order those who are not affluent and powerful are more tempted to rebel, or to take what is not theirs, than those who are—who need not take what they already have. Hence, the burden of the law falls most heavily on the least privileged: the threats and punishments of the criminal law are meant to discourage those who are tempted to violate it, not those who are not. Marxists are as right in saying that the criminal law is addressed disproportionately to the poor as Anatole France was in his witticism: "the law in its majestic equality forbids rich and poor alike . . . to steal bread." However, that discovery is about as interesting as the disclosure that the prohibition law was meant to restrain drinkers rather than the teetotalers who imposed it. The criminal law would be redundant if it did not address those tempted—by taste or social position—to break it.

Quinney also asserts that with socialism "law as we know it" will disappear, for "the crime problem" will be solved "once society has removed all possibility of hatred" (August Bebel). Trotsky held similar views: under socialism

> . . . man will be incomparably stronger, more intelligent, more subtle. His body will be more harmonious, his movements more rhythmical, his voice more musical; his style of life will acquire a dynamic beauty. The average type of man will rise to the level of an Aristotle, Goethe, Marx. From this mountain crest, the new peaks will rise.[8]

Bebel and Trotsky had no experience of socialism when they wrote. Richard Quinney must be congratulated for managing to preserve or regain his innocence, untained by the available theoretical and practical experience. Bereft of Quinney's innocence, I do not foresee a society—socialist or otherwise—in which men will not quarrel and envy each other, wherefore the criminal law will have to restrain them and protect the social order against those who are, or feel, disadvantaged by it. At present the societies which claim to be socialist seem to use legal punishments more than others.[9] I see no reason for maintaining that future socialist societies—whatever form of socialism they adopt—will need criminal law any less.

---

[7] Richard Quinney, *Critique of Legal Order: Crime Control in a Capitalist Society* (Boston: Little Brown & Co., 1974).

[8] Leon Trotsky, *Literature and Revolution*, (New York: Russell & Russell, 1957).

[9] Solzhenitsyn's *Gulag Archipelago* is only the latest illustration of this well-known phenomenon.

BLACK CRIME RATES

Crime among blacks occurs at a rate about 10 times higher than among whites, when blacks and whites are compared as groups. Most crimes are intraracial. The victims of violent crimes are almost as often black as the criminals. (The victims of property crimes committed by blacks and of assaultive crimes concerned with property, such as robbery, are more often white.) Some figures may give an idea of the gross difference. In 1970 blacks in the United States accounted for about 60 percent of all arrests for murder and, according to the FBI's figures, for 65 percent of the arrests for robbery.[10] (Blacks constitute 12 percent of the population.) The difference between black and white crime rates may well be explained by different environments. What has been said in the preceeding section should prevent confusion of such an explanation with a justification for individual offenders.

However, simple comparisons of black and white crime rates are misleading. They ignore the fact that a greater proportion of blacks are young and poor, and the young and poor of any race display the highest crime rates. In other words, the age- and income-related variances must not be attributed to race. The age-specific crime rates of blacks are only slightly higher than those of whites on the same socioeconomic level.[11] The remaining difference cannot be attributed to racially discriminating law enforcement.[12] What discrimination there is may lead in the opposite direction. Crime is less often reported in black communities, and

police are less inclined to arrest blacks for crimes against blacks than they are to arrest whites for crimes against whites.

The difference in crime rates should not come as a surprise. Blacks have been oppressed for a long time. Many are recent migrants from rural to urban areas who have the usual difficulties of acculturation faced by most immigrants. Their access to the labor market was, and still is, limited because of lack of training due to past discrimination. All this has some effect on the legitimate opportunities available to them and, as importantly perhaps, on the ability of individuals to utilize what opportunities there are.

Thus, we should expect a somewhat higher crime rate for blacks, and no explanation in *current* economic terms is needed. Such an explanation would not be supported by the available data. Between 1960 and 1970, the medium income of white families went up 69 percent; that of black families doubled. Whereas only 3 percent of black families earned more than $10,000 a year in 1951, 13 percent did so in 1971.[13] Thus disparity between the income (and the social status) of blacks and whites, though it remains considerable, has been diminished even faster than the difference between white poor and nonpoor. The difference between black and white crime rates has not decreased. Clearly the crude economic explanation—poverty—won't do. Possibly resentment of the remaining disparities has not decreased as these disparities have become fewer and less considerable. Resentment, then, could have prevented the black crime rates from falling as blacks become less deprived and the

[10] F. B. Graham, "Black Crime: The Lawless Image," *Harper's Magazine*, September 1970, p. 64.
[11] See M. A. Forslund, "A Comparison of Negro and White Crime Rates," *Journal of Criminal Law, Criminology and Police Science* 161 (June 1970); E. R. Moses, "Negro and White Crime Rates," in M. E. Wolfgang et al., eds., *The Sociology of Crime and Delinquency* (New York: John Wiley & Sons, 1970); R. M. Stephenson and F. R. Scarpitti, "Negro-White Differentials in Delinquency," *Journal of Research in Crime and Delinquency* 5 (July 1968).
[12] See D. J. Black and A. J. Reiss, Jr., "Police Control of Juveniles," *American Sociological Review* 35 (January 1970); E. Green, "Race, Social Status and Criminal Arrest," *American Sociological Review* 35 (June 1970).

[13] The figures used are in dollars of constant purchasing power, that is, they exclude the effects of inflation; they are taken from Ben J. Wattenberg and Richard M. Scammon, "Black Progress and Liberal Rhetoric," *Commentary*, April 1973, p. 35.
[14] For teenagers, the economic picture is darker. And teenagers account for much crime. One-third of black teenagers were unemployed in 1971, against 15 percent of white teenagers. The high unemployment rate probably contributed to high crime rates in both cases, and the difference in the unemployment rate of white and black teen-

black-white difference in economic and social status become smaller.[14]

Continuing cultural differences, created by historical circumstances, probably contribute to the difference in crime rates of blacks and whites as well; but we know too little as yet to usefully describe, let alone explain, these cultural differences. Phrases such as "the culture of violence" merely describe what is yet to be understood.[15] Surely crime is largely produced by the life styles generated by the subcultures characteristic of those who commit it. But does this tell us more than that crime is produced by a crime-producing subculture?

ENVIRONMENT AND PERSONALITY

What are we to conclude? Many people, black and white, living under the conditions ordinarily associated with high crime rates—such as poverty or inequality—do not commit crimes, while many people not living under these conditions do. It follows that these conditions are neither necessary nor sufficient to cause crime. Crime rates have risen as poverty and inequality have declined. It follows that high crime rates need not depend on more poverty or inequality and are not remedied by less. More resentment may increase crime rates even when there is less poverty—but resentment is hard to measure and may increase with improving conditions, as was pointed out by Alexis de Tocqueville.[16]

Since the incidence of crime among the poor is higher than among the nonpoor, it is quite likely that when combined with other ingredients—not always easily discerned—poverty and inequality do produce high crime rates, probably by affecting motivations and temptations. Thus, poverty may be an important element—though neither indispensible nor sufficient by itself—in the combination that produces high crime rates and explains the variance among groups. But recognition of the importance of poverty as a criminogenic condition should not lead us to neglect individual differences. Enrico Ferri, unlike some of his latter-day followers, did not neglect them. He wrote:

> If you regard the general condition of misery as the sole source of criminality, then you cannot get around the difficulty that out of the one thousand individuals living in misery from the day of their birth to that of their death, only one hundred or two hundred become criminals. . . . If poverty were the sole determining cause, one thousand out of one thousand poor ought to become criminals. If only two hundred become criminals, while one hundred commit suicide, one hundred end as maniacs, the other six hundred remain honest in their social condition, then poverty alone is not sufficient to explain criminality.[17]

THE LEGAL AND THE SOCIAL APPROACH

Surely it is futile to contrast environmental (social) with individual (psychological) causation, as though they were mutually exclusive alternatives. Instead, we might ask in quantitative terms:

1. How much of the variance in crime rates—among social groups, or between two time

agers contributed to the difference in crime rates. The high teenage unemployment rates may be caused at least in part by minimum wage legislation, which requires that teenagers be paid a minimum, which often exceeds what their production is worth to employers. (The minimum wage rate for most other workers rarely is above what they are worth to employers.)

[15] Ghettoization does not explain much, for, except for black ghettoes, the incidence of crime in ghettoes (ethnically segregated slums) is low. In Chinese or Jewish ghettoes there was little crime. On the other hand, variances in crime rates everywhere are associated with ethnic differences.

[16] Democracy in America. For example:

"It is natural that the love of equality should constantly increase together with equality itself, and that it should grow by what it feeds on. . . ."

". . . The mere fact that certain abuses have been remedied draws attention to the others and they now appear more galling; people may suffer less, but their sensibility is exacerbated. . . ."

[17] Enrico Ferri, *The Positive School of Criminology*, ed. Stanley E. Grupp (Pittsburgh: University of Pittsburgh, Press, 1968), p. 60.

periods—is controlled by specific differences in social conditions?

2. Which of these (a) can be changed; (b) at what cost, monetary or otherwise?

3. At what cost can we then reduce the crime rate in general, or the variance, by changing social conditions? What specific social change is likely to bring about what specific change in crime rates and in variances?

To illustrate: if we assume that X percent of the variance between black and white crime rates is explained by the lower employment rates of black males, then we might be able to predict that a rise of X percent in the employment rate of black males would lead to a decline of X percent in the crime rate or in the variance. There are all kinds of pitfalls in such a simplified model. Employment rates, for instance, are determined by a variety of factors. Richard Cloward came to grief by assuming that employment rates are determined exclusively by employment opportunities.[18]

Still, in the apt words of Enrico Ferri: "Certain discreet shelters arranged in convenient places contribute more to the cleanliness of cities than fines or arrests."[19] Ferri meant public urinals. But the principle applies to any change in the social or physical environment, and the questions it poses are always: (1) What is the ratio of the cost of the change in social conditions to the benefit (the reduction in crime rates) compared to the ratio of a change in other variables (for example, expenditures on police; higher or more regular punishments) to the benefit (the reduction in crime rates)? (2) Given these ratios, which change is preferable in view of other merits or demerits?

Parking violations can be reduced by better policing, higher fines, and more public garages. Very high fines would help, but may not be tolerable. More public garages will help, but may be too costly. Without some punishment for violation, there would be no incentive to use public garages, and without some legitimate opportunity, it is likely that the law will be violated unless punishments are extremely severe and certain. The alternatives— "improve social conditions" and "increase punishment"—are not mutually exclusive. They are cumulative. The question is, which combination promises the greatest benefits at the least cost.

[18] See Daniel Patrick Moynihan's *Maximum Feasible Misunderstanding* (New York; The Free Press, 1969) for an analysis of these pitfalls.

[19] Enrico Ferri, *Criminal Sociology* (New York: Agathon Press, Inc., 1917), p. 24.

SECTION III

THE BIOLOGY AND PSYCHOLOGY OF CRIME

Biological explanations of crime have been developed, with varying degrees of acceptance, for almost 200 years. We offer only one study out of an increasing body of serious research on inherent physiological or genotypic studies that are now emerging. Dalgard and Kringlen, in an attempt to separate the influence of heredity from that of later environmental forces, examine a sample of identical and fraternal twins born in Norway, who had attained the ages of 40 to 50 by the time of the investigation. After a detailed analysis of the populations under consideration and by using various measures of criminality, they conclude that there were negligible differences in criminality between identical twins (with the same heredity) and the more usual type of twins, who do not have exactly the same heredity but, like identical twins, share similar environments. These findings lead the authors to doubt the importance of hereditary factors in criminality.

Without question a large segment of American society believes that, in some unspecified manner, criminals are psychologically distinctive from law-abiding, conventional persons. In fact, an appreciable proportion of professionals who deal with criminals also evince similar ideas. Although the evidence thus far does not confirm these beliefs, new, carefully designed research does make some modest claims regarding psychological variations. Conventional wisdom and some early research have suggested a causal tie between learning disabilities (LD) in children, school failure, and juvenile delinquency. The first selection in this section deals with a government project that attempts to ascertain the validity of the claimed link between LD and delinquency. The data do not support such a link—the delinquent behavior of LDs and other children being very similar. But it does appear, the authors conclude, that somehow LD children are treated differently and that their cases are more likely to be brought to the attention of the criminal justice system.

Finally, the selection by Silverman and Dinitz examines the manner in which compulsive masculinity, race, and matriarchal family structures may be associated. They conclude that black delinquents rate themselves as more "manly" than white delinquents do, and that delinquents from female-based homes are more hypermasculine than delinquents from other types of households.

8

CRIMINAL BEHAVIOR IN TWINS

ODD STEFFEN DALGARD AND EINAR KRINGLEN

Particularly in the psychiatric literature it has been maintained that genetic factors play a central role in the etiology of crime, but during the last 20 to 30 years, with increasing delinquency and violence in the Western countries, there has been a weakening of the genetic hypothesis in criminology. A significant number of investigations have shown how delinquency and criminal behaviour are related to psychological, social and cultural factors. However, even though today one is apt to stress psychosocial factors in the etiology of crime, it is nevertheless common to suppose that hereditary factors play a role, at least in certain types of criminal behaviour. For instance, it is reasonable to assume that typical juvenile crime, which varies in accordance with social conditions, is largely environmentally determined, whereas more serious crime, such as grave violence and sexual assaults, is more individually determined and perhaps even genetic in origin. Crime is a cultural and legal concept and accordingly what is considered crime varies to some extent from country to country. In order to entertain the idea that crime could have a genetic origin, one has, of course, to assume that crime is linked to certain personality characteristics, such as aggressive tendencies or deficient ego control.

Source: "A Norwegian Twin Study of Criminality," *The British Journal of Criminology* (July 1976), **16**:213–232. Reprinted by permission.

THE TWIN METHOD

The study of the relative contributions of genetic and environmental factors in human behaviour can best be carried out by the classic twin method. This method is based on the existence of two types of twins: *monozygotics* (MZ) and *dizygotics* (DZ). Whereas MZ twins are supposed to be identical in hereditary endowment, DZ twins are no more alike genetically than common sibs. Thus all differences in MZ have to be attributed to the environment in the widest sense of that term, whereas differences in DZ, on the other hand, may be due to both hereditary and environmental factors.

Through a comparison of concordance figures in MZ and DZ with regard to certain traits, one might arrive at an impression of the relative significance of hereditary and environment for the trait in question. A pair is called *concordant* if both twins in a twin-pair harbour the same trait or illness, *discordant* if they are dissimilar, for instance if one twin is criminal and the other is not. Significantly higher concordance figures in the group of identical twins have usually been regarded as evidence in support of a hereditary background of the traits concerned. Conversely, if a characteristic is chiefly environmentally determined, one would expect similar concordance rates in MZ and DZ. In the case of epidemics where genetic differences are far less important than environmental ones, one would expect clustering in families but no marked difference in concordance rates for MZ and DZ. The same would be true for criminality in the case of environmentally causative origin.

GENERAL METHODOLOGICAL PROBLEMS

We shall not here discuss methodological problems but we would like to draw attention to a few common sources of error in twin research and make some general statements with regard to interpretation of data.

The results of twin studies are debatable if the following requirements are not fulfilled:

a. The sampling must be based upon complete series of twins. *Cf.* Rosenthal's (1962) theoretical discussion and Kringlen's (1967) empirical research in the field of schizophrenia.
b. The separation of MZ and DZ same-sexed twins must be reliably carried out. Particularly in small samples is blood- and serum-typing necessary.
c. The concept of concordance must be clearly defined and the method of computing concordance given, since there are different measures of concordance (Allen *et al.*, 1967).

Higher concordance figures in MZ than in DZ have usually been regarded as proof of hereditary disposition for the trait concerned. Such an interpretation is, however, based on the following assumptions:

a. The environmental conditions are in general similar for MZ and DZ pairs. This assumption is obviously not true. Zazzo (1960) and others have shown that the environment of MZ pairs is more likely to be closely similar than the environment of DZ pairs.
b. The frequency of the trait concerned is not higher in MZ than in DZ pairs. Christiansen's (1968) data throw doubt on this assumption with regard to criminality since he found that MZ twins were more frequently imprisoned for crime than DZ twins.

PREVIOUS CRIMINOLOGICAL TWIN STUDIES

Table I gives a summary of previous twin studies, along with the present one, with regard to concordance in crime.

Lange (1929) studied 30 pairs of same-sexed (male) twins and observed that 10 of 13 MZ were concordant, whereas only 2 of 17 DZ displayed concordance. Concordance was defined as offences which lead to imprisonment. Lange obtained his sample of criminal same-sexed twins from prisons, from registered convicted psychopaths, and from his own psychiatric hospital. In addition to the 13 MZ and the 17 DZ of the same sex he learned by chance of ten opposite-sexed twin pairs. The zygosity—monozygotic or dizygotic—was determined by means of somatic measurements, photographs and fingerprints. As a rule the author himself examined personally both twins in a pair. In his monograph Lange gives a fairly detailed description of all the MZ pairs. He concluded his famous study by stating that heredity plays a major role in crime under contemporary conditions.

LeGras (1933) found that all four of his MZ were concordant whereas the five DZ were discordant with regard to criminality. He investigated both psychotic and criminal twins and collected his sample by writing to heads of asylums, prisons, state working colonies and correctional institutions as well as by a search of the university psychiatric-neurological department in Utrecht. Where the twin pairs were similar in appearance they were investigated by means of the Siemens' method (Siemens, 1924), whereas in cases of dissimilarity they were considered dizygotic and investigated further by mail only.

Rosanoff *et al.* (1934) obtained their relatively large sample of twins both from mental and penal institutions. The sample was divided into three groups: criminal adults, *i.e.* persons 18 years or over who had been sentenced by a criminal court; juvenile delinquents, *i.e.* boys and girls who had been placed on probation or had been committed to a correctional insti-

TABLE I Pairwise Concordance for Criminality in Previous and Present Twin Studies[a]

	MZ		DZ—same sex		DZ—opposite sex	
	No. of pairs	Per Cent con- cordance	No. of pairs	Per Cent con- cordance	No. of pairs	Per Cent con- cordance
	13	76.9	17	11.8	10	10.0
Lange 1929, Germany	4	100.0	5	0.0	—	—
LeGras 1933, Holland	37	67.6	28	17.9	32	3.1
Rosanoff et al. 1934, U.S.A.	31	64.5	43	53.5	50	14.0
Kranz 1936, Germany	18	61.1	19	36.8	28	7.1
Stumpfl 1936, Germany	4	75.0	5	40.0	10	20.0
Borgstrom 1939, Finland	28	60.7	18	11.1	—	—
Yoshimasu 1961, Japan	5	60.0	—	—	—	—
Tienari 1963, Finland	81	33.3	137	10.9	226	3.5
Christiansen 1968, Denmark						
Dalgard and Kringlen 1976,	49	22.4	89	18.0	—	—
Norway[b]	31	25.8	54	14.9	—	—

[a] Only concordance rates for adult criminals are included in the table. Some studies include female same sex twin pairs, i.e. Rosanoff, Kranz, Stumpfl, and Christiansen.
[b] Broad and strict concepts of crime, respectively.

tution; and children with behaviour disorders who had not been in conflict with the law. It is unclear to what degree the twins were personally seen by the research team. Concordance for the adult group was 67.6 per cent in MZ and 17.9 per cent in same-sexed DZ, whereas only 3.1 per cent of the opposite-sexed DZ were concordant. Concordance rates in juvenile delinquents were 93 per cent in MZ, and 80 per cent in DZ of the same sex, and 20 per cent in DZ opposite-sexed. Concordance in children was 87 per cent in MZ, 43 per cent in same-sexed DZ and 28 per cent in opposite-sexed DZ.

Kranz (1936) sampled from several prisons and thus obtained 552 pairs of twins. However, the majority had to be excluded, 127 pairs because they were in fact not twins, 202 pairs because one of the partners had died, and 97 pairs because of uncertain zygosity diagnosis or uncertain concordance. The author combined Siemen's similarity method with blood testing in determining the zygosity of the remaining same-sex subject twin-pairs and Kranz himself investigated most of the twins personally. Concordance in MZ and DZ of the same

sex was 64.5 per cent and 53.5 per cent respectively, whereas the concordance figure for opposite-sexed DZ was considerably lower, namely 14 per cent. In his comprehensive monograph Kranz discusses the zygosity diagnosis of several pairs in detail, and he gives a thorough description of the life histories of both MZ and DZ pairs.

Stumpfl (1936) collected his sample from several prisons as well as from the register of "biological criminals." Zygosity was determined by photographs and physical measurements. The author investigated most of the twins personally and supplemented his data by information from relatives and official sources. The concordance rates of this study fall into the same pattern as we have observed for the Rosanoff and Kranz studies, concordance figures being highest in MZ and lowest in opposite-sexed DZ with the same-sexed DZ falling in between (61.1–36.8–7.1 per cent).

Borgstrom (1939) reported that three of his four MZ pairs were concordant compared with two out of five DZ same-sexed pairs. Only two out of ten opposite-sexed DZ pairs were concordant.

Yoshimasu (1961) studied 46 same-sexed (male) twin pairs and observed that 17 of 28 MZ and two of 18 DZ were concordant. The author was aware of the significance of representative sampling but could not obtain a complete series because of no access to a twin register. Zygosity was based on various measures, and on blood-typing. We have not been able to obtain Yoshimasu's original report.

Tienari (1963) in his large-scale twin study of various types of psychopathology reported that six of 15 MZ pairs were concordant with regard to psychopathic behaviour, and three of five MZ were concordant with respect to manifest criminal behaviour.

Christiansen (1968) based his study on the Danish twin register, which includes virtually all twins born in Denmark between 1870 and 1910. Nearly 6,000 pairs of twins where both twins had survived the age of 15 were checked against the central police register and/or the local police registers. Zygosity diagnosis was based on a modified similarity test which previously had been controlled by a thorough blood and serum testing. In his 1968 paper the author reported that 35.8 per cent of the 67 male MZ pairs were concordant, *i.e.* both twins had been recorded in the official penal register, in contrast to 12.3 per cent concordance in 114 male DZ pairs. In the female group the concordances were 21.4 per cent in 14 MZ pairs and 4.4 per cent in 23 DZ pairs. In the group of opposite-sexed DZ pairs the concordance was 3.5 per cent.

The studies reviewed above consistently show a higher concordance for MZ than for DZ twins, a finding which supports the genetic hypothesis. However, the differences in concordance figures in MZ and DZ are in some studies slight and statistically not significant. Furthermore one also observes a difference in concordance between same-sexed DZ and opposite-sexed DZ, a finding which indeed emphasises the significance of environmental factors. Finally, the 1968 study and the results of the present one deviate considerably from the general pattern previously reported. Not only

is the difference in concordance for MZ and DZ small in these last studies but the concordance in MZ is considerably lower than reported earlier. In fact discordance is more pronounced than concordance.

We shall now present some findings from our own study, reverting later on to these other studies. We shall then try to explain the observed differences in concordance figures and will argue that the recent studies which show that genetic factors play a minimal role in the etiology of crime are more reliable, essentially due to improved sampling.

THE PRESENT INVESTIGATION

The aim of this investigation was first of all to arrive at "true" or representative concordance figures for MZ and DZ twins with regard to criminality in order to elucidate the relative contributions of heredity and environment in antisocial behaviour. In addition, we wanted to study in more detail the developmental histories of MZ twin-pairs discordant for crime in order to throw light on individual predisposing factors. Finally, our aim was to study nosological aspects of behaviour. Given an MZ criminal twin, what spectrum of behaviour can one observe in the MZ co-twin?

In order to reach our aim, the investigation was from the start planned in two steps. To begin with, we wanted to study the total sample of twins in a crude manner. Afterwards we intended to carry out a more intensive study of a sub-sample focusing attention on discordance. In this selection we shall report our methods and findings regarding the first part of the study and accordingly address ourselves to the problem of concordance figures.

SAMPLE

A twin register comprising all twins born in Norway between 1900 and 1935 had previously been compiled by one of the authors (Kringlen, 1967). This register contains the names and dates of birth of approximately 66,000 twins, *i.e.* 33,000 pairs. In the present investigation the names of all male twins born in the period 1921 to 1930 were checked against the national criminal register at December 31, 1966. We thus obtained a sample of 205 pairs of twins who had passed the main risk period for serious crime: 42 pairs where one twin had died before age 15 were excluded from the sample. In addition, 24 pairs were excluded for other reasons (*cf.* Table II). Female twin-pairs and opposite-sexed twins were not included in the investigation because the low frequency of reported crime for women would have required an unusually large basic twin population to afford a sufficient sample, and hence considerable secretarial work. Thus we are left with a sample of 139 twin-pairs where according to the national criminal register one or both of the twins had been convicted. Local directories enabled us to ascertain the addresses of the subjects, whereupon the twins were approached personally for blood test and interview.

ZYGOSITY DIAGNOSIS

The zygosity diagnoses were in most cases based on blood and serum typing. The following systems were employed: ABO, MN, CDEce. Hp, Gc, PGM, K, SP, and C_3. Identicalness on all these systems was considered evidence of monozygosity. The dizygotics were classified as such when only dissimilar on at least two factors. All pairs were thus not tested on all systems. By such a thorough testing, the zygosity diagnosis is rendered almost 100 per cent correct (Juel-Nielsen *et al.*, 1958). In case it was not practically possible to have blood samples taken from both twins, the zygosity diagnosis was determined by comparing the twins with regard to such physical categories as similarity of external appearance, colour of eyes and hair, shape of face, and height. Finally, in all cases we obtained information with respect to identity confusion as children. Research has shown that simple questions such as "Were you mixed up as children? Were you considered alike as two drops of water?" can determine the zygosity correctly in over 90 per cent of cases (Cederlöf *et al.*, 1961). Accordingly, even though blood tests were not available in all cases, there is no reason to believe that many if any twin pairs have been misclassified.

Table III gives the zygosity diagnosis of the sample.

INTERVIEW AND SUPPLEMENTARY INFORMATION

The main part of the personal investigation was carried out in 1969–71. The twins were, of course, geographically distributed throughout the country so the home visits had to be made by private car, airplane, and sometimes boat to reach remote places.

Information about the life history of the twins was obtained through a semi-structured interview which lasted one to one-and-a-half hours. Each twin was usually interviewed once either by an advanced medical student or by the authors. The interview covered such items as childhood and adult biography, and included present social background, somatic and mental health status, as well as criminal career. In addition each twin was asked to describe

TABLE II Survey of the Sample

Number of original twin pairs		205
Excluded from original sample due to		
death of one twin prior to age 15	42	
unknown address	10	
other reasons	14[a]	66
Number of pairs in final sample		139

[a] Six pairs by death of both twins, two pairs due to their living in the most northern part of the country, two pairs were in fact not twins, two pairs could not be located, two pairs were living abroad.

TABLE III Zygosity Determination of Same-Sexed (Male) Twin Pairs

Zygosity diagnosis	Blood-tested	Not blood-tested	Total
MZ	33 pairs	16 pairs	49 pairs
DZ	49 pairs	40 pairs	89 pairs
Unknown	—	1 pair	1 pair
Total	82 pairs	57 pairs	139 pairs

his co-twin. Sometimes it was possible to obtain information from siblings and/or parents as well, so that the data could be constantly corrected and supplemented. In some cases, interviews with both twins could not be obtained, because one of the twins was dead, lived in an inaccessible location, was at sea or abroad. Table IV shows the extent of personal interviewing. In close to 70 per cent of cases both twins in a pair were interviewed. In only four pairs did we not obtain a personal interview with either twin.

In most instances we were able to study the legal case material of convicted twins. This was crucial in order to arrive at an objective picture with regard to criminal life. Usually the interviewer studied the legal case material before he interviewed the twin so as to facilitate discussing the case with the subject. In case of so-called judicial observation, we were permitted to study the psychiatric documents. We would also like to add that the total sample has been checked against the psychosis register and, in case of medical treatment or hospitalization, additional information has been obtained.

RESULTS

SURVEY OF THE SAMPLE

First we shall give a description of the sample by age, civil status, social class, mental health, and crime committed (omitting one pair with uncertain zygosity diagnosis). Then we shall report the concordance figures for various types of crimes, and finally some data with regard to discordance.

TABLE IV   Extent of Personal Interviewing

	MZ Pairs	DZ Pairs	Total Pairs
Both twins	35	58	93
Only one twin	12	29	41
Neither	2	2	4
Total	49	89	138[a]

[a] One pair with unknown zygosity diagnosis excluded.

Of the 276 twins, *i.e.* 138 pairs, 248 were alive at the time of investigation; 11 had died of accidents, ten of somatic diseases, three by suicide, and four could not be traced. All subjects were men in the age group 40–50 years at the time of investigation, with a mean age of 44.9 years (44.8 years in MZ and 45.0 in DZ).

Table V, on social class, shows some over-representation of classes V and VI compared to the general population. More than 50 per cent work as factory workers, small-holders and fishermen, and only 5.4 per cent belong to the upper social strata. On the other hand, most of the people have an occupation, only 3.3 per cent being without durable jobs or on social security. There is no significant difference in social class distribution for MZ and DZ.

As to civil status there is a slight over-representation of never-married in the sample compared to the general population (17 per cent versus 13.5 per cent), and the rate of divorce is somewhat increased.

Of the subjects 65 per cent had elementary schooling as the only formal education, which corresponds closely to Christie's (1960) figures for a 1933 cohort of Norwegian criminal males. The corresponding figure for the general population of that cohort was lower, namely 48 per cent with only elementary school.

TABLE V   Distribution According to Social Strata

	No.	Per cent
I. Professionals in high positions, executive, managerial	3	1.1
II. Professionals in lower positions, higher employees, businessmen	12	4.3
III. School-teachers, technicians, employees	23	8.3
IV. Skilled workers, lower employees, farmers	66	23.9
V. Unskilled workers, small-holders, fishermen	158	57.3
VI. Day labourers, others without a stable job	9	3.3
Unknown	5	1.8
Total	276	100.0

Table VI gives an impression of the mental health status of the subjects. A rather conservative classification has been employed based on a global evaluation of subjective and objective symptoms as well as social functioning. We were able to evaluate 262 subjects of whom the majority were functioning satisfactorily, socially, and most of the subjects were without marked neurotic symptoms, such as pain, tensions, irritability, anxiety or depression. 15 per cent had moderate but clear-cut neurotic or psychopathic traits and some did not function adequately socially, *i.e.* did not work or were hospitalized or imprisoned. Only 7.6 per cent had serious symptoms such as psychotic symptoms or severe alcohol or drug problems, some of these combined with grave social dysfunction. In other words, in this male population, age 40–50 years, 20–25 per cent could be said to have been seriously disturbed mentally, a figure which is commonly reported in investigation on the general population.

With regard to alcohol consumption, we obtained reliable information on 262 subjects. Of these, 33 per cent had an alcohol problem and drank too much according to rather liberal standards, but only 13 per cent could be considered chronic alcoholics. According to various studies, the risk of developing alcoholism

in the male Norwegian population is around 8 per cent.

Table VII shows the types of crime committed by the group. As one can see, theft/burglary is the most common crime, followed by traffic law violation. Crime involving violence is, for instance, rather uncommon, consituting barely 10 per cent.

Thus, this sample of male twin pairs where the index twin is in the Criminal Register does differ slightly from the general population with regard to certain epidemiological variables. They seem to have a lower social class distribution; they seem to have received a less-than-normal degree of education; they are to a lesser degree married; and frequency of alcoholism seems higher in this group than in the general population. However, these differences are by and large of a minor nature.

CONCORDANCE FIGURES IN TWIN STUDIES

Concordance is usually defined as persistent manifestation of similar traits in both twins. A pair is labelled concordant if both twins have

TABLE VI Global Evaluation of Mental Health

	No.	Per cent
1. No symptoms, adequate social functioning	129	77.5
2. Slight symptoms, adequate social functioning	74	
3. Moderate symptoms, adequate social functioning	15	
		14.9
4. Moderate symptoms, some social impairment	24	
5. Serious symptoms, some social impairment	9	
		7.6
6. Serious symptoms, grave social impairment	11	
Total	262	100.0

TABLE VII Type of Crime Committed[a]

Reason for conviction	No. of persons	Percentage
Theft, burglary	70	32.6
Violation of motor vehicle law	53	24.7
Violation of vagrancy law	18	8.4
Violence	17	7.9
Treason during World War II	17	7.9
Sexual assault on children	11	5.1
Deceit, fraud	11	5.1
Violation of military criminal law	7	3.3
Indecent exposure	3	1.4
Threats of bodily harm	2	0.9
Intoxication	2	0.9
Incest	2	0.9
Rape	2	0.9
Robbery	1	0.5
Total	215	100.5

[a] Some persons were convicted for several types of crime.

the same illness or same behaviour, for instance if both are criminals, discordant if one twin is criminal and the co-twin is not. The concept of concordance implies a dichotomy which is not always acceptable. Accordingly, in the case of measurable traits, concordance is usually expressed as the average intra-pair difference. In psychiatry the view has gained ground that there is no qualitative distinction between mental health and illness in general. Therefore dichotomies are often drawn arbitrarily or the reference is, for instance, to partial concordance, as when one twin is schizophrenic and the co-twin is borderline schizophrenic.

There are different ways of computing concordance rates (Allen *et al.*, 1967). The *direct pairwise method* is simple and most used when comparing concordance in MZ and DZ. By this method one simply calculates the percentage of concordant pairs in the sample. The *proband method* is more useful when one also wishes to compare incidences (concordances) in siblings. (Proband is the name given to index cases in a genetic investigation.) The proband concordance is the proportion of afflicted twins or sibs who have an afflicted partner. In other words it is the morbidity rate of the partners of affected twins. By this method each affected pair doubly ascertained counts twice. Concordance is not a correlation in the usual sense since the number of twin pairs in which neither is a criminal is usually not accessible.

Direct pairwise concordance is obtained according to the formula $(c/c + d)$ where c is the number of concordant pairs and d is the number of discordant pairs. The proband concordance is ascertained by this formula: $(c + x)/c + x + d)$ where x is the number of pairs represented by two independently ascertained cases, and c and d as defined above.

Table VIII gives concordance rates for MZ and DZ when a broad concept of crime is employed. Crime is here defined as legally punishable behaviour reported to the Criminal Register. As the table shows, the figures yield high rates for proband concordance in both MZ and DZ, but the pairwise concordance shows the higher ratio MZ/DZ, namely 1.24 against 1.20. The concordance rates in MZ are higher than in DZ, but the difference is slight and statistically not significant. (The 95 per cent confidence interval for the difference between concordance rates included 0; See Dixon and Massey, 1969, p. 249.)

Table IX gives concordance rates when a more strict concept of crime is employed. Crime here is defined as anti-social acts which would be considered crimes in most countries, such as crimes of violence, crimes involving sexual norms, crimes against property. Here the difference in concordance rates between MZ and DZ increases, although the difference is still not statistically significant ($p > 0.05$).

In Table X the sample is split up according to various types of crime. For crimes related to theft and burglary which have the highest incidence, the pairwise concordance is 19.1 per cent in MZ and 18.5 per cent in DZ, practically no difference at all. With regard to other types

TABLE VIII   Concordance with Respect to Criminality, Employing a Broad Concept of Crime [a]

Zygosity	Total pairs	Concordant pairs	Discordant pairs	Pairwise concordance	Proband concordance
MZ	49	11	38	22.4 %	36.7 %
DZ	89	16	73	18.0 %	30.5 %
MZ/DZ				1.24	1.20

[a] Including, for instance, crime according to the motor vehicle law, the military law, and cases of treason during World War II.

TABLE IX Concordance with Respect to Criminality, Employing a Strict Concept of Crime[a]

Zygosity	Total pairs	Concordant pairs	Discordant pairs	Pairwise concordance	Proband concordance
MZ	31	8	23	25.8%	41.0%
DZ	54	8	46	14.9%	25.8%

[a] According to the criminal law, including: violence, sexual assault, theft and robbery.

of crimes the numbers are so small that no conclusion is indicated with regard to concordance, except that the general pattern seems to be that of discordance in both MZ and DZ.

Thus the data do show higher concordance figures in MZ and DZ with regard to criminal behaviour. However, the differences reported are of a minor character, and statistically not significant. The natural conclusion would appear to be that, if there does exist a genetic disposition to criminal behaviour, the disposition is a weak one. Even such a modest conclusion, however, is based on the underlying assumption that the environmental conditions for MZ pairs do not differ from those of DZ pairs, an assumption which today cannot be accepted. MZ twins receive, in fact, more similar external environmental influence than do DZ, because they are treated more often as a unit and are seen together more. Consequently higher concordance figures in MZ may not be the result of heredity only. Table XI shows clearly that the MZ pairs have been treated more frequently as a unit and have experienced more extreme closeness and interdependence than the DZ pairs. In the MZ group, for instance, 92 per cent of the pairs felt they had been brought up as a unit as against 77 per cent of the dizygotic group. In the MZ group 94 per cent had been dressed alike in childhood as against 74 per cent of the DZ pairs. A still clearer difference is revealed when one compares the subjective feeling of emotional closeness and mutual identity. Most of the MZ pairs, namely 86 per cent, had felt an extreme or strong interdependence compared with 36 per cent of the DZ. Expressed another way, only 13 per cent of the MZ group felt that in childhood and adolescence they had been no more close than non-twins sibs, whereas 64 per cent of the DZ pairs had felt so.

Let us examine the implications of these findings with regard to concordance figures. In Table XII we have compared the concord-

TABLE X Concordance for Similar Type of Crime in Monozygotic and Dizygotic Twins

Type of crime	MZ		DZ	
	Concordant pairs	Discordant pairs	Concordant pairs	Discordant pairs
Theft, burglary	4	17	7	31
Violence, robbery with menace	1	4	1	12
Deceit, fraud	0	5	0	6
Sexual offence against children	2	2	0	5
Exhibitionism	0	1	0	2
Rape	0	0	0	1
Incest	0	1	0	1
Total	7	30	8	58

TABLE XI   Twin Relationship and External Environment in MZ and DZ Twins

Twin relationship as children and as adolescents	MZ pairs	DZ pairs	Total pairs
Brought up as a unit	45	67	112
Brought up differently	4	20	24
Unknown	0	2	2
Dressed alike	46	64	110
Dressed differently	3	23	26
Unknown	0	2	2
Extremely strong closeness	14	5	19
Strong closeness	28	27	55
Slight closeness, as "sibs"	7	57	64

ance figures in MZ and DZ according to degree of psychological closeness, *i.e.* strong or weak intra-pair interdependence. The table shows that the previously observed difference in concordance between MZ and DZ now almost disappears in the group of twins who have experienced a close relationship. Thus when one compares MZ and DZ who have more or less experienced the same environmental influences the difference in concordance figures vanishes. The second row in the table speaks against this hypothesis. However, one is inclined to de-emphasize this observation since the numbers concerned are very small.

How then can these factors influence the concordance rates? Most likely, similar external milieu and mutual identification lead to similarities in personality, including the shared criminal tendencies. For the same reason, the twins in a pair, as adults, operate together as a unit, and accordingly carry out criminal acts together. However, the significance of these factors must not be exaggerated. One has to bear in mind that, even in MZ and DZ with rather similar external environment, discordance is more conspicuous than concordance.

Table XIII shows that twins of MZ and DZ concordant pairs to a large extent operate together in criminal acts. We have also data showing that a relatively larger number of twin pairs who work together during acts of crime have been closely connected in childhood. This applies particularly MZ pairs; however, the numbers are small and not statistically significant.

DISCORDANCE

We have shown in this study that the difference between MZ and DZ with regard to concordance rates in crime is negligible. Even in MZ discordance is more conspicuous than concordance. But why the discordance? Our information is as yet not sufficient to throw much

TABLE XII   Concordance for Crime in the Strict Sense in Twins with Respect to Intra-pair Interdependence

Degree of closeness	MZ		DZ	
	Concordance	Per Cent	Concordance	Per cent
Extreme or strong	6/26	23.2	3/14	21.4
Moderate or weak	2/5	40.0	5/40	12.5
Total group	8/31	25.8	8/54	14.9

TABLE XIII Degree of Contact with Co-Twin During Criminal Act in Concordant Pairs

Degree of togetherness	MZ	DZ	Total
Always together in the same act	7	3	10
Partly together in the same act	1	9	10
Never together in the same act	8	4	12
Total	16	16	32

light on this question. We will therefore just give a few conclusions based on our preliminary findings and revert to this problem in a later paper.

First, one observes that the criminal twin has belonged as an adult to a lower social class and has been more often somatically and mentally ill, and more often classified as an alcoholic, than his co-twin. Furthermore, one finds differences in personality characteristics in both MZ and DZ, *e.g.* the criminal twin in discordant pairs has been the more suspicious or sceptical by nature, the more restless and anxious, the more dominant and self-assertive. If these differences occurred only in the DZ but not the MZ group they might be ascribed to genetic factors. However, since the differences are present in both MZ and DZ pairs they have to be ascribed to environmental influences in the broadest sense of that term, *i.e.* they could be due to organic perinatal factors or to psychosocial factors after birth. But since there is no correlation between criminal behaviour in adult life and birth order, birth weight and physical condition in infancy, such differences in personality and life outcomes as alcoholism and criminality must be psycho-social in origin.

Finally a reservation: one should bear in mind that the figures on which we based our observations are small, and in many cases the actual extent of intra-pair differences has not been fully explored and tabulated. The differences reported here are statistically significant in only a few cases, and accordingly one should at this time regard them as hypotheti-

cal, interesting observations which will have to be more carefully investigated.

GENERAL DISCUSSION

In a sample obtained from the Norwegian criminal register we have observed very slight differences in concordance rates in MZ and DZ twins with regard to crime. Since MZ twins experience a more similar upbringing and an identity with each other stronger than that of DZ twins, we have compared groups of monozygotic with dizygotic twin pairs who by and large have experienced this same close twin relationship and report the same type of upbringing with regard to dressing and treatment by the parents. In such a comparison the difference in concordance between MZ and DZ practically disappears altogether. These findings lead us to conclude that *the significance of hereditary factors in registered crime is non-existent.*

One could, of course, object that by focusing attention only on registered crime one misses the unreported and unconvicted crime. Could it not be that several of the co-twins of registered criminals in fact are also criminals and accordingly the reported concordance figures are minimum figures? Obviously our figures are minimum figures in this respect. However, in our interviews we tried to obtain information with regard to criminal behaviour in the co-twin, and furthermore there is no reason to believe that we should have missed disproportionately more MZ co-twins than DZ co-twins with criminal records. Thus even if one accepts the possibility that the real figures should be higher, there is no reason to believe that the relative difference in concordance rates between MZ and DZ is affected by this source of error.

Our results are clearly at variance with most of the twin literature on crime. In several of the more comprehensive earlier studies the concordance rates found are considerably higher for MZ than for DZ twins. Table XIV shows the results of the major studies, excluding investigations with smaller samples. As one can observe, the figures for DZ vary considerably, with a range of 11–53 per cent. In MZ there is a more uniform pattern, with concordance in the range of 61–77 per cent. However, in all the previous studies, except Kranz, there is a clear-cut difference between MZ and DZ.

Why then do the more recent studies from Scandinavia, by Christiansen and ourselves, deviate? To answer this question we have to examine the crucial factors related to sampling and zygosity diagnosis. It is evident that sampling is important in concordance studies of twins. If the sampling is unsystematic and uncontrolled the likelihood of obtaining disproportionately more concordant than discordant pairs is increased.

It goes without saying that the probability of being brought to the attention of investigators is greater for concordant pairs than for the less conspicuous discordant cases. If the probability of finding a twin in an institutional population is p and the members of concordant pairs are discovered independently, the probability of catching a discordant pair is p and the probability of finding a concordant pair is: $p + p - (p \times p)$. For instance, if p is 0.6, then the probability of finding a discordant pair is 0.6 and $0.6 + 0.6 - (0.6 \times 0.6) = 0.84$ for a concordant pair. In reality the difference in probability is most likely greater because the twins in concordant pairs are often not reported independently.

It is also obvious that the establishment of correct zygosity diagnosis is of importance, particularly when one is dealing with small samples as one usually does in twin research. Recent experimental studies have shown that there is a tendency to diagnose MZ as DZ when bloodtesting is not employed. As there are more discordant than concordant DZ in the various studies, this source of error will have the effect of inflating the concordance rate in MZ.

Why, then, is the proportion of MZ considerably higher than expected in earlier studies, namely 45 per cent in the Lange study, 57 per cent in Rosanoff's, 42 per cent in Kranz's, and 49 per cent in the study by Stumpfl? (The Japanese study is a special case since the twin population of Asia differs from the European one.) In the Christiansen study the proportion of MZ in same-sex twins is 37 per cent and in the present study 36 per cent, numbers which correspond fairly well with expected frequencies for the normal population of twins. We have no satisfactory explanation to offer. Could

TABLE XIV Pairwise Concordance Figures for Criminality in MZ and DZ in Relation to Two Critical Variables[a]

Investigator	MZ Concordance %	DZ Concordance %	Sampling complete Unselected sample	Zygosity diagnosis Blood and serum typing[b]
Lange 1929	76.9	11.8	No	No
Rosanoff et al. 1934	67.6	17.9	No	No
Kranz 1936	64.5	53.5	No	Yes
Stumpfl 1936	61.1	36.8	No	No
Yoshimasu 1961	60.7	11.1	No	Yes
Christiansen 1968	33.3	10.9	Yes	Yes
Dalgard and Kringlen 1975	25.8	14.9	Yes	Yes

[a] LeGras, Borgstrøm and Tienari have been excluded because of small samples, cf. Table I.
[b] Kranz employed a limited number of blood groups; Christiansen based his zygosity diagnosis on a modified similarity test based on a questionnaire, but this method had previously been controlled by thorough blood and serum testing.

it be that an uncontrolled sampling without access to a regional or national twin register will automatically obtain relatively more MZ than DZ same sexed twins since the first group are considered by most people to be more interesting subjects?

In reviewing the major twin studies with respect to crime one notes that Lange, Rosanoff, Kranz, Stumpfl and Yoshimasu did not obtain unselected complete series of criminal twins as Christiansen and the present authors did. Neither did they secure their zygosity diagnosis through blood tests to the same degree as did the Scandinavian investigators. Let us, however, examine the various studies in more detail.

SAMPLING

Lange obtained twins from resident populations of both a prison and a mental hospital, and he also included in his sample convicted psychopathic probands registered by a research institution, twins resident in prisons in Bavaria on a certain day, as well as any other twin-pairs in the convict's family. By such a method he was theoretically likely to obtain relatively more concordant than discordant pairs because concordant pairs have a greater chance of being found. However, since Lange does not give figures for the original population of inmates it is difficult to know how successful his sampling was.

Rosanoff and co-workers sampled a series of institutions, such as psychiatric hospitals and clinics and penal and correctional institutions. The investigators do not give a detailed account of the sampling technique. It is, however, evident that the sampling was uncontrolled and unsystematic, and accordingly one would expect to find relatively more concordant than discordant pairs.

Kranz obtained the major part of his sample from Prussian prisons. Every inmate of all the jails in that region had been asked on a certain day if he was a twin. The author supplemented his original sample by inquiring of every recently-admitted prisoner in six penal institutions in a specific area over a one-year period whether he was a twin. According to the author this last series had not been obtained by continual registration. Nevertheless, most likely Kranz by his sample secured from the outset a rather unselected group of criminal twins. However, because of later exclusion of a large number of pairs, the representativeness of his final sample might be questioned. Whereas his original material consisted of 552 pairs of twins, after excluding 427 of them for a variety of reasons, he was left with only 125 pairs. It is noteworthy that he left out a total of 97 pairs because of uncertain zygosity diagnosis or uncertain concordance. Since we are not given more detailed information concerning this group it is difficult to evaluate its impact on the final sample.

Stumpfl also seems to have obtained, at the outset, a rather unselected sample of twins by collecting 550 twin-pairs from consecutively admitted convicts of German prisons and from the files of a research institute in Bavaria. However, the author states that he investigated only 65 of these pairs more thoroughly, and the reason for selection was "availability," which of course is a dubious criterion with regard to sampling. Thus it is impossible to have any idea how this selectivity might affect concordance figures in MZ and DZ.

Yoshimasu tried to obtain a complete unselected series of criminal twins, but according to himself he did not succeed. His sample most likely would contain a preponderance of concordant cases.

Christiansen, in contrast to earlier investigators, had access to a national twin register and thus an unselected sample of criminal twins could be located. By such a sampling method the probability of identifying more concordant than discordant cases is negligible.

Our own investigation followed, in principle, the Danish method. All male twins of the national twin register born 1920–29 were checked against the central criminal register. Thus a complete and representative sample of criminal twins was obtained.

In summary, then, *from a sampling point of view we might conclude that previous studies, due to possible sampling errors, most likely obtained a preponderance of concordant pairs, which would render too high concordance figures in MZ and DZ twins.* Any real difference in concordance figures between MZ and DZ will accordingly be artificially increased due to deficient sampling. The Danish and Norwegian studies, however, were able to avoid these sampling problems and thus the results of these studies are more reliable.

ZYGOSITY

Lange relied on physical measurements, photographs and fingerprints, but for part of his sample he only obtained superficial information due to uncooperativeness of the twins. Accordingly there is a risk that some of his MZ twins have been classified as DZ.

Rosanoff *et al.* investigated the largest sample, but methodologically their study is far from satisfactory. Not only was the sampling unsystematic but it is quite unclear how the zygosity diagnoses were established. Most likely a sort of similarity method was employed and, as noted before, this will lead to misclassification of some MZ.

Kranz is the only one of the earlier investigators who, to some extent, employed blood grouping. The blood groups most used were the ABO and MN systems, which today are considered very reliable. If twins in a pair differ on any of these systems, they are without doubt dizygotic. The opposite is, however, not true since same-sexed DZ may in fact both have blood group A in 10 per cent. He also used the similarity method of Siemen and in some cases he had access to photographs of the twins. Thus there is no reason to believe that many same-sex twin pairs were misclassified.

Stumpfl employed only the similarity method and thus one would assume that some of his MZ might have been classified as DZ. The proportion of MZ is, however, considerably higher than one would expect. This could of course be due to the fact that he studied twins who

were "available," and one might then infer that MZ were more available than DZ.

Yoshimasu seems to have employed both the similarity method and blood tests and thus the zygosity diagnosis of his sample is likely to be reliable. The proportion of MZ in his sample seems very high but according to vital statistics corresponds rather well with the expectation for Japan.

Christiansen studied a sample where zygosity had been established by a modified similarity test. The method had been tested out previously by comparing a group of same-sexed twins where thorough blood and serum typing had been performed. By this method probably not more than 5 per cent of the sample falls into the dubious group, so only a couple of the basic MZ pairs might theoretically have been incorrectly classified as DZ.

With respect to our own study we shall refer the reader to our previous account. Suffice it to say that interview questions concerning identity confusion in childhood, photographs and blood tests were all used to establish zygosity. In fact 60 per cent of the sample were blood-tested. In case of misclassification this applies most likely to some MZ who might have been wrongly diagnosed as DZ. Table III might support such an assumption since 40 per cent of the blood-tested pairs are MZ whereas only 30 per cent of the non-blood-tested pairs have been so classified. These reservations should, however, not affect the concordance figures to a significant degree.

CONCLUSION

Our data and review of the literature suggest that previous studies of criminal twins probably observed too great a difference in concordance rates between MZ and DZ due to sampling errors and unreliable zygosity diagnosis. Here we would like to emphasise the fact that the number of twin pairs of different zygosity is in most previous studies relatively small and, accordingly, a shift of two or three cases from one group to the other would produce different concordance rates. An unsystematic, uncontrolled sampling procedure will include disproportionately more concordant than discordant cases, and zygosity determination without blood and serum grouping tends to classify MZ pairs as DZ.

Compared with previous investigations the present study and Christiansen's study have been able to collect large samples and avoid sources of error due to deficient sampling and zygosity diagnosis. Accordingly the results of these studies probably give a better picture of the relative significance of heredity and environment in crime than did previous studies.

The concordance rates in the Christiansen study were 33.3 per cent in MZ and 10.9 per cent in DZ of the same sex. In our study the difference between MZ and DZ is still smaller, namely 22.4 per cent in MZ and 18.0 per cent in DZ, when a broader concept of crime is employed, and 25.8 per cent and 14.9 per cent. when a more strict concept of crime is used. These differences between MZ and DZ are not impressive compared with previous twin studies, but are still clear-cut. Since MZ pairs usually are brought up more similarly than DZ, this slight difference in concordance rates could be partly explained on these grounds. In our study we have been able to show that the difference in fact disappears almost completely when this "twin relationship factor" is controlled for. In other words, the difference in concordance rates between MZ and DZ is partly due to environmental factors. The consistent difference in concordance rates between same-sexed and opposite-sexed DZ also supports this conclusion (*cf.* Table I).

SUMMARY

In an unselected sample of 138 pairs of same-sexed male twins, age 40–50 years, who were obtained through the national twin and criminal registers of Norway, concordance with respect to registered crime was slightly higher in monozygotic (MZ) than in dizygotic (DZ) twins. Employing a broad concept of crime—

including violation of the motor vehicle law and treason during World War II—concordance was 11/49 or 22.4 per cent in MZ and 16/89 or 18.0 per cent in DZ. With a more strict concept of crime, concordance was 8/31 or 25.8 per cent in MZ and 8/54 or 14.9 per cent in DZ.

However, since MZ pairs experience a more similar upbringing than DZ pairs, we compared groups of MZ and DZ who by and large had been exposed to the same type of environmental influences in childhood and adolescence. In such a comparison the difference in concordance almost completely disappears. These findings support the view that *hereditary factors are of no significant importance in the etiology of common crime.*

These observations and conclusions are at variance with most of the earlier twin studies in criminality. However, it has been demonstrated by a review of the older literature that previous studies in this field, owing to various sources of error, gave results in which the genetic factor was over-estimated. The present study seems to have avoided the pitfalls of unrepresentative sampling and uncertain zygosity diagnosis and has therefore arrived at considerably lower concordance figures in MZ with respect to crime.

REFERENCES

Allen, G., Harvald, B., and Shields, J. (1967). "Measures of Twin Concordance." *Acta genet.* (Basel) **17**:475–481.

Borgstrøm, C. (1939). "Eine Serie von Kriminellen Zwillingen." *Arch. Rass. ges. Biol.* **33**:334–343.

Cederløf, R., Friberg, L., Jonsson, E., and Kaij, L. (1961). "Studies on Similarity Diagnosis in Twins with the Aid of Mailed Questionnaries." *Acta genet.* (Basel) **11**:338–362.

Christiansen, K. (1968). "Threshold of Tolerance in Various Population Groups Illustrated by Results from Danish Criminological Twin Study." In: de Reuck, A. V. S. (ed.), *The Mentally Abnormal Offender.* Boston: Little, Brown & Co.

Christie, N. (1960). *Unge Norske Lovovertiedere.* Oslo: Universitetsforlaget.

Dixon, W. J., and Massey, F. J. (1969). *Introduction to Statistical Analysis*. New York: McGraw-Hill.

Gottesman, I. I., and Shields, J. (1972). *Schizophrenia and Genetics*. New York: Academic Press.

Juel-Nielsen, A., and Hauge, M. (1958). "On the Diagnosis of Zygosity in Twins and the Value of Blood Groups." *Acta genet. (Basel)* **8**:256–273.

Kranz, N. (1936). *Lebensschicksale Krimineller Zwillinge*. Berlin: Springer.

Kringlen, E. (1967). *Heredity and Environment in the Functional Psychoses*. Oslo: Universitetsforlaget and London: Heinemann, 1968.

Lange, J. (1929). *Verbrechen als Schicksal. Studien an Kriminellen Zwillingen*. Leipzig: Thieme.

LeGras, A. M. (1933). "Psychose und Kriminalität bei Zwillingen." *Z. ges. Neurol. Psychiat.* **144**:198–222.

Rosanoff, A. J., Handy, L. M., and Plesset, I. R. (1934). "Criminality and Delinquency in Twins." *J. Crim. Law Criminol.* **24**:923–934.

Rosenthal, D. (1962). "Problems of Sampling and Diagnosis in the Major Twin Studies of Schizophrenic Twins." *J. Psychiat. Res.* **2**:116–134.

Siemens, H. W. (1924). *Die Zwillingpathologie, Ihre Bedeutung, ihre Methodik, ihre bisherigen Ergebnisse*. Berlin: Springer.

Stumpfl, F. (1936). *Die Ursprünge des Verbrechens, dargestellt am Lebenslauf von Zwillingen*. Leipzig: Thieme.

Tienari, P. (1963). "Psychiatric Illness in Idential Twins." *Acta Psychiat. Scand.* **39**: suppl. 171.

Yoshimasu, S. (1961). "The Criminological Significance of the Family in the Light of the Studies of Criminal Twins." *Acta Criminol. Med. leg. jap.* **27**: 117–141. Cited after *Excerpta Criminologica* **2**:723–724, 1962.

Zazzo, R., (1960). *Les Jumeaux, Le Couple et la Personne*. Paris: University of France Press.

9

LEARNING DISABILITIES AND JUVENILE DELINQUENCY[1]

INGO KEILITZ, BARBARA A. ZAREMBA, AND PAUL K. BRODER

INTRODUCTION

During the last few years, the connection between learning disabilities (LD) and juvenile delinquency (JD) has caught the interest of an increasing number of parents, juvenile justice personnel, educators, and researchers in several disciplines. In particular, the phenomenon of learning disabilities has attracted the attention of individuals in the field of juvenile justice who have witnessed the disordered learning behavior of many of the youths who become involved in the juvenile justice system. Similarly, parents and educators in the field of learning disabilities have frequently viewed juvenile delinquency as a particularly disturbing probable consequence of learning disability. While most observers agree that many youths in trouble have learning problems, the issue of the actual existence and nature of a link between LD and JD has not been resolved.

In response to the increased interest in this area, the Office of Juvenile Justice and Delinquency Prevention of the U.S. Department of Justice initiated an ambitious effort to shed some light on the issue of the LD/JD link. In 1975 the American Institutes for Research (AIR) were commissioned to: summarize the current theory and knowledge about the relationship between LD and delinquency; draw preliminary conclusions; and make policy recommendations based on these conclusions. The AIR study concluded that the existing literature neither firmly establishes nor completely disproves a relationship between learning disabilities and juvenile delinquency, but that the pattern of learning problems among delinquents warrants further study (Murray, 1976). Furthermore, the AIR study found various problems in previously reported investigations of the LD/JD link; among them: (1) the absence of comparative studies of the prevalence of LD in adjudicated delinquent and officially nondelinquent populations; (2) definitional, diagnostic, procedural, analytic, and presentational difficulties with the investigations, precluding reliable estimates of the prevalence of learning disabilities; and (3) the ab-

Source: "The Link Between Learning Disabilities and Juvenile Delinquency: Some Issues and Answers," *Learning Disability Quarterly* (Spring 1979), **2**:2–11. Reprinted by permission.

[1] This research was supported by Grants Numbers 76-JN-99-0022, 76-NI-99-0133, 76-JN-99-0021, 78-JN-AX-0028 and 78-JN-AX-0022 from the Office of Juvenile Justice and Delinquency Prevention, U.S. Department of Justice. Points of view or opinions in this paper are those of the authors and do not represent the official position or policies of the U.S. Department of Justice. Thanks are due to Paul B. Campbell, Loretta Weingel-Fidel, B. Claire McCullough, W. Vaughan Stapleton, and William McClory for their critique of an earlier version of this manuscript.

Further information regarding this study may be obtained from the authors at the National Center for State Courts, 300 Newport Avenue, Williamsburg, Virginia 23185.

sence of studies comparing the development of learning disabled and nonlearning disabled children. The report recommended a research initiative to determine the prevalence of LD among populations of juvenile offenders and nondelinquents in several parts of the country. The study also recommended a project to test the value of treatment programs for remediating learning disabilities as an aid to rehabilitation of juvenile delinquents.

This article describes the research and development which have resulted from the AIR recommendation. This effort, which is funded by the Office of Juvenile Justice and Delinquency Prevention, was begun in October, 1976, and is slated for completion in August, 1980. To date, it has produced preliminary LD prevalence estimates, attempts at resolving definitional issues in learning disabilities and delinquency, and preliminary observations about the link between LD and JD.[2] The purpose of this article is to summarize these early findings. Following a general overview, the topics of definition, prevalence, and the LD/JD relationship will be discussed.

OVERVIEW OF THE LD/JD PROJECT

The LD/JD project is a large-scale, complex, field-research effort, involving the development of an LD classification procedure, a study of the prevalence of LD, a remediation program focused on the learning disabled delinquent, and an evaluation of that program. The project is being conducted jointly by two grantees: the Association for Children with Learning Disabilities (ACLD) and the National Center for State Courts. The program is being conducted in the metropolitan areas of Baltimore, Maryland; Indianapolis, Indiana; and Phoenix, Arizona.

While the ultimate goal of the program is to provide information that will assist in the de-

velopment of informed policy regarding learning disabilities and delinquency prevention, the research and development program has several major objectives:

(1) The determination of the prevalence of LD in groups of adjudicated delinquent and officially nondelinquent 12- to 15-year-old boys;

(2) an exploration of some of the definitional issues concerning learning disabilities;

(3) the establishment of an instructional (remediation) program for selected groups of 12- to 17-year-old boys and girls who have been adjudicated delinquent an classified as learning disabled;

(4) an evaluation of the effectiveness of the remediation program with respect to resulting changes in the participants' academic achievement and delinquent behavior; and

(5) the follow-up of youths in the officially nondelinquent public school sample, to determine changes in delinquent behavior and the relationship of these changes to LD.

While ACLD is responsible for the instructional program, the National Center for State Courts is responsible for program evaluation, as well as for the other research components of the project. For the purpose of classification into learning disabled and nonlearning disabled subsamples, Educational Testing Service (ETS) of Princeton, New Jersey, contracted with the National Center to perform the diagnostic evaluations of the adolescents in the study. Figure 1 schematically shows the study design.

In the spring and summer of 1977, after parental consent had been obtained, the educational records of 1,778 boys and girls between the ages 12 and 17, including 1,381 12- to 15-year-old boys (984 officially nondelinquent public school students and 397 adjudicated delinquents) were reviewed for indicators of LD. Individual assessments were made of those youths whose records did not preclude

---

[2] The first phase of the project was conducted at Creighton University and ended on August 31, 1978. The two-year continuation of the research and evaluation components is being conducted by the National Center for State Courts.

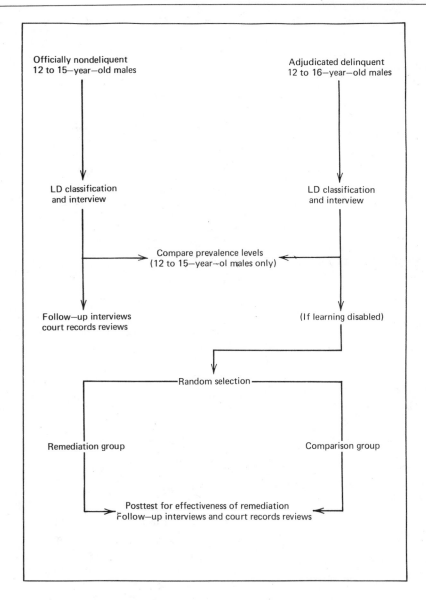

FIGURE 1. Schematic representation of study design.

a classification of learning disabled. The assessments consisted of individual testing that measured several key aspects of ability and academic achievement. In addition, during interviews with each youth whose records were reviewed, other data were gathered, such as questions about personal characteristics and family background, attitudes toward school, and self-reported delinquent activity. The principal LD prevalence estimates in this study are being based on data obtained only from the boys between the ages of 12 and 15, inclusive; however, the remediation program ncludes both boys and girls between the ages of 12 and 17.

From a sample of approximately 260 adjudicated delinquent youths who were classified LD, half were randomly selected for inclusion in the remediation program, while the remainder were assigned to a comparison group. (Additional record reviews and diagnostic assessments of 12- to 17-year-old delinquent youths were conducted in the summer and fall of 1978, in order to increase the sizes of the demonstration program's remediation and comparison groups. As a result, approximately 160 additional learning disabled delinquent children have been placed in the treatment and comparison groups of the program.) At the end of the demonstration program in the summer of 1979, the youths in both groups will be retested, and the changes in academic achievement and delinquent behavior of the youths in the remediation group will be compared to those of the youths in the comparison group, in order to evaluate the effectiveness of the remediation program.[3]

---

[3] Once a youth is classified learning disabled and placed in the remediation group, an instructional plan based on the diagnostic recommendations and additional formal and informal assessments is prepared by a learning disabilities specialist. The individualized program is written for student-preferred learning patterns (i.e., auditory, visual, motor, or a combination thereof), and includes appropriate teaching techniques. The remediation program is based on an academic treatment model. As such, it focuses directly on school subjects and the improvement of academic skills. The goal of the program is to meet with each youth in an instructional setting for the equivalent of four class periods

DEFINITIONAL ISSUES

Neither "learning disabilities" nor "juvenile delinquency" have operational definitions of widespread acceptability. Consequently, the project depended greatly on the formulation of acceptable operational definitions of both concepts. This section describes attempts to address these definitional issues.

LEARNING DISABILITIES

Learning disabilities is a concept that is talked about in many different ways. The field is rife with ambiguities and contradictions (e.g., Coles, 1978). This study has focused on basic discrepancies between ability and achievement, as suggested in the definition of LD formulated in 1968 by the National Advisory Committee on Handicapped Children. Learning disabilities has been conceptualized in this study as being characterized by pronounced intrapersonal differences in ability to perform a variety of verbal, quantitative, and manipulative tasks, presumably because of some nonobvious interference with the process of receiving information, utilizing it in cognitive process, or communicating the results of cognition. Only those subjects whose learning performance displayed such discrepancies and were not adequately explained by such factors as physical handicaps, mental retardation, or severe emotional disturbance were classified learning disabled (Barrows, Campbell, Slaughter, & Trainor, Note 1).

In the LD classification process ETS employed two procedural steps. The first was to review educational records in order to exclude those children whose educational performance was within the range of normal expectation, or who could be categorized as mentally retarded, physically handicapped (e.g., hard of hearing, deaf, visually impaired), or severely

---

per week for at least one school year. The instructional program is not designed to duplicate or to replace the educational programs offered to the youths by local schools; rather, it is designed to permit the assessment of the effects of particular treatment variables on measures of LD and delinquency.

emotionally disturbed. If available achievement scores differed by the equivalent of at least two years (a T-score difference of 10 points) from available ability scores on one or more tests, or from one another, the child was referred for further assessment. Educational records also were reviewed for the presence of a recorded clinical diagnosis of learning disabled, evidence of hyperactivity, unusually illegible handwriting, perceptual test performance indicating possible malfunction, and, if grades were available, for uneven grade profiles, including abrupt changes in profile character. These characteristics were grounds for referring the youth for diagnostic assessment.

The second step involved diagnostic assessment. After the completion of record reviews, youths whose records did not preclude a classification of learning disabled were given a series of diagnostic tests. The tests which were used as a basis for the classification decision included the *Wechsler Intelligence Scale for Children (Revised)*, the *Key Math Diagnostic Arithmetic Test*, the *Woodcock Reading Mastery Test*, and the *Bender Visual-Motor Gestalt* (Koppitz scoring). In addition to the conventional scoring of the WISC-R, the Witkin factors were also used. These consist of Analytic Functioning, Verbal Comprehension, and Attention Concentration.[4] The approach employed in the diagnostic assessments basically focused on discrepancies within and between ability and achievement profiles, supplemented by perception measures and test-situation observations, as indicators of LD.

Although the rules behind the LD classification decision based on the test results were

stated explicitly, some latitude for judgment by the diagnostic assessors was intended. However, considerable variability evidenced in cross-site protocol checks argued for more precise explication of the rules. Accordingly, the role of clinical judgment was limited to the initial categorization of observations applying to behavior during the WISC-R administration and the youth's general behavior in the testing situation. Specific requirements for the LD classification decision were stated sequentially as a series of discrete "yes" or "no" questions, considering each as an element of data in a decision algorithm.

These rules have been described in detail by Campbell (Note 2). Data for each adolescent were entered into a computer and, after a sequential examination of each step of the decision process, an LD classification was made. The decision process involved assigning points based on significant differences among the achievement and ability scores considered in each step. That is, the process moved through a series of steps, systematically considering the differences between the math and reading scores, and between the reading or math scores and the Witkin factors. Behavioral observations made during the administration of the assessment battery also were considered in the point assignments.

The definition utilized in our study, then, is one of positive classification of LD by assessment of discrepancies between measures of abilities and achievement, and by exclusion of children with other particular handicapping conditions. However, the definition is not based upon particular assumptions concerning the causes of LD.

JUVENILE DELINQUENCY

Historically, defining juvenile delinquency has been problematic. Disagreements concerning the conceptualization and measurement of delinquent behavior have made estimates of its incidence, as well as comparisons among estimates, difficult. Many of the problems stem from variations among statutes and treatment

---

[4] The WISC-R was reported in two forms: as conventionally reported in Verbal (V) and Performance (P) subscores and in terms of the Witkin factor scores—Analytic Functioniong (AF), Verbal Comprehension (VC), and Attention Concentration (AC). The AF score is composed of the Block Design, Picture Completion, and Object Assembly subtests. The VC score is composed of the Vocabulary, Information, Comprehension, and Similarities subtests. The AC factor combines the scores from the Digit Span, Arithmetic, and Coding Subtests (Witkin, Dyk, Faterson, Goodenough, & Karp, 1974). The test battery is described more fully in Barrows et al. (Note 1).

of juvenile offenders from one jurisdiction to another, as well as from the fact that many referrals to the juvenile justice system are handled informally. Just as it was necessary to develop an operational definition of LD, it was necessary also to develop a general research definition whereby each youth could be classified as delinquent or nondelinquent for purposes of assignment to samples within the study.

A two-step analysis was undertaken (Greguras, Broder, & Zimmerman, Note 3). The initial step in the analysis, which involved an examination of alternative approaches to defining delinquency, led to the conclusion that legal criteria were more workable than behavioral criteria as the primary basis for classifying participants. (However, a self-reported delinquency scale was also used in the study.) The second step was the identification and analysis of various points of penetration into the juvenile justice system (e.g., police contact, arrest, etc.) to determine the degree of involvement considered to be the most feasible for this study.

Each identifiable point of penetration into the juvenile justice system was analyzed according to four criteria. First, the point had to be common to, and clearly identifiable in, the court system records of all three project sites. Second, the point could not be so far into the system that it sharply limited the potential sample size. Third, the point of penetration had to be far enough into the system that the reluctance on the part of the court to the release of youths' names (directory information) for the purposes of obtaining informed consent could be allayed. Finally, the point of penetration had to be such that the youths had clearly manifested delinquent behaviors on at least one occasion.

After considering the various factors, the primary criterion chosen for the operational definition was adjudication by a juvenile court. The juveniles could have been adjudicated for a delinquent act (an act which, if committed by an adult, would be a crime) or a status of-fense (an act which, if committed by an adult, would not be a crime, e.g., habitual truancy). Adjudication is an identifiable point of penetration into the juvenile justice system which is common to all three sites and which satisfies the need for a sample large enough to ensure the reliability and validity of research findings.

PREVALENCE OF LEARNING DISABILITIES

Many estimates of the prevalence of learning disabilities have been made using various types of testing batteries and criteria. The prevalence of LD in the general population has been estimated at between 7 and 10 percent (Myklebust & Boshes, Note 4; Graydon, 1978; Murray, 1976). Prevalence estimates of LD among juvenile delinquents, on the other hand, generally have been higher and have varied more widely; e.g., 26 percent (Comptroller General of the United States, 1977), 32 percent (Duling, Eddy, & Risko, Note 5), 49 percent (Podboy & Mallory, Note 6), 50 percent (Poremba, 1967), and 73 percent (Swanstrom, Randle, Livingston, Macrafic, Caulfield, & Arnold, Note 7).

As stated before, approximately 1,300 12- to 15-year-old boys in the metropolitan areas of Baltimore, Indianapolis, and Phoenix were included in the full classification procedures of the prevalence study. According to the computer algorithm every youth was classified as either learning disabled or nonlearning disabled. Using that means of classification, 16 percent of the officially nondelinquent, public school youth and 32 percent of the adjudicated delinquent youth of the same age and sex were determined to have learning disabilities (see Table I).

While the classification of proportionately more delinquent adolescents than public school youths as learning disabled is not sufficient evidence to establish LD as a causal factor in delinquency, the difference between the prevalence estimates indicates that a relationship does exist and justifies an investigation into its

TABLE I Estimates of LD/JD Prevalence[a]

Category	Records[b] Reviewed	Learning N	Disabled %
Public School	984	161	16
Juvenile Delinquent	397	127	32

[a] Table adapted from Campbell, 1978 (Note 2).
[b] These cases presented sufficient data to make a LD/non-LD decision.

precise nature. Also, the finding that 16 percent of the officially nondelinquent children are learning disabled is not without educational policy significance. This figure considerably exceeds previous estimates. If this estimate withstands further scientific scrutiny, it may have important implications for school officials and legislators.

THE LINK BETWEEN LEARNING DISABILITIES AND JUVENILE DELINQUENCY

Three conditions of cause and effect generally are required to establish a causal relationship (Cook & Campbell, 1976). The first, temporal antecedence, is the requirement that the cause must precede the effect; in this case, LD must precede the effect; in this case, LD must precede juvenile delinquency. The second, covariance of cause and effect, is the requirement that the effect must vary as the cause varies in magnitude and direction. The third is the absence of a competing viable hypothesis. These conditions have not been met in previous research; the postulated causal relationship between LD and JD remains without rigorous support. Yet, for many, the relationship between learning disabilities and juvenile delinquency seems obvious and compelling.

The two most prominent explanations for the link between learning disabilities and juvenile delinquency have been called the "school failure rationale" and the "susceptibility rationale" (Murray, 1976). The first proposes that the child's learning difficulties lead to classroom failure which, in turn, leads to a greater probability of delinquency. The second proposes that learning disabled children possess "a variety of socially troublesome personality characteristics" which make them "susceptible" to delinquent acts. Both hypotheses assume intermediate effects, such as the development of a negative self-image, association with peers prone to delinquency, and general impulsiveness, which lead to delinquent activities and, subsequently, to entry into the juvenile justice system. The literature commonly describes the LD/JD link as follows:

> Two things come into play in explaining how learning disabilities contribute to delinquent behavior. Frustration in school often leads to aggressive behavior. The child becomes more and more frustrated as his needs go unmet and the aggression spreads to all facets of his life. He calls attention to his unmet needs by delinquent behavior. Secondly, because many learning disabled children are impulsive and lack good judgment, they are unable to anticipate the consequences of their acts. They often cannot control their behavior and they do not learn from experience (Unger, 1978, p. 27).

Of all the hypotheses suggested in the literature to explain the chain of events leading from learning disabilities to juvenile delinquency, the school failure hypothesis is cited most frequently. The strong, consistent finding that juvenile delinquents have records of lower-than-average school achievement makes this explanation appealing (see Bernstein, 1978; Comptroller General of the United States, 1977; Elliott & Voss, 1974; Graydon, 1978; and Mauser, 1974).

If, indeed, there is a relationship between LD and JD, a higher prevalence of specific learning disabilities should exist among juvenile delinquent youth than among nondelinquent youth. But, at the time of Murray's (1976) review, this seemingly simple hypothesis remained untested; no attempt had been made to test comparable delinquent and nondelinquent samples at the same time, with the same instruments, and in a manner sufficiently objective to preclude diagnostic biases. Moreover, there had been no clearly specified operational definition of learning disabilities that could have been used among these different populations.

The preliminary results of the prevalence study summarized above, as well as previous studies, strongly suggest that proportionately more adjudicated delinquent youths have learning disabilities than nonadjudicated youths. Proponents of a causal LD/JD link generally share a common notion, namely that the learning disabled child is more likely to engage in delinquent behavior and, therefore, is more likely to be adjudicated delinquent, than his/her nonlearning disabled peer. It is our investigation of precisely this notion which has led us to question the school failure and susceptibility rationales and to propose an alternative hypothesis concerning the relationship between LD and JD (Zimmerman, Rich, Keilitz, & Broder, Note 8).

It was hypothesized that learning disabled children would report greater frequencies or different varieties of delinquent activities than nonlearning disabled children. Our sample of officially nondelinquent public school and adjudicated delinquent youth, classified as to the presence of LD, were asked to report the delinquent behaviors in which they engaged.[5]

[5] The self-reported delinquency questionnaire consisted of 28 items concerning behaviors ranging from relatively minor, status-type offenses to delinquent behaviors of a serious nature, as well as questions pertaining to police pick-up. For each behavior, the participants were asked to report the frequency with which they had engaged in it, both overall and during the past year. More information about the self-report scale is contained in papers by Broder and Zimmerman (Note 9), and Zimmerman and Broder (Note 10).

Somewhat surprisingly, the data suggest that learning disabled and nonlearning disabled children engage in the same types and number of delinquent activities. Table II shows the percentage of children in both the nondelinquent, public school, and delinquent samples who reported having ever engaged in behavior falling into seven offense categories. The reported delinquent behaviors of learning disabled and nonlearning disabled children are highly similar in all categories. A review of the official records of the officially delinquent sample revealed the same pattern. Table III shows the percentage of children who were adjudicated for offenses in each of the seven categories. Those children who are adjudicated delinquents tend to be convicted of the same types of offenses, regardless of whether or not they are learning disabled.

The school failure hypothesis and the susceptibility hypothesis both purport to explain why learning disabled children are more likely than nonlearning disabled children to engage in delinquent activities. Our data do not support these hypotheses about the LD/JD link. If it is accepted that learning disabled and nonlearning disabled children engage in the same delinquent behaviors, our data do not support the school failure hypotheses, the susceptibility hypothesis, or any other hypotheses that propose differences in learning disabled children's delinquent behaviors.

TABLE II   Percent of Children Reporting Acts in Seven Offense Categories

Offenses	Public school		Juvenile Delinquent	
	LD	Not LD	LD	Not LD
Status	83	86	95	96
Miscellaneous	63	72	88	88
Alcohol	64	73	85	87
Drug	20	23	72	69
Automobile	25	25	68	69
Criminal	18	18	80	74
Violent	50	49	77	78
Mean	46	49	81	80

TABLE III Percent of Delinquents in Each Offense Category

Offense	LD	Not LD
Status	36	35
Miscellaneous	33	30
Alcohol	3	1
Drug	6	4
Automobile	8	6
Criminal	38	46
Violent	15	16

If a greater prevalence of learning disabilities exists among adjudicated juvenile delinquents than among public school children, and if it is accepted that learning disabled and nonlearning disabled children behave comparably, then a "different treatment" rationale may be proposed as a general hypothesis that is consistent with the above data to explain the link between learning disabilities and juvenile delinquency. That is, it may be argued that learning disabled and nonlearning disabled children engage in essentially the same behaviors but that, somewhere in the juvenile justice system, learning disabled children are treated differently from nonlearning disabled children. It is possible that differential treatment and the consequent greater likelihood of adjudication result from evidence of the child's failure in school, from a reaction to something about the child himself/herself, or both. This is in line with the thinking that suggested the school failure and susceptibility rationales. However, the different treatment hypothesis asserts that, for whatever reason, the LD child is treated *differently* for the *same* delinquent behavior.

*

REFERENCE NOTES

1. Barrows, T. B., Campbell, P. B., Slaughter, B. A., & Trainor, M. L. (1977), *Psychoeducational diagnostic services for learning disabled youths: Research procedures.* Unpublished manuscript, Educational Testing Service.

2. Campbell, P B. (1978). *The Definition and Prevalence of Learning Disabilities.* Paper presented at the meeting of the Fifteenth International Conference of the Association for Children with Learning Disabilities, Kansas City, Mo. (March).

3. Greguras, F. M., Broder, P. K., & Zimmerman, J. (1978). *Establishing an Operational Definition of Juvenile Delinquency* (Tech. Rep. 13). Omaha: Creighton University, Institute for Business, Law and Social Research, (March).

4. Myklebust, H. B., & Boshes, B. (1969). *Minimal Brain Damage in Children* (Final report, U.S. Public Health Service Contract 108-65-142). Evanston, Ill.: Northwestern University Publications (June).

5. Duling, F., Eddy, S., & Risko, V. (1970). *Learning Disabilities of Juvenile Delinquents.* Unpublished manuscript, Department of Educational Services, Robert F. Kennedy Youth Center, Morgantown, W.Va.

6. Podboy, J. W., & Mallory, W. A. (1977). *The Diagnosis of Specific Learning Disabilities Among a Juvenile Delinquent Population.* Unpublished manuscript, Sonoma County (California) Probation Department.

7. Swanstrom, W., Randle, C. Livingston, V., Macrafic, K., Caulfield, M., & Arnold, S. (1977). *Blue Earth/Nicollet Counties Prevalence Study.* Unpublished manuscript, Dodge-Fillmore & Olmsted County Community Corrections Learning Disabilities Research Project, Rochester, Minn.

8. Zimmerman, J., Rich, W. D., Keilitz, I., & Broder, P. K. (1978). *Some Observations on the Link Between Learning Disabilities and Juvenile Delinquency.* Manuscript submitted for publication.

9. Broder, P. K., & Zimmerman, J. (1978). *Establishing the Reliability of Self-Reported Delinquency Data.* Unpublished manuscript, National Center for State Courts, Williamsburg, Va.

10. Zimmerman, J., & Broder, P. K. (1978). *Deriving Measures of Delinquency from Self-Report Data.* Manuscript submitted for publication.

REFERENCES

Berstein, S. (1978). In N. P. Ramos (Ed.), *Delinquent Youth and Learning Disabilities.* San Rafael, Cal.: Academic Therapy Publications.

Coles, G.S. (1978). "Learning Disabilities Test Battery: Empirical and Social Issues." *Harvard Educational Review* **48**:313-340.

Comptroller General of the United States (1977). *Learning Disabilities: The Link to Delinquency Should Be Determined, but Schools Should Do More Now.* Washington, D.C.: General Accounting Office.

Cook, T. D., & Campbell, D. T. (1976). "The Design and Conduct of Quasi-Experiments and True Experiments in Field Settings." In M. D. Dunnette (Ed.), *Handbook of Industrial and Organizational Research*, Chicago: Rand McNally, 1976, 223-326.

Elliot, D. S., & Voss, H. L. (1974). *Delinquency and Dropout*. Lexington, Mass: Lexington Books.

Graydon, J. (1978). In N. P. Ramos (Ed.), *Delinquent Youth and Learning Disabilities*. San Rafael, Cal.: Academic Therapy Publications.

Mauser, A. J. (1974). Learning Disabilities and Delinquent Youth." *Academic Therapy* **9**(6), 389-400.

Murray, C. A. (1976). *The Link Between Learning Disabilities and Juvenile Delinquency: Current Theory and Knowledge*. Washington, D.C.: U.S. Government Printing Office.

National Advisory Committee on Handicapped Children (1968). *Special Education for Handicapped Children* (First annual report). Washington, D.C.: U.S. Department of Health, Education, and Welfare.

Poremba, C. (1967) "The Adolescent and Young Adult with Learning Disabilities: What Are the Needs of Those Who Deal with Him?" In *International Approach to Learning Disabilities of Children and Youth: Selected Papers from the Third Annual Conference of the Association for Children with Learning Disabilities.* San Rafael, Cal.: Academic Therapy Publications.

Unger, K. V. (1978). "Learning Disabilities and Juvenile Delinquency." *Journal of Juvenile and Family Courts.* **29**(1), 25–30.

Witkin, H. A., Dyk, R. B., Faterson, H. F., Goodenough, D. R., & Karp, S. A. (1974). *Psychological Differentiations.* New York: John Wiley and Sons.

10

COMPULSIVE MASCULINITY AND DELINQUENCY

IRA J. SILVERMAN AND SIMON DINITZ

Although the Sociological, Psychological, psychiatric, and particularly the psychoanalytic literatures are replete with references to the relationship between compulsive masculinity and delinquency, there are no definitive, and few empirical studies of this concept.

The introduction of the concept of compulsive masculinity into the sociological literature is generally attributed to the work of Talcott Parsons. Parsons (1947) specifically related the occurrence of compulsive masculinity to the emergence of the mother-dominated household as an increasingly characteristic type of familial organization. The primacy of the instrumental role of the father as breadwinner compelled the mother to assume the principal responsibility for the socialization of the children. Thus, boys initially identify with and depend upon their mothers as primary role models. However, at adolescence, boys must repudiate their feminine identification because they are destined to become adult males, not females. Parsons considers the behavior that results from the boy's repudiation of this feminine identification to be marked by a kind of reaction formation involving compulsive masculinity.

Source: "Compulsive Masculinity and Delinquency: An Empirical Investigation," *Criminology* (February 1974), 11:498–515. Reprinted by permission of the publisher, Sage Publications, Inc.

In summary, Parsons argues that the female-dominated household has negative consequences for male development because it creates anxiety about maleness; this anxiety, in turn, is transformed into compulsive masculinity. The latter, it should be added, tends to promote antisocial and and aggressive conduct.

Taking the work of Parsons as his points of departure, Toby (1966) has further elaborated the concept of compulsive masculinity. Toby (1966: 20–21) believes that the compulsive masculinity hypothesis can explain violent behavior among certain types of adolescent boys. He hypothesizes that violent behavior would be more prevalent among boys (a) from matriarchal homes (especially black boys), (b) who grow up in households in which it is relatively difficult to identify with a father figure, (c) whose physical and social development toward adult masculinity is slower than their peers, (d) of working-class rather than middle-class background.

Rosen (1969) has reviewed the clinical literature to determine whether there is any empirical basis for the Parsonian conceptualization. Although he found some evidence for the development of sexual anxiety and compensatory masculinity among boys from female-based households, no link between this behavior and delinquency was demonstrated.

One recent study, omitted in Rosen's review of the clinical literature, lends considerable empirical support to the Parsonian formulation. This study, which investigated the relationship between masculinity and father presence or absence from the home, was conducted by Barclay and Cusumano (1967). Using more subtle perceptual measures of masculinity, these researchers were able to get beneath the "he-man" facade of their subjects and tap their basic orientation. They found that boys from father-absent homes made higher, more feminine scores than boys with fathers. Barclay and Cusumano suggest that this finding provides evidence of the existence of a compensatory drive toward hypermasculinity among boys from father-absent homes. Moreover, they contend that this drive results in the development of exaggerated masculine interest and characteristics.

Rosen (1969) has also reviewed the sociological literature on matricentric families and fatherless homes. Based on his examination of the literature, he concluded that the absence of a father fails to account for a significant portion of male delinquency.

Recent emphasis on compulsive masculinity has focused chiefly on nonwhite boys and is tied to the research on the lower-class black matriarchal family. In fact, the lower-class black family structure is normally cited as an illustration not only of the emergence of the female-based household, but also of the consequences of this household organization for problems of masculine identification.

Moynihan (1968), in particular, has called attention to the "pathological" nature of the black matriarchal family. From his point of view, the female-based black family is highly generative of much aberrant, inadequate, and antisocial behavior frequently observed in the lower-class black community (Rainwater and Yancy, 1967: 67).

Kenneth Clark has also spent considerable time studying the lower-class black family structure. He feels that the dominance of the black family by the female, in conjunction with the society's relegation of the black male to a menial and subservient position, has had profound influence on the means available to the black male for maintaining self-esteem. Denied the opportunity for achievement in business, politics, and in industry, the black male feels compelled to base his self-esteem on the kind of behavior that tends to support a stereotyped picture of the black male—sexual impulsiveness, irresponsibility, verbal bombast, posturing, and compensatory achievement in entertainment and athletics (Clark, 1965: 70).

Moreover, the all-too-frequent absence of the black male from the home has had especially profound implications for the male children; the black boy has no strong male role figure to emulate. As a result, males come to regard the maintenance of stable family life as unmasculine. In fact, Clark (1965: 71) points out, the young black man comes to gauge his masculinity by the number of girls he can attract and conquer.

Liebow's (1967) recent study of a group of lower-class black males lends some empirical support to Clark's thesis. Based on his street corner research as a participant-observer, Liebow concludes that lower-class, female-based households have resulted from the black male's failure to be able to carry out his duties and responsibilities as husband and father. Liebow (1967: 216) also found evidence to support the contention of Clark and others that black males validate their manliness through sexual conquest.

Hannerz (1969) has also developed a thesis of the black male's conception of self by observing life in a black neighborhood. Based on his observations, Hannerz takes issue with those who hold that the black matriarchal homes cause young boys to be deficient or uncertain about their masculinity because their fathers are absent or peripheral in household affairs. He contends that black boys can and do learn the nature of the male role from (a) observing the behavior of their mothers' more or less steady boyfriends; (b) the reactions of adult females in the home to their behavior; (c) peer-group reinforcement of the images of masculinity gleaned from the home.

Based on his research, Hannerz (1969: 17) concludes that "the behavior of the street corner male is a natural pattern of masculinity with which ghetto dwellers grow up and which to some extent they grow into."

Although there has been a great deal of discussion about the role played by the black matriarchal family in juvenile delinquency, only Rosen (1969) has actually examined this relationship empirically. Rosen examined the relationship between the factors of father absence, sex of main wage earner, main decision-making, and most influential adult on the one hand and delinquency on the other for a sample of 921 black males aged 13–15 who resided in lower-class, high-delinquency areas. He concluded (1969: 175) that "the factor of matriarchy may be only one of numerous 'original causes' which 'push' a lower class Negro male into delinquency, thus accounting for the small association for matriarchy and delinquency."

While Moynihan and others have considered how the life situation of the black boy generates problems of masculinity, others have related the life situation of the lower-class boy—regardless of color—to problems of masculinity.

Miller (1966) has studied lower-class life and found that an exaggerated emphasis on masculinity, which he calls toughness, represents only one of several concerns of lower-class culture. Miller (1966: 140) considers the toughness component to include the following characteristics:

> Physical prowess, evidenced both by demonstrated possession of strength and endurance and by athletic skill; "masculinity," symbolized by a distinctive complex of acts and avoidances (bodily tatooing, absence of sentimentality, non-concern with "art", "literature," conceptualization of women as conquest objects, etc.); and bravery in the face of physical threat.

From Miller's point of view, this emphasis has emerged because a significant proportion of lower-class males are reared in predominantly female households and lack a consistent male figure with whom to identify and from whom to learn essential components of a "male" role. He concludes (1966: 140) that "since women serve as primary objects of identification during preadolescent years, the almost obsessive lower class concern with masculinity probably resembles a type of compulsive reaction formation." Moreover, Miller considers this focal concern of toughness, along with the other focal concerns of lower-class culture—trouble, fate, autonomy, and smartness—to account for much of lower-class delinquency.

Fannin and Clinard (1965) investigated the differences between lower- and lower-middle-class white delinquents in conception of self as a male, and behavioral correlates of such differences. They found that lower-class boys conceived of themselves as being tougher, more fearless, powerful, fierce, and dangerous than the middle-class delinquents, who, on the other hand, saw themselves as being more loyal, clever smart, smooth, and bad. Moreover, these self-conceptions were found to be related to specific types of behavior. The "tough guys" significantly more often committed violent offenses, fought more often, carried weapons, had lower occupational aspirations, viewed dating primarily as a means to sexual intercourse which was achieved by conquest, and stressed physical prowess and callousness.

Fannin and Clinard (1965: 213) feel that their data suggest that "a significant proportion of offenses involving physical violence may be committed by delinquents who stress certain masculine traits in their self-conceptions as males which help to channel and legitimate such violence." Moreover, they feel that "self conception may act as a closure factor restricting the possibilities of behavior to a narrowed universe."

In addition to examining the etiology of compulsive masculinity, special concern has been devoted to the relationship between compulsive masculinity and violent behavior.

Wolfgang and Ferracuti (1967: 259) posited the existence of a subculture of violence in which masculinity is a focal concern. This subculture is not restricted to the United States, nor to the Latin American countries where the concept of machismo is a dominant cultural theme. "Machismo," as defined by Wolfgang and Ferracuti (1967), involves the equation of maleness with overt physical aggression.

Furthermore, based on a thorough analysis of the research on violence both here and abroad, these authors conclude that most violent behavior can be explained by the existence of this subculture of violence. They define the subculture of violence as a complex of values, attitudes, and material traits that have violence as their central theme. Violence is evident in the life style, socialization processes, and interpersonal relations of groups that possess this value cluster (Wolfgang and Ferracuti, 1967: 140). Moreover, the subcultural ethos of violence is most prominent among males in the limited age groups ranging from middle to late adolescence (1967: 158–159).

Finally, concern with compulsive masculinity and the violence that results from it is certainly more than an academic concern, as evidenced by the establishment of the National Commission on the Causes of and Prevention of Violence (1969).

This paper will report on one part of a study undertaken to examine some of the hypothesized aspects of compulsive masculinity. The particular contributions of this paper will be in examining how the factors of family situation and race relate to some of the hypothesized aspects of compulsive masculinity.

METHOD

In order to examine the relationship between compulsive masculinity, race, and matriarchal home, a study was conducted of a representative cross-section of the population at the Fairfield School for Boys, the largest Ohio Youth Commission operated facility for delinquent boys.

The sample for this study was drawn from five of the fifteen cottages at Fairfield. These particular cottages were chosen because they represent a cross-section of the institutional population.

Each of the boys in these cottages was administered a questionnaire which included a compulsive masculinity index, the Lykken Scale, and the Zuckerman Scale.

The compulsive masculinity index was used to measure the boys' self-identification with tough behavior (e.g., weapon-carrying maintaining a reputation as a tough guy) and sexual athleticism.[1]

The Lykken Scale was included to measure impulsiveness and proneness to activities that are high risk in nature and excitement oriented. It also measures general hostility (for a detailed description of the Lykken Scale, see Lykken, 1957).

The Zuckerman Scale was included in this study to measure field dependency—tendency to be effected by environmental influences including peer pressures—a variable Barclay and Cusumano (1967: 35) found to be highly correlated with compulsive masculinity (for a detailed description of this scale, see Zuckerman, 1964).

Finally, each respondent was also asked to rate himself and all the other boys in his cottage according to how manly he considered himself and each other boy to be. The ratings for himself and each of the others involved circling a number on a continuum from one to ten (least to most). The second part required the respondent to rate himself and each boy in the cottage according to how tough he considered each one (including himself) to be. Again, these ratings for himself and each of the others

---

[1] This scale was developed by the researcher because there was no measure of "compulsive masculinity." For detailed discussion of the development of this scale, see Silverman (1970).

involved circling a number on a continuum from one to ten (least to most).

Furthermore, the cottage supervisor, two cottage officers, and the cottage social worker were also asked to rate each boy on a continuum from one to ten, according to how tough and how manly they considered each boy to be. The purpose of these ratings was to obtain a measure of the consistency or discrepancy between a boy's conception of his own masculinity and toughness, and the conceptions of his masculinity by all other boys in the group, and by the cottage staff.

Some 284 boys ranging in age from fourteen to nineteen with the median at seventeen were studied and evaluated. Of these 53.9% of the boys were white. Moreover, institutional records showed that the mother-based home was the modal type of household (34.9%) for this sample with natural parent families (24.3%) ranking second and biological and stepparent families (2.89%) ranking third.

FINDINGS

RACE

A comparison of the white and black delinquents' self-ratings on manliness showed that the black boys rated themselves significantly higher (more manly) than the white boys. The mean self-rating of the black delinquents was 7.0 as compared to the white delinquents whose mean self-rating score was 6.4 (based on a range of 0–9). Also, on the toughness self-ratings, the black delinquent boys rated themselves higher (tougher) than the white boys. The means were 6.0 and 5.6 respectively. A similar pattern was found on the compulsive masculinity index. The black delinquents had a higher mean score on this index than the white delinquents. The mean scores were 15.3 and 14.1 respectively (based on a range of 0–32; see Table I).

Moreover on manliness, the black delinquent boys were rated significantly higher by

TABLE I   Mean Scores on Manliness and Toughness Ratings and the Compulsive Masculinity Index, and Discrepancies in Self and other Ratings, by Race

| | Mean scores | | Discrepancy scores | | |
Race	Self-Rating	Group rating	Boy-group	Boy-cottage staff	Boy-social worker
Manliness					
White	6.4 [a]	4.3 }[b]	2.1	2.0	1.2
Black	7.0	4.8	2.2	1.7	1.1
Toughness					
White	5.6	3.4	2.2	1.8	1.0
Black	6.0	4.0	2.0	1.3	.9
Compulsive masculinity index	Mean Ratings				
White	14.1				
Black	15.3				

[a] p < .05.
[b] p < .001.

their cottage mates than the white delinquents. The mean scores were 4.8 and 4.3, respectively. This pattern was also evident on the group toughness rating (see Table I).

An examination of the discrepancy scores on the manliness rating scale revealed that black delinquent boys held perceptions of their own manliness that were slightly closer to those of the other evaluators. On both boy-group and boy-social worker comparisons, the white delinquents had slightly lower mean manliness discrepancy scores.

On the other hand, the pattern of discrepancy scores on the toughness rating scale was exactly the opposite. On toughness, the black delinquents' perceptions of their own toughness were more consistent with those held by their cottage mates, the cottage staff, and their social workers than were those of the white delinquent boys (see Table I).

Finally, all three groups of evaluators rated the delinquent boys lower on both manliness and toughness than they perceived themselves to be, with the social worker more closely approximating the delinquent boys' self-perceptions than the other two sets of evaluators.

Data from this study also supported the hypothesized differences in black and white proneness for excitement-oriented, high-risk activities, hostility, impulsiveness, and field dependency.

The black delinquent boys had higher mean Lykken scores than the white delinquents, indicating greater impulsiveness, hostility, and proneness to engage in excitement-oriented high-risk activity than white delinquent boys.

An examination of the Zuckerman Scale scores by race revealed that the white delin-

quents had significantly higher mean scores than the black delinquents, suggesting greater black field dependence. (Zuckerman found field dependence to be negatively correlated with his scale.) Moreover, since Barclay and Cusumano (1967) have indicated that field dependence is related to "compulsive masculinity," this finding provides additional evidence for the hypothesis concerning race and "compulsive masculinity."

TYPE OF HOUSEHOLD

An examination of the delinquents' self-ratings on the manliness index revealed that delinquents coming from female-based homes had a mean manliness score of 6.8, which ranked high compared with delinquents from other types of households. On the toughness variable, delinquent boys from mother-based homes rated themselves significantly higher than delinquents from other types of family situations (see Table III). Similarly, the mean scores of delinquents from mother-based homes on the compulsive masculinity scale disclosed that these delinquents had high mean scores (14.4) compared to delinquents from other types of households.

Moreover, the group rated the delinquent boys from mother-based households the highest on both manliness and toughness. On manliness the mother-based delinquents received a mean high rating of 4.7, which was significantly higher than that received by the father-based delinquents who had a low mean group rating of 4.0. This same pattern also prevailed on the toughness ratings. However, here, mother-based delinquents received a mean rating that was significantly higher than the delinquents coming from father-based and surrogate-parent homes. The mean group rating for the mother-based delinquents was 3.9, as compared with 3.3 received by both the father-based and surrogate-parent delinquents.

Table III shows that delinquent boys from mother-based homes had mean manliness discrepancy scores—boy group, boy-staff, boy-social worker—that were generally low com-

TABLE II Mean Scores on the Lykken Scale and the Zuckerman Scale, by Race

Race	Mean Lykken scale score	Mean Zuckerman scale score	
White	13.6	13.5	} a
Black	14.3	11.0	

a p < .001.

TABLE III   Mean Scores on Manliness and Toughness Ratings and the Compulsive Masculinity Index, and Discrepancies in Self and Other Ratings by Type of Household

	Mean scores		Discrepancy scores		
Type of household	Self-rating	Group rating	Boy-group	Boy-cottage staff	Boy-social worker
Manliness					
Natural parents	6.5	4.6	1.9	1.5	.8
Parent and stepparent	7.0	4.6	2.3	2.3	1.6
Mother-based	6.8	4.7	2.1	1.7	1.2
Father-based	6.1	4.0 }ᵃ	2.1	1.9	1.3
Surrogate	6.7	4.1	2.6	2.3	1.2
Toughness					
Natural parents	5.1	3.6	1.5	1.0	.2
Parent and stepparent	5.7 }ᵃ	3.6	2.1	1.6	1.0
Mother-based	6.2	3.9	2.3	1.7	1.2
Father-based	5.7	3.3	2.4	1.7	1.7
Surrogate	5.6	3.3	2.3	1.3	.8

Compulsive masculinity index

	Mean ratings
Natural parents	14.2
Parent and stepparent	16.0
Mother-based	14.4
Father-based	13.9
Surrogate	13.8

ᵃ p > .05.

pared with delinquents from other types of households. Thus, of the six household types examined, delinquent boys from mother-based homes held perceptions of their manliness that were relatively consistent with those of their evaluators. On the toughness discrepancy scores, delinquents from mother-based homes had perceptions of their toughness that were relatively discrepant from those held by their evaluators.

It is interesting to note that on both the manliness and toughness dimensions, delinquents from natural-parent homes had conceptions of themselves that were the most consistent with those of their cottage mates, the cottage staff, and their social worker.

Data from this study also provided some support for the hypothesized differences in hostility, impulsivity, proneness to engage in excitement-oriented, high-risk activities, and field dependence of delinquent boys from matriarchal homes and from other types of households.

Delinquents from mother-based homes did not have appreciably different mean Lykken scores as compared with delinquent boys from other types of households. On the Zuckerman Scale, however, delinquents from mother-based homes had the lowest mean score when compared with delinquents from other types of households. There is thus some support for Barclay and Cusumano's (1967) findings that delinquents from mother-based homes were more field dependent than delinquents from father-present homes.

Following the explanation of field dependency provided by Barclay and Cusumano (1967), this finding indicates that delinquent boys from mother-based homes are more likely to be susceptible to situational, including peer-group, pressures and to be more hypermasculine in orientation than boys from other types of households.

Moreover, further evidence of the role played by mother-based homes in generating problems of compulsive masculinity is provided by the fact that on the Zuckerman Scale, delinquent boys from father-based homes had the highest mean scores when compared with delinquents from other households, while it will be recalled that mother-based delinquents had the lowest scores on this scale. Thus, father-based delinquents are theoretically least field dependent, while mother-based boys are the most field dependent. One explanation for this finding is that when mothers are absent from the home, fathers spend more time with their sons, allowing the boys to observe them in a wider variety of situations. Thus, these boys may develop more accurate conceptions of manliness than boys from other types of households, who have limited or no interaction with their fathers.

DISCUSSION

THE FEMALE-BASED HOUSEHOLD

Data from this study clearly suggested that delinquent boys from female-based households were more hyper-masculine than delinquents from other types of households. That is, the self-ratings of the mother-based-house-hold boys on the three direct measures of compulsive masculinity showed that these delinquent boys (a) had the most exaggerated perceptions of their own manliness and toughness; (b) placed great emphasis on tough behavior—drinking, weapon-carrying, kicking a fallen opponent, maintaining a reputation as a tough guy (compulsive masculinity index); (c) emphasized sexual athleticism—conceptualization of women as conquest objects (compulsive masculinity index); (d) were more impulsive (Lykken Scale); (e) were more hostile (Lykken Scale): (f) were more predisposed to engage in excitement-oriented, high-risk activities (Lykken Scale); and (g) were overly predisposed to peer pressures (Zuckerman Scale). These findings lend support to the Parsonian thesis that the mother-based home generates problems of compulsive masculinity, which in turn promote antisocial and aggressive conduct.

As Parsons and his interpreters have suggested, the development of problems of compulsive masculinity among boys from female-based homes can be traced to the period of adolescent development when boys must adopt masculine self-definitions and roles. Two factors probably interact to make this transition difficult. First, since these boys have no father in the home, their mothers have to play both roles—a most difficult assignment. Second, these boys have had no stable male model from whom they could learn the socially acceptable attributes of manliness. What develops when these boys realize that they must repudiate their earlier identification with their mothers is a type of reaction formation. In other words, boys from female-based households may tend to become preoccupied with appearing to be "real men" in their own eyes as well as in the eyes of others. In the absence of a consistent and middle-class male model, these boys come to believe that being a "real man" involves stressing aggressive masculine traits such as toughness, sexual athleticism, and daring, and they seek to convince both themselves and others of their superior manliness and toughness.

These data may imply that an exaggerated male self-concept may act as a closure factor, restricting the possibilities of behavior to a narrowed universe, as suggested by Fannin and Clinard (1965). In other words, delinquent boys may come to regard antisocial and aggressive conduct as the only means by which to maintain an image of being a "real man." The argument set forth here represents one possible explanation for the seemingly greater "compulsive masculinity" among delinquent boys from female-based households than delinquents from other types of households. However, much more research is necessary before this Parsonian conception can be accepted as more than a sensitizing theme for viewing the delinquency problems of boys from mother-based homes. It is suggested that future research explore (a) the consequences of the female-based household for male development—e.g., between delinquent boys and nondelinquent boys; and (b) the role of the masculine self-concept in delinquency.

THE BLACK BOY

Data presented in this study have also shown that black delinquents as a group define themselves as being more manly and tough than white delinquents in the same training school. It will be recalled that on the various instruments and scales, black as compared with white delinquents (a) considered themselves to be more manly and tough, (b) placed more emphasis on tough behavior, (c) emphasized sexual athleticism, (d) were more impulsive, (e) were more hostile, (f) were more predisposed to engage in excitement-oriented, high-risk activities, and (g) were more predisposed to peer pressures for deviant behavior, based on the various scales and measures used.

The Parsonian interpretation of compulsive masculinity among boys from female-based homes certainly applies to black boys from matriarchal families. In fact, the lower-class black family structure is normally cited as an illustration, not only of the emergence of the female-based household, but also of the consequences of this household organization for problems of masculine identification.

However, in addition to the mother-based home, the black male's menial and more subservient status in American society has done much to foster a male definition which centers around toughness, sexual athleticism, and antisocial and retreatist behavior. The fact that the black male has been denied the opportunity for achievement in business, politics, and industry has compelled him, as well as other disadvantaged males generally, to base his self-esteem on contracultural norms, including those subsumed under the heading of compulsive masculinity.

It may well be that disadvantaged males become preoccupied with maintaining an image of themselves as real men through antisocial and aggressive behavior since the alternative to this facade is an acceptance of oneself as a failure. Certainly, if this is the case, the hypermasculinity of the black delinquents represents a normative subcultural definition of manliness.

This study has shown, as predicted, that black delinquents rate themselves as being more masculine than white delinquents. It is suggested that future research involve two interrelated studies. Research should be conducted on the impact of subservient social position on self-concept as a male. In addition, it is necessary to study the coping behavior techniques of the majority of black boys from matriarchal families who do not become delinquent.

CONCLUSION

In general the data from this study have provided some empirical support for the theoretically posited relationship between the factors of race, matriarchy, and compulsive masculinity.

However, this study has not been able to address itself to various issues that are of great importance in evaluating the etiologic significance of compulsive masculinity in delinquent behavior. For example, is compulsive masculinity endemic to low socioeconomic adolescents as such (Miller, 1966; Toby, 1966), or only to those of lower-class background who become delinquent? How are boys able to maintain exaggerated self-concepts of their manliness and toughness in the face of interaction with "significant others" who judge them far less masculine and tough? To what extent are the self and other definitions of masculinity derived from and related to the various physique types and to such other "hard" measures as physical strength, maturational status, and agility? If machismo or compulsive masculinity are learned life styles, how might these styles be converted into more socially acceptable channels? Finally, is it possible to develop a treatment program for delinquents which capitalizes on these self-perceptions and life style definitions?

Much, obviously, remains to be done.

REFERENCES

Allen, H. (1969). "Bio-Social Correlates of Two Types of Anti-Social Sociopaths." Ph.D. dissertation. Ohio State University.

Barclay A. G., and D. R. Cusumano (1967). "Testing Masculinity in Boys Without Fathers." Trans-Action 5 (December): 33–35.

Clark, K. (1965). Dark Ghetto: *Dilemmas of Social Power*. New York: Harper & Row.

Fannin, L. F. and M. Clinard (1965). "Differences in the Conception of Self as a Male Among Lower and Middle Class Delinquents." *Social Problems* 13 (Fall): 205–214.

Hannerz, A. (1969). "Roots of Black Manhood." *Trans-Action* 6 (October): 112–21.

Hardt, R. H., and G. E. Bodine (1965). "Development of Self-Report Instruments in Delinquency Research: a Conference Report." Syracuse, N.Y.: Syracuse Univ. Press.

Liebow, E. (1967). *Tally's Corner: A Study of Negro Street-Corner Men*. Boston: Little, Brown.

Lykken, D. T. "A Study of Anxiety in Sociopathic Personality." *J. of Abnormal and Social Psychology* **55**:6–10.

Miller, W. B. (1966). "Lower Class Culture as a Generating Milieu of Gang Delinquency, pp. 137–150 in R. Giallombardo (ed.) *Juvenile Delinquency: A Book of Readings*. New York: John Wiley.

Moynihan, D. P. (1968). "The President and the Negro: the Moment Lost," pp. 431–460 in R. Perracci and M. Pilisuk (eds.) *The Triple Revolution: Social Problems in Depth*. Boston: Little, Brown.

National Commission on the Causes and Prevention of Violence (1969). *To Establish Justice. To Insure Domestic Tranquility*. Washington, D.C.: Government Printing Office.

Parsons, T. (1947). "Certain Primary Sources and Patterns of Aggression in the Social Structure of the Western World." *Psychiatry* **10** (May): 167–181.

Rainwater, L., and L. Yancy (1967). *The Moynihan Report and the Politics of Controversy*. Cambridge: MIT Press.

Rosen, L. (1969). "Matriarchy and Lower Class Negro Male Delinquency." *Social Problems* **17** (Fall): 175–189.

Silverman, I.J. (1970). "Compulsive Masculinity and Delinquency." Ph.D. dissertation. Ohio State University.

Toby, J. (1966). "Violence and the Masculine Ideal: Some Qualitative Data." *Annals of the Amer. Society of Pol. and Social Sci.* **364** (March): 19–27.

Wolfgang, M. E., and F. Ferracuti (1967). *The Subculture of Violence: Toward an Integrated Theory of Criminology*. London: Associated Book Publishers.

Zuckerman, M. (1964). "Development of a Sensation-Seeking Scale." *J. of Consulting Psychology* **6**:477–482.

SECTION IV

THE SOCIOLOGY OF CRIME

Attempts to ascertain basic causes of crime by researchers in various disciplines show much variability in "fashionable" modes of explanation. Early in the twentieth century, biological studies seemed to have offered the greatest promise. In the period from the 1920s through the 1940s, psychological and psychiatric investigators were both abundant and comparatively prestigious. Although there has been a resurgence of biological studies, the bulk of research into the causes of adult criminality and juvenile delinquency has been made within a sociological frame of reference in recent decades.

A dominant, inordinately important feature of modern American society is the obsession with winning or "being Number One." One tragic result of this mania is depicted in Woodley's selection on the Soap Box Derby. As American as apple pie, the desire to win the annual race at Akron, Ohio by use of Yankee ingenuity led to sophisticated skullduggery and the dishonest manipulation of car specifications as well as help from unauthorized adults.

Rosen and Nielsen survey, in great depth, the major sociological variable of family structure, as previous research has related it to juvenile delinquency. They summarize, and more importantly, recalculate the data produced by several major studies of broken homes. They conclude that a broken home, no matter how it is defined, has a very weak relationship, with little explanatory value, to juvenile delinquency.

The next item deals with the central social institution of education. Elliott, in a major study of delinquency and school dropouts, finds that, contrary to what is frequently believed, although school dropouts have consistently higher police contact rates and self-reported delinquency than their fellow students while they are in school, after leaving school, their involvement in serious offenses declines substantially. In addition, Elliott finds that, in contrast, graduates are involved in more offenses than dropouts, once out of school.

There has been much made of the new "female criminal" and her relationship to the Women's Movement. By use of a body of self-report data, Weis concludes that, in spite of predictions by "liberation" theories of increasing similarities in the criminal behaviors of males and females, women are no more violent today than they were a decade ago. Modest increases in some categories of female crime cannot be clearly laid at the door of the increasing assertiveness and independence of women.

Hindelang addresses the crucial topic of racial differences in crime rates. Using data secured from the National Victimization Surveys, he finds evidence, supportive of official crime statistics findings, that the higher black arrest rate is probably due to their heavier involvement in criminal offenses rather than the result of selection biases in the criminal justice system.

A topic of continuing importance, and no little fascination, is gang life and gang behavior. Erlanger's article dissects Los Angeles Chicano gangs, particularly with respect to the central concepts of "machismo," courage and dignity, and recent feelings of estrangement resulting in an increase of gang violence. By direct participant observation and analytic induction, West focuses on what he terms "serious thieves"—a neglected type of criminal somewhere between the amateur and the professional. By observing them over a long period of time, he collected data on the social process of becoming a thief and ultimately "retiring" when pressures of arrests, available jobs, marital possibilities, and maturation make being a thief less attractive.

The highly publicized indifference and failure to "get involved" on the part of most urbanites when they are confronted with street crime is tested in an ingenious experiment by Takooshian and Bodinger. They describe the consequences of setting up a simulated situation on city streets where bystanders witnessed what they thought was a thief (a research assistant of the authors) breaking into cars. The conclusions are both pessimistic and intriguing.

11

THE IMPORTANCE OF BEING NUMBER ONE

RICHARD WOODLEY

The all-American soap box derby will once again be run in Akron, Ohio, in August. But it will be a smaller, cheaper, surely more honest shadow of its former self. The thirty-seven-year-old Derby lost its virginity in a sinful caper last year and almost fell apart.

It will be remembered that last year's winner, fourteen-year-old Jimmy Gronen, was disqualified when an electromagnet was discovered in his racer. The magnet, mounted in the nose, drew the nose against the metal starting gate and caused the car to be yanked ahead when the gate flopped down to start the race.

That incident, and subsequent evidence of rampant skullduggery over the years, caused the Akron Chamber of Commerce to withdraw its sponsorship, asserting that the Derby had become a victim of "cheating, fraud, and hoax."

The befouling of the venerable Derby was not, to be sure, the idea of the children who aspired to its crown, but of the adults who guided the innocents in the childhood game of coasting downhill in a homemade wagon. The proclaimed villain in this case was Jimmy Gronen's guardian uncle, Robert B. Lange, Sr.,

who was earlier known for his development of the admired plastic-shell ski boot bearing his name. For violating the sanctity of the Derby ("It's like discovering that your Ivory Snow girl has made a blue movie," commented a prosecutor), Lange, forty-eight, of Boulder, Colorado, was ordered by a Colorado court in a "nonjudicial" bargain to pay $2,000 to a boys' club. The judge said Lange owed an apology to the youth of the nation.

But Lange admits only a "serious mistake in judgment," and avers that cheating has been so rife that all he did was to even his nephew's odds in a dirty system. In fact, when I talked to him not long ago, he was inclined to sue those responsible for disqualifying his nephew without banishing others who had cheated in the same race.

If mores may be defined as the accepted mode of behavior which does not threaten the stability of the community, it is more important to define the community than the mores. The withdrawal of the Chamber of Commerce, combined with information from many others involved with the Derby for many years, confirms that Lange, however wrong in his actions, is right in his assessments. The sponsor of the first thirty-five championships was Chevrolet, which deftly and without substantive explanation withdrew its sponsorship before the 1973 race. It is widely inferred that

Source: "How to Win in the Soap Box Derby," *Harper's Magazine* (August 1974), **249:** 62–66, 67–69. Copyright © 1974 by Richard Woodley. Reprinted by permission of Paul R. Reynolds, Inc.

Chevrolet, while probably not condoning the growing wickedness in the competition, at least turned a deaf ear and blind eye to the problem.

And so the scandal blew, with its fallout, and the Derby, for which children aged eleven to fifteen supposedly build their own $75 racers that supposedly conform to construction rules and supposedly coast unaided down the 954-foot macadam track called Derby Downs, fell prey to what seemed to be a national malaise: winning, being everything, is worth doing anything to achieve. The Derby, like the Presidency, will likely survive, because enough people want it to. At the last minute, the Akron Jaycees picked up the interim sponsorship, and the Derby is scheduled to run in Akron on August 17, with a new rule book and tighter controls. The intention is to return the Derby— which had become sophisticated and expensive, with fiberglass racers, adult engineering, and meddling old grads—to the kids. Such a retreat to morality is publicly welcomed by all; whether such a basic Derby might be too mundane to attract sustaining interest remains to be seen.

A FAMILY EVENT

Lange's son, Bobby, Jr., won the race in 1972, the same year that Jimmy Gronen, because of the lengthy hospitalization of his widowed mother, joined the Lange family, Jimmy won the 1973 race in a car almost identical to Bobby's. Bobby's car disappeared mysteriously from the Lange basement shortly after the scandal about Jimmy's magnet broke. Lange figures that somebody must have just swiped it but insists that it contained no magnet. He admits, however, that it was an illegal car in other ways, as was Jimmy's.

No scandal was hinted at prior to Jimmy's championship race. The pre-race week had gone smoothly; the 138 local race winners— including 19 girls, and entrants from Venezuela, West Germany, and Canada, were greeted with customary hoopla by Akron.

There was a police escort into town, welcoming kisses, and ritualistic donning of Derby T-shirts and beanies. The contestants were then deposited at the YMCA's Camp Y-Noah for four days of fun before the championships. Their racers had been impounded for safe-keeping at Derby Downs.

Akron was a good host, as it has been for the American Golf Classic, the Firestone-PBA Tournament of Champions for bowlers, big-time spelling bees, and other events which have made the "Rubber Capital of the World" (Firestone, General Tire, B. F. Goodrich, Goodyear Tire) a hub of all-American activities, of which the All-American Soap Box Derby— the "World's Gravity Grand Prix"—was just about the grandest family event of the year. There was a giant parade with bands and Marines and celebrities.

Prior to and during the race heats, contestants milled nervously around their racers in the paddock area. The cars were nothing like what the children's parents had made in earlier years. They were smooth racers, so slender and streamlined that drivers who had grown a bit between their local races in June and July and these finals in August had to wedge themselves in slowly. Many of the models were designed in "layback" style: the drivers were almost lying down, their eyes just visible over the cockpit.

There were differences in design—such as between the high-tailed layback and the "sit-up" models—and they were painted all manner of colors, with the sponsors' names professionally lettered on the sides, along with the drivers' names and car numbers. But beyond that, there was an enforced similarity. Their overall length could not exceed 80 inches, their height no more than 28 inches, their width no more than 34¾ inches, and the wheelbase could not be less than 48 inches. Total weight of car and driver could not exceed 250 pounds. Any metal in the car was to be a functional part of the construction; no welded parts were permitted.

All entrants had been issued a brand-new

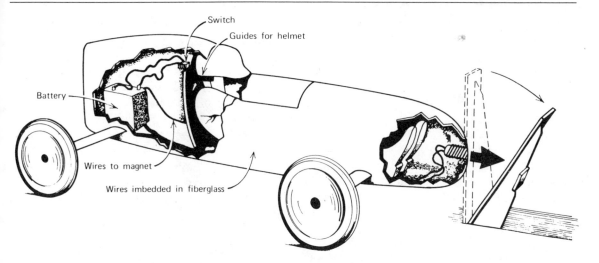

set of computer-matched official gold Soap Box Derby championship wheels to replace the red ones on which they had won in their local towns. They were to be placed on official Soap Box Derby axles, and neither wheels nor axles were to be tampered with in any way.

The rule book stated the whole reason for the Derby to the contestants: "The Soap Box Derby is for YOU. You must build your own car. You must not let adults or anyone else work on your car. You may accept advice and counsel from adults in the design and construction of your car`. . ."

James H. Gronen first raced in the forty-sixth two-car heat. (The official records: "Fourteen-year-old Jim, who is called 'Big Jim' by his friends, is 4-feet, 11-inches tall and weighs 68 pounds. He lost in the first round of the double-elimination Boulder race when a broken steering cable caused him to hit a curb. The damage was repaired and he raced on to victory. He likes skiing, sailing, and motorcycles.") His green fiberglass layback number 12 was carefully walked down the hill to the starting line and set in position in Lane 2 beside the entry from Nashville. The noses of both cars, angled downhill, rested against the spring-loaded steel flaps which rose out of the shimmering macadam.

On signal, the starting flaps dropped forward and the cars rolled, gathering speed to between thirty and thirty-five miles per hour by the time they crossed the finish line. Jimmy Gronen won in a time of 27.48 seconds. On subsequent heats through the afternoon, Jimmy beat cars from Lancaster, Ohio; Appleton, Wisconsin; Columbus, Georgia; and Winston-Salem, North Carolina. In the semifinal, Jimmy beat the Ossining, New York, car with a 27.63 time. In the final, he beat Bret Allen Yarborough of Elk Grove, California, though with his slowest time yet, 27.68.

When Jimmy was presented the trophy, his long, wispy blond hair tossing beneath his helmet edge in the breeze, the braces on his teeth sparkling in the sun, he said simply with a smile, "I was hoping that I'd win." He was also given a gold ring and a $7,500 college scholarship.

When Jimmy received his trophy, there was, amid the cheering, a solidly audible round of boos. Spectators were curious about why Jimmy's times had strangely worsened with each heat. People were showing the officials pictures they had taken of the starts, claiming they showed the Gronen car leaping head. And during the heats, it was said, officials had caught Jimmy cheating by buffing his tires on the pavement, and had made him substitute a new set. They had drilled in his car to remove excess weight. And what was this about some cars having been disqualified before the race, and then somehow reinstated? People wondered whether Jimmy's car was in fact Bobby's car from the year before. It was rumored that the Lange cars had cost over $20,000 to build, that they were constructed by experts at the Lange ski factory and were tested in a wind tunnel.

Derby officials began looking over the Gronen car. An inspector found a small button in the headrest, drilled through the headrest, and found wires and a battery. The car was taken to Goodyear Aerospace, near Derby Downs, and X-rayed. That was how the hunk of metal, the magnet, was discovered in the nose. To activate it, Jimmy would have leaned his helmet back against the switch in the headrest. Officials later found a second switch, formed by two supports under the cowling which covered the steering wheel, turned on by Jimmy pulling them together with his thumbs.

On Monday, Chamber of Commerce officials called in the press and announced news of the magnet and Jimmy's disqualification. Bret Yarborough was declared the new champion, and each of the following eight finishers was moved up a notch. The press leaped on the story, spreading the scandal across the nation in a mix of chuckles and pronouncements. In Putnam County, New York, Derby Director Ronald Mills, whose daughter, Diane, had been moved up to second place, said, "It's just unbelievable that anyone would want that ego trip that bad." Andy Noyes, father of now-third-place winner Chris, said, "Let's give the Derby back to the kids, where it belongs."

CHARGES OF CORRUPTION

Gronen's car was immediately locked in a bank storage room (as evidence, should there be lawsuits or criminal charges), and the Chamber of Commerce clammed up. Prosecutors in Akron and Boulder quickly began hearing from people from all over, some anonymously, who described other cheating. Akron Prosecutor Stephen Gabalac said, "If the Chamber doesn't come out swinging now, even the golfers

won't want to come here. The whole town is besmirched."

And then Lange issued a statement admitting responsibility for sanctioning the magnet, which Jimmy had installed. He asserted that both Jimmy and Bobby had built their own cars and that no significant expense went into them except in the permissible "area of advice and counsel." He admitted that Bobby's car had been tested in a wind tunnel, which, he said, was neither uncommon nor illegal.

Then he leveled his charges: "Anyone participating in derby races with eyes and ears open would soon learn, as I did, that . . . the Derby rules have been consistently and notoriously violated by some participants without censure or disqualification." He said it was "common knowledge" that eleven-year-olds cannot build winning racers, and that "it is all that some mechanically inclined and dexterous fourteern- or fifteen-year-old boy can do to carry out the superfine mechanical construction and machine work required." That was why, he said, there were adult professional builders who "build cars for sale to participants or race the cars themselves with young, lightweight drivers, who are known as chauffeurs. Early in my experience one of the professional builders offered to build a car for my son for $2,500, which I promptly refused because I felt the true value of the derby would come from my son's own efforts."

"After seeing my nephew work hundreds of hours to build his own car," Lange said, "knowing that he would be competing in Akron against professionally built cars, and against cars that would be in violation of the official rules, and having heard and believing that some fast cars in Akron would be equipped with a magnetic nose, I determined that he should build and install a magnetic nose so as to be competitive. I knew that this was a violation of the official Derby rules and consider it now to be a serious mistake in judgment."

As prosecutors continued to receive information of violations, at year's end the Chamber abandoned the race with its "cheating, fraud, and hoax" statement. Later on, I went to see Lange in Boulder.

Lange is a convivial, hospitable man with a smooth manner and modish style, with a moustache, and hair down over his ears. He still carries athletic leanness (he was a swimmer at Harvard and skis and surfs often now). His wife, Vidie, a graphic artist, is similarly lean and friendly and modish, with long blond hair. We sat in the living room of their spacious, ranchstyle house, where we could look out through the glass wall upon the sparsely grassed, yellow foothills of the Rockies. From time to time, their son Bobby, grown tall and gangly, and their nephew Jimmy Gronen, shorter and stockier, stopped by for bits of chat. But at Lange's request, to protect the boys from any further involvement, they were not included in the general Derby discussion.

Lange's ski and ski-boot company was bought in 1972 by the Garcia Corporation. Last summer Lange became inactive as president of his division, though he remains a consultant and draws a $90,000 salary. The Lange factory is in nearby Broomfield, and it is there and in a machine shop in Boulder, as well as in the Lange garage, that the boys built their racers.

"I'm sure that not one Derby official in Akron believes for a second that they built their cars," Lange said, "but they did. Most people violate that rule, but I think the most important thing of all, the most exciting thing for the boys, was the thrill of building their cars and running them down the hill."

Lange's involvement with the Derby, aside from a brief try as a boy, goes back to 1970, with Bobby. "He built a car and lost right here in Boulder. He worked hard on it, but we didn't know anything, and he didn't have a chance."

He went to Akron to visit that year's championship, and then to Detroit, where Chevrolet had the winning cars on display. Through casual conversations and careful examination and measurement and photography of the cars, he began to learn about the technology, aerodynamics, and mechanics. Good alignment, he decided was it. Also, it seemed to him that wooden cars, such as Bobby's first, built in the dry climate of Boulder, would be slowed by absorbing moisture in the dampness of Akron. At a special Soap Box rally in Detroit, he also began to learn of the dark side of the Derby.

"A bunch of us got together and just got to talking, and I began to realize that a lot of these cars just weren't built by kids. These men were building them. One guy said, 'Well, there are drivers and there are builders.' I learned about souping up wheels. They use all kinds of solvents to expand the tires, then when they come back they're faster. I don't know the full technology about the tires, but they have to be resilient, so that when you go over a tiny bump, the tire kind of pushes back. The flex on the wheels sets up vibrations, and if the car vibrates properly, it goes a lot faster. And there are ways of working on bearings. I also learned that most people do not win with official Derby axles. One guy, a production-line worker, was building axles in his spare time and selling them all over the country. He was bragging about it."

"Were these guys telling you how to cheat?" I asked.

"They were telling me how to *win*," Lange said. "They were just doing me a favor. They don't feel it's cheating; it's so common it's just part of the game. These are ordinary guys, lots of engineers, not rich or anything. It's their life. They just live and die Derby. They probably thought, 'We'll give Lange a little bit of help, but he's never going to be any real problem.' Because I was coming out of nowhere, you know. They knew I wasn't a builder."

DESIGNED TO WIN

Lange's first step along the trail toward scandal occurred four years ago in Detroit, when he paid about $20 for a set of illegal axles for Bobby's second car. That car was made of fiberglass, which wouldn't absorb moisture, and had a metal T strip down the mid-bottom to which the axles could be bolted for sure and precise alignment. Lange made a "female" fiberglass mold from which the fiberglass top and bottom halves, which were identical, could be shaped. "But we didn't work on vibrations that year," Lange said. "We didn't realize how important that was." The second car was a great improvement, but it was beaten in Boulder.

Now, however, Derby was deep in Lange's blood; his competitive nerves were alive. He took Bobby to Anderson, Indiana, where one of the biggest wildcats is held annually after Akron, and Bobby's car was second fastest of about 130 cars. At first he thought they might just make some minor alterations for the coming season, but they actually needed a whole new car for the 1972 derby, which would be Bobby's third try.

"I didn't work on constructing Bobby's car, but I spent a lot of time designing. Bobby was too far back in that car. Having your weight where you want it is probably one of the most important things in the race. Live weight is high in the center of gravity, whereas dead weight you can put where you want it, which is in the back. Since the car is running at a tilt most of the way, weight in the rear has more drop, so you have more energy in your car. The whole principle is to add dead weight back up the hill, and to balance that you slide the boy forward. Ideally, from an energy standpoint, you would put all your weight over the rear wheels. But that advantage would be overcome by friction when you get down on the flat, friction on the tires and the bearings that takes the resiliency out. So you have to have a balance. I have four slide scales, like doctors' scales, and you put one wheel on each scale so you get it just right,"

Also, the car was not aerodynamically correct. "A friend of mine who works at Cal Tech said that what we had was fine in water but was not fine in air doing under fifty miles an hour. The nose has to be rounded, like a tear drop. So when we got the car ready, we shipped it out to California, and my friend put it in the Cal Tech wind tunnel. You mount it

up on pins and put fine pieces of thread all over the sides so you can see the airflow, what the laminar flow is and so forth. Computers measure the drag. Aerodynamics is only a small percentage in importance, but at the finish line you're looking for inches."

Lange also applied his ski knowledge. "I had come up with a new theory of the vibration in the car that really made it go fast, just like a downhill ski. If it gets too much oscillation up and down, it goes slow. Even a smooth surface has very slight undulations. Get a ski trip that's too stiff, and it doesn't undulate right. In the suspension of a derby car, the rear is solid, but if the front gets too solid, or too floppy, it goes slow. The oscillations load and unload the bearings as it goes downhill. You want that action in there, but it has to be just right. We worked on the vibrations by moving the attachment points back and forth, so that all of a sudden we had the right oscillations, and the car just kind of took off.

"And, of course, I was a super-expert in fiberglass, and a super-expert in machining things so they stay in line. I designed a jig just like an engine-block jig, to hold the car while you work on it, where you can lock it in and spin it all around, where the spindles of the axles are kept absolutely square and parallel all the time, and you don't knock it out of line in assembly."

Bobby milled a square end on the T alignment bar, pushed an axle against it, drilled and tapped, and put the dowel pins in. Then he slid the T into the length of the body and assembled the car in the jig, then took it out and balanced it on the scales, making it about ten pounds heavier in the rear. Following the guidance from the wind tunnel, he worked out subtleties in the shape with automobile-body putty.

"The molding was done here in our garage," Lange said, "but all the metalwork and assembly were done in the factory, right out in front of everybody, by Bobby. He learned to run all the machines, and somebody there would just check the setups. Bobby would go down there at 3:30 and work till 10:00 almost every night for three straight months. He loved it."

In order to accommodate the added deadweight without exceeding the 250-pound limit, Bobby was dieting and exercising. "He trained down from 123 to 106," Lange said. "I had him running three miles a day."

With everything honed, shaped, balanced, squared, light, firm, and quick, Bobby won the 1972 Boulder race easily ("There isn't much derby knowledge here, compared with some places where it's really hot and heavy. If you can't win the Boulder race easily, you won't do anything in Akron"), and went on to Akron.

In the course of watching Bobby win the championship, Lange lost whatever faith he had in the honesty of the Derby. "I still didn't know all the things that were really going on until Bobby got into the zoo. I learned right away that a kid can't leave his car for a minute, because of the sabotage there. You don't have to do much—just put a little linseed oil in a guy's bearings, and he's out of the race. And then Bobby had all these stories about guys not building their cars. Guys had illegal welded parts, double-drilled axles, they were juicing wheels—just putting some kind of stuff on their hands, like a spitball pitcher, to rub 'quickies' on their tires.

"And the big talk about the magnets was around. There was supposed to be a car in that race with a magnet, faster than Bobby's, but he cracked up. The whole thing made me sick. After Bobby won, Vidie and I were both glad we were through with that mess."

When Chevrolet dropped its sponsorship, a special Organizational Board of the Derby was set up, to seek a sponsor and perhaps develop new rules. Lange served on it. "I was through, but I wanted to see the place cleaned up, an entirely different kind of race. But I think in everybody's mind at that point was not to rock the boat, not to do something that would cause the whole race to collapse."

Then the Akron Chamber of Commerce took over, and there were no rule changes for 1973.

That same summer, Jimmy Gronen moved from his home in Dubuque, Iowa, to live with the Langes. Jimmy had never built a racer, and through the following fall and winter showed no interest. "Then in March," Lange said, "Jimmy suddenly asked if he could build a car. I was absolutely shocked."

It was a time, Mr. and Mrs. Lange agreed, for soul-searching. "I was fighting with myself," Vidie Lange said. "The boys enjoyed it so much, building the cars. It's a terrible turmoil in your house, all this sanding, all this fiberglass everywhere. I wondered whether the race was as bad as I thought it was, or whether I was just angry because of the turmoil."

In the end, it was Vidie who encouraged the building of yet one more racer. "When you introduce another person into your house," she said, "you try very hard to make him a part of your family and do the things for him you're doing for your other children."

"So finally we decided to do it," Bob Lange said. "I think it did a great thing for my relationship with Jimmy. But time was so short—just three months before the local race, and you really need about six. So we said we'll design a car that Jimmy can build, but the only way we could get it done in time was to use Bobby's mold—which was not illegal—and built one that was essentially the same. Even so, it would be nip and tuck. Bobby had had three years' experience working in a machine shop. I told Jimmy he just couldn't be a machinist in such a short time. We had to take shortcuts, everything was simplified. Where Bobby used five bolts, Jimmy used three—stuff like that. There was nothing much new we tried to do, just tried to get in the damn race. The only thing we did, since he was so much smaller than Bobby, was to move him further forward in the car. And where Bobby's car was about ten pounds heavy in the rear, we made Jimmy's about forty. He weighed about ninety pounds, but he was chubby, so he started his diet right away."

They made axles, and for weight in the rear

Lange used epoxy mixed with buckshot. "Technically the axles were illegal. I knew they couldn't pass a hardness test. But they had never done anything about that anyway. I don't call the buckshot and epoxy illegal; I designed it so they couldn't call it illegal."

Since the car was virtually the same as Bobby's, there was no wind-tunnel test. They assumed they would get to Akron with it. As expected, despite an accident in an early heat, Jimmy won the Boulder race as easily as Bobby had. And, as they had done with Bobby's car after the Boulder race, they brought Jimmy's car home to paint and letter it for Akron. (It is technically illegal to bring a car home after winning the local race, but the practice is common. Lange didn't want the car touched by "some yokel" who might somehow jar the car out of alignment.)

Then came the magnet. "We had done everything," Lange said. "I had Jimmy down to weight, the car balanced the way I wanted. I knew we had a fast car. But we also knew what we were up against. I had files on other cars. A guy from Michigan told me he had a car that was a whole car-length faster than Bobby's, for example. And we knew the Elk Grove car was going to be superfast. So we said, 'What else can we do? How can you make a car faster? Have we done everything?' We discussed theory. Jimmy came up with some ideas, Bobby with some."

The idea that recurred, although Lange doesn't recall who brought it up first, was a magnet. "Vidie probably would have shot us if she had known we were kicking that around. The year before at Akron, all the builders I talked with knew all about magnets. It wasn't anything new at all. It certainly wasn't *my* idea. I had heard a story about one guy who had a magnet, and somebody turned it on and left it on so it wore down before the race. I'd heard about an inspector measuring a car with a steel tape measure when, bang! it stuck to the thing. They made the driver remove the magnet, but they let him run. We knew Jimmy would be running against all those chauffeurs

in professionally built cars, and maybe other cars that had magnets, so we figured that in order to be competitive we would probably try one. It was the only thing we could think of. I figured even if they detected it they wouldn't throw him out, just make him disconnect it."

NO MORAL CRISIS

Given the situation at Akron, Lange did not consider the immorality of using a magnet. "These boys had sat in on meetings with builders. They knew what was in those cars. Our attitude toward the Akron race was that it was one big wildcat, and we were in it. There was no moral crisis for Jimmy. He had been around all these super-illegal cars and saw the whole business. The scene was there, he didn't create it. Jimmy wanted to win the race."

Moreover, he said, he wasn't even sure it would work. And if it did, it would be no greater advantage than good axles, wheels, balance, and all the rest. "There's a lot of things I'd rather have than a magnet. What's more of an advantage than having a guy that's been building racers for eighteen years? Who's kidding who about advantage? You call a magnet a secret motor? You're pulling a secret motor in if you add a pound, because your weight is your motor. I don't go along with the magnet being a different type of thing from the other things that are just commonly being done. Sure, I take full responsibility for it because I'm the one that should say yes or no. But I had never seen a magnet, or how they were designed. The kids designed it, and Jimmy put it in. They learn all that stuff in science class in school. All you need is a little ingenuity."

And so Jimmy put the battery in the tail fin, and ran copper wires on either side along the inside seam, where the top and bottom halves were joined. Using a stick to reach the recesses of the fuselage, he glued strips of fiberglass over the wire. He cut a hole in the nose. He bolted together four small pieces of iron, totaling about three inches in length, wrapped them with the wires, laid them in the hole, filled in around them with fiberglass resin and body putty, sanded the metal head smooth to the nose, and painted it over so that there was no visible seam or metal. The entire inside of the car was coated with black primer, which obscured any view. Lange said his only contribution was to suggest the second fail-safe thumb switch under the cowling to protect against the battery running down if one switch was turned on by accident, say, in shipping.

They tested the magnet once, by putting an I beam across the nose and trying to putt the car forward. "You could feel it," Lange said, "but it wouldn't make the car move. And the battery's got to sit for a month, so there's no point in wearing it down by testing it. It's either going to work, or it's not going to work. Anyway, nothing would substitute for a bad car. Jimmy's was a super car without it. As it turned out, he would have won anyway, but at the time I didn't think he could win without the magnet."

And then they went to Akron, where Jimmy was to win. They were attended by controversy from the beginning. Before the races, several cars, including Jimmy's were listed for disqualification for having illegally hard axles, but officials backed down and allowed all the cars to run, just as Lange had supposed they would. During the races, officials took Jimmy's first set of wheels away because he had been working on them with his hands, and buffing them. Then they drilled in his car to remove some of the buckshot weight, while Jimmy wept in frustration. "Friends kept running up to me," Lange said, "and saying how much the officials were hassling Jimmy. I said, 'He's all right, he's a big boy, you know.' "

And finally Jimmy won it all, just before losing it all, and he said he didn't even have a chance to turn on the thumb switch for the last championship run.

Lange believes that part of the reason for singling out Jimmy for harsh treatment was jealousy from other builders they beat. Also, the Akron Chamber of Commerce, he felt, "wouldn't have made such a big issue over the thing" if it had been aware of what had been going on for years. "As a matter of fact," Lange said, "since Jimmy won about five guys have called me and said they used magnets."

The swirl of claims, charges, rumors, and denials continues. This year at Akron, the contestants will have to demonstrate their skills by duplicating "selected steps in the construction of their car"; "female" fiberglass molds of the Lange type, which can be reused, are prohibited (next year fiberglass may be banned altogether); the insides of the cars, from nose to tail, must be accessible to permit inspection for such things as magnets.

The case of the Soap Box Derby scandal is closed, more or less. Jimmy has not returned his trophy or accepted his disqualification. Lange says his nephew has been quite philosophical. "Sure, he was upset. He said, 'Here they're calling me a cheater, when these other guys are more cheaters than I am.' " But, he said, Jimmy's friends have been "super," and people in general have been sympathetic because "they know what was going on."

I agreed with Lange that to discuss all this with Jimmy would exacerbate old wounds and expose him to further painful publicity, and I wished not to do that. I came away with a sense of charm and spirit within the Lange household, and warmth in the relationships with their children, and I prefer to trust that sense.

But I cannot shake a certain melancholy. Perhaps Jimmy Gronen did not adapt to cheating as easily as all that. When he sat poised in his racer at the top of Derby Downs, with the knowledge of what he was doing, the fear of detection, the hope of winning, the faith in his guardian uncle, and the memories of the past year, he must have felt at least a transient pang of utter loneliness. And I wonder how often that stab has recurred, and will, at odd times, to different stimuli, with varying intensities, and whether winning was worth so scarred a heritage from the age of fourteen.

12

BROKEN HOMES

LAWRENCE ROSEN AND KATHLEEN NEILSON

Considerable attention has been focused on the family as a contributing factor in delinquency. Three major approaches have been utilized to explicate the relationship between familial factors and delinquency. Respectively, these orientations emphasize: (1) deviant structural configurations, (2) deviant familial relationships, and (3) the transfer of deviant norms.

The "deviant structure" orientation focuses on delinquency as a result of the child being nurtured in a household that has deviated from the "ideal" or normative family structure in a given society. According to this perspective, one would expect that in American society, a child living in a "broken home" would, for a variety of related reasons, tend to become delinquent, since this is a departure from the predominant and ideal arrangement of a nuclear family with both parents present. The second approach that emphasized deviant familial relationships assumes that the type of familial interaction will have an effect on the subsequent behavior of the child. Factors such as too much love or lack of love, too harsh or too lax discipline, lack of familial solidarity, emotional inconsistency, etc., will often result in rebellion, psychological difficulties, and personality problems, with a subsequent increased probability of delinquency. The final orientation—the transfer of deviant norms—

Source: Selection especially written for this volume.

focuses on the differential socialization of children and their resultant tendencies toward either conforming or delinquent behavior. According to this perspective, delinquents would be taught to favor violation of societal norms and juvenile statutes whereas nondelinquents would internalize respect for societal norms and juvenile statutes.

This selection evaluates the empirical evidence that addresses itself to the effect of one aspect of the family structure—the presence of a "broken" or "intact" home—on delinquency.

CONCEPT OF A BROKEN HOME

The definition of a broken home that is most commonly employed in the delinquency literature refers to a home that is characterized by the absence of at least one natural parent because of death, desertion, divorce, or separation. However, some variations can be found, such as the absence of either a natural *or* a stepparent or even absences that may be temporary in nature (e.g., absences resulting from institutional commitment or occupational opportunities away from the home). The definition of a broken home can also be restricted so that only divorce, desertion, and/or separation are utilized as reasons for the break.

All conceptions of a broken home, however, include two major dimensions: (1) the absence of a parent or parents, and (2) the reason for the absence. Thus the variability in the definition of a broken home is a consequence of the extension or restriction of the concept in terms of which parent or parents are absent or the reasons for the absence. In order to evaluate the literature systematically on this dimension, it seems appropriate to avoid the more restrictive definitions of broken homes and to employ a more general one. For purposes of this study, a broken home simply refers to a family that is characterized by the absence of at least one parent (natural or step).

REVIEW OF THE LITERATURE

The literature in delinquency exhibits a considerable amount of controversy concerning the relative importance of the broken home as a contributing factor of delinquency. Peterson and Becker (1965), for example, argue strongly for its importance:

> . . . the substantial relationship between delinquency and broken homes remains as one of the overriding facts any conception of delinquency must take into account. (p. 69)

On the other hand, a harsh criticism of this position is posited by Mannheim (1965):

> No other term in the history of criminological thought has been so much overworked, misused, and discredited as this. For many years universally proclaimed as the most obvious explanation of both juvenile delinquency and adult crime, it is now often regarded as the ''black sheep'' in the otherwise respected family of criminological theories, and most writers shamefacedly turn their backs to it. (p. 618)

A perusal of the literature indicates that the once popular position that broken homes are instrumental in the development of delinquent behavior has waned somewhat in recent years. The predominant position among contemporary criminologists seems to be that broken homes are of *secondary* importance for understanding juvenile delinquency.

Despite this view among the professionals, it seems that the public tends to believe that the broken home is a major cause of delinquency. This is an understandable concern, considering that the prevalance of broken homes has increased substantially since the middle of the 1960s. In 1974 there were approximately 2.5 million more children (below the age of 18) living in households with at least one parent absent than in 1965. In 1974 it was estimated that approximately 11.8 million children were residing in broken homes (U.S. Bureau of the Census, 1974:111–112). Thus, if the broken home is a major cause of delinquency, a sizable number of the youths in the United States could be adversely effected.

Because the studies have varied widely in terms of defining delinquency and broken homes, sampling procedures, research design, and data analysis, it is somewhat difficult to find an adequate base for comparison. Although it is nearly impossible to consider all the conditions of research, we decided to invoke the following criteria for inclusion of eligible studies for review:

1. A comparison group of nondelinquents must have been included in their research design.
2. The data must have been presented in sufficient detail so that a ϕ^2 (phi square) could be computed.
3. The delinquent group did not consist solely of institutionalized youths. (There is evidence that family structure is a factor in the judicial decision to commit a juvenile to a correctional institution. By using only an institutional population, there is a decidedly possibility that the proportion of broken homes would be somewhat inflated.)[1]

In addition to these requirements we also decided to use the same statistical measure of strength of association, namely ϕ^2. This was deemed necessary to provide a common base of comparison. Most studies have relied either

[1] Richard S. Sterne (1964), P.M. Smith (1955). The Gluecks' (1950) study, although utilizing an institutional population of delinquents, was included because it is widely cited.

on percentage differences of χ^2 (chi square). Each is inadequate for our purposes. Percent differences do not adequately measure strength of asssociation. In addition, exclusive reliance on χ^2 (or other inferential tests of association/no association) are inappropriate because of the variable sample sizes between studies. Thus, all the studies were reanalyzed by computing a ϕ^2 as well as χ^2 for purposes of assessing inferential probability. Since almost all of the studies meeting this criteria were conducted on males, the findings for Table I relate only to males (females are discussed in a subsequent section).

Despite the variation in time, locale, sample size, nature of population, definitions of both delinquency and broken home, and in basic research design, the conclusion is clear: the strength of the relationship is very small (even though in nine studies a significant level of at least 0.05 was reached).

A word is in order concerning the two stud-

TABLE I Summary of Studies Investigating "Broken Home" and Male Delinquency

Researcher	Year published	N	Association	
			ϕ^2	$\chi^{2\ a}$
Shaw and McKay[b]	1932	8953	0.004	40.28
Weeks and Smith[c]	1939	2449	0.012	24.49
Carr-Saunders, et al.[d]	1944	3925	0.019	74.57
Glueck and Glueck[e]	1950	1000	0.078	78.50
Nye[f]	1958	1160	0.005	5.80
Browning[g]	1960	164	0.096	15.69
Morris[h]	1964	112	0.014	1.57
Hardt[i]	1965	164	0.022	3.66
Hardt[j]	1965	191	0.015	2.92
Tennyson[k]	1967	320	0.007	2.21
Tennyson[l]	1967	217	0.009	1.87
Koval and Polk[m]	1967	873	0.009	7.60
Rosen[n]	1968	866	0.012	10.13
Rosen, Lalli, and Savitz[o]	1975	532	0.025	12.66
Rosen, Lalli, and Savitz[p]	1975	502	0.004	1.78

[a] All χ^2 values are for one degree of freedom. Significant values are: for 0.001 level, 10.83; for 0.01 level, 6.64; and for 0.05 level, 384.

[b] Clifford Shaw and H.D. McKay (1932). Delinquents are from Juvenile Court in Chicago, 1929–1930. The nondelinquents, ages 10 to 17, were sampled from public schools in Chicago. The delinquency rate of the control group was not checked; therefore it is not known how many delinquents were in the control group. "Broken home" defined as at least one parent absent because of death, desertion, divorce, separation, or confinement in an institution.

[c] H.A. Weeks and Margaret G. Smith (1939). Delinquents are from Juvenile Court in Spokane, Washington. The nondelinquents are a random sample of public secondary school students, Spokane Washington, 1937, having no court record. The age of delinquency is 7 to 18 years. Definition of "broken home" same as that given by Shaw and McKay (footnote 2).

[d] A.M. Carr-Saunders, H. Mannheim, and E. Rhodes (1944). Delinquents (ages 7 to 17) are taken from those appearing before court in 1938 in selected cities in England (including London). The nondelinquents were chosen by asking the head teacher at the school at which the delinquent attended for a youth who would be similar to the delinquent youth. The matching variables were age and residence. "Broken home" defined as at least one natural parent absent because of death, separation, or divorce.

[e] Sheldon Glueck and Eleanor Glueck (1950). The sample of delinquents was taken from correctional schools and the nondelinquents from Boston public schools in 1939. The delinquents and nondelinquents were matched for age, intelligence, and ethnicity. "Broken home" is one "broken by separation, divorce, or prolonged absence of a parent."

ies (the Gluecks and the Browning), which seem to have a typically high ϕ^2 value (although both values were below 0.10). The Glueck's study, using 500 institutionalized boys as its delinquents, may well have involved an administrative bias of disproportionate commitments from broken homes to juvenile institutions. A second possible reason for the relatively high association stems from the matching design employed by the researchers (thus giving them an equal number of delinquents and nondelinquents). ϕ^2 is af-

fected by the marginals in such a manner that its values are maximized when there is a 50-50 split. A reordering of the Glueck's data to give a split of 30 percent delinquents and 70 percent nondelinquents (which is closer to the other studies listed in Table I) yields a ϕ^2 of 0.018 (still significant at the 0.0001 level).[2] The

[2] A similar reordering for all the other studies in Table I not having approximately a 30–70 split on the dependent variable, although producing some changes in the ϕ^2 failed to effect the conclusion of a very weak relationship between the two variables. (Not a single recomputed ϕ^2 value exceeded 0.025.)

---

[f] F. Ivan Nye (1958). The sample was selected from high school students in three "medium-sized" towns in Washington in 1955. The measurements of delinquent group being those scoring highest on the delinquency scale. The association values noted include stepparents in the intact family; a reconstruction of the broken home definition to exclude stepparents yields a ϕ^2 of less than 0.001 and χ^2 of 1.16.

[g] Charles J. Browning (1960). The youths were chosen from a population that was white, at least third generation Americans, Protestant, Catholic or no religion, enrolled in public schools, and living in a common court jurisdiction within Los Angeles (no date given). The mean age of the youths in the sample was 15. The delinquents were defined as those having a court record and whose most serious offense was auto theft or truancy (the analysis divided delinquency into most serious and least serious). The nondelinquents were those who had no record or truancy for the year of the study. The proportion of delinquents was 66.5%. "Broken home" defined as a "boy not living with both of his natural parents."

[h] Ruth Morris (1964). Very little information is given concerning the selection of both delinquents and nondelinquents, other than the fact that they were selected as a match for white female delinquents with two or more police contacts in Flint, Michigan. The matching variables were social class, intelligence, grade in school, and age. Broken home defined as at least one parent absent.

[i] Robert H. Hardt (1965). The study was conducted in 1963 in a city of 250,000 located in "the center of one of the major metropolitan areas in a Middle Atlantic state." Delinquents were defined as having a record or a "suspected" or "alleged" delinquent in the Central Registry of Juvenile Police Contacts. Both the delinquents and nondelinquents were seventh-, eighth- and ninth-grade students attending parochial and public schools. Broken home defined as father absent.

[j] Ibid. The sample is the same as noted in footnote except that delinquency was defined as self-report.

[k] Ray A. Tennyson (1967). Delinquency was membership in a gang defined as "troublesome" by the "Program for Detached Workers of the YMCA of Chicago." (This sample was not a random one.) The nongang members were suggested by the YMCA workers. An intact home was a response by the youth of either "both parents continuously" or "mostly both parents" to the question, "Whom did you live with when growing up?"

[l] Ibid. Same as footnote k, but the sample was white boys.

[m] John P. Koval and Kenneth Polk (1967). Sample taken from one high school and a non-probability selection of "dropouts" residing in a "small city" in Lane County, Oregon (no date given). Delinquency was defined as a court or police record, with family structure being characterized only as "natural family intact."

[n] Lawrence Rosen (1968). Sample of black youths, 13 to 15 years old, drawn by an area sampling technique, residing in a low-income, high-delinquent, predominantly black area of Philadelphia in the summer of 1963. Delinquency was defined as at least one apprehension by the juvenile authorities. "Broken home" was simply the absence of at least one parent.

[o] Lawrence Rosen, M. Lalli, and L. Savitz (1975). Sample of black youths attending public schools in Philadelphia in 1970, age 13. Delinquency was defined at least one official contact with police or juvenile court. Broken home was defined as the absence of at least one parent.

[p] Ibid. A sample of white youths, age 14, attending public school or a ninth grade in Catholic school in 1971. Delinquency and broken home same as in footnote o.

Browning study seemed to employ the least systematic procedure of all studies used. The nondelinquents were not selected on a probability basis, and the delinquents chosen were only those who had either committed a truancy (a "less serious" offense) or auto theft (a "serious" offense).

To a limited extent, other issues have been researched. The major ones are sex, social class, race, and age. (In analyzing these issues we have referred to studies that do not meet the criteria given above. This was necessary because, for the most part, these studies contain the only available empirical evidence on these issues.)

SEX

As already indicated, the major portion of studies meeting our criteria for inclusion in this review have researched male subjects. There are a few studies of females but, for the most part, they have simply compared broken home rates of male and female delinquents. (Weeks, 1940; Monahan, 1957; Chilton and Markle, 1972; Datesman and Scarpitti, 1975.) All of these studies have found that the proportion of broken homes was greater for female delinquents than male delinquents. This has, of course, led all the authors to conclude that the broken home is of greater importance in the etiology of delinquency for females. (The usual theoretical argument is that the family is of greater salience for females in terms of affectional needs, status, role definition, and control. Therefore any disruption or problem in the family would have greater consequence for the behavior of females.) However, reaching such a conclusion on the basis of this kind of evidence is hazardous because of the unequal delinquency rates of males and females. (The implicit assumption of the kind of data analysis employed in these studies is that the delinquency rates are equal.)

We are aware of at least two studies that meet our criteria. Using a sample of delinquent white girls in Flint, Michigan with two or more police contacts and a group of nondelinquents matched for age, intelligence, social class, and school grade,[3] Morris (1964) found a relatively large difference in delinquency rates between girls residing in broken homes and those coming from intact homes ($\phi^2 = .279$; $\chi^2 = 31.75$). The second study by Nye (1958), used a self-report measure of delinquency and also found sizable differences in delinquency rates ($\phi^2 = 0.037$; $\chi^2 = 42.81$). Both studies exhibited stronger associations for females than for males in their sample (see Table I).

There is also some evidence on the effect of type of offense. Weeks (1940), when controlling for type of offense and source of referral to juvenile court, found that the difference in broken home rates between male and female delinquents was appreciably reduced. He thus argued that the reason for the higher rates of broken homes for female delinquents was due both to the larger incidence of juvenile status offenses (runaway, truancy, ungovernability) for females, and the greater likelihood of parents referring their daughters to juvenile court for these types of offenses. Datesman and Scarpitti (1975) also found some important differences between black and white delinquents in this regard. For the black delinquents the incidence of broken homes was greater for females, for person and property offenses; the reverse was true for juvenile status offenders (although this difference was not statistically different). For the white delinquents the broken home rates was greater for females, for the person and juvenile status offenders, but about equal for property offenders.

As we will argue shortly, these differences between males and females may be more a consequence of the differential likelihood of delinquency in the general population for these groups instead of a differential impact of broken homes.

---

[3] No information was given on how the nondelinquents were selected.

RACE

Both Toby (1957) and Chilton and Markle (1972) have, on the basis of general juvenile court statistics, argued that the broken home has a stronger association with delinquency for whites than for blacks. However, the two studies [by Tennyson (1967) and Rosen et al. (1975)] that have data for blacks and whites show very little if any difference between whites and blacks in this regard (see Table I). In fact, the one study (Rosen et al., 1975) with a representative sample of youths exhibits a slightly higher relationship for blacks than for whites.

AGE

Two studies have investigated the issue of age. Toby (1957), in reexamining the Shaw and McKay data, has argued that the broken home is more important for the younger males. However, our reanalysis of the same data does not support this conclusion. The ϕ^2 values for the 10 to 12-year-olds[4] was exactly the same as 13 to 17-year-olds.[5]

Chilton and Markle (1972) found a slightly higher incidence of broken homes for the 10

---

[4] This age group is, one assumes, what Toby meant by preadolescent (he never actually defined the age range) when he characterized the association between "broken homes" and delinquency as "considerable" for "preadolescents." A computation of ϕ^2 for the 10 to 11-year-old group would have been unfeasible because of the extremely small proportion (2.7%) of delinquents in that group.

[5] This generalization is true only for the Shaw and McKay data with its given age distribution and differential delinquency rates by age. (The rates were about 5% for the 10 to 12-year-olds and 32% for the 13 to 17-year-olds.) One may well ask what the relationship between delinquency and "broken home" would be if the delinquency rates were the same for both age groups. Reconstructing the data for the 10 to 12-year-olds to yield an identical delinquency rate as the 13 to 17-year-old group (the effect is similar to standardizing the age distribution of the delinquents on the basis of the nondelinquents, a procedure that Toby argues Shaw and McKay should have followed) gives a ϕ^2 of 0.019. Although this finding now supports Toby's assertion of a differential age effect, the value of ϕ^2 for the younger group is still quite less than the "considerable association" claimed by Toby.

to 13-year-old delinquents than those aged 14 to 17 years.

SOCIAL CLASS

The evidence for this area is extremely sparse. Chilton and Markle (1972) report a higher proportion of broken homes for the children from the low-income families. The major difficulty in interpreting this finding is that the broken home rates in the general population also decrease as family income increases.

Week and Smith (1939), using fathers' occupations as a measure of social class, found a slightly higher relationship between the two variables for professional and white collar boys ($\phi^2 = 0.025$; $\chi^2 = 7.0$) than the boys with laborer and unemployed fathers ($\phi^2 = 0.016$; $\chi^2 = 7.21$). Utilizing the Warner I.S.C. scale as measure of social class, Rosen, Lalli, and Savitz (1975) researched this issue separately for whites and blacks. The data are presented in Table II. For the white youths all associations were nonsignificant. However, the ϕ^2 values would indicate that the broken home has more impact for the lowest social class group. The findings for the black youths are somewhat more mixed. The χ^2 values show that relationship is only significant for the lowest social class. The ϕ^2 values, on the other hand, would

TABLE II Relationship Between Broken Home and Delinquency for Social Class Level (Warner I.S.C.) for White and Black Males

Social class (Warner)	N	ϕ^2	χ^2
		Blacks	
Low	249	0.019	4.86
Middle	171	0.011	1.87
High	112	0.027	3.03
		Whites	
Low	78	0.028	2.22
Middle	155	0.008	1.26
High	269	0.006	1.50

Source: Rosen, Lalli, and Savitz (1975).

lead us to conclude that the relationship is of some importance for the highest income level.

DISCUSSION

As we have already indicated, there are major problems in reaching any firm conclusions on the basis of such a review because of the variability in research design and sampling strategies. Most studies that have used comparative nondelinquent groups have not used representative samples. Some studies have looked at total juvenile court populations and contrasted them with total population statistics (Monahan, 1958; Chilton and Markle, 1972). Consequently, it is possible that the findings (especially with respect to age, race, and sex) are artifacts of artificial sampling constraints and reversed dependent probabilities (i.e., the likelihood of family status for a delinquent rather than the reverse of delinquency status for family types). The primary interest should focus on the relationship between family structure and delinquency in the total population with whatever proportion of delinquency and broken homes naturally occur in that population. It is clear that many of the studies reviewed do not allow for any reasonable conclusion in this regard. This is especially true of those studies that use only delinquents as their research population (e.g., Chilton and Markle, 1972).

As a way of attempting to gain a more adequate approach to this problem, we simulated what the relationship between delinquency and family structure might be in the total U.S. population by utilizing data provided by Chilton and Markle (1972). In their study they used data from all youths having contact with juvenile and county courts of Florida in the first four months of 1969. As a comparison, they utilized data for the total U.S. population of 10 to 17-year-olds for 1968. Utilizing this same data, it is possible to compute ϕ^2 values for different assumed general delinquency rates. The simulated data are presented in Table III and can be viewed as holding true for the total

United States if one is willing to assume that delinquents processed in Florida and for whom information on family structure was available (such information was not available for 40% of the delinquents) are representative of all delinquents in the United States.

The data in Table III are given for two conditions of delinquency likelihood: a value of 3%[6] and 10%. For each condition, both a ϕ^2 value and a set of dependent probabilities are computed. The first two columns in Table III give the probability of finding a broken home for delinquents and nondelinquents, respectively.

The $Pr\ (B/D)$ is the usual statement made when one is simply using a delinquent population. (This is what, for example, can be found in the Chilton and Markle study). Since family structure is seen as the cause of delinquency, the more appropriate dependent probabilities are those given in the last two columns, namely $Pr\ (D/B)$ and $Pr\ (D/I)$.

Several kinds of issues can be examined in this table. First we examine the table for the delinquency rate of 3% (i.e., every group listed in the table would have a 3% delinquency rate). The relationship for broken home and delinquency is very real for all children ($\phi^2 = 0.012$) and consistent with the majority of studies listed in Table I. As the general delinquency rate increases, the strength of the relationship increases. Thus the ϕ^2 value for the total group for a 10% delinquency rate increases to 0.042. If one looks at the $Pr\ (D/B)$ and $Pr\ (D/I)$ columns for both delinquency levels, one can clearly see that delinquents are more likely to come from broken homes than they are from intact homes for all demographic groups. And, among the broken home group, females, whites, and the very young have slightly higher likelihoods of delinquency rates. These are some conclusions as reached by most researchers, but it is quite

[6] The rate of 3% is the usual incidence rate cited nationally for all youths 7 to 17 years of age. The usual prevelance figure is 10 to 15%. Since the Chilton and Markle study is using incidence of delinquency, the more appropriate reference is the 3% value.

TABLE III   Simulation of Broken Home Delinquency Relationships for Selected Demographic Groups for Assumed General Delinquency Rates of 0.03 and 0.10

	$Pr (D) = 0.03$					$Pr (D) = 0.10$				
		Pr					Pr			
	ϕ^2	B/D	B/N	E/B	D/I	ϕ^2	B/D	B/N	D/B	D/I
Total	0.012	0.40	0.16	0.07	0.02	0.042	0.40	0.14	0.24	0.07
Male	0.012	0.40	0.16	0.07	0.02	0.042	0.40	0.14	0.24	0.07
Female	0.015	0.44	0.16	0.08	0.02	0.057	0.44	0.14	0.26	0.07
Black	0.002	0.58	0.43	0.04	0.02	0.010	0.58	0.41	0.14	0.07
White	0.008	0.30	0.12	0.07	0.02	0.028	0.30	0.11	0.23	0.08
Black male	0.002	0.58	0.43	0.04	0.02	0.010	0.58	0.41	0.14	0.07
White male	0.008	0.30	0.12	0.07	0.02	0.028	0.30	0.11	0.23	0.08
Black female	0.004	0.60	0.42	0.04	0.02	0.013	0.60	0.41	0.14	0.07
White female	0.015	0.38	0.12	0.08	0.02	0.061	0.38	0.10	0.29	0.07
Age 10-13	0.023	0.45	0.14	0.09	0.02	0.077	0.45	0.12	0.30	0.06
Age 14-17	0.006	0.38	0.18	0.06	0.02	0.026	0.38	0.17	0.20	0.08

Key: D = Delinquent
N = Nondelinquent
B = Broken home
I = Intact home
Pr = Probability

Source: Analysis based on data presented in Chilton and Markle (1972).

clear that they are contingent on the assumption that the groups being compared have the same general delinquency rate. This is, of course, not a viable assumption: females have higher rates than males, blacks have higher rates than whites, and the older delinquents have higher rates than the younger ones. Therefore, a more appropriate comparison can be made by comparing across both general delinquency levels in Table III. In comparing males with females, for example, it is more realistic to consider the values for females at the 3% delinquency level with the values for males at the 10% level. In that comparison, one can see that the broken home is of greater relevance to males than females. In other words, males from broken homes have a higher delinquency rate than females from broken homes. The ϕ^2 values also support the same conclusion. The conclusions are similar for race and age: broken homes seem more strongly related to delinquency for blacks and for the older age

group. These findings with respect to sex, race and age are the opposite from those reached by Toby (1957) and Chilton and Markle (1972).

Once more we should stress, however, that broken homes are weakly related to delinquency for all groups. (Not a single ϕ^2 value was above 0.1 in Table III.)

Of course, the actual values of ϕ^2 and the dependent probabilities will be contingent on the actual delinquency rates in the population; however, the usefulness of this type of simulation does indicate that conclusions based on artificial constraints on sampling and inappropriate dependent probabilities can possibly lead to faulty generalizations about the relationship between delinquency and broken homes in the general population.

CONCLUSION

A variety of possible explanations can be forwarded to account for the lack of a strong relationship between broken homes and delinquency. The most obvious explanation for this fact is that the family may not be a major contributing factor in terms of delinquency. Social structural or social process variables (delinquent value systems, opportunity structures, subcultures, etc.) may be the main determinants. Another possibility allows for the importance of the family as an independent variable for delinquency, but emphasizes the "quality of family interaction" instead of the family structure per se as causative. Finally, the crude research designs and statistical measures employed in almost all of the studies of broken homes and delinquency may have combined to offer conclusions that are at best questionable.

In conclusion, the information compiled in this report illustrates that the concept of broken homes, no matter how it is defined or measured, has little explanatory power in terms of delinquency. Since, for the most part, the studies included here have had difficulties both in conceptualizing and measuring the broken home concept and in controlling for significant variables, such as age at the time of the break and subsequent arrangements after the break, it is impossible to rule out completely the factor of broken homes as contributing to the etiology of delinquent tendencies. Until these problems are resolved, the relevance of broken homes for delinquency is not totally disproven. The most one can say at present is that the empirical evidence does not support the thesis that the broken home is a significant factor in the development of delinquent tendencies.

REFERENCES

Browning, C. J. (1960). "Differential Impact of Family Disorganization of Male Adolescents." *Social Problems* 8:37–44.

Carr-Saunders, A. M., H. Mannheim, and E. Rhodes (1944). Young Offenders. New York: MacMillan.

Chilton, R. J., and G. E. Markle (1972). "Family Disruption, Delinquent Conduct and the Effect of

Subclassification." *American Sociological Review,* **37**:33–55.

Datesman, S. K., and F. R. Scarpitti (1975). "Female Delinquency and Broken Homes." *Criminology,* **13**:33–55.

Glueck, S., and E. Glueck (1950). *Unravelling Juvenile Delinquency.* New York: Commonwealth Fund.

Hardt, R. H. (1965). "Delinquency and Social Class: Studies of Juvenile Deviations or Police Disposition." Unpublished paper presented at Eastern Sociological Meetings, New York.

Koval, J. P., and K. Polk (1967). "Problem Youth in a Small City," pp. 123–138 in Malcolm W. Klein (Ed.). *Juvenile Gangs in Context.* Englewood Cliffs, N.J.: Prentice-Hall.

Mannheim H. (1965). *Comparative Criminology.* Boston: Houghton-Mifflin Company.

Monahan, T. P. (1957). "Family Status and the Delinquent Child: A Reappraisal and Some New Findings." *Social Forces,* **35**:250–258.

Morris, R. R. (1964). "Female Delinquency and Relational Problems." *Social Forces,* **43**:82–89.

Nye, F. I. (1958). *Family Relationships and Delinquent Behavior.* New York: John Wiley and Sons.

Peterson, D. R., and W. C. Becker (1965). "Family Interaction and Delinquency," p. 69 in Herbert C. Quay (Ed.). *Juvenile Delinquency.* Princeton, N.J.: D. Van Nostrand pp. 63–99.

Rosen, L. (1968). The Delinquent and Non-Delinquent in a High Delinquent Area. Unpublished doctoral dissertation, Temple University.

Rosen, L., M. Lalli, and L. Savitz (1975). "City Life and Delinquency: The Family and Delinquency." Report submitted to National Institute for Juvenile Justice and Delinquency Prevention. Law Enforcement Assistance Administration. Unpublished.

Shaw, C., and H. D. McKay (1932). "Are Broken Homes a Causative Factor in Juvenile Delinquency?" *Social Forces,* **10**:514–524.

Smith, P. M. (1955). "Broken Homes and Juvenile Delinquency." *Sociology and Social Research,* **39**:307–311.

Sterne, R. S. (1964). *Delinquent Conduct and Broken Homes.* New Haven, Conn.: College and University Press.

Tennyson, R. A. (1967). "Family Structure and Delinquent Behavior," pp. 57–69 in Malcolm W. Klein

(Ed.), *Juvenile Gangs in Context*. Englewood Cliffs, N.J.: Prentice-Hall.

Toby, J. (1957). ''The Differential Impact of Family Disorganization.'' *American Sociological Review,* **22**:402–412.

U.S. Bureau of the Census (1974). Current Population Reports; Special Studies, p. 23, No. 54: Social and Economic States of the Black Population in the United States.

Weeks, H. A. (1940). ''Male and Female Broken Home Rates by Types of Delinquency.'' *American Sociological Review,* **5**:601–609.

Weeks, H. A., and M. G. Smith (1939). ''Juvenile Delinquency and Broken Homes in Spokane, Washington.'' *Social Forces,* **18**:48–59.

13

DELINQUENCY AND SCHOOL DROPOUT

DELBERT S. ELLIOTT

INTRODUCTION

The focus of this selection[1] is on the relationship between delinquency and dropout. Our concern over this relationship grew out of a larger study testing a general theoretical explanation of the causes of delinquent behavior and dropout, which viewed these two behaviors as alternative responses to failure experiences at school. This postulated relationship between school failure and delinquency or dropout led to an expected relationship between delinquency and dropout that appeared to be at odds with the current view that dropout leads to an increasing likelihood of delinquency.

Relying heavily on Cloward and Ohlin's work in *Delinquency and Opportunity* (1960), we propose that the crucial conditions for delinquency are goal blockage or failure to achieve personal goals, extrapunitiveness, normlessness, and exposure to delinquent persons or groups. A similar set of variables and casual sequences provide a parallel explanation of

high school dropout: dropout involves failure to achieve personally valued goals, intrapunitiveness, social isolation, and exposure to dropouts or pro-dropout influences. Because of the central place occupied by the school in the lives of young people, we argue that it is the most important context in the generation of delinquent behavior, and we thus postulate that delinquency and dropout are alternative responses to limited opportunities and goal failure experienced primarily in the social context of the school.[2]

While both delinquency and dropout are considered responses to failure experiences encountered at school, they are postulated to involve different explanations or rationalizations for failure, and different forms of personal alienation. The way in which an individual explains his or her failure basically determines what that person will do about it

Source: Selection especially written for this volume.

[1] This selection is an adaptation from D. S. Elliott and H. L. Voss, *Delinquency and Dropout* (Lexington, Mass.: Lexington Books, D.C. Heath and Company, 1974, Chapter 5) and is reprinted here by permission of the publisher. The larger study was supported by grants MH 07173 and MH 15285 from the Center for Studies in Crime and Delinquency, MIMH.

[2] The findings from the larger study confirmed this hypothesis. For males in particular, the school was the critical social context in the generation of delinquency and dropout; for females, both the school and home were important contexts for delinquency. Utilizing the theoretical variables identified here, the multiple correlation of the postulated variables and self-reported delinquency frequency scores was 0.54 for males and 0.50 for females. R values for gains in delinquency across the study period were 0.44 and 0.40 R values for dropout were 0.41 for both males and females. In all of these analyses, the temporal order of predictor and criterion variables were maintained (i.e., they were genuine predictive analyses).

(Cloward and Ohlin, 1960). Those who attribute the blame for their difficulties to unjust or arbitrary institutional arrangements, discriminatory practices on the part of teachers, administrators, or other students, or some other external feature of the school context are most likely to adopt a delinquent response to their failure. Their explanation for failure provides a justification for criticizing, attacking, and ultimately withdrawing their sense of moral commitment from the normative system. Extrapunitiveness is thus postulated to be a conditional variable in the relationship between school failure and delinquency. It explains why some youths experiencing difficulties at school become alienated from conventional norms and adopt delinquent means for achieving their goals while others do not.

Not all persons experiencing goal failure at school attribute their problem to the policies, practices, and situations encountered in this setting. If personal inadequacy—lack of discipline, effort, or intelligence—is considered the source of failure, then the outcome is pressure either to change oneself or to develop techniques to protect oneself from a feeling of personal inadequacy. An intrapunitive or impunitive explanation of failure implies acceptance of the legitimacy of conventional norms, not alienation from them. Apart from developing greater personal competence, there are two possible adaptations for persons who attribute blame to themselves: the individual may lower his or her aspirations and engage in a form of passive compliance to the norms, or withdraw from efforts to achieve presumably unattainable goals. In the context of the school, students who adopt the first solution are referred to as "low achievers" or "poorly motivated" students; students who adopt the latter solution are referred to as truants and dropouts. Dropping out of school is one alternative for youths who are failing to achieve valued goals and who assume personal responsibility for this problem.[3] We thus postulate that dropouts

tend to be intrapunitive or impunitive and develop feelings of social isolation and/or powerlessness in response to their failure at school.

In summary, delinquency and dropout are viewed as alternatives available to those experiencing failure and frustration at school. On the one hand, they may remain in school and attempt to deal with their failure by attacking the system of norms that they believe to be the cause of their difficulties, expressing their resentment and rejection of this system and those who attempt to enforce its norms. On the other hand, they may leave school, retreating from the situation that produces the failure and frustration. Once out of this context, there is little or no need to attack the school or the normative system it represents.

Several hypotheses concerning the relationship between delinquency and dropout follow logically from this explanation. First, the act of leaving school should reduce school-related frustrations and alienation and thereby lower the motivational stimulus for delinquency. To the extent that perceived failure in school provides a motivational stimulus for delinquency, dropout should lead to a decreasing probability of delinquency. While this expectation is consistent with our theoretical position, it is important to note several complicating factors. A youth's prior involvement in the delinquent subculture or the experience of official labeling as a delinquent may provide continuing motivation for delinquency. In this case, the hypothesized relationship would hold only for those dropouts who were not subcultural delinquents and were not labeled, either formally or informally, as delinquent persons prior to leaving school. In addition, failure in school may be repeated in the dropout's out-of-school experience; he or she may trade failure in school for failure in the economic context. In essence, the same motivational stimulus is involved, but failure is experienced in a different social context from that postulated here as the most relevant for delinquency. It is also possible that the school is an effective agent of social control because it regulates and super-

---

[3] There is some evidence that dropouts lower their aspirations immediately prior to leaving school (Krane, 1976).

vises so much of the normal activity of adolescents. If there is a constant level of motivation for delinquency among juveniles attending school and out-of-school, then the absence of the restraints imposed on youths by the school will result in a higher rate of delinquent behavior among dropouts. The absence of restraints may compensate for a lower motivational stimulus for delinquency among dropouts with the result that in- and out-of-school delinquency rates for dropouts would be comparable. Writers who adopt a control perspective argue that this one factor should produce higher rates of delinquency among dropouts (Cervantes, 1965; Haskell and Yablonsky, 1970; Schafer and Knudten, 1970; Simpson and Van Arsdol, 1967; Havinghurst, 1963). Control theorists generally avoid the issue of instigation to delinquency, whereas we have postulated variables that may positively motivate youths toward delinquent behavior, whether restraints are present or absent. Although we argue on theoretical grounds that departure from school should reduce the motivational stimulus for delinquency, it may not follow that the rate of delinquency will diminish with dropout if any of the above factors are operative. Nevertheless, even in the presence of these possible complicating factors, we would not expect an *increasing* delinquency rate to be a consequence of dropout.

Second, we postulate that while dropout should not lead to an increasing probability of delinquency, a high involvement in delinquency should lead to an increased likelihood of dropout. If we assume that delinquency is a response to frustrations encountered in the school context, then those frustrated students who remain in school and attempt to deal with their frustration by attacking the school's system or norms and values should encounter increasing conflict with school authorities and an increasing risk of suspension or expulsion. Not all of the students' depredations will occur within the school. However, we assume that adolescents involved in serious and frequent delinquent behavior outside the context of the

school will rarely be models of propriety in school. Nor does the school operate in a vacuum; students labeled delinquent by the police or courts are likely to be considered troublemakers by school personnel. Although their withdrawal from school may often be involuntary, adolescents who are disruptive in school or are involved in delinquent acts should have a relatively high probability of being classified as dropouts. In essence, we are arguing that dropout provides a satisfactory resolution of the school failure problem, whereas delinquency does not; a delinquent response to school failure complicates the difficulty and increases the likelihood of some type of exit from the school system.

PRIOR RESEARCH

Consistently higher rates of official delinquency among high school dropouts in comparison with the general youth population or high school graduates have been reported—dropouts have three to four times more police contacts than graduates (Cervantes, 1965; Elliott, 1961, 1966; Shafer and Polk, 1967; Schreiber, 1963a, 1963b; Simpson and Van Arsdol, 1967; Jeffery and Jeffery, 1970; Bachman et al., 1971; Hathaway and Monachesi, 1963; Hathaway, Reynolds, and Monachesi, 1969). In fact, Schreiber (1963b) found the delinquency rate for dropouts to be ten times higher than the rate in the total youth population or among high school graduates. Clearly, these studies have established an association between official delinquency rates and dropout. However, the temporal order of this relationship has not been determined, nor has a causal relationship been demonstrated. In all but one of the studies cited, police arrests or court contacts were employed to measure delinquency, and we are concerned about the appropriateness of official records as a measure of delinquent behavior (Kitsuse and Cicourel, 1963; Gold, 1963; Short, 1958). Furthermore, with three noteworthy exceptions, the temporal sequence between delinquency and dropout was not examined or controlled in these studies; instead, the investigators employed *ex post facto* designs and failed to note the relative frequency of arrest or court appearance before and after the point of dropout. Nor have juveniles who differ with respect to their involvement in delinquent behavior at some point in time been compared in terms of subsequent rates of dropout. Schreiber (1963b) and Jeffery and Jeffery (1970) have been careful to note that existence of a correlation or an association between dropout and delinquency is not sufficient grounds to argue for a specific causal relationship. Unfortunately, most writers have assumed that dropout causes greater involvement in delinquency; the folk adage, "idle hands are the devil's workshop," has been translated into a simple scientific proposition.

The only known studies in which rates of delinquency before and after dropout are compared are those of Elliott (1966), Jeffery and Jeffery (1970), and Bachman et al., (1971). Elliott reports that delinquents who dropped out had a higher official referral rate while in school than after dropout. He also notes that male dropouts had a lower police contact rate than males in school. Elliott's study was retrospective and involved a small sample. Because the study was exploratory, a substantial number of subjects who left the area during the study period were excluded from his analysis. Consequently, his conclusions must be considered tentative. Furthermore, the measure of delinquency that Elliott employed was based exclusively on official police records. Nevertheless, Elliott's study casts doubt on the common assumption that dropping out of school leads to greater involvement in delinquency.

Jeffery and Jeffery (1970) employed a rather unique research design insofar as the temporal sequence of dropout and delinquency is concerned. They compared the rates of delinquency of dropouts before and after entry into a special school program. The investigators' primary purpose was evaluation of a special educational program designed to help dropouts pass the GED, but they included a comparison of the dropouts' official delinquency contacts before and after entering the program. They conclude: "The number of weeks a student (dropout) was in the project did not deter him from delinquent conduct; in fact, the longer a student was in the project the higher the chances of delinquency" (Jeffery and Jeffery, 1970:8). The exact nature of the comparison they made is not clear, nor do they discuss the types of controls utilized for variable lengths of time in the program. If dropouts who return to school differ from all dropouts or the general population of youth, Jeffery and Jeffery's results cannot be generalized beyond the universe of dropouts who subsequently return to school. Such limitations suggest, that we view their conclusion with caution, but it consistent with Elliott's finding that higher rates of delinquency are associated with school attendance, not dropout. The study by Bachman et al. (1971) provides more compelling evidence. This study involved a representative national sample of tenth-grade boys and a longitudinal design following these boys through their normal years of high school to graduation. For dropouts in this study, measures of delinquent behavior were obtained before and after dropping out. The results indicate that the boy who is likely to drop out of school is involved in far above average levels of delinquency before dropping out. In fact, level of involvement in delinquency was found to be the strongest predictor of future dropout. An examination of delinquency rates after dropout indicated a continuing involvement in delinquency, but there was ". . . no evidence whatever that dropping out *increased* their rate of delinquency" (Bachman et al., 1971:123). Unfortunately, the self-reported measures of delinquency employed in this study involved different "periods of risk," and the pre-post comparisons involved different time periods, rendering it difficult to determine if the actual *rate* of delinquency changed. It was clear, however, that dropouts showed no *relative* increase in delinquency after they dropped out.

Although the above evidence is limited, it appears consistent with the expectations derived from our theoretical scheme. A more detailed analysis of the relationship is clearly needed: one that utilizes both official and self-reported measures of delinquency, controls for the temporal order of delinquency and dropout, and considers out-of-school conditions such as unemployment and marriage.

DESCRIPTION OF THE STUDY

In this research, a type of cluster sample was used in which the basic sampling unit was a school instead of a person. We sampled only in the purposive selection of eight schools to guarantee inclusion of students with a wide range of social, economic, and racial or ethnic characteristics. All of the schools were located within two metropolitan areas; seven of the schools were located in southern California, and the other was in the northern part of the state. All students who entered these schools as ninth graders in September 1963 comprised the target population. From the available pool of 2663 students, we encountered five student refusals and did not obtain parental permission to interview 41 others. Thus, the study population consisted of 2617 students.

The research design was longitudinal. Initial observations were obtained when the study population entered the ninth grade, and additional observations were obtained annually until the usual date for graduation from high school for the cohort. Limitation of the study population to a single academic class "controls" the effects of age or maturation. We attempted to make personal contact with each respondent in the original cohort during each of the four annual data-gathering phases. Included in this effort were those students who dropped out as well as those who transferred to another school. In addition to the annual students questionnaires or interviews, a parent of each subject was interviewed in the first year of the study, and relevant information from

school, police, and court records was obtained for each subject.

Even though completion of a longitudinal study involves considerable expense and presents a number of special data-gathering problems, the nature of our problem required use of this type of design if we were to assess postulated cause-effect relationships. The first observations were calculated to precede dropout and extensive involvement in delinquent behavior in order to permit accurate determination of the temporal order of events. As is often the case with research in the behavioral sciences, neither the independent nor dependent variables could be manipulated artificially; it was essential to take repeated measurements through time and to relate previous measurements to subsequent differences while controlling for those factors known to be relevant. A longitudinal design permits a more adequate test of expected relationships than a cross-sectional design. On the other hand, a fundamental problem in longitudinal studies involves the loss of subjects over the course of the project. To minimize case attrition because of residential mobility, we developed elaborate tracking techniques. As a result, the attrition over the four-year study period was less than 10 percent.

MEASURES OF DELINQUENCY AND DROPOUT

A self-reported measure of delinquent behavior similar to that utilized by Short and Nye (1957) and Bachman et al. (1971) was employed as the basic measure of delinquent behavior. The study population reported an average of ten delinquent offenses over the study period on this scale (male $\bar{X} = 12$; female $\bar{X} = 7$). Considering the total study period, no significant race or class differentials in frequency of offense were found on the self-report measure, although there was an indication that those with lower social-class backgrounds or minority group statuses had a relatively higher involvement in delinquent behavior during the junior high school years and a relatively lower involvement during the high school years than did Anglos and those from higher SES backgrounds.

A second measure of delinquent behavior involved the number of police contacts (investigation reports) for persons in the study. A total of 1486 police contacts were recorded for the study population prior to June 1967 (end of twelfth grade). This resulted in a mean of 0.869 contacts for males and 0.253 for females. The analysis of police contact reports revealed the expected race, sex, and class differentials with minority groups, males, and those with lower socioeconomic statuses having disproportionately high police contact rates. With respect to these characteristics, the study population appears quite similar to other populations studied.

A comparison of self-reported offenses and police contact reports (limited to ten offenses on the self-report measure) revealed that overall there were fewer than five police contacts for every 100 self-reported offenses. The ratio of police contacts to self-reported offenses varied by sex, race, and social class with males, minority groups (particularly blacks), and lower-class subjects encountering a relatively greater risk of a police contact for each self-reported act.

Three separate dropout measures were developed: dropout status, attendance status, and graduate status. The dropout was defined as a person who left school for one or more consecutive months without transferring to another school. By the end of the study, 558 (21 percent) persons were classified as dropouts. Since dropouts were in school for some part of the study and frequently returned to school at some later point (there were 130 reentries), attendance status referred to the subject's presence or absence from school during each specific year of the study. The graduate status measure reflected the final educational outcome (at the termination of the study) clas-

sifying subjects as graduates and nongraduates. Graduates comprised 79 percent of the original cohort. Nongraduates included 2 percent who were still attending school and 19 percent who were out of school at the termination of the study. Approximately 10 percent of those classified as dropouts were also classified as graduates.

FINDINGS

Persons classified as dropouts at the end of the study had a substantially greater number of recorded police contacts and reported considerably more delinquent behavior than did the graduates. The mean number of police contacts for dropouts was approximately four times higher than the average for graduates. A similar pattern exists with respect to police contacts for serious offenses, although the dropout-graduate ratio for females is somewhat lower, (3:1).

The police contact rates for dropouts and graduates appear to be consistent with the findings of previous research. Using juvenile court records, which are less inclusive than police contact reports, Schreiber (1963b) reported a 10:1 dropout-graduate ratio. For comparative purposes the proportion of graduates adjudicated delinquent was 0.03; the comparable figure for dropouts was 0.17. Restricting the analysis to adjudicated delinquents, we still observe differences between dropouts and graduates substantially lower than the ratio reported by Schreiber.

Involvement in delinquent behavior was also measured by self-reported delinquency, and differences between graduates and dropouts were statistically significant and substantial. Male dropouts reported a mean of 16.82 offenses; in comparison, male graduates reported an average of 10.59 delinquent acts. Comparable figures for females were 8.74 and 6.33. Although the means for dropouts were consistently higher than those for graduates, in no case did the mean for dropouts exceed the mean for graduates by a factor of 2. The relative differences in dropout-graduate ratios suggest that there is, given a constant number of delinquent acts, a higher risk of official action for dropouts than graduates.[4]

Both the official and self-report measures of delinquent behavior support the conclusion that dropouts have been involved in more delinquent behavior than graduates, although the differences on the self-report measure are not nearly as dramatic as those based on official police contacts. Dropouts are also more likely to have been adjudicated delinquent.

Having established the association between delinquency and dropout, we turn now to a consideration of the nature of this relationship. There are four alternative, although not mutually exclusive, ways in which delinquency and dropout could be associated. If dropout is treated as the causal variable, then it is possible that dropout increases or decreases the probability of delinquent behavior. On the other hand, if delinquency is considered as the causal variable, then delinquency may increase or decrease the probability of dropout. The effect of dropout on delinquency can be determined by comparing the dropouts' in- and out-of-school delinquency rates; in this way support may be provided for either the first or second hypothesis. In a similar manner, we compare the dropout rates of subjects with high and low rates of delinquency to ascertain the effect of delinquency on dropout; this approach may provide evidence in support of either the third or fourth alternative. The hypotheses within each of the pairs are mutually exclusive. However, the alternatives in the first set are not necessarily inconsistent with the hypotheses in the second set; for example, delinquency could lead to dropout which, in turn, could produce increasing or decreasing rates of delinquency.

[4] This finding is consistent with the observation that dropouts are disproportionately drawn from among lower-class and minority youths. See Chapter IV, *Delinquency and Dropout*.

THE EFFECT OF DROPOUT ON DELINQUENCY

If dropping out of school leads to increased delinquent activity, a comparison of delinquency rates while dropouts are in and out of school should provide evidence in support of such a causal sequence. In- and out-of-school rates of police contact during each study period[5] are presented in Table I. In this table dropouts are categorized according to the period in which they left school. Dropouts in Period II (hereafter cited as DO IIs) left school sometime during the second period (early ninth to mid-tenth grade), and the number of days in and out of school during this period had to be calculated for each dropout, as did the number of police contacts prior to and subsequent to his or her leaving school. Individually, DO IIs contributed a variable amount of time and number of police contacts to the in-school and out-of-school rates during Period II. Similarly, dropouts in Periods III, IV, and V (hereinafter cited as DO IIIs, IVs, and Vs, respectively) have in-school and out-of-school rates for the period in which they left school. The vertical line in Table I represents the point of dropout; values on the left side of the table are in-school rates, and those to the right are out-of-school rates. Because the dropouts are categorized according to the period in which they left school, a comparison of the dropouts' rate of police contact within any particular time period requires examination of the diagonal cells. For comparative purposes, police contact rates by study period are also shown in the first row of Table I for graduates who were in school throughout the study.

Comparison of police contact rates of dropouts and graduates in Period I clearly demonstrates that, with the exception of those

[5] The study was divided into five time periods: Period I—prior to the first annual questionnaire; Period II—between first and second annual questionnaires (early ninth to mid-tenth grades); Period III—between second and third questionnaires (mid-tenth to mid-eleventh); Period IV—between third and last questionnaires (mid-eleventh to late twelfth grades); and Period V—after the last questionnaire.

TABLE I Total Police Contact Rates,[a] by Subjects In and Out of School

	In school					Out-of-school				
Periods: Graduates (N = 2142)	I 0.19	II 0.19	III 0.27	IV 0.20	V 0.19					
Periods: DO V (N = 65)	I 0.10	II 0.47	III 0.60	IV 0.68	V 1.12	V 0.43				
Periods: DO IV (N = 195)		I 0.55	II 0.48	III 0.74	IV 0.81	IV 0.41	V 0.00			
Periods: DO III (N = 106)			I 0.71	II 0.71	III 1.64	III 0.30	IV 0.01	V 0.00		
Periods: DO II (N = 109)				I 1.00	II 1.70	II 0.94	III 0.32	IV 0.10	V 0.00	

[a] Mean number of police contacts per 1000 days. The summer period from June 15 to September 15 is excluded. For this analysis Period I was assumed to have started in September 1959, when the cohort's mean age was 10 years.

dropping out late in their junior or senior year (DO Vs), dropouts had substantially higher contact rates prior to the start of the study. In Period I the rate for respondents who were to drop out in the following year (DO IIs) was five times higher than the rate of eventual graduates. Only one category of dropouts, the DO Vs, had a rate lower than the graduates, and this category, which contained 65 subjects, included 13 dropout reentries and 52 respondents who tenaciously remained in school almost to the date of graduation. Furthermore, dropouts consistently had higher police contact rates than graduates for every period they were in school; the rates for dropouts were never less than twice the rate of graduates in any single time period. The case of the DO IIs was particularly impressive. While in school during Period II, their rate was nine times higher than the police contact rate of graduates. These data are consistent with the findings reported by Elliott (1966); they demonstrate forcefully that dropouts have higher in-school rates of police contact than graduates.

For each category of dropouts the police contact rates increase with time while they are in school. Furthermore, the highest rate for each category is observed in the period in which dropout occurs. The pattern is similar regardless of when the subjects dropped out; that is,

the rate of police contact increases steadily and peaks in the last period the subjects are in school. In contrast, among graduates the rate increases somewhat from Period II to Period III, but then declines to the earlier level in Periods IV and V. Among the graduates the magnitude of the rate changes with time is slight, particularly in comparison with the changes observed in each dropout category. The dropouts' increasing involvement with the police while they are in school is not accounted for by the general trend observed in the total population. The higher initial or prestudy police contact rates and the accelerating rates through time are also observed for serious police contacts.

The out-of-school rates for dropouts indicate a dramatic reversal of the in-school trend. In the period in which dropout occurs, the rate for out-of-school police contacts is approximately one-half the magnitude of the in-school rate for DO IIs and IVs; the out-of-school rate declines even more sharply among DO IIIs and Vs. For each category of dropouts the rate systematically declines in the period after which dropout occurred, and it continues to decline in subsequent time periods. In the later periods the police contact rates are substantially lower than the comparable rates for graduates. In Periods IV and V, the out-of-school police contact rates for dropouts are close to 0. The figures for Period V must be treated as tentative approximations, because this was a short time period. Nevertheless, these data support the conclusion that dropping out of school is associated with decreasing, instead of increasing out-of-school rates of police contact. Dropouts who have been out of school for a relatively short time have higher rates of police contact than prospective graduates who are still in school. It is not until Period IV that the official delinquency rates of DO IIs and IIIs reach a level lower than the rates of future graduates. From the standpoint of a causal argument, the most important finding is that dropping out of school is associated with a decreasing involvement with the police.

Use of the self-measure instead of police contacts produces similar findings, as shown in Table II. This analysis is limited to a comparison of graduates with DO IIs who did not return to school, because these dropouts were in school during nearly all of their junior high school years, but were out of school for all of their senior high school years.[6] Thus, the first self-report measure covers the period these dropouts were in school, while the second coincides with the period they were out of school. On the other hand, graduates were in school continuously throughout the junior and senior high school years. Because the length of the two periods is identical, means are used instead of rates.

In Table II, males and females are considered separately to control for the established differences in delinquency rates by sex. It is also assumed that the effect of dropping out might be different for males than for females. During the junior high school years, male dropouts report a mean of 8.57 offenses in comparison with 3.88 for graduates; female dropouts and graduates report 4.40 and 2.47 offenses, respectively. Even greater differences are observed for serious offenses during the junior high school years. Male dropouts report more than three times as many serious offenses as graduates. These differences are all significant statistically. These data are consistent with the findings based on police contacts and indicate that, while in school, dropouts have substantially greater involvement in delinquent activity than graduates.

A comparison of the means for male dropouts reveals a decline from 8.57 self-reported offenses while in school to 8.13 after dropping out of school. This represents a 5 percent average decrease in raw scores. The comparable rate of change for female dropouts is a decrease of 4 percent. Substantially greater decreases are observed in the means for serious offenses, -28 percent for male and -57 percent for female dropouts.[7] While the decrease in the total number of offenses is slight, it is, nevertheless, clear that the high rates of delinquency among the dropouts cannot be attributed to their dropping out of school. The dropouts reach a high level of involvement in delinquency prior to leaving school, but once they are out of school, their total offense rates decline slightly, and their involvement in serious offenses declines substantially.

While the dropouts' involvement in delinquent behavior decreased from the junior to the senior high school years, graduates reported an increasing number of delinquent

---

[6] In Period II (early ninth to mid-tenth grade) 109 subjects dropped out of school. Fifty percent ($N = 55$) of these dropouts failed to complete the fourth annual questionnaire and thus had missing data for the second self-reported delinquency measure. The means in Table II for senior high school and the residual gain means in the text are based on an N of 54. A check for possible selectivity in this loss provided no evidence of a selective loss with respect to prior delinquency scores. This loss did not affect the police contact measures, as official records were searched in the appropriate geographical areas for all dropouts and graduates whether or not they completed each of the annual questionnaires; except for eight cases, the whereabouts of all subjects were known, even if interviews were not completed.

[7] Unfortunately, year-by-year changes are not reflected in the self-reported delinquency measure, and the systematic decline observed in police contacts for each year out of school cannot be replicated with these data. Nevertheless, the findings based on the two measures of delinquency are consistent—there is a decreasing involvement in delinquency after dropout.

TABLE II   Mean Number of Self-Reported Delinquent Acts and Percentage Change Scores for Dropouts in Period II and Graduates During Junior and Senior High School, by Sex

	Males						Females					
	Junior high		Senior high		Percentage change		Junior high		Senior high		Percentage change	
	Total	Serious	Total	Serious	Total	Serious	Total	Serious	Total	Serious	Total	Serious
	Means		Means		Percentages		Means		Means		Percentages	
Dropouts	8.57	3.59	8.13	2.60	−5.1	−17.6	4.40	1.17	4.21	0.50	−4.3	−57.3
Graduates	3.88	0.99	6.76	1.71	+74.2	+72.7	2.47	0.43	3.83	0.67	+55.1	+55.8
t test	3.90[a]	3.71[a]	0.85	1.00			2.74[a]	2.31[b]	0.61	−0.54		

[a] $p < 0.01$.
[b] $p < 0.05$.

acts. The change from a mean of 3.88 total offenses for males in junior high school to 6.76 delinquent acts in senior high school represents a 74 percent average increase in raw scores. A similar increase is observed for serious offenses. Female graduates also report substantially more delinquent acts in senior high school than in junior high school; their average increase exceeds 55 percent for the total number of offenses as well as for serious offenses. Given the sizable increases in delinquent behavior among graduates, the declining rates for dropouts assume even greater importance, because they represent a trend counter to the one occurring in the general population.

In terms of raw scores the dropouts' self-reported delinquency declined slightly after they left school. With the exception of serious offenses among females, in the senior high school period the dropouts' mean self-report scores were slightly greater than the means for graduates, although the differences were not significant. In view of the dropouts' significantly more extensive involvement in delinquency while in school, we would have predicted higher rates of delinquency for the dropouts during the high school years, even if they had not dropped out of school. The use of residual gain scores allows for a comparison of dropouts and graduates in terms of self-reported delinquency scores in which the effects of prior delinquency have been partialled out.

The residual gain score for dropouts represents the difference between their out-of-school delinquency score and an expected score based on their prior delinquency level. Similarly, the residual gain score for graduates reflects the difference between their high school score and a predicted score based on their prior delinquency in junior high school.

A comparison of mean residual gain scores indicated that dropouts reported fewer offenses than expected while graduates reported slightly more than expected.[8] Both male and female dropouts reported an average of approximately one less offense than expected, given their prior self-reported delinquency scores. The slightly higher self-reported means for dropouts than graduates in the high school years are thus explained by the dropouts' initially higher involvement in delinquency. Once they leave school, dropouts commit fewer offenses than students in school with similar levels of prior delinquency.

Whether delinquency is measured in terms of police contacts or self-reports, similar patterns are revealed: (1) dropouts show a high level of involvement in delinquency while they are in school, and their involvement declines after they leave school; (2) there is limited in-

---

[8] Mean residual gain scores were as follows: dropout males, −1.37; dropout females, −0.70; graduate males, +0.06; graduate females, +0.04.

itial involvement in delinquency on the part of graduates, but it generally increases in the high school years; and, finally, (3) the rates of delinquency for subjects out of school are no greater—and possibly slightly lower—than the rates for students in school. Because these findings are contrary to the widely accepted belief that dropout leads to an increasing risk of delinquent activity, it is necessary to consider the possibility that the relationship is spurious. The findings we have presented on the relationship between delinquency and dropout are consistent with the results of earlier research; in this study the dropouts' involvement in delinquency is substantially greater than the participation of graduates in delinquency. The fact that these data also confirm a higher in-school and a lower out-of-school delinquency rate makes it unlikely that this finding is due to some unique feature of the study population.

With respect to the measure of delinquency based on police contacts, it might be argued that the lower out-of-school rate is simply a consequence of a decrease in visibility, which accompanies dropout. We do not deny that dropout may affect the visibility of delinquent acts, but it is unlikely that this could explain the decrease in delinquency among out-of-school youths, in view of the fact that a similar finding was produced when a self-report measure, unaffected by visibility to the police, was employed. Furthermore, the finding that lower-class and minority-group youths have a higher risk of police contact contradicts this possibility, because these youths contribute disproportionately to the dropout categories. If operative, the effect of police bias would be to exaggerate estimates of delinquency among dropouts in comparison with graduates. Another possibility is that if school officials frequently initiate police action, then those in school are more visible. However, school-related offenses such as truancy are not included in this analysis, and in less than one-half of 1 percent of the police departments' investigation reports are school personnel identified as the source of the complaint. This corroborates

Elliott's (1966) finding that the school is rarely the agency that initiates action resulting in a police contact. It does not appear that differential visibility can account for the decreasing police contact rate among dropouts.

While the problem of spuriousness can never be resolved, the observed relationship between delinquency and dropout cannot be explained by class or sex differences among dropouts and graduates or by differential visibility. Two additional facts support the conclusion that the relationship is not spurious—the police contact and the self-report measures produce consistent findings, and the overall rates are similar to those reported in earlier studies.

THE EFFECT OF DELINQUENCY ON DROPOUT

The observation that dropouts have significantly higher police contact and self-reported delinquency rates while in school than graduates appears to be consistent with our expectation that delinquency increases the probability of dropout. However, it does not demonstrate that subjects who were highly involved in delinquency at the beginning of the study or in a particular time period have a greater likelihood of dropping out than respondents with limited involvement in delinquency. To ascertain the effect of delinquency on dropout, we compared the in-school to out-of-school transition rates of subjects stratified according to prior involvement in delinquency (Davis, 1963). Comparison between the strata indicates the relative probability of dropout during a given period for subjects with and without police contact at the beginning of that period; in this analysis the size of each stratum is held constant, as are differences in initial marginal frequencies. The in-school to out-of-school transition rates for subjects with no police contacts and juveniles with one or more police contacts at the beginning of each period are presented in Table III. For convenience of reading the rates are stated in percentages.

TABLE III   In-School to Out-of-School Transition Rates, by Time Period, Stratified by Police Contact (Percentages)

| | Period | | | | | | | |
| | II | | III | | IV | | V | |
Police contact[a]	Rate	N	Rate	N	Rate	N	Rate	N
One or more police contacts	0.8	308	1.0	418	2.1	464	1.0	464
No police contacts	0.3	2307	0.4	2082	0.7	1876	0.4	1652
t value	4.55[b]		5.45[b]		8.75[b]		5.26[b]	

[a]Persons were classified as being in one or the other of these strata at the beginning of each successive time period. Subjects with no police contact at the beginning of Period II could be in either strata at the beginning of Period III. However, respondents who entered the "one or more" strata at any given point remained in it in subsequent time periods.

[b]$p < 0.01$.

The transition rates for respondents who experienced police contact are consistently higher than for juveniles with no official record. For each study period the probability of dropout is more than two times greater for those who experienced police contact than for respondents with no police contact. In Period IV, these probabilities differ by a factor of 3. These data offer strong support for the hypothesis that official contact with the police increases the likelihood of dropout.

In school to out-of-school transition rates for respondents with high, moderate, and low levels of self-reported delinquency at the beginning of the study are presented in Table IV. These transition rates reflect the probability of dropout over the entire study period. The data confirm that extensive involvement in delinquent behavior, whether or not it leads to official action, increases the probability of dropout. The transition rates of subjects with high initial self-reported delinquency scores are

TABLE IV   In-School to Out-of-School Transition Rates, by Sex, Stratified by Self-Reported Delinquency in Period I (Percentages)

Self-reported delinquency 1[a]	Males	Females	Total	N
High	3.5	3.3	3.3	775
Moderate	1.6	2.4	2.0	804
Low	1.1	1.4	1.3	1038
t values				
High versus moderate	6.55[b]	2.57[b]	6.36[b]	
High versus low	8.57[b]	6.55[b]	10.77[b]	
Moderate versus low	2.13[c]	4.08[b]	4.22[b]	

[a] The membership in each strata was determined at the beginning of the study on the basis of total self-reported delinquency scores for Period I and could not be readjusted for each period, as was the case with police contacts. For both sexes, those with less than two offenses were considered low; those with two to four offenses, moderate; and those with five or more offenses, high. These cutting points were used to trichotomize the initial self-report scores for each sex.

[b] $p < 0.01$.

[c] $p < 0.05$.

more than double the rates of respondents with low scores; more than one-third of the respondents with high initial self-report scores dropped out of school prior to graduation. The direction and magnitude of the differences in Table IV are similar to those in Table III. Together, these data offer impressive support for the hypothesis that delinquency leads to dropout.

The expected relationship between delinquency and dropout is not a simple one: delinquency increases the probability of dropout, which in turn decreases the probability of delinquency. Measures of delinquency based on police contacts and self-reports provide evidence in support of this causal sequence. These relationships were postulated in our theoretical scheme and support the basic proposition that the school is the critical social context for the generation of delinquent behavior.

DELINQUENCY AND POST-DROPOUT EXPERIENCES

Earlier, we suggested that dropouts' decreasing involvement in delinquency would depend on several contingencies in their out-of-school experiences, particularly employment and marriage. Dropout should reduce the motivation for delinquency to the extent that the dropout makes a satisfactory adjustment in the adult, working community. Should he or she encounter difficulty in obtaining a job, establishing new friendships, and making the transition into an adult role, one type of failure has simply been trade one for another, and we would not anticipate any dramatic decrease in motivation for delinquent behavior.

The circumstances of youths after they have dropped out of school vary widely. The unemployed, unmarried, out-of-school teenager probably comes closest to fitting the popular conception of the aimless, drifting high school dropout. On the other hand, males who are steadily employed and married, as well as females who are married, are viewed as having successfully entered conventional adult roles

in the community, and we would not expect continued involvement in delinquent behavior. It was therefore hypothesized that dropouts who were employed and married should be less delinquent than unmarried and unemployed dropouts.

In Table V the rate of police contact for out-of-school dropouts by sex, marital status, and employment status is presented. For Periods II, III, and IV, subjects who were out of school were jointly classified with respect to marriage and employment; the rate of police contact during each period was determined for respondents in each category. Subjects who were employed or married for the major part of a given time period were classified as employed or married for that period. Respondents who were married or employed for less than one-half of the period and subjects unmarried or unemployed for the entire period were classified as unmarried and unemployed.[9]

While out of school, male dropouts had 25 official police contacts, and female dropouts had 8 contacts. Thus, this analysis involves only 33 offenses. An examination of the rates reveals that for males marital status is the variable most highly associated with police contact. The police contact rate for unmarried males is more than three times the rate for married males. The rate for unemployed dropouts is also greater than for employed dropouts, but the difference is small. As expected, males who were unmarried and unemployed had the highest rate of police contacts, whereas married and unemployed males had the lowest rate. The finding must be viewed with caution, because there were very few cases of this type;

[9] The rates do not accurately reflect relatively short shifts from one marriage-employment category to another *within* a given time period, as all offenses in a particular time period are attributed to the single category that characterized the subject for the majority of the time involved. The rates in Table V reflect the total experience of dropouts in various marriage-employment categories through time; a given dropout may have contributed to the unmarried-unemployed rate for Period II, the unmarried-employed rate for Period III, and the married-employed rate for Period IV.

TABLE V Police Contact Rates[a] for Out-of-School Dropouts, by Sex, Marital Status, and Employment Status

	Married	Unmarried	Total
Males			
Employed	6.1	14.9	11.8
Unemployed	0.0	17.5	15.9
Total	5.1	15.4	13.3
Females			
Employed	4.0	2.4	3.0
Unemployed	1.8	6.2	3.1
Total	2.1	4.7	3.0
Total			
Employed	5.2	10.2	8.6
Unemployed	1.8	11.7	6.0
Total	2.6	10.9	7.0

[a] The number of police contacts per 100 dropouts in each marriage-employment category. The number of dropouts involved by period are as follows: Period II, 80; III, 136; IV, 484.

most of the married male dropouts were also employed. Nevertheless, it is clear that marriage and not employment is the critical variable.

In general, the same conclusions apply to female dropouts, but the limited number of police contacts they experienced forces us to view these findings as highly tentative. Again, the highest rate is found in the unemployed-unmarried category. The rate for unmarried females is more than twice the rate for married females, but there is no difference in the rates according to employment status. The lowest rates are found in the married-unemployed and the employed-unmarried categories. The first of these presumably describes the typical housewife; the second depicts the career woman. Either marriage or employment presumably is a deterrent to delinquency, but marriage and employment apparently do not work together to deter delinquency for female dropouts. Dropouts who do not marry or obtain employment appear to have the greatest risk of police contact.

Combining the males and females, we confirm the importance of marital status—the de-linquency rate of unmarried dropouts is four times higher than the rate of married dropouts. The rate of police contact for all employed dropouts is higher than for unemployed dropouts; however, this is due primarily to the large number of married and unemployed females who have very limited involvements with the police.

An analysis employing self-reported delinquent behavior revealed relationships similar to the ones observed with the police contact measure. Marriage again appeared to be a more important variable than employment; the mean self-reported delinquency score of those in the unmarried category was more than two and one-half times the score of married dropouts. This difference was found for both male and female dropouts. It also appears that unemployment is associated with higher levels of self-reported delinquency for married and unmarried males, as well as for unmarried females. In no case are these employment differences as large as the ones observed for married and unmarried dropouts. The number of cases is small, but the relationships are similar whether self-report or police contact data are employed, and this consistency lends credence to the general finding.

SUMMARY

Analyzing the effect of dropout on delinquency, we find that dropouts consistently have higher police contact rates; than graduates for every period they are in school, and these rates increase with time while they are in school. However, the police contact rate systematically declines in the period after which dropout occurs, and it continues to decline in subsequent time periods. In the later periods the rates are substantially lower than the rates for graduates. Use of the self-report measure produces similar findings. The dropouts reach a high level of involvement in delinquency prior to leaving school, but once they are out of school, their involvement in serious offenses declines substantially, and the total number of offenses reported declines slightly. In comparison, graduates report an increasing number of delinquent acts, as well as serious offenses, with time. Whether delinquency is measured in terms of police contacts or self-reports, similar patterns are revealed. The rates of delinquency for those out of school are no greater—and possibly lower—than the rates for students in school. The relationship between delinquency and dropout cannot be explained by class or sex differences among dropouts and graduates or by differential visibility.

The expected relationship between delinquency and dropout is observed; delinquency increases the probability of dropout, which in turn decreases the probability of delinquency. This causal sequence is supported with measures of delinquency based on police contacts and self reports. For each study period the probability of dropout is more than two times higher for those who experienced police contact than for subjects with no police contact. Extensive involvement in delinquent behavior, whether or not it leads to official action, increases the probability of dropout.

The dropouts' out-of-school experiences with respect to marriage and employment are related to their involvement in delinquency. With marriage and employment, the dropout makes the transition from adolescence into conventional adult roles. It is this factor, we suggest, that accounts for the general decline in the dropouts' rates of delinquent behavior. This interpretation is consistent with the finding that marriage is a more significant deterrent for delinquency than employment, since marriage is a less ambiguous indicator of adult status than employment, particularly when sporadic and part-time employment to some extent characterize student roles.

The employment-delinquency relationship is more complex than the association between marriage and delinquency. Unemployed males and unmarried females have consistently higher police contact and self-reported rates of delinquency. For married females, the opposite is true, girls with jobs have higher rates than unemployed females. In part, then, the lower rates of delinquency observed among dropouts may be attributed to changes in marital and employment status that follow dropout.

REFERENCES

Bachman, J. G., S. Green, and I. D. Wirtanen (1971). *Youth in Transition, Volume III: Dropping Out—Problem or Symptom.* Ann Arbor, Mich.: Institute for Social Research.

Cervantes, L. F. (1965). *The Dropout.* Ann Arbor, Mich.: University of Michigan Press.

Cloward R., and L. E. Ohlin (1960). *Delinquency and Opportunity: A Theory of Delinquent Gangs.* Glencoe, Ill.: Free Press.

Davis, J. A. (1963). Panel analysis: Techniques and Concepts in the Interpretation of Repeated Measurements. Unpublished monograph. Chicago: University of Chicago National Opinion Research.

Elliott, D. S. (1961). Delinquency, Opportunity and Patterns of Orientations. Unpublished Ph.D. dissertation. Seattle: University of Washington.

——— (1966). "Delinquency, school attendance and dropout." *Social Problems* **13**:307–314.

Gold, M. (1963). *Status Forces in Delinquent Boys.* Ann Arbor, Mich.: University of Michigan.

Haskell, M. R., and L. Yablonsky (1970). *Crime and Delinquency.*, Chicago: Rand McNally and Company.

Hathaway, S. R., and E. D. Monachesi (1963). *Adolescent Personality and Behavior.* Minneapolis: University of Minnesota Press.

Hathaway, S. R., P. Reynolds, and E. D. Monachesi (1969). "Follow-up of the Later Careers and Lives of 1,000 Boys Who Dropped Out of High School." *Journal of Consulting and Clinical Psychology,* **33**:370–380.

Havighurst, R. J. (1963). "Research on the School Work-Study Program in the Prevention of Juvenile Delinquency." In William R. Carriker (Ed.). Washington, D.C.: U.S. Government Printing Office.

Jeffery, C. R., and I. A. Jeffery (1970). "Delinquents and Dropouts: An Experimental Program in Behavior Change." *Canadian Journal of Corrections* **12**:47–58.

Kitsuse, J. I., and A. V. Cicourel (1963). "A note on the Use of Official Statistics." *Social Problems* **11** (Fall):131–139.

Krane, S. (1976). School Dropout: A Response to Aspiration Opportunity Discrepancy? Unpublished monograph. Boulder: University of Colorado (June).

Schafer, W. E., and K. Polk (1967). "Delinquency and the Schools." In President's Commission on Law Enforcement and Administration of Justice, Juvenile Delinquency and Youth Crime. Washington, D.C.: U.S. Government Printing Office, pp. 222–277.

Schafer, W. F., and R. D. Knudten (1970). *Juvenile Delinquency*. New York: Random House.

Schreiber, D. (1963a). "The Dropout and the Delinquency." *Phi Delta Kappa* 44:215–221.

——— (1963b). "Juvenile Delinquency and the School Dropout Problem." *Federal Probation* 27:15–19.

Short, J. F., Jr., and F. I. Nye (1957–58). "Reported Behavior as a Criterion of Deviant Behavior." *Social Problems* 5:207–213.

Short, J. F. (1958). "Extent of Unrecorded Juvenile Delinquency: Tentative Conclusions." *Journal of Criminal Law, Criminology, and Police Science* 49:296–302.

Simpson, J. E., and M. D. Van Arsdol, Jr. (1957). "Residential History and Educational Status of Delinquents and Non-delinquents." *Social Problems* 15:25–40.

14

THE INVENTION OF THE NEW FEMALE CRIMINAL

JOSEPH G. WEIS

A variation of the general social control theory of crime has emerged which attempts to integrate the apparent changes of women's position in the straight and criminal worlds. It asserts that apparent increases in the prevalence and variety of criminal behavior among women are a consequence of their "liberation." A concomitant of this view is a new image of the female criminal—a more versatile and serious offender who is equally adept at committing property crimes and acts of violence. The "new female criminal" is personified in media accounts by Bernardine Dohrn, Susan Saxe, the Manson women, Katherine Anne Power, Emily Harris, Patty Hearst, and other atypical female offenders. This perspective on female crime has been sold in the mass media, legitimated by criminologists like Sir Leon Radcinowicz, Francis Ianni, and Freda Adler, and supported by many control agents, including Chief Ed Davis of the Los Angeles Police Department who believes that the women's movement has triggered "a crime wave like the world has never seen before."

Contrary to mass media, pop-criminological,
and system agent impressions, data on the changing status of women in society and both "official" and "unofficial" data on crime among women show that the relationship between the women's movement and changes in female criminal behavior is tenuous. The tenuous nature of the relationship can be traced to theoretical progenitors, reliance on official crime statistics, logical errors of inference, and questionable interpretations of data, especially regarding the proposed causal relationship between "liberation" and crime. This paper will examine empirically three current theoretical perspectives on female crime which address changes in the roles and criminal behavior of women. National arrest data and self-reports of delinquent behavior show that the "new female criminal" is an invention and that the women's movement cannot be held responsible for changes in female criminal behavior which data indicate simply have not happened.[1]

[1] Whether there has been and is "liberation" among women, particularly among female criminals, is, of course, the other empirical question which deserves equal attention in research into the relationship between "liberation" and crime. However, the extent and the nature of the changing status of women will not be addressed in this paper because of space limitations and the fact that it is not essential logically to an empirical examination of the proposed relationship. See Simon (1975) for a recent discussion of the changing status of women. She suggests that women have not made the kinds of occupational, political, and social gains that would signal pervasive "liberation."

Source "Liberation and Crime: The Invention of the New Female Criminal," *Crime and Social Justice* (Fall-Winter 1976), **3:** 17–27. Copyright © Crime and Social Justice, P.O. Box 4373, Berkeley, CA, 94704. Reprinted by permission.

* Revised version of a paper presented at the Pacific Sociological Association Meeting, March 27, 1976, San Diego, California.

THEORIES OF FEMALE CRIMINAL BEHAVIOR

The dominant theories of crime (e.g., anomie, cultural transmission, conflict) are essentially theories of lower-class, male criminal behavior.[2] They typically disregard middle-class and female crime as relevant research and theoretical problems, primarily because they are anchored in official measures of crime which suggest that both middle class and female criminality are relatively neglible and insignificant. When pressed to account for other-than-lower class, male criminal behavior, criminologists tend to rely on psychologistic theories that impute some pathological difference to the criminal such as some abnormality of sex-role socialization, identification, or performance. Ironically, a substantial part of the theoretical literature on female crime and delinquency mirrors Cohen's (1955) explanation of middle class *male* delinquency as being a protest against femininity and a means of alleviating sex-role confusion or anxiety.[3]

Theories of female crime and delinquency can be characterized as *sex-role* theories. These female-specific theories are a consequence of the apparent empirical inadequacy of the dominant male-specific theories, the sexism which has helped to place female crime outside of the domain of professional criminological inquiry in the face of overwhelming evidence that sex may be the most powerful causal variable available, the ideological and theoretical sexualization of female behavior, both conventional and criminal, and of the fact that women's identity, adequacy, and moral worth have been anchored historically in sex-role performances. Female criminal behavior signifies a "spoiled identity"—a failure to adhere to cultural standards of proper feminine role performance. Of course, this theoretical perspective serves particular ideological functions. It stereotypes women offenders as sexually psychologically, and socially inadequate and abnormal. It reinforces existing social relationships between men and women by depicting "good" women as exemplars of feminine cultural standards and "bad" women as fallen from grace. And it also discredits the women's movement in the proposition that it is a breeding ground for female crooks and thugs because participants actively reject feminine stereotypes in the struggle for sexual egalitarianism. Female criminals, as well as participants in the women's movement, are sex-role inferiors to "conforming" (or oppressed) women.

In general, theories of female criminal behavior have been sexualized, psychologized, and syllogized. Beginning with the biological theory of Lombroso (1899), elaborated in the psychological theory of Freud (1905, 1931, 1933), and modernized in the current theory that women's "liberation" causes female crime, a theoretical perspective has developed which claims that female crime is a product of the masculinization of female behavior. Female criminals are more "masculine" than noncriminal females, biologicaly, psychologically, and socially. In social psychological terms, female criminal behavior is a concomitant of *role reversal.*

According to Lombroso (1899), the female offender has a "virile cranium," an overabundance of body hair, and constitutional anomalies and brain capacity which are more similar to those of a man than to a noncriminal woman.[4] Freud (1933) psychologizes the anatomy is destiny theory. Those women who cannot "adjust" to their absence of and longing

[2] These theories are not addressed in this paper, primarily because they are male-specific and do not address the relationship between "liberation" and crime among women.

[3] Cohen (1955:163) does not address the delinquency of middle class girls because of imputed negligibility and because of the assumption that socialization within a female-centered household leads to proper female role identification. There is no sex-role anxiety and, therefore, nothing to react against or to disavow.

[4] See Klein (1973) for an informative discussion of Lombroso and other theoreticians of female crime and delinquency. The biological basis of the masculinization of female behavior has been reiterated by Spaulding (1923), Healy and Bronner (1926), the Gluecks (1934), and most recently by Cowie, Cowie, and Slater (1963) who propose that the observed "markedly masculine traits" of delinquent girls can be traced to chromosomal abnormalities.

for a penis in culturally prescribed manner of dutiful sexual performance and motherhood, attempt to acquire symbolic masculinity by aggressively rebelling against their "natural" feminine roles. They engage in behavior (conventional and criminal) which they believe signifies masculinity in order to compensate for their lack of an anatomical sign of maleness. They deny their female role and femininity and identify with the male role and masculinity. In short, they "attempt to be a man" (Klein, 1973:17).[5]

With the emergence of the women's movement in the late sixties came a more sociological version of the masculinization or role reversal theory—what might be called the *"liberation"* theory of female crime.[6] Its most visible exponent proposes that "the social revolution of the sixties has virilized (!) its previously or presumably docile female segment" (Adler, 1975:87). With the "increasing masculinization of female social and criminal behavior" has come an increase in the frequency and variety of their criminal activity (Adler, 1975:1, 42, 251). That is, "Women are committing more crimes than ever before. Those crimes involve a greater degree of violence" (Adler, 1975:3). The more the position of women in society approximates the position of men, the more alike become their conforming *and* criminal behavior.

The move toward sexual egalitarianism is also viewed as being responsible for the emergence of "the new female delinquent." It is proposed that "the emancipation of women appears to be having a twofold influence on female juvenile crimes. Girls are involved in more drinking, stealing, gang activity, and fighting behavior in keeping with their adoption of male roles" (Adler, 1975:95). They are becoming more violent, while the image of the girlish petty property offender and shoplifter is fading to the point where it is "likely to become almost as uncommon as the male shoplifter" (Adler, 1975:96, 165). Once again, female criminal behavior is a consequence of the masculinization of female behavior.

A variant of the masculinization, role reversal, or women's "liberation" theory is what might be called the *human "liberation"* or *role convergence* theory of criminal behavior. It postulates that the simultaneous masculinization of female roles and feminization of male roles—a convergence of sex-role expectations—is responsible for assumed differences in lower and middle class delinquency and for imputed similarities in the delinquent behavior of middle class boys and girls. Wise (1967) suggests that in the middle class "female delinquency closely resembles male delinquency in form and quantity" because middle class boys and girls are more exposed than their lower class peers to a convergence of male and female role definitions and expectations in the family, in school, and in their class culture. The apparent petty and nonviolent character of middle class delinquency is attributed to the more pervasive feminization of middle class boys as compared to working class boys and to the masculinization of middle class girls.[7] Middle class boys are (and have been) more like girls, and middle class girls are becoming more like boys.

Unlike either of the "liberation" theories (women's or human), the *sexism, role validation,* or *opportunity* theory of female criminal behavior proposes that it is an illegitimate expression of femininity rather than a symbol of masculinity. Beginning with Thomas (1923), the

---

[5] The general features of the psychological masculinization of female behavior have been reiterated by Payak (1963), Konopka (1966), and Vedder and Somerville (1970).

[6] Throughout the paper, the term "liberation" refers to the rather narrow, liberal definition used by these contemporary "liberation" theorists. They seem to use it to mean *cultural liberation*—emancipation from sex-role constraints—and ignore the broader questions of whether sexual egalitarianism is meaningful and even possible in a society where there is pervasive class and race inequality. The structural meanings of "liberation" are not addressed by these theorists.

[7] This is in a sense a synthesis of Cohen's (1955) theory of middle class male delinquency and the role reversal theory of female crime.

notion emerged that female criminals are not sex-role abnormals. Instead of denying "femininity"and becoming more masculine, they are validating their "femininity" illegally. They engage in role expressive and role supportive criminal behavior (cf. Grosser, 1952), such as sexual misconduct, shoplifting, and other types of delinquent behavior which are extensions of their female role. Pollak (1950) proposes that the crimes that women commit are less likely to be detected because they are concomitants of traditional female roles, such as teacher, secretary, domestic, clerk, nurse, or housewife, which act as effective "covers" for low visibility and typically female crimes such as shoplifting, forgery, embezzlement, and petty theft. Davis (1961) offers a functionalist explanation of prostitution as an illegitimate extension of the female sex role. Prostitution is the illegal role analogue of marriage for women. Hoffman-Bustamante (1973) proposes that female criminal behavior is consistent with female role expectations and with sex-role-determined opportunities to commit certain types of crimes (e.g., prostitution, shoplifting). Or as Klein and Kress (1976:41) have suggested, the "class structure of sexism . . . is reproduced in the illegal marketplace." Women occupy and perform roles in the straight and criminal worlds which are defined by their sex-determined *lack* of opportunity: "They are no more big-time dope dealers than are they finance capitalists." In short, female criminal behavior is an illegitimate expression of legitimate female role expectations and opportunities. Rather than being a reflection of symbolic masculinity (or "liberation"), it is an alternative means of female role validation (or oppression).

The remainder of the paper will examine the women's "liberation" (role reversal), human "liberation" (role convergence), and sexism (role validation) theories of female crime in light of (1) recent careful analyses of national arrest data and (2) the self-reported delinquent behavior of 555 eighth and eleventh grade girls and boys in an upper-middle class suburban community. The evidence suggests that the sexism model is more valid than the "liberation" theories of female crime and juvenile delinquency.

OFFICIAL MEASURES OF FEMALE CRIMINAL BEHAVIOR

The masculinization, role reversal, or "liberation" theories of female crime are based on a syllogism: (1) crime is a typically male phenomenon; (2) females are apparently committing more, and more serious, crimes; (3) therefore, females, especially those involved in crime, are more like males. In a syllogism, if one of the premises is false, the conclusion does not follow. For the purposes of discussion, premise number one will be accepted as essentially true. However, premise number two is not essentially true. The "new female criminal" seems to be a product of the collective imaginations, perhaps wishes, of misguided observers and analysts. The official crime statistics upon which *they* base *their* claims show that women are still typically nonviolent, petty property offenders.

Contrary to mass-media and pop-criminological impressions, recent careful analyses of Uniform Crime Report (UCR) data show that the "proportion of female arrests for violent crimes has changed hardly at all over the past two decades" (Simon, 1975:46) and, in fact, has decreased for murder-man-slaughter and aggravated assault (Hoffman-Bastamante, 1973:121). The percentage of men arrested for violent crimes has increased about four times as much as the percentage of women. On the other hand, there have been rate increases for women in certain types of property offenses— the proportion of women who have been arrested has increased three times as much as the proportion of men involved (Simon, 1975:38–39). However, the increases have come primarily in *larceny* (viz. shoplifting; cf. Cameron, 1964, who has estimated that 80 percent of female larceny arrests are for shoplifting) and secondarily in *fraud* (viz. "bad checks" and embezzlement) and in *forgery* (viz. "naive" check forgery; cf. Lemert, 1971, who has estimated that 75 percent of forgery arrests are of naive check forgers).[8] These are the traditionally "female" offenses which have been tied to the consumption role of women as houseworkers (cf. Klein and Kress, 1976). They occupy similar sex-determined roles in the legal and illegal marketplaces: they move from shopper to shoplifter, from cashing good checks to passing bad ones, from taking aspirins to popping bennies and barbs, from being a welfare mother to being accused of welfare fraud, and so on.

Unfortunately, official crime statistics are questionably valid, especially for adult and juvenile females. The under-representation of females in official statistics can be attributed either to sex differences in criminal involvement or to the favored differential handling of women within the criminal justice system. Either their behavior is different or they elicit different behavior from system agents because the sexual double standard, paternalism, or the chivalry factor (cf. Thomas, 1923; Pollak, 1950; Reckless and Kay, 1967; Nagel and Weitzman, 1972; Chesney-Lind, 1973; Rogers, 1972; Singer, 1973).[9] Self-report studies have shown that there is a great deal of "hidden" criminal behavior (Short and Nye, 1957; Clark and Haurek, 1966; Wise, 1967; Gold, 1970; Hindelang, 1971; Weis, 1973), but that, contrary to what Pollak (1950) and others have suggested, there are important and significant sex differences in the relative prevalence, incidence, and seriousness of criminal involvement. However, they also show that the pattern of involvement is similar; for example, boys and girls tend to commit similar kinds of delinquent acts. Self-

report data gathered by the author suggest similar relationships, which undermine further the "liberation" theory of female crime and support the sexism, role validation, or opportunity model.

THE PREVALENCE, INCIDENCE, AND PATTERNS OF DELINQUENT BEHAVIOR

The findings reported here represent a part of the data gathered in a larger, two-year community study of middle class delinquency (cf. Weis, 1973). A variety of research techniques were utilized, including interviews, field observations, role plays, an attitude survey, prestige rankings, secondary data analysis, and an anonymous self-report survey of delinquent behavior which will be the focus of analysis.

An anonymous, paper and pencil, self-report questionnaire was administered to the subjects by the author and colleagues in classrooms during the course of one school day. The questionnaire was similar to others which have been used to ascertain the involvement of young people in a variety of proscribed activities (e.g., Porterfield, 1946; Murphy, Shirley, and Witmer, 1946; Short and Nye, 1957, 1958; Nye, Short, and Olson, 1958; Dentler and Monroe, 1961; Hindelang, 1971; Hindelang and Weis, 1972). The survey consisted of thirty-four delinquent acts, and the subjects were asked to report the number of times they had engaged in each of the activities during the past three years.[10]

Table 1 shows the percent of the four sex-grade populations admitting to the commission of each of the acts at least one time within the past three years and the within-grade sex ratios of the percentage of participants involved in each offense. Those acts which have been committed one or more times by the largest percentages of subjects are curfew viola-

---

[8] Also contrary to media and pop-criminological fictions, the proportion of women arrested for drug violations has decreased since 1958 (Hoffman-Bustamante, 1973).

[9] The under-representation of girls, especially middle class girls, in the juvenile justice system does not mean that they are treated more leniently after they do enter the system. In fact, some of the cited studies show that they are treated more harshly, especially for sexual conduct.

[10] Parenthetically, Gold (1966, 1970) also used a three-year time frame. It was chosen here for one reason: it locks the reported activities of the older subjects into their first three years of high school and of the younger subjects into their intermediate school years.

TABLE 1   Percent Committing Acts One or More Times

	11th grade			8th grade		
	Boys	girls	Ratio	Boys	girls	Ratio
Curfew Violation	97.5	93.7	1.04	88.1	79.3	1.11
False ID	20.8	12.0	1.73	16.8	14.4	1.17
Sent Out of Class	64.8	58.5	1.11	78.3	64.9	1.21
Petty Theft (<$2)	57.3	40.1	1.43	62.2	48.6	1.28
Medium Theft ($2-$50)	24.5	14.1	1.74	34.3	15.3	2.24
Grand Theft (>$50)	8.8	0.0	8.80	6.3	3.6	1.75
Gambling	79.9	49.3	1.62	82.5	39.6	2.08
Driving without License	55.3	54.9	1.01	51.0	41.4	1.25
Drinking Alcohol	91.8	83.1	1.10	71.3	57.7	1.24
Drunk on Alcohol	82.4	68.3	1.21	54.5	38.7	1.41
Individual Fighting	43.4	2.8	15.50	65.0	13.5	4.15
Group Fighting	11.3	0.0	11.30	11.9	6.3	1.87
Concealed Weapon	25.8	1.4	18.43	37.1	10.8	3.44
Individual Weapon Fight	3.8	0.7	5.43	7.7	2.7	2.85
Group Weapon Fight	1.9	0.0	1.90	4.9	1.8	2.72
Marijuana	62.9	54.2	1.16	40.6	24.3	1.67
Cheating	86.2	92.3	.93	86.0	90.1	.95
Illegal Entry	20.8	2.1	9.90	19.6	8.1	2.42
Driving While Intoxicated	53.5	37.0	1.45	8.4	4.5	1.87
Vandalism Private Property	36.5	6.3	5.79	46.2	23.4	1.97
Vandalism Public Property	36.5	12.7	2.87	40.6	20.7	1.96
Cut Class	86.2	87.3	.99	58.0	55.0	1.05
Cut School	68.6	68.3	1.00	31.5	18.9	1.67
Hit and Run	27.1	19.7	1.38	4.2	0.9	4.67
Joyriding	14.5	5.6	2.59	7.7	9.9	.78
Stealing Money	33.3	23.2	1.44	48.3	33.3	1.45
School Probation	5.0	2.1	2.38	8.4	9.0	.93
School Suspension	7.5	2.1	3.57	13.3	3.6	3.69
Out All Night	51.6	26.1	1.98	31.5	16.2	1.94
Shoplifting	39.4	35.9	1.10	57.3	42.3	1.35
Shakedown for Money	4.4	0.0	4.40	4.2	0.9	4.67
Drag Racing	64.2	25.4	2.53	11.9	7.2	1.65
Defacing Walls	20.2	19.7	1.03	31.5	37.8	.83
Sneaking In	76.7	54.9	1.40	67.1	52.3	1.28
	N = 159	N = 142	$\bar{X}$ = 3.15	N = 143	N = 111	$\bar{X}$ = 1.95

tion, cheating in school, gambling, being sent out of class, and drinking alcohol, while grand theft, individual or group fighting with weapons, shaking people down, and being placed on school probation or suspension have been committed by very small percentages of all four of the subject populations. The most popular offense for eleventh grade boys and girls and for eighth grade boys is curfew violation, ranging from 97.5 percent of the eleventh grade boys to 88.1 percent of the eighth grade boys violating curfew on at least one occasion.

Among eighth grade girls, cheating in school is the most pervasive offense with 90.1 percent admitting the commission of this proscribed act. Not unexpectedly, more boys engage in various kinds of fighting than girls, and a large proportion of eighth grade boys engage in fights with another individual (65.0 percent) than eleventh grade boys (43.4 percent). However, an almost equal percentage (11.3 and 11.9 percent) of eleventh and eighth grade boys have participated in fights where there were more than two combatants.

Contrary to the popular image of the young, female petty-thief and shoplifter, more boys than girls engage in the theft of items worth less than two dollars and in stealing merchandise from stores. Again, the eighth grade boys have the highest proportion of participants in these two activities (62.2 and 57.3 percent), followed by the eleventh grade boys (57.3 and 39.4 percent), the eighth grade girls (48.6 and 42.3 percent), and finally the eleventh grade girls (40.1 and 35.9 percent). For many of the delinquent acts, the older girls are the *least* "delinquent." Of the four groups, they are the only one with zero scores on some of the delinquent acts: not one eleventh grade girl reported participation in grand theft, group fighting, group weapon fighting, or shaking someone down for money.[11]

These data generally indicate, as others have found for middle class populations, that (1) the percent of boys involved in delinquent behavior, with some exceptions, is greater than the percent of girls involved at any age-grade, and (2) older adolescents tend to "mellow" or become less involved in delinquent behavior with age (Vaz, 1965; Wise, 1967; Hindelang, 1971). The greater delinquent involvement of boys holds with the following exceptions: (1) more eleventh grade girls (92.3 percent) *and* eighth grade girls (90.1 percent) cheat in school than eleventh grade boys (86.2 percent) and eighth grade boys (86.0 percent); (2) a larger percentage of eleventh grade girls than boys cut class (87.3 versus 86.2 percent); (3) more eighth grade girls (37.8 percent) than eighth grade boys (31.5 percent), eleventh grade boys (20.2 percent), and eleventh grade girls (19.7 percent) have admitted to defacing walls. The percentages of boys and girls within each grade who engage in sex-shared social activities like

violating curfew, drinking alcohol, getting drunk, and smoking marijuana are very similar.

Unfortunately, the number of youngsters within a population who report that they have committed an act one or more times provides no indication of the *frequency* with which the identified participants commit the offenses. Table 2 shows that those delinquent acts which are committed with the greatest frequency are curfew violation, smoking marijuana, cheating in school, cutting class, and drinking alcohol. Those acts with the lowest frequencies of commission are grand theft, group fighting, fighting with weapons against another individual or as part of a group, burglary, hit and run, being placed on probation or suspended by school authorities, and shaking others down for money. The act committed most frequently is curfew violation, ranging from a high mean of 221 times for eleventh grade boys to a low mean of 35 times for eighth grade boys.

The second and third most frequently committed acts for eleventh grade boys and girls are smoking marijuana and drinking alcohol. For the eighth graders there is a sex difference: gambling and cheating in school rank two and three for the eighth grade boys, while cheating in school ranks two and cutting class and shoplifting are tied for third for the eighth grade girls. Contrary to what the number of offenders data indicate, girls do engage in shoplifting more frequently than boys. Even though the eighth grade boys have the largest percentage of participants in shoplifting, the eighth grade girls have the highest mean frequency of shoplifting (12.4), followed by the eighth grade boys (7.3), eleventh grade girls (7.1), and eleventh grade boys (4.7).

These data also indicate that boys engage in delinquent behavior more often than girls. The boys within each age-grade have higher mean frequency scores than the girls with the following exceptions: (1) eleventh grade girls, on the average, engage more often than eleventh grade boys in cutting school (10.6 versus 8.7), stealing money (6.2 versus 4.3), and shoplift-

---

[11] The listed sex ratios for these offenses are the percentage of eleventh grade boys committing the act. Of course, this makes the sex ratio smaller than it actually is for these offenses. However, this "conservative" estimate of the ratios preserves the integrity of computations based on these data.

TABLE 2 Frequency of Commission

	11 Boys		11 Girls		8 Boys		8 Girls	
	X	sd	X	sd	X	sd	X	sd
1. Curfew	221.21	251.19	250.12	216.34.	35.42	86.08	66.09	214.11
2. False	2.18	9.68	.35	1.26	.83	3.31	.52	2.51
3. Sent	2.97	4.69	2.33	5.26	7.11	12.49	4.18	8.55
4. Ptheft	6,28	11.70	2.27	4.68	6.55	18.62	2.92	9.97
5. Mtheft	1.93	6.37	.63	2.13	1.62	5.07	.74	2.94
6. Gtheft	.49	4.04	.00	.00	.36	2.15	.08	.44
7. Gamble	28.76	67.98	5.47	12.63	25.33	89.11	2.71	5.77
8. Drivel	8.95	22.37	6.04	18.71	11.92	50.10	4.47	12.31
9. Drink	75.82	152.84	54.95	106.45	11.56	25.08	5.56	11.43
10. Drunk	62.76	145.67	37.36	64.54	8.16	21.30	3.34	11.20
11. Ifight	3.18	16.25	.17	1.69	5.56	25.60	.91	7.10
12. Gfight	.49	2.80	.00	.00	.39	1.57	.13	.62
13. Weapon	9.90	80.54	.07	.65	14.41	49.75	.27	1.13
14. Ifitew	.11	.84	.01	.08	.30	1.33	.05	.35
15. Gfitew	.09	.85	.00	.00	.08	.53	.02	.21
16. Grass	187.27	311.11	109.03	269.90	20.24	61.22	11.72	75.86
17. Cheat	22.98	52.00	27.87	90.05	21.26	50.95	42.02	113.69
18. Burgle	.95	2.77	.04	.31	1.33	5.05	.21	1.06
19. Drived	28.66	107.21	7.02	31.19	.72	4.63	.24	1.40
20. Vand Pr	2.13	4.81	.66	5.14	2.42	5.49	1.39	5.43
21. Vand Pu	2.44	6.13	.28	1.08	2.05	6.88	1.21	5.27
22. Class	38.81	97.99	29.90	53.37	6.69	33.87	14.16	96.04
23. School	8.72	14.62	10.68	28.70	3.44	25.18	1.92	10.69
24. Hitrun	.43	1.51	.35	1.15	.27	2.24	.01	.09
25. Joyride	1.04	4.74	.21	1.37	3.85	41.67	1.42	9.68
26. Steal	4.37	18.52	6.25	43.47	4.07	12.18	2.21	7.78
27. Proba	.05	.25	.02	.14	.27	1.18	.13	.47
28. Suspen	.33	1.99	.02	.14	.30	1.40	.05	.29
29. Night	5.62	16.50	1.35	5.09	2.42	7.89	.66	2.42
30. Shop	4.77	12.19	7.16	58.52	7.36	26.77	12.47	94.79
31. Shakm	.13	.87	.00	.00	.18	1.33	.02	.28
32. Drag	7.60	16.03	1.45	8.52	1.87	11.86	.13	.56
33. Deface	.95	4.00	.58	1.72	2.18	7.20	2.36	6.36
34. Sneak	11.14	21.48	8.02	58.53	667.	12.98	2.58	5.90
	N = 159		142		143		111	

ing (7.1 versus 4.7); (2) eighth grade girls violate curfew (66.0 versus 35.4), cheat in school (42.0 versus 21.2), cut class (14.1 versus 6.6), shoplift (12.4 versus 7.3), and deface walls (2.3 versus 2.1) more frequently than do eighth grade boys.

Although more boys are more frequently involved in delinquent behavior than girls, the *pattern* of involvement is very similar for the four subject populations. Table 3 shows that within each group the rank-order of the mean frequencies of participation in various proscribed acts is very similar[12] The rank-order correlation coefficient for all four groups is .903 (p<.000). The rank-order correlation coeffi-

[12] The act with the highest mean frequency is assigned the rank of 31. Three items (3, 27, 28) are the responses of school officials to behavior in which a subject might engage. Consequently, some analyses and tables will contain 31 variables.

TABLE 3 Patterns of Delinquent Involvement Rank Orders and Rank Correlations of Acts

Variable	(A) 11 boys	(B) 11 girls	(C) 8 boys	(D) 8 girls	Group ranks compared	k	x^2	p<	R
1. Curfew	31.0	31.0	31.0	31.0	A,B	2	56,211	.002	.968
2. False	12.0	11.0	8.0	11.0					
3. Ptheft	18.0	18.0	20.0	23.0	C,D	2	51,209	.009	.924
4. Mtheft	10.0	14.0	10.0	13.0					
5. Gtheft	5.5	2.5	5.0	5.0	A,C	2	53,117	.005	.941
6. Gamble	26.0	19.0	30.0	22.0					
7. Drivel	21.0	20.0	26.0	25.0	B,D	2	53,876	.004	.948
8. Drink	29.0	29.0	25.0	26.0					
9. Drunk	28.0	28.0	24.0	24.0	A,B,C,D	4	97,872	.000	.903
10. Ifight	14.0	8.0	19.0	14.0					
11. Gfight	5.5	2.5	6.0	6.5					
12. Weapon	22.0	7.0	27.0	10.0	N = 31				
13. Ifitew	2.0	5.0	4.0	4.0	df = 30				
14. Gfitew	1.0	2.5	1.0	2.5					
15. Grass	30.0	30.0	28.0	27.0	R = Friedman's (1937) rank correlation ratio				
16. Cheat	24.0	26.0	29.0	30.0					
17. Burgle	8.0	6.0	9.0	8.0					
18. Drived	25.0	22.0	7.0	9.0					
19. Vandpr	11.0	15.0	14.5	16.0					
20. Vandpu	13.0	10.0	12.0	15.0					
21. Class	27.0	27.0	22.0	29.0					
22. School	20.0	25.0	16.0	18.0					
23. Hit run	4.0	12.0	3.0	1.0					
24. Joyride	9.0	9.0	17.0	17.0					
25. Steal	15.0	21.0	18.0	19.0					
26. Night	17.0	16.0	14.5	12.0					
27. Shop	16.0	23.0	23.0	28.0					
28. Shakm	3.0	2.5	2.0	2.5					
29. Drag	29.0	17.0	11.0	6.5					
30. Deface	7.0	13.0	13.0	20.0					
31. Sneak	23.0	24.0	21.0	21.0					
	N = 159	142	143	111					

cients for *sex-differences* within the eleventh and eighth grades are .968 (p<.002) and .925 (p<.009), respectively.[13] In short, those acts which are committed by boys also tend to be committed by girls and in a similar rank-order of frequency of commission. The rank-order correlation coefficients for *age-differences* within each sex are .941 (p<.005) for the two grades of boys and .948 (p<.004) for the two grades

of girls. Again, whatever differences in the percent involved or mean frequency of involvement may appear between the age categories, there is a similar pattern of delinquent involvement.

FACTOR ANALYSIS OF SELF-REPORT DATA

Given that the rank-order data indicate *similarities* in the patterns of delinquent involvement among the four groups *and* that the data on the percentage of participants and the mean frequency of participation show some sex and

---

[13] Hindelang (1971) found a rank-order correlation coefficient of .925 for lower-middle and middle class male and female adolescents across 24 items of delinquent behavior, and Wise (1967) reports one of .871 across 35 items for middle class male and female groups of adolescents.

age *differences*, in order to ascertain better the patterning and/or variation in the statistical relationships among the delinquent acts, a full cycle cluster analysis was performed (Tyron, 1966, 1967; Tyron and Bailey, 1966, 1970).[14] The general objective of cluster analysis is to determine whether a large number of variables can be "clustered" together into a smaller number of subsets of variables. The analyst attempts to group variables which are similar to each other in the same cluster and to isolate clusters which are as different from each other as possible: that is, to extract clusters with minimum within-cluster variation and maximum between-cluster variation. Hopefully, the resultant clusters will represent a conceptually simpler depiction of relationships among the variables in the correlation matrix.[15]

Tables 4 and 5 show that there is a surprising similarity in the variable composition of the clusters of delinquent acts which were extracted for the boys and girls.[16] The first cluster of variables for both groups is identical, except for one variable—using a false identification—which was not included in the girls' factor because of an insufficient factor loading. This cluster has been designated *Social* because the activities which comprise it revolve around "social" situations or activities of one sort or another. The *Property* factor includes acts of property theft and destruction, and it is also similar for boys and girls, except for two variables which are absent from the girls' factor: vandalizing private property had an inadequate factor loading, and grand theft is one of the four delinquent acts which no eleventh grade girl committed. An *Aggression* cluster contains every item related to fighting for the

TABLE 4   Three Factor Solution (Boys)

Factor	Variable	Fc	h²	r̄
Social	Drink	.899	.855	.557
	Drunk	.880	.810	.546
	Grass	.722	.598	.447
	School	.707	.501	.438
	Class	.706	.509	.437
	Drived	.682	.472	.423
	Sneak	.607	.379	.376
	Curfew	.580	.340	.360
	Night	.559	.324	.347
	Drivel	.500	.263	.310
	Drag	.491	.274	.304
	Cheat	.484	.275	.300
	Gamble	.455	.229	.282
	False	.402	.207	.249
	Reliability = .904 Domain Validity = .951			
Property	Mtheft	.800	.639	.527
	Ptheft	.778	.650	.513
	Burgle	.679	.462	.448
	Shop	.662	.456	.436
	Steal	.629	.407	.415
	Vand Pu	.609	.377	.401
	Vand Pr	.588	.382	.387
	Gtheft	.525	.358	.346
	Reliability = .868 Domain Validity = .931			
Aggression	Gfight	.831	.697	.510
	Ifitew	.611	.384	.375
	Gfitew	.525	.289	.322
	Ifight	.488	.255	.299
	Reliability = .721 Domain Validity = .847			

Fc = Oblique factor coefficient
h² = Communality
r̄   = Average correlation with definers

boys, but it could *not* be extracted for girls since so few girls engage in fighting. (It is included for the purpose of symmetrical rather than rigorous statistical analysis.)

Tables 6 and 7 show that these clusters reproduce a substantial proportion of the original relationships among the variables in the correlation matrices (Boys = .939; Girls = .909), and the *social* factor accounts for most of the variance (Boys = .779; Girls = .834). This suggests that the clusters may not be as independent of each other as they appear to be. Two of the three factors are highly correlated

[14] See Hindelang and Weis (1972) and Weis (1973:380–407) for a detailed description of the application of cluster analysis to self-reported delinquency data.

[15] The data entries were transformed to their natural log so extremely high scores did not distort mean values and statistical computations.

[16] Complete cluster analyses were performed for eleventh grade boys and girls only because of the limits of resources and the fact that cluster analysis uses up a great deal of machine time.

TABLE 5   Three Factor Solution (Girls)

Factor	Variable	Fc	h²	r̄
Social	Drunk	.845	.735	.506
	Drink	.807	.671	.484
	Class	.783	.614	.469
	School	.679	.482	.407
	Drived	.679	.507	.407
	Grass	.668	.448	.401
	Sneak	.631	.473	.378
	Curfew	.513	.334	.307
	Drivel	.468	.227	.281
	Cheat	.450	.213	.270
	Night	.443	.204	.266
	Gamble	.442	.197	.265
	Drag	.384	.191	.230

Reliability = .887 Domain Validity = .942

Property	Shop	.846	.722	.510
	Ptheft	.729	.534	.440
	Mtheft	.679	.466	.409
	Burgle	.551	.417	.332
	Steal	.415	.179	.250
	Vand Pu	.397	.175	.240

Reliability = .789 Domain Validity = .888

Aggression	Ifight	1.000	1.000	1.000

Reliability = 1.000 Domain Validity = 1.000

Fc = Oblique factor coefficient
h² = Communality
r̄ = Average correlation with definers.

TABLE 6   Statistical Properties of Three Factor Solution (Boys)

	Social	Property	Aggression
Social	(.779)	.543	.271
Property	.481	(.900)	.378
Aggression	.218	.298	(.939)

Diagonal = Cumulative proportion of mean square of raw correlation matrix exhausted by the three successive dimensions
Above = Correlations among oblique cluster domains
Below = Correlations of raw cluster scores with each other

TABLE 7   Statistical Properties of Three Factor Solution (Girls)

	Social	Property	Aggression
Social	(.834)	.062	−.077
Property	.503	(.901)	.051
Aggression	−.072	.045	(.909)

Diagonal = Cumulative proportion of mean square of raw correlation matrix exhausted by the three successive dimensions
Above = Correlations among oblique cluster domains
Below = Correlations of raw cluster scores with each other

with each other. The correlations among the oblique cluster domains indicate that for the boys (.543) and girls (.602) the *Social* factor is closely related to the *Property* factor. And the correlations of *Aggression* with the other factors, though not as high, are higher for the boys than for the girls. For the boys, *Aggression* is more closely related to the *Property* factor (.378) than to the *Social* factor (.271). For the girls, *Aggression* is negatively related to the *Social* factor (−.077) and barely related to the *Property* factor (.051).

DISCUSSION

A number of conclusions can be drawn from the different analyses of the self-report data. *First*, there is a substantial amount of "hidden" female *and* male delinquent behavior. The often-cited 1:6 ratio of male to female arrestees is twice as large as the mean ratio of 1:2.56 self-reported participants in delinquent behavior. *Second, the offenses which are most often committed are more petty than serious, such as curfew violation, cheating in school, drinking alcohol, smoking marijuana, cutting class, being sent out of class, and gambling. These acts are included in the Social cluster. Third,* more boys are more frequently involved in most delinquent acts. There are significant sex differences in the prevalence, incidence, and seriousness of delinquent involvement. There are only a few offenses in which girls are more involved than boys, and they tend to be school-related or petty property offenses. *Fourth,* the patterns of delinquent involvement by sex and age are similar. The extracted clusters of delinquent acts are also similar, with the notable exception that no *Aggression* cluster could be generated for the girls. The girls are almost completely nonviolent, and there seems to be a small subpopulation of boys who are doing most of the fighting. *Social* types of delinquent behavior characterize the involvement of boys and girls, "versatility" rather than "specialization" best describes their delinquent involvement, but the boys are involved in a greater variety of delinquent behavior, which includes more serious kinds of offenses.

These conclusions tend to substantiate the sex-role determined opportunity theory. The "liberation" theories (role reversal and role convergence) predict more similarities in the delinquent behavior of boys and girls than the data indicate. Even though the sex ratio is smaller than official data suggest, there are still substantial sex differences in delinquent involvement. Boys and girls are *most similar* on the *Social* offenses which are committed typically with members of the opposite sex in social situations (e.g., drinking, curfew violation, smoking marijuana) or are committed in a context—the school—where boys and girls have the same opportunity to commit them (e.g., cutting class, cheating). The school can be viewed as the adolescent analogue of the labor market in the *opportunity* theory of female crime: "increased participation in the labor force provides women with more opportunities for committing certain types of crimes. As those opportunities increase, women's participation in larceny, fraud, embezzlement, and other financial and white-collar crimes should increase" (Simon, 1975:19). The delinquent behavior exhibited in these contexts (social and school) does not reflect masculinization but, rather, heterosexual sociability and equal opportunity to commit delinquent acts.

Where girls are *more involved* than boys, the offenses are not "typically masculine" but,

again, are related to sex-shared social situations (curfew violation), the school (cheating, cutting class, cutting school), or they are the "typically feminine" property crimes (shoplifting, stealing money).[17] Shoplifting is role expressive and supportive delinquent behavior, as is stealing money. Shoplifting is the illegitimate adolescent female analogue of the "consumption" role of the adult middle class female (almost 80 percent of the mothers of the subjects occupy the consumer role of houseworker). It expresses this female consumption role and supports the feminine role in that the goods taken are usually clothes, cosmetics, and other items which are used in role maintenance (cf. Grosser, 1953; Cameron, 1964). The money is usually stolen from parents in small amounts and is used to consume those commodities which are perceived as necessary to the enhancement of a particular identity among adolescent peers, including boys and girls.

The girls are *least involved* in the "typically masculine" offenses included in the *Aggression* factor: individual fighting, group fighting, individual fighting with weapons, and group fighting with weapons. The boys are not particularly violent, but the girls are virtually nonviolent. If "liberation" is operative, one would expect *some* significant violent behavior among girls. Instead they behave in keeping with the cultural expectations of the nonviolent female.

These conclusions from the self-report data support the sex-role-determined opportunity theory, but they are not conclusive because they are synchronic. A diachronic analysis is essential to a more rigorous examination of the relationship between the *process* of "liberation" and changes in delinquent behavior over time. Self-report studies of delinquent behavior which span the period from 1960-1971, the decade during which one should expect intensive and pervasive "liberation," masculinization, and role reversal, particularly among middle class

---

[17] Eighth grade girls "deface walls" very slightly more often (2.36 to 2.18) than eighth grade boys. But it is also age-specific; eleventh graders rarely participate (.95; .58).

women and girls (cf. Adler, 1975; Simon, 1975; Hoffman-Bustamante, 1973) provide the basis for a crude examination of this relationship.

A comparison of self-report studies of delinquent behavior conducted around *1960* (Clark and Huarek, 1966), *1964* (Wise, 1967), *1968* (Hindelang, 1971) and *1971* (Weis, 1973), shows that the mean sex ratios across all delinquent acts and for theft and aggression items have not changed in the direction predicted by the "liberation" theories for this time period. The sex ratios across *all* offenses[18] are relatively stable from 1960–1971 (2.71,[19] 2.00,[20] 2.56, and 2.55), contrary to the expectation that they would get smaller during the period of supposedly intense "masculinization." If one looks at *theft*, where arrest statistics do show increases for females during this period, the radio has *increased* (1.40, 2.00, 3.09, and 2.88)[21]—the opposite from what one would predict from role reversal or role convergence theories. The *aggression* ratios show little change from 1964 to 1968 and substantial change from 1968 to 1971 (3.41, 3.34, and 8.00),[22] but, again, in the direction opposite to that predicted from the "liberation" theories. The data suggest that boys became more violent and/or girls became less violent during this period. The findings of these four self-report studies corroborate the longitudinal analyses of UCR arrest data for

---

[18] The number of items in each study: Clark and Huarek = 38; Wise = 35; Hindelang = 24; Weis = 34.

[19] This is the sex ratio for the middle class suburban community ("upper urban") in the Clark and Huarek (1966) study. The mean ratio for all four communities (upper urban, rural farm, lower urban, industrial city) in the study is 2.31.

[20] This ratio is computed from Table 2, Wise (1967:186).

[21] All of these ratios are for compilations of theft items. The first consists of theft items which are not all specified by Clark and Huarek; the second consists of thefts of things of little, medium, and large value; the third consists of thefts of items worth less than ten dollars and more than ten dollars; the fourth consists of thefts of items worth less than two dollars, between two and fifty dollars, and more than fifty dollars.

[22] No sex differences are given by Clark and Huarek (1966), nor by Clark and Wenninger (1962), for acts of aggression. All of the ratios given are for a compilation of individual and group fighting.

females (Hoffman-Bustamante, 1973; Simon, 1975).

CONCLUSION

Both official arrest statistics and self-reports of delinquent behavior show that the "new female criminal" is more a social invention than an empirical reality and that the proposed relationship between the women's movement and crime is, indeed, vacuous. Women are no more violent today than a decade ago and the increase in property offenses suggest that the sexism which still pervades the straight world also functions in the illegal marketplace. For example, increases in larceny, embezzlement, and fraud reflect sex-determined opportunities to commit these kinds of crimes—both now and before women's "liberation" became a viable social movement. The proposed relationship between "liberation" and crime now seems more absurd than at face; after all, the women's movement is dedicated to stopping and preventing the kinds of exploitation and victimization which comprise many criminal, as well as noncriminal, activities and relationships. Thus, the sexism model fares better than "liberation" theory in light of the data, but the evidence and conclusions cannot be considered conclusive because first, there are other plausible explanations of the observed changes in patterns of female crime which are beyond the scope of the three sex-role theories of female criminal behavior examined in this paper, and second, the differential involvement in crime of the sex-role emancipated (i.e., the "liberated") and the sex-role constrained (i.e., the oppressed) has not been examined by "liberation" theorists nor herein.

Other plausible explanations include the possiblity that the increase in certain categories of property offenses reflects a depressed economy and concomitant widespread unemployment, particularly among women who are entering or returning to the job market or who may have greater demands placed upon them than in the past to support their households.

Or the increase may be related to the changed material conditions of consumption over the past two decades. The ever-increasing reliance on self-service marketing and credit purchasing, especially the proliferation of credit cards, makes larceny, forgery, and fraud more possible and probable among those who are the primary consumers.

To test rigorously the competing theoretical positions, one must also focus on the conclusion of the syllogism upon which "liberation" theory is based. *Are "liberated" women more criminal than those who are not "liberated?"* This simple examination of relative criminal involvement has not been done, even within the context of the theories examined in this paper which imply narrow, liberal definitions of "liberation" to mean breaking sex-role shackles. There is anecdotal information which indicates that female criminals are more oppressed than noncriminals and that the benefactors of the women's movement are typically white, middle class, and conformists, but one cannot specify the relationship between the women's movement and crime. If one takes a broader, more radical view of what "liberation" means, one is faced with the possibility that its achievement is impossible within our political economy. This means that theories other than the current sex-role theories are needed to account for whatever changes have occurred in patterns of crime among women. Until these theories are formulated and appropriate empirical relationships are elaborated, the final burial of the assertion that there is a positive relationship between "liberation" and crime may be delayed. For now, though, it can be put to rest on a syllogistic fallacy.

REFERENCES

Adler, Freda (1975). *Sisters in Crime: The Rise of the New Female Criminal.* New York: McGraw-Hill.

Cameron, Mary Owen (1964). *The Booster and the Snitch.* New York: The Free Press.

Carter, Robert M. (1968). Middle Class Delinquency: An Experiment in Community Control. Report to the President's Committee on Juvenile Delinquency and Youth Development. School of Criminology: University of California, Berkeley.

Chesney-Lind, Meda (1973). "Judicial Enforcement of the Female Sex Role: The Family Court and the Female Delinquent." *Issues in Criminology* 8, 2:51–69.

Clark, John P., and Edward W. Huarek (1966). "Age and Sex Roles of Adolescents and Their Involvement in Misconduct: A Reappraisal." *Sociology and Social Research* **50**, 4:495–508.

Cloward, Richard A., and Lloyd E. Ohlin (1960). *Delinquency and Opportunity: A Theory of Delinquent Gangs.* Glencoe, Illinois: Free Press.

Cohen, Albert (1955). *Delinquent Boys: The Culture of the Gang.* Glencoe, Illinois: Free Press.

———(1957). "Middle-Class Delinquency and the Social Structure." Paper delivered at the American Sociological Association Annual Meeting, August. Pp. 203–207 in Edmund W. Vaz (ed.), *Middle-Class Juvenile Delinquency.* New York: Harper & Row, 1967.

Cowie, John, Valerie Cowie, and Eliot Slater (1968). *Delinquency in Girls.* London: Heinemann Publishers.

Davis, Kingsley (1961). "Prostitution." Robert K. Merton and Robert A. Nisbet (eds.), *Contemporary Social Problems.* New York: Harcourt, Brace, Jovanovich.

Dentler, Robert A., and Lawrence J. Monroe (1961). "Social Correlates of Early Adolescent Theft." *American Sociological Review* **26** (October):733–743.

Dunphy, Dexter C. (1969). *Cliques, Crowds and Gangs: Group Life of Sydney Adolescents.* Melbourne, Australia: F. W. Cheshire.

Freud, Sigmund (1905/1938). *Basic Writings of Sigmund Freud.* A. A. Brill (ed.), New York: Modern Library.

———(1931/1950). *Female Sexuality.* London: Hogarth.

———(1933) *New Introductory Lectures on Psychoanalysis.* New York: Norton.

Glueck, Eleanor and Sheldon Glueck (1934). *Four Hundred Delinquent Women.* New York: Alfred A. Knopf.

Gold, Martin (1970). *Delinquent Behavior in an American City.* Belmont, California: Wadsworth.

Grosser, George (1952). Juvenile Delinquency and Contemporary American Sex Roles. Unpublished doctoral dissertation. Harvard University.

Healy, William and Augusta Bronner (1962). *Delinquents and Criminals: Their Making and Unmaking.* New York: Macmillan.

Hindelang, Michael J. (1971). "Age, Sex, and the Versatility of Delinquent Involvements." *Social Problems* **18,** 4 (Spring): 522–535.

Hindelang, Michael J. and Joseph G. Weis (1972). "Personality and Self-Reported Delinquency: An Application of Cluster Analysis." *Criminology* **10,** 3 (November):268–294.

Hoffman-Bustamante, Dale (1973). "The Nature of Female Criminality." *Issues in Criminology* **8,** 2:117–136.

Klein, Dorie (1973). "The Etiology of Female Crime: A Review of the Literature." *Issues in Criminology* **8,** 2:3–30.

Klein, Dorie, and June Kress (1976). "Any Woman's Blues: A Critical Overview of Women, Crime and the Criminal Justice System." *Crime and Social Justice* **5:**34–49.

Konopka, Gisela (1966). *The Adolescent Girl in Conflict.* Englewood Cliffs, N.J.: Prentice-Hall.

Lemert, Edwin (1971). *Human Deviance, Social Control.* Englewood Cliffs, N.J.: Prentice-Hall.

Lombroso, Cesare (1899/1920). *The Female Offender.* New York: Appleton.

Miller, Walter B. (1958). "Lower Class Culture as a Generating Milieu of Gang Delinquency." *Journal of Social Issues* **14**(3):5–19.

Millett, Kate (1970). *Sexual Politics.* New York: Doubleday.

Murphy, Fred, M. M. Shirley, and Helen L. Witmer (1946). "The Incidence of Hidden Delinquency." *American Journal of Orthopsychiatry* **16** (October):686–696.

Nagel, Stuart S. and Lenore T. Weitzman (1972). "Double Standard of American Justice." *Society* **19** (5):18–25

Nye, F. Ivan, James F. Short, Jr., and Virgil J. Olson (1958). "Socio-Economic Status in Delinquent Behavior." *American Journal of Sociology* **63** (January):381–389.

Payak, Bertha (1963). "Understanding the Female Offender." *Federal Probation* **27:**13–21.

Pollak, Otto (1950). *The Criminality of Women.* Philadelphia: University of Pennsylvania Press.

Porterfield, Austin (1946). *Youth in Trouble.* Fort Worth, Texas: Leo Potishman Foundation

Reckless, Walter C., and Barbara A. Kay (1967). The Female Offender. President's Commission on Law Enforcement and Administration of Justice. Washington, D.C.: U.S. Government Printing Office.

Rogers, Kristine Olson (1972). "For Her Own Protection: Conditions of Incarceration for Female Juvenile Offenders in the State of Connecticut." *Law and Society Review* (Winter):223–246.

Short, James F., Jr., and F. Ivan Nye (1957). "Reported Behavior as a Criterion of Deviant Behavior." *Social Problems* **5** (Winter):207–213.

———(1958). "Extent of Unrecorded Juvenile Delinquency: Tentative Conclusions." Journal of Criminal Law, Criminology, and Police Science **49,** 4 (December):296-302.

Simon, Rita James (1957). *Women and Crime.* Lexington, Massachusetts: Lexington Books.

Singer, Linda R. (1973). "Women and the Correctional Process." *American Criminal Law Review* **11,** 2:295–308.

Spaulding, Edith (1923). *An Experimental Study of Psychopathic Delinquent Women.* New York: Rand-McNally.

Thomas, W.I. (1923). *The Unadjusted Girl.* New York: Harper & Row.

Tyron, Robert C. (1966). "Unrestricted Cluster and Factor Analysis, with Applications to the MMPI and Holzinger-Harman Problems." *Multivariate Behavioral Research* **1** (April): 229–244.

———(1967). User's Manual of the BC TRY System. (Mimeo) Berkeley: Department of Psychology.

Tyron, Robert C., and Daniel E. Bailey (1966). "The BC TRY Computer System of Cluster and Factor Analysis." *Multivariate Behavioral Research* **1** (January): 95–111.

———(1970). *Cluster Analysis.* New York: McGraw-Hill.

Vaz, Edmund W. (1965). "Middle-Class Adolescents: Self-Reported Delinquency and Youth Culture Activities." *Canadian Review of Sociology and Anthropology* 2, **1** (February):52–70.

Vaz, Edmund W. (ed.) (1967). *Middle-Class Juvenile Delinquency.* New York: Harper & Row.

Vedder, Clyde B., and Dora B. Somerville (1970). *The Delinquent Girl.* Springfield, Illinois: Charles C. Thomas.

Weis, Joseph G. (1973). Delinquency Among the Well to Do. Unpublished doctoral dissertation, University of California, Berkeley.

Wise, Nancy B. (1967). "Juvenile Delinquency among Middle-Class Girls," in Edmund W. Vaz (ed.), *Middle-Class Juvenile Delinquency*, pp. 179–188. New York: Harper & Row.

15

RACE AND CRIME

MICHAEL J. HINDELANG

INTRODUCTION

One of the most important theoretical questions facing criminology is whether, and to what extent, race is related to involvement in common law personal crimes.[1] Perhaps because of the sensitivity of this question, assertions and speculations about this relationship have outdistanced the research attention focused on it. Despite the limited research on the relationship between race and common law personal crime, this relationship is central to many contemporary criminological theories, and therefore it deserves the empirical attention that must be given to any important theoretical question.

Most sociological theories of crime agree that blacks are disproportionately arrested for common law personal crimes but disagree about the extent to which *arrest* data are indicative of disproportionate offending behavior vs. criminal justice system selection biases. Although most sociological theories of crime can accommodate a race-crime relation in arrest data, it is possible to conceive of these theories as falling along a continuum in terms of the proportion of variation in racial differences in rates of arrest that is attributed to differential *involvement* in common law crimes vs. differential *processing* by the agents of the criminal justice system. For purposes of discussion, "low" on the continuum will refer to theories which attribute very little of the variation in racial differences in rates of arrest to differences in the involvement of blacks and whites in common law crimes. "High" on the continuum will refer to theories which attribute much of the variation to actual behavioral differences between blacks and whites.[2]

Theories which fall at the higher end of the continuum suggest that concomitants of race, such as cultural or economic factors, are etiologically related to involvement in criminal activity. Characteristic of theories in this range on the continuum is Wolfgang and Ferracuti's (1967) subculture-of-violence thesis. In the *Subculture of Violence*, the authors observe:

> Statistics on homocide and other assaultive crimes in the United States consistently show that Negroes have rates between four and ten times higher than whites. Aside from a critique of of-

Source: "Race and Involvement in Common Law Personal Crimes," *American Sociological Review* (February 1978), **43**:93–109. Reprinted by permission.

* Special gratitude is due to Michael R. Gottfredson who offered critical comments on several drafts of this paper.

[1] Included among the common law crimes are murder, rape, robbery, assault, burglary, larceny, and arson; the first four of these are designated personal common law crimes in this discussion. See Blackstone (1778) and Clark and Marshall (1967).

[2] In a paper on minorities as victims of police shootings, Goldkamp (1977) has presented a dichotomous characterization of labeling theories vs. theories that predict greater involvement of blacks in violent crimes.

ficial statistics that raises serious questions about the amount of Negro crime, there is no real evidence to deny the greater involvement that Negroes have in assaultive crimes. . . . There is reason to agree . . . that whatever may be the learned responses and social conditions contributing to criminality, persons visibly identified and socially labeled as Negroes in the United States appear to possess them in considerably higher proportions than do persons labeled white. Our subculture-of-violence thesis would, therefore, expect to find . . . [widespread] learning of, resort to, and criminal display of the violence value among minority groups such as Negroes (1967:264).

Thus, although Wolfgang and Ferracuti (1967) acknowledge the difficulties in using official police statistics to investigate the relationship between race and crime, they nonetheless conclude that blacks are disproportionately *involved* in assaultive crimes. More generally, the theories of Merton (1938) and Cloward and Ohlin (1960), because of their emphasis on structural impediments to the achievement of success goals via legitimate avenues, are also consistent with the hypothesis that blacks will have rates of involvement in common law criminal activity which exceed those of whites.

Theories which fall toward the middle of the continuum include those commonly referred to as conflict theories. These theories suggest that laws are enacted to protect the interests of the more powerful segments of society, and hence many of the activities that are criminalized are activities in which less powerful persons (blacks, the poor, the young, etc.) are disproportionately involved. Although such theories generally imply or state that blacks and other less powerful members of society will be disproportionately *involved* in common law criminal activity, these theories strongly emphasize that the overrepresentation of blacks in arrest statistics is considerably influenced by enforcement practices that discriminate against the less powerful.

Within the conflict group, it is perhaps Bonger (1916; 1943) who places highest on this continuum. In *Criminality and Economic Conditions*,

Bonger (1916:379) suggested that in "every society which is divided into a ruling class and a class ruled, penal law has been principally constituted according to the will of the former." Under capitalism, individuals are encouraged to use any means available, including criminal activity, to obtain material goods. Furthermore, the widespread poverty that abounds under capitalism "kills the social sentiment in man, destroys in fact all relations among men" and fosters criminality (1916:436). After having studied prison statistics in the United States, he concluded that:

> Crime among Negroes is significantly higher than among whites. It is three or four times higher among the men, and four or five times higher among the women. To me this appears to eliminate the idea that actual criminality among Negroes is no greater than among whites. (1943:43)

It was Bonger's (1943) view that the higher rate of crime among blacks was attributable to the unfavorable economic circumstances in which blacks were disproportionately found.

Because of a greater emphasis on differential enforcement, other conflict theorists place lower on the continuum than does Bonger. Quinney (1970:129–30), for example, notes that "the differences in arrest rates are not, however, due entirely to the fact that Negroes may be involved more than whites in law-violating behavior, but that in similar situations Negroes are more likely than whites to be apprehended." Chambliss (1969:856) and Chambliss and Seidman (1971) emphasize that the "administration of the criminal law is a highly selective process and involves the use of a wide range of discretion" that results in "systematic bias in law enforcement." Although most of their discussion of such biases is couched in terms of lower-class persons, many of their examples are of discrimination against blacks. They observe that such persons are "more likely to be scrutinized and therefore to be observed in any violation of the law and more likely to be arrested if discovered under suspicious circumstances" (Chambliss, 1969:86; see also Chambliss and Seidman, 1971:322–46). In general, the conflict theorists are careful not to deny that personal characteristics such as race are related to involvement in criminal behavior but tend instead to focus on power-related differentials in enforcement which introduce an unspecified proportion of contamination into arrest statistics.

At the lowest point on the continuum, those who subscribe to the labeling perspective in its most extreme form are found. Those at this pole argue that there are no demographic, sociological, or psychological correlates of involvement in criminal behavior but rather that any differences in arrest rates along social, demographic, or other dimensions are attributable to biases in official processing. Characteristic of this position is the thesis presented by Chapman (1968:4) in *Sociology and the Stereotype of the Criminal*:

> . . . 3. That apart from the factor of conviction there are no differences between criminals and non-criminals.
> 4. That criminal behavior is general, but the incidence of conviction is controlled in part by chance and in part by social processes which divide society into the criminal and non-criminal classes, the former corresponding to, roughly, the poor and under-privileged.

Lemert (1967:24), in his discussion of "the new deviance sociology"—Lemert (1951), Tannenbaum (1938), Kitsuse (1964), Goffman (1961), Erikson (1962), Becker (1963)—notes,

> In extreme statements deviance is portrayed as little more than the result of arbitrary, fortuitous, or biased decision-making, to be understood as a sociopsychological process by which groups seek to create conditions for perpetuating established values and ways of behaving or enhancing the power of special groups.

Lemert's exception to this extreme position places him more toward the middle of our continuum, in light of his observation that "striving to validate a conception of deviance as pri-

marily a definitional phenomenon overlooks the way in which the societal reaction varies with *objective differences in behavior, its context, and its consequences*" (1967:21, emphasis added).

This brief review of contemporary sociological theories relevant to the question of the relationship between race and crime demonstrates that although all of these theories can accommodate higher arrest rates for blacks than whites, they differ substantially in the extent to which such racial differences are attributable to objective differences in behavior. Because each of these positions claims support from research findings, it is necessary to turn our attention to that body of research.

PRIOR RESEARCH

OFFICIAL DATA

Among the sources of official data on race and crime, the Federal Bureau of Investigation's *Uniform Crime Reports* (UCR) is the most extensive. In the UCR, characteristic of arrestees, including race, are published for the United States in the aggregate. These data for 1975 show that in relation to their representation in the general population (about 11%), blacks were substantially overrepresented among arrestees for murder and nonnegligent homicide (54%), forcible rape (45%), robbery (59%), aggravated assault (40%), burglary (28%), larceny and theft (31%), and motor vehicle theft (26%). For all of the remaining (Part II) offenses, blacks constituted 22% of the arrests (Kelley, 1976).

Police data were used by Mulvihill et al. (1969) to investigate the relationship between race and crime in a study published under the auspices of the President's Commission on the Causes and Prevention of Violence. Data were gathered on a probability basis from offense and arrest reports in police files in 17 large cities covering all regions of the United States. The authors report that the race of the offender was black in 72% of the criminal homicides, in 74% of the aggravated assaults, in 70% of the forcible rapes, in 85% of the armed robberies, and in 81% of the unarmed robberies (Mulvihill et al., 1969:271–83).

Wolfgang et al. (1972:Table 5.3) in their *Delinquency in a Birth Cohort* use as their criterion recorded police contacts of their cohort when the subjects were 7 through 17 years old. For the offenses of homicide, rape, robbery, and aggravated assault, the number of contacts per 1,000 cohort subjects was 139.9 for nonwhites and 9.2 for whites. For the remaining offenses (burglary, larceny, and auto theft), the number of contacts per 1,000 cohort subjects, was 476.6 for the nonwhites and 124.0 for the whites.

These official data from the UCR, the Violence Commission study, and the Wolfgang et al. (1972) cohort study are typical of comparisons of the offending of whites and blacks as measured by a variety of official data (arrest data, victim reports to the police, and police contacts). Theorists at the higher end of the continuum use such data as evidence of disproportionate involvement by blacks in the common law crimes. Theorists at the lower end of the continuum, by definition, argue that such official data are reflective of differential selection patterns, and hence they rely heavily on research data that are generated independently of the criminal justice system to support their arguments—typically data on self-reported involvement in illegal activities. To date, such studies have focused almost exclusively on juveniles.

SELF-REPORT MEASURES

Relatively few self-report studies have compared the extent and nature of delinquency among whites and blacks. Three of the earliest research efforts to do so were those of Chambliss and Nagasawa (1969), Gould (1969), and Hirschi (1969). In the Chambliss and Nagasawa (1969:73) study, lower-class white, black, and Japanese high school boys responded to self-reported delinquency questionnaires; in addition, juvenile court records were canvassed to ascertain the official delinquency status of the respondents. Despite the finding that

blacks had an official delinquency rate that was substantially higher than that of whites, when self-reported delinquency was used as the criterion, whites were found to have a slightly higher rate than blacks. Similarly, Gould (1969:330) studied junior high school boys in Seattle and found that although race (white vs. nonwhite) was moderately related to official delinquency in the usual direction (theta = .46), race was virtually unrelated (theta = .07) to self-reported delinquency on equivalent offenses.

In his study of more than 800 black and 1,300 white boys in California high schools, Hirschi (1969:Table 14) found that the former were more likely than the latter (42% vs. 18%) to have police records. When self-reported delinquency was used as the criterion, however, 49% of the blacks and 44% of the whites reported one or more delinquent acts. Once again, the racial differences for official delinquency were found to be much greater than for self-reported delinquency.

In two national studies, Gold and his colleagues (Williams and Gold, 1972; Gold and Reimer, 1975) made sex-specific comparisons of the self-reported delinquent behavior of black and white respondents. In the first study, a national probability sample of 736 white and 101 black respondents, 13 to 16 years old, was interviewed in 1967; in the second study, a national probability sample of 481 white and 67 black respondents, 13 to 16 years old, was interviewed in 1972. For both years and sex groups, whites and blacks reported involvement in 17 delinquent behaviors with similar *frequencies*. When the *seriousness* of eight items amenable to the Sellin-Wolfgang (1964) seriousness scoring procedure were tallied, the seriousness-weighted rate of self-reported delinquency was slightly greater for black males than for white males for both years.[3]

---

[3] For the 1967 results, Williams and Gold (1972:215) report Mann-Whitney U-test p-levels for racial comparisons on seriousness of .49 and .06 for females and males, respectively. For the 1972 results (Gold and Reimer, 1975: Tables 3 and 4) comparable U-tests are not reported. How-

The research findings on racial differences in offending behavior can be summarized succinctly: studies using official measures of criminal and delinquent behavior (e.g., arrests) have repeatedly found that blacks have markedly higher rates of arrest than do whites. However, studies using self-report measures of illegal behavior (almost exclusively illegal behavior of juveniles) have found that blacks and whites report only minimal differences on self-report inventories. This discrepancy between the self-report results and the official results requires some explanation and ultimate resolution, especially in light of the theoretical controversy. Thus, it is essential that a third source of data be brought to bear on this question.

THE PRESENT STUDY

VICTIMIZATION SURVEYS

Victimization surveys, in which representative samples from the general population are asked to report on victimizations they may have suffered during a specific reference period, provide data on the relationship between race and common law crime that are independent of criminal justice system selection biases. In these surveys respondents are asked to tell interviewers about victimizations, regardless of whether or not they reported them to the police.

The data used here derive from a national survey of victims of crimes, undertaken by the U.S. Bureau of the Census under the sponsorship of the U.S. Department of Justice, com-

monly referred to as the National Crime Panel (NCP).[4]

There are two parts of the NCP—a national probability sample of households (and individuals) and a national probability sample of businesses. In a period of six months, six independent probability samples of households and businesses are interviewed (see LEAA, 1976 for a fuller description of sampling techniques). For purposes of estimating victimizations occurring during 1974 (the data to be used here), a total of approximately 80,000 housing units and other living quarters as well as approximately 17,000 businesses were selected for the sample (Law Enforcement Assistance Administration [LEAA], 1976:45).

From the 80,000 housing units selected to make victimization estimates for 1974, interviews were completed in about 65,000. The majority of the 15,000 housing units in which interviews were not obtained were found to be vacant, demolished, converted to nonresidential use, or otherwise ineligible to be sampled (LEAA, 1976:46). Overall, "interviews were obtained in about 96% of all eligible housing units, and about 99% of the occupants of these households participated in the survey" (LEAA, 1976:46).

In the survey of households there are three types of respondents: household respondents, self-respondents, and proxy respondents. The household respondent, usually the head of household, answers such questions as whether the residence is owned or rented and what is the family income. In addition, the household respondent answers questions about victimizations affecting the entire household, such as burglary and vehicle theft.

Self-respondents are all household respondents 14 years of age or older. In addition to background information (e.g., age, sex, and

ever, because the mean racial difference in seriousness rates for females is smaller in 1972 than in 1967 and the mean racial difference in seriousness rates for males is larger in 1972 than in 1967, we infer (in light of the 1967 U-test results) that in 1972 the racial difference for males is probably significant beyond the .06 level and the racial difference for females probably has a p-level of greater than .49. This inference depends, of course, on the assumption that the standard errors in seriousness rates are comparable across years. See Gold (1970:79) in which black-white differences in the seriousness and frequency of self-reported delinquency are not significant when SES is controlled.

[4] A good deal of developmental work in the area of surveying victims of crime was undertaken by the U.S. Bureau of the Census and others prior to the implementation of the National Crime Panel. For the sake of brevity, this research will not be reviewed here, but the interested reader is referred to Hindelang (1976: Chaps. 2 and 3) for a summary of this research.

education), each of these household members is asked a series of "screen" questions designed to elicit whether or not the person has been the victim of a crime of rape, robbery, assault, or personal larceny during the preceeding six months. After all screen questions have been asked, a series of detailed incident questions is asked about each victimization uncovered in the screen questions. Proxy respondents are used to elicit the same information about household members 12 and 13 years old and for individuals who are physically or mentally unable to answer for themselves. Thus, the estimates derived in the household portion of the survey are national estimates for those 12 years of age or older.[5]

In the commercial portion of the survey, the owner, manager, or someone knowledgeable about the affairs of the business is interviewed about robbery and burglary victimizations occurring during the reference period. As in the household portion of the survey, the screen method is used to elicit victimizations and is followed by a detailed incident report. Businesses eligible for interviews, but in which interviews were not completed, amounted to fewer than 1% of those eligible (LEAA, 1976:60).

[5] Some personal victimizations are classified as series victimizations and an incident report is completed only for the last crime in a series of crimes. To be counted as a series victimization *all* of the following criteria must be met:
  (a) the respondent must be unable to recall the details of the victimizations in the series well enough to report on the circumstances of each victimization separately;
  (b) the victimizations must be of a similar type; and
  (c) there must be at least three victimizations to constitute a series.
Series victimizations are tabulated separately from nonseries victimizations and tend disproportionately to be either assaults, more likely simple than aggravated, or household larcenies under $50 (LEAA, 1976:51). I have excluded series victimizations from the analyses for two reasons: (1) because detailed information, such as the perceived race of the offender is collected only for the last crime in a series, details of series crimes are not known; and (2) because the respondent may not have reported accurately on the time of occurrence, it is less certain that these events fall within the reference period. In 1973, about 5% of the personal victimizations reported to interviewers were classified as series victimizations. See Hindelang (1976: App. F) for a discussion of some of the problems inherent in the use of series data.

The data derived from the interviews are then weighted to give estimates for the nation (see LEAA, 1976: App. 1 and 2 for a detailed discussion of the weighting procedures and standard errors). The estimates used here are for incidents rather than victimizations. In the former, one incident is counted for each event uncovered during the survey regardless of the number of victims involved in the crime, whereas in the latter, one victimization is counted for each person victimized during an event. The incident weight assigned to each sample case is adjusted in those cases in which an event involved more than one victim because such cases would have more than a single chance of being included in the sample (LEAA, 1976:49–50). The mean incident weight for the crimes studied here (rape, robbery, aggravated assault, and simple assault) in the household portion of the survey is about 1,023.

Because the UCR arrest data include business robbery arrestees in tables on the race of offenders, it was necessary also to include business robberies in the NCP data. This was accomplished by combining the results on the race of offender in business incidents from the 1974 NCP with those for personal robberies.

RESULTS

In the course of the interview, respondents who had been confronted by offenders were asked a series of questions about the offender(s), including the number of offenders involved and the sex, race, and estimated age of the offender. The data presented here have been tabulated according to the responses to these questions. Before proceeding to the findings, it is necessary to discuss briefly how they were generated.

Each incident reported to survey interviewers was weighted by the number of offenders that the victim reported was involved in the incident.[6] Incidents in which the number of

[6] As noted above, each incident had a weight that was inversely proportional to the probability of appearing in the sample. It was actually this incident weight that was weighted by the number of offenders that the victim reported having been involved in the incident.

offenders was unknown or not ascertained or in which there was a group of offenders of mixed races (i.e., in which some were white and some were black or of other races) were excluded from analysis. It was necessary to exclude incidents in which the number of offenders was unknown because in such cases the victim was not asked the race of the offender(s). It was necessary to exclude incidents involving multiple offenders of mixed races because victims were not asked how many offenders were from each racial group. Of the total estimated number (8,130,059) of incidents of robbery, rape, and assault elicited by the survey for the 1974 calendar year, 3% or 210,824 were excluded from the analysis because they met at least one of the exclusionary conditions noted above.

The analyses presented here are limited to robbery, rape, and assault because it is in victimizations of these types that the victim is confronted by the offender and hence is able to report on the offender's characteristics. In the crimes of burglary, household larceny, and vehicle theft, the victim usually does not see the offender during the commission of the crime and therefore cannot report on the offender's personal characteristics.

The UCR annually publishes data on the racial characteristics of arrestees. It is possible to compare the racial characteristics of offenders as reported by victims in the 1974 national sample of the National Crime Panel to the racial characteristics of arrestees as reported in the 1974 UCR. If there are substantial biases in the UCR data for *any* reason, we would expect, to the extent that victimization survey reports are unbiased, to find large discrepancies between the UCR arrest data and victimization survey reports on racial characteristics of offenders. Specifically, the theories at the lowest point of the continuum predict a very substantial overrepresentation of blacks in the population of UCR arrestees, whereas theories at the highest point of the continuum predict a very small overrepresentation of blacks in arrest statistics

when compared with victimization survey reports.[7] Furthermore, the former theories (low on continuum) would predict a small overrepresentation of black offenders in victimization survey reports relative to the representation of blacks in the general population, whereas the latter (high on continuum) would predict a very substantial overrepresentation. The victimization survey reports are thus an independent measure of the involvement of whites and blacks in rape, robbery, and assault—a measure that cannot be affected by the kind of contamination with which theorists falling at the lower end of the continuum contend police data are rife.[8]

The UCR victimization comparison for 1974 are presented in Table 1. Both sources follow the U.S. Bureau of the Census convention of counting Spanish-Americans as white; "other races" include American Indian, Chinese, and Japanese. As expected, for each of the offenses shown, the ratio of offenders in incidents reported by victims in the survey to the number of UCR arrestees is large. This results primarily from three factors: first, the victimization survey data include many crimes that have not been reported to the police; second, even for reported crimes, the clearance rates for these offenses are small;[9] third, the UCR data on race of arrestees in 1974 were based on reports of police agencies covering an estimated population of 124 million persons rather than on the entire population (211 million), whereas the victimization survey results are estimates of victimization experiences of the entire U.S. population 12 years of age or older.

For convenience, the discussion will focus on the results for blacks. Table I shows that

[7] It should be noted here that this comparison will be sensitive not only to biases on the part of police but also to such potential biases as would be introduced if white victims were more likely to notify the police when victimized by black offenders.

[8] Some of the limitations of victim survey data are discussed later.

[9] In 1974, 51% of the forcible rapes, 63% of the aggravated assaults, and 27% of the robberies were cleared by arrest (Kelley, 1975:43).

TABLE 1 National Comparisons between Uniform Crime Reports (UCR) and National Crime Panel (NCP) Estimates[a] for Race of Arrestees and Offenders, 1974

		White	Black	Other	Total
Rape	NCP	60%	39%	1%	
		(125.890)	(82,873)	(1,847)	210,609
	UCR	49%	48%	3%	
		(7,665)	(7,482)	(453)	15,600
Robbery	NCP	34%	62%	4%	
		(797,246)	(1,465,838)	(105,587)	2,368,671
	UCR	35%	62%	3%	
		(31,477)	(55,728)	(2,210)	89,415
Aggravated Assault	NCP	66%	30%	4%	
		(1,473,341)	(659,814)	(93,044)	2,226,199
	UCR	56%	41%	2%	
		(75,136)	(54,870)	(3,330)	133,336
Simple Assault	NCP	66%	29%	5%	
		(2,204,576)	(969,432)	(150,572)	3,324,580
	UCR	61%	37%	2%	
		(154,757)	(92,417)	(6,337)	253,511
Representation in General Population		88%	11%	1%	

[a] Weighted by number of offenders in incident.
Source: UCR data, Kelley (1975:191). General population data, U.S. Bureau of the Census (1975a).

the UCR and the victimization data are identical for the crimes of robbery: 62% of the victimization survey offenders and 62% of the UCR arrestees were reported to have been black. For the remaining crime categories (rape and assault), in relation to the victimization reports, blacks are overrepresented by about ten percentage points in the UCR arrest data. Thus, for the crimes of rape and assault, but not for robbery, these results are consistent with the hypothesis that a small proportion of the white/black discrepancy in arrest rates is attributable to selection bias of some sort. The nature of this selection bias and some competing hypotheses will be discussed below.

In 1974 an estimated 88% of the U.S. population was white, 11% was black, and 1% was of other races (U.S. Bureau of the Census, 1975a:26). Regardless of whether the UCR or the victimization survey data are taken as the indicator, blacks are substantially overrepresented in relation to their representation in the general population. This overrepresentation is by a factor of three or three and one-half times for assault, about four times for rape, and more than five times for robbery. In light of these data, it is difficult to argue that blacks are no more likely than whites to be *involved* in the common law crimes of robbery, forcible rape, and assault. At the same time, in UCR arrest data for assault and rape, blacks are found with a greater relative frequency than victimization survey data would predict, under the assumption that race-linked biases have not been introduced at some point in the arrest selection process.

Both the NCP and the UCR data can be dichotomized into groups of offenders (or, in the case of the UCR, arrestees) under 18 years of age and 18 years of age or older. Although not shown in tabular form, these results closely parallel those reported in Table I.[10] Thus, both among adults and juveniles, blacks are substantially overrepresented in relation to their representation in the general population regardless of whether the NCP data or the UCR data are used.

One major source of potential bias in the UCR data, one that is independent of the actions of criminal justice functionaries, is differential reporting of crimes by victims to the police. It is possible that the UCR/NCP differences, as reported in Table 1, are attributable not to discriminatory enforcement patterns but rather are attributable to victims' reporting to the police offenses committed by blacks proportionately more often than offenses committed by whites. Because research has demonstrated that offenses of these types almost exclusively come to the attention of the police through victim reporting (Reiss, 1971; Hindelang and Gottfredson, 1976), the reporting decision obviously affects arrest patterns; offenses not reported to the police almost certainly will not result in an arrest.[11]

The data in Table 2 indicate that when only those NCP victimizations which the victims told interviewers were reported to the police are considered, blacks are found to constitute 47% of the NCP rape offenders as compared with 48% of the UCR rape arrestees (Table I). For both aggravated and simple assault, on the other hand, there is a slightly greater discrepancy between the NCP and the UCR percentages when only those NCP crimes which victims said were reported to the police are considered. For instance, 26% of the offenders involved in aggravated assaults which victims said were reported to the police were black, whereas 41% of the aggravated assault arrestees were black. If we operationally define criminal justice system selection bias as the discrepancy between the proportion of blacks involved in victimizations which victims said were reported to the police and the proportion of blacks among UCR arrestees, then these data suggest that there is virtually no criminal justice system selection bias for either rape or robbery but that there is such bias for assault, especially aggravated assault. Thus, once the victim's reporting (to the police) behavior is taken into account, differences between NCP crimes reported to the police and UCR data on arrestees remain only for assault.

SOME NCP MEASUREMENT PROBLEMS

It is essential to note at this point that the crime of assault is the NCP crime which has the most measurement difficulties. In reverse record checks (U.S. Bureau of the Census, 1970a; 1970b; LEAA, 1972), checks in which victims are selected from police files and ideally interviewed on a double-blind basis by Bureau of the Census interviewers, assault has been found to be the most poorly measured offense in the sense that: (a) assault victims from police files are more difficult, for a variety of reasons, than other victims to locate and interview: (b) of those victims who are interviewed, a smaller proportion of assault victims than other victims from police files mention having been victimized when they are interviewed.

In the three reverse record check studies, assault victims selected from police files had the lowest rate of completed interviews, about three out of five. Furthermore, among those victims selected from police files with whom interviews were completed, assault victims consistently had the poorest "recall" rate, that

---

[10] For the UCR data, see Kelley (1975:192–3). Forcible rapes committed by offenders under 18 years of age are relatively rare; the number of NCP sample (unweighted) cases is very small (23 cases).

[11] In a small proportion of victimizations (about 3% of the victimizations in the NCP data), the police do come across the crime in progress. In addition, it is possible for police to discover incriminating evidence in the possession of an offender (e.g., another person's wallet) even though the victim may not have reported it to the police.

TABLE 2 Race of Offender in National Crime Panel Estimates[a] (1974) by Whether the Crime Was Reported to the Police

	White	Black	Other	Total
	Rape			
Not Reported to Police	66% [b]	33%	1%	100%
	62% [c]	48%	68%	56%
	(78,058)	(39,442)	(1,261)	(118,762)
Reported to Police	52%	47%	1%	100%
	38%	52%	32%	44%
	(47,832)	(43,431)	(585)	(91,848)
Total	60%	39%	1%	100%
	100%	100%	100%	100%
	(125,890)	(82,873)	(1,847)	(210,609)
	Robbery			
Not Reported to Police	38%	57%	5%	100%
	47%	38%	42%	41%
	(370,800)	(550,378)	(44,405)	(965,583)
Reported to Police	30%	65%	4%	100%
	53%	62%	58%	59%
	(426,445)	(915,454)	(61,182)	(1,403,081)
Total	34%	62%	4%	100%
	100%	100%	100%	100%
	(797,245)	(1,465,832)	(105,587)	(2,368,664)
	Aggravated assault			
Not Reported to Police	62%	33%	5%	100%
	43%	52%	53%	46%
	(629,837)	(341,198)	(49,123)	(1,020,158)
Reported to Police	70%	26%	4%	100%
	57%	48%	47%	54%
	(843,503)	(318,617)	(43,921)	(1,206,041)
Total	66%	30%	4%	100%
	100%	100%	100%	100%
	(1,473,341)	(659,814)	(93,044)	(2,226,199)
	Simple assault			
Not Reported to Police	65%	31%	4%	100%
	64%	69%	64%	65%
	(1,401,374)	(669,775)	(95,904)	(2,167,053)
Reported to Police	69%	26%	5%	100%
	36%	31%	36%	35%
	(803,202)	(299,657)	(54,668)	(1,157,527)
Total	66%	29%	5%	100%
	100%	100%	100%	100%
	(2,204,576)	(969,432)	(150,572)	(3,324,580)

[a] Weighted by number of offenders in incident.

[b] Row percent.

[c] Column percent.

is, the smallest proportion of known victims who reported to survey interviewers that they had been victims of the crime selected from police files. For example, in completed interviews in all three studies combined, 88% of the burglary victims, 80% of the robbery victims, and 67% of the rape victims reported the crime selected from police files to survey interviewers; however, only 47% of the assault victims did so. In addition, it was found that when the offender was known to the victim, especially when the offender was *related* to the victim, the rate of "recall" was smaller than when the offender was a stranger (LEAA, 1972). This finding is important for two reasons. First, among the crimes studied here, assault is the most likely to involve nonstrangers.[12] Second, victimization data suggest that nonstranger victimizations account for a larger proportion of black than of white victimizations.[13] For example, in the NCP data used here, 32% of the white victims and 48% of the black victims were reportedly victimized in aggravated assaults by nonstrangers.[14] If we assume that the "recall" problem for assaults in victimization surveys is comparable for nonstranger victimizations suffered by both blacks and whites, it follows that the *total* number of assaults suffered by black victims will be underestimated in victimization data more so than those suffered by whites because blacks apparently are victimized by nonstrangers in a greater proportion of the assaults than are whites. In light of this and because the victims in assaults are likely to be victimized by persons of the same race (Hindelang, 1976:184–6), we can infer that the victimization data on assault probably underestimate the proportion of black offenders.

[12] This holds generally whether victimization survey data or police data on offenses known are used. See Hindelang (1976: Table 7.16).

[13] Of course, the victim-offender relationship affects the data, because, as noted above, the "recall" rate in victimization data is related to the relationship between the victim and the offender.

[14] Nonstrangers include family members and other relatives, persons well-known to the victim, and casual acquaintances of the victim.

SUMMARY AND CONCLUSIONS

These results demonstrate that both the victimization data and the official arrest data show blacks to be substantially overrepresented, in relation to their representation in the general population, as offenders/arrestees for the common law crimes of forcible rape, robbery, and assault. Both data sources show that this disproportionality is greatest for robbery, followed by rape, aggravated assault, and simple assault. Furthermore, both sources of data show virtually the same percent figure for robbery but for the remaining three crimes the official data show a somewhat greater proportion of black offenders than do the victimization data. The discrepancy for rape is accounted for by the finding that rapes involving black offenders are more likely to be reported to the police than are rapes involving white offenders. When only those rape victimizations that are reported to the police are examined, there is virtually no difference between the two sources. Parenthetically, it should be noted that the UCR/victimization survey similarity for robbery maintains when only victimizations reported to the police are studied. For both aggravated and simple assault, however, the NCP/UCR discrepancy is slightly greater when only victimizations reported to the police are examined. For the reasons noted above, the NCP data on assault must be viewed with less confidence than the NCP data for robbery and rape.

In general, the results on the disproportionate involvement of blacks in rape, robbery, and assault as shown in these nationwide victimization data are much more congruent with studies that have used police data than with studies that have used self-reports of offenders. This is true even when the data for offenders reported by victims to be under 18 years of age, the age group most often studied in self-report research, are examined separately.

There are several reasons why the self-report studies discussed earlier may be incompatible with the NCP and UCR data.[15] First, with the exception of Gould's (1969) study, these self-report studies did not examine official and self-reported offenses of comparable seriousness; the self-report studies are weighted toward the least serious offenses. Second, with the exception of the Gold (1970; Gold and Reimer, 1975; Williams and Gold, 1972) studies, the self-report studies drew samples from in-school populations; the higher dropout rates for blacks than for whites means that this sampling approach results in a race-linked sampling bias. Third, the Gold studies, which increasingly are the studies most often cited by those arguing that black/white differences are minimal, had numbers of blacks that are certainly too small for reliable conclusions in a national survey (1967: 53 black males, 48 black females; 1972: 33 black males, 34 black females), especially in light of the relative rarity of all but the most trivial illegal behaviors.[16]

These findings may indicate that at its current level of methodological development, the self-report technique is simply inadequate for assessing racial differences in rates of involvement in serious offenses. Even if the self-report technique itself were well developed from a methodological point of view, it would be necessary to use sample sizes much larger than those used in self-report studies to date in order to estimate reliably correlates of involvement in serious offenses.

Earlier, I discussed a continuum along which selected criminological theories fall in terms of the proportion of variation in arrest statistics which they attribute to involvement in criminal

activity. It was noted that because all of these theories can accommodate the higher black arrest rate for common law personal crimes, it is necessary empirically to disentangle involvement in these crimes from selection biases in criminal justice processing. To the extent that a small percentage of the racial disproportionality in arrest rates is attributable to racial disproportionality in offending behavior, theories at the lower end of the continuum (e.g., labeling) are supported and theories at the higher end of the continuum (e.g., subculture of violence) are not. If the victimization data as reported in Table 1 are taken as a measure of involvement in rape, robbery, and assault and the UCR arrest data are taken as a measure of involvement in these crimes *plus* selection biases,[17] then the discrepancy between the two data sources can be taken as a measure of selection bias. The ratio of the percentage of black offenders in the NCP data to the percentage of black arrestees in the UCR data is an index of the proportion of the arrest percentage that can be attributed to criminal involvement; the complement can be attributed to selection bias. For robbery this ratio

---

[15] In the course of discussing theoretical perspectives above, some of the shortcomings of official data were suggested by the theorists. For critiques of police data see Doleschal and Wilkins (1972) and Wolfgang (1963).

[16] For example, the mean number of burglaries reported during the three years prior to the interview was .06 for the white males and .09 for the black males in the 1972 study. Also in 1972, more than one-quarter of the males had total Sellin-Wolfgang (1964) seriousness scores of zero. See Nettler (1974) and Reiss (1975) for some recent discussions of suggested methodological shortcomings of the self-report method.

[17] These biases include those introduced by differential reporting of offenses by victims to the police as well as criminal justice system selection biases. It should be noted here that the UCR data may also reflect statistical biases due to the fact that not all police jurisdictions report arrest data to the FBI. For data on offenses, the UCR received reports from jurisdictions covering 94% of the U.S. population in 1974. The published UCR arrest data are broken out only for cities, suburban areas, and rural areas. Because the offense data cover almost all of the U.S. population, we can examine the extent to which the arrest data come disproportionately from city, suburban, and rural areas by examining the ratio of the U.S. population covered by agencies that report arrest data (Kelley, 1975: Tables 44, 49 and 54) to the U.S. population covered by agencies reporting offense data (Kelley, 1975: Table 13). These ratios are .72 for the cities, .72 for the suburban areas, and .51 for the rural areas. Thus, rural areas are underrepresented in the national arrest data. However, the total number of arrests in rural areas for rape, robbery, and assault (26,000) is relatively small in relation to the total number of arrests in all reporting areas for these crimes (490,000), and even if adjustments were made for the underrepresentation of rural areas, the effect on the aggregate figures would not be substantial.

(62% ÷ 62%) is 1.0, indicating that none of the arrest percentage can be attributed to selection bias. The ratios for the remaining offenses are .84 for rape, .78 for simple assault, and .73 for aggravated assault. This indicates that for these crimes some of the arrest percentage can be attributed to selection bias but, by far, most of the arrest percentage appears to be attributable to the substantially greater involvement of blacks than whites in these crimes.

The complements of these ratios can be thought of as an index of selection bias. These selection biases can be decomposed into criminal justice system biases (differential police patrols, closer scrutinizing of blacks by police, greater propensity of police to arrest blacks once contact has been made, etc.) and victim reporting (to the police) biases. By using the data in Tables 1 and 2, the ratios discussed above can be recomputed, using in the numerator only those incidents which victims said were reported to the police. For example, in rapes elicited in the NCP survey which victims said were reported to the police, offenders were black in 47% of the cases (Table 2). In the UCR arrest data, blacks constituted 48% of the rape arrestees. This ratio for rape is (47% ÷ 48%) .98. The comparable ratio is 1.05 for robbery, .63 for aggravated assault, and .70 for simple assault. The complements of the ratios reported in the previous paragraph can be taken as a measure of all selection biases, that is, criminal justice system and victim reporting biases. The complements of the ratios reported in this paragraph can be taken as a measure of selection biases exclusive of victim reporting biases. For aggravated assault the first complement is .22 and the second is .37, which suggests that criminal justice system biases are more pronounced than they first appear once victim reporting biases are taken into account. For rape, the first complement is .16 and the second is .02, which suggests that for this crime category almost all (.16 − .02 = .14) of the deviation of the UCR from NCP data is attributable to the reporting biases of victims rather than to criminal justice system selection bias.

These results suggest that criminal justice system selection bias may be greatest for aggravated and simple assault and may be negligible for rape and robbery. At the same time, these data indicate that such biases account for much less of the racial disproportionality for these crimes than does differential involvement. These results do not support the heavy theoretical emphasis on differential selection manifested in the theories at the lower end of the continuum.[18] Rather, these data suggest that theories of criminality must give more attention to explaining disproportionate involvement (or noninvolvement) in common law personal crimes among blacks and whites, as do those theories higher on the continuum.

Of course, there are some measurement problems that may affect the victimization survey results. For example, victims' reports of the racial characteristics of offenders may be affected by popular stereotypes of the criminal. Furthermore, persons of Spanish heritage may be reported by some victims to be black. Because Spanish heritage persons in the general population are counted as white by U.S. Bureau of Census convention, this potential definitional difference may artificially inflate the disproportionality of blacks among the NCP offenders. It is also possible that white victims, who in assault and rape are likely to be victimized by white offenders, underreport their victimizations to survey interviewers. On the other hand, as noted in the discussion above, available evidence indicates that race-linked biases in the measurement of assault in victimization surveys may tend to undercount black

---

[18] It should be stressed that I am not arguing that these results by any means indicate that racial discrimination in the criminal justice system should cease to be a cause for concern. There is evidence within the data of racially discriminatory enforcement and, obviously, any racial discrimination in the mechanisms by which people enter the criminal justice system is objectionable and demands attention. The argument being made is that it appears that these data seriously question sociological explanations which attribute most of the racial disproportionality in arrest data to differential selection rather than to differential involvement.

offenders. Furthermore, there is some evidence that the most undersampled respondent group consists of young black males (U.S. Bureau of the Census, 1975b), who would be expected to be victimized in these crimes by black offenders. In any event, it is unlikely that biases in the victimization surveys linked to the race of the offender would be of such a magnitude that the substantial overrepresentation of blacks in the offender population would disappear.

The results of this study have important theoretical implications. The analysis indicates that theories at the lower end of the continuum are incapable of accounting for these victimization survey results which show a much higher rate of involvement for blacks than for whites in these common law personal crimes; the data from two independent sources (victimization surveys and arrest data) are in close agreement with each other and in sharp disagreement with the predictions of labeling theory, particularly in its extreme form (e.g., Chapman, 1968). As one moves from the lower to the higher end of the continuum, the predictions of the theories become increasingly compatible with the results. Conflict theory, which is nearer to the middle of the continuum than labeling theory, is somewhat compatible with the results in that it predicts racial differential in involvement in common law personal crimes because the more powerful (white) segments of society will have legislated against those activities in which the less powerful (black) segments of society engage disproportionately. However, many conflict theorists (e.g., Chambliss, 1969; Chambliss and Seidman, 1971; Quinney, 1970) also strongly emphasize that power differentials result in differential processing by agents of the criminal justice system. Although there was evidence of bias in police processing for assault, there was virtually none for robbery and rape.

Theories at the higher end of the continuum are most consistent with the data. These theories, such as Merton's (1938) anomie theory, Cloward and Ohlin's (1960) opportunity theory, or Wolfgang and Ferracuti's (1967) subculture-of-violence theory are quite compatible with large racial differentials in involvement in common law personal crimes and *comparatively* small racial differentials in police processing.

It is much more difficult, in light of the findings, to choose among theories at the higher end of the continuum than it is to reject, as incompatible with the data, theories at the lowest end. For example, these findings could easily be interpreted within the differential ooportunity perspective because the NCP and UCR data indicate that the greatest racial differences in involvement are for the economically motivated crime of robbery.[19] Blocked access to legitimate avenues for material achievement (e.g., Merton, 1938; Cloward and Ohlin, 1960) can be readily invoked to account for the higher rate of black involvement in robbery. Although differential opportunity might seem less capable of encompassing the higher rates of black assault and rape, several strain theorists have suggested mechanisms to account for violent crime. Cloward and Ohlin (1960:171–8) postulate the existence of a subcultural adaptation to blocked opportunities that is organized around violent behavior. In this conflict subculture, ". . . violence is the keynote; its members pursue status ('rep') through the manipulation of force or threat of force" (1960:20). Under conditions conducive to the development of conflict subculture:

. . . tendencies toward aberrant behavior become intensified and magnified. These adolescents

---

[19] Another NCP property crime, personal larceny, also shows greater racial differences than those found for assault and rape. A small proportion of larcenies involve a confrontation between the victim and the offender and are differentiated from robberies in that they do not involve force or the threat of force—for example, a purse snatch in which force is not threatened or directed at the victim. The UCR arrest tables do not separate larcenies of this type from larcenies in which there is no personal confrontation between the victim and the offender; the NCP data on larcenies that do involve such a confrontation cannot reasonably be compared with the UCR arrest data. However, the 1974 NCP data reveal that 69% (estimated N = 230,091) of the offenders in face-to-face larcenies were black.

seize upon the manipulation of violence as a route to status not only because it provides a way of expressing pent-up angers and frustrations but also because they are not cut off from access to violence by vicissitudes of birth. In the world of violence, such attributes as race, socioeconomic position, age, and the like are irrelevant. . . . (1960:175).

Similarly, Cohen (1955) suggests a strain model which links school failure with an increased probability of engaging in negativistic, nonutilitarian, and malicious behavior. One important emphasis of the anomie theorists which cannot be ignored in accounting for differential rates of violent behavior is their emphasis on the frustration that accompanies blocked opportunities and the use of violence as status-conferring.

On the other hand, those subscribing to the subculture-of-violence perspective have argued that blacks are more likely than whites to be members of the violent subculture and hence are more likely than whites to accept and expect violent behavior in social interactions (Wolfgang and Ferracuti, 1967: Curtis, 1975). To the extent that the crimes studied here, that is, rape, robbery, and assault, are construed to be violent crimes, the results are interpretable within this subcultural perspective. It should be noted, however, that despite the fact that robbery has been defined by some as a violent crime (e.g., in the Uniform Crime Reports; Mulvihill et al., 1969), the primary aim of robbery is to deprive a person of property, whereas assault and rape, if completed, necessarily involve bodily harm to the victim. Among the personal crimes studied here, the least violent crime (robbery) shows the greatest racial difference,[20] and the more violent crimes (assault and rape) show a smaller racial difference. Subculture-of-violence theorists argue, however, that much violent crime is intraracial, particularly blacks victimizing blacks. It may be that intraracial crimes of assault and rape are undercounted in both the NCP and UCR

data because, according to this subcultural theory, they are more accepted and expected by blacks in social interactions and hence are less often construed as crimes and/or reported to either the police or to survey interviewers as crimes. Of course, the resolution of this speculation is well beyond the scope of the data.

By the definition of the continuum used here, the theories at the higher end all predict racial differences in involvement in common law personal crimes and the data are not sufficient for choosing among these competing explanations. However, the results do strongly indicate that research attention in this area should focus on these competing (higher-end) explanations of the differential involvement of blacks and whites in common law personal crimes. Is the differential attributable to the disparity between the socioeconomic status distributions of blacks and whites as Bonger (1943) has suggested or to actual or perceived differences in structural impediments to the achievement of success goals via legitimate avenues (e.g., Merton, 1938; Cloward and Ohlin, 1960)? Are these differences due to cultural factors as Wolfgang and Ferracuti (1967) argue? Or is the explanation to be found in the historical maltreatment of American blacks? Only further research specifically designed to assess these and other hypotheses can shed additional light on these questions.

Throughout this paper, substantial care has been taken to limit the discussion to common law crimes of forcible rape, robbery, and assault. The NCP data now available only address common law crimes. For the crimes of burglary, household larceny, and vehicle theft, which are also included in the NCP surveys, offender characteristics are generally unavailable because these crimes do not typically involve a face-to-face confrontation between the victim and the offender. Clearly, these results cannot be extrapolated beyond the specific crimes to which the analyses were addressed. If the differential involvement in white-collar offenses, organized crime, corporate crime, or consumer fraud had been studied, the results might have

---

[20] Similarly for personal larceny (see fn. 19).

been very different. Obviously, these data and analyses shed no light on racial differences in crime generally.

As Nettler (1974:126) has noted:

. . . caution is required in the interpretation of differentials in crime rates between whites and nonwhites. In the light of the sad history of racial relations, it is difficult to make comparisons today of the relative importance of the alleged causes of any differences in observed behaviors.

Although research on this question is difficult for a variety of reasons, the results of this study suggest that it is incumbent upon social scientists to give long overdue research attention to such basic questions as these.

REFERENCES

Becker, Howard S. (1963). *The Outsiders: Studies in the Sociology of Deviance*. New York: Free Press.

Blackstone, William (1778). *Commentaries on the Laws of England*. 8th ed. Oxford: Clarendon Press.

Bonger, Willem (1916). *Criminality and Economic Conditions*. Tr. Henry Horton. Boston: Little, Brown.

———(1943). *Race and Crime*. Tr. M. Hordyk. Montclair: Patterson-Smith.

Chambliss, William (1969). *Crime and the Legal Process*. New York: McGraw-Hill.

Chambliss, William, and Richard Nagasawa (1969). "On the validity of official statistics: a comparative study of white, black, and Japanese high school boys." *Journal of Research in Crime and Delinquency* **6**:71–7.

Chambliss, William, and Robert Seidman (1971). *Law, Order, and Power*. Reading, Pa.: Addison-Wesley.

Chapman, Dennis (1968). *Sociology and the Stereotype of the Criminal*. London: Tavistock.

Clark and Marshall (1967). *A Treatise on the Law of Crimes*. 7th ed. New York: Holt.

Cloward, Richard, and Lloyd Ohlin (1960). *Delinquency and Opportunity: A Theory of Delinquent Gangs*. New York: Free Press.

Cohen, Albert (1955). *Delinquent Boys*. New York: Free Press.

Curtis, Lynn (1975). *Violence, Race, and Culture*. Lexington: Lexington Books.

Doleschal, E., and Leslie Wilkins (1972). *Criminal Statistics*. Rockville, Md.: Center for Studies in Crime and Delinquency.

Erickson, Kai (1962). "Notes on the Sociology of Deviance." *Social Problems* **9**:307–14.

Goffman, Ervin (1961). *Asylums*. New York: Anchor.

Gold, Martin (1970). *Delinquent Behavior in an American City*. Belmont, Ca.: Brooks/Cole.

Gold, Martin, and David Reimer (1975). "Changing Patterns of Delinquent Behavior Among Americans 13 through 16 Years Old." *Crime and Delinquency Literature* **7**:483–517.

Goldkamp, John (1977). "Minorities as Victims of Police Shootings: Interpretations of Racial Disproportionality and Police Use of Deadly Force." *Justice System Journal* **2**:169–83.

Gould, Leroy (1969). "Who Defines Delinquency: a Comparison of Self-Reported and Officially-Reported Indices of Delinquency for Three Racial Groups." *Social Problems* **16**:325–36.

Hindelang, Michael (1976). *Criminal Victimization in Eight American Cities: A Descriptive Analysis of Common Theft and Assault*. Cambridge, Ma.: Ballinger.

Hindelang, Michael, and Michael Gottfredson (1976). "The Victim's Decision Not to Invoke the Criminal Process." Pp. 57–78 in W. McDonald (ed.), *The Victim and the Criminal Justice System*. Beverly Hills: Sage.

Hirschi, Travis (1969). *Causes of Delinquency*. Berkeley: University of California Press.

Kelley, Clarence (1975). *Crime in the United States*. Washington, D.C.: U.S. Government Printing Office.

———(1976). *Crime in the United States*. Washington, D.C.: U.S. Government Printing Office.

Kitsuse, John (1964). "Societal Reaction to Deviant Behavior: Problems in Theory and Method." Pp. 87–102 in Howard Becker (ed.), *The Other Side: Perspectives on Deviance*. New York: Free Press.

Law Enforcement Assistance Administration, U.S. Department of Justice, National Institute of Law Enforcement and Criminal Justice, Statistics Division (1972). *San Jose Methods Test of Known Crime Victims*. Statistics Technical Report No. 1. Washington, D.C.: U.S. Government Printing Office.

———(1976). *Criminal Victimization in the United States*. Washington, D.C.: U.S. Government Printing Office.

Lemert, Edwin (1951). *Social Pathology*. New York: McGraw-Hill.

——(1967). *Human Deviance, Social Problems and Social Control*. Englewood Cliffs: Prentice-Hall.

Merton, Robert (1938). "Social Structure and Anomie." *American Sociological Review* **3**:672–82.

Mulvihill, D., M. Tumin, and L. Curtis (1969). A Staff Report Submitted to the National Commission on the Causes and Prevention of Violence. Crimes of Violence, Vol. 11. Washington, D.C.: U.S. Government Printing Office.

Nettler, G. (1974). *Explaining Crime*. New York: McGraw-Hill.

Quinney, Richard (1970). *The Social Reality of Crime*. Boston: Little, Brown.

Reiss, Albert Jr. (1971). *The Police and the Public*. New Haven: Yale University Press.

——(1975). "Inappropriate Theory and Inadequate Methods as Policy Plagues: Self-Reported Delinquency and the Law." Pp. 211–22 in N.J. Demerath, Jr., Otto Larson, and Carl F. Schuessler (eds.), *Social Policy and Sociology*. New York: Academic Press.

Sellin, T. and M. Wolfgang (1964). *The Measurement of Delinquency*. New York: Wiley.

Tannenbaum, Frank (1938). *Crime and the Community*. New York: McGraw-Hill.

U.S. Bureau of the Census (1970a). "Victim Recall Pretest (Washington, D.C.): Household Survey of Victims of Crime." Mimeographed. Suitland, Md.

——(1970b) "Household Survey of Victims of Crime: Second Pretest (Baltimore, Md.)." Mimographed. Suitland, Md.

——(1975a). *Statistical Abstract of the United States*. Washington, D.C.: U.S. Government Printing Office.

——(1975b). "Comparison of the Second State Ratio Factors Produced in the National Crime Survey and the Current Population Survey." Mimeographed memorandum. Suitland, Md.

Williams, Jay, and Martin Gold (1972). "From Delinquent Behavior to Official Delinquency." *Social Problems* **20**:209–28.

Wolfgang, Marvin (1963). "Uniform Crime Reports: a Critical Appraisal." *University of Pennsylvania Law Review* **111**:708–38.

Wolfgang, Marvin, and Franco Ferracuti (1967). *The Subculture of Violence: Toward an Integrated Theory in Criminology*. London: Tavistock.

Wolfgang, Marvin, Robert Figlio, and Thorsten Sellin (1972). *Delinquency in a Birth Cohort*. Chicago: University of Chicago Press.

16

MACHISMO AND GANG VIOLENCE[1]

HOWARD S. ERLANGER

The subculture of violence thesis sees values relating to violence as playing an important causal role in the generation of violent behavior. Subcultural values, it is argued, define certain circumstances and stimuli that appropriately evoke physical aggression, especially on the part of young black and Hispanic males. Within the subculture, failure to respond violently to physical or verbal challenge may well lead to negative sanctions, while violent response to such challenges is said to be supported, encouraged and at times directly required (Wolfgang and Ferracuti, 1967).

By and large, the literature relating to the subculture of violence thesis has concentrated on two questions. The first of these is an empirical question: Can the hypothesized value differences be demonstrated? What little evidence exists on the issue is mixed; several stud-

Source: "Estrangement, Machismo and Gang Violence," *Social Science Quarterly* (September 1979) 60(2):235–248. Reprinted by permission University of Texas Press.

[1]This research was supported in part by funds granted by the National Institute of Mental Health, and in part by funds granted to the Institute for Research on Poverty, University of Wisconsin pursuant to the provisions of the Economic Opportunity Act of 1964. Work on this project and preparation of this paper would not have been possible without the advice and assistance of Fred Persily. Of the many other persons who contributed to this project I would especially like to thank Monte Perez and Steve Sanora for their comments and support, and Marilyn Zeitlin and Nick Danigelis for their work on earlier phases of the research.

ies (e.g., Ball-Rokeach, 1973; Erlanger, 1974) suggest that the differences do not exist, while others suggest that they do (e.g., Ferracuti et al., 1970; Ferracuti and Wolfgang, 1973). The second question is more theoretical: Assuming that the value differences do exist, should they be regarded as the product of a semiautonomous subculture (as implied, although not unequivocally, in the work of Wolfgang and Ferracuti [1967]), or should they be regarded as an adaptation to situational exigencies induced by social structure (a position explicitly taken by Cloward and Ohlin [1960] in their discussion of the "conflict subculture" and by Curtis [1975] in his elaboration of Wolfgang's model)? This paper attempts to advance discussion on both of these questions, in the specific context of the Chicano barrios of East Los Angeles. It concludes that, while subcultural values of the barrio may be different from those of Anglo society and may exist independently of Anglo society, they do not directly require or condone violence. Rather, behavior is a product of the way in which structural conditions limit the expression of these values.

In the study of Chicano life, a major theme has been that of manliness, or machismo. Many popular accounts of machismo portray it as encompassing a strong emphasis on sex-role differentiation, with a concomitant emphasis on physical aggressiveness. The materials reported on here suggest, however, that a machismo orientation, if it does exist, is not nearly as narrow in content as portrayed in the literature. Rather, the subcultural trait understood as machismo seems to be one that can contribute to physical aggression, but one that does so only indirectly and under certain structural conditions.

One set of these structural conditions appears to be political conditions in the community. The usual state of political affairs in East Los Angeles is one in which Chicano youth experiences a feeling of estrangement. This estrangement fosters a strong identity with the peer group in the immediate neighborhood (barrio) because the peer group is the most readily available source of identity. The consequence is a strong consciousness of turf, which in turn greatly increases the potential for conflict and thus for violence. However, these structural conditions can change, as they did in roughly the period from late 1967 to early 1972, when a strong, locally based political movement succeeded in greatly reducing the level of estrangement. For this period there is evidence of a change in group identity, the opening of different avenues for the expression of machismo and a reduction in the incidence of gang violence. Then, as the movement subsided, gang violence increased.

METHOD

The interpretations presented in this paper are based on more than 35 open-ended interviews. About two-thirds of the respondents were Chicano males aged 15 to 30 who lived in one of the barrios of East Los Angeles and who were participating or had participated extensively in gang activity. This age range allows an assessment of both the contemporary situation and that of the middle and late 1960s. These respondents came from many different gangs, including those generally considered to be the toughest in East Los Angeles. The remaining respondents were persons with a comprehensive knowledge of the community and the events discussed in this paper. These included police and probation officials, community program directors and political figures.

As a case study with a small, nonrandom sample, this study is of necessity exploratory and its findings tentative. It does not purport to be an empirical test of the subculture of violence thesis, but rather is an attempt to develop an explanation that, while compatible with the thesis' stress on values, offers a different understanding of the role of values in determining outcomes. Its object then, is to urge a broadening of the range of future inquiries into the subculture of violence.

THE COMMUNITY

In East Los Angeles the number of persons of Mexican heritage, numbering one million or more, is comparable to the population of Guadalajara or Monterey and is substantially exceeded only by Mexico City. Governmental authority is divided among several jurisdictions, but many of the Chicano residents (especially in the barrios near the central city, where a very high percentage of the residents in the barrios are Chicano) view East Los Angeles as a single community. The sections nearest the central city are the oldest and also the poorest, and in these areas the income per capita and the mean educational level are among the lowest in the Los Angeles area, as low or lower than in the black ghettos of Watts and surrounding areas.

East Los Angeles is divided into numerous subcommunities; contrary to common Anglo usage, Chicanos use the term *barrio* to refer to these subcommunities or neighborhoods rather than to the community as a whole. In the barrios nearest the central city, most male youth belong to the barrio gang, which bonds together all those who wish to be part of the group. In the more affluent barrios, gang membership is somewhat less common. There are subdivisions (some formal, some informal) of each gang, and a member spends virtually all his free time associating with this subgroup.

THE MEANING OF MACHISMO

Studies of Chicanos and Latin Americans have placed great emphasis on machismo, or manliness, which is reputed to be a cultural trait predisposing men to an exaggerated sense of honor, hypersensitivity, intransigence, sexual promiscuity, callousness and cruelty toward women, physical aggression and lack of respect for human life (see, e.g., Aramoni, 1971; Burma, 1970). There is a substantial literature attacking many of the negative stereotypes of Chicanos (see especially Hernandez, 1970; Romano, 1968) and some that deals with the machismo stereotype (see, e.g., Alvarez, 1973; Montiel, 1971). However, the relationship of machismo to physical aggressiveness has not been studied directly.

For all the Chicanos interviewed, machismo meant having courage, not backing down or being ready to fight. Without further inquiry, these phrases would most likely be taken as connoting physical aggression. However, to those interviewed, violence in itself was not directly a macho trait. For example, each respondent was asked whether César Chavez—a Chicano who eschews all forms of physical aggression, goes on hunger fasts, allows himself to be arrested, etc.—had machismo. Almost all respondents knew of Chavez, and all of these strongly felt that Chavez did have a good deal of machismo. It is particularly noteworthy that most of the respondents stressed that Chavez did indeed fight, and rejected a presentation of him as a man who wouldn't fight. Thus, fighting, being strong and having machismo can be much broader than simply physical aggression. The following response is representative:

> I don't know [Chavez] personally, but from what I hear about him and what I've read about him, I don't think he'd [pause]. If somebody came up to him and slapped him, I think he'd try [pause]. He wouldn't fight back you know, but he'd fight back in words, not with fists.

Several of the older respondents resented the use of the word *machismo* and complained

that it was being misused by Anglos. One of the more articulate respondents stated.

> We get [machismo] slapped on us all the time by the *gabachos* [whites]. They use it more than we do—"He's a macho dude." We've been stereotyped to death on that.

The interviews thus suggest that the core values of the subculture are not directly concerned with violence, but rather with defense of self in a much more abstract sense. Although it is true that defense of personal dignity can be a justification for physical fighting, it is also true that Chavez, one of the heroes of the subculture, refuses to engage in physical aggression. In this subculture, it appears that violence results not from the definition of certain situations as appropriate for or demanding a violent response, but rather from the blocking of alternative avenues to the maintenance of dignity, a broader value. This interrelationship between subcultural values and the structural conditions under which they are expressed is elaborated in the following section.

ESTRANGEMENT AND INTERPERSONAL VIOLENCE IN THE GANG CONTEXT

THE EMERGENCE OF ESTRANGEMENT

From the time of the American conquest of the northern territories of Mexico in 1848, persons of Mexican heritage living within the United States have been subject to economic and cultural domination by Anglos. Moore (1970), for example, has suggested that the model of internal colonialism is especially appropriate for the analysis of the Chicano experience. The historical experience of the Chicano in the United States has been well documented and need not be reviewed here.

The record of discrimination against Chicanos in East Los Angeles is also well documented, and the educational situation faced by Chicanos has been particularly unsatisfactory. All those interviewed attended school—both public and parochial—in which Chicanos were punished for speaking Spanish, even among themselves in the schoolyard. Many reported that their first confrontation with Anglo authorities was over language. For example:

> They asked, "What's his name?" and someone said, "His name is Juan," so right then my name changed to John. "Well, now he'll be called John because that's his American name."

Many respondents reported a general atmosphere in school in which Chicano students were not respected or seen as having much potential. The general validity of these observations was corroborated by a Chicano teacher who grew up in an East Los Angeles barrio, went to college and then taught elementary school in the same barrio. He reported that he was quite successful in school and college and that through that period of his life he questioned why other young Chicanos could not do for themselves what he felt he had done for himself. However, once he became a teacher and got a view of the school system from the inside, he fundamentally changed his evaluation of the process. After a year of teaching, he wondered how he had ever made it.

> I heard teachers saying out in the field, "You goddamn Mexican" to another teacher who was umpiring. . . . I heard teachers reprimand kids who were speaking Spanish in the hallways . . . and this was supposed to be a time when they were teaching Spanish in school already. I heard teachers saying, "What do you expect of these kids? We can only give them so much."

The school is just one place where the young Chicano is confronted with negative images of his culture. From an early age the Chicano is bombarded with the message that his language, culture, food and habits are inferior and should be changed to conform to those of the Anglo. This is not to say that every Chicano has the same experience but rather that this has been the most common experience over the years. The domination of Chicanos has resulted in their feelings that they are living in an environment controlled by an Anglo structure that they cannot affect. Political action to change these circumstances is difficult because of gerrymandering and because of widespread feelings that there is little prospect that meaningful change will come about. These feelings of powerlessness, exclusion and absence of control over the conditions of one's existence can be summed up as estrangement.

THE RESULT OF ESTRANGEMENT

A major consequence of the estrangement just described is the emergence of a strong identification with the immediate environment—the peer group and the barrio. Adolescent youth particularly are faced with the need to expand identity beyond the family. In the estranged environment the peer group in the barrio, who share the same feelings and experiences, are the most readily available source of identity.

The interviews indicate that this identification is equal to that with the family and is much more intense than that with religion, with political entities (Los Angeles, California, United States) or, except under certain circumstances discussed below, with the Chicano people as a whole. The following exchange with a 21-year-old probationer, talking about the period just before he was incarcerated, illustrates how deep the attachment to the barrio is:

Q. What I'm trying to figure out is which was more important? What would you consider more serious—an insult to you or an insult to the barrio you were a part of at that time?

A. Probably the barrio—the neighborhood.

Q. The barrio was more important?

A. Yeah, there's people I've seen who have given up their lives for the neighborhood. I've seen people die. . . .

Q. Literally die?

A. Yeah, yelling out, like *"Qué vivas!"* [Long live the neighborhood!]

In the estranged setting, the gang member who shouts the name of his barrio with his last breath has, from the point of view of the gang, shown his courage and dignity in one of the few ways open to him. Youth in the barrio are rejected by Anglo society, and that society is rejected in turn, for it demands that they surrender their cultural identity in order to gain positive recognition. Thus most young Chicanos come to rely on the peer group for this recognition. The respondents reported that it is critical that status in the gang be based on attributes that can be reached by anyone—for example, the machismo qualitites of courage, dignity and readiness to fight. Since other outlets for demonstration of these attributes are blocked in the barrio, the pursuit of them is often in the context of physical confrontation. But many respondents reported that even in such confrontations the important personal quality is the willingness to fight, more than physical prowess per se:

> I went to this other school when I moved. The first day I went in and right away I started pinpointing who's who—you know, the pecking-order type thing. And the second day that I was there, there was a [gang] already there—little kids, you know, you run around together. So I was jammed: "Where you from?" and all that kind of stuff. And he says, "Well, you're going to have to fight one of us. No, not one of us, you're going to have to fight this dude." I was scared as hell, but I had to go along with the program. But luckily I didn't have to fight. . . . I didn't have to fight with them, but because I wanted to fight with them I was accepted by that clique.

There are many scenarios that push the willingness to fight over the brink into actual fighting. The most frequent and important instigators of gang fights are violations of barrio turf, either physically or symbolically. The gang establishes control over the physical territory that constitutes the barrio, and defends it against all intrusions. A teen-age male may by challenged to identify his barrio at any time. If he responds, and identifies his barrio as one that is on unfriendly terms with that of the challenger(s), physical conflict will usually ensue, and the fight can escalate to involve large

numbers of young men from the two barrios. Gang members also do not tolerate outsiders—especially from a rival gang—dating a woman from their barrio, even if she is unattached and even if they meet on another turf. Horowitz and Schwartz (1974) present a useful microsociological account of the processes through which the concern with turf and with honor can lead to violent clashes. The reports of the respondents were similar:

> You know, when a kid is down and if you attack the only things that he has going for him—namely, his manliness, his machismo; his home boys, his barrio—that's all he has. When you attack that you're attacking him to the quick—what else does he have?

This interpretation of the nature of Chicano gang activity differs from that of Suttles, whose study of the Addams area of Chicago included Chicano barrios there. Suttles (1968) sees "named street corner groups," or gangs, as growing out of a distrust of strangers. No resident can possibly know all the others, and street corner groups provide "one of the ways in which the residents can be grouped together to reduce [the] problem of indeterminacy." These groups may act to control their area, protecting outsiders in such a way that conflict may ensue. In East Los Angeles, it does not appear that barrio-based gangs result from the simple lack of information about others. Rather, they emerge from the absence of other avenues to achieve identity and power. Control over the physical space of the barrio seems to be sought less for the purpose of reducing uncertainty than for the sense of power it conveys. This can be most clearly seen when (as discussed in the following section) structural circumstances change and these needs are fulfilled through other means.

POLITICAL ACTION AND THE DECLINE OF ESTRANGEMENT

Much can be learned about normal patterns and the basis for them when these patterns are disrupted. Such a situation existed in East Los Angeles in the late 1960s and early 1970s, when there was a broadly based political movement in the community.

THE MOVEMENT

Contrary to the impression of many writers, Chicanos have been involved in political activity directed at changing their life circumstances for over a century (Guzman, 1968). However, the period from late 1967 to early 1972 marked a particularly intense period of political activity in East Los Angeles, a period that will be referred to as the movement period. The issues in East Los Angeles were similar to those in other minority communities across the country—for example, Chicano control of the schools and of the social and law enforcement agencies operating in the community, greater recognition of Chicano needs by the Catholic church, and development of economic independence through governmental assistance and through the development of an independent local economic base. Basic to these issues was Chicano pride and a quest for unity and power.

Key events during the movement in East Los Angeles included walkouts from the city schools, a moratorium protesting the disproportionate Chicano fatalities in the Vietnam War, protest of allocation of Catholic church funds to construction of churches in West Los Angeles rather than to social programs in the barrios, protests against police treatment of Chicanos, and a protest at a state educational conference. These events involved thousands of people, and some culminated in violent clashes between police and Chicano demonstrators and bystanders.

THE EFFECT OF THE MOVEMENT ON ESTRANGEMENT

From its inception the movement involved large numbers of Chicano youth. Walkouts were held at almost every high school and several of the junior high schools in the community, with large numbers of students participating. The interviews indicate that gang members were not immediately involved in the movement, but many of the gang youth felt that they were receiving repercussions from the police for movement activities and as a consequence decided to become directly involved. One of the better known movement leaders reported that as the movement progressed, not only were gang members involved, but the relationship between them and others, especially college youth, was fundamentally changed:

> It put a whole positive connotation into being [a gang member], the thing is that the movement said everybody is a worker in the movement, no matter who they are. And that gave them less social alienation, so they could go to meetings with college students, whereas before they couldn't, because they felt that definite alienation. They could go to meetings with anybody, 'cause the movement says, "We need you too. Because you're a Chicano too, and you're not some weirdo."

Besides generating unity among youth in the barrios, the movement generated pride and a feeling of power. The heightened sense of pride and Chicano identity was perhaps expressed best by a respondent who was released from prison on a pass for El diez y seis de septiembre, Mexican Independence Day:

A. When I come out, the Chicano convict organization calls me, sticks a button on me, says, you're with us, brother, blah, blah, . . . They have a parade every year and we'll bring up the ranks. As far as I could look back, all I could see was Chicanos. . . . I'm on a pass from Soledad. I still had to go back to prison. I was just out on a pass.

Q. That day?

A. Ya. You know what, a pride went over me, I don't think I've had it since.

The sense of power is shown in an incident that occurred early in the movement, during the school walkouts:

> That was the first time I saw students dealing with the principal on an equal level. And they were telling him, "Hey, . . ." because they were

coming from a sense of power, 'cause the students were out there, and these [leaders] were the ones that could tell the students to come back. And the principal knew that, and he sat there and we dealt with the issues on a negotiating basis. So that gave us a whole sense of power that we didn't have before.

CHANGE IN GANG VIOLENCE DURING THE MOVEMENT PERIOD

The validity problems of official statistics are well known and need not be repeated here. The validity of data for gang-related violence is even more questionable because there is usually no complainant, and for a variety of reasons police officers are aware of a large number of assaults among gang members for which they do not make arrests. According to law enforcement officials in Los Angeles, records of gang-related violence prior to 1973 are particularly inaccurate. Hence, in order to determine the rate of violence before, during and after the period of intense movement activity, the qualitative impressions of more than a dozen law enforcement officials knowledgeable about the trend of gang violence in East Los Angeles were sought. These included representatives of the Gang Squad of the Los Angeles Police Department, Youth Authority officers and supervisors in East Los Angeles, and probation officials. All of these law enforcement officials recalled a marked decline in the amount of fighting between gangs and between individuals within the gangs during the movement period. In addition, older gang members were virtually unanimous in reporting a sharp drop in violence during the period. Gang members whose lives were essentially unaffected by the movement were the exception, not the rule.

PROCESSES THROUGH WHICH THE MOVEMENT AFFECTED GANG VIOLENCE

The movement affected the level of gang-related violence primarily by changing the ideas of those youths affiliated with it, and by changing the environment experienced by those who were not affiliated with it.

For gang members personally involved in the movement (in varying degrees, from serving as leaders to being just loosely affiliated), reduction of fighting came from the heightened sense of efficacy and from a commitment to the principle that all Chicanos are brothers and should not fight each other. For those youths, the focus was on *carnalismo* (brotherhood), which to our respondents connoted the feeling of pride and unity:

A. *Carnalismo* to me would be having people unite, being brothers to each other, so they can relate to each other, know what's happening, and to more or less carry each other.

Q. Is that affected by the *movimiento*?

A. To me it is because, once you're *carnal* to someone else in the *movimiento*, you've got someone to go with to push that movement. The *carnalismo* is like sticking together. You're united, you're united! That's your *carnalismo* right there.

The feeling of *carnalismo* existed prior to the intense period of the movement, but it was only expressed on the barrio level, and could not be effectively used to defuse a confrontation. Chicano gangs from different barrios did not cooperate except in confrontation with a non-Chicano group, for example, the police. During the movement, *carnalismo* took on special significance. Because courage and dignity were achieved in other ways through the movement, barrio youth were less likely to take affront at the actions of others. In the following exchange, the respondent was asked about the effects of the movement:

A. We'd go to parties during the movement, like fundraisers at a certain house. All the gangs would be there. If there was an argument between one guy and another from another barrio the first thing anyone would say would be, "Hey man, don't go hitting your brother," and the fight would cease right there and then. And they'd go. "Forget the barrio and being from Hazard [a particular rough barrio] and all that bullshit."

Q. Was there a different kind of identification then? They didn't really forget the barrio, did they?

A. No. But they tried not to use the barrio against one another. "I'll respect your barrio and you respect mine."

In expanding their identity from the barrio to the broader Chicano community, several hundred gang members joined groups that maintained some of the characteristics of the gang but that were community rather than barrio based. The members of these groups became soldiers of the movement rather than soldiers of the barrio. This was a way of maintaining courage and dignity while transcending interbarrio conflicts. Probably the best-known example of an organization of this type was the Brown Berets.

For gang members not directly affiliated with the movement, the effects were more indirect. These youths often found that, although their ideas and feelings did not change, other barrio youth, both in their gang and in others, were much less interested in fighting. The experience of one respondent well illustrates this situation. Now in his twenties and still a member of one of the toughest barrio gangs, he was never a part of the movement, does not have a clear idea of what the issues were or why the events took place, and does not feel that the movement affected his sense of being Chicano. But although his ideas and self-concept were unchanged by the movement, his life style was profoundly affected. He remembered the movement period as one in which the types of actions that would otherwise be provocative did not evoke a combative response. For example, he reported that during the movement period he dated a girl whose brother was a member of a gang with which his gang has had an intense rivalry for over 30 years, but that he suffered no repercussions. Although he would have been willing to fight if challenged for this action, the challenge did not

occur, and in general he reported that a high degree of freedom of movement between the two barrios existed. This is because those youths who were affiliated with the movement were playing by the new rules of *carnalismo*, and did not support their comrades who played by the old rules.

ALTERNATIVE EXPLANATIONS

The foregoing indicates that there was a decrease in interpersonal violence during the intense period of activism in the barrio, and that the key elements of the movement that led to this effect were the increase in political consciousness and the feeling that Chicanos were going to change their life conditions for the better. This section considers whether the effect on violence can properly be attributed to the new sense of power. Possible alternative explanations for the reported reduction in fighting can be divided into those stressing factors that were external to the movement and those stressing nonpolitical consequences of the movement.

The most likely factor outside of the movement that could account for the observed relationship would be a major change in employment opportunities. If the movement were to coincide with very favorable economic conditions for Chicanos, then it could well be that material benefits, rather than ideological change, led to reduced levels of interpersonal violence through reducing the amount of idle time, getting people a bigger stake in the system or whatever. Although the late 1960s was a period of relative prosperity, the economic situation of the Chicano in the barrio, especially that of gang youths (including those interviewed), was not significantly affected.

This is not to deny that the economic conditions of the 1960s may have substantially contributed to the milieu in which the movement developed. But these conditions themselves could not alone be responsible because there have been similar periods of relative prosperity since World War II in which gang violence did not notably change. For example, one respondent, who had extensive experience working with gang youth and who himself belonged to a gang when he was younger, reported that the only fluctuations he was aware of were seasonal, with periods of intense violence followed by lulls. Having worked with gang youth for a long time, he could "almost gauge when it's going to happen." Except for the extended period at the height of the movement, he knew of no other period of more than a few months in which there was a sharp decrease in gang fighting in East Los Angeles.

There are several plausible nonpolitical consequences of the movement that could be considered as contributing to the decline in gang violence. One might argue that the activities of the movement provided sufficient excitement so that violent interpersonal action was not necessary. But if it were simply the excitement of the movement that was having the effect, then nonparticipants would not be affected, and there would not have been any reason for appeals to *carnalismo* to stop a fight that was about to start. Similarly, it might be argued that the political movement simply kept people busy, without regard to the content of what they were doing, and thus they simply had less time to fight. Again, the contrary evidence is that the movement was not that time-consuming, except for the relatively few leaders, and that this alternative explanation would not explain the effect on nonparticipants.

It may well be true that when people are busy they are less likely to fight, and many barrio programs have been based on this premise. Gang workers have promoted car clubs, mural programs to paint over barrio *placas* (graffiti including the gang name and the name of the person who drew it) and a wide variety of recreational projects. However, at best these programs work only during the actual period of activity, and they do not affect people who are not directly involved. They are different from the movement in that they do not change the relationship of the individual to the outer world or fundamentally change the milieu of a community.

CONCLUSION

Chicano culture places a strong emphasis on values such as courage and dignity for males, but how these values are manifested in behavior depends heavily on the broader context in which people function. In an estranged setting, these values can lead to a high incidence of physical confrontation, but in a nonestranged setting, the evidence from this case study suggests that they do not. Virtually the only time within the memory of those interviewed in which there was a viable opportunity for the expression of courage and dignity outside of the gang setting for the masses of Chicano youth was during the movement period of late 1967 through early 1972. During this period identity with the broader community became primary and a sense of power to influence the institutions affecting the community emerged. As a result, gang-related violence decreased markedly.

In subsequent years the intensity of the movement lessened. The last movement events attracting thousands of people occurred in late 1971, and ended in violent confrontations with the police. Remnants of the movement live on, but the sense of power has lessened considerably, and with it the community identity transcending that of the individual barrios. As one of the movement leaders observed in an interview:

> We thought the limits of the struggle were just getting Chicanos together and then everything else would follow. Now we have greater information to work behind and we realize that that's not the case. We can still effect change, but it's going to come through different directions. . . . Now we still have potential power, but I think we're more realistic.

A sense of estrangement has returned, and even though appeals to *carnalismo* can sometimes be effective, gang violence has been on the upswing. In recent years the degree of violence has been greater than in the early 1960s, in part due to the greatly increased availability of weapons.

To the extent that the interpretations presented here are generalizable, they suggest that discussion of the relationship between violence and values needs to be broadened to include the possibility that violence may not flow from values that directly encourage it, but may instead occur when structural circumstances prevent achievement of related values. And, if correct, they also speak to the need for linking theories of deviance to theories of power and its distribution, a need that has been articulated in the conflict approach to criminological theory and in political interpretations of collective action, but that has received only recent attention in the explanation of the behavior of juvenile delinquents. In considering whether the theory developed here can be generalized, the focus of attention must be on the relationship between estrangement and gang behavior. Thus, if the political consciousness and involvement of gang members were unaffected by local or national social movements, their level of estrangement would remain high, and fundamental changes in gang life would not ensure. (See, for example, the discussion of black gangs in Chicago in Short [1974].) If, on the other hand, reduction in estrangement occurred from any source, political or not, we would expect noncomitant changes in the day-to-day life of the estranged.

REFERENCES

Alvarez, Rodolfo (1973). "The Psycho-Historical and Socioeconomic Development of the Chicano Community in the United States," *Social Science Quarterly* 53 (March): 920–42.

Aramoni, Aniceto (1971). "The Machismo Solution." In Bernard Landis and Edward S. Tauber (eds.), *In the Name of Life: Essays in Honor of Erich Fromm.* New York: Holt, Rinehart and Winston, pp. 100–7.

Ball-Rokeach, Sandra (1973). "Values and Violence: A Test of the Subculture of Violence Theses." *American Sociological Review* **38**: 736–50.

Burma, John H. (1970). "A Comparison of the Mexican American Subculture with the Oscar Lewis Culture of Poverty Model." In John H. Burma (ed.), *Mexican Americans in the United States: A Reader.* Cambridge, Mass.: Schenkman, pp. 17–28.

Cloward, Richard A., and Lloyd E. Ohlin (1960). *Delinquency and Opportunity: A Theory of Delinquent Gangs.* New York: Free Press.

Curtis, Lynn (1975). *Violence, Race, and Culture.* Lexington, Mass.: Lexington Books.

Erlanger, Howard S. (1974). "The Empirical Status of the Subculture of Violence Thesis." *Social Problems,* **22** (December): 280–92.

Ferracuti, Franco, Renato Lazzari and Marvin E. Wolfgang (eds.) (1970). *Violence in Sardinia.* Rome: Bulzoni.

Ferracuti, Franco, and Marvin E. Wolfgang (1973). *Psychological Testing of the Subculture of Violence.* Rome: Bulzoni.

Guzman, Ralph (1968). "Politics and Policies of the Mexican American Community." In Eugene P. Dvorin and Arthur J. Misner (eds). *California Politics and Policies.* Palo Alto, Calif.: Addison Wesley.

Hernandex, Deluvina (1970). *Mexican American Challenge to a Sacred Cow.* Los Angeles: University of California, Chicano Studies Center.

Horowitz, Ruth, and Gary Schwartz (1974). "Honor, Normative Ambiguity, and Gang Violence." *American Sociological Review* 39 (April): 238–51.

Montiel, Miguel (1971). "The Social Science Myth of the Mexican American Family." *Voices:* 41–47.

Moore, Joan W. (1970). "Colonialism: The Case of the Mexican Americans." *Social Problems* 17 (Spring): 463–72.

Romano, Octavio Ignacio V. (1968). "The Anthropology and Sociology of the Mexican-Americans: The Distortion of Mexican-American History." *El Grito* 2 (Fall): 13–26.

Short, James F., Jr. (1974). "Youth, Gangs and Society: Micro- and Macrosociological Processes." *Sociological Quarterly* 15 (Winter): 3–19.

Suttles, Gerald D. (1958). *The Social Order of the Slum: Ethnicity and Territory in the Inner City.* Chicago: University of Chicago Press.

Wolfgang, Marvin E., and Franco Ferracuti (1967). *The Subculture of Violence; Toward and Integrated Theory in Criminology.* London: Social Science Paperbacks.

17

THE CAREERS OF SERIOUS THIEVES[1]

W. GORDON WEST

The policy oriented questions of how persons become and cease being criminals have long been central to research on crime and delinquency. Although many studies of criminals lump all miscreants together, thus hopelessly confusing issues by failing to recognize that legal proscription is often the main feature shared by different criminals, it would seem advisable initially to focus separately on different types of offenders. [Clinard and Quinney, 1973 (e.g., rapists, forgers, and traffic violators)] Of the various types of criminals, thieves would seem to be a prime focus for such research, since they cause great material concern to the civil authorities, and directly challenge the moral order by (often inadvertently) questioning the legitimacy of the distribution of property and the social relationships incumbent upon property. Officials statistics [e.g., Statistics Canada, 1969;] indicate that about eighty per cent of the specified violations of the Criminal Code in Canada involve theft. Of the twenty to twenty-five per cent of reported incidents cleared, about forty per cent of those convicted are juvenile, the model age is 15–17 years, most are working-class in origin, and the majority are males. Yet there are very few studies of thieves, and almost no studies of those Canadian thieves who figure so prominently in the official statistics. In particular, existing research reports fail to document how persons become typical thieves, how they lead their careers and what becomes of them in later life. This is a remarkable deficiency, given the social policy value of such knowledge about such a prominent group of criminals.

This paper reports on the careers of serious thieves; more detailed descriptions of their occupational activities and social cohesion are available elsewhere. [West, 1974; West, 1977] The youths studied are so located and treated within society that they experience a major common problem—lack of acceptable employment opportunities. When this is combined with access to thieving, they may choose to become thieves unless restrained by conventional bonds (such as a spouse, a good job or school plan, or their self-concept). Serious thieves lack these conventional restraints. Most who become thieves, acquire these commitments later and cease thieving. Moreover, the mistakes which seem inevitably to occur in pursuing the occupation result in multiple convictions and prevent its being a life-long career. Shifting situations and new bonds make serious theft a very short-term occupation and a desirable occupation for a specific age group only.

Source: "The Short Term Careers of Serious Thieves," *Canadian Journal of Criminology* (1978), **20**(2): 169–170. 173–190. (Editorial adaptations.) Reprinted by permission.

REDRESSING RESEARCH DEFICIENCIES

. . .Research on thieves has had a peculiar focus substantively. Subjects in case studies and intensive interview research are usually rare professional thieves, who are interesting as extreme cases, but hardly typical of the thieves of most concern to the police. [Klein, 1974] Alternatively, self-report surveys probably gather data more indicative of petty theft activities, which almost everyone seems to have committed—but which are also of minor concern to the police. The large groups of more-than-amateur but less-than-professional thieves are left unstudied, although they are of most concern socially.

In Canadian law, a thief is one who is convicted of taking another's property without his permission.

(1) Everyone commits theft who fraudulently and without colour of right takes or fraudulently and without colour of right converts to his use or to the use of any other persons, anything whether animate or inaminate, with intent.

    (a) to deprive, temporarily or absolutely, the owner of it or a person who has special property or interest in it, of the thing, or of his property or interest in it,

    (b) to pledge it or deposit it as security,

    (c) to part with it under condition with respect to its return that the person who parts with it may be unable to perform, or

    (d) to deal with it in such manner that it cannot be restored in the condition in which it was at the time it was taken or converted.

(2) A person commits theft when, with intent to steal anything, he moves it or causes it to move or to be moved, or begins to cause it to become moveable.

(3) A taking or conversion of anything may be fraudulent notwithstanding that it is effected without secrecy or attempt at concealment.

(4) For the purposes of this Act, the question whether anything that is converted is taken for the purpose of conversion, or whether it is, at the time it is converted, in the lawful possession of the person who converts it is not material.

Martin, et al., 1972: Section 283

My concern is focussed on actors labelled as thieves rather than acts labelled as theft. [Lemert, 1967d] Using a "sensitizing concept" approach [Blumer, 1969] I have operationally defined "serious thieves" as those persons having all the following characteristics:

    (a) being recognized and labelled by themselves as thieves;

    (b) being recognized and labelled by their peers as thieves;

    (c) having been officially convicted by courts or labelled by police as thieves;

    (d) having gained at least $500 in profit from theft within a two-year period or less, making at least $100 or at least one-third of their total income from theft during any single month in which they were actively thieving (1971–2 figures). These criteria distinguish the subjects from petty or amateur thieves. In addition, serious thieves are distinguished from professional thieves:

    (e) they do not have as highly developed skills, such as safe-cracking, confidence racketeering, pickpocketing, or counterfeiting;

    (f) serious thieves are non-migratory;

    (g) serious thieves can rarely "patch" ("fix") cases that come to the attention of the police;

    (h) as a result, serious thieves spend two-thirds to three-quarters of their time locked up (compared with one-quarter to one-third of professionals' time) if they continue thieving for more than a couple of years;

(i) serious thieves make much less money, talking of "scores" of hundreds of dollars rather than thousands.

In practice, this definition gave me thieves who appeared adequately to represent the major characteristics of those figuring most prominently in the official court records. They specialized in six types of theft: shoplifting, house-burglary, commercial burglary, "clouting", [2] vehicle theft, and fraud/forgery. Such thieves adopted an occupational perspective towards their activities. Rather than being "irrational" (committing theft for "kicks," to provide reactions, to destroy property, to symbolize rebellion, to express neurotic or psychotic drives, etc.), these thieves organized their activities efficiently along business lines to maximize profit both in acquisition and distribution.

They were skilled at perceiving situations which one can turn into a moneymaking theft propositions by stealth and deception. Customers (consumers, legitimate merchants, and "fences") were selected with care. During the couple of years preceding 1971, the thieves studied averaged approximately $50 profit from their activities during a work week of two to twenty-five hours, a figure comparable to their income from full-time legal jobs available. They averaged $7,000 profit each over their careers, collectively profiting by some $250,000 (a figure which is ten to fifty per cent of the gross retail value of the goods stolen).

BACKGROUND

In describing background factors of the thieves studied, I am able to elaborate some antecedent or concommitant "causes" of becoming a thief (not "thieving") of the kind described. All thieves in the sample lived in, or grew up in, a lower and working class area of Toronto.[Garner, 1971; Mann, 1968; Butler, 1970] The neighbourhood has a high density of population, large families, and fifty to sixty per cent of the household heads are unemployed. Twenty-eight to forty-five per cent of the families in the area are female headed.[see Lorimer and Phillips, 1971] The neighbourhood youths associated in loose peer clusterings-[Lerman, 1967; Rogers, 1945] but these groups are not the highly structured gangs described in many American studies. [Short and Strodtbeck, 1965] Although the area is known to the police as a high-crime district, the theft ratio when compared with a middle class suburb falls from 5:1 in official statistics to 1½:1 in Byles' self-report questionnaire study.[1969] This study will address the puzzle implied by such data: that although everyone seems to steal, it is generally working class youths who become occupants of the status "thief."

The families of the forty thieves intensively interviewed tend to have handicaps to full participation in urban Toronto:[Lodhi and Tilly, 1973] only fourteen of the forty have both parents who were native-born, urban raised, and English speaking.[Clark, 1976] Almost all, however, are Anglo-Saxon or French Canadian. The families of all thieves studied are working-class or lower-class in occupational ranking; half are single-parent families.

The thieves themselves are disadvantaged in numerous ways. They completed only 8.4 years of schooling on the average, and all but 6 were dropouts at the time of interviewing. Thirty-six of the forty had been in low non-academic school streams.[see West, 1975] Thirty-three of the forty had committed petty theft as juveniles, thirty-five had been charged as juveniles (twenty-seven with theft offences) and eight had been incarcerated. The thieves who had left school had spent an average of forty to forty-five per cent of their time unemployed by the time of the interviews, and ninety-one per cent of them were unemployed at least twenty per cent of this time. The jobs they obtained were low paying (averaging $65-70/week in 1971) and low status menial ones, such as printers' helpers, delivery-boys, etc. They had difficulty maintaining employment, averaging 7.5 months per first job, and 3.9 jobs in the average time of three years between school-leaving and interviewing. In sum, they all had economic problems. All thieves studied were male, and they averaged 18.8 years at the time of the interviews, ranging from 15 to 23 years. These characteristics of the sample studied closely approximate those of official thieves as indicated in police and court data.

Since self-report studies[Box, 1971] indicate few behavioural differences regarding theft between social strata, the above factors may best be seen as more relevant to the elaboration (by youths and officials) of non-distinguishing petty acts of theft into the status of "serious thief" than simply as causes of "theft".

SOCIALIZATION

Not all persons sharing the background situations of the youths studied become thieves. Access (recruitment, training, and colleagues) is required to perform as a serious thief; it may be conceived as a necessary intervening variable.[Cloward and Ohlin, 1960] Some persons who have access remain constrained by conventional bonds (such as a spouse, a good job, or their self-concept).

(A) RECRUITMENT

How did these youths become occupational thieves? To join any social organization, the organization must first exist, it must be visible, entry to it must be available, and the individual must either be compelled or desire to participate.

Numerous studies[Mann, 1968; Shaw and McKay, 1972] attest that thieving of the type practised by the serious thieves described here is prevalent in lower and working-class areas. My own data tend to corroborate this:

C—You'll find almost everybody around . . . is into that some. L, X, T, Q, little C, C. Now Q is small, he sold a $26 pair of pants for $2. I sold them for $5-10. Depends on who the guy is. All this stuff I'm wearing is hot. Some, though, like M and X or S, or K or C or the H's, they're into it big. They take a place for everything, Me. I'm mostly into boosting clothes. [Interviewee, May 2, 1972]

It is, of course, possible that individuals could create theft organizations if they didn't previously exist, but it is much easier to merely join an already-existing institution where problems and methods of operation have already been worked out with some success.

For an institution to draw new recruits, its existence must be visible to them.[Becker, 1974: 66–72; Becker 1970: 248] As theft is a highly visible occupation in a lower or working-class community, most adolescents know at least one peer who steals. Theft is in the very air.

In the restaurant, S came in with a shirt up his sleeve, offered to sell it to me for 3 or 4 bucks as it was marketing for 6 retail. He'd just picked it up.[Group Observation, May 10, 1972]
Talked to E and F his friend. They are 10 and 14 respectively.
Me—You steal then?
E—Sure, if I need it. Anytime I want something and I don't have money. I took the axle cleaners for my bike. Or a radio. Or this knife from a hardware store.
Me—Many on the street steal?
F—Put it this way—its hard to say who doesn't. Almost everybody takes something. Maybe a few people don't. (They named some). The I's take everthing. We went away on holidays last year and our record player was gone.
E—Adults and kids all over the street steal. If they see what they want, they try to take it.[Group discussion, July 20, 1972]

The data presented earlier indicate how difficult access to legitimate jobs is for the youths studies. By sharp contrast, theft is open to their participation. There are no age or academic restrictions. There is no closed-shop unionism.

Me—How did you start doing this (Car theft)?
N—We first just took them for fun—joy-rides. Now we got into speed and needed bread, so then we decided to check them out, and saw stuff. I hung around and watched the older guys. Didn't go with them, just watched and listened to E and them. It seemed easy, so I tried it. I remember the first time, I was so nervous. I just drove off the lot and the guy ran out, and I just barrelled at him and he dove out of the way,

that's how I established my nerve. You don't need any skills, just learn to drive. I never truly taught others, but maybe they just picked it up from listening to me.Interview, Dec. 17, 1971

The primary social formation through which recruitment to occupational theft takes place is the loosely structured peer group. Leadership is usually spread over a number of individuals, often depending on mood and activity. Obligations are rarely imperative and membership boundaries are somewhat vague. Groups coalesce and disperse; individuals drift in and out of them, alone or in pairs. Almost all the neighbourhood youths have committed some petty varieties of theft during childhood. They are usually caught and "labelled as secondary deviants."Lemert, 1967b A great many teens thus know of the existence of theft through at least one peer who is thieving as an occupation. The symbiotic relationship between some older and younger clusters facilitates contact between peer groups and the potential recruits are able to meet the already-initiated.

K—Well, we hit it a few weeks or months ago. Just walking by and we needed cash for dope or something, and had this little C kid with us. We threw him in the shoot for clothes, and told him to bring back all the suits, so he did. I had five, and the rest of us (about 5) had about the same. Got 200 for them, I did. We gave the kid 5 for his work and he was happy.Interview, Nov. 3, 1971

There is no segregation of peer cluster members according to occupations; friendship lines do not replicate occupational lines. Thus, most teens do not need to *befriend* somebody to find a "partner in crime": They *already* know one.

Me—How did you start doing it?
C—I need money and E said, "come along," so I went. We pretty much kept it quiet and to ourselves you know, we didn't want a lot of guys in on it . . . He pointed out a few things and I guess that along the way, I showed other guys too.Interview, March 16, 1972

Learning within a friendship group probably facilitates the educational process.

(B) TRAINING

The basic skills required are learned from peers or older people in the neighbourhood. While the technical refinement of all but a few are low-level (the main exceptions being lockpicking and the "conning" required in forgery and some shoplifting), they are required for the job.

C—I took a locksmith course by mail, I can use a plastic shim to slide locks pretty good, and I got a master key and pick. I can make them. So I practise that. I'm good at thinking of ways into places. Like I delivered to a jewellery shop and wired their burglarized window by making an extra circuit below the window, so when you broke in through the glass later at night, the alarm doesn't go cause the circuit isn't broken. A lot of guys would never think of that. You sort of go around looking for places like that, things you can do. You pick places that are franchises, cause often the boss isn't there all the time, and he has to leave cash around to open in the morning. It's usually in a standard place. Some little guy who owns his own shop, he either takes the money in and out with him, or he hides it in a shoebox or some weird place, and you can't find it.Interview, May 2, 1972

To be a successful thief, it is essential to "learn the angles," to develop a certain perspective or world-view. Good thieves are constantly "on the prowl," "casing" potential jobsites, inspecting escape routes, assessing likely gains to be made, etc. Their *world* is different than non-thieves'; physical objects, buildings, and people assume a different meaning for them than for other people.

Over with E at 7:30.
We went driving over to downtown. Cased around the back alleys. On the way I jotted notes. E joked—You better have a good alibi if the cops stop us.
And indeed, we were somewhat suspicious looking—what are you doing when you go down alleys and look over buildings? "We would make a good insurance sales team or security outfit. . ."
It was very noticeable how a thief is *continually* assessing places. You evaluate each shop or establishment for what it likely contains which

you can turn into money or useful goods; you examine all the shops as well for ways in. Look for ways out. Judge the risk involved. And the appropriate times. The kids also have mentioned over and over again that each place is different, each place has its particular thing. I now see that that really is true.Observation, June 12, 1972

This orientation is developed over years of cultivation.

The thief also has to develop contacts, a series of relationships with supporting others. He needs colleagues, in most cases, who will "cut him in" on jobs, angles, or "hot tips," warn him when "the heat is on," and lend him money when he gets down on his luck. He needs reliable fences and customers, who are aware of constrictions on his work and know how to "play his game" or interact with him to minimize risks and maximize gain.Shover, 1973 An understanding lawyer is useful as well.

> Me—Where do you get rid of it?
> S—I just sell it around. Like the shirt today. It's not hard. L and E, they get orders. They took me to some guys, some kids and some adults—you'd be surprised how many adults will buy stuff. Most of them, I just know where they are and what they look like, not their names. I learned them from E and L.Interview, May 10, 1972

Training in an illegal occupation, however, entails special problems. Apprenticeship training in theft is often anticipatory: it takes place unselfconsciously among juveniles engaging in theft-as-a-lark.

> Me—How did you get into stealing stuff?
> C—I been shoplifting since I was 11 or so. I used to take watches. Started off big. I just been doing more of it lately—in the last year.Interview,November 25, 1971

> E—I just had pulled a few jobs as a kid. I left school and couldn't find work. So I needed some cabbage. Tried it a bit. After that first few times, you lose your fright and it becomes like any other job—a routine. You become cooler and better at it.Interview, June 6, 1972

All of these job-traits are learned over a period of years as the lower or working-class boy

is growing up. Any youthful, spontaneous escapadesLemert's primary deviation, 1967d will be interpreted by some people in his community differently than if he lived in a middle-class area.Cicourel, 1968; Emerson, 1969; Piliavin and Briar, 1964 The storekeeper and policeman will perceive him as a potential delinquent, a young thug, and treat him accordingly. His more worldwise peers may consider him a "chump" or "sucker" for getting caught, confessing, playing for small stakes, etc., and will inform him of "the real score," and tell him how to "really do it right."

> Me—How did you learn to do all this stuff?
> K—I mainly taught myself. Listen to guys around. You'd pick up hints.
> Think of it a lot and get new angles. Like the jack on the barred windows.
> We'd always be casing places.Interview, January 21, 1972

The peer group thus functions in training as well as in recruitment.

The boy who starts thieving as a juvenile has a period of grace in which to serve his apprenticeship and develop skills. Throughout the legal process, potential labellers are more likely to release him because of his youth. In particular, the juvenile court (in Toronto at least) will give him many more "chances" than adult courts would. At age 16, by legal fiction, he can continue his career with a new clean record. (After conviction in adult court, however, his juvenile record may be retrieved for consideration in sentencing.) The consequences of apprehension are much greater after age 16, but so are his skills and the potential rewards.

(C) COLLEAGUESHIP

Only within relationships with colleagues is the young person able to enact roles as a thief. Other thieves not only recruit and train him, they also are the very "vehicle" through which he realizes his potential identity as a thief. No serious thief of the type described carried on his work without colleagues.

As indicated above, the serious thieves studied have known at least some of their work colleagues for a number of years as peer group associates. Such colleagues offer emotional support and a continuing affirmation of the thief's sense of personal worth in his private as well as business life.^{Cameron, 1964: 167; Jackson, 1969: 81}

> K—I mean, we were partners. Cause you get scared—especially at first. You don't know what's up. You're out alone at night and its spooky. But if you did it alone, there'd be no hassles like arguing over when to pull another "score." And nobody to fink out and nobody to blame but yourself. And you'd have twice as much money.^{Interview, June 6, 1972}

The colleague group exercises some weak control over who joins their ranks.

> C—We pretty much kept it quiet and to ourselves you know. We didn't want a lot of guys in on it. N and his brother had a good racket going unloading railroad cars and selling the hot goods. I just learned last summer that he's being doing that for a while.^{Interview, March 16, 1972}
>
> N—X horses around too much. If he didn't find what he was looking for, he'd tear the place apart. Q talks too much, makes a lot of noise.^{Interview, December 17, 1971}

Since, however, the groups are so loosely structured, someone who wants very much to thieve can usually find somebody who will join him. Although some youths talked of developing special techniques on their own, I know of none who were serious thieves who did not associate regularly at some point early in their careers with at least one other thief. Being asked to join an activity by a significant other entails some social obligations which go beyond the specific task at hand.

Many jobs are carried out in partnership. Sometimes an elementary division of labour is apparent. Car and house-thieves co-operate with forgers and fraud artists by selling them the identification and credit cards necessary for their trade. Occasionally, a car-thief will rent his hot car to transport a burglar's or shoplifter's stolen goods. A good lock-picker or "heavy" can establish himself as a key member of one or many teams. Like the eminent surgeon, he attains a position of some power and prestige among colleagues.

> T—I'm usually the heavy—to do the muscle stuff. Pull off locks with tools, or just break them out of the wood, or you can strip them off with pliers. Then I keep watch, and if there is anybody around, stall them or fill them in. That's how I got asked along at first.^{Interview, December 13, 1971}

On some particular jobs, different tasks are assigned to partners who have no highly-developed specialty. One person may "keep six" or watch for intruders, another may wait in a "getaway" car. One shoplifter covers for another by distracting clerks.

> K—Usually there'd be two of us, sometimes three. One guy would get us in, usually me. Then another, he might keep six outside, like you'd have a system of taps or barks. He'd be hiding, but watching. Two sounds would mean somebody coming, three the cops, and four run or something like that. He might bark or tap an old broom. Mostly see, "somebody" is just an old drunk in the alley. That guy would hail the cab or drive the car too. A good partner? You got to have somebody trustworthy. Not to rat. To divvy up stuff evenly. A guy who'll back you and can fight. A fast runner. Maybe a guy who's got skills, with locks or keys or something. Again, K was the best.^{Interview, January 21, 1972}

Many "on-the-job" roles are unskilled and every thief is expected to be able to play them well.

Although I have no comparable data on middle class youths, my conjecture is that few become serious thieves as described here (although they steal almost as frequently while they are juveniles).^{Byles, 1969; Vaz, 1965} Such youths are much less likely to be afflicted by the background factors (especially unemployment) which make conventional activities less attractive than theft. Studies of middle class communities^{e.g., Seeley, et al., 1956} do not report that access factors are present there. In any case, these access factors are necessary and not sufficient "causes."

AGING AND RETIREMENT

Should a person take advantage of his access to serious thieving, he will attempt to solve his economic difficulties by organizing his stealing into an occupation. Almost inevitably, however, he will commit critical mistakes which will precipitate a career crisis within two or three years. Serious theft is a short-term occupation for the thieves studied.

> Mrs. M.—Most of them steal for a year or maybe a few. Like C was doing it for years. They get caught in 9 or 10 months or so. A few never do, but most of them get busted eventually. Now the older ones, like my Q and N have found nice girls and settled down. But I don't know if C and the other younger ones will. They're wilder and into dope in ways the older boys never were. I really think it's worse around here now. . . . And then when they get a girl and a job, they slow down or stop. I don't know any of above 25 who are still making their money as a thief.[Interview, August 5, 1972]

The twelve thieves interviewed who were still active had been so for an average of twenty months. the twenty-eight who had "retired" had practiced theft for an average of twenty-eight months. The longevity of their involvement in this occupation compares favourably with the short-term pattern of their involvement in other, legitimate employments. Why is the occupation pursued for so short a period?[Lemert, 1967b: 53]

In a few cases, physical ability to enact the behaviour required may deteriorate. The thief may lose agility, speed, special techniques and attributes (such as a size small enough to squeeze through windows). Particularly easy jobs may become closed off.

> S—I had the key to North—a master that guy I know got off a janitor in a fight. I worked until they changed the locks. . . .[Interview, December 13, 1971]

The serious thief loses desirable key social attributes which facilitate doing theft. Aging almost invariably implies an accumulated arrest record.

Economic success is only moderate among the thieves studied (although quite comparable to their legitimate jobs). Partly because of low skill levels, any one "score" offers only minimal profit, and committing an increasing number of infractions eventually results in arrest. Although these thieves are able to "work" the police and courts to their advantage, they are not able to "lay a patch" or "fix" cases in the strong sense described by professional thieves.[Sutherland and Conwell, 1937] When a charge is laid, these thieves generally have recourse only to those ploys available to the ordinary citizen (legal aid, bargaining on pleas, presenting extenuating circumstances, etc.) The main exceptions occur when they are able to coerce local neighbourhood witnesses, or when they (rarely) are able to trade information ("rat out") for a lesser charge.

First and second convictions usually result in probation or short sentences of a couple of months. Incarceration serves as a forced holiday, as well as a "business convention" among colleagues. In addition, it serves as a confirmation of a previously ambiguous identity and a "state licence" which is recognized both by colleagues and the public.

After the arrest, the thief is no longer anonymous and further arrests have much greater negative consequences.

> K—I just got clothes there now, like these pants.
> Me—How come you cut that out?
> K—Well, the heat is on me. I don't want to get sent up. So I want to lay low you know. I'm already on probation. And they almost caught me on that thing with the cheque, and now the mischief, so I want to take it easy.[Interview, November 3, 1971]

After being sent up a few times, prison terms dramatically increase in length to assume a substantially different nature. If the person continues thieving, he almost certainly will spend a large proportion of his days imprisoned. (Even "professionals," by their own accounts, seem to spend a quarter or third of their time incarcerated).[Sutherland and Conwell, 1937; Jackson, 1969; King, 1972; Miller and Helwig, 1972]

Me—How many you know who are still into theft?

C—About 30 I suppose, ranging in age from 20 to 60 years of age.

Me—How come they didn't stop?

C—They got nothing to stop for. No wife—none of them are married. None of them have good jobs.

Me—They can hack time okay, they don't mind being sent up?

C—Oh, that's bullshit. Sure they hate doing time. they can do it, but they don't like it. Only when they got out, theft is still the best thing for them. They forget about the jail and have a good time while they're out.

Me—How successful are they in staying out—What percentage of their time are they free?

C—Not much. Maybe a third on the outside and two-thirds inside. I don't know any of those 30 who are successful in staying out. Maybe some of the oldest guys, guys in their 50's are. But they don't make much, are very cautious. And the cops seem to go easy on them.

Me—There are no pros you know who spend only a quarter of their time inside, pull a few bit scores for big money.

C—No, nobody is that good. Maybe it is getting harder too—all the alarm systems and stuff.^{Group} Interview, July 17, 1972

He can no longer continue being a serious thief. In this career crisis, three options are open to him:

1. He will become a "jailbird," a convict, if he continues to behave as a serious thief. For some who have few outside ties, this institutionalized life may be palatable.

Me—It seems that of the guys I've talked to here, most by the time they're 20, have stopped theft pretty well. You haven't. Why not?

K—Most other guys they get responsibilities and they decide to cut it out. They get a job or married and a family. Me, I ain't got no responsibilities, see. Just me. So who gives a shit what I do. As far as I'm concerned, this country is totalitarian anyway. . . But I'll shake my time. Like my brother said, you make your bed and you got to lie in it. "If you can't shake the time, don't do the crime."

Me—You think you'll continue like this?

K—I dunno. I might find a woman. See, then I'd settle down. I wouldn't want no kids of mine doing all this stuff like I been doing. I'd box his ears good.

Me—Even though you talk about it being okay as a thief?

K—Look, even me, I don't like jail. I don't think my kids should go there. . . . I'll just keep on going the way I am, stealing all my life.^{interview, June 13, 1972}

Two of my interviewees have become "jailbirds," spending over half their lives since in prisons. They continue to act as serious thieves when released, precipitating further incarceration. If they have no outside conventional commitments, such as a family or a good job (see below), this option may be the path of least resistance. The longer they continue in this life, the harder it becomes to change and assume a conventional status.

2. A second option is to switch to a safer criminal occupation. Twenty of my forty thieves have "moonlighted," trying other criminal jobs at various times during their career and five of the retired thieves made their living by other criminal pursuits. Age may bring increasing skill or a different status which allows a person to make a living with less risk of arrest.

One may move into a small but profitable "service industry" crime such as bootlegging, bookmaking, fencing, bondsmaking, or loansharking.

S—See, what I want to do is just set myself up behind the scenes. Not boosting the stuff, so I can't easily get caught, but making deals and favours. Becoming a fence a lot.

Me—Tell me about that.

S—It's mostly what I've been doing to survive over the last year. Kids pick up stuff, shoplifting or from b and e's or cars say. They get rid of it to you. Or sometimes you ask them if they take something take X cause you can get rid of it. You take it and tell the guy you'll sell it for a price. Say he's got a tv worth 200 new. You pay him $30, telling him you'll get $35 for it. You make $5 he thinks. Only you sell it for $40 and make an extra $5. Then the guy you sold it to sells it to a customer who'll use it for 70 . . . The direct theft was shot for me. I wanted to keep doing staff, but safer. I met these guys who fence stuff too. And I know maybe now—9 or 10 thieves who deal through me.^{Interview, December 23, 1971}

These small "service industry" crimes allow—indeed require—the person to maintain and develop community ties. Since they are crimes without victims, they are difficult to prosecute; most such entrepreneurs combine them with a legitimate occupation.

Almost none of the thieves studied had been able to move into elaborate confidence or fraud rackets (which border on legitimate business and hence are difficult to prosecute) nor were they able to become expert professional thieves (who minimize chances of apprehension by pulling only a few big jobs a year). Few role models exist and the relations between serious (or "amateur") thieves and professionals were so weak I had great difficulty contacting any professionals.[3] Sutherland and Conwell, 1937: 21, 198

3. The third option is to go "straight," Twenty-one of twenty-eight interviewees who have stopped thieving have become "conventional." By age 20, if not earlier, a thief usually finds the attractiveness of a legal life has increased as the negative sanctions of an illegal one mount.

(a) He often finds a woman he loves and desires to be with; he shares her expectation that he support her and their children economically. If he opts for this fate, the possibility of incarceration must be avoided. Thieving and a stable marriage seem incompatible.^{Becker, 1974: 114; King and Chambliss, 1972: 76; Box, 1972: 244} As well, a married man needs a larger income than that available as a serious thief.

> Me—What you figure you got to lose by beaking the law?
> K—A lot now, My girlfriend, the kid. I got to support them, It's my baby, not T's.^{Interview, March 13, 1972}

Twelve of the twenty-one "reformed" thieves have married, compared with only one of the twelve active thieves.

(b) Coincident with this development, the thief usually finds some legitimate jobs become more available to him because of his greater age and accumulated work experience. ^{Box, 1972:245; King and Chambliss, 1972: 126, 140}

> C—When N got caught, both E and I figured we had jobs we liked and didn't need it that bad, and we didn't want to get sent up. I'd do it again if I got desperate, but I don't think I will. ^{Interview, March 16, 1972}

These jobs may be tolerable if not interesting, and offer a favourable increase in earning over theft. Further schooling or formal training may be available; some government programs even offer subsistence support during training.

> Me—Now you're cooling out—How come?
> N—I guess I'm just getting older. I don't need as much money now I'm over the quick (amphetamines). And I got nailed and did time. It'll be bigger next time. I got more going for me. A job here, one maybe lined up that I'd like as a printer. And more people doing stuff for me now. The recreation program here and C talking to me. So I got more out here. And I'd lose more if I was caught. ^{Interview, December 17, 1971}
> Me—You said you're clean these days, How come?
> C—Well the boosting is riskier—I'm too well known, Cops always look out. The keys we got are not good. I could still do the b and e's. But not too many come up. The cars—I got sent up. I'll grab big time if I go again. So it's hard. Not too much money to be made there really, and it's risky. There's no place really to move up bigger, unless you start pulling really fancy big jobs, and then the chances of getting caught are bigger cause the cops put on more heat to solve them and the time is bigger if you get pinched. And I want to sort of settle down, get a job. Like this one lined up at the employment service is to do shit at work first, around the factory, to see if I'm a good worker, and then they'll put me into printing stuff too and an apprenticeship. I'll make better bread than the 50 a week from boosting. I won't really get out of crime altogether.^{Interview, December 15, 1971}

Fifteen of the twenty-one "reformed" thieves

had found legal employment. Three others have returned to school.

(c) It is evident that changing motivations and self-conceptions are likely to accompany the above changes in occupation and marital status. Some thieves report a simple desire to "settle down". They have had enough of strange hours, violent escapes, and nervous tension.[Lemert, 1967a; Sutherland and Conwell, 1937: 184n]

N—Did pull b and e's. Ya, we did a lot of them. Mainly when I was 16, 17. I didn't give a shit then. I could be cool. Now, I don't think I'd have the parts. I'd be paranoid, afraid of every sound. I guess I pulled 40 or so in the couple of years. But its hard to guess. We'd go every night for a while, then slack off, not need money, or be scared for a bit.[Interview, May 15, 1972.]

K—The cops were hot after me too. Always looking out you know. It's a strange life too. You're always nervous. Cause there's always something they can pin on you. You never know what's gonna happen. That makes it exciting too, but it gets to you after a while.

Me—Any of the other guys still in it?

K—Not that I know of, of guys around here.[Interview, January 21, 1972]

Only in three of the twenty-one "reformed" cases have changed motivations been present without an accompanying wife, job or school-plan.

TABLE I Conventional Bonds and Criminality

	Active criminals		Reformed criminals	
	Number	%	Number	%
Without bonds (Woman, job, school plan)	17	89	3	14
With bonds (Woman, job, school plan)	2	11	18	86
Total	19[a]	100	21	100

[a] Consisting of 12 thieves, 2 convicts and 5 others.

CONCLUSION

Using participant observation methods and analytic induction. I have focussed on the careers of serious thieves, who seem to be the most numerous thieves of material consequence (in distinction from petty amateurs and rare professionals). By observing over an extended period, I collected longitudinal data on the social process of becoming a thief and retiring.

Situational adjustment[Becker, 1970] seems a useful concept in explaining this process of personal change. The thieves studied lacked social advantages and had problems from an early age in dealing with formal organizations such as schools, police, and employers. Their community provided recruitment, training, and colleagues required to be a serious thief. However, when their situations change, and accumulated arrests, suitable jobs, conventional marital relationships, and changed self-concepts make being a thief less attractive, they abandon the status.[4] The same three factors which "insulate"[Reckless and Dinitz, 1967] a person from becoming a serious thief are also associated with ceasing crime as a life-style. "Going straight" does not mean that a person will never commit another crime as an isolated act, but rather that he will no longer occupy the status of criminal (secondary deviant). Indeed, it is often "good citizens" desire to satisfy their own wants and their willingness to aid criminals (by placing illegal bets, buying "hot goods," "setting up" their factories for break-ins, etc.) that encourages crime to persist.

As practiced, serious theft is a short-term occupation. In demonstrating that such thieves quit when conventional commitments are acquired, the study corroborates control theory and survey research on recidivism.[e.g., Durkheim, 1951; Hirshi, 1969; Waller, 1974; and Box, 1971] Although the major precipitating factors are economic, this study modifies "vulgar" Marxist analysis by incorporating other social factors, such as attachments to spouses

The study also refutes crude statements of labelling theory[Nettler, 1974: 202ff] which claim that mere labelling causes behaviour; in this study, multiple convictions are more likely to result in abandonment of the deviant status when conventional commitments are present.[Bordua, 1967] Incarceration acts as a deterrent *if* combined with these restraining bonds. Nonetheless, it should be clear that an interaction perspective on deviance has been central to the analysis.[Becker, 1974] By incorporating the actors' viewpoints, it has been necessary to depict them as creating their own world by exercising well within situations of external constraint,[Matza, 1969] The fact that most of these thieves "cool out" refutes "psychological" or "type of person" explanations of the activity, in favour of a social situational one.

This exodus from the status suggests that crime in Canada, or more specifically Toronto, may differ from illegal activities as practised elsewhere. Since Toronto has comparatively uncorrupted police and little "organized" professional crime, there is less access to professional adult criminal statuses for serious thieves. The peer group structure is markedly different so that descriptions of American gangs[Short and Strodtbeck, 1965; Cloward and Ohlin, 1960] are simply inappropriate. Situational adjustments in later life seem more readily available, perhaps because of the lack of ethnic barriers for these youths (most are majority group white Canadians). Nonetheless, the enduring structural disadvantages of this age, sex, socio-economic

status group[Ross, 1975; Greenberg, 1975; Committee on Youth, 1971] suggest that "serious thief" will remain an attractive status for new, younger recruits.

FOOTNOTES

1. This article is based on my Ph.D. dessertation (West, 1974). My thanks to Norm Nurmi for typing assistance: to Howard S. Becker, John I. Kitsuse and Allan Schnaiberg for their comments on earlier drafts; and to Northwestern University, The Canada Council, O.I.S.E., and Queen's University for financial assistance. Earlier versions were presented at The Conference on Youth, Society, and The Law (Queen's University, June 1976) and the Annual Meetings of the Canadian Sociology and Anthropology Association (University of New Brunswick, June 1977).

2. "Clouting" consists of stealing goods in transit from delivery vans or warehouses.

3. This difficulty experienced initially as a research problem of access seems to me good evidence of a substantive finding.

4. Considerations of causality become intriguing here. The empirical evidence indicates that it is unlikely that either stopping being a thief or marrying/working routinely precedes the other. I could not, for instance, tease from the data support for the claim that merely having a job prevented theft; the job must be perceived by the actor as "good" both in the sense of providing adequate pay and being worthwhile retaining. Different actors go through different sequences of weighing the factors in their minds as they change the meanings of terms (e.g., marriage) for themselves. I take this as a paradigmatic example of Blumer's concern with interpretive practices in his arguments against "variable analysis."[Blumer, 1969]

REFERENCES

Becker, H. S. (1974). *Outsiders*. Toronto: Collier-Macmillan, revised edition.

——— (1970). *Sociological Work*. Chicago: Aldine.

Blumer, H. (1969). "The Methodological Position of Symbolic Interactionism." In his *Symbolic Interactionism*. Toronto: Prentice-Hall.

Bordua, D. (1967). "Recent Trends: Deviant Behaviour and Social Control." *Annals of the American Academy of Political and Social Science* **369** (January) 149–63.

Box, S. (1971). *Deviance, Reality, and Society.* Toronto: Holt, Rinehart, and Winston.

Butler, J. (1970). *Cabbagetown Diary.* Toronto: Peter Martin.

Byles, J. (1969). *Alienation, Deviance, and Social Control.* Toronto: Interim Research Project on Unreached Youth.

Cameron, M. O. (1964). *The Booster and The Switch.* Toronto: Collier-Macmillan.

Cicourel, A. V. (1968). *The Social Organization of Juvenile Justice.* New York: Wiley.

Clark, S. D. (1976). "The Disadvantaged Rural Society: New Dimensions of Urban Poverty," in his *Canadian Society in Historical Perspective.* Toronto: McGraw-Hill Ryerson.

Cloward, R. and L. Ohlin (1960). *Delinquency and Opportunity.* Toronto: Collier-Macmillan.

Clinard, M. B. and R. Quiney (1973). *Criminal Behaviour Systems: A Typology* Toronto: Holt, Rinehart and Winston

Committee on Youth (1971). *It's Your Turn . . .* Ottawa: Information Canada.

Durkheim, E. (1951). *Suicide.* Toronto: Collier-Macmillan.

Emerson, R. (1969). *Judging Delinquents.* Chicago: Aldine.

Garner, H. (1971). *Cabbagetown.* Richmond Hill, Ontario: Simon and Schuster.

Greenberg, D. (1975). "Coming of Age in Delinquency: A Theoretical Synthesis" Unpublished manuscript, Sociology Department, New York University.

Hirchi, T. (1969). *Causes of Delinquency.* Berkeley: University of California Press.

Jackson, B. (1969). *A Thief's Primer.* Toronto: Collier-Macmillan.

King, H. and W. Chambliss (1972). *Box Man: A Professional Thief's Journey.* Toronto: Harper (Fitzhenry and Whiteside).

Lemert, E. (1967a). "An Isolation and Closure Theory of Naïve Check Forgery." In his *Human Deviance, Social Problems and Social Control.* Toronto, Prentice-Hall.

———— (1967b). "The Concept of Secondary Deviation." *Ibid.*

Lerman, P. (1967). "Gangs, Networks, and Subcultural Delinquency." *American Journal of Sociology.* LXXIII (July): 63–72.

Lodhi, A and C. Tilly (1973). "Urbanization, Crime, and Collective Violence in Nineteenth Century France." *American Journal of Sociology.* LXXIX, 2 (September)

Lorimer, J. and M. Phillips (1971). *Working People.* Toronto: James Lewis and Samuel.

Mann, W. E. (1968). "The Social System of a Slum: The Lower Ward, Toronto." In his *Deviant Behaviour in Canada.* Toronto: Social Science Publishers

Matza, D. (1969). *Becoming Deviant.* Toronto: Prentice-Hall.

Miller, B., and D. Helwig (1972). *A Book About Billie* (retitled *Inside and Outside*). Ottawa: Oberon.

Nettler, G. (1974). *Explaining Crime.* Toronto: McGraw-Hill Ryerson.

Piliavin, I., and S. Briar (1964). "Police Encounters with Juveniles." *American Journal of Sociology* LXX (September): 206–214.

Reckless, W. C., and S. Dinitz (1967). "Pioneering with Self-Concept as a Vulnerability Factor in Delinquency." *Journal of Criminal Law, Criminology, and Police Science LVIII,* 4.

Rogers, K. (1945). *Streetgangs of Toronto.* Toronto: Ryerson.

Ross, M. (1975). "Economic Conditions and Crime—Metropolitan Toronto 1965–72." *Criminology Made in Canada II,* 2: 27–41.

Seeley, J., *et al.* (1956). *Crestwood Heights.* Toronto: University of Toronto Press.

Shaw, C., and H. D. McKay (1972). *Juvenile Delinquency and Urban Areas.* Chicago: The University of Chicago Press.

Short, J., and F. Strodtbeck (1965). *Group Process and Gang Delinquency.* Chicago: University of Chicago Press.

Shover, N. (1973). "The Social Organization of Burglary." *Social Problems XX.* 4: 499–514.

Sieber, S. (1973). "The Integration of Fieldwork and Survey Methods." *American Journal of Sociology,* LXXXIX (May).

Statistics Canada (1969). *Census #93–609*. Ottawa: Information Canada.

Sutherland, E., and C. Conwell. (1937). *The Professional Thief*. Chicago: University of Chicago Press.

Vaz, E. (1965). "Middle-Class Adolescents: Self-Reported Delinquency and Youth Culture Activities." *Canadian Review of Sociology and Anthropology II*, 1 (February).

Waller, I. (1974). *Men Released From Prison*. Toronto: University of Toronto Press.

West, W. G. (1974). *Serious Thieves: Lower-Class Adolescent Males in a Short-term Deviant Occupation*. Unpublished Ph.D. Dissertation. Northwestern University, Evanston, Ill.

———— (1975). "Adolescent Deviance and the School" *Interchange 6*, 2: 49–56.

———— (1977). "Serious Thieves: Lower-Class Adolescent Males in a Short-term Deviant Occupation." In E. Vaz and A. Lodhi (eds.) *Crime and Delinquency in Canada*. Toronto: Prentice-Hall.

18

BYSTANDER INDIFFERENCE TO STREET CRIME

HAROLD TAKOOSHIAN AND HERZEL BODINGER

No problem seems to press more heavily on the minds of urban Americans than crime. A survey by *The New York Times,* for example, confirms the finding of many others, that New Yorkers far and away cited rampant street crime as the City's number-one problem (Carmody, 1974). A more recent survey found the problem of crime intrudes even into New Yorkers' dream-life: "A full third (of their dreams) were dominated by a feeling of naked fear, of being chased, or of being victimized by crime" (Milgram, in Duncan, 1977: 58). Indeed, objective social indicators justify this concern, since per capita crime rate is consistently higher in urban than in nonurban areas (Fischer, 1976), and has been accelerating much faster in cities than noncities since the close of World War Two (U.S.F.B.I., 1978).

It is perplexing that urban crime almost always remains unsolved. Urban criminals are as elusive as they are pervasive. They are rarely apprehended. The popular media image of the hard-nosed police officer who "gets his man" contrasts sharply with the all too common and frustrating experience of urban victims who are told by the police that they will never again see their stolen car, bicycle, or valuables, or

that the mugger will probably never be found (Dominick, 1973). Indeed, New York City's analysis of its own Police Department records found that hardly 2 percent of reported street crimes result in the arrest of a suspect, which leaves 98 percent of street crimes unsolved (Greenwood, 1969).[1]

How is it that street criminals in the city so commonly elude apprehension or detection—even in public areas during daylight hours? Three possible explanations may be offered: (a) Perhaps street criminals act when no others are present. (b) Perhaps criminals act with others present, yet are skilled at remaining unseen. (c) Perhaps others are present and see the crime, yet simply do not intervene.

This field experiment inquires into the third possibility above. What is the reaction of bystanders (pedestrians and police) who view an apparent street crime?

Though some prior research has inquired into bystander reactions to crime, it does not relate at all to the very real problem of *street* crime. This prior research has been limited to crimes in a *laboratory* (Schwartz & Gottlieb, 1976), or *store* theft (Bickman, 1979; Bickman & Green, 1977; Steffensmeier, 1975; Latane &

Source: "Street Crime in 18 American Cites: A National Field Experiment." Paper presented at American Sociological Association (August 1979), Boston. Reprinted by permission of the authors.

[1] Even this low 2 percent apprehension figure is likely to be inflated. Consider that many street crimes go unreported (Block, 1974), and a suspect arrested for one crime may be induced to confess to others as well.

Darley, 1970). There are crucial differences between these and street crime.[2]

This, then, is an unprecedented exploratory investigation, which tentatively hypothesizes that urbanites do not intervene when confronted with a suspicious criminal act performed in a public area—which would explain Greenwood's 1969 finding that only 2 percent of street larcenies result in an arrest.

METHOD

A common and serious street crime was simulated: forcibly breaking into a parked car. A "suspect" surreptitiously inspects a row of parked cars in the Central Business District (Gibbs, 1960) of Manhattan. (See Figure 1: Precincts 10, 13, 17, 19, 20, 23, 24, Midtown North and Midtown South.) Then the suspect produces a wire hanger, anxiously forces the door of one of the cars for a minute of more, removes a valuable large object (CB, TV set, camera, or fur coat), locks the door again, and hurries away.

Meanwhile, a recorder inconspicuously notes the dress, and features of the suspect, time of day, location, duration, number of passersby and police officers, and so on. The dependent measure (bystander response) is recorded for each trial into one of four categories:

1. *Ignore.* Observers give the suspect no more than a passing glance.
2. *Notice.* Observers stop, stare, point, or somehow react without directly interacting with the suspect.
3. *Intervene.* Observers ask the suspect if it is his/her car, or stop the break-in.
4. *Other.* Any uncategorized response.

The early research (phase 1) was limited to midtown New York City, while phase 2 included repetition of precisely the same pro-

cedure in 17 cities in North America, to determine a general urban response.

RESULTS

During the crimes in Manhattan (phase 1), 31 suspects[3] broke into parked cars 214 times. The research was then expanded to 17 major cities in the United States and Canada (phase 2), in which suspects[4] forcibly entered parked cars 167 times—9 or 10 times per city.

PHASE 1: MANHATTAN

At first, suspects were understandably upset in publicly breaking into the car and removing valuables within sight of pedestrians and police. A majority of them predicted they would be stopped during their first break-ins, and they seemed to be holding their breath during the initial trial or two, waiting for a tap on the shoulder and a challenge by a passerby: "Is that yours?" Even the minority who forecast they would not be stopped showed visible signs of tension during the initial crimes. They reported uneasy stomach, shaking hands, trembling, fear, and a desire to quit the research.[5]

Indeed, elaborate precautions were taken from the outset to allay such fears. A key was

---

[2] Note the sharp difference in the eyes of the onlooker between a street crime like breaking into a car versus a shoplifting. In a shop, the witness (a) in an enclosed environment; (b) sees an object of small value; (c) stolen from an impersonal owner.

[3] Our thanks to all 31 suspects in phase 1: Margaretha Van den Berg, Herzel Bodinger, Barbara Cohen, Franklin Hampton, Alice Lilly, Teresa Diak, Valerie Hendrix, Carol McCalla, Jeanne Russo, William Rydquist, Katherine Shaw, Allan Summer, Ida Vega, Mitchell Cherry, Cathy Carr, Joan Clemente; Kathy Helton, Karen Hickey, Ethel Wingers, Helayne Cohen, Sharon Cohen, Felix Martinez, Theresa Concert, Jacqueline Bonnafour, Maureen Doyle, Mary Huehner, Mary Ann Krieger, Charliann Lander, Gloria Mazurek, Susan McGrath, Harold Takooshian.

[4] Our thanks to all nine suspects in phase 2: S. Schmueli, I. Saban, U. Hatuka, N. Datner, B. Ben Shimol, V. Noga, H. Bodinger, C. Colon, V. Toth.

[5] The "suspects" were enrolled in a social psychology class, and volunteered to participate in this research rather than some other project of their own selection. Indeed, a majority of the suspects were victims of authentic street crimes, who shared a genuine interest in learning the results of the experiment. It might also be noted here that an actual crime was never committed during this research. The autos and property belonged to members of the research team, and proper papers were always on hand to verify this if necessary.

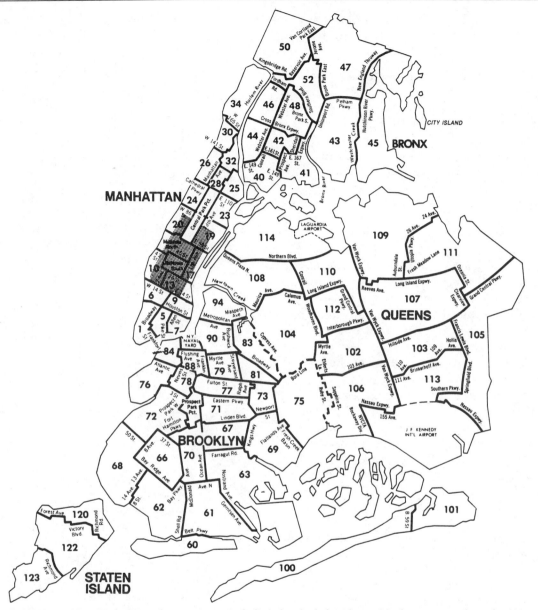

FIGURE 1. New York City police precincts, including the shaded midtown Manhattan area where the 214 simulated crimes were performed.

positioned on the dashboard of the locked car, so a challenged suspect could point out that his/her key was mistakenly left inside. The suspect also had the auto registration ready to produce on a moment's notice. Recorders were stationed nearby to insure that no mishap should occur with the suspect alone.

These precautions proved wholly unnecessary, even from the very first trial. The recorder wrote:

Trial no. 1 . . . A black youth tapped the suspect's arm as he was breaking in, said "Hey baby, this is my schtick," took the hanger and succeeded in breaking in, watched the suspect remove the portable TV and relock the door, then he asked for a "tip" as the suspect walked away with the TV.

This reaction—helping the suspect—was unforeseen. Such a response was recorded as an uncategorized "other," whenever the passerby helped the suspect remove property without asking if it belonged to the suspect.

The 214 Manhattan break-ins resulted in a low rate of interference with the suspect's action: *20.1 percent* "other" (helping), *44.9 percent* ignore, *32.2 percent* notice, and *2.9 percent* intervene. Among over 3000 passersby in the 214 trials, 6 questioned the suspect.

By far, the modal response of observers—police as well as pedestrians—was to *ignore* the incident. This supports Milgram's (1970) notion of urban overload, that the urbanite becomes accustomed to filtering out stimuli that are unrelated to his own survival needs. The great majority of passersby on even the most crowded streets gave the anxious suspect no more than a blank passing glance.

The minority of passersby who tangibly *noticed* the suspect would stop, stare, snicker, and often seemed to deliberate for a minute or more about what to do. Yet this typically ended in their casually walking away, without approaching the suspect at all. Though such passersby seemed concerned, they also seemed too confused about how to curtail the suspect's action.

Those who *aided* the suspect usually (though not always)[6] assumed the suspect owned the car and property, even in instances when a shabby man would remove a woman's purse. If questioned, suspects did not claim it was their car, but instead remained silent or made unclear statements like "I want to get the camera" or "Let's see if you can get in before the

---

[6] In at least four cases, passersby clearly perceived the suspect as a thief when they offered to help. One young man watching two female suspects take a camera wanted to join them and help clean out the other materials on the car seat. In another incident, a young man warned the suspect that a policeman was approaching so the suspect should be careful not to be caught.

police pass by!" Though helpers were likely motivated by good intentions, it remains an upsetting thought that a genuine thief might rob someone's auto while surrounded by a crowd, and members of the crowd actually step forward to offer their unquestioning assistance.

Of the six cases of *intervention*, three were by police, and three by pedestrians. One young man asked the suspect, "Does that car belong to you?" A teenage black girl asked the suspect, "Is that your camera? (No answer.) I'm going to stay here until a policeman passes by, unless you get away from that car!" Though a number of police officers forced open the car door for a suspect without demanding identification, three policemen requested to see the auto registration while they helped to pry open the car window.

There was a discernible shift in suspects' feelings during the course of the research. Many of the suspects' initial tension subsided, to be replaced by surprise, boredom, entertainment, or even anger. One suspect noted after 15 trials:

> It was getting boring. Nothing was happening, and I felt I was wasting time. Nobody was reacting, no matter how furtive or how outrageous I acted.

Another suspect's reaction differed:

> I wanted someone to stop me, to say "Hey you, get away from that car!" I've been ripped off several times, and I'm sorry to see how easy it must have been (when they) stole my car.

Two researchers interviewed nonresponsive witnesses after the theft, to learn their reasons for not intervening.

Since the rate of nonintervention began appearing from the initial trials, we began to spin tentative explanations and to adapt the basic procedure as we went along, in order to increase the rate of intervention:

Perhaps passersby viewed the suspect as the owner of the car. Such *reinterpretation* of a crisis is a common finding among researcher on "helping behavior" (Latane & Darley, 1970;

Huston & Korte, 1976). Efforts were made to reduce this reinterpretation of the crime. (a) A shabby 14-year-old acted as the suspect; no passerby ever stopped her, though a number offered to help her remove the TV set. (b) Suspects simultaneously broke into two adjacent parked cars; despite the peculiarity of the scene, observers did little more than stare, and one group commented to the recorder ". . . Yes, this is a high crime area, and these things are always happening." (c) In 15 cases, a "victim" conspicuously parked her car within 20 feet of curbside bystanders, left before a stranger ambled by, broke into her car, and hurried away with her camera or coat. Again, the rate of intervention by bystanders was almost nil, though noticing was higher than average.

Perhaps observers were *afraid* to intervene. We stationed a uniformed policeman 100 feet down the block from a car being forced open. Pedestrians did not inform the policeman that they had noticed a suspicious break-in going on. This fear notion, too, seemed inadequate to explain the phenomenon of nonintervention in street crimes.

Before concluding that urbanites do not intervene in street crimes such as this car break-in, we might well ask: Is New York typical of most American cities? We know, for instance, that New York is exceptionally high (the highest) in rate of reported violent crimes per 100,000 and that one of every 20 cars parked on New York streets was reported stolen in 1977 (U.S.F.B.I., 1978). Perhaps there is a higher rate of intervention in other cities, of which New York's 3 percent rate is atypical?

PHASE 2: 17 CITIES

As part of a cross-country musical tour, the second author replicated the same break-in procedure in 17 cities in North America. These were sampled from all parts of the U.S. and Canada (see Figure 2). The midtown area was selected using a procedure suggested by Stanley Milgram (personal communication): we asked our local contact where is the approximate center of the city, where a visitor might

go to be most likely to bump into a local friend whose address he does not have? So, for instance, we sampled the Loop in Chicago, Market Street in San Francisco, and CBD areas comparable to mid-Manhattan.

We found the cross-country rate of urban invervention was *10.8 percent*—over three times the Manhattan rate (Chi-square = 9.27 at 1 df, p < .005). To be sure, this rate varied greatly among cities. There was 0 percent intervention in five of them (Baltimore, Buffalo, Toledo, Miami, Ottawa), up to 25 percent in one (Phoenix), and 20 percent in four others (Chicago, Los Angeles, San Francisco, and Fort Lauderdale). The recorder often noted the police (who were responsible for over half the interventions in phase 2) had greatly different attitudes from city to city: in some they seemed indifferent, while in others their style of policing seemed oriented towards control of their environment. This concurs with others' findings of cross-city variation in police and pedestrian behavior (Wilson, 1976; Takooshian, Haber & Lucido, 1977).

Phase 2 of this research was not designed to test each one of the 17 cities separately, and the modest sampling of 9 or 10 trials per city may be an unreliable score on a per-city basis. Nevertheless, the overall result from 167 trials in phase 2 yields two findings: (a) New Yorkers were far less likely to confront a potential street thief than those in other cities by a significant factor of 1-to-3. (b) The rate of intervention nationally, 10.8 percent, is still a small fraction of the number of times passersby let the suspicious incident go unchallenged.

DISCUSSION

These findings seem to expose an urban problem as serious as the rising rate of street crime: namely, urbanites' refusal to react to this street crime. In 9 of 10 cases, no one stepped out from the passing crowd to question someone behaving in a suspicious manner, and the nonresponse was greatest in the largest of the cities, New York.

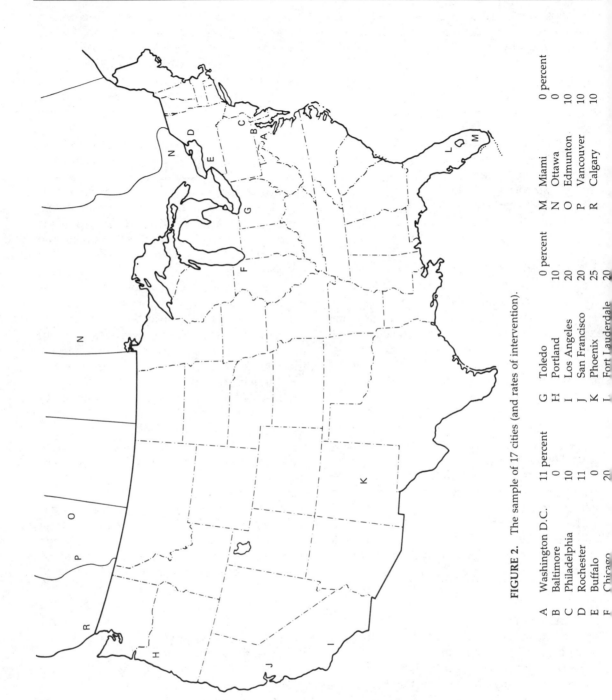

FIGURE 2.   The sample of 17 cities (and rates of intervention).

A	Washington D.C.	11 percent	G	Toledo	0 percent	M	Miami	0 percent
B	Baltimore	0	H	Portland	10	N	Ottawa	0
C	Philadelphia	10	I	Los Angeles	20	O	Edmunton	10
D	Rochester	11	J	San Francisco	20	P	Vancouver	10
E	Buffalo	0	K	Phoenix	25	R	Calgary	10
F	Chicago	20	L	Fort Lauderdale	20			

This nonresponse might be more systematically probed in a couple of ways by future researchers.

1. Experimental Variations. Would suburbanites or ruralites show comparable nonresponse to street crimes? Would residents of urban neighborhoods (outside the CBD) be more likely to intervene upon a suspect acting suspicious on their "turf"? To what extent do the suspect's personal features (race, sex, age, dress) influence his image as a thief? In contrast to the laudable deluge of helping research since the tragic death of Catherine Genovese in New York in 1964, we have yet to investigate with equal care bystander intervention in crimes.

2. Social Action. In place of local experiments on "saturation policing," in which the police presence is increased in a limited area of the city (Wilson, 1976), it is equally possible to increase citizen involvement via a community mass-media campaign: informing citizens of the crime problem, what to do when viewing a suspicious incident, information on if and how to intervene, etc. Although LEAA-sponsored neighborhood projects have attempted to boost citizen involvement (Froetschel, 1978), there has been no attempt known to the present researchers to monitor success using pre and post measures of local response to suspicious incidents. The present authors feel the ethics and practicality of such a social action effort warrant exploration.

REFERENCES

Bickman, L. (1979). "Interpersonal Influence and the Reporting of a Crime." *Personality & Social Psychology Bulletin* 5:32–35.

Bickman, L. and S. Green (1977). "Situational Cues in Crime Reporting." *Journal of Applied Social Psychology* 10:1–18.

Carmody, D. (1974). "How New Yorkers feel about New York," *The New York Times*, 14 January 146: 1.

Block, R. (1974). "Why Notify the Police: A Victim's Decision to Notify the Police of an Assault. *Criminology* 11:555–569.

Dominick, J. (1973). "Crime and Law Enforcement on Prime-Time Television." *Public Opinion Quarterly* 37:241–250.

Fischer, C. (1976) *The Urban Experience.* New York: Harcourt Brace Jovanovich.

Froetschel, S. (1978). "ACT ONE: Crime Prevention Is up to You." *Our Town,* 12 November 9:5.

Gibbs, J. (1960). *Urban Research Methods.* Princeton: Van Nostrand.

Greenwood, P. (1969). An Analysis of the Apprehension Activities of the New York City Police Department. New York: New York City Rand Institute report #R-529-NYC.

Huston, T., and C. Korte (1976). "The Responsive Bystander: Why Does He Help?" In T. Lickona (ed.), *Handbook of Moral Development.* New York: McGraw Hill.

Latane, B and J. Darley (1970). *The Unresponsive Bystander: Why Doesn't He Help?* New York: Appleton Century Crofts.

McCaghy, C., P. Giordono and T. Henson (1977). "Auto theft: Offender and offense characteristics." *Criminology* 15:367–386.

Milgram, S. (1970). "The Experience of Living in Cities." *Science* 167:1461–8.

Schwartz, S., and A. Gottlieb (1976). "Bystander Reactions to a Violent Theft." *Journal of Personality and Social Psychology* 34:1188–1199.

Steffensmeir, D. (1975). "Levels of Dogmatism and Willingness to Report a 'Hippie' and 'Straight' Shoplifter." *Sociometry* 38:282–290.

Takooshian, H., S. Haber, and D. Lucido (1976). "Responses to a Lost Child in City and Town." Paper presented at the annual meeting of the American Psychological Association, Washington.

Takooshian, H., S. Haber, and D. Lucido (1977). "Who Wouldn't Help a Lost Child?" *Psychology Today* 10:67, 68, 86.

U.S. Federal Bureau of Investigation (1978). Crime in the United States, 1977. Washington, D.C.: Government Printing Office.

Wilson, J. (1976). *Varieties of Police Behavior: The Management of Law and Order in Eight Communities.* New York: Atheneum.

Duncan, S. (1977). "Mental Maps of New York." *New York,* 19 December 10:51–62.

SECTION V

ORGANIZED CRIME

Although many ventures into theory have proved to be sterile, some valuable speculation and research have developed regarding two forms of criminal behavior: the competent, experienced criminal, sometimes referred to as the "professional criminal," and criminals who band together within a formal organizational framework to maximize collective efficiency, safety, and profits: the so-called "organized-crime offender."

One of the most persuasive statements on work capabilities, talents, and skills of career criminals is that of Letkemann in his description of offenders who engage in crimes involving face-to-face confrontation with their victims. In this selection, he deals with the experienced bank robber. The importance of pre-event planning and subtle, psychological alternatives in victim-management strategies during the robbery are very clearly and dramatically presented.

The major sources of illegal income of persons in organized crime are by common attribution, lending money at usurious rates (loansharking), and illicit gambling. Seidl's dissertation is the most detailed and least stereotyped investigation yet made of loansharking. Viewing the activity from an economic perspective, the author portrays the borrower-lender agreement, the collection process, and the two types of borrowers: the "rationed" and the "unrationed." Horse betting is examined in a selection from a recent investigation by a Select Committee of the U.S. House of Representatives. The testimony reveals how horse races have often been "fixed" by the use of electrical devices, illegal drugs, "ringer" horses, and the deliberate "pulling" of horses.

The cliche "crime doesn't pay" may be applied with accuracy to amateurish activities of the occasional or young criminal. But what of the real "pro"? How much does he actually earn (tax-free, of course) in a year? This interesting question has rarely been investigated. The selection by Plate attempts to estimate not only incomes of various criminal specialities but also some of their illicit overhead expenses.

Although it is a very "American" sort of crime and quite common, auto theft has been understudied by criminologists. The selection in this section is an explanation, in the words of professional thieves, describing step-by-step the techniques used to steal and dispose of automobiles. For a number of years it has been contended that one continuing threat posed by organized crime consisted of their infiltration into legitimate businesses. One example of this tactic is revealed in MacMichael's description of the manner in which notorious and widely feared members of organized crime, such as Johnny Dio and Thomas Eboli, infiltrated the kosher meat and bagel industries in New York City.

By an anthropological study of the Lupollo family, Ianni describes the rules of appropriate conduct in organized crime, which center primarily around the concepts of family loyalty, "acting like a man," and secrecy; and the ways organized crime families enforce these codes of behavior among their members.

19

THE SKILLED BANK ROBBER

PETER LETKEMANN

INTRODUCTION

The information received from the forty-five subjects interviewed for this study includes comments on a wide variety of criminal behavior. Without wishing to provide yet another detailed typology of crimes, I believe it is useful to differentiate between those crimes committed surreptitiously and those involving direct confrontation with the victim. The one involves the taking of property without the owner's consent or knowledge, the other involves the demand for property and its being "given" to the thief by the victim. Roughly speaking, this follows the legal distinction between burglary and robbery. The primary difference sociologically is that robbery involves direct interaction between thief and victim, whereas burglary does not. It follows, therefore, that the skills associated with robbery must include those necessary for the management and manipulation of people. This is not to minimize the importance of mechanical and technical skills, but to indicate that victim confrontation adds an additional dimension to the skills necessary for success in nonsurreptitious crime. Sutherland points out that, in terms of status, professional thieves distinguish between those criminals whose work depends primarily on manual dexterity as opposed to those whose work depends on "wit, 'front' and talking ability":

. . . burglars, robbers, kidnappers, and others who engage in the "heavy rackets" are generally not regarded as professional thieves, for they depend primarily on manual dexterity, or force. A few criminals in the 'heavy rackets" use their wits, "front" and talking ability, and these are regarded by the professional thieves as belonging to the profession.[1]

The inference, as I see it, is that violent crimes, for example those involving the threat or use of violence by way of weapons are thought to require little or no ability to manipulate people. Since the mechanical skills, besides the ability to use a gun, also appear to be minimal, the robber appears to share neither the social skills of the con artist, nor the technical skills of the burglar.

My subjects recognized that some lines demand greater ability in conning the public (obviously, for example, con artists) and that some lines involve no contact with the public at all. Among the latter, however, are some lines, such as burglar-alarm experts who, although not in face-to-face contact with the public, speak of their work in terms of their ability to outsmart the public. The same is true of safe-

Source: Crime as Work. Spectrum Books. Englewood Cliffs, N.J.: Prentice-Hall, Inc., 1973, pp. 90–116. Reprinted by permission of Prentice-Hall, Inc., Englewood Cliffs, N.J. (Editorial adaptations.)

[1] Sutherland, Edwin, *The Professional Thief*, Chicago: Univ. of Chicago Press, 1937, p. 198.

crackers, who violate the ultimate symbols of financial security. Therefore, although the manual aspect of the above lines varies (the safecracker doing much more purely physical labor), each is perceived as an intellectual rather than a physical conquest.[2]

It is my purpose to analyze the accounts given by armed robbers, with a view to discovering the assumptions on which the robber proceeds and the skills used in the action.

Just as safecracking was used to illustrate various dimensions of burglary, so group bank robbery will be used here to illustrate facets of robbery. This choice is partly arbitrary, for similar basic patterns can be seen in general armed robbery as well. To focus on bank robbery, however, provides a useful contrast with our previous discussion of safecracking, which is also used to extract money from banks. My subjects frequently suggested that the increasing difficulty of burglarizing a bank is the cause for the rise in bank robberies.

In terms of organization, robbery may involve a highly organized group of persons working as a team; on the other hand, it may be a loose, temporary liaison between several persons, or it may take the form of a lone gunman doing a stick-up. The victims may also vary, from banking institutions to the corner grocer or a lone pedestrian.

*

My choice of group bank robbery enables us to look both at the interaction between the group and the bank employees, and at the sociological processes within the group itself. The group formation, the testing of loyalties, and the allocation of responsibilities will be dealt with later under the more general topic of teaching and learning criminal skills. In this chapter, we will look at the act of group rob-

[2] There are exceptions to this, and examples of snobbishness can be documented. For example, no. 35, who was a burglar, recalled his difficulty in opening his first safe. I asked why he had not sought advice from an experienced safecracker. "I wasn't that much interested in it," he said. "Actually, I just rate a safecracker, even the best, only as a laborer." (no. 35)

bery itself, so that the technical, organizational, and social skills involved may be documented and described before we ask how they are learned and transmitted.

PRE-EVENT PLANNING

If the group is a loose, temporary liaison initiated by a transient robber, the choice of partners will be made at least partly on the basis of the skills required for a particular job. If the group is a coalition of some duration, various responsibilities will be understood and fulfilled by members prior to the event itself. Legal, medical, and financial arrangements may or may not form a part of an individual's prerobbery preparation, depending on his experience and ability to pay.

The only tools you basically need then are masks and guns?

Oh no. Definitely, you need more than that. Now this is where organization is the big thing. You see, well—first of all you've got—well, I was shot. Well, I'm shot, see? Now just supposing I'd have got away, where am I going to go? St. Paul's Hospital? Am I gonna go to St. Mary's Hospital? General Hospital? Oh no—I've gotta have a doctor. You've gotta, so therefore you've gotta have a doctor. You've gotta take care of all these things. You just don't—you've gotta have, in case you go to jail, you've gotta have a lawyer. You've gotta have all these things taken care of long before you go into planning a bank job. Well, where would I have gone if I'd have got shot? Well, I couldn't have stayed in a hotel room, bleeding like a sieve. Right away, if I'd have got out, I'd have just phoned my doctor so and so, and said, "I'm here, get up here right away!" You see, you've gotta pay them off, you see. There's lots of them in Western City. Same also if I'd have got caught, I would have needed a lawyer right away, quick. Things like that. You've got to take care of all these things.

What about bail money?

Oh, I had that all taken care of. Bail money was taken care of. (no. 7)

It may be for reasons such as these that organized criminals tend to operate within specific areas, despite the fact that such operation draws "heat" on them. The transient criminals enjoy anonymity, but must choose partners from among relative strangers, and sacrifice the insurance provided by arrangements with doctors, lawyers, and bondsmen.

The bank will have been cased beforehand by the one who initiated the robbery. He may or may not have consulted with a partner (before the casing) as to the feasibility of the job. In cases of transient, two-, or three-man groups, casing may be done by all members of the group as they drive leisurely down the streets. In all cases of bank robbery related to me, no member of the group was entirely "cold" (for example, had not as much as seen the bank to be done). The general procedure is for the one who initiated the job to case the place, decide on a suitable time, and then take his partners with him on a dry run the day before the hold-up.

Okay. let's say it's the day before—the day before you want to do this. What do you have to do the day before?
Well, we usually get our car the night before, and we—well, we naturally check over our weapons. We go through the dry run so to speak, you know. The best exit out.

Do you do that with your own car?
Oh yes.

Do you make any drawing at that stage?
No.

But you're all together at this time, right?
Right.

Do you spend the night together?
We have at times, yeh. But not all the time, not all the time. We—usually, if we're gonna meet in the morning we just sort of casually saunter into a coffee shop, just like the working stiff, you know. Saunter in and have a cup of coffee. And before you know it there's three of us there and we have our coffee and then we saunter out.

And your car is ready to go?
Yeh, that's right—it's all been taken care of.

When did you get this car?
The night before.

And it's a stolen car?[3]
That's right.

Suppose the cops are looking for that car by that time?
That's very unlikely, because we have the plates and that all doctored up.

At what point do you decide who does what?
Well, it's pretty well understood; like you always have one who makes the suggestion, "Let's rob a bank." So, naturally, if you're going to rob a bank, you make the suggestion, you're the one who's going to lay the groundwork for it. So they—well, they just more or less accept you as the leader. (no. 7)

Bank robbers rely heavily on the architectural uniformity of banks. Banks are frequently located on street corners, and this is convenient for getaways. Glass doors permit the robber-doorman to see who is coming in, whereas, as a robber noted, the persons coming in have more difficulty seeing through the glass because of light reflection. The present trend toward low counters, possibly motivated by the bank officials' desire for a more personal and less prisonlike atmosphere, is looked upon favorably by bank robbers:

What about the height of the counter? Is this a factor?
Well, sometimes you see, you might have to jump the counter. Well, if you get some of these real high counters, well—they're tough to get over. Well, you lose a few seconds by getting over the counters, and some of these banks, like, they have these gates like, with—well, you can't reach over and open them because the catch is too far down, so therefore you've got to jump over this counter, you see. The lower the counter, the better I like it. You just hop over the—and hop back, and also you can see just exactly what the man is doing with his hands at all times. (no. 7)

Just as architectural uniformity is assumed, so the presence of mechanical alarm systems is assumed. The use of hidden TV cameras and

[3] Later no. 7 stated:
You never steal your own car—you have somebody do it for you, and pay them off. There's no use incriminating yourself in a car theft, when you're gonna pull a bank job. Therefore, it's worth to you to give some fellow a hundred dollars to get you a car. What's a hundred dollars of the bank's money? Nothing! (no. 7)

other devices (the presence of which are advertised with warning stickers) are not a deterrent to the experienced bank robber because he will be "covered" (wearing a mask) anyway, and so he cares little whether he is seen only by bank personnel on the scene or by others via TV. Since the presence of alarm systems is taken for granted, they are neither "cased" nor the object of special attention. The robber assumes they are in working order and that they have gone off the moment he enters the bank.

Although these purely mechanical factors are assumed constant, other factors vary and may affect the difficulty of doing a bank. Some of these may be assessed beforehand. The disposition of the manager is inferred by his apparent age. Those robbers who prefer to deal with as few employees as possible may make daily observations as to the most opportune time. No attention is paid to the number of customers in a bank, except insofar as this indicates the probable number who may wish to enter the bank during the robbery. Persons wishing to enter at this time are much more of a risk to the robber than those already inside. The danger lies in the customer noting that something is wrong before he, or she has entirely entered. Such a customer cannot be prevented from leaving at that point, and becomes the first "alarm." When this happens, the doorman will call his men out immediately.

The safecracker who wants to do a bankjob assumes the presence of money at all times. Primarily, he must consider the *technical* availability, which involves the architecture of a building permitting an "in," the make of the safe, and so forth. The bank robber, on the other hand, must consider the *immediate* availability of money. Unless he is planning a rural robbery, during which he will have time to rob the vault as well as the teller's tills, the bank robber expects to take only what is in the tills.[4] He assumes that the amount carried in tills

---

[4] Larger banks, with more tills, are preferred because of their greater cash potential.

varies according to day of the week, time of day, and paydays.

The following outline was presented by no. 41:

> The time—on a Monday, if possible. On a Friday, people withdraw for the weekend: Only got two thousand six hundred dollars on a Friday from three cashiers. Business deposits on Monday—each cashier will have no more than five thousand dollars—some under the box, some above. Businesses need change for the weekend, they don't want to deposit till Monday. On Saturday banks are closed. Businesses may make a night deposit—if so, that deposit will also be counted on Monday morning (no. 41).

The bank robber may plan his robbery on the basis of inferences made from the location of the bank:

> If a bank is near factories, you can be sure it will carry a lot of cash on paydays, which as a rule are on Friday. (no. 39)

Given a suitable commercial context, the thief may wish to assess more specifically the economic potential, particularly with reference to its temporal fluctuations:

> So you see, there's quite a few mills around here, so I sat down and bought some beers for a couple of guys who work in mills, and just in conversation, you know, kind of—the conversation got around to working in these mills and that, and I mentioned that I knew a guy who worked at the mill and who could—and the guy owed me some money and I asked them when—when does this group get paid. I'd like to collect. I'd like to catch him on a day he gets paid. So they told me. So I figured, well, a lot of these guys cash their cheques here and more do on Thursdays than on Fridays, so sure enough I went down the next—the following week on Thursday, and sure enough, and they came around like a couple of trained rats. So I said, the money's there all right—I'll get it here. (no. 2)

While interviewing an urban bank robber I had little success in having him respond to the question, "What time of day is the best time to hit a bank?" He finally responded by saying,

"Well, you can't tell, you see—you may not be able to find a parking spot." He noted that sometimes robbers are obliged to cruise around the block repeatedly before a suitable parking spot materializes. The urban bank robber can neither double-park nor park some distance from the bank. The problem of parking, which may be only an annoyance to the shopper, is a vital consideration to the bank robbers. Furthermore, banks, in order to draw customers by providing parking space, also draw unwanted "customers."

The urban parking consideration makes further planning difficult. Knowledge of police patrol must be synchronized with uncertain parking opportunities, which vary within the urban setting. One robber pointed out that parking is seldom a problem in the suburbs. In those instances where parking violations are anticipated, the robber follows what he considers to be "normal" parking violations, that is, violations that will not attract attention. Just as persons in law enforcement offices construct concepts of the "normal" or "typical" crime, so it is assumed by the robber that the layman distinguishes between routine parking violations and atypical ones:

Suppose you can't find a parking spot?
Oh, we double-park. You see, in these small towns, especially country towns, you see, we're driving a pickup truck; if people see a truck double-parked, motor running, they think it's a farmer who's gone into the bank for a minute—so it takes away all suspicion. We make sure it's an old truck, but with a fairly good motor in it. (no. 8)

*

DIMENSIONS OF VICTIM MANAGEMENT

The skills required for crimes involving the avoidance of the victim are significantly different from the skills required for crimes involving victim confrontation. Surreptitious crimes tend to revolve around mechanical competences, whereas crimes involving victim confrontation revolve around victim manage-

ment. The term "management" is chosen to differentiate this process from what might be termed "victim manipulation," as in confidence games.[5]

My focus on victim management is not intended to obscure other differences, nor to suggest that criminals develop mechanical or social skills to the exclusion of the other; I have earlier pointed out that thieves may engage in both types of crimes. The focus arises, instead, from the distinctions made by the criminals themselves, and from inherent differences in mechanical versus social skills.

1. SURPRISE AND VULNERABILITY

The bank robber relies on surprise to bring about momentary mental and physical paralysis of bank employees.

> The door would fly right open and the people inside, they freeze! (no. 28)

Such paralysis is crucially important to the bank robber: it allows him quickly to take up his position in the building; further, he hopes to be able to back all cashiers away from their counter before they have had a chance to regain enough composure to push an alarm button.

Criminals believe that bank employees' susceptibility to surprise and their consequent vulnerability varies with the time of day and the day of week. A bank robber insisted mornings are the best time:

> *Okay. now that time of day?*
> Always in the morning. Catch them by surprise. They've still got sleep in their eyes and sort of hung over if they drink. Catch them by surprise. About ten o'clock. (no. 7)

A bank robber who preferred Monday mornings, said:

> On Monday, everybody's asleep; not asleep, but not going anywhere. People are dull. On Mon-

---

[5] Under some conditions victim manipulation develops into a situation of victim management. Erving Goffman, "On Cooling the Mark Out," *Psychiatry* 15, no. 4 (November 1952).

day, people are not on the street in the morning—people are either asleep or at work. (no. 41)

The criminal is also aware that his surprised victim is not in a position to react efficiently, even if he should try to. A burglar involved in the "live prowl" stated:

Were you prepared in any sense in the event of being caught?

Well, you don't think of that. Course I always made sure, like you say, that there were ways out. 'Cause I never thought of being cornered by anyone there, because most people when they wake up, they're stunned, you know, anyhow; they're not that wide awake, so you're wide awake, you know. You're going to get out of the place. (no. 21)

This resembles the bank robber's inducement of near hysteria in order to create an imbalance in the degree of rationality the robber and the victims are respectively capable of.

In addition, the victim is not equipped with the skills required to reverse his position of weakness, even if he should recover from his surprise:

But in the long run, your chances of ever using a gun on a professional thief are very small—you're better off without a gun—you'll probably get your head shot off because he's doing something he does every day and you're doing something you've never done before.[6]

2. ESTABLISHING AUTHORITY AND MANAGING TENSION

The initial moment of surprise and shock is the first step in establishing a robber-victim relationship. During this time, the entire group may be herded into one corner of the bank, or ordered to lie prostrate on the floor. In either case, the posture and physical location of the victims are such as to enhance the robber's control over them.

Once having established control, some robbers encourage the return of rational thought to the victim, while others prefer to extend the state of shock until the robbery is completed.

[6] Martin, J. B. *My Life in Crime*, New York: Signet Books, 1952, p. 69.

In either case, the particular style adopted seems to be a matter of personal preference rather than a choice based on features of the specific robbery itself. Through experience, robbers adopt a style they find effective in managing the victim. The robber quoted next seeks to maintain victim management by continuing the state of shock in his victims.

. . . the door would fly right open and the people inside, they freeze. You know, when there's a big smash around everyone they freeze on the spot and look around, whether it's a joke or not. And you see them guys, you know; and they have hoods on their heads, and the gun, you know. And then there's one command—"Hit the ground!" you know—"Hit the dirt!"—I don't know how to say that—"Hit the floor—bunch of dogs! " you know. That's the way we say that: "Fuckin' dog, hit the floor, or we kill each and everyone of you!" you know. So they are froze there—their reaction is one of very extreme fear and they drop on the floor and sometime we select the strongest person—the manager especially or another teller which is very big—a six footer, or something like that, you know. And we won't say a word, we just walk up to him and smash him right across the face, you know, and we get him down. And once he's down the people, the girls especially, they look at him and they say, "My God—big Mike, he's been smashed like that—I'd better lay down too, and stay quiet." You know—it's sort of like psychology, to obey us immediately, everybody will follow the leader. The manager is the leader, and I see you go down—Jesus Christ, I'm going to follow you—I'm going down too, you know! (no. 28)

Another bank robber, in contrast, is anxious to avoid hysteria:

That's how I used to operate. I'd stand right there and the manager and the whole works at bay. I might have them lay down on the floor, 'cause you couldn't just have them standing there with their hands up, because it's too noticeable. You just walk in, and anyone you think is going to panic, well you just talk real quiet to them and you say, "Don't panic and everything will be all right; just take it easy and there'll be no trouble, see?"

Did you use to fire any shots into the ceiling or anything like that?

No—I used to talk very softly—I'd talk very softly, very quietly, and I'd never raise my voice. I always figure that if you holler and show panic, it would make the people panicky. If you just walk in quietly, just like you're transacting ordinary business, it kinda reassures the people that you know exactly what you're doing, and that you mean them no harm. But if you go in there hustling and bustling and firing and shooting, you're going to have people start to scream, and everything else. And it's pretty hard to hold back people screaming no matter what pressure they're under.

But isn't there the problem that if you speak softly there may be someone at the back at an adding machine . . .?

Oh well, they automatically know. You don't speak that softly. You know, when we walk in we say, "This is a holdup!" and they automatically hear you. But then after that you just sort of—no worry, no rush, It's just a matter of routine—load up the money, and your shopping bags and go out. Oh, we make sure that everybody hears you, that's for sure. We don't just walk in there and say, "Well this a holdup, hand over the money," We give a good bellow when we walk in.[7] (no. 7)

Bank robbers emphasize self-confidence as the key to successful bank robbery. They directly relate self-confidence to the ability to control people who are under stress. The manner in which this confidence is communicated is secondary, but it essential that it be communicated.

Number 45 stressed the importance of making it clear to those in the bank that his group "meant business."[8]

They can tell by the sound of your voice, by what you say and how you go about things, whether or not you mean business. If you're shaking they'll know.[9] (no. 45)

The role of "voice" in establishing authority and in managing tension is considered critical to bank robbery, and to armed robbery in general. The methods used are visual (masks, hoods), auditory (vocal commands), and physical.

So what would you say are the dangers in this kind of an operation?

Uh—well, panic on the part of the store owner.

What forms can that take?

Uh—I've experienced a man literally freezing—couldn't speak. He just pointed to show where the money was.

So that didn't cause you much trouble?

No, no. But on occasion I've had women scream.

What do you do in that case?

Well, on a couple of occasions I've just belted them on the side of the head with the pistol.

Knock them out or what?

No.

So that's one way of dealing with women who scream?

Or slap them in the face with the fist. The man I worked with was well over six feet and a very powerful built man with a deep resonant voice, and I saw him just with a loud voice, and with the tone of his voice, he would bring people out of a shock state.

Is the manner in which you speak very important?

Very much so—yeh—you have to be positive at all times.

Did you ever have any trouble, let's say, with a woman who wouldn't cooperate?

I didn't, no. (no. 27)

Another example regarding the use of language:

Now, her mother and brother they were at the back of the bank, you know, of the house, and

---

[7] This is similar to the approach used by the robber described in "The Heist . . ." by DeBaum. On page 74, he states:

"So far as may be, the mob are calm and polite on the job. 'Cowboying' or the wild brandishing of pistols and shouting of orders in all directions is frowned upon; fear has made more heroes than courage ever has."

DeBaum pays detailed attention to some aspects of victim management in armed bank robbery. [Everett DeBaum, "The Heist: The Theory and Practice of Armed Robbery," *Harpers* 200 (February 1950): 69–77.]

[8] This raises the question of why bank personnel find it difficult to accept the reality of a robbery.

[9] Number 45 was described to me by other criminals as "very good in banks," and as having a "very good voice for banks."

they heard that, because, you know, my talking during a bank holdup is very different from the talking we have now—it's full of tension and very commanding, you know. In order to impress the people as much as we possibly can. (no. 28)

What bank robbers seem to be describing has certain similarities with what Max Weber has defined as "charisma." Robbers refer to these qualities, such as voice and physical build, as inherent, rather than as techniques that might be learned. It is more difficult, however, to delineate the various dimensions of what robbers refer to as "confidence." Some clues have been provided; in crime, as elsewhere, success breeds success:

And you were pretty sure that you could keep this up without trouble?
Oh yes, definitely—most of the guys that I've met, and I've met a tremendous amount of criminals, you know, that were involved in a bank robbery, and we feel very confident; as a matter of fact, anyone who does two banks and he succeeds going all through and he has no police suspicion on him, he becomes over confident, you know. You say, "Well, now I'm a master criminal and I know how to do it. They didn't catch me, they're not aware that I'm working on it, and everything goes smoothly—it will work forever like that." You know, you get confident like that. (no. 28)

Number 28 points out that confidence can be dangerous, encouraging false notions of immunity from danger. Yet it appears to be precisely this confidence that facilitates successful robbery. In a sense, the robber cannot afford to consider possible or even probable consequences of his action, lest such considerations deprive him of the confidence needed to complete the task successfully.

Number 40 noted that, objectively and rationally, the probability of a prison sentence ought to deter the criminal. He added, however, that the criminal cannot afford to consider these matters, particularly just before a holdup, because he will lose his confidence. At that stage, it is rational *not* to consider failure, since by so doing you will bring it upon yourself all the more surely.

Although the degree of tension felt by a robber appears to vary from person to person, it is clear that he must manage his own tension beside his victims'. Number 28 said he is very tense before a holdup, whereas to no. 7 it was just "like getting up and having a shave and having coffee and going to work."

The ability to manage one's own tension affects work roles. It is generally agreed that it is essential for the door-man to be armed but that the other accomplices can do without weapons. Only those who have demonstrated their ability to control themselves will be given guns:

> The man with experience carries the gun; the reason he carries the gun is that he won't pull the trigger right away. Everybody is nervous; if a guy is too nervous you don't give him a gun—it's too dangerous. (no. 39)

Another stated:

> Getting the money is the easiest job for the least experienced or nervous person. (no. 41)

Experienced criminals may demand that less experienced partners be unarmed, or armed with less effective weapons. An experienced burglar who worked with two less experienced partners insisted they carry knives rather than guns:

> You think twice with a knife. A person going with a gun, if he has to use it, he'll use it right away, whereas a person with a knife, if he can dodge it, he will. Say, for instance, if you saw a guy in the place, instead of panicking and blowing the guy's head right off, with a knife you can move back into the shadow, and you don't panic, you just relax. With a gun you're likely to shoot the guy, with a knife you gotta stab him which means you come in close contact with him to stab him. (no. 10)

Ability to manage their own fears is also requisite for the driver of the holdup car, particularly when it is necessary for the driver to remain in the car during the holdup. His opportunity to leave the scene in relative safety is in stark contrast to the situation of his partners. Whether or not the driver remains in the car appears to be related both to the reliability of the driver and the degree of pressure he is exposed to:

In the old days, they used to leave the driver of a bank car outside, and most times they'd come out and the car would be gone! Now, you take the driver with you and he's the first one out.

Do you think that is why they take the driver with them?
Definitely, no other reason. (no. 15)

Another respondent:

You leave the motor running?
Yes.

With no one in the car?
That's the way I would do it. Sure, because if something happens and this guy panics and takes off with the car—which has happened, but not to me. (no. 36)

Experienced bank robbers feel their work is made more difficult, and the victim's situation more dangerous, by the tendency of the mass media to depict bank robberies as phony, "toy gun stuff." Robbers feel they are now constrained first of all to convince their victims the event is "not a joke." This may require more brutal action on their part than they would otherwise need to use. They need to convince any potential "heroes" among their victims that they cannot be subdued, TV dramas to the contrary.

The establishment of authority is no doubt enhanced by the display and use of weapons. The discussion above is intended to indicate, however, that the gun is only one of various persuasive devices used by robbers. This is not to deny that the successful use of other resources such as loud commands and physical violence is possible only because he has a gun. Nevertheless, much of the robber's activity during a robbery is necessitated only because he does not want to use his gun. He is, therefore, rightly dismayed at the condescension of those who fail to appreciate that his techniques revolve around the nonuse, rather than the use of guns.

Such condescension is obvious in the statement of a con man serving a sentence for armed robbery:

He had great pride in his previous achievements as a con man but said that anyone could stick a gun in a sucker's belly and get some money and that anyone who did this and landed in prison for it should feel ashamed.[10]

If guns are carried for purposes of intimidation only, then why not use toy guns? The answers were unanimous: "It's too dangerous—you've got nothing to protect yourself with." (no. 39) Such protection may be needed because of police or potential heroes among robbery victims. Robbers have only contempt for the hero type, whose action is considered irrational and extremely dangerous. Whenever the robber meets resistance from his victims and is forced to shoot, he is almost certainly going to "win," given his experience and advantageous position. Such "winning," however, has serious legal implications. Also, the scuffle will likely disrupt the orderly retrieval of money, forcing him to leave empty-handed. The bank robber does not want trouble—he wants money:

Well, this is where the public makes an awfully tragic mistake. It's a tragic mistake and I think maybe there would be a lot less people getting shot in holdups if people were just told that the money is there—give it to the man and leave it to the police. And you've seen in the paper time and time again where people have been shot chasing them down the street. Mind you, they may catch the odd one, but they've only got to shoot one man and it's tragic, you know what I mean. And actually I don't want to shoot anybody, but if it's me or you, you're going first, I'll tell you that right now. (no. 7)

Although the robber will hesitate to use his gun on a civilian, confrontation by police is seen as resulting inevitably in a "shootout."

---

[10] Sutherland, *Professional Thief*, p. 42.

"Why not put your hands and surrender when cornered?" I asked. That seemed incomprehensible: "They'd mow you down. They can just say we resisted arrest." (no. 39)

Bank robbers do not anticipate resistance from a single patrolman but are prepared for it should it occur. Such resistance would be interpreted as a stupid "hero act," similar to a civilian's:

> Have you ever heard of a smart detective getting shot? No, the only ones you ever hear of getting shot are some dumb patrolmen. What do you think so-and-so [a detective] would do if he pulled up alongside a car and a guy raised a chopper? [Submachine gun] You think he'd be a hero? No—he's got brains. He'd get away from there as fast as he could. But he'd eventually find out who that was. Where a dumb patrolman hasn't got enough sense to do that." [11]

Police are expected to arrive in a group, or more likely, to be waiting in the bank. The experienced robber, however, does not expect to be apprehended while at work. If he is to have "trouble," he expects it upon arrival at the bank, or after he has left. To meet it upon arrival indicates an information leak, considered by robbers as their most serious uncontrollable contingency.

The successful management of victims during a robbery demands the continuous and correct interpretation of the victim's behavior. As such, it is important the robber understands correctly the non-verbal communication that is going on—a particularly difficult task, since the degree of tension encourages abnormal behavior. Robbers pointed out numerous examples of bizarre behavior on the part of the victims. The most common observed in banks took the form of bank customers offering their own valuables to the robbers, presumably to enhance their own chances of survival. On the other hand, some customers will go to great lengths to hide their own wallets, rings, and jewelry. Such actions must be interpreted as a threatening move. When this occurs, the robber may issue a warning, or shoot. One respondent, an experienced robber, said he was in prison now because of an error he had made in this regard:

> The guy wouldn't stop moving—I didn't know what he was doing, so I let him have it. Later, I found out he was just trying to hide something under a rug.

---

[11] Martin, *My Life in Crime*, p. 100.

20

LOAN-SHARKING

JOHN M. SEIDL

DEFINING CRIMINAL LOAN-SHARKING AND ITS ILLEGAL ASPECTS

Criminal loan-sharking comprises three major elements. The first is the lending of cash at very high interest rates by individuals reputed to be connected with underworld operations. With few exceptions, interest rates are much higher than those available at legitimate lending institutions. The second element is a borrower-lender agreement which rests on the borrower's willingness to pledge his and his family's physical well-being as collateral against a loan. The corollary of the borrower's willingness is the lender's willingness to accept such collateral with its obvious collection implications. The third element is a belief by the borrower that the lender has connections with ruthless criminal organizations. The borrower is induced to repay his loans based on this reputation and his expected needs for future loans. If loan-shark reputations and future loan needs are inadequate repayment incentives, however, the lender is willing to resort to criminal means to secure repayment.

*

Interest charges which borrowers pay for loan-shark funds are not a function of supply and demand or marginal cost and marginal revenue relationships. Rather they are traditional prices which have been established over time. There is a small-loan rate which is charged by loan-sharks who work industrial plants, docks, construction sites, and neighborhoods catering to blue collar and lower middle class borrowers. Individual loans ranging from $50.00 to $1000.00 are common for these small (in capital assets) loan-sharks; an average loan is probably somewhere between $150.00 and $400.00

The street corner loan-shark racket of the 1920's and 1930's was known as the "6 for 5" racket.[1] Twenty percent continues to be an important element in the small-loan charge today. The rate in some urban areas for small-loans is 20 percent per week—"6 for 5." The interest charges—called "vig," "vigorish," or "juice" by borrowers and lenders alike—is due each week as long as the principal is outstanding. The principal can be reduced only in lump-

---

[1] "6 for 5" means that the interest on a five dollar loan for one week is one dollar. Thus if a borrower repays the principal and interest in one week on a five dollar loan, he repays six dollars. If he does not desire to repay the principal, he pays weekly interest which is one dollar or 20 percent per week. Turkus and Feder, 1951, pp. 120–125; Boehm, *New York Journal American*, February 19, 1940, p. 7; Stanton, *New York American*, November 7–9, 1935; "Loan-Shark Victim Driven Insane: Four More Shylocks Go to Prison," *Bronx Home News*, December 3, 1935, p. 1; People v. Faden, 271 N.Y. 435; 3 N.E. (2nd) 584 (1935); aff'd. 247 App. Div. 777; N.Y. Sup. 405 (1936).

Source: *Upon the Hip: A Study of the Criminal Loan Shark Industry.* Ph.D. Dissertion, Harvard University, 1968, pp. 20–31, 39–40, 45–59, 88–94. (Editorial adaptations.) Also published by U.S. Department of Justice, Law Enforcement Assistance Administrator, December 1969. Reprinted by permission of author.

sum or, in some cases, half-lump-sum payments.[2]

[One] major element of criminal loan-sharking is the borrower-lender agreement. It is not easy to borrow money from a loan-shark. A potential borrower must first find an illegal lender. For someone acquainted with the underworld this is not a difficult task; he already knows a loan-shark or at least someone who can "steer" him to one. For an individual not acquainted with the underworld, finding a loan-shark is more difficult. He must look for a "steerer" or "shill"[3] who can introduce him to a loan-shark. "Steerers" normally work in service jobs requiring the continuous meeting of people: For example, bartenders, taxi drivers, hat check girls, elevator operators, barbers, and doormen.[4]

One can also try to find a loan-shark by first looking for a bookmaker. Normally wherever there is a "bookie," there is a loan-shark nearby to whom the "bookie" can direct a potential borrower. The advantage of beginning the search with a "bookie" is that "bookies" are more plentiful and people are more familiar with bookmaking organizations than with loan-shark organizations.[5]

Generally loan-sharks do not solicit business. Borrowers seek loan-sharks. There are exceptions to this general rule. Loan-sharks normally attend large dice and card games run by the underworld to provide losers with an on-the-spot lending service.[6] Some loan-sharks also solicit business in banks approaching potential borrowers whose loan requests have been turned down.[7]

Once a potential borrower makes the acquaintance of a loan-shark, it is still not easy to obtain a loan. For the first loan, the new borrower must have a "voucher" or guarantor. The guarantor must be known and trusted by the loan-shark. The guarantor normally guarantees only the principal in a transaction, although in some cases he may have to guarantee both interest and principal.[8] Once a loan has been successfully negotiated and all or a part of it repaid, the borrower has established his credit with the loan-shark; a guarantor is

---

[2] Twenty percent per week is the most common charge in some urban areas. It is not the only charge. In some cases borrowers can negotiate small-loans for five or ten percent per week, but this is normally on a second or succeeding loan. The important understanding is that a borrower does not shop for low lending rates. Loan-sharks do not compete for each other's customers. A variation in lending charges is a matter between borrower and lender and depends upon their personal relationship.

[3] "Steerers" or "shills" direct potential borrowers to loan-sharks. Depending upon their relationship with the loan-shark and the borrower-lender transaction that follows the introduction, "steerers" may or may not receive a "finders fee." New York State Commission of Investigation, 1965, pp. 27–28. Interviews, New York: Disbarred Attorney; Dominic; Salerno; Philadelphia; Mark; Members of the Intelligence Section; Boston: Doyle, Members of the Intelligence Section; Members of the Special Service Unit; Chicago: O'Donnell, Siragusa.

[4] Same as above.

[5] New York State Commission of Investigation, 1965, p. 35; *Burroughs Clearing House*, April 1965, p. 41. In many cases there is a business relationship between "bookies"

and loan-sharks. "Bookies" have been known to sell selected customer debts to loan-sharks. They sometimes require a heavy bettor, who has "a lot on the cuff" (substantial credit betting), to borrow from a loan-shark to pay off his gambling debt. Interviews, New York: Salerno; Dominic; Jimmy; Disbarred Attorney; Cronin and Procino; Detroit: Piersante, Swartzendruber; Boston: Detective Edward Twohig, District No. 4, Boston Police Department; Members of the Special Service Unit; Members of the Intelligence Section; Chicago: Duffy, Peterson; Philadelphia: Members of the Intelligence Unit.

[6] The loan-shark at a gaming session is often referred to as "the man with the box" or "the man with the bank." Interviews, New York: Salerno; Kelly; Disbarred Attorney; Boston: Howland; Members of the Intelligence Section; Detroit: Paul Komives; attorney in a private law firm, formerly Assistant U.S. Attorney and Counsel for a One Man Grand Jury of Wayne County that investigated criminal organizations; Piersante; Chicago: O'Donnell.

[7] This is a prevalent practice in the New York garment district owing to the seasonal nature of garment manufacturing, the small capital stock of most firms, and the need for cash to meet payrolls, suppliers, etc. One loan-shark would get "a nod of the head or a wave of the hand" from a bank official to indicate a potential borrower in immediate need of cash who had been refused credit by the bank. New York State Commission of Investigation, 1965, pp. 68–70. Interviews, New York: Tyler; Disbarred Attorney.

[8] Infrequently the guarantor is required to pay off a loan when the actual borrower leaves the area or makes himself unavailable in some other manner. Interviews, New York: Disbarred Attorney; Jimmy; Dominic; Philadelphia: Mark; Kevin; Thomas; Ted. All law enforcement officials interviewed pointed out the need for a guarantor on the initial loan from a loan-shark.

no longer needed for second and successive loans.[9]

The amount of money a loan-shark desires to or is able to lend a borrower varies. It can be a function of the loan-shark's personality, his evaluation of the borrower's repayment capabilities, or the organizational constraints imposed upon him. Some loan-sharks arbitrarily decide, without reliance upon meaningful economic facts, what amount they will lend a customer.[10] Some loan-shark organizations run credit and asset checks on potential borrowers. They can accomplish this, with connections, through legitimate credit channels; or the organization can attempt to make the check with its own resources. Credit checks are run most often in large-loan transactions when portions of a business are offered as collateral.[11]

Many loan-sharks will lend only that amount which they believe a borrower can afford to repay. They determine repayment capabilities based upon the borrower's income or his expected profits as a result of the loan.[12] Some loan-sharks attempt to lend the borrower a little more than he can afford to repay so that he becomes "hooked." The "hooked" borrower is continually in debt to the loan-shark. Oftentimes the size of a customer's weekly payment to the loan-shark requires that he borrow new money on payday to supplement his already depleted earnings. Some borrowers are never able to repay the principal, because weekly interest payments make saving for the principal payment impossible.[13]

There is never any misunderstanding between the loan-shark and the borrower about

their relationship or the collateral for the loan. Seldom does any paper pass between borrower and lender;[14] a handshake usually confirms the bargain. The borrower realizes that he is offering his body and his family's well-being as collateral. He must understand, if he seeks the loan-shark and then secures the proper guarantor. Loan-sharks usually make the relationship clear in their first meeting with a potential borrower. In some cases the underlying threat is communicated subtly; in other cases it is made explicitly clear.[15]

[Another] major element of criminal loan-sharking is the collection process. Two important generalizations must be discussed before turning to the more detailed aspects of collection procedures. A loan-shark organization's reputation for violence and ruthlessness is the most important factor inducing borrowers to repay their loans.[16] An organization's reputation may stem from a number of things; but from the borrower's viewpoint reputation is a function of two perceptions—of the loan-shark

---

[9] Same as above.

[10] Interviews, New York: Disbarred Attorney.

[11] New York State Commission of Investigation, 1965, p. 29. Interviews, New York: Dominic; Detroit: Olzlewski and DePugh; Cleveland: Successful Defense Attorney; Boston: Members of the Intelligence Section; Members of the Special Service Unit.

[12] Interviews, New York: Dominic; Jimmy; Philadelphia: Mark; Ted; Thomas; Kevin; Cleveland: Successful Defense Attorney.

[13] Interviews, New York: Salerno; Kelly; Cronin and Procino; Winthers; Chicago: Duffy; O'Donnell; Siragusa.

[14] Paper does pass between the borrower and lender on rare occasions. A loan-shark in Philadelphia always required new borrowers to give him a check made out to cash for the total principal on the first loan; this was in addition to the okay of a guarantor. The checks were seldom cashed. They served as a continual inducement to borrowers to make their payments. Interviews, Philadelphia: Davis; Mark; Ted; Kevin; Thomas.

[15] The Disbarred Attorney (Interviews, New York) told the author that his partner left no misunderstanding about the collateral that the borrower was putting up. He explained the possibility of beatings should there be collection problems. The borrowers in Philadelphia (Interviews, Philadelphia) all said that their loan-shark matter-of-factly warned them when he handed them money, "If you can't make the payments, don't take the money." Everyone the author interviewed regarding loan-sharking agreed that there is never any misunderstanding in the borrower-lender agreement about collateral.

[16] This point was emphasized by all the individuals interviewed by the author. The borrowers stressed that repayment was a function of a loan-shark's reputation and their anticipated needs for future loans. Interviews, New York: Jimmy; Philadelphia: Mark; Kevin; Thomas; Ted. Dominic and the Disbarred Attorney (Interviews, New York) stressed this point emphasizing that the loan-shark works hard to establish and maintain his reputation which is his key collection tool. All the law enforcement officials interviewed also agreed that reputation was a loan-shark organization's greatest asset in the collection process.

from whom he borrows and of the organizational structure and operational methods of the loan-shark industry.[17]

There are a number of important factors which affect a borrower's perceptions of his loan-shark. The physique, appearance, and demonstrated or rumored physical prowess of the loan-shark and his associates are important factors.[18] Arms carried by the loan-shark and his associates as well as their demonstrated or rumored willingness to use them are important factors.[19] Foreboding qualities about the loan-shark's temperament, character, or attitudes that are made known directly or indirectly to the borrower affect his perception of the loan-shark from whom he borrows.[20] Finally, the loan-shark's connections with criminal organizations, whether they be real or imagined, are an important ingredient in the borrower's perception of his loan-shark.[21]

[17] Interviews, New York: Dominic; Jimmy; Disbarred Attorney; Philadelphia: Ted; Kevin; Thomas; Mark.

[18] Law enforcement officials and other people acquainted with the underworld interviewed by the author maintained that loan-shark associates who act as enforcers reveal their trade merely by presenting themselves. It is probable that if violence is required in the collection process enforcers not known to the borrowers will be used. Associates of loan-sharks, nevertheless, are chosen for their appearance as well as their skill to insure that implicit and explicit threats are as effective as possible. Interviews, New York: Salerno; Disbarred Attorney; Kelly; Chicago: Siragusa; Duffy; O'Donnell; Boston: Doyle; McClain; Members of the Intelligence Section; Detroit; Piersante; Olzlewski and DePugh.

[19] A loan-shark organization was lending money in a large book binding factory in New York. The plant had two shifts and a different loan-shark worked each shift. The loan-shark who worked days was about six foot four inches tall and weighed 260 pounds. He utilized his physical appearance and rumored toughness to establish his reputation. The loan-shark who worked nights was a slightly built individual who carried a Beretta; this was the subject of many rumors within the plant and was instrumental in establishing his reputation. In addition, it was rumored that the loan-sharks were connected with a large-scale criminal organization headquartered in Greenwich Village. Interviews, New York: Members of the C.I.B.

[20] Interviews, New York: Disbarred Attorney; Salerno; Kelly; Cronin and Procino; Detroit: Olzlewski and DePugh; Boston: Howland; Doyle; Chicago: Siragusa; O'Donnell.

[21] See n. 3, p. 51. The Philadelphia borrowers (interviews, Philadelphia) all pointed out that they personally liked the brothers who loaned them money; however, a

A borrower's perception of the loan-shark industry is the second important factor in the establishment of a reputation. This perception hinges on the borrower's previous contacts with the underworld and his exposure to criminal organizations and their enforcement methods through communications media.[22] If the reputation is formidable, it makes the loan-shark's job easy by removing many of his potential collection problems.[23]

A second important generalization about the collection process is that the use of actual violence is minimized. Potential violence causing fear and anxiety is utilized whenever necessary to motivate delinquent borrowers. Actual violence can become counter-productive from an organizational standpoint, however, for it may bring increased scrutiny of loan-shark activities by public, law enforcement, or underworld elements. It also hampers lending profitability. It makes repayment more difficult for the individual who is victimized from customers who now view the risks of borrowing differently.[24]

third brother, rumored to an be important member of the large-scale criminal organization in South Philadelphia, was supposedly backing the other two brothers. This rumor helped to establish a fearsome reputation for the loan-shark brothers. The importance of underworld connections in the establishment of a reputation was pointed out by most of the law enforcement officials interviewed by the author.

[22] The borrowers interviewed by the author all referred to the ruthless violent enforcement methods of loan-sharks as an accepted fact. When questioned about their own knowledge of these enforcement methods, they all cited newspapers, magazines, rumors, etc., to support their beliefs. Typical of their answers was, "Everybody knows about loan-sharks and the way they operate." Interviews, New York: Jimmy; Philadelphia: Mark; Thomas; Kevin; Ted.

One borrower was aware of these methods from first-hand experience as a result of repayment troubles. Interviews, New York: Jimmy.

[23] Same as n. 2, p. 50.

[24] Interviews, New York: Salerno; Kelly; Disbarred Attorney; Dominic; Detroit: Olzlewski and DePugh; Piersante; Boston: Howland; Doyle; McClain; Members of the Intelligence Section; Members of the Special Service Unit; Philadelphia: Rizzo; Members of the Intelligence Section; Cleveland District Office, Internal Revenue Service; Providence: Stone.

The detailed aspects of the collection process can be described in terms of six steps.[25] The first step is the weekly payment meeting between the borrower and the lender. These meetings are on the same day every week, sometimes at a specific time. The meetings not only provide for the collection of payments, but they also establish borrower-lender rapport.[26] Some loan-sharks are not interested in establishing a special relationship with their borrowers. In these cases, payments may be made at a drop with no meeting between borrower and lender.[27]

The first step in the collection process is the only step that many borrowers are personally acquainted with. Should they miss a weekly payment, however, they will become aware of the second step. A loan-shark moves quickly to establish contact with a delinquent borrower reminding him of his obligation. The type of

reminder is not standard and depends upon the size of the loan outstanding, the borrower's previous record, and the loan-shark's psyche. Reminders at this stage are usually pleasant, but the loan-shark does penalize the borrower for his tardiness. Normally the penalty is a fine which is added to the already late payment. In some cases, a loan-shark will fine a borrower by increasing the principal.[28]

Harassment is the third step and likely the first aggressive action the loan-shark takes to induce repayment from delinquent borrowers. This can take the form of a continuously ringing telephone at the borrower's home in the early morning hours or constant telephone interruptions at work. It can include circumstances contrived by the loan-shark to embarrass the borrower in public.[29]

Implicit threats are used next to induce repayment. The loan-shark accompanied by enforcers, whose appearances easily reveal their occupations, may visit a delinquent borrower's home or place of employment. Phone calls are made to members of the borrower's family. Callers simply state their name and ask that the borrower be reminded of a specific appointment which is important if business troubles are to be averted. General demonstrations

Chicago is an exception to the rule of minimum violence. Chicago loan-sharks are more violent than the loan-sharks in any of the other cities visited by the author. They are much quicker to explicitly threaten delinquent borrowers and to resort to physical beating in the collection process. Peterson, *A Report on Chicago Crime for 1965*, 1966, p. 99; "River" and "Stone" Cases, Files of the Intelligence Division, Chicago Police Department; Statement of loan-shark victim to a State's Attorney, October 18, 1963, Files of the Intelligence Division, Chicago Police Department. Sandy Smith *Chicago Sun Times*, November 18, 1965, pp. 3–4; "Loan-Shark Gang Bared in Chicago," *New York Times*, January 16, 1966; Illinois Crime Investigating Commission, *Report of the Proceedings Held and Evidence Taken at a Hearing Before the above Entitled Commission*, January 1966, three volumes. Interviews, Chicago: Duffy; Siragusa; O'Donnell.

[25] The six steps are a general characterization of the collection process in as comprehensive a manner as possible. They are analogous to the steps on an escalation ladder in any type of dispute. Every collection dispute need not include all six steps nor does each step have to take place as described. There are a number of factors which shape the specifics of a collection situation. Especially important factors include: The borrower, the lender, the loan-shark organization, the underworld, and the sum of money involved.

[26] New York Commission of Investigation, *Testimony of Public Hearing Loan Shark Investigation*, December 1964; Illinois Crime Investigating Commission, January 1966. Interviews, New York: Disbarred Attorney; Dominic; Jimmy; Salerno; Detroit: Piersante; Olzlewski and DePugh.

[27] Statement of loan-shark victim to a State's Attorney, October 18, 1963, Files of the Intelligence Division, Chicago Police Department. Interviews, Philadelphia: Ted; Thomas.

[28] New York State Commission of Investigation, December 1964, pp. 38–43, 124–135, 136–162, 164–192, 378–416; Illinois Crime Investigating Commission, January 1966; "Stone," "Farm," and "River" Cases, Files of the Intelligence Division, Chicago Police Department. Interviews, New York: Disbarred Attorney; Dominic; Jimmy; Members of the C.I.B.; Salerno; Kelly; Detroit: Piersante; Olzlewski and DePugh; Boston: Doyle; McClain; Members of the Intelligence Section; Members of the Special Service Unit; Providence: Stone.

[29] A large-loan loan-shark in New York would harass his delinquent customers unmercifully after they had missed one or, at the most, two payments. He would do anything to infuriate the borrower, so he would pay just to get the loan-shark off his back. The loan-shark would spit in a delinquent borrower's face in public, call him vile names in front of his wife, or ring his doorbell or phone in the early hours of the morning. Interviews, New York: Disbarred Attorney. Also New York State Commission of Investigating Commission, January 1966. Interviews, New York: Salerno; Kelly; Dominic; Jimmy; Philadelphia: Kevin; Thomas; Boston: Members of the Special Service Unit; McClain.

of violence are also used by loan-sharks. The demonstration is not directed specifically at a borrower, but rumors circulate which indicate that the violence was the work of a loan-shark or his associate.[30]

Explicit threats directed at various aspects of the borrower's psyche are the fifth step in an escalating collection process. Usually the borrower is threatened with violence against his own person or against his family, relatives, or property. The language is raw and vulgar frequently communicated to a wife who is unaware of her husband's borrowing. The threats portend property destruction, physical beatings, accidents, torture, or death.[31]

Sometimes loan-shark organizations use demonstrations of violence to explicitly threaten a delinquent borrower. A bombing or a fire preceded by a warning and followed by threatening pressure is an effective method.[32] Oftentimes loan-shark organizations will claim responsibility for underworld violence which is none of their doing; they adopt it and utilize it skillfully as a demonstration of their willingness to act violently when sufficiently provoked.[33]

Some loan-shark organizations use a class "B" movie technique to threaten victims. They pick up a delinquent borrower and take him "for a ride" in a big black cadillac or its equivalent. Usually the destination is the waterfront.

Here the borrower is verbally threatened as well.[34] When violence is required, loan-sharks often use it to explicitly threaten other customers. If a delinquent borrower is beaten, other borrowers may be required to observe the result of the enforcer's treatment.[35]

Actual violence, the sixth step, is used when loan-shark organizations feel that a borrower is *not trying* to meet his obligations. A key consideration is the size of the outstanding loan; for at some point, especially in the large-loan business, the loan-shark must consider the credibility of his own reputation and that of his organization.[36]

Violence related to delinquent borrower's repayment problems can be very harsh and painful. The weapons most often used are enforcers' fists and feet. Other weapons used are iron pipes, brass knuckles, baseball bats, bicycle chains, sledge hammers, and razor blades.[37] Most loan-shark violence involves physical beating which may or may not be severe enough to include broken limbs. The intentional murder of delinquent borrowers, however, is extremely rare.[38]

Throughout any period of payment delinquency, a loan-shark continues to increase the repayment burdens of an already overburdened borrower with the assessment of fines. There are provisions within most large-scale criminal organizations for adjudication in cases

---

[30] New York State Commission of Investigation, December 1964; Illinois Crime Investigating Commission, January 1966. Interviews, New York: Dominic; Jimmy; Salerno; Disbarred Attorney; Detroit: Olzlewski and DePugh; Boston: McClain; Doyle; Chicago: Siragusa; O'Donnell; Providence: Stone.

[31] Same as n. 1, p. 55. Also *Burrough's Clearing House*, April 1965, p. 41. Typical threats include showing the borrower two sticks of dynamite and telling him his house will be blown up without regard to his wife and children; or warning the victim that his daughter may have an accident on her way home from school. "Two Plead Not Guilty to Loan-Shark Charges," *Boston Herald*, October 28, 1966, p. 12.

[32] New York State Commission of Investigation, December 1964, pp. 494–504; Interviews, New York: Salerno; Detroit: Piersante; Boston: Doyle; Providence: Stone.

[33] Interviews, Detroit: Olzlewski and DePugh; Boston: Howland; Doyle; Members of the Intelligence Section.

[34] Interviews, Detroit: Olzlewski and DePugh.

[35] Statement of loan-shark victim to a State's Attorney, October 18, 1963, Files of the Intelligence Division, Chicago Police Department. Interviews, Chicago: O'Donnell; Boston: Doyle.

[36] Interviews, New York: Jimmy; Dominic; Salerno; Disbarred Attorney; Detroit: Piersante; Olzlewski and DePugh; Boston: Doyle, Members of the Special Service Unit; Members of the Intelligence Section; Philadelphia: Mark; Thomas; Kevin.

[37] Sandy Smith, *Chicago Sun Times*, November 18, 1965, p. 3; *Burrough's Clearing House*, April 1965, p. 41; "Enforcers Back Up Loan Sharks," *Boston Globe*, March 17, 1963, p. 1; Illinois Crime Investigating Commission, January 1966. Interviews, Chicago: Siragusa; Duffy; O'Donnell.

[38] Interviews, New York: Disbarred Attorney; Salerno; Kelly; Detroit: Olzlewski and DePugh; Piersante, Boston: Doyle, Members of the Special Service Unit; Members of the Intelligence Section; Chicago: O'Donnell; Duffy.

where the borrower *strongly* feels that the loan-shark's claims are completely out of proportion to what is owed. These disputes normally arise after interest payments have been made for a long time and total much more than the original principal. A "sit-down" or meeting is held presided over by an underworld figure of greater recognized importance than any of the participants to the dispute. He arbitrates the dispute normally prescribing a lump sum settlement to be paid by the borrower within a given time period.[39]

*

Rationed borrowers desire more credit in the upperworld than legitimate lending institutions are willing to supply or than they think legitimate lending institutions are willing to supply. In either case, they turn to loan-sharks to supplement their credit needs. Some rationed borrowers are unaware of the legitimate lending alternatives available to them. Thus they do not fully exploit upperworld lending possibilities.[40] Other rationed borrowers are aware of legitimate alternatives but fail to contact lending agencies. They believe their requests will not receive favorable consideration.[41] Most rationed borrowers, however, do

not possess the required creditworthiness, based upon present lending laws and practices, to secure the loan they desire.[42] Unrationed borrowers, on the other hand, can secure needed credit in either the upperworld or the underworld. They borrow from loan-sharks because of the peculiar lending service offered.[43]

The peculiar lending service offered by loan-sharks is an important factor which stimulates loan demand among rationed and unrationed borrowers. Its importance is easier to isolate in unrationed borrower demand, because it is obvious that these individuals borrow from a loan-shark due to the lending service he offers.[44] The service also entices rationed borrowers who not only appreciate the availability of funds but the convenient lending methods of loan-shark organizations. Many rationed borrowers would not pay the loan-shark charges for an unduly formal and complex lending service.[45]

Four important characteristics comprise the loan-shark lending service. The importance of each characteristic varies with individual borrowers. The first characteristic is (a) secrecy. No one needs to know about the loan including

---

[39] Testimony of Assistant District Attorney Frank Rogers, New York State Commission of Investigation, December 1964, pp. 46–47. Interviews, New York: Disbarred Attorney; Salerno; Kelly; Detroit: Piersante.

[40] Some borrowers do not know the lending alternatives available to them; some do not visit every legitimate lending institution that is available. If a borrower is turned down once or twice, he probably assumes that he will be turned down by all lending institutions. Yet there is a percentage of rationed borrowers who could have secured needed credit in the upperworld if they had explored completely all possible upperworld alternatives. Large-loan borrowers are less likely to be unaware of lending alternatives than small-loan borrowers because of their different educational and occupational backgrounds. Interviews, New York: Disbarred Attorney.

[41] This seems reasonable especially if in the past borrowers have had questionable credit ratings or unpleasant experiences with lending institutions. One large-loan and one small-loan borrower interviewed by the author borrowed from loan-sharks because each believed his request

for money from legitimate lending institutions would not receive favorable consideration. It also should be noted that they preferred the loan-shark lending service to upperworld lending techniques. Interviews, Philadelphia: Mark; Thomas.

[42] Most law enforcement officials interviewed believed that loan-shark borrowers were predominantly poor credit risks who borrowed in the underworld because they could not secure credit elsewhere. Of the three small-loan borrowers interviewed by the author, only one admitted that he had initially borrowed from loan-sharks because he believed he could not secure credit at legitimate lending institutions owing to his creditworthiness. Interviews, Philadelphia: Thomas.

Large-loan borrowers, on the other hand, are predominantly rationed borrowers who are unable to secure loans because of upperworld lending institutions' creditworthiness criteria. Interviews, New York: Jimmy; Dominic; Disbarred Attorney.

[43] Interviews, New York: Jimmy; Dominic, Philadelphia: Mark, Thomas; Ted; Kevin.

[44] Interviews, Philadelphia: Ted; Kevin, Mark; Thomas.

[45] Interviews, New York: Jimmy; Philadelphia: Thomas.

the borrower's family, his neighbors, his employers, or his creditors.[46]

(b) Second, the loan is made on an informal basis.[47] The borrower is not kept waiting[48] or interviewed by "stuffy" or "pompous" loan officials. He is not required to fill out long complicated forms which is particularly embarrassing for individuals without language facility. Secret screening of a borrower's credit history or personal background is unusual in a small-loan transaction and not too common in large-loan transactions. The borrower is seldom subjected to an overt credit investigation among his friends, neighbors, fellow employees, or employers. The loan-shark borrower does not require a formal co-signer, nor does the borrower need to offer material collateral usually required by institutional lenders.[49]

Third, the loan is made quickly and conveniently.[50] The speed with which one is able to secure a loan depends upon one's previous dealings with a loan-shark. Customers who have successfully borrowed from a loan-shark can secure successive loans quickly. Those who have underworld connections will not find it too difficult to negotiate an initial loan. Customers without underworld connections will find securing an initial loan more troublesome. The convenience factors are almost always present in a loan-shark transaction. Proceeds of the loan are cash and usually made available to the borrower immediately. Oftentimes the loan-shark comes to the borrower, visiting his place of business or neighborhood.[51] Seldom does a borrower have to travel far to meet his loan-shark. Hours of operation are not a problem; loan-sharks lend money every day and night of the week.[52] Many loan-sharks even simplify repayment procedures for borrowers by personally collecting from them on payday.

---

[46] The importance of secrecy was stressed by all loan-shark borrowers interviewed. Interviews, New York: Jimmy; Philadelphia: Ted; Kevin; Thomas. In some cases, there was a desire to hide spending habits; in other cases, there was a desire to hide a thin week in sales and commissions. One small businessman desired to hide the regular purchase of new inventory from his wife. Interviews, Philadelphia: Mark.

[47] The informal aspects of the loan-shark service were emphasized as an important positive feature by all borrowers interviewed. One unrationed borrower, who claimed he could have negotiated a loan with either a bank or a finance company, just did not like to go through the red tape involved in borrowing in the upperworld. Interviews, Philadelphia: Kevin; Thomas; Mark; Ted; New York: Jimmy.

[48] Allen Jung concluded in a study of personal finance company attitudes toward borrowers that there ". . . was [a] desire of loan representatives to keep prospective borrowers waiting in a private office." The reasons for using this tactic against borrowers was not clear. Jung concluded that loan officials probably believed that waiting had a psychological effect upon the borrower which increased the chances of negotiating a profitable loan. Jung also pointed out that attitudes among loan officials in banks were "completely different." Jung. *Public Opinion Quarterly*, Fall 1961, pp. 414–416.

[49] The informal aspects were of special interest to the author, for it appears that borrowers preferred to honor an informal commitment rather than a formal one. All the borrowers interviewed believed they had incurred an obligation to pay their loan-shark, because the loan-shark had provided them with an important service. The loan-shark had taken a definite risk lending money on a handshake while minimizing red tape. This obligation to pay was in addition to repayment motivations induced by loan-shark

reputations and borrowers' anticipated needs for future loans. Small-loan borrowers believed it would be easier to discuss repayment troubles; as a result of sickness, family problems, or loss of work; with their loan-shark than with an impersonal credit department or lending agency. Large-loan borrowers believed their obligation stemmed from the risk taken by a loan-shark when he lends large sums so informally. They held factors in special contempt because of their reputedly high interest charges yet their unwillingness to accept risk by completely tying up a debtors' assets. Interviews, New York: Jimmy; Dominic; Philadelphia: Mark; Thomas; Kevin; Ted.

[50] The loan-shark borrowers interviewed by the author stressed speed and convenience as important components of the loan-shark lending service. All the borrowers were regular customers, so they could obtain their loans quickly and easily. Interviews, New York: Jimmy; Philadelphia: Mark; Kevin; Ted; Thomas.

[51] Interviews, Philadelphia: Mark; Ted; Thomas; Kevin.

[52] One borrower told a story of being in a night club in North Philadelphia; he was somewhat drunk. It was 11:30 p.m. a few days before Christmas. Outside it had been snowing since late afternoon. He had run out of money and called his loan-shark. The loan-shark came out in the snow from South Philadelphia to lend the borrower $200 on the spot. The borrower told the author, "I would gladly pay $40 interest over 10 weeks for a service like that. Where else could I borrow $200 at that time of night under those conditions?" Interviews, Philadelphia: Thomas.

Mark, an antique dealer and loan-shark borrower, illustrated the convenient nature of loan-shark borrowing. When he read or heard about a sale that he wanted to attend, he would call his loan-shark and ask to meet him at the corner of 15th and Chestnut Streets in downtown Philadelphia. Mark could request that the meeting take place within an hour or within a week depending upon the circumstances. The loan-shark would arrive as requested, hand Mark an envelope with the needed cash, and Mark would go on to the sale. It is interesting that Mark seldom checked the contents of the envelope. He was certain he could trust his loan-shark.[53]

The fourth important characteristic of the loan-shark lending service is the regular availability of funds. Loan-sharks provide a continuous source of available cash for borrowers who meet their repayment schedules. The borrower does not need to worry about the effect of tight money on his borrowing potential, nor need he worry over the frequency of his borrowing. As long as he meets his payments, the loan-shark is willing to keep him supplied with loans.[54]

[53] Interviews, Philadelphia: Mark.

[54] Availability was emphasized by all borrowers interviewed. Two borrowers admitted that easy availability meant they borrowed more money than they need or would have borrowed if it had been harder to negotiate a loan. One stated that he stayed in debt to the loan-shark when he knew he was the only one in the automobile agency borrowing. He believed that if he stopped borrowing the loan-shark would stop visiting the agency and he would "lose his angel." Interviews, Philadelphia: Kevin;

21

FIXING HORSE RACES

SELECT COMMITTEE ON CRIME, U.S. HOUSE OF REPRESENTATIVES

RACE FIXING

Because horseracing and other forms of legalized gambling can affect the integrity of State government, they should be the best policed of activities. We have determined that inadequate security at many thoroughbred tracks and harness raceways has led to race fixing which threatens not only the integrity of the industry in which the sport is sanctioned but that of the State itself.

This committee has heard of schemes as simple in design as that of a dishonest jockey hoping an electrical charge applied to his mount will put him into the winner's circle.[1] We have also heard of elaborate conspiracies in which an entire race was effectively tied up by knocking out half the field of horses with drugs.[2]

Fixed races have been discovered at both thoroughbred, or flat tracks, and harness raceways. What has come to public attention, we fear, are only the most flagrant examples of a significant problem which the industry chooses

[1] Hearings before the Select Committee on Crime entitled "Organized Crime in Sports (Racing)" (hereinafter referred to as "hearings"), testimony of Alexander MacArthur, pt. 2, pp. 527–528.

[2] Crime Committee Hearings, testimony of Bobby Byrne, pt. 3, pp. 1103–1139.

Source: "Organized Criminal Influence in Horseracing," Report by the Select Committee on Crime, 93rd Congress, 1st Session, House of Representatives. Report No. 93–326 (June 25, 1973), pp. 1–10,14 (Editorial Adaptations.)

not to face due to its misguided desire to protect the image of the sport.

*

An attempt to prod a horse through the jolt of an electric whip at an Illinois track focused attention on the need to inspect equipment as well as horses at the track. The jockey involved was not a newcomer to the sport but Lane Suire, the country's fourth ranked rider. MacArthur said:

> There was a collision coming into the homestretch on the third race. . . . One jockey [Suire] was injured . . . one horse had to be destroyed for a broken leg. It was a pretty good collision out there.

*

It was directed to our attention by one of the ground personages, that he picked up a whip out there. Upon examination he saw that this whip had what appeared to be a battery device in it. I might add the men told me a very sophisticated one. * * * Because of the suggestion of an irregularity, I immediately asked the steward, the chief State steward, Ted Atkinson, to go in and indulge in some important curiosity and then check the jockeys' quarters in other racetracks. And I am advised and regret to inform you that in Fairmont, Ill., that night, we entered the jockey quarters and conducted a search and found another one of these devices in the footlocker of another jockey.[3]

*

MR. PHILLIPS. Essentially a device to speed a horse up and help fix the race; is that correct?

MR. MACARTHUR. It is a device very definitely engineered to increase the speed of the horse. Besides the moral aspect of it, which is plenty in my book, because I won't even allow a cattle prod to be used on my cattle because it stresses them. I think it is a terrible way to treat an animal that is supposed to be your friend.[4]

*

MR. FITZGERALD. . . . I have studied the betting pattern of the race. The horse's name was "Little Solaris." It was appropriately priced at where it belonged, and it is our belief that he [Suite] inadvertently touched this device to the horse. He certainly would not have deliberately done so at the turn. He was in a crowded condition at a turn and he wouldn't normally do this, but we suspect he brought the whip down along the side of the horse and the prongs touched the horse and the horse veered, as the pictures illustrate, into other horses, tripped, went down, broke his leg; had to be destroyed there. . . .[5]

*

In another incident, a nine-State, 12-track fraud in which superior or "ringer" horses were substituted under the names of slower thoroughbreds was described by witness Paul Berube, an investigator for the Thoroughbred Racing Protective Bureau. The scheme was such a substantial financial undertaking that

"it would be my opinion that organized crime is definitely involved in perhaps the financing of this whole operation," Berube told the committee.[6]

Berube's testimony underscored the need for Federal statutes to make such schemes, which can be interstate in character, subject to heavy fines.

Six horses running under 12 different identities had one thing in common—the fraudulent foal certificates under which they ran were of slower thoroughbreds. (Foal certificates contain information about the animals and are comparable to birth certificates for humans). The "ringer" or substitute horses ran in at least 41 races at the 12 different tracks. Some ringers finished as much as seven lengths in front of the field. Berube named nine States in which he detected the use of forged foal certificates and substitute horses: Michigan, New Hampshire, Massachusetts, Rhode Island, New Jersey, Pennsylvania, Maryland, Delaware, and Florida. He also named a total of 12 tracks at which the practices were detected: Hazel Park, Rockingham Park, Suffolk Downs, Narragansett Park, Atlantic City, Garden State Park, Liberty Bell, Bowie, Laurel, Pimlico, Delaware Park, and Florida Downs.[7]

Berube testified that the 18-month period in which the scheme was in operation covered the period from November 1970 to March of 1972. "Of the races in which ringers were run, there were at least 14 winners."

*

The committee also heard about an incident which occurred on June 6, 1971, in which many of the 17,900 patrons on a "hot June Monday night" rioted at Yonkers Raceway in New York. The Yonkers race became the target of a Federal investigation by the New York Strike Force on Organized Crime whose chief, Daniel P. Hollman, had no authority to act unless

[3] Hearings, testimony of Alexander MacArthur, pt. 2, pp. 527–528.
[4] Id., p. 528.
[5] Hearings, testimony of Gerald F. Fitzgerald, pt. 4, p. 1838.

[6] Hearings, testimony of Paul Berube, pt. 2, p. 780.
[7] Id., p. 780.

there was evidence of some interstate violation involved. The possibility that the race had been fixed was so apparent, however, that Hollman decided to look into the case to determine whether there was any interstate activity on which to charge a violation when it became apparent State officials were not going to act.

[The fans] rioted after a particular fifth race, and they had good reason to riot. They had been "had" by inside information, as far as they were concerned. They didn't know where it was, what had happened, but they knew they had been had and a good many of the fans rioted.

*

What sparked the rioting was this: The fifth race went off. I think it was a pace of 1 mile. There were eight horses in the race.

They came around the second time, and the No. 6 horse, "Moonstone Bay" won, and No. 7 "Mr. Ace," finished second. The exacta paid a very low amount, $42.60, which was about a hundred dollars less than what it should have paid. And this is what triggered that riot.[8]

This meant that a higher percentage of bettors were holding exacta tickets than the odds would dictate. As it turned out, a number of the ticket holders turned out to be drivers, trainers and others with access to the paddock area. Several holders of large blocks of winning tickets never cashed them in, presumably when it was discovered that an investigation was underway. One unknown purchaser of a block of twenty-two $20 tickets to this day hasn't claimed them. "Those tickets are worth $10,000," Hollman said. "In all the history of Yonkers, they know of no other situation where that has occurred.[9]

*

. . . Syndicate enforcer Joe Barboza gave the committee a chilling rundown of the muscle

tactics he employed on jockeys in New England on behalf of mobster Henry Tamello to fix races. Barboza testified that New England crime boss Raymond Patriarca had once boasted of owning "half of the horses in New England" through third party fronts—an obvious accounting error.

Barboza testified:

Tamello, Patriarca's right-hand man, had five jockeys under his control.

MR. BRASCO. Do you know whether or not Mr. Tamello ever asked these jockeys to do anything in terms of any race they were riding in?

MR. BARBOZA. All I know is that after he would talk to them, he would say that he got them to pull the races for him.

Barboza related an example of the tactics he said Tamello used to intimidate jockeys to the point where they would pull horses for him. This particular incident took place in the Ebb Tide bar located near Suffolk Downs. Barboza said Tamello told him to corner a jockey who owed a $1,500 bar tab to Castucci—

and start to pressure him and I will come in there and I will stop you. Don't hurt him, but just really come on strong.

So I went in there and said, "You owe $1,500, you know . . . to the Ebb Tide. Richard Castucci. How come you haven't paid him? You may be a good strong guy, you know, you have all kinds of publicity, you think you are a bad man as far as riding horses," and so forth. "Everybody caters to you but I am not catering to you. * * * I pulled out a knife and put it at his throat and said I was going to slice it. And Henry came in and said, "What's this? What's going on?" Henry says, "Get away from him. He's a good kid. Are you crazy?" I said, "He owes Richard Castucci $1,500 and he hasn't paid."

Henry Tamello says, "I want to pay for him. I am telling you, don't bother this kid any more. He can do anything he wants in here.

---

[8] Hearings, testimony of Daniel P. Hollman, pt. 2, p. 646.

[9] Id., p. 657.

I want to cover his tab, pay his tab," and so forth.

I walked out of the cloakroom. Henry Tamello stayed there with the jockey maybe 15–20 minutes, and he came out, and he had a jockey that was going to pull horses for him.[10]

*

MR. BYRNE.   At one particular meet alone we would have access to like a dozen jockeys. But we used two key ones. Two key jockeys, three key jockeys, and they would be buddy-buddy. Remember, them kids, some of them are making good money. But the average jockey, he doesn't make any money.[11]

So a guy, like the same guys again—he has got a weakness for money. He wants to make money. He says, "Gee, look, these guys ride around in big cars, good clothes, living in the best. Here I am out among the horses all day long for a 10-percent piece of the purse, and probably a little workout in the morning. I have to get up early in the morning." You know, they say, "I have got to get with this, I want to go where the money is."[12]

MR. PHILLIPS.   In relation to some of this money, was some of it paid to jockeys to hold horses?[13]

MR. BYRNE.   Right. Some jockeys you can buy cheap and others, one guy in particular, he is expensive. Other jockeys will do it. Like one jockey we had, he had no qualms, he knew we would take care of him. And if we made a score, and we were using the jockeys and trainers, we made a score, we would take care of him. He never had to worry about money. We didn't give him too much because the more you give them, the more they want. If you give them a couple hundred

now, they want $400 next time. So if he asked for $200, you give him $150.[14]

*

Byrne explained that he and his cohorts obtained the drug from a cooperative veterinarian—that veterinarian had been previously barred from Rhode Island racetracks.

MR. PHILLIPS.   In all of these situations where you actually hit [drugged] the horse, the horse ran out of the money?

MR. BYRNE.   Definitely, out of the money.

MR. PHILLIPS.   In every case?

MR. BYRNE.   It was working so good that we have, like our four live ones, and we would stand on the backstretch at different tracks, or at the top of the stretch, and we used to bet among ourselves who was going to buy the beer and lunch and how the four live ones were going to finish, and we have the winning tickets in our pocket.

*

MR. PHILLIPS.   In a 10-horse race you leave four, and an eight-horse race you leave four or three?

MR. BYRNE.   We leave three. Our practice is to leave three in an eight-horse field.[15]

*

MR. PHILLIPS.   How did you actually hit him, with a hypodermic needle?

MR. BYRNE.   Right. In the neck, You could hit him in three places. You could hit him in the neck, or breast, or rump. But the most effective place to hit him is right in the neck, because it travels, it travels faster. This particular drug we use, it travels, it hits them faster. For the first half-hour it is noticeable that the drug is in there because the horse is standing there like he is drunk. After that it wears off and he is kind of dopey.

---

[10] Hearings, testimony of Joseph Barboza, pt. 2, p. 737.
[11] Id., p. 1106.
[12] Id., p. 1106.
[13] Hearings, question by Chief Counsel Joseph A. Phillips, pt. 3, p. 1101.

[14] Hearings, testimony of Bobby Byrne, pt. 3, p. 1102.
[15] Id., pp. 1092–1093.

But it hits his brain and his heart. It flows through the blood stream fast; whereas the other places it takes a little bit longer. It is effective, but not as good as in the neck. The neck is the best place to hit him with it.

Depending on the circumstances at the time, you might—like depending on the race and the time you get to this horse, how many cc.'s of this drug you would use. Like, say, the best time to hit, say it is like a race is going to come off after 4:30 or 5 o'clock. The ideal time to hit a horse with 5 cc.'s of this drug is between 8 and 10 o'clock. And by the time he goes to race, he can go to his post position and no one notice nothing, You couldn't detect it without a test on him. You could surmise.

They run out a few trainers that are pretty sharp, but they would have a hard time. There are certain things they look for, but if you hit it right and enough dosage, they will never detect it. And they don't check the losers. That is why people think we were hitting favorites, I mean hitting the horse to win. But what we were doing was hitting them to stop them.

We didn't want them to win and they never check the ones who lose the race. They only check the winners.[16]

[16] Id., p. 1091.

22

CRIME PAYS

THOMAS PLATE

This may well prove a troubling chapter to many Americans. For it will indicate how much money can be made by a professionally dishonest person. Unfortunately, as you will see, crime really does pay.

At the outset, it bears stating that underworld salaries not only are comparable with those in other industries, but, because of the tax dodge, actually are superior in many categories. It should not be surprising, then, that the crime profession regularly manages to attract to its ranks some outstanding talent. This infusion of fresh young blood helps the underworld maintain its edge in its war on legitimate people.

The Internal Revenue Service, for example, has estimated that the underworld annually accepts about twenty billion dollars in wagers—admittedly, a conservative estimate—and that about 6 or 7 percent of this gross is retained as pure profit. This handsome profit margin helps to underwrite the high salaries and enticing commissions of the underworld employee.

Most criminals work on commission. Thus, ultimately, the criminal's income depends on how hard he works and the take on each job. Sometimes the number of jobs over time fluctuates wildly, making annual estimates difficult.

Source: Crime Pays. New York: Simon & Schuster, 1975. Copyright © 1975 by Thomas Plate. Pp. 87–108. Reprinted by permission of Simon & Schuster, a division of Gulf & Western Corporation.

Here are some brief sketches showing how much money some successful professional criminals can make in the various rackets.

NUMBERS RUNNER

A numbers runner is in the employ of a gambling combine. His work role is to accept bets from people in their homes or places of employment. His income is based on a percentage of the take. The actual take depends somewhat on the organization he's working for, but in general he gets between 15 and 25 percent of all bets he takes; from 33 to 50 percent of the losses of a new customer; and a 10 percent tip from the customer when he or she wins. If a numbers runner handles five hundred dollars in action each day, then his daily salary, as it were, would be roughly one hundred dollars, (This is an absolutely tax-free sum.)

BURGLAR

The burglar also works for a percentage of each score, the difference going to the fence, or criminal receiver. Burglary income varies tremendously. One Dorchester, Massachusetts, burglar manages only fifteen thousand a year, plus welfare; a New York burglar, who lives in Westchester County, and who commutes to New York once or twice a week to commit his foul deed, does considerably better. Here is how he did during 1972. The information is based on an interview conducted by a friend.

In January, four scores for a net (after overhead, largely, the occasional tool or transportation cost; most of the merchandise was fenced) of two thousand; February, three scores for thirty-five hundred; March, five scores for twelve hundred; April, three scores for two thousand; May, three scores for three thousand; June, three scores for one thousand (a bad month); July, two scores for four thousand; August, none (vacation); September, one score for three thousand; October, two scores for two thousand; November, one score for six thousand; December, none (vacation).

Total income for 1972 for this Westchester County burglar was $28,700.

Again, this is a tax-free sum. Twenty-eight thousand dollars of untaxed income is the spending-power equivalent of perhaps forty thousand dollars, at today's tax rates. Forty thousand dollars is a tremendous salary in this country. I know of bank vice-presidents who make considerably less than that.

To cover up illicit income, many criminals bank a large percentage of their profit and live more or less on welfare or unemployment. So the average American is hit in two ways: he not only is deprived of tax revenue from the criminal, but in some cases has his tax money appropriated for the purpose of paying the criminal's welfare checks.

JEWELRY FENCE

This is a highly specialized occupation. There are not too many of them, and most of them are simultaneously legitimate businessmen, that is, they run their fencing operation out of a regular jewelry store or exchange. Also, in New York and several other big cities, the jewelry fences exist at the sufferance of the reigning syndicate executives; in this way, any big jewelry heist in that city has to be approved by the bosses, who naturally take their cut (more of this later), because if it weren't, the

burglars would have great difficulty fencing the take.

Jewelry fencing is highly profitable. One big fence on the West Side of Manhattan reportedly cleared three hundred thousand one year—just on fencing.

PORNOGRAPHY STORE CLERK

This one is a real shocker. In New York, along 42nd Street, there are dozens of dirty book and peep-show stores. Many, if not all of them, are owned by organized crime interests. A simple clerk in these stores can earn up to five hundred a week in straight salary, plus a percentage of the gross after a certain level. He is also provided with a lawyer in the event of a bust. So, if he works for a full year, as many do, then splits for Europe or the West Coast, he makes twenty-five thousand a year—the equivalent of perhaps a taxable income of thirty-eight thousand for a single man under current schedules.

MUSCLEMAN

A muscleman is usually a member of the enforcement area of a criminal outfit. His job is to enforce law and order, as the bosses so define it. Some musclemen work on a free-lance basis—that is, they are known as leg busters and hit men, and so on.

How much a muscleman actually makes depends, obviously, on how active he is. For breaking a man's leg, a muscleman will charge anywhere from one hundred to a thousand dollars. For serving as an armed guard on a robbery team—i.e., riding shotgun—a man can get one hundred fifty dollars for an hour's work. For protecting an organized crime card game for a night, one hundred dollars. For a straight hit (murder), the cost varies from a thousand dollars to fifteen thousand. The very best hit men value their services exorbitantly, so that the fifteen-thousand figure is probably close to the average. However, a contract killer who is on the payroll of a criminal organization may not get anything per hit—just his salary, which will probably be in high five or low six figures, easily.

LOAN SHARK

"Loan sharking," Angelo De Carlo, the New Jersey mobster, once said inadvertently into an FBI tape recorder, "is the strongest racket in

Criminal Salaries*
(Estimates Based on the Experience of Successful Criminals)

Job	City	Estimated Annual Gross
Peep-show clerk	New York	$ 20,000 (tax-free)
Hotel burglar (pick man)	East Coast	$ 75,000 (tax-free)
Pickpocket	Miami	$ 20,000 (tax-free)
Numbers runner	Harlem	$ 26,500 (tax-free)
Numbers controller	Brooklyn	$ 60,000 (tax-free)
House burglar	Long Island	$ 25,000 (tax-free)
Burglar (industrial)	Westchester County	$ 75,000 (tax-free)
Bank robber	East Coast	$ 24,000 (tax-free)
Shoplifter (booster)	Washington	$ 15,000 (tax-free)
Drug distributor	Los Angeles	$ 27,000 (tax-free)
Hit man (contract, nonsalaried)	Chicago	$ 75,000 (tax-free)
Loan shark	New York	$125,000 (tax-free)
Drug importer	Miami	$165,000 (tax-free)
Pornography Store owner (sex shows, films magazines)	New York	$120,000 (tax-free)
Mob lieutenant	New York	$125,000 (tax-free)
Securities thief (airports)	East Coast	$100,000 (tax-free)

* These figures are rough estimates of the gross income of fourteen successful criminals for a minimum of one year over the last five years. They are not mean figures, averages, or necessarily even representative incomes. In fact, they were chosen precisely for the purpose of illustrating the point that crime can indeed pay. The estimates, in each case, used at least two sources, and usually three, to arrive at the income over a one-year period. Usually one of these sources was the criminal himself. In all instances, the estimates are skewed toward the conservative figure, and the final list was circulated among professional criminals and law enforcement officials in an effort to make sure that none of the data is out of line. Of course, the list must be read with some skepticism. It is impossible to determine beyond any possibility of doubt the income of a criminal, if only because by necessity his income gathering remains secretive. I.R.S. statements, even if they were available, would be unrevealing. Still, as gross estimates for working criminals, the list is as factual as it can possibly be made and, at least among the experts to whom it has been shown, well within not only possibility but more importantly, past experience, as revealed by I.R.S. cases against professional criminals. Also, several of the figures in the chart were coordinated with published testimony, including Congressional hearings on organized crime. For instance, in the hearings before the Permanent Senate Subcommittee on Investigations in June of 1971, a criminal convicted for mail theft gave testimony regarding his activities as a securities thief. (His testimony was corroborated by a staff member.) "My share of the loot my partners and I stole in a four-year period," he said, "came to approximately $1 million." This would average out to $250,000 per year. However, professional criminals consulted argued that this (1) seemed too high and (2) was not in the least representative. On this basis, the experience of another criminal, who admitted to an average income of $100,000, seemed more appropriate for the chart. In the same vein, I have quoted one professional drug distributor in Los Angeles as making $27,000 a year. Virtually all sources, on both sides of the fence, suggest that this figure might be misleading, since it seems relatively low. However, it is a real figure.

the world . . . better than numbers or anything else, and cleaner."

By "better," the convicted gangster means "more profitable." A good loan shark puts one hundred thousand dollars out on the street in loans to hard-up addicts, businessmen, criminals, and so forth, and by the end of the year realizes a pure profit of one hundred and fifty thousand dollars.

This is because of the interest rates. The usual loan shark interest on a loan is 20 percent per week. If I borrow one hundred dollars from a loan shark, I pay him twenty dollars per week until I pay back the original principal.

On a longer-term loan, I might pay 1½ percent interest per week, or 78 percent a year.

Established loan sharks are easily six-figure-a-year professionals.

STREET PEDDLER OF DOPE

Once again, tremendous variation here. Often this man or woman is just scraping by.

MARIJUANA IMPORTER/WHOLESALER/RETAILER

One marijuana entrepreneur I know also holds down a full-time job as a drug salesman with a pharmaceutical firm. In this capacity, the young man is a traveling salesman. He sells over the counter for his firm and under the counter for himself. He clears about thirty thousand dollars a year, and much of the money is stashed in out-of-state banks.

We should note, morosely, that salaries in the straight world are generally not so good. Besides, anyone who is on salary is subjected to the cruel straitjacket the income tax system. The only people who seem to be able to beat this system, then, are the very rich, or the crooks. Of course, in some cases the two are identical.

. . . AND NOW FOR THE OVERHEAD

Criminals are the first to argue that their overhead costs are just like those of any other business. These costs are somewhat more bizarre than those, say, of the corner delicatessen. But the principle is the same—which, in plain English, is that you can't get something for nothing.

A list of these costs that a criminal might bear in mind include monetary ones as well as those that cannot possibly be measured in dollars and cents.

PSYCHOLOGICAL OVERHEAD COSTS

Davey* is so paranoid that he hates to walk to his car. He gets up in the morning and thinks, Maybe I can do everything by phone, never have to leave the house. Then he remembers that his phone is tapped—or so he thinks. Maybe, he thinks further, I shouldn't even get out of bed. Then he remembers that this is no use either: the police have planted a bug in one of his bedposts—or so he thinks.

Davey is a typical narcotics criminal. There are thousands of them in the trade, and just about all of them, understandably enough, have the same complaint. I'm being bugged, I'm being watched, I'm being followed, I'm in big trouble. What can I do? They look at a utility repairman on a telephone pole and see an FBI man taking notes. They see a suspicious guy at one end of the bar and won't even go to the men's room, because it'll give the man a better shot at him.

This is the paranoid world of the professional criminal. Now, there are overhead costs and there are overhead costs. It may be that the ones that cannot be qualified into dollars and cents are the most painful of all.

Sometimes crime exacts a tremendous toll. The fear of detection and arrest can be a living hell. Perhaps the price is worth paying, per-

---

* Davey is not his real name.

haps not. But it is one that professional criminals pay all the time.

Of course, Davey doesn't do what seems obvious, I think, to you—that is, get out of the business. The money is just too good to be true. Last year he managed to clear one hundred thousand dollars, after expenses and other overhead costs. Still, there's no way of measuring the psychological toll on Davey over the long run.

The psychological wear and tear come from not knowing what lurks around the corner. The straight businessman who goes to work every day, puts in his eight hours five days a week, comes home bored, perhaps, but at least he has the satisfaction of some security against sudden, absolutely unexpected turns in fortune.

The criminal has no such psychological security. He is at the mercy not only of his luck on the job, but also of the police, and of fellow criminals as well. If a professional criminal trespasses on another criminal's territory, there may be consequences. Criminals suspected of informing police face instant retribution if discovered. Criminals who are truly doing well in their line of work face the jealousies of those who are not. Although the crime business is not as violent as portrayed in television and movies, still, it is entirely possible that some frustrations may be vented at the end of a gun barrel.

The question of whether there is honor among thieves is important in this context. Among criminals who respect each other greatly there is a considerable sense of mutual integrity. But among relative strangers and outright competitors, there is very little of the Ten Commandments indeed. This is why Davey says, "Whoever said there was honor among thieves didn't know what he was talking about." Davey feels this way perhaps because in the drug world there are so many newcomers to the business that there is no sense of community whatsoever. In more established trades, the situation may not be quite so bad.

Here again there is an exception to the rule. For some reason, the book-making business seems rife with animosity and subterfuge. As an investigator of organized gambling in the State of New York once observed, "Bookmakers cheat not only the public but one another. As one bookmaker stated, he would never trust the word of another bookmaker. Bookmaking partnerships are notoriously fragile, with constant changes in personnel. Some bookmakers absolutely refuse to deal with certain others. Bookmakers give one another false odds and point spreads. . . . They inform police against competitors not approved by organized crime whom they wish to drive out of business." With minor modification, this general description of the bookmaking business applies to the drug world as well.

For all this, criminals seem prepared to pay the psychological overhead costs in return for what they regard as relative freedom from the straightjacket of the normal world. The very thought of a nine-to-five job reassures the criminal that he is doing the best for himself after all. And, remember, the vast majority of these criminals making very good money indeed have no higher education whatsoever. In fact, many of them have no lower education to speak of, either, and would be limited to low-paying menial jobs were it not for their involvement in crime.

I recall once being on a talk show in New York with the brilliant crime novelist George Higgins, himself a former assistant United States Attorney in Massachusetts and an exceedingly knowledgeable person about the criminal life. The hosts of the show were two very nice ladies who, I believe, were adept at throwing teas among New York's higher society. At one point in the discussion, one of the hosts complained that she could not understand for the life of her why any young man would become a criminal. George Higgins then asked her what she would do if *she* had a choice between an $80-a-week job as a car-washer or a three-hundred-dollar-a-week job as a numbers runner. The fine lady said she'd definitely be a car-washer. Then she asked Higgins, who is as quick as he is direct, what he would do.

Said Higgins, "I wouldn't work in the car wash."

THE POLICE

Here we break down the overhead cost into several categories.

First, there is the complete police investigation. This can cost the criminal a great deal, especially in lost time; the criminal getting wind of the trouble ahead may simply leave town for a long vacation. This can be tremendously costly to the criminal whose business has built up a certain momentum. (Usually, the criminal will go right about his business, hoping for the best.) Then, there is the police bribe. This can be measured in dollars and cents and, indeed, is often an integral part of an operation.

In the past few years police investigations have gotten quite sophisticated. The police have been forced to upgrade themselves, in part by court decisions restricting gang-buster techniques that served in the past, in part by the growing sophistication of the professional criminal. In any event, full-scale police investigations now are almost entirely restricted, in the big cities, to major criminals.

Criminals in narcotics, burglary and even gambling can still do a modest business and not draw the boys decked out in the utility-man overalls on a telephone pole across the street, tapping the phone, or the technicians in the panel truck with the peephole shooting Vista-Vision films. But as the size of the business increases, the criminal has to realize that he becomes a plum for the cops.

Here is what can happen to a criminal, assuming the cops in his area are *not* on the take.

1. The police can open a preliminary investigation. This will entail a record check, some interviewing, a few phone calls to registered

The Office Hours of the Criminal

Day burglar (apartments, homes)	11 A.M.–2 P.M.
Night burglar (hotel)	6:30–11 P.M. (dinner and theater hours)
Night burglar (house)	12 A.M.–5 A.M.
Booster (department store shoplifter)	12 P.M.–2 P.M. (crowded lunch hour)
Fence (general merchandise)	Any time (but especially 5 A.M.–12 P.M., When the hijackers come in)
Drug dealer	Any time (but especially on weekends, when federal narcotics cops are off)
Mugger	11 A.M.–2 P.M. (old ladies shopping) 5 P.M.–7 P.M. (tired secretaries) 12 A.M.–4 A.M. (inebriated businessmen)
Auto thief	Any time

informants (of which all municipal police forces have thousands)—that sort of thing.

2. Police initiate visual surveillance. This means they are serious. Police don't generally sit in unmarked cars for hours upon hours unless they are onto something. This is usually the beginning of the end.

3. Police obtain authorization from a judge to wiretap or bug a suspect's office or home. In order for the police to be permitted to use wiretap testimony in court against the defendant, the police must first obtain a court order for the electronic surveillance. Of course, nothing can stop the cops from putting in eavesdropping equipment without a court order if they want to; and if the purpose is simply to find out what the criminal is up to, they can always go to the judge for official approval of a second tap. However, putting in a tap or bug without a court order is strictly illegal, but some cops do it all the time. Whether the electronic surveillance is authorized or not, however, the use of this equipment means that the investigation is deadly serious and that the cops won't give up until they've got something—if only to prove to their bosses that

they knew what they were doing and to justify the expense of the surveillance, which is very high.

4. Police will work on an associate of the criminal. They will make an incriminating case against this associate, then offer him a deal. In return for testimony against the guy he is working for—the higher-up—the police will see to it that the prosecutor and the judge are lenient.

   For the police, this is a terrific deal. They nail a lot of criminals this way. They get the smaller fish to point the accusing finger at the big fish, like John Dean, the former White House counsel, making accusations against President Nixon.

   There is only one problem with this kind of deal. Sometimes the smaller fish invents his story. To get himself off the hook, he weaves out of whole cloth an incriminating tale about another criminal, on whom police have placed a high priority. Sometimes police and prosecutors even coach the accuser, helping him to invent this damning story. Of course this is unethical but it is done a great deal. Ambitious prosecutors often descend to the same level as the very criminals they seek to incarcerate. For example, in the thirties, Lucky Luciano, the boss of the American Cosa Nostra, was set up in this way. He was indicted and convicted on the charge of fostering white slavery, or prostitution. The prosecutor was Thomas E. Dewey, later to become Governor and even later Presidential nominee of the Republican party. Luciano was guilty of many violations of law, but one thing that was beneath him—as it remains beneath top-level criminal bosses today—is the prostitution rackets. A former high official of the New York Police Department once admitted to me that Luciano had, in fact, been "set up."

5. Police sometimes go one step further. They actually plant incriminating evidence on the premises of the criminal. This is common in narcotics cases. They break into the criminal's residence or place of business, plant a stash of dope, return the next day with a search warrant, discover (surprise!) the damning evidence, and arrest the suspect. They will do this because

   a. they know that the criminal has been doing such-and-such, but they have not been able to catch him red-handed and are frustrated.

   b. they are shakedown artists; they will use the planted evidence to elicit a bribe.

   c. they are absolutely desperate for an arrest because the pressure is on from headquarters for a "crackdown" or the captain has been breathing down their necks for the past few months or they are genuine law-and-order nuts who believe that any means justifies the end of putting the bad guys where they belong, behind bars.

6. Police do nothing even slightly unethical and go to the district attorney with absolutely hard, professionally obtained evidence. In this event—and it is an event that does occur—the criminal had better get himself a good lawyer. When the cops actually take the trouble to put together a good, clean, thorough case, they can do one tremendous job.

Taps and bugs are the criminal's true bane. When a piece of listening equipment has been legitimately installed, it can be devastating. Although many criminals today insist that they no longer converse freely on the phone, or even in the office, some of them must, because the cops keep putting taps in, and they keep picking up some great stuff on the tape recorder.

Here are a few excerpts from a wiretap transcript. The tap was put in under court order. The New York detective had gone to a judge, with the district attorney at his side, with a so-called wiretapping affidavit. This a long, tortuous document, which seeks to justify to the judge violation of the citizen-suspect's Constitutional right to privacy. The affidavit contains a summary of the investigation, the alleged activities of the suspect, and the reason why electronic surveillance must be used. In the particular affidavit from which these quotes are taken, the detective adds portions of a transcript from a previous tap. I found these excerpts fascinating, and I pass them along to show you not only how criminals talk to one another but how detailed is the information given a judge on an application of this sort.

EXCERPT ONE

The detective, in the affidavit, explains to the judge that in recent months there has been a relative shortage of heroin on the street in New York. Then he quotes from a conversation between two Cosa Nostra narcotics dealers about the shortage.

FIRST DEALER: "I don't know, we doing something wrong, or what? I don't know what the fuck it is."

SECOND DEALER: "I don't hear of any—I don't hear of anybody scoring. This Jack says, 'Forget about it, it's clean,' he's clean out. Anybody scoring, maybe one. They bring it around in person."

The detective explains to the court that "I don't hear of anybody scoring" means that the Cosa Nostra member doesn't know of anyone obtaining large amounts of narcotics, and that the only people actually receiving narcotics are getting it from criminals who operate independently: "Anybody scoring maybe one (that is, one kilogram), they bring it around in person."

EXCERPT TWO

The detective also pointed out to the judge that this was a sophisticated trafficking organization, and that the members sought to insulate themselves from lower-level dealers who might be under police surveillance. In this conversation, we see that the dealers are not very happy about having to associate with a certain Jack, who it turns out is a heavy narcotics user and who has several times been arrested.

DEALER THREE: "We gotta worry about Jack. I told him to call only in an emergency, you know."

DEALER TWO: "Yeah, 'cause he got in trouble and everything."

DEALER THREE: "So I made him drive me downtown. Then I say, 'You dirty cocksucker, I told you (inaudible) only in an emergency. The only fucking thing you worried about is whether I got something or not!'"

The detective points out to the judge that Jack apparently had called up to inquire whether he could buy some dope.

The dealer's irritation with "Jack" was further expressed in an overheard conversation on September 29, 1972, around nine o'clock in the evening.

NUMBER TWO: "Jacks wants five. I was going to give him the whole five tomorrow, okay?"

NUMBER ONE: "I wouldn't"

NUMBER TWO: "Well, I say let's do it. He's got headaches. They're on him all the time. He's got the I.R.S."

UNIDENTIFIED MALE: "I.R.S.?"

NUMBER TWO: "Yeah, he's on the spot."

NUMBER THREE: "I.R.S."

NUMBER TWO: "It's (the heat is) all on this guy, all on this guy."

NUMBER ONE: "You know, I hate to see, I hate to see it happen, so many times (inaudible) . . . fall out a fucking window, I swear to God."

NUMBER TWO: "He should run away, didn't we tell him that?"

Incidentally, they never did execute Jack. The cops arrested him before they had the chance.

The simplest way of dealing with the cops is to buy them off. Many criminals believe that most cops can be persuaded from duty by a percentage of the take. In return for the bribe, the cop either sabotages an ongoing investigation, fails to complete an arrest, makes an improper arrest—deliberately, so that the case will be thrown out of court—or offers testimony at the trial in such a way as to undermine the credibility of the prosecution's case. I say this is the easiest way. Given the cost of today's lawyers, it may also be the cheapest.

Criminals often take out insurance policies, or licenses with the local precinct. In return for a percentage of the action, the criminal enterprise is insured against arrest or is guaranteed adequate warning in case of a headquarters-ordered crackdown. The insurance policy is called a "pad" by the police, and in some police forces the pad is regularly collected, a representative of the police actually making the rounds of the clientele much like a newsboy collecting for his papers.

The chart on the next page is an historic document. I have seen very few like it in my research. Yet I am sure it represents absolutely typical criminal bookkeeping. Ordinarily, a profit-and-loss statement of a gambling combine, complete with entries for "payoffs to police," would get burned before the police raided. This one didn't. In figuring the picture today, allow for the enormous decline in the value of the dollar over a forty year period.

Some criminals pay off the police in information about other criminals, rather than in money. These informants, who are well situated in the profession, meet regularly with police officers, usually detectives, to brief them on news of the underworld. In return, the cops may issue these informants what is in effect a license to operate. These licenses are issued only to *productive* informants. As a result of this information, it may be said that a very high percentage of police arrests of professional criminals can be attributed to information from these licensed criminals.*

* The number of criminals actually licensed by police to make a living in this way is quite extraordinary. This is primarily because in the United States there is so much activity in the crime world that the police can barely keep up with it all. Without the help of these double agents, the police would be totally left behind.

Thus a certain percentage of the criminal world in a metropolitan area is not only known to the police, but subsidized by them. This percentage is in effect an arm of the police department. A certain percentage of every burglary, every narcotics transaction, every hijacking and so forth is not only known, but tacitly approved, by police officers.

ATTORNEY'S FEES

Upon arrest, the criminal immediately secures an attorney. If the criminal is unconnected with a formal crime organization, then he'll have to retain one himself. Otherwise, the ring will provide one. A major fringe benefit of being attached to a ring is the automatic appearance of the ring's attorney at your arraignment. Even criminals who are not so affiliated tend to have a lawyer on retainers so they don't have to fish around at the last minute.

The attorney's fee probably constitutes the most expensive overhead cost of the criminal life. Very good criminal lawyers are *very* expensive. One attorney who represented an East Coast fence in 1974 was rumored to *start* his fee in a major criminal case at $25,000. One professional criminal once told me that in his opinion, the real criminals in the American way of crime are the criminal lawyers. "They never lose," he said. "The more crime there is, and the more court cases, the more money they make. The guys really making the dough in this game are the lawyers. My son asks me what he should be when he grows up, I tell him go to a law school and be a lawyer so I can retire early on his first million."

It can even be claimed that the high cost of legal talent contributes to the frequency of crime in America. On the face of it, it is an astounding, even incredible argument, but it is one that criminals make frequently. It goes something like his (I am paraphrasing an acquaintance of mine from Miami who deals in dope):

"You get busted, the first thing to do is to find a good shyster lawyer. He's going to cost a lot of bread. Where do you get the bread to afford a high-priced lawyer? You go out and score. I sell dope, another guy steals a car, another guy a bank. Add it all up, and you got these fancy lawyers making for a new crime wave. And don't think they don't know it. Why do you think they keep asking for postponements and adjournments and all of that legal crap? To give their client more time to get up the bread, that's all. They're going to make a deal with the D.A. anyway, rather than go to trial. All they care about is their fee. And they know there's only one way for us to get it, and that's do our thing. And don't tell me to go to Legal Aid. Those guys are for the birds. I know one Legal Aid lawyer, he told his client where to find a fence for his next job . . . Listen, everyone is in this thing together. Lawyers, crooks like me, judges, it's all one big game.

Precisely what lawyers do with their exhorbitant fees puzzles some criminals. The cynical ones—that is most criminals—believe that where the fee is $25,000, the judge gets about ten thousand and the prosecutor five. How much truth there is to their allegations has never been proven. Although one hears in courthouse circles rumors that such-and-such a judge can be "reached," evidence supporting the allegations is almost always nonexistent.

Whether or not some judges are corrupt, the fact is that criminals do tend to go to jail from time to time, their sentence being the major nonmonetary cost of doing business. Usually their lawyers seek to negotiate a light sentence for their client in return for pleading guilty. Usually such requests are granted. Criminals' trials are generally quite lengthy, and exceedingly costly, and everyone involved in the criminal justice system seems to prefer the easy way out by reaching an out-of-court settlement. In a sense, the pleabargaining system is a game of mutual bribery. The criminal bribes the prosecutor and the judge by offering to save them a lot of trouble; the judge and prosecutor bribe the criminal by offering to save him some time.

The Gambling Business in Historical Perspective: The Overhead Costs

The Balance Sheet for Gambling Operations in Cook County, Chicago for the Month of July 1941. (Until uncovered by investigators, this sheet was seen only by Jake Guzik, Frank Nitti, Edward Vogel and Murray Humphreys, four top underworld leaders.)

1. Gross earnings from slots, gambling houses, et cetera in Cook County outside of Chicago		$ 322,966
2. Overhead cost/Payoffs to Police, prosecutors, politicians		$ 26,280
3. Net profit (gross minus all overhead, including payrolls and graft)		$ 221,674
4. Annual projects:		
	Gross	$3,875,592
	Protection	315,000
	Projected net	$2,660,000

Note: The records consisted of six sheets of loose-leaf ledger. The bribe takers were noted in code, such as "Skid," "O.G.," "Tub."
Source: Chicago Tribune, October 25, 1941.

Plea bargaining is an atrocious perversion of justice and should be halted immediately. Even criminals secretly agree with me that plea bargaining is a joke.

JUDGES AND THE COURTS

Criminals are not deterred by stiff sentencing or harsh laws. When a stiffer narcotics law was put into effect in New York State on September 1, 1973, proponents of the tough law predicted that in short order the drug dealer would be forced out of the state. On the face of it, the prediction seemed reasonable.* The penalties

* On the contrary, I would argue that longer prison terms are undesirable precisely because prison contributes to crime rather than cures it. Prisons are not rehabilitation centers, but graduate schools in crime. They do not make the bad guy into a good guy, but reinforce every criminal instinct and talent that the offender has. If a man enters prison as a relative amateur, by the time he comes out there's a very good chance that he has been converted into a professional by peer-group pressure, as well as the opportunity to learn new tricks of the trade from the accomplished performers.

for dealing were the harshest in the nation, and it was thought that by raising the drug dealer's cost of doing business, he could be driven out of business. In actuality, the theory behind the law was reasonable, but the calculation was naive; what happened was that in comparison to the profit in the drug trade, the overhead costs were being only marginally increased. Crime still paid in New York for the narcotics dealer, even if the overhead went up somewhat. Indeed, there is some reason to believe that the higher overhead costs were simply passed on to the drug consumer in the form of higher retail prices for heroin, cocaine and marijuana.

If the possibility of prison shapes the behavior of criminals in any respect at all, it is perhaps in their choice of line of work. Criminals are very much aware of disparity in sentencing and will take several factors into calculation, if possible, before embarking on a score. One factor is the likelihood of detection and conviction for the crime in the area in which they are working. Another is the estimated sentence they will receive upon conviction.

In New York City, for example, there is a tremendous difference in both these factors, and criminals try to keep up on developments. They do this not by reading *The New York Times* or scholarly studies of sentencing, but by reflecting upon the experience of unfortunate colleagues.

One sentencing study in New York shows the possibility of a jail term per type of crime and the likely sentence for that crime. One such study showed that between May 1 and October 31, 1972, if you had been convicted in federal court, you would have had the following chance of going to jail:

In the following chart, which professional criminals are generally aware of, the list of offenses is arranged in a different order. This list tells the criminal what the average sentence was per violation.

If the crime was	The time was (average)
Bank robbery	70 mos.
Narcotics	62 mos.
Securities theft	57 mos.
Rackets and Extortion	47 mos.
Guns, sale of	28 mos.
Interstate theft	18 mos.
Counterfeiting	15 mos.
Bail jumping	10 mos.
Income tax evasion	6 mos.
Gambling	3 mos.

Please keep in mind that these charts refer to the experience of criminals who are *caught*. Most professional criminals are *not* caught.*

If caught and convicted and the crime was	Chances of some sort of time were
Securities theft	100%
Bank robbery	83%
Narcotics trafficking	77%
Bail jumping	67%
Rackets and extortion	56%
Interstate theft (hijacking, etc.)	55%
Counterfeiting	52%
Guns, sale of	50%
Gambling	37%
Income tax evasion	35%

* The figures presented above are statistical means and averages. In reality, there is a tremendous disparity in sentencing in the federal courts, and professional criminals know this better than anyone. A recent study of fifty federal judges in New York, Connecticut and Vermont illustrated the dimensions of the problem. A questionnaire was distributed to the judges, who were requested to sentence a number of hypothetical cases. In one "case," a union official was convicted on a nine-count extortion indictment. Under law, he could have received up to twenty years on the main charge, and up to $75,000 in fines. One judge "sentenced" him to the full twenty years and $65,000 in fines. Another levied a mere three-year sentence and no fine at all. Judges who are routinely "soft" on certain crimes are deliberately sought out by criminal lawyers—that is, every effort is made to get their client's case before the least punitive jurist for the particular offense in question.

The balance sheet shows the following:

1. Many crimes pay well.
2. The payoff is enhanced by the fact that the take is off-the-books; the money is tax-free. Every dollar in criminal take is the functional equivalent, for argument's sake, of at least a dollar fifty in legitimate income. (I recall once going out on a raid of a "massage parlor" with police. As one officer was handcuffing one of the girls, he said to her, "Why don't you give this all up and come work as my secretary at the precinct house?" The girl, who could not have been older than twenty-one, laughed and replied, "Sure, if you'll pay me five hundred a week—and *off the books!*—sure.")
3. The overhead costs are sometimes exceedingly high, especially in terms of personal freedom, but the money is good, too. When the criminal balances the equation, he comes up with the result that profits exceed overhead (and venture capital) costs by a margin sufficient to make the profession very attractive indeed.
4. Unless the overhead costs can be made staggering beyond belief—and it is difficult to see how this might be done consistent with the Bill of Rights—profits will always exceed overhead. Crime will pay.

23

PROFESSIONAL CAR THEFT AND CHOP SHOPS

PERMANENT SUBCOMMITTEE ON INVESTIGATIONS, U.S. SENATE

**TESTIMONY OF "JOHN SMITH"
ACCOMPANIED BY
ROBERT BURGER, ESQ.**

SENATOR PERCY. I want to advise you of your rights and obligations as a witness before this subcommittee. First you have the right not to provide any testimony or any information which may tend to incriminate you. If you do so testify, anything you say here may be used against you in any other legal proceeding.

*

MR. SMITH. My name is John Smith. Currently I am serving a 5–year sentence for conspiracy to transport in interstate commerce a stolen motor vehicle. The conviction resulted from my involvement in a major vehicle theft ring consisting of 40 to 45 individuals and five salvage yards that operated in nine States and Mexico. This criminal operation was responsible for 1.500 motor vehicle thefts.

I have personally stolen over 700 American-made cars in my life. At the time of my conviction, I could steal almost any American-made car in less than 90 seconds, and could

steal most in 40 to 50 seconds. I have also stolen Porsches, Volkswagens, and two Mercedes-Benz cars, each in under 3 minutes. The rewards from vehicle theft can be staggering, some individuals in my group earned close to $200,000 in 1977.

Growing up, I developed a strong interest in automobiles. After I graduated from high school, I held a number of jobs in the automotive field, including working as an automobile painter's helper, a line mechanic, and a general body man. In 4 or 5 years, I learned a great deal about automotive repair and body work.

In 1964, hoping to find more lucrative employment, I moved my family to southern California where I worked as a mechanic for local automobile dealerships. While living in southern California, I discovered that I could earn a substantial amount of money legitimately rebuilding salvage automobiles on my own. I could rebuild and sell about two cars a month working no more than 20 hours a week in my spare time.

After a few months of operation, my business was running pretty smoothly; however, with a family to feed, I was consistently looking for ways to increase my volume and profits. One day in 1966, after I had left a salvage yard that stocked spare parts, two men approached

Source: "Professional Motor Vehicle Theft and Chop Shops," Hearings Before the Permanent Subcommittee on Investigations, 96th Congress, 1st Session, U. S. Senate, 1980. Pp. 59–80. (Editorial adaptations.)

me on the street and asked me if I wanted to buy some inexpensive Corvette parts. They offered me a terrific deal on these parts; for instance, I was offered a set of bucket seats for $150 when the going rate at area salvage yards was $350. Other parts were also offered to me for less than half the going rate. I knew by the price of the parts that they were probably stolen but I needed the parts, and I knew I could not afford to buy them at legitimate prices. I decided to buy the stolen parts because they were not marked with any traceable factory numbers. No one could prove that these parts were stolen. I paid cash for the parts, and used them to rebuild a salvage Corvette.

Until these two thieves approached me, all my automobile dealings had been legitimate. Yet, the price of the "hot parts" was too good to turn down, and I continued to buy from the thieves. The idea of stealing cars for profit started to sound good to me because of the big money to be made. It seemed to me that anyone with common sense who wouldn't take stupid risks could get away with stealing cars. Within a few months, I had stolen my first car, a 1965 Corvette and had retagged it with the salvage from a wrecked 1965 Corvette. This was the start of a long and profitable relationship with a number of salvage yards in the southern California area.

During 1966 and 1967, I dealt primarily in legitimately rebuilding automobiles. Yet it became more and more tempting for me to buy stolen parts and even entire stolen cars. I also started to illegally rebuild and retag cars. For me, the risk in all this was minimal. I would carefully sanitize the stolen parts by removing all identification numbers, papers, and markings from the stolen merchandise.

In the midst of my illegal enterprise, I continued to work full-time at an automobile dealership. Yet as time went on, I paid less attention to my legitimate auto work. I leased two commercial garages and hired an old friend to do body work for me. Finally, in late 1967, I quit my legitimate job and started my own business in a garage behind my house. I legitimately rebuilt two or three cars per month and illegally retagged about one car a month. I dealt primarily in popular middle-sized models, including Camaros, Firebirds, Chevelles, and Corvettes. During 1968, I retagged about 40 cars.

I returned to my hometown in the spring of 1969, but became bored with the lifestyle there. I came back to southern California and started working for a legitimate rebuilding shop where I remained for about 2 or 3 months. I quit the job because I decided to start my own retagging operation. To carry out the operation, I rented a six-car commercial garage under a false name. An old friend, whom I had known since we were kids, and I started retagging cars together.

We rebuilt about four to six cars a month, half of which were illegal retags. I also stole cars pretty regularly and made good money from these easy thefts.

We did some of our work in my friend's own garage. Unfortunately for us, one of his neighbors got suspicious and called the police. In late 1970, the local police caught us red-handed with parts from a 1970 Chevy pick-up truck. Due to a technicality—the police neglected to obtain a proper warrant—the charges against us were dropped. But that arrest blew my cover, and the police arrested me on an unrelated 2-year-old warrant for auto theft. Eventually, I was sentenced to 1 year of weekend incarceration. I served 14 weekends of that sentence.

Even though my partner quit working with me after we were busted in his garage, I continued to work by myself out of my own shop for almost 5 months. I tried to stay straight and rebuild just enough cars to live on, but when money got tight I again started retagging. Because of my past record, I knew the police were probably watching me, so I had other people do most of my illegitimate buying and selling. Still, in early 1971, the police and the National Auto Theft Bureau came to the shop asking if they could look over my place. Certain that I had cleaned all the cars on the lot, I let them enter the shop. Unfortunately, the police found an air-powered impact wrench I had bought from a guy who had stolen the wrench and done a poor job of changing the numbers. I knew that I was in real trouble at this time. Two months later I was sentenced to 9 months in prison for receiving stolen property. I served 6 months and 10 days of that term. After the arrest in early 1971, too many auto theft investigators in southern California knew my name, and they wanted me out of the business.

In late 1975, I went back home for 3 to 4 months. Early in 1976, an old friend talked me into returning to the auto theft business. The financial temptation still held a powerful sway over me.

In 1976, I moved back to California and started dealing in stolen vehicles again. I also operated a small retag business involving six people and directed the illegal activities of three major retaggers in California and Texas and five wrecking yards in Texas, Colorado, New Mexico, and California. I stole cars and pickup trucks for my own business and for sale to others. I supplied parts and documents to other retaggers, helped locate drivers, body men, and rebuilders for my main accomplices, and found buyers for dozens of illegally rebuilt vehicles.

Eventually, this theft ring involved 40 to 50 individuals and was responsible for 1,500 to 2,000 vehicle thefts. By the end of 1976, I was the leading vehicle identification number, or VIN, package dealer in the Southwest. These packages were used to provide a new, clean identity for stolen vehicles. Members of my ring purchased VIN packages and also bought, sold, and retagged vehicles in New Mexico, Colorado, Louisiana, Texas, Arizona, California, Nevada, Oklahoma, Washington, and Mexico. In 1976 and 1977, I personally retagged about 60 pickup trucks, about a third of which were sold in Mexico. By 1977, the whole operation had gotten so big that many of the people working for me did not know each other. However, all of the people knew that I was in charge.

*

SENATOR PERCY. Mr. Smith, according to your statement this morning, you have stolen more than 700 cars during a 12-year period as an auto thief. You also stated you started out legitimately rebuilding wrecked cars and made a fair living at it. Could you tell the subcommittee why you turned to crime, specifically stealing cars. Did you intend to earn a better living or was it the simplicity of the crime that attracted you?

MR. SMITH. Well, I was looking it over and it was very easy to steal automobiles. I could see there was big money involved in it and I was right.

SENATOR PERCY. In 1966, you purchased for the first time, stolen auto parts that were not marked to any traceable factory numbers. Of course, no one could prove the unmarked parts were stolen. If the police had identified these first stolen parts you purchased, would you have continued in your illegal activities?

MR. SMITH. No, sir, I wouldn't have taken the risk of being arrested with those numbers on those parts. Even if parts are numbered and you remove the numbers from those parts, you will still be arrested for having vehicle parts with altered serial numbers in your possession.

SENATOR PERCY. While you were dealing in stolen cars and parts in southern California, about what percentage of salvage yards there dealt in hot or stolen parts?

MR. SMITH. I would say approximately 50 percent of the yards.

SENATOR PERCY. What is the basis of your estimate?

MR. SMITH. I have owned half interest in two yards in southern California in my 12 years of living there. The vehicle dealers I bought parts from were also associated with other dealers. We all knew one another.

SENATOR PERCY. Two areas seem to lead to encouragement of this fast-growing industry; these are the lack of vehicle identification numbers on hot parts, and the retag operation giving a clean title to a stolen vehicle. We have had a definition of retagged cars. Could you take us step by step through the retag operation?

MR. SMITH. OK. First you go out and buy a salvaged vehicle or, if you know a wrecker that will just sell you the identity off of the salvaged vehicle, that is really all you need. You really need the frame that has the secret, secondary numbers on it, you need the motor and transmission for cars, the VIN number stamped on them and you need the identification plate, Federal sticker, for some of the cars from 1970, up, the license plates, the registration and the title and to fix the identification plates for the vehicle.

SENATOR PERCY. How long did that whole operation take you?

MR. SMITH. If I wanted to do a real sanitary job on it, it will take around 8 hours.

SENATOR PERCY. How could you be sure no one detected a switch?

MR. SMITH. If you do a real neat job, even an auto theft specialist cannot detect the job.

SENATOR PERCY. Could you talk about the rosette rivets which are not supposed to be available to the public? How did you obtain rosette rivets?

MR. SMITH. I had friends working in General Motors production plants and I could go over and hang around the bars, shoot pool with the guys that worked in there on their lunch break and get to know them and they would bring me those rivets out without any problem.

SENATOR PERCY. Let's backtrack. What is a rosette rivet?

MR. SMITH. A rosette rivet is a little rivet that has a head design on it, kind of like a rose or a cauliflower, and it is a special built rivet made out of stainless steel material and the manufacturers that manufacture them will not sell them to the general public. They are only sold to the automobile manufacturers and they use those rivets to attach the public VIN plate to all the American-made automobiles.

SENATOR PERCY. Could you tell us something about the confidential VIN's, where they are located, and how confidential they actually are? The VIN is the vehicle identification number.

MR. SMITH. Correct. OK, if you are in the business of rebuilding cars and in the salvage business, those numbers are not very confidential at all. They are stamped usually on the frame rails, on the top of the frame rails, approximately 2 feet apart and some of the cars have them stamped in the cowl which is always in the same place on the cowl for General Motors Firebirds and Camaros and you will find the big Lincolns and T-Birds have a confidential number stamped under the dashpad on them.

SENATOR PERCY. What other things would you do to insure that you would not get caught?

MR. SMITH. The automobile manufacturers scatter broadcast sheet numbers all through the vehicle. These are sheets of paper about the size of this right here and they have all the description of the accessories, color interior, and all, everything that is going into that vehicle, type engine, transmission. Up in the top corner they will have the vehicle identification number typed in there and they hide them in the seats, throw them under the carpet, put them on top of the gas tanks, stuff them down around the front fenders. They are liable to be anywhere on those cars.

You have to go through those cars with a fine tooth comb to be sure that you get all those out. Some cars, people find as high as 20 broadcast sheets; some vehicles I have not found any in.

You have to be real clean, looking for gas receipts and any torn paper that might have a telephone number or address on it and if the police impound that car at a later date, they can check and get back to the people to find out where that came from.

SENATOR PERCY. Almost any car has certain personal belongings in it, an article of clothing, coat, suitcase, whatever it may be. When those cars contain personal effects, what would you do with them?

MR. SMITH. I went to the city dump.

SENATOR PERCY. You would do what?

MR. SMITH. I would take them all to the city dump. I wouldn't want to have anything around my person.

SENATOR PERCY. In other words, if you found a $40 or $50 sweater, you would just destroy it, get rid of it?

MR. SMITH. Get rid of it.

SENATOR PERCY. In other words, the profit margin on which you were operating was so great that these belongings which might be valuable to the individual whose car was stolen, were simply discarded. Otherwise the car might be identified as stolen if those items could be identified. Is that correct?

MR. SMITH. That is correct. It would be stupid to take a chance of having a $40 sweater get you busted with a $4,000 profit, you know. It just doesn't make sense.

*

SENATOR NUNN. You have stated that you operated a nine State vehicle theft ring. Where were your operations? What states were covered?

MR. SMITH. OK. Texas, Louisiana, Oklahoma, Colorado, Arizona, California, Nevada, and Mexico.

SENATOR NUNN. Did your operation deal with salvage yards and body shops in each State where you operated?

MR. SMITH. Yes, sir.

SENATOR NUNN. Could you estimate how many yards and shops you dealt with?

MR. SMITH. I would say approximately from 50 to 100 for the yard that I ran. I dealt with at least 100 people.

CHAIRMAN NUNN. Did you transport stolen cars and parts from State to State?

MR. SMITH. No. I have used common carriers, like freight companies, to ship commercial carriers; you know, to ship the parts around, and I would hire drivers to drive the cars to different States.

CHAIRMAN NUNN. Would they know that they were dealing with stolen automobiles?

MR. SMITH. They never asked any questions.

CHAIRMAN NUNN. What kind of vehicles did you steal and retag most often?

MR. SMITH. Most often I would say Ford pickup trucks.

CHAIRMAN NUNN. Why?

MR. SMITH. They are the prime target for re-taggers and auto thieves both. They have a very high retail and wholesale value. They have no motor and transmission numbers on the vehicles. The ID tag is held on the Ford truck with a little push-on aluminum rivet. It is very easy to change, and they have two secret or confidential numbers that are stamped on the right frame rail that is very easy just to change that rail in a truck. If you change the rail, you change the main portion of the identification on that vehicle. They are very easy to steal. The ignition pulls out of them very easy.

CHAIRMAN NUNN. Did you use these vehicles for chop shop operations? Did you chop them up and sell the parts or did you sell them as a whole?

MR. SMITH. I sold mine, the biggest part of mine, as a whole.

CHAIRMAN NUNN. If they had had vehicle identification numbers on the motor and transmission, would that have made any difference in your operation?

MR. SMITH. Yes, it would. With identification numbers stamped on those engines, Chevrolet trucks, I would deal with Chevrolet trucks, but I had to either buy the salvaged motor and transmission to go with those trucks or either buy new short blocks and transmission cases to put in all the guts of the stolen motors. So I would be sure that I wouldn't be having an engine number and a transmission number that had even been altered. At the least I wouldn't mess with any of those engines that had been altered after getting burned in 1967 with that Corvette.

CHAIRMAN NUNN. Was your operation as profitable on Chevrolets when you had to go

to that kind of trouble as it was with the Ford pickups?

MR. SMITH. No, sir, it wasn't.

CHAIRMAN NUNN. At that time what kind of VIN marking did Ford provide for its pickups?

MR. SMITH. They had a frame rail, they had the confidential numbers stamped on the frame rail, which is on the right side. It is stamped in two places, one place is up underneath the hood, real near the radiator on the front, and the other one is right underneath the passenger seat.

They have the public VIN number, which is on the floor, it is held on with real lightweight aluminum rivets and they have a Federal sticker on the cap. That is all the ID on a Ford truck.

CHAIRMAN NUNN. What was the scope of your operation at its peak in terms of money involved? How much money was involved in your overall operation?

MR. SMITH. Hundreds of thousands of dollars.

CHAIRMAN NUNN. What would you guess in a year? Did you keep good books, did you know what you were doing in terms of money, or would you just be estimating?

MR. SMITH. No. We never kept any records.

CHAIRMAN NUNN. What would be your best estimate of the most money you made in a year? Let's divide it into two questions. Let's talk about the whole ring, and then you personally. How much would your ring profit in a year? And then how much would you personally profit in a year according to your best estimate?

MR. SMITH. It is really hard for me to separate that. Excuse me. I lived a very high life style and I never kept records of money. It would be hard to say how much I really made.

CHAIRMAN NUNN. Would it be in the hundreds of thousands of dollars in a year or would that be too high?

MR. SMITH. That probably wouldn't be too high, no, sir.

CHAIRMAN NUNN. It would not?

MR. SMITH. No, sir.

SENATOR PERCY. Is that tax free?

MR. SMITH. Yes, sir.

*

SENATOR COHEN. Perhaps you could relate your experience about the process you used in going about stealing a car.

MR. SMITH. . . . I had a key cutter. I would take the door lock out of the passenger side of the car and put another dummy lock in it.

SENATOR COHEN. . . . How do you take a door lock out?

MR. SMITH. I would take a little hand drill with an eighths inch bit on it, drill right to the right side of the lock, about an eighth of an inch away, right across the center, and I have an ice pick or punch-awl and stick in that hole, flip that spring clip off of the lock and pull the lock out, put another dummy lock in the door, so no one could tell the hole was left in the door there you know.

I would walk off to my car, sit down and tear the lock apart and read the tumblers in it and cut a key for it.

SENATOR COHEN. How long would that take?

MR. SMITH. It would take about 30 seconds to flip that keeper off. I would be around, I would be outside the car less than half a minute and I would walk away, just leave it sitting and in the Chevrolets, they had the key code stamped right on the door lock, from, well the 1965, 1964, and up until 1969. I could just read the code off of it and I had a code book.

SENATOR COHEN. Where did you get the code book?

MR. SMITH. I bought the key cutter, Curtis-Mathis Key Machine, and the code book and everything came with it. I bought it through a salvage yard.

*

MR. SMITH. OK. So General Motors then, in 1970, quit putting key codes on their door locks, but I was familiar. I could read the key tumblers anyhow, the key codes, so that really didn't bother me any. So in 1969, I guess they probably slowed a lot of amateurs down, they put that locking system on the steering column and the transmission, in the steering wheel lock and they moved the key ignition cylinder from the dash up to the steering column. But General Motors kept the same door lock and the same ignition cylinder, the one key worked it up until 1973.

*

MR. SMITH. . . . In 1974 General Motors came down again and they switched to where it took a separate key to unlock the door from the steering column. So when they came out with those two key systems like that, I got busy and invented a puller that was a finger-type puller that flipped the chrome ring off of the ignition cylinder and clamped this puller on it and put a bolt in the back end of it and extracted that lock just like pulling, kind of like pulling a cork out of a wine bottle.

When I would get that whole key cylinder and everything out, I would just drop it down in the steering column and turn the car on and everything would be unlocked just like using your own key.

So, General Motors after they found out that the thieves were stealing those cars like that, in 1977 they quit making that top of that ignition cylinder to where you could get hold of it with that puller. They made it smooth on the top. So I got busy again and invented another tool that was like a hole saw, with a garret plate and I would use a little electric power drill and drill around this little hard button that they put inside of these things. Back up to 1972 I believe General Motors put little hard buttons about the size of a dime down there where your key slot goes, so you can't put a screw in there.

It is so hard, the screw won't screw into that metal. So you have to crack that, break it out, then I would use this screw system which you could use a slide hammer to break the cylinders out in these General Motors in 1977. But it is awful noisy. So I made another tool that I would screw in and I had a bolt on the back side of it, I would run that nut down on the back side and it would pull that cylinder out, extract it the same way as my puller for the '74 to 76's can, only I attached the puller into the switch by screwing the screw down into the switch itself.

*

SENATOR PERCY. Before you go into the demonstration, there is one aspect that you haven't touched on yet. Of the 70 cars that you were personally involved in stealing, which would probably come to a retail value in excess of $5 million, you have mainly talked about techniques that you call blue-collar techniques. Did you ever engage in any other techniques in stealing automobiles?

MR. SMITH. Yes, sir. I have another technique of getting those General Motors cars. I call this a white-collar technique.

*

SENATOR PERCY. . . . Could you describe what a white-collar technique would be?

MR. SMITH. Yes, sir. You will find very common, that a lot of dealerships like to put their name on the vehicle on a little chrome tag or something. You know, stick them on the deck lid or on the license plate frame brackets. They will always give this to a customer and they will have their name, the company name and address on those brackets.

*

. . . If you had bought a Cadillac say from Supreme Cadillac, they give you a license plate bracket that fits around your license plate on the car. They will have the name of that company on it. So you will know that that car has come from that dealership. You know, that that dealership keeps service records on that automobile. So you see a car you want, you get the license number off of it, write it down, you go to the Department of Motor Vehicles and ask them for a teletype readout on this vehicle and they will give you that teletype readout, and it will give you the name and address of the registered and legal owner on that car.

So I would wait until approximately 4 or 4:30 in the afternoon, after I had the people's address and name—

SENATOR PERCY. Why would you wait until late in the afternoon?

MR. SMITH. I would use the excuse to call down to the dealership. I know it's late in the afternoon, everybody's busy and getting ready to go home, wanting to quit work for the day. I would call the dealership and get hold of the service writer and tell him that I am Joe from Joe's locksmith, and I have a customer of his down here at the mall and she has lost her keys while shopping, and would he be kind enough to give me the key codes off of her service record so I don't have to detain her and charge her $35 to tear the steering column down on her Cadillac. I will charge her a couple of dollars for cutting her a key and send her on the way.

They are more than happy to give you those key codes. He will give me the key codes over the phone and I will go cut a key for the car, then I can steal the car out of the driveway; with the keys to the trunk and the ignition both.

SENATOR COHEN. . . . I believe the witness talked about the VINs, and that there were at least two confidential VINs, . . . on most automobiles?

Before you answer, the reason I would like to inquire, is how did you discover the confidential source of information? How long would it take, assuming we impose more requirements, more VINs, how long do you think it would take for organized crime to detect that code?

MR. SMITH. OK. Myself, when a new year model would come out, if I am specializing, retagging certain cars, Corvettes, Rivieras, or trucks, as soon as I seen a current year model wrecked at a salvage pool, I would put a high bid on it, buy that car and take it to my shop and tear it apart with the help from some of my employees, and personally I would inspect every piece on that car and I would find out where they put those secondary numbers on it. I have found out that—well, during my operation, General Motors, it is common for them to put two secondary numbers on those vehicles and when I found them, I felt comfortable that I had found the only ones that were on that car.

SENATOR COHEN. Was there ever an establishment of a ring inside the automobile manufacturers that would disclose this code to organized car thieves?

MR. SMITH. Not the people that I dealt with. Like I say, we would tear those cars down and find out where they were for our own benefit.

A lot of people you can't trust what they tell you anyhow.

*

[NOTE.—Mr. Smith demonstrates how to defeat the ignition and steering column lock of a 1978 General Motors Chevrolet Malibu. For purposes of demonstration, a 1978 steering column has been mounted on a stand. Mr. Smith uses a screwdriver to pry off the chrome key-guide which covers the ignition cylinder. Then, using a cork-screw-like device which extracts the ignition cylinder . . . Mr. Smith replaces it with an ignition cylinder for which he has the key . . . With the replacement ignition cylinder in place, Mr. Smith merely turns the key to "start," releasing the steering-column lock.]

MR. BERK. Mr. Smith, can you explain step by step as you are going through this demonstration exactly what you are trying to do?

*

MR. SMITH. First thing you do when you get in the car is take a screwdriver. See this is cracked up through here, and cracked up through here. I fractured that so hard, when it breaks it usually, fractures three or four places. The next thing I have to do is get a piece of this out. I don't need to get the whole thing out. As long as you get half of it out, there it is. That sucker was a rough one. OK, you can see what that does. This is all plastic they put in this thing, that is the reason we were having the problem. I ripped that whole plastic out instead of breaking this end off.

If this column is made out of pot metal, it will break this off in about two turns of this, it will go crack, come out real fast and easy.

MR. BERK. Mr. Smith, could you tell the Senators and the audience how long it has been since you have stolen a car and how long it took you when you were in the business to steal this type of vehicle?

MR. SMITH. It's been about 19 months since I have been around.

*

MR. BERK. How much time did it take you on the average to steal that type of vehicle?

MR. SMITH. Approximately 3 minutes on one of these 1977 type vehicles.

*

. . . Any General Motors. I will have another key, a substitute, in my pocket like this.

CHAIRMAN NUNN. Wouldn't you say this differs from the normal?

MR. SMITH. You see that housing right here, that thing is made out of plastic. General Motors has made that housing there out of plastic, I guess, to save a little cost in manufacturing. But you can see how this thing pulled.

CHAIRMAN NUNN. To keep it from breaking off as easy?

MR. SMITH. Yes; just pull the whole thing out. Like a plow, this is what holds that cylinder in, it's a spring-loaded foot right here. When you put this thing in, drop it in the cylinder, that little foot right there goes down and jumps down into a notch down in the bottom of this column. This thing was made out of pot metal. It will break this off through here, and comes out real easy.

You noticed I was having a lot of problems getting it out.

SENATOR PERCY. You still did pretty well.

MR. SMITH. That's a little change on the different models. You need to stay out and be active in this business to keep up with them. They will constantly change on you.

*

SENATOR PERCY. Mr. Smith, maybe you can tell us what you are going to demonstrate here.

[NOTE.—Mr. Smith demonstrates vehicle theft techniques with a 1979 Ford Zephyr. A cut-away of the driver's side of the passenger compartment, including door, cowl and steering column, has been mounted on a platform constructed for the demonstration. Mr. Smith uses a thin, notched metal strip known as a "slim jim" to unlock the door and gain entry to the vehicle. Once inside the vehicle, he uses a greased rubber key to turn the ignition lock to "start," releasing the steering column lock. An alternative to this method is pointed out by Mr. Smith: removal and disassembly of the passenger door lock yields information enabling a thief to cut a key to fit both the door lock and the ignition lock of Ford Motor Co. automobiles. Mr. Smith demonstrates a key-cutting device similar to the one which he has used for this purpose.]

MR. SMITH. This is a 1979 Ford Zephyr. I am going to demonstrate to you how you use this tool here, that is called a slim jim. You slide it down in here to unlock the vehicle. I will show you how to use this lock pick to turn the ignition on and after I show you that, I'll also show you how to take the door lock out of these Fords, which has the same door-lock key that fits the ignition. I will show you how to cut a key for it, how I use the key to get into this car with it.

SENATOR COHEN. Before you go any further, would the placement of this handle way down, hidden away from the coat hanger, prevent you from doing that?

MR. SMITH. No, sir. See, what I got down here is the arm that works the back of this switch right here. It's real simple to do, do you want to try it? Just take that rod and slide it down in there, kind of push it to the side a little bit. See this mark on it right here, pull it back up. Just a minute, you see this mark, this scratch, keep it right in the center of this door handle and get it level with this chrome right in here. There you go. Pretty simple?

That is with the original key for that car. This is a lock pick, this is what they call—this is what they call a rubber key. It's got a rubber in it right in here. We slide this in the car and that turns it on.

MR. MAYER. Can you tell us if this key can be used on other Ford products, or is it particular to this one here?

MR. SMITH. I would say this key right here would work on, I would say 70, maybe 80 percent, maybe even more of the Ford products, this thing right here will get it.

See this little gadget here, If you have any problem getting it to turn on, work this thing up and down and what it does is forces this rubber down into the tumblers, lines them up. Keep pressure to the right.

CHAIRMAN NUNN. Most professional automobile thieves have this type—

MR. SMITH. Not that I know of, I don't think so.

SENATOR PERCY. You don't have a patent on that?

MR. SMITH. No. I will take this door lock—

CHAIRMAN NUNN. Can that usually be prevented by the manufacturer?

MR. SMITH. Like General Motors, they put an extra key—it makes it real hard to hit with a lock pick. Ford has only got four or five depth cuts—

CHAIRMAN NUNN. You couldn't do this on a GM car.

MR. SMITH. It would be a lot harder. Let me show you guys one more thing. Could somebody give me a pair of pliers? . . .

SENATOR COHEN. Did one of those automatic alarm systems prevent you from doing that?

MR. SMITH. If the alarm was on the car, I wouldn't want to get into it, because it would set the alarm off. After I get in this car—see, Ford doesn't even have a protector over this clip that holds this door lock in. If my key pick wouldn't work, I would take and ease this slip out of this thing, take this door out, see. That way you wouldn't disturb or scratch the door. That puller we used on that 1978 Chevrolet, I will screw in here and screw that nut down, it will pull that lock straight through this clip.

I will never have to open the car door to turn the interior light on. Also, when I get this door locked up, see this rod right there, I would push this rod, push that rod down as I unlock the door. This is what you got on awhile ago, you pushed this lever right here.

CHAIRMAN NUNN. When you took that out, you would use it to make a key?

MR. SMITH. Yes; I would take this off.

CHAIRMAN NUNN. They have the same key that fits this as the ignition.

MR. SMITH. Right, the same key that fits your door lock fits the ignition. See, Chevrolet changed this in 1974.

CHAIRMAN NUNN. So, having two different keys, different from the door and ignition helps prevent theft?

MR. SMITH. It does.

CHAIRMAN NUNN. It makes it a little more difficult?

MR. SMITH. Yes. After I take this door lock out, I take it to my car. I sit down, tear this lock apart, take the tumbler out of it and cut a key with this cutter, come over here, and make it work. If you all want to come over here, we will sit and do this. This is just a general locksmith operation.

SENATOR PERCY. The committee will stand in recess for 5 to 10 minutes until the vote is over. Then we will be back and finish up with our witness.

*

[Brief recess.]

*

[Mr. Smith demonstrates vehicle theft techniques with a 1979 Ford pickup truck. A cutaway of the driver's side of the passenger compartment, including door, cowl, and steering column, has been mounted on a platform constructed for the demonstration. Mr. Smith uses two wire hooks to unlock the "swing wing" window and gain entry to the vehicle. Once inside, he uses a corkscrew like device . . . to extract the ignition cylinder, inserting in its place another ignition cylinder which he carries with him, together with its key. With the replacement ignition cylinder in place, Mr. Smith merely turns the key to the "start" position, releasing the steering column lock.]

MR. SMITH. This is a 1979 Ford pickup truck. This is my specialty in my business. I go up to these vehicles, slide a lock in here, a wire in here, push this button in. You have to push that button in to get it to release because it keeps this lock—I flip that up like that, open the swing wing, I will roll the window down. On these Ford trucks and Chevrolet pickups, a lot of them have burglar alarms that activate when you open the door.

I will first come up to them and rock them like this to see if they don't have the rock alarm. Some of them you can see the alarm buttons on them so I won't open the door, I will just crawl through the window. That way I don't disturb any alarms.

I'll crawl through, go on in and get to the ignition cylinder system in it right here. I will

show you that works there. I will use this tool to extract the ignition cylinder out of the lock.

Earlier Fords, like 1977 models, it's real simple to pull the harness off of the back and just plug another substitute switch in. There you go. The same with this thing here, I can have another key in a cylinder that works. You can see how weak that is, right where it breaks these little ears off of these things. It holds the cylinder in this switch. It's real simple to pull that out.

SENATOR PERCY. Now that, again, that is no more than a minute.

MR. SMITH. It's real quick.

SENATOR PERCY. That time includes climbing through the window if there is an alarm system?

MR. SMITH. Yes sir.

MR. MAYER. Mr. Chairman, Mr. Smith has not stolen any motor vehicles since his arrest in early 1979, and thus has not been able to study in detail the latest antitheft designs used by the major auto makers on 1979 and 1980 motor vehicles.

At this point, Mr. Smith is prepared to demonstrate the use of one of the latest tools designed to defeat 1979 and 1980 model General Motors vehicles' antitheft devices. It's called the GM force tool.

Inside sources in Chicago inform us that this tool is now widely used by professional thieves. The tool was obtained from Mr. Fred Jarm, an experienced motor vehicle repossessor, who was subpenaed by the subcommittee. Through his firm, Repossessors Supply, a division of Credit Industry Associates in Arlington Heights, Ill., he markets the GM force tool as a device for repossessors and salvage dealers.

Mr. Jarm successfully demonstrated the use of the tool to Mr. Smith only yesterday. Today Mr. Smith will attempt to defeat the antitheft devices on a 1979 Chevrolet Malibu, using the GM force tool.

Once again, Mr. Chairman, it should be noted that the 1979 demonstrator ignition systems are identical to those coming off the major motor vehicle manufacturer assembly lines today.

[NOTE.—Mr. Smith demonstrates vehicle theft techniques with a 1979 General Motors Chevrolet Malibu. A cutaway of the driver's side of the passenger compartment, including door, cowl, and steering column, has been mounted on a platform constructed for the demonstration. Mr. Smith uses a "slim jim" to unlock the door and gain entry to the vehicle. Once inside, he uses a screwdriver to pry off the chrome key-guide which covers the ignition cylinder. This reveals the flange which circles the exposed end of the ignition cylinder—a flange with two gaps on opposite sides of the key hole. Mr. Smith then demonstrates the use of the "G.M. Force Tool," designed with two metal "ears" to fit into the gaps in the flange of the ignition cylinder. By applying pressure and torque to the tool, Mr. Smith breaks the restraining bolt which holds the ignition cylinder in place, twisting the entire starting mechanism to release the steering column lock and turn the ignition lock to "start".]

MR. SMITH. Again, we will get into this car with this slim jim. This is another tool that's used to run down by the window and trip the lock. General Motors in 1979 put a shield over this door lock that is supposed to prevent this, but you'll see here that it doesn't prevent it. Once we get inside the vehicle—this is a new tool that a guy has designed. It's real impressive to me. We will show you that the ignition works with the key. I need a small screwdriver, please. We will use a screwdriver to flip this cone off. You take this tool. This tool right here, see these dog ears on it right here, they slip into this General Motors—General Motors made two indentations that made it perfect for this tool to fit into. You make sure that you get her lined up just right, tap it on there real good. That's all it takes.

24

ORGANIZED CRIME, KOSHER MEAT, AND BAGELS

DAVID C. MACMICHAEL

NEW YORK

The recent New York State hearings into the legitimate business activities of organized crime and the continuing Waterfront Commission investigations provide a large amount of material on the subject.

The New York State Investigative Commission report, "An Investigation of Racketeer Infiltration into Legitimate Business," purports to show that through the use of personal and economic threats organized criminals are coming to infiltrate and control a wide variety of businesses in New York in a way that "endangers the economy and welfare of the people of this city and state." Unfortunately, the Chairman of the Commission pointed out, not only is fear preventing victimized businessmen from seeking the aid of law enforcement, but some businessmen shameful to say, are actually inviting criminal participation in their businesses.

[Several] cases were presented during the hearings:

*

[One] case examined in some depth by the Commission was that of the kosher meat in-

Source: *The Behavior of Organized Crime Figures in Legitimate Business.* Stanford, Ca.: Stanford Research Institute (December 1970) pp. 30–31; 34–40. (Editorial adaptations.) Reprinted by permission of the author.

dustry. In the last ten years or so innovations in meat packaging have resulted in rabbinical authorization for kosher meats properly wrapped in plastic to be handled and displayed without previously required ritual precautions. The result has allowed the sale of kosher meat products in all groceries, meat markets, delicatessens and so forth and produced a minor boom in the kosher meat business. While the long established firms occupying "high or moderate competitive positions in the industry," to quote the New York State Commission report, enjoyed the benefits of the boom without any special effort, a number of new firms attempting to secure positions in the cheap and lower quality end of the market were not above employing as salesmen people with organized crime backgrounds in order to place their products in markets which are not infrequently owned or controlled by identified members of Mafia (or Cosa Nostra) families.[1]

---

[1] Testimony at the hearings brought out clearly the fact that stores of this sort serve as important outlets for highjacked meat. More than a quarter of a million tons of meat are highjacked in the New York area annually and the ability of men like Gambino to sell stolen meat at below market prices gives them, naturally, a great competitive edge. As one witness who had had to close a store in close competition with one of Gambino's candidly testified this situation was very good for the consumer but tough on the meat packers.

One such firm was the American Kosher Provisions Industry (AKPI) owned by a Hyman Kleinberg. In 1959 he saw himself losing business to his chief competitor, Consumer Kosher Provisions, Inc. and guessed that the latter's employment of Max Block,[2] former President of the Amalgamated Meatcutters Union who had recently been ousted after exposure by the McClellan Committee as a labor racketeer, might have something to do with the situation. Nothing simpler than to hire Block away at a higher salary ($50,000 a year) and also one Lorenzo Brescio, a member of the Vito Genovese Mafia family and a former bodyguard for Lucky Luciano. With the assistance of these two, AKPI soon outstripped Consumer and the latter firm was in desperate straits by 1963.

In that year the notorious John Dioguardi (John Dio) was released from the Federal Penitentiary at Atlanta where he had been serving a term for extortion. Dio, a member of the Lucchese family, wielded enormous power in the Teamsters Union,[3] and Herman Rose, the owner of Consumer, hired him as a salesman because, as Rose stated to investigators, people like Dio had the entree to the big food chains.

With Dio's help Rose first tried to negotiate a merger with AKPI. When this attempt failed in 1964, Rose decided that the best tactic for Consumer was to go into bankruptcy, which occurred in January 1965, and that another previously dormant corporation of his First National Kosher Provisions, should take up the struggle with AKPI. Dio later was convicted of bankruptcy fraud in connection with the demise of Consumer, but for the next several years he led First National in a conquest of the low-priced kosher meat business in New York. Eventually, his own salary reached

$250,000 a year, and by January 1966 he succeeded in driving AKPI into bankruptcy.

According to the investigations of the Nassau County District Attorney, William Cahn, Dio's success as a salesman was based almost totally on his ability to guarantee labor peace to those supermarket chains which took his product and dropped AKPI's. This conclusion is supported by the statements of supermarket executives who testified, usually anonymously and on the Commission's promise that the names of their firms would not be revealed.

For purposes of this study there are several interesting aspects to the kosher meat case. First, the legitimate owners of the companies vied for the services of organized crime figures who, they believed, could give them a competitive advantage. Second, a fierce competition developed between two firms, each with a leading organized crime racketeer in an important position. With the exception of the abortive attempt at merger of AKPI and Consumer in 1964 there was no appearance of conspiracy by organized crime *as such* to control the market. Third, the competition was only rarely based on considerations of price, quality, or service but almost entirely on which competitor was better able to prevent supermarket labor disputes from arising. Fourth, one of the firms did engage in a fraudulent bankruptcy as a competitive tactic. (And, incidentally, that fraud was rapidly detected and resulted in a return to prison for Dio.) Finally, there was no indication that the consumer suffered through increases in cost or reduction in quality except at the time Consumer was going into bankruptcy and deliberately reduced quality and service in order to hasten the loss of accounts.

Interestingly enough, although the struggle involved two different Mafia families no violence was reported throughout. Also it has to be inferred that markets owned or controlled by other organized crime were involved as purchasers. Unfortunately, the testimony at the hearings did not reveal what tactics were used to persuade them to take one brand or another.

---

[2] Block is, or was, also the owner of the Black Angus restaurant in Manhattan, an eatery famous for its food and infamous as the preferred gathering place for the organized criminals of New York.

[3] Dio had been important in James Hoffa's successful effort to topple David Beck and gain the presidency of the International Brotherhood of Teamsters.

The case of the bagel shops again involved organized crime figures (including the ubiquitous John Dio) in the expanding market for traditional Jewish food specialties. Most of the testimony introduced at the New York hearings established clearly that such racketeers as the late Thomas Eboli (Tommy Ryan) and Gerardo Catena established a number of bagel shops and, further, that they employed the services of John Dio in getting their products introduced into leading supermarkets.

Once again, however, the careful reader of the testimony is struck by the absence of evidence regarding price gouging, violence, or fraud in the conduct of these businesses. Of particular interest is the testimony of Harold Fleishmann, representing Local 338 of the Bagel Bakers Union, regarding his successful efforts to unionize the Mafia-owned shops.

Fleishmann's first experience with this new type of owner occurred in 1964 when he got word that a new shop, the Bagel Boys, was opening in Brooklyn. The owners, later identified as members of the Genovese Mafia family, at first expressed no interest in the union. Told by Fleishmann they would be picketed they offered him a bribe which he refused. Then they offered to sign a contract with the understanding that they need not abide by it. This offer, too, was refused. That night one of the union officers received a telephoned threat against his family. This was ignored (and no attempt was ever made to carry out the threat) and the next day union pickets were on the scene.

The picket line was successful, the picketers even distributing free bagels to dissuade prospective customers from entering the shop. After a few days of this the Bagel Boys owners' announced that they had signed with another union. This turned out to be a phony under a notorious hoodlum named Benny Ross. The union continued picketing, informing the public of Ross' background, and the Bagel Boys made another try, announcing a contract with a racketeer-controlled jewelry workers union.

This too, was exposed, and eventually the shop signed with Local 338.

Fleishmann testified that the experience was repeated several times during ensuing months. In every case the shop either signed or gave up the fight and went out of business. There was only minor violence at any time—a fistfight on one occasion; someone threw hot water on a picket on another—and after the incident mentioned above, no additional threats.[4]

Other testimony on the bagel business dealt with the activities of the ubiquitous John Dio in getting his friends in the supermarkets to buy the products of his friends in the bagel business. However, there was no evidence to show price gouging or delivery of poor quality goods. On the contrary, Dio assisted one Ben Willner of W&S Bagels to introduce his machine-made product with the result that retail bagel prices in the metropolitan area dropped more than 15 percent.

There is reason to suspect, although no testimony was introduced alleging this, that Willner's eventual bankruptcy and the consequent sale of his plant to Thomas Eboli at a time when Eboli and his associates were organizing an interstate bagel operation (Bagel U.S.A.) represented a classic takeover. However, the evidence presented to the Commission might as well have supported an opposite contention. Dio several times introduced Willner to his highly placed friends in the big market chains in order that the bagel maker could solicit them, unsuccessfully, for loans to stay in business.

In bagels, as in kosher meats, there was competition between firms with organized crime

---

[4] Testimony during the hearings revealed that at the time of the events described here bagel bakers were the highest paid bakery workers in the United States. The standard union contract provided a wage of $210.00 a week plus generous pension benefits. It was not unusual for bagel bakers to make $15,000 to $17,000 annually. One of the owners described by the Commission as a racketeer, complained bitterly about high labor costs and makework practices imposed by the union.

connections. In Teaneck, New Jersey, in 1965 a Bagel Boys shop planned to open at a location coveted by an established bagel bakery. When representatives of the rivals met it developed that the Eboli-backed Bagel Boys were not the only ones with Mafia support. The New Jersey family boss Gerardo Catena was a silent partner in the established firm. Eventually the two agreed to allow Bagel Boys to open a retail shop in Teaneck but to refrain from engaging in wholesale operations in the area. It was also revealed that not only did Bagel Boys try to violate this agreement by seeking wholesale outlets but that both parties were paying John Dio to use his influence in gaining them access to the major supermarkets. However, in no case was violence threatened or employed.[5]

The Commission hearings show Mafia bagel

bakeries as rather ordinary small businesses, plagued by labor problems, haggling and competing over business sites, and paying off to the man with connections in order to distribute their products. One even sees Thomas Eboli's son, Xavier, taking such a personal interest in Bagel Boys that he waits on customers and works parttime as a baker in various shops until his annoyed father makes him quit to pay more attention to his insurance brokerage business.

The amounts of money involved in bagel baking are apparently small. Investments of $500, $1,000, and $1,500 dollars are the rule. Dio reportedly got $10,000 to introduce Bagel Boys to the larger supermarkets in New Jersey. When Bagels U.S.A. went public in late 1968 the business was capitalized at $300,000. With regard to the incorporation of Bagels U.S.A. it should be noted that in early 1970 the bad public character of the people involved in the corporation caused the Securities and Exchange Commission to prohibit the circulation of the firm's prospectus.

---

[5] The deCarlo and de Cavalcante transcripts reveal the wide extent of competition between Mafia families in the greater New York area. One conversation has deCarlo envying Chicago, Detroit, and Cleveland which each have only one family so that the members are able to make a decent living.

25

RULES OF CONDUCT IN "CRIME FAMILIES"

FRANCIS A. J. IANNI

We began our study of the Lupollo family with two basic questions in mind: How is the family organized to achieve shared goals? What are the techniques of social control used to motivate members in that pursuit? In the last two chapters, we have described the family's organization as we saw it. Now we turn to the code of rules which not only shapes the behavior of family members but also distinguishes the "good" or successful member from the less-successful one. In the sense we use it here, control within social systems begins with values which establish preferential guides to action. Ultimately, it comes to take the form of specific rules which attempt to apply those values to everyday situations. Thus, while values direct behavior, it is the rule which states which actions will be approved and which forbidden. Rules also carry with them sets of sanctions to be applied when they are broken.

Before we describe the Lupollo family's code of conduct, . . . it may be worthwhile to look at the code of rules which other investigators have found applicable to Italian-American criminal syndicates. Like the popularly known pattern of organization and roles we discussed

earlier, these rules of conduct have usually been derived by analogy. That is, rather than looking directly at the behavior of criminal-syndicate members and extrapolating a code from their words and actions, investigators have tried to apply to syndicates codes drawn from observations of other groups.

CODES OF RULES DERIVED BY ANALOGY

"THE MAFIA CODE"

One favorite analogy for the code of conduct in Italian-American criminal syndicates is the "code of the Mafia." The report of the Task Force on organized crime, for example, reasons that since "there is great similarity between the structure of the Italian-Sicilian *Mafia* and the structure of the American confederation of criminals it should not be surprising to find great similarity in the values, norms, and other behavior patterns of the two organizations."[1] Continuing with this reasoning, the report then goes on to present two summaries of "the *Mafia* code"; one statement was made in 1892, the other in 1900.

Source: *A Family Business: Kinship and Social Control in Organized Crime* by Francis A. J. Ianni, with Elizabeth Reuss Ianni. © 1972 Russell Sage Foundation, New York, pp. 135–149. (Editorial adaptations.)

[1] The President's Commission on Law Enforcement and Administration of Justice, *Task Force Report-Organized Crime: Annotations and Consultant's Papers*, Washington, D.C.: Government Printing Office, 1967, p. 47.

1. Reciprocal aid in case of any need whatever.
2. Absolute obedience to the chief.
3. An offense received by one of the members to be considered an offense against all and avenged at any cost.
4. No appeal to the state's authorities for justice.
5. No revelation of the names of members or any secrets of the association.

1. To help one another and avenge every injury of a fellow member.
2. To work with all means for the defense and freeing of any fellow member who has fallen into the hands of the judiciary.
3. To divide the proceeds of thievery, robbery and extortion with certain consideration for the needy as determined by the *capo*.
4. To keep the oath and maintain secrecy on pain of death within twenty-four hours.[2]

The report notes that "the *Mafia* code" is quite similar to the tenets of American organized criminals—loyalty, honor, secrecy, honesty, and consent to be governed, which may mean "consent to be executed." As the report freely admits, "the *Mafia* code" is similar to the code of any secret organization, from Mau Mau to the Irish Republican Army, and even to public organizations opposed to existing authority and seeking to overthrow it.

Unless the premise of direct descent of Italian-American criminal syndicates from the *Mafia* is accepted, there seems to be no more reason for attributing these reported similarities in behavioral code to *Mafia* origins than to the general behavioral needs of all secret organizations opposed to existing power. The antiquity of the reports used to reconstruct the *Mafia* code also reduces the utility of the analogy. Again, unless it is assumed that the early immigrants to the United States brought the code from Sicily and that it remains largely

unaffected by American culture, then it would seem more sensible to compare the current codes of behavior in Sicilian *Mafia* and Italian-American crime syndicates.[3]

THE CODE OF AMERICAN PRISONERS

The Task Force Report and more recently both Donald Cressey and Ralph Salerno also find striking similarities between the behavioral code of organized-crime syndicates and the code of prisoners in American penal institutions.[4] Both Salerno and Cressey recognize the similarity of the prisoners' code to that of underground organizations in general, and see the similarity as growing out of similar needs to control behavior.

THE CODE OF ORGANIZED-CRIME FAMILIES

While each of the major sources admits the absence of any codified set of rules in organized-crime families, all present descriptive lists drawn either from analogies with the code we have just described or from the experience of the writers in observing organized criminals. Cressey holds that the "thieves' code" is essentially the conduct code for organized-crime families:

1. Be loyal to members of the organization. Do not interfere with each other's interest. Do not be an informer. . . .
2. Be rational. Be a member of the team. Don't engage in battle if you can't win. . . . The directive extends to personal life.
3. Be a man of honor. Respect womanhood and your elders. Don't rock the boat. . . .
4. Be a stand-up guy. Keep your eyes and ears open and your mouth shut. Don't sell out. . . . The "stand-up guy" shows courage and "heart." He does not whine or complain in the face of adversity, including punish-

---

[2] *Ibid.*, p. 47; The first summary was taken from Ed Reid, *Mafia*, New York: New American Library, 1964, p. 31, and the second from A. Cutrera, *La Mafia ed i Mafiosi*, Palermo, 1900.

[3] CF. Francis A. J. Ianni, "Time and Place as Variables in Acculturation Research," *American Anthropologist*, Vol. 60, No. 1, February 1958, pp. 39–45.

[4] Donald Cressey, *Theft of the Nation*, New York: Harper and Row, 1969; Ralph Salerno and J. S. Tompkins, *The Crime Confederation*, New York: Doubleday and Co., 1969.

ment, because "If you can't pay, don't play."

5. Have class. Be independent. Know your way around the world. . . .

Ralph Salerno derives his list from study of organized crime during a career with the New York City Police Department:

1. Secrecy. Most members reveal as little as possible to the police, but the silence of the "Cosa Nostra" segment of organized crime has been so complete that until the famous Apalachin meeting in November 1965, many law-enforcement officials doubted its very existence.

2. The organization before the individual. As in the case of secrecy, this rule is one that many in the outside world subscribe to. In military service the individual is expected to put the good of the organization ahead of his own, even if his life depends on it. Our gallery of national heroes is made up of people who made such a choice; the heroes of organized crime are those who went to the death house with their mouths shut.

3. Other members' families are sacred. In most social groups it would be considered unnecessary to specifically prohibit members from making seductive approaches to their associates' wives and daughters. But "Cosa Nostra" is an organization of Italian-Americans and as Luigi Barzini has observed, all Italian males, married and unmarried, are in a constant state of courtship. The rule helps protect the organization from vendettas over such "matters of honor." It makes it possible for a member to be inattentive to the female relatives of another member without this lack of interest being considered unmanly. This sense of chivalry does not, of course, extend to the families of strangers. They can, and often are, taken advantage of.

4. Reveal nothing to your wife. There are three reasons for his rule. In the first place, a member might become estranged from his wife and since "Hell hath no fury . . . "—it is important that she not know anything that she could use to hurt him. Keeping wives in the dark about illegal activities diverts law enforcement attention from them and the rest of one's family. The overall policy that business is not discussed with one's wife is part of a general desire to dissociate the home and family from criminal activities.

5. No kidnapping. The rule against kidnapping [of other members] for ransom is probably a holdover from Sicily where this form of coercion and extortion was widespread.

6. You don't strike another member. This is another rule designed to avoid internal vendettas that could easily arise if an argument were allowed to turn physical. The restraint of often fiery temperaments that it demands is a graphic demonstration of the authority that the code carries.

7. Orders cannot be disobeyed. While self-explanatory, this rule is much broader than similar injunctions found in military or religious organizations. Orders must not only be obeyed, they must be properly carried out. Going through the motions, or hewing to the letter of one's instructions is not enough. This is true even though orders are not detailed or explicit.

8. Promotions and Demotions. Members are promoted in rank—soldier to *capo* to underboss etc.—to fill vacancies created by death, illness, and retirement. The rank of a member who is in prison, however, is kept by him, though his job may be performed by a substitute until he is paroled. At the same time, all members of the same rank are not necessarily equal. A highly successful soldier, for example, may operate a number of different businesses or rackets and have many people working for him. His economic power and influence will tend to make him more important than his technical rank would indicate.

9. Transfers. The majority of members spend

their lives within the same family or group. The rules and traditions encourage this loyalty. Under special circumstances, though, there can be a transfer to a family in another jurisdiction.

10. All arguments to higher authority. Most of the disputes that are important enough to go to higher authority involve business practices, sales territories, new operations and the like.

11. Always be a stand-up guy. A "stand-up guy" is by definition, a man who lives by the rules and, if necessary, will die for them. He keeps his mouth shut to the police, he puts the organization ahead of himself, he respects the families of others. He is a man of honor who can be relied on. In the parlance of those in the Confederation he "has character," he is true to the code. In other words, the injunction, be a stand-up guy epitomizes what the code says a real man should be.

12. Justice. The law is the basis for the administration of justice, which is handled within each family. The authority for judgments comes down from the boss in the same way that it might from the village chief of a primitive tribe. The boss, however, does not personally preside except in very serious cases.[5]

All these attempts to define the "code of the *Mafia*" are based on a fundamental, unproven assumption—for there to be a single "code" which covers *all* Italian-American criminal syndicates, there must be a single national organization. Any code of rules must be derived from some shared set of values; the only way *the* "code of the *Mafia*" could exist would be in the context of a unified organization. Cressey, Salerno, and the others assume that such an organization exists. We found no evidence for it in our study of the Lupollo family and our data are limited to what we were able to see and hear. Thus we have investigated the code of the Lupollos, *not* the code of the *Mafia*.

[5] Salerno and Tompkins, 1969, pp. 111–128.

Our method was to observe and record behavior and then to seek regularities that had enough frequency to suggest that the behavior resulted from the pressures of the shared social system rather than from idiosyncratic behavior. We also questioned family members and others about rules, usually by asking why some member of the family behaved in a particular way. Thus, our reconstruction of rules of conduct comes both from our own observations and from the explanations of observed behavior given by the people living under those rules.

In the Lupollo family as in the card game of bridge, there are two levels of the rules. There are game or ground rules, which structure the game, and then there are informal rules for playing the game intelligently. Similarly, in the Lupollo family there are those basic rules which structure the framework of acceptable conduct, and those supplementary rules which define who plays the game well and who plays it poorly. We found three basic ground rules for behavior in the Lupollo family: (1) primary loyalty is vested in "family" rather than in individual lineages or nuclear families, (2) each member of the family must "act like a man" and do nothing which brings disgrace on the family, and (3) family business is privileged matter and must not be reported or discussed outside the group. These three rules are basic for maintaining membership within the group, but each subsumes a number of informal rules which explain why some members are more successful at the game than others.

THE LUPOLLO CODE OF CONDUCT

RULE 1. LOYALTY TO THE FAMILY

Several studies of family structure among Italians both in the United States and overseas have reported that what seems at first an *extended family*—a unit which extends horizontally and vertically to include all kin in a socially and economically self-sufficient unit—is actually an *expanded family*, nuclear families in separate households who maintain close social relationships but do not function as an integrated economic unit.[6] Among the impoverished peasants in the south of Italy, this has always been a matter of necessity rather than choice. Poverty and the scarcity of land precluded any holdings large enough to sustain extended families except among the nobility or land-owning classes. When the peasant migrated, the new conditions of his life also precluded common residence or joint economic enterprise for the vast majority. The Lupollo family, however, while they live as separate households, are an integrated extended family in every sense. They are economically and socially self-sufficient and do not venture far outside the family group. Friends of individual members either become part of the family circle or are seen only occasionally.

It is to the extended Lupollo family (which includes the Alcamo, Salemi, and Tucci lineages) that primary loyalty is given. On the surface, at least, this loyalty supercedes loyalty to lineage and even to individual nuclear families, and is expressed in a number of ways. Members speak of the family as a unit; they are almost completely dependent on friendship, business, and social relations within the family circle; they tend to settle in physical proximity to other family members. Most fundamentally, however, this loyalty finds expression in the closeness that members feel for the family and for one another.

Once Bobby Lupollo and I talked about how close members of the family were with one another. Bobby had remarked that he thought running was better exercise than basketball, that he was going to mention this to his cousin Freddy, and that perhaps Freddy and Bobby could then get Tommy and Paulie to start jog-

ging in a "running club." I asked Bobby why it was that he usually thought of his relatives whenever he mentioned starting some new social or business venture:

> Our family is very close like all Italian families, but ours is even closer than most. Ever since I could remember everything we did was done together. If I decided that I wanted to go to the circus, my father [Joey Lupollo] would get Tommy or Freddy to go with us, too. Even when we were dating we used to go to the same places together. I was Tommy's best man when he was married and he was mine. When I was in college I was a pledge in a fraternity—no, two different fraternities—but never became a brother because I didn't have anything in common with the other fellows. Even now that we are married we go out together, not because our wives get along together so well—they don't and Linda [Bobby's wife] is always after me to make new friends. It's because we were raised more like brothers than like cousins. Look, I can stand naked in front of you [we were in the dressing room at an athletic club] and I can stand naked in front of my wife but I can't stand naked in front of the two of you, not without all of us feeling ashamed or my wife saying that I'm some kind of a crude guinea bastard. It's something like that with my cousins. I can say and do things in front of them that I wouldn't say or do even in front of my wife, because we're close. If I find a good business deal or see a movie that I like I always think about how they would like it too. We're a family that believes in sticking together. All Italians are that way but when it comes to business we're more like Jews than like Italians. I know that if I tell Tommy about a good deal he'll remember me when he finds a good one. Even my father is that way with Pete Tucci and he doesn't like him too much.

As Bobby's remarks indicate, the bonds which we normally associate with the nuclear family are, among the Lupollos, generalized beyond, into the extended family relationship which has been produced by the merger of personal and social interests with economic interests. This conforting sense of family is accepted by all of the fifteen members of the central family. Basil Alcamo—with Paulie, the

[6] Cf. Donald Pitkin, "Land Tenure and Farm Organization in an Italian Village," Unpublished Ph.D. Dissertation, Harvard University, 1954, p. 114; Herbert Gans, *The Urban Villagers*, Glencoe: The Free Press, 1962, pp. 45–46; and Philip Garigue and Raymond Firth, "Kinship Organization of Italianates in London," in Raymond Firth (ed.), *Two Studies in Kinship in London*, London: Athlone Press, 1956, p. 74.

most alienated from the family—often explains business or social arrangements which run counter to his own idea of good practice by the phrase "it's in the family." He resents Joe's old-fashioned business ideas, but he never expresses any thought of striking out on his own, nor does he refuse to go along with what he considers bad deals arranged by Joe. He protests, but only toward his "brothers" in his same age-grade rather than to Joe and his peers or to the younger family members, and he eventually accepts the decision like any dutiful "son." How much he complains to his father, Phil, and whether Phil is responsive to his complaints has not been determined; but publicly he submits to the family authority structure just as other members do. Paulie, on the other hand, never protests openly. In private conversation, however, he complained to me of the favoritism shown the Lupollo and Alcamo lineages at the expense of the Salemis.

One revealing deviation from the injunction to maintain family loyalty occurred when Freddy married Monica, a woman of Irish descent, against his parents' wishes. Soon after their marriage in 1967, they began socializing with her friends and their husbands. By 1968, the "defection" had become a problem in the family. The family's reaction included harsh and biting comments about Monica, her ancestry, and Freddy's lack of masculinity in letting her "lead him around by the balls." Their extra-familial friendships were frowned upon. Phil Alcamo commented that whenever the women of the family gathered they talked of Monica and her airs. According to Phil, who got the information secondhand from his wife (who is also non-Italian), the women's comments ranged from "she thinks we're not good enough for her" to speculation that Monica was not interested in her friends, but in their husbands. Freddy's mother bore the brunt of the collective displeasure. Finally, in exasperation and embarrassment, she would join in the chorus of disapproval and her most caustic comment was always ". . . she says she wants to give me respect, I don't need respect from

her, I'm not her mother." This pressure had its effect. Freddy and Monica began turning more toward the family and gradually dropped their outside associations. After that, Phil thought Monica was not so bad "for an Irish."

The rule of loyalty to the family includes a number of subsidiaries. The most important among these is "no outside business interests which might conflict with the family." Here are two situations exemplifying this rule and its application.

In early 1968, Tony Lupollo bought a tract of land on the Toms River in New Jersey, and planned to build a motel-marina. Although the land had been purchased through Brooklyn Eagle Realty, Tony's business venture was a private one. By early 1969, ground had been broken for the motel and some of the marina piers had already been built. Then, in the summer of 1969, trouble developed over the township's zoning ordinances. News of the difficulty reached Joe Lupollo. Joe was furious at Tony because his own interests in New Jersey would be jeopardized by any dispute involving a member of the family, and because, according to Phil, "Tony never had the balls or the head to tell his father he was doing it." Later in 1969, Phil said that Tony had sold the land at a loss and that a good way "to get his ass up" would be to ask him when the motel would be finished.

The second incident took place in early 1970, and involved Joe's son Marky, who is considered to be a poor judge of business. Marky decided that since New York was without an Italian discotheque, whoever started one would make a killing. For weeks he talked of nothing but how he would set it up, with Italian singing stars and rock groups coming over to play, and how people of all ages would flock to it. One night at dinner, Marky commented on the possibility of getting a well-known Italian singer to come over for the opening of the club, which he had already named "The Villa," Joe turned to him and said (in Italian), "I don't want to hear anymore about the club, now or ever again." Later, Phil Alcamo explained that "anyone with any sense should realize that a nightclub is the one sure way of getting into trouble, since all kinds of bums go to nightclubs and just like Joe Namath you can find yourself associated with people you don't know and who don't owe you anything." His mother (Phil said) had always told him that "If you go around with a cripple you learn to limp." Marky never mentioned "The Villa" again.

A second subsidiary to the rule of family loyalty calls for mutual aid to other family members. There are no status differences in who can call upon whom for aid. In the two years of this study, there were situations in which a member with high prestige called upon a lower-prestige member for help, as well as those in which a high-prestige member helped a person with lower-prestige. The explanation is always given in terms of family. For example, Phil gave several thousand dollars to Tony after the motel-marina fiasco. When his son Basil took him to task, pointing out that Tony could have gotten it from his father and that gratitude was not one of Tony's outstanding virtues, Phil answered simply, "he's family, Basil, how can I say no?"

A third subsidiary rule says, "Don't interfere in the business of another family member." It is an expression of the security which comes with family membership. In its most basic form, it is the insurance which goes with knowing that others will not interfere in one's best interest so long as you do not give them cause to distrust you. The rule is expressed in many ways. Pete Tucci is the best example within the family of the importance of "playing the game" properly in this area. He has no base of power other than his relationship with his father-in-law, Joe Lupollo. Since none of his children have gone into the family business, he has no paternal relationship which would allow him to call on others for support, and yet the vulnerability of his position obviously does not worry him. His role in managing the food-processing sector of the family business is an important and lucrative one, which would be profitable to any other member—better connected—who craved it. Yet, so long as Pete does not try to move into someone else's area, he is secure. No one really thinks very highly of him—he is considered little more than "Joe's boy" in the business—but he does not have the role of isolate. He is *a member of the family*, and as long as he gives it his first loyalty he enjoys its collective security.

The basic rule of loyalty to the family over all else and the subsidiary rules which define the way to use the rule to one's best advantage give the family a group solidarity against anyone or anything outside the family. While the younger members of the family do not seem to show it as belligerently as their parents and grandparents, it is still an important behavior guide for them. They are known in the Italian-American community as members of the family, and without exception they see the future of that organization as their own.

The rule of loyalty does not ensure smooth social relationships within the family. There are squabbles, and rivalries, and cliques, and the various lineages do stick together; but the family as a unit absorbs these differences and continues to function. When there are attacks from outside the group, the force of family cohesion comes into play and the divisions disappear.

Not all members of the family use the rules equally well. Those with high respect or prestige show more awareness of and conformity to the subsidiary rules than those with low respect or prestige. Only when someone seems to be ignoring the rule of loyalty itself, as when Freddy began finding new friends and when Tony got involved in the potentially troublesome motel-marina, is the question of loyalty raised. Marky's desire to start the Italian nightclub was simply considered foolish and everyone could laugh at it; Freddy and Tony actually lost some respect as a result of their actions, and group pressure was exerted to bring them back into line.

RULE 2. "ACT LIKE A MAN."

The concept of "being a man" goes by many names in the Lupollo family. At various times it is expressed as "being a stand-up guy," or "having balls." At the same time, however, the notion of being a man carries with it a distinct sense of humility and willingness to accept decisions, even when they are troublesome to ego, without resort to complaints, whines, or other unmanly actions. In fact, the rule of being a man seems so close to the concept of *omertà* found in the south of Italy that it is tempting to assume that *omertà* is its origin. To one who has watched both systems in operation, however, it is logical to conclude that both *omertà* and the injunction to be a man are part of the social contract created when a group of men bond themselves together in a secret society. In such bonding, the alliance demands that each man depend on the others in the group to protect their common interest, and to act like a man in the company of other men.

The importance of being a man within the Lupollo family is part of the code for each generation, and no one escapes its demands. But the demands differ according to one's status in the family. Generally, the higher the status the more important it is to present a public image of self-control, willingness to accept decisions, and interpersonal power which demands respect from others. Being a man is also mediated in non-"business" relationships. Joe Lupollo, for example, is stern and authoritarian even with his grandchildren in all matters related to the family business, but he is permitted to show grandfatherly concern for them in social and personal relationships even in public. The younger members of the family have learned to read the particular role he is playing and to react accordingly. Freddy, for example, will actually tease his grandfather about his oldfashioned suits and shoes in front of other members of the Lupollo lineage, but whenever members of other lineages or persons outside the family are present he is respectful and correct in relations with Joe. This same pattern of situational determination of the content of the requirement to be a man is true throughout the family between father and son, godfather and godson, and brothers.

In many ways, the behavior involved is similar to the Chinese or Oriental concept of "face." That is, just as "losing face" is a much more obvious and observable social and behavioral feature than gaining it, so those behaviors and group reactions which appear when someone is *not* being a man are more obvious in the Lupollo family than the behaviors and reactions appearing when someone *is*. In this negative aspect, it appears that being a man has two different dimensions, one primarily social and one primarily personal. The social aspect of being a man is part of the awarding of respect within the family and, while it does characterize family members to outsiders, it is much more obvious and important within the group itself. It is the *groups'* valuation of the individual member in terms of how they define him as a man worthy of trust and so respect. Since group functioning depends on mutual trust and confidence that other family members will perform in ways appropriate to being a man, behaviors which are not so defined can cause serious problems for the individual and the group. During this study, only one incident occurred which approached a loss of respect and consequent loss of status for a family member. Early in 1969, Joe's son Marky evidently entered into a business arrangement with Albert Cuccio, who is a cousin of Domnick Maisano of the East Harlem De Maio family. Marky kept it from his father and other members of the family. In the spring of that year Marky left for Florida and did not return until late June. One of the younger members of the family told me that Marky had gone away for a while because his father was so furious with him that it was best to "keep out of the old man's sight" for a while. Joe was particularly upset because Cuccio was reputedly involved in the drug trade, and thus Marky had possibly compromised the family by being seen with Cuccio. What made matters worse for Marky was that he had behaved badly when confronted by his father and his Uncle Charley. Marky apparently tried to implicate his brother Joey and refused to take responsibility for his own actions. Evidently just being seen with Cuccio was sufficiently dangerous that his subsequent refusal to admit his error was viewed as cowardly and disruptive of family discipline. Marky's son Tommy was particularly upset, because some of the criticism spilled over to him.

While we have little information on even this case of loss of status within the group as a result of behavior contrary to the requirement to be a man, we venture to suggest these rules: (1) loss of respect within the group can come from behavior defined as contrary to the requirement to "be a man" and (2) such loss reaches beyond the individual to affect his closest relatives and associates. Being a man in this collective sense means earning and keeping the respect and trust of one's associates. In the case just described, Marky violated the first rule of family loyalty by endangering the group through association with a reputed drug baron and then, having been discovered, did not accept the responsibility for his actions and lost the respect of his fellows for not acting like a man.

There is a second dimension to being a man which is personal in that it is part of an individual's "reputation." While the social aspect of being a man is essentially internal to the group and suggests that the individual can be depended upon to behave in a fashion which will not bring danger or disgrace to the group, the reputational aspect of being a man is much more a matter of his image outside the family. In earlier chapters some of these external "reputations" were described—Freddy's being a "ladies' man" and Phil Alcamo's being an "astute political animal." Such reputational aspects of "being a man" can change without any great effect on the person's role within the family, for they are part of the individual's role

in the *external* environment. They can be enhanced or diminished, changed by personal effort or clever maneuvering, and even borrowed through association with the right people. The social aspect of being a man, however, is not only defined within the group, it is maintained or lost as a whole. After Marky returned from Florida, his position within the group seemed to have diminished to the point that it created serious personal and social difficulties for him.

The reputational aspect of the injunction to be a man is supported in family legendry by numerous oft-told tales of family members or their associates who have shown that peculiar combination of personal courage mixed with humility which is defined as being a man. In one such story, the protagonist, a relative of the Salemi lineage who was known as *"Don Cece,"* was picked up by the police in front of one of the storefront social clubs in Greenwich Village for questioning. One of the police officers, a detective inspector, knew enough about the importance of respect in the world of the families that he decided to shame *Don Cece* (who was then in his early sixties) by having two patrolmen beat him to the ground and handcuff his hands behind his back. When they lifted him to his feet, his face was bloody and his glasses had been knocked off onto the sidewalk. One of the patrolmen, somewhat abashed by what he had done, picked up the glasses and started to put them back on *Don Cece's* nose, but *Don Cece* turned his head aside and said (in Italian for the benefit of his audience), "I have seen and remembered all I need to this morning." The Lupollos always tell the story in the same manner that second- and third-generation Italian-Americans tell tales of their immigrant forebears' courage, endurance, and simplicity in face of the adversity of the ghetto. Here, however, the moral is very obviously not the stoic perseverance of the peasant immigrant but the refusal of someone in a family to allow himself and so his family to be publicly shamed.

RULE 3. THE RULE OF SECRECY

The third set of conduct rules fit under the basic rule that family business matters are privileged and are not to be reported or discussed outside the group. An obvious reason for secrecy in the Lupollo family is their involvement in illegal activities. But even in the legitimate business enterprises the degree of secrecy goes beyond that found in other business organizations. This could be explained by the linkages between the illegal and legal activities, except that secrecy extends even beyond legitimate business activities, to include the social and personal behavior of individual members of the family. This extension of secrecy is manifest in a number of characteristic behaviors among family members. The most obvious is that family members use a jargon made up of words and phrases which have meaning only to family members. Some of the "code" refers to business activities. The family-controlled Absford Linen Service, for example, is always called "the Long Island place" or "Vince's place" (Vincent Corallo is the owner of record) in conversation. The same approach is used with personnel: Vincent Corallo is referred to as "the fellow in Long Island" or "Patsy's brother-in-law." But the jargon carries over into all conversation, and even when social or kinship relations are being discussed the same descriptive terms are used. In addition, in the second and third generations (but less so in the fourth generation), Italian and Sicilian words and phrases are used in their original meanings as part of a conversation in English. Marky, for example, might say to Patsy, "I know that guy from meeting him a couple of years ago and he is a real *cafone* (idiot)." The use of Italian and Sicilian terms in English sentences is not an uncommon practice among other Italian-Americans of the same generations, but here it combines with the use of jargon to provide a shared language which serves to protect the conversation from those not part of the group.

There is another function of secrecy in the Lupollo family beyond concealing or obscuring information. In Sicilian *Mafie*, the differentiation of individuals as members or outsiders is one of the purposes of secrecy. Those individuals who share the secrets are fellow members; those who do not are outsiders. Secrecy in this sense serves as a bonding mechanism among the members of the group. Not only does it assign individuals to a membership or outsider status, it establishes a comaraderie among group members. In the Lupollo family, this shared sense of membership excludes those members of the various lineages who are not part of the family business and all female members of the lineages as well. Rosa Parone, who is Phil Alcamo's sister and operates the family-related Melrose Cigarette Company, is the only women who has any contact with any of the family businesses, and most of the actual business operation is actually handled by her son James. Even the brothers and sisters of members are excluded. Usually, where one part of a group joins together and agrees to hold certain secrets in common, the action invites hostility from those who are not members. In the Lupollo family, however, this does not seem to be so.

Finally, secrecy serves as a means of establishing and maintaining dominance and social distance not only between family members and nonmembers but within the family as well. Some secrets are more secret than others, and are shared by only some members of the group. In part this circumstance relates to the structure of authority in the family. Joe Lupollo and his brother Charley have access to all family information; some they share with other members, but some they do not. In part the differentiation is an outgrowth of the relationship between the respect-rating structure of the group and secrecy. There are some members of the family who enjoy low respect and do not have access to as many secrets. But in part it is also the natural result of the various power networks, which make for greater confidentiality among some members than others.

In the Lupollo family, despite the cardinal importance of the basic rule that loyalty to the family comes before loyalty to lineage, there seems little question that, for example, Phil Alcamo and his son Basil share a father-son confidentiality, as do Joe Lupollo and his favorite son Joey.

Every business organization has secrets of some kind. Business practices, tactics, and strategy to some degree are always private and privileged information. A difference in the Lupollo family business, however, is that the rule of secrecy is more inclusive than in most business operations, and violations are considered independent acts against the collective welfare of the group. The injunction against disclosure of information is not specific to the illegal sectors of the business operations, but cover virtually all areas of the family operations. The preferred behavior is not just reluctance to disclose business secrets which might aid competitors, but complete silence in the face of any inquiries, formal or informal, official or private, about business affairs. In a sense, then, this rule reflects not only the businessman's reluctance to make business matters public, but also the strength of the bond among family members which defines all others as "outsiders." Here again it is the kinship bond, both real and fictive, which effectively serves as the basis of enforcement; to violate the injunctions against disclosure of information is not a bad business practice, it is an act of disloyalty to the family. And family in this context excludes wives, those members of the various lineages who are not directly involved in the family business, and all others.

ENFORCING RULES OF CONDUCT

Rules of conduct are meant to be enforced, and a system of sanctions always has to be established. Previous studies of organized crime have stressed the coercive sanctions or the allocation of punishments, including death, as the principal means of control in Italian-American criminal syndicates. It would be naïve to

suggest that such sanctions do not exist in the Lupollo family, but this study did not produce any evidence of them. Within the family, the canon of reciprocity forms the motive force behind rules of conduct. Individuals within the group have obligations toward others and, in turn, have expectations concerning how others will relate to them. Because the group is small and close primary relationships exist within the group, violations of the rules of conduct are not frequent. Where they do occur, they tend to be idiosyncratic behaviors rather than outright disobedience. This shared understanding of what is right and what is wrong in terms of behavior keeps conflict over rules at a minimum. And, since in groups of this type rules tend to be enforced only when something provokes enforcement, it is usually sufficient for the offending behavior to become public within the group for behavior to become appropriate once again. Thus in the examples of rule violation we described earlier—Freddy's turning outside the family for friendship and the actions of Patsy and Marky that jeopardized the welfare of the group—it was sufficient for group attention to be focused on the violations. There are, however, some members of the family who blow the whistle on infractions of rules with some consistency. Joe Lupollo, as head of the family, seldom intervenes except when his anger is aroused—as when he felt Marky was behaving foolishly in attempting to open a nightclub— or where an infraction is of such magnitude that his authority is questioned. Generally, Charley Lupollo questions the behavior of other family members. Usually this is done publicly without much rancor, as any uncle or father might do in a traditional Italian-American family. What is different is that Charley takes the initiative for citing rule infractions in every area of behavior, from business practices to social protocol, and he acts in the name of his brother Joe. This surrogate position is obvious both in his approach to the erring family member and in the reaction of the miscreant. Charley will, for example, chide Patsy for being late to some gathering and suggest that Joe expected everyone to be there on time. Patsy's response will differ depending on whether Joe is scheduled to be there or not; in neither case, however, will Charley pursue the point. He lets his suggestion that Joe will be offended serve as warning enough.

In addition to Charley, Phil Alcamo and Joey Lupollo are also frequent critics of rule violators. Phil usually cites rule violations on the part of members of the next lower generation in the family—Patsy, Marky, Basil and so on—while Joey reserves his criticism for the younger members of the group, who are also his next-generation relatives. Our limited experience with rule violation and consequent enforcement makes it difficult to differentiate rule enforcers in the family with any certainty, but it seems that Charley's role as Joe's surrogate is a fairly formal one, while Phil is acting as an informal rule enforcer as a result of his age and respect ranking in the group. Joey, on the other hand, acts both in his role as heir-apparent and as the role model for his younger relatives within the family.

SECTION VI

SEXUAL AND DRUG-RELATED CRIMES

The relationships between drugs and crime is a topic that has aroused great public concern since the late 1960s. The dope-crazed "junkie" is a vivid figure in the media and in much popular speculation about the roots of crime. What is known and what is mythologized about the "junkie" who necessarily engages in income-producing crimes to support a costly habit is sorted out by Gettinger in his article on addicts and burglary. A true, objective, and frightening depiction of "a day in the life" of a street addict is given by Agar. The endless round of hustle, copping, and getting off exemplifies an existence so narrow and so cruel, and yet so prevalent even to this day.

Rape is an ancient offense, but recent concern, fueled by the women's rights movement, has mainly centered on the victim and the manner in which she is handled within the criminal justice system. A large number of polemic articles and books have appeared but, incredibly, there have been very few careful studies that seriously examine the rapist himself. The Queen's Bench Foundation pilot study of 164 rapists is a limited but admirable examination of the general demographic characteristics of the rapists and some fascinating, if tragic, data on the elements of the sexual assault itself, particularly factors that go into the selection of the rape victim by the assailant.

Holmstrom and Burgess analyze the manner in which rapists use, not only physical force but linguistic manipulation in controlling the victim before, during, or after the rape. The final selection describes the subtle verbal games played by prostitutes and vice squad officers (the former trying to protect herself from arrest and the latter trying to construct a good "pinch") and by the same prostitutes with their customers to maximize their earnings.

26

IS THE JUNKIE/BURGLAR A MYTH?

STEPHEN GETTINGER

It is no secret that the property-crime problem is really a heroin problem. After all, people who become involved with heroin usually become addicted to it. And addiction is very expensive; it costs $50 to $200 or more each and every day. And since it is impossible to hold a job while using heroin, addicts must turn to crime—usually robberies and burglaries—to get money. Therefore, anything that cuts down on addiction, especially locking addicts away in jail where they cannot hurt anyone, will cut crime drastically.

These beliefs underlie California's Heroin Impact Program, and they are the credo of most detectives in narcotics and property-crime units across the country. Yet every "fact" in the preceding paragraph is false, or at least open to serious question, according to those who have studied the heroin problem closely. The research concludes that:

- No one knows how many people use heroin.
- Most people who use heroin are not addicted to it.
- Many of them support their use without resorting to predatory crime.
- The cost of maintaining a heroin habit is much lower than thought.

Source: "Addicts and Crime," *Police Magazine* (November 1979), 2(6):42–45. Copyright © 1979 by Police Magazine and Criminal Justice Publications, 116 West 32 St., New York, NY 10001. Reprinted by permission.

- While many heroin addicts do steal, it is not at all certain that they steal because they are heroin addicts; rather, heroin use may be part of a criminal lifestyle.
- It is not at all clear how any type of law enforcement affects heroin use.

Many of our beliefs regarding heroin are as outdated as "Reefer Madness" depictions of marijuana-crazed teenagers chopping up their parents with hatchets, experts say. And law enforcement agencies have frequently succumbed to the temptation to use the public's fear of heroin as a justification for increased expenditures.

In 1976, federal officials said that an $18-billion "crime cost" was directly associated with heroin use. But this total was 25 times as great as the total amount of property stolen and unrecovered for that year throughout the U.S. This kind of numerical legerdemain has infected local police departments, as demonstrated by the Sacramento and San Mateo figures regarding heroin "costs" to their communities.

The same exaggeration extends to other statistics. In 1971, to justify his "war" on heroin, President Richard Nixon asserted that the number of heroin addicts had risen precipitously, from 68,000 in 1969 to 559,000 in 1971. Governor Nelson Rockefeller of New York, perhaps the champion heroin fearmonger of recent times, once broadcast heroin-crime figures that would have had each resident of New York City robbed or mugged seven times each year.

"In this field, more than any other, lying with statistics has become a way of life," warned a guide for reporters put out by the Drug Abuse Council, a private study group.

The absurdity of some of the statistics was documented in detail by journalist Edward Jay Epstein in a 1977 book, *Agency of Fear*. Epstein showed how the assertion by the federal Bureau of Narcotics and Dangerous Drugs that the number of addicts had grown from 68,000 to 559,000 in two years reflected a politically inspired change in record-keeping. Previously, the BNDD had included in its figures only those individuals who had come to the attention of public agencies. Under pressure from the Nixon administration, it was decided that for each of these there were also another 7.2 addicts who escaped notice.

Epstein saw a conspiratorial purpose in Nixon's efforts to establish a powerful anti-drug agency: "If Americans could be persuaded that their lives and the lives of their children were being threatened by a rampant epidemic of narcotics addiction, Nixon's advisors presumed that they would not object to decisive government actions such as no-knock warrants, pretrial detention, wiretaps, and unorthodox strike forces."

Other observers are willing to admit that there was indeed an increase in heroin use during the 1960s and 1970s. But most experts agree that we do not really know how many addicts there are. The National Institute on Drug Abuse uses the figure of 450,000, but its figures represent conjecture, not identifiable individuals.

One popular formula for counting addicts is based on the number of drug-overdose deaths. This is one of the few reliable figures, particularly in New York, where half of the addicts in the country are thought to reside. Some researchers have concluded that there is one death per 100 addicts per year. Others have

asserted that the ratio of deaths to addicts is closer to one per 1,000.

Other computations are based on the amount of heroin imported into the country each year. Two respected researchers noted that 5,500 tons of heroin were seized by law enforcement agencies in a recent year. If that represents ten percent of the total—a generous estimate—then that amount of heroin could support as many as 4.5 million active users, they said.

One thing most researchers agree on is that many heroin users are not true addicts. Studies disclose that there are many "chippers" and "joy/poppers" who regulate their habits well. Epidemiologist Leon Hunt concluded that only one heroin addict in ten is a daily user—the same ratio as that of alcoholics to those who drink. A study by the Hudson Institute found that less than a quarter of those classified as "addicts" by law enforcement agencies used more than $25 worth of heroin per day.

Perhaps the most sophisticated analysis of the structure of the heroin marketplace was done by Mark Moore, an associate professor of public policy at the Kennedy School of Government at Harvard University. Based on a review of the evidence, he concluded that the number of users in New York City was between 70,000 and 150,000—about half the commonly used figures. Moreover, he asserted in his book *Buy and Bust* that only 32 percent of that number were true addicts, and another 25 percent were "drug dependents" who used regularly but were not much involved in predatory crime. More than 17 percent were dabblers or joy-poppers, who used smaller amounts of drugs for short periods of time.

The cost of a daily habit is another area of dispute. Most police estimates range from $50 a day to $200 or, for a few dealer/users, even $500. But Alan Parachini, a reporter who spent several years studying drug problems for the national Drug Abuse Council, called these figures a "lie." He said that "in my experience the amount of money is anywhere between five and ten percent of the advertised figures."

One reason for the uncertainty about the real

cost of a heroin habit is that while addicts or users may occasionally spend a large amount of money on drugs every day, they do not do so for very long. Mark Moore noted that "users spent from one-third to one-fourth of their time in jail, hospitals or treatment programs." A junkie may go on a "run" of heavy daily usage lasting several months, but seldom longer. Moreover, when an addict cannot come up with money to buy his day's supply, the researchers say, he is as likely to substitute a cheaper drug or do without as he is to steal.

There is no arguing with the fact that heroin addicts commit crimes. After a review of the literature on how addicts support themselves, Moore concluded that about 84 percent are involved in crime of some kind. But he found that 32 percent support their habits by selling narcotics to others—transactions that go on mostly within the drug culture and do not affect the public at large. Only 37 percent supported themselves through burglary and other property crimes. Only seven percent supported themselves through robbery; this crime requires a degree of personal involvement and command that most addicts cannot muster.

The amount of violence and property crime committed by addicts has always been exaggerated by law enforcement officials, some researchers have concluded. David Musto, a Yale professor who is the author of the authoritative history of narcotics control, *The American Disease*, warns: "Narcotics are assumed to cause a large percentage of crime, but the political convenience of this allegation and the surrounding imagery suggest the fear of certain minorities, and make one suspicious of this popular assumption."

The connection between crime and heroin is apparently even more tenuous with joy-poppers. After studying many addicts, Leon Hunt and Norman Zinberg wrote: "Contrary to conventional wisdom, occasional heroin users hold jobs, live in stable families in conventional communities, and manifest none of the outward signs of social distress associated with the 'junkie' addict."

Even when heroin addicts commit crimes, researchers say that they do not necessarily commit them *because* they are drug addicts. A great number of studies have concluded that people engage in crime independently of heroin use. They note that most heroin addict/criminals were involved in thefts *before* they became addicted.

The Lakewood (Colo.) Police Department came to the same conclusion after interviewing a large number of incarcerated burglars for a 1977 crime-prevention project. "Surprisingly," their report said, "we did not find many burglars who were heavy users. They admitted that they had committed a great number of burglaries in order to obtain cash for their habits, but they also admitted that they had begun committing burglaries before ever becoming addicted to drugs."

To be sure, heroin use does exacerbate crime: People commit more crimes after taking up the drug, and they commit fewer crimes after abandoning it.

The National Commission on Marijuana and Drug Abuse, in its 1973 report, evaluated the evidence this way: "Criminal behavior is not a by-product of dependence but results, as does drug dependence itself, from psychological and social deviance which predates dependence. This conclusion challenges the theory that drugs cause crime. . . ."

The commission went on to note that "the drug most often associated with violence is alcohol." Others have also suggested that if we need to look for a crime-causing drug, we should look no further than the neighborhood bar.

In 1967, the President's Commission on Law Enforcement and the Administration of Justice warned: "To commit resources against [drug] abuse solely in the expectation of producing a dramatic reduction in crime may be to invite disappointment."

The succeeding 12 years have certainly been filled with disappointment. An enormous amount of money has been spent on combatting drug abuse. The federal budget for drug enforcement alone increased from $36 million in 1969 to $257 million in 1974—with precious little to show for it. Crime rates and drug abuse increased exponentially.

This raises the question of whether law enforcement can have any impact on drug use, and whether its efforts in that area have any impact on crime rates. "Street-sweeping" programs like the Heroin Impact Program are nothing new; a dozen national and local campaigns against drug addiction have been waged during this century. Generally the results have been meager.

New York, which has the worst drug problem in the country, has been the scene of many of these efforts. The most famous such crackdown in recent times rested on the so-called Rockefeller drug laws, which went into effect in 1973. They reversed the policy of diverting street-level users into treatment programs, instead decreeing life sentences for all sellers of drugs and fobidding plea-bargaining for all significant felonies.

In 1977, a major evaluation sponsored by the Association of the Bar of the City of New York and the Drug Abuse Council confirmed what most people in the criminal justice system already knew: The laws were a dismal failure. The report concluded that, after three years:

- Heroin use, by whatever measure one used, was as widespread in mid-1976 as it had been in 1973.
- The pattern of use was the same as in other comparable cities.
- Serious property crime of the sort often associated with heroin users increased sharply between 1973 and 1975. The rise in New York was similar to increases in nearby states.
- The law was expensive to implement, costing approximately $32 million in three years.
- While the total number of people sent to prison on drug charges did rise, the chance of an arrested heroin offender going to prison were the same as they had been before the law.

The Rockefeller drug laws were aimed mostly at major drug dealers. In 1977, the New York City police reversed course and initiated a program to sweep the streets of addicts. The effort was started after a dealer tried to sell drugs to Mayor Abraham Beame as the diminutive, white-haired mayor emerged from a van from which he had been observing the open hawking of drugs on a Harlem street corner. The department assigned 170 officers to Operation Drugs, at a cost of $5 million. In a little more than two years, 19,000 arrests were made. But in the end only 848 people were sentenced to jail terms in excess of the time they served in jail awaiting trial. The average sentence for them was 60 days. "And that's with the harshest drug laws in the country," commented Sterling Johnson, New York City's special prosecutor for narcotics.

Johnson, who in his five years as prosecutor had handled some 6,500 narcotics cases, is pessimistic about the effectiveness of street-level drug control strategies. "I liken it to a sink: You turn on a faucet and the water runs over the sink and onto the floor," he said. "You can mop and mop until hell freezes over and not do anything." Johnson believes in dividing resources equally between low, middle and high levels of trafficking.

There is even evidence that, in some circumstances, tough narcotics-law enforcement can be counterproductive. A study of heroin use in Detroit, for instance, asserted that in the early 1970s, every ten-percent increase in the price of heroin produced a 2.2-percent decrease in heroin use. But it also inspired a 2.9-percent increase in property crimes. Some studies of methadone maintenance programs, as described by Charles Silberman in his book *Criminal Violence, Criminal Justice*, concluded that "by freeing young addicts of the need to spend most of their time 'chasing the bag,' methadone apparently gave them more time and energy to commit predatory crimes."

And, in what might serve as a warning against street-sweeping programs Bruce Bullington observed in *Heroin Use in the Barrio* that whenever Chicano addicts "find themselves in situations or crises which they define as pressure-inducing, such as family fights, parole troubles, or police hassles, they tend to 'go off the deep end' and use drugs to the extent of their ability."

In the end, there is a delicate balance between narcotics control and property-crime control. After all, it is narcotics control itself that leads to property crime by addicts by raising the price of drugs beyond what they can afford. The National Commission on Marijuana and Drug Abuse pointed out that "society must decide what concerns it most. If dependence-related crime is the main concern, then it should remove or modify the current restrictions on the availability of dependence-producing substances, particularly the opiates. If, on the other hand, society's major concern is to reduce the incidence and dependence and minimize its adverse effect on the public health and welfare, it should continue to restrict availability."

Given the probability that this dilemma is not likely to be resolved soon, what strategy should law-enforcement agencies adopt?

In his book, Mark Moore considered several approaches:

- the "good citizen" model, which relies on education and the moral impact of law to discourage heroin use;
- the deterrence model, which tries to frighten people out of heroin use by stiff penalties;
- the inconvenience model, which makes it difficult to find narcotics.

"Of these models, the strongest case can be made for the inconvenience model," Moore wrote. He chose this model largely because it offered the best hope of preventing potential users from getting heroin to experiment with.

Increasing inconvenience, Moore noted, is much more feasible for smaller cities—such as those that have instituted HIP programs—than for large urban areas. "In effect, narcotics enforcement can prevent heroin use in Richmond, N. J., but not in Harlem," he wrote.

27

A DAY IN THE LIFE OF A STREET ADDICT

MICHAEL AGAR

PROBLEMS IN LEXICAL VARIATION

The terminology of heroin addicts is difficult to analyze systematically. The addicts are regionally and racially heterogeneous. There are, of course, other dimensions of heterogeneity, although these two alone are sufficient to make the point. Although urban heroin addicts share many of the same situations and problems, their speech can vary. Whereas some terms are specific to the addict culture nationwide, others are used in nonaddict cultures, and still others may be specific to a regional, racial, or other subgroup. To give a quick example, *junkie* is a well-established term. *Jones*, on the other hand, is not. In Boston, *jones* is a "heroin habit"; in Detroit, it refers to "heroin" itself.

*

HUSTLING

To *cop*, the *junkie* needs *bread*, but *hustling* is certainly not the only way to get it. Like the *square*, the *junkie* could hold a legitimate job, using his wages to purchase heroin. Alternatively, he could sell his car, his furnishings, or even his home to raise cash to support a habit.

Source: Ripping and Running; A Formal Ethnography of Urban Heroin Addicts. New York: Seminar Press, 1973. Pp. 43–56. (Editorial adaptations.) Reprinted by permission.

In fact, a progression from legitimate support to support through illegal activities (*hustling*) fits one popular stereotype of the addict.

In many cases this is a false picture. First of all, an addict who does not *hustle* is not a *street junkie* or *stone dope fiend*. By definition this type usually obtains his *bread* from *hustling* activity. Second, almost all the *junkies* who assisted in this study were competent *hustlers* before they became *street junkies*. Rather than being driven into *hustling* activity due to increasing costs, they applied previous skills while developing more as well. . . . In fact, several *street junkies* claimed that the newer *junkies* are more likely to enter *the life* without prior *hustling* experience. Such incompetence makes them more dangerous and unpredictable.

As already implied, *hustling* skills are not restricted to *street junkie* culture. *Hustles* provide an alternative source of financial support and are used by numerous different groups for this purpose. . . .

Due to time limitations on this study, *hustles* were not given the detailed analysis that is applied to *copping* and *getting-off*. Two specific *hustles*, the *burn* and the *rip-off*, are treated in detail because of their relevance to *junkies* engaged in the *cop* or *get-off* events. On the whole though, the domain of *hustles* is neglected here. Since *hustling* is the activity least specific to *street junkie* culture, and since other sources are available, that area was sacrificed to the pressures of time.

Although no extensive analysis was done, some preliminary interviewing did touch on the domain of *hustles*. A tentative discussion might be appropriate to familiarize the reader with some of the alternatives available and some of the considerations important in selecting among them.

A *hustle* can be operationally defined as the set of responses to any of the following queries in a context where the respondent knows that the questioner knows that he is a *street junkie:*

1. What's your game?
2. What's your thing?
3. What do you do?

There are undoubtedly other forms taken by the query; these three are examples.

Although most *junkies* will give only one response to the queries, this does not imply that they actively practice only one *hustle*. Most have a primary *hustle*, but will draw on a wider *hustling* repertoire as the opportunity arises. An earlier analysis of folkloristic material suggests that diverse *hustling* ability is an attribute of high status. . . .

Numerous different *hustles* are used by *street junkies*. Perhaps the most common are *stealing, dealing, pimping,* and *confidence games*. *Prostitution* is often used by females, but it is not discussed here. Again, high status accrues to the individual who can draw from all categories of *hustling*. In conversations with *junkies,* frequent mention of a "click-click" mind occurred. The metaphor emphasized that the good *junkie's* mind never stops working. Any situation in which he finds himself can be exploited by the clever *junkie* toward the attainment of money or *dope*.

The categories listed above include several more specific categories of *hustles*. . . . *Confidence games,* as their name suggests, are routines where the *junkie* obtains the confidence of the target of the *game,* or the *mark*. Basically, the *game* convinces the *mark* that he will receive something for his money or ser-

vices, when in fact the *junkie* has no intention of delivering. *Confidence men,* whether *junkies* or not, must be good intuitive psychologists with poise and a sense of authority. They must correctly "read" the *mark* and immediately formulate a strategy to encourage his trust.

Confidence games vary. Some, for example, are *played* for what the *mark* has in his pocket (*short con*), whereas other entice the *mark* to obtain money for a large investment (*long con*). Some are used by a *con man* operating alone, whereas others rely on teams. Perhaps the most frequent kind of *con game* used by the *street junkie* is the *burn*. This term has been used to label events where an insufficient amount of heroin is given for the money. Actually, this is only one kind of *burn,* but the most frequent in *junkie-junkie* interaction.

When the domain is enlarged to include *burns* usually directed toward *squares,* several other types appear. One is the *Murphy,* where a *mark* is sold the services of a prostitute who never shows up. Another is the *hot TV game*. In this form of the *burn,* the *junkie* enters a bar or other neighborhood setting and talks about the availability of an inexpensive color TV. Eventually some potential *mark* approaches him, and the *junkie* tells him that the set is *hot* ('stolen'). Usually, the *mark* remains interested because of the inexpensive price tag.

At this point, the *junkie* instructs the *mark* to follow him. They drive to a large appliance warehouse where several trucks are loading shipments in plain sight of the *mark*. The *junkie* tells the *mark* to wait and enters the warehouse. He approaches a driver who is loading his truck and asks him for a match, converses about the weather, etc. This occurs in sight of the *mark,* sitting in his car across the street. The *junkie* returns to the *mark's* car and tells him that the deal is arranged.

The *mark* is to give the *junkie* the money for the TV. The *junkie* will give it to the driver. When the driver leaves, the *mark* should follow him until in a quiet neighborhood. The driver will stop and give the *mark* his new color TV set, reporting it stolen from his truck when he returns to the warehouse. The *mark* will have his TV, and the *junkie* and the driver will share the money.

Of course, no such thing will occur. The *junkie* does not know the driver, but he must get the *mark's* confidence to get his money. This is the crucial moment of the *game*, since the *mark* must be absolutely convinced to release his money. A person who is *hip* would suggest that he hold the money and give it to the driver when they stop in the quiet neighborhood, but if the person was *hip* he probably would not have been chosen by the *junkie* as a *mark*.

The *junkie* must now demonstrate his psychological proficiency. He must decide what sort of tactic to follow with the *mark* to reassure him—kindness, anger, disgust, disinterest—all are possible tactics. Assuming the *mark* gives him the money, the *junkie* reenters the warehouse, again converses innocuously with the driver, smiles and waves to the *mark*, and leaves the scene. Eventually, the truck will leave with the *mark* following, and sooner or later the *mark* will realize that he has been *burned*.

This example of a *burn* is included to illustrate the general mechanisms of the *confidence games*. A second category of *hustles* is labeled *dealing*. As noted by Preble and Casey . . . there are many different kinds of *dealers*. At the higher levels are importers of nearly pure heroin, men who are never *junkies* and whose life centers on luxury. At the lowest level is the *junkie* who sells a few *bags* to support his own habit. Numerous levels exist between these two. For the *street junkie*, an involvement with *dealing* extends only to an occasional purchase of some heroin for quick resale. If a *street junkie* moves up a level or two in the dealing hierarchy, he is no longer a *street junkie*. The two categories are contrasted in conversations, as in "I'm no big time *dealer*; I'm just a *junkie* like you." A *dealer's dope* is purer and less expensive. His life is easier in that his *hustle* comes to him; he occupies a seller's market. On the other hand, he runs a higher risk of arrest,

incarceration, and robbery from *street junkies*. For the *street junkie*, then, *dealing* is only an occassional, low-level affair.

The *junkie's* involvement in *pimping* is similar to *dealing*. As with *dealers*, there are different kinds of *pimps* who operate on different levels. At the highest level are those with a number of attractive, high-priced girls who serve elite clientele. At the lowest level is a *pimp* with one girl who is physically unattractive and available at low cost. Again, *street junkies* tend toward the lower end of the scale. The most frequent form of *pimping* is to have one *old lady* who works the *streets* and turns her *bread* over to the *junkie*. Often, the *old lady* is a *junkie*, too.

Finally, there is the category of *stealing*. The kind of *stealing* practiced by *street junkies* varies. Some methods are very simple and straightforward. For example, there are different forms of *boosting* ('stealing property') such as *till-tapping* ('stealing from cash register') or *tail-gating* ('stealing from a parked delivery truck'). Other kinds of *stealing* are more complicated, as in the form of breaking and entering called *crib-cracking* ('entering homes'). This form of stealing often involves skills related to lock picking, signals that the residents are absent, and so on.

There are also forms of *stealing* which involve the presence of a victim, such as *dipping* ('pick-pocketing'). Another example of this type of *stealing* is the *rip-off*. The *rip-off* involves direct physical confrontation where goods or money are stolen by threatening the victim. Different forms of the *rip-off* include simply grabbing the valuable object, such as a purse, and running, or using a weapon like a knife or pistol to force the victim to surrender. As with the *burn*, the kind of *rip-off* that will concern us here is the type related to *junkie-junkie* interaction, where one may *rip-off* another for his *bread* or *stuff*.

In picking a particular *hustle*, a *junkie* will consider several aspects. First, certain *hustles* require certain kinds of personal skills that not all junkies have. *Confidence men*, as mentioned earlier, must be poised, authoritative, and quick-witted. *Pimps*, it is said, must be *cold*, capable of concealing and controlling emotion in the face of their *prostitutes'* demands or pleas. *Dealers* must also be *cold*, to resist the pleas of sick *junkies* who do not have enough to *cop*. *Junkies* who want to steal from others in a face-to-face situation must display some bravado to cower their victims. If a *junkie* is not prepared or not able to display these attributes, he is less likely to choose the *hustle*.

Of course, other attributes of the *hustle* are also important. Some, like the *confidence game*, pay off in cash, which can then immediately be used to *cop*. Others, like *boosting*, result in property, which must then be exchanged for cash (*fenced*) before *copping*. Another factor involves risk, both in the possibility of arrest and in the chance of being attacked by other *junkies*. *Dealing*, for example, is high in risk on both counts. *Dealers* must constantly guard against arrest, and they are frequent targets of a *rip-off* by junkies. As we have seen though, *dealing* pays off in providing the most reliable, highest quality source of *stuff*.

Two final factors that might be mentioned include length of penal sentence and payoff. Again, *dealing* and *boosting* provide good contrasts. *Dealing* pays well, but the *dealer* risks a sentence of several years if apprehended. *Boosting*, on the other hand, pays much less, but carries only a misdemeanor charge in most cases. In short, there are several attributes of *hustles* that are considered by a *junkie* when he selects a particular one. To repeat, this discussion is only to familiarize the reader with the broad outlines rather than providing a systematic analysis.

Hopefully, this section gives the *square* some feeling for the variety of *hustles* and process of selecting among them. Since this book is an analysis of events among *street junkies*, the only *hustles* that receive extensive treatment are the *burn* and the *rip-off*. These two are the most likely ones that one *junkie* would use against another while *copping* or *getting-off*; hence, they appear as topics in conversations. . . .

COPPING

Copping ('scoring, making a connection'), in the context here, refers to a category of events where the desired outcome is the exchange of money or goods for heroin. In its broader sense to *cop* can be glossed as 'to get', as in to *cop* some food. Furthermore, one could exchange money/goods for other drugs and correctly label the event *copping*. For the *street junkie*, though, *copping*, as contrasted with *hustling* and *getting-off*, usually refers to *copping* heroin.

The individual from whom one *cops* is called a *dealer* (*the man, connection*). Although *dealers* may operate in numerous settings, such as bars or pizza parlors, most either deal on the streets (*street dealer*) or in an apartment or house (*house connection*). Since this is not an analysis of *dealers*, reasons for selecting the streets or a house as a setting by *dealers* will not be examined. The *street dealer* and *house connection* are not the only kinds of heroin *dealers* . . . although they are the usual kind dealt with by the *street junkie*. Whichever *dealer* is contacted, the units of exchange must be known. *Junkies almost always use cash for their purchase; dealers will seldom accept goods as payment, since the trouble in fencing ('illegally selling') the material is not worth the effort.*

The *junkie* finds his heroin, or *stuff* (*smack, skag, shit, jones, boy*), packed differently from region to region (see Table I). The largest amount he usually purchases is a *bundle* or a *spoon*, costing around $30.00. Larger units,

TABLE I. Sample of Heroin Packaging from Three Cities

Type of packaging	New York	Los Angeles	Detroit
Bag	$2, $3, $5	$10, $20	—
Cap	—	—	$1
Spoon[a]	$25	$35	$5
Half-load	$30	—	—
Half-quarter	—	—	$30

[a] Obviously the New York *spoon* is a larger measure than the Detroit *spoon*.

such as the *piece* ('ounce'), are usually purchased only by *dealers*.

Unfortunately, it is difficult to describe the packaging system precisely. Quality, quantity, and price can vary, sometimes across a wide range. Lingemann, for example, estimates that *bags* of heroin can vary from 1% to 80% heroin. The rest of the mix usually contains milk sugar or other easily soluble powders resembling heroin and quinine, which tastes and gives a *rush* (glossed later) like heroin. A *dealer* will *cut* ('adulterate') the heroin as much as he can without losing customers. Since this amount varies from *dealer* to *dealer* and from day to day, quality concommitantly varies.

Quantity also varies. *Dealers* sometimes give a *short count* by removing a small amount from each unit. Furthermore, *dealers* are often not overly precise when they divide the heroin for packaging. Similarly, price can vary. For example, in 1969 a *bag* that cost $5.00 in New York cost $10.00 in Boston. Generally, the more distant an area is from the point of entry, the more middlemen are involved in the transaction. Thus, either the price will increase, or the quality will decrease through additional *cuts*.

Within an area, prices can rise in the event of a shortage of heroin, or *panic*. Prices can also vary in different neighborhoods. For example, one New York informant reports that a *trey* ($3.00 *bag*) can vary in price $1.00 either way. A Caucasian who is afraid to *cop* in Harlem can purchase the *bag* for $4.00 in a "safe" area, whereas the *junkie* who is known in Harlem can purchase it for $2.00.

For these and other reasons, the packaging system is a loose system at best. The *street junkie* must learn through experience if a quantity is acceptable as a member of the category. Furthermore, although visual inspection offers some clues to quality, he must learn to *taste* ('take a small fix') a small amount and judge the quality from physical sensations. Table I gives the units usually found in New York, Los Angeles, and Detroit. The *bag* and the ½ teaspoon *spoon* are classified by price; there is the *deuce* ($2.00), the *trey* ($3.00) the nickel ($5.00),

and the *dime* ($10.00). In Los Angeles, heroin is sometimes packaged in folded *papers* or *balloons*. The *cap* is a small gelatin capsule. Larger units in Table I include the *half-load* ('15 treybags') or the *half-quarter* ('⅛ ounce').

The next level, now shown in the table, is represented by the *bundle* ('25 nickel bags') or the *quarter-piece* ('¼ ounce'), each selling for about $70.00 to $80.00. Although it would be advantageous to buy at this level, since the more you buy, the lower the price, most *junkies* cannot do so. Since the abstinence syndrome begins 4 to 6 hours after the last injection, time pressure impedes the accumulation of large sums of money.

GETTING-OFF

The final event category considered here is labeled *getting-off (taking-off, shooting up, fixing)*. The desired outcome in all of these events is the injection of the dissolved heroin into a vein. To *get-off*, the *junkie* must have the necessary paraphernalia. Among these are the set of *works* (*outfit*). There is some disagreement as to just what is included in the *works*. All agree that it must include a hypodermic needle or *spike* (*pin*) and either a *gun* ('hypodermic syringe') or a *dropper* and *bulb*.

The *spike* size is usually 26 gauge. The *dropper* may be an ordinary glass eyedropper or a dropper from Murine, a commercially available eye relaxant The Murine *dropper* may be preferred because the 26 *spike* fits snugly over the end. Because of its relatively small size, though, many will not use it. Since most *junkies* have some trouble getting a *hit* ('needle into the vein') they want to use all the heroin they intend to in one *fix*. This often requires more volume than the Murine dropper can provide. Thus, many will prefer the larger *dropper*.

If the ordinary *dropper* is used, some thread is wrapped around the tip to ensure a snug fit with the *spike*. Another type of collar is the *Gee*, a strip of paper torn from a $1.00 bill and similarly wrapped. Rather than using the standard rubber *bulb*, the *bulb* from a baby pacifier is removed and fastened to the top of the *dropper*. The larger *bulb* is preferred, since it increases both the pressure that can be used to *draw up* the heroin and the total volume of the *works*.

Although some *junkies* use a *gun*, most will not for two reasons: First, the injection must usually be administered with one hand, since the other usually holds the *tie*. The *dropper* is much easier to handle with one hand than is the *gun*, especially if one wants to *boot*. Second, most addicts must probe to get a *hit*. With the *dropper*, a *hit* is indicated when the pressure in the vein forces some blood into the *works*. This is called a *flag (register)*. With a *gun*, the *junkie* must pull back on the plunger to test for a hit. This often jerks the *spike* out of the vein. Thus, unless a *junkie* has good *ropes* ('veins') that are easy to *hit*, he will prefer the *dropper*.

Three other items are included in the *outfit* by some informants. A small piece of wire is useful to clean the *spike* if it becomes clogged. A razor blade may be included to open heroin packaged in *balloons* (as in Los Angeles), or to divide a quantity into equal piles. *Cotton* may be carried and used to filter the dissolved heroin into the *works*. The *cotton* catches the undissolved material and minimizes the possibility of clogging the *spike*. Others may use part of a cigarette filter or a piece of Kleenex for this filtering process. In addition, the *junkie* will need a *cooker*. This can be any small, nonflammable receptacle in which the heroin can be dissolved. Two frequently used *cookers* are a spoon with the handle bent to prevent spillage or a bottle cap with a hairpin handle attached.

Finally, the addict needs a *tie*, unless he has exceptionally good *ropes*. A *tie* is any flexible material that can be applied like a tourniquet to force the veins to stand out. This facilitates getting a *hit*. Some examples of *ties* are a belt, a nylon stocking, or a thin piece of cord. If a belt is used for an injection into the arm, for example, the belt is wrapped around the mid-upper arm and cinched tightly. The *junkie*, who is sitting, then leans forward on the elbow of the belted arm with the belt running under the

elbow to the left hand. Held tightly, the veins bulge and the right arm is free to use the *works*. By releasing his grip, the tension on the belt is relaxed.

This is only one example. There are different ways of using different *ties*. Furthermore, the arm is not the only area for injection. Any vein can be used, for example, in the hands, legs, or feet. Some *hit* in the neck, and there are rarer cases who use a vein in the tongue. Other veins are usually used sooner or later, since constant use of one vein usually results in venal collapse. Furthermore, unsterile needles or accidental subcutaneous injection may cause abscesses, also necessitating a move to another spot.

Given the necessary equipment, the addict must know how to use it. First he must *crack the bags* and place the heroin in the *cooker*. The *works* are filled with water, and the water is squirted into the *cooker*. He then heats the mixture over a burning match or candle to dissolve the heroin. The *cooker* is set on some surface and the cotton (or other filter) is dropped into the mixture. The tip of the needle is placed in the cotton and the mixture is drawn into the *works*. The *tie* is applied, and the addict probes for a vein until the *flag* comes up. Usually, he then loosens the *tie* to ensure that the needle does not slip out. He can then *shoot-up* the entire *fix*, or he can *boot (jack, milk.)*

If he *boots*, he shoots in a fraction of the fix, then releases the *bulb*, thus drawing in blood. He then reapplies pressure to the *bulb, shooting* the blood-heroin mixture (*gravy*). He can continue to *boot* until the *works* are empty of heroin. He may do this for one of two reasons. First, he may want to test the quality by fixing a bit at a time. Second, he may want the multiple *rush* (glossed later) that comes with *booting*. The disadvantages of *booting* include the possibility of clogging the needle as a mixture cools. Finally, one can *boot*, obviously, only when one has adequate time to do so.

As the drug first enters the body, the *junkie* experiences the *rush (flash*, 'initial physiological effects'). The *rush*, as well as the other physical effects discussed later, are usually said to be impossible to describe to a *square*. The *rush* is sometimes compared to a "driving force" or to an orgasm. Two important implications of the *rush* should be noted. First, popular knowledge has it that heroin use has no effect on a *junkie* after his tolerance builds up. While this is true for some effects (to be discussed), it is not for the *rush*. Unless he has purchased a *blank* ('bag of fake heroin'), the *junkie* experiences the *rush* no matter how addicted he is. A second implication is that intravenous injection is preferred because it is a means to a quicker, better *rush*. *Snorting* ('sniffing heroin like snuff') and *skin-popping* ('subcutaneous injection') are possible techniques of administration, as is simple ingestion. But none of these produce a *rush* as rapid or powerful as intravenous injection.

A second kind of effect is the *high*, described as a feeling of general well-being. This effect (and the *nod*, discussed later) decreases with increased tolerance. That is, as the *junkie* becomes more addicted and acquires a higher tolerance to heroin, it takes increasing amounts to make him *high*. The *high* is longer lasting than the *rush*, though the length of time varies with the tolerance of the *junkie* and the dosage.

A third effect is the *nod*, usually described as a state of unawareness, a kind of chemical limbo. *Nods* can vary from *light* to *heavy*. A *light nod* produces such effects as slightly dropping eyelids and jaw, whereas a *heavy nod* is a state of complete unconsciousness. The *nod* is less frequent than the *high*, since a higher dose of heroin relative to the *junkie's* tolerance is necessary to bring it about.

A fourth effect, . . . is the feeling of being *straight*. A *junkie* is *straight* when he is not sick. If the *fix* removes whatever withdrawal symptoms the *junkie* is experiencing, then it gets him *straight*. Four to six hours after the injection, symptoms of withdrawal begin to appear (runny nose, watery eyes, chills among others) and continually worsen until another shot is administered.

Unless he has purchased a *blank* the *junkie* will get a *rush* and get *straight*. Depending on the amount in his *fix* and the quality [i.e. *garbage* ('poor quality'), *decent* ('normal'), or *dynamite* ('high quality')], he may get *high* and possibly *nod* If the dose is too high or the quality too good, he may *O.D.* ('overdose') and die.

28

THE RAPIST

QUEEN'S BENCH FOUNDATION

RESEARCH METHOD

This research was initiated as a pilot study to explore the dynamics of sexual assault from the perspective of the sexual offender. To date prevention information has evolved exclusively from victim accounts and analysis of crime reports; studies of rapists have focused on psychodynamics of offenders and treatment. Our research is directed towards understanding what precipitates a man to rape a particular woman, and what stops him.

As with the victim study, this research analyzed incidents of completed and deterred sexual assault, and in particular it focused on (1) factors contributing to commission of the crime, (2) characteristics of the crime scenes, and offender and victim behaviors before, during, and after the assault, (3) methods of resistance used by rape and attempted rape victims, (4) differences between completed and deterred sexual assaults, and (5) the relationship between resistance and injury.

Inquiry was guided by a series of specific questions:

1. What is a man seeking when he rapes or attempts to rape?
2. Does a rapist plan his attack?
3. Is a victim selected beforehand? If so, why is a particular woman selected?

4. Does an assailant perceive the woman he attacks as having influenced[1] his commission of the crime?
5. To what extent does his decision to rape include violence?
6. In the assailant's perception, is the amount of violence influenced by the victim? If so, to what extent?
7. What factors cause intensification of the degree and type of violence inflicted upon the victim?
8. What factors are associated with deterrence of rape?
9. How does an assailant respond to victim resistance?
10. How does an assailant account for his rape or other sexual assault?
11. Finally, what ideas do rapists have for ways in which a victim can deter a rape attack; and what can women do to avoid being raped?

Because injury and possibility of death are major issues in considering resistance to rape, this study concentrated on offenders who used "excessive violence" in commission of the assault, (i.e., force or threat of force exceeding the violence of rape itself). Special attention was addressed to factors pertinent to exacerbation of aggression and violence: what trig-

Source: *Rape Prevention and Resistance.* San Francisco: Queen's Bench Foundation, 1976, pp. 59–76, 79–87, 92–94. (Editorial adaptations.) Reprinted by permission.

[1] "Influence" is used here in a neutral sense, not to impute blame on the victim. It reflects the *assailant's perception* of the chain of events and factors which affected his commission of the crime.

gered the violence, was the injury intentional, what types and degrees of injury were inflicted, and what might victims have done to prevent infliction of injury?

The selection of excessively violent rapists for the study provided important insights regarding victim injury, however, it must be remembered that the research findings reflect the choice of this sample population: If the research had included non-excessively violent rapists, the correlations of violence with other elements of the attacks would have been significantly reduced. What was important in this study was the exploration of the factors which influenced violence *in those cases where it occurred.*

The lack of prior research on rapists determined the exploratory nature of this study. This report is therefore a compilation of the data received in response to a series of more detailed questions encompassing the issues outlined above, a discussion of the significant relationships between certain variables in the study identified through data analysis, the identification of those variables that seemed to impinge most significantly upon violence and deterrence, and finally, a few suggested hypotheses and tentative explanations for key trends observed in the data.

DEFINITIONS

For the purpose of this study, specific meanings were assigned to the following terms:

1. "Rape" was defined as forced vaginal or anal penetration of a woman, or forced oral copulation (fellatio and cunnilingus).
2. "Attempted rape" was an assault which stopped short of vaginal or anal penetration or oral copulation, but in which the assailant's intent (through verbal or physical indications) to commit such an act was clear.
3. "Excessive violence" meant force or the threat of force excessive of that necessary to accomplish a rape and exceeding the violence of rape itself, e.g., serious bodily harm to the victim, use of a lethal weapon, strangulation or other forms of force which might result in serious bodily harm or death but

which do not necessarily leave noticeable injuries, prolonged beating of the victim; severe restriction of the victim's physical movements by binding or physical force, etc.
4. "Deterrence" signified the interruption of a specific attack (i.e., rape was not accomplished).
5. "Prevention" was used in a larger sense, to mean the curbing of rape attacks in general, before the inception of particular incidents.
6. Mentally Disordered Sex Offenders (MDSO) is defined by Section 6300 of the Welfare and Institution Code of California, as "any person who by reason of mental defect, disease, or disorder is predisposed to the commission of sexual offenses to such a degree that he is dangerous to the health and safety of others."

DATA COLLECTION

The interview method was the primary data collection technique, supplemented by a review of participant's medical records which contained information on the offense described during the interview. Unlike a self-administered questionnaire (which is often met with a low response rate among research participants), the interview approach seemed to hold greater potential for a high response rate and for comprehensiveness and clarity in responses. Since the research was exploratory in nature, the interview format allowed an opportunity for the interviewer to probe and to raise other questions in order to assist the participant in recollecting details of the assault and to clarify obscure or inconsistent responses. The review of participants' medical charts was useful for the verification of background data on the offender and the offense.

Development. Two types of research instruments were used: an interview schedule and data sheets for the background information from the offender's records. Preparation of the interview protocol was preceded by a detailed examination of Queen's Bench Foundation's 1975 interviews with rape victims and a review of the available literature on rapists. The draft interview schedules were submitted to the Research Committee at Atascadero State Hospital. (This committee includes hospital staff who have conducted research on sex offenders and who have supervised therapy programs for rapists; their comments aided the refinement of the interview schedules.) The final format was approved by the Research Committee prior to implementation of the research.

The interview schedule was partially structured, with the majority of the questions open-ended. The schedule included 49 questions arranged in three broad categories:

1. A series of background questions covering demographic variables, age, ethnicity, education, etc., and prior criminal record (both sexual and non-sexual offenses).
2. The participant's account of the rape incident, followed by specific questions regarding the assault, arranged sequentially: what was happening in the participant's life *immediately prior to the rape*; what factor led to the attack itself; why was a particular woman selected; what signalled the beginning of the rape; how did the victim respond; what violence was used; and what injuries were inflicted.
3. Questions regarding victims' resistance and rape deterrence in the specific case under investigation, and prevention of rape in general.

Administration. Research staff met with the sex offenders selected as eligible for the study (see "Subject Population" below) to explain the purpose, nature, and procedures for the research, and to answer questions regarding the study. The voluntary nature of the research was stressed, and participants were offered $2.50 to participate. Offenders who chose to participate in the research signed consent forms and were scheduled for interviews.

The research was conducted over a period of four days at Atascadero State Hospital. Interviews, each lasting between one and two hours, were conducted by six women staff members of Queen's Bench Foundation; 3 interviews were conducted in Spanish. For security purposes, all but three interviews were conducted in a large multi-purpose room, however, the individual interview tables were several yards apart to insure full privacy during the interviews. The remaining three interviews were conducted in private rooms connected to the wards; one interview was conducted under maximum security. With the permission of the participants the majority of interviews were audio-taped.

Confidentiality. Stringent precautions were taken to preserve confidentiality, both to protect the offender from misuse of information and to reduce bias in the data collection. The questions were limited to only those offenses for which the participant had been *charged*, and all names mentioned during the interviews were erased from the audio-tapes. All interview schedules and data sheets are identified by numbers, and no list exists to match participants names to those numbers. Access to research materials is limited to Queen's Bench Foundation staff, Atascadero State Hospital, and those deemed to have legitimate research interests.

SUBJECT POPULATION

Contacts with the California Department of Corrections and Department of Health resulted in the selection of Atascadero State Hospital as the most feasible site for research with a rapist population.

Atascadero State Hospital has a current population of approximately 1,000 men, including approximately 18% of all convicted rapists in California. It is a maximum security institution specializing in particular in the treatment of mentally disordered sex offenders (MDSO's). The offender/patients are returned to the courts when the hospital recommends their release from the hospital, either because they have improved and are not a danger to others or because they are *not* improved and are still a danger but would not benefit from further treatment.

Of the hospital's total population, 16.4% (164 patients) are rapists. A brief demographic summary follows:

1. MDSO's comprise 42% (420) of the total population. Of these, 55% are pedophiles (child molesters); 40% are rapists; and 5% are other sexual offenders, e.g., exhibitionists, voyeurs, etc.
2. The remaining 58% (580) are categorized as not competent to stand trial. This group included those men whom the courts have declared not guilty by reason of insanity or not able to stand trial, transfers from the Department of Corrections for purposes of accommodation, and conservatees, i.e., men who are unable to provide themselves with clothing and shelter.

Because the researchers anticipated severe psychiatric disorders among the offenders, this possible sample bias was closely investigated. Hospital authorities assured us that despite the MDSO (Mentally Disordered Sexual Offender) classification of the offender/patients, the men at Atascadero were (with few exceptions) not seriously mentally disordered and that they were fully capable and suitable for participation in the study.

The research sample was necessarily clustered in type, i.e., it included all the men at the hospital who fell within the excessively violent rapist category. Because of the particular sentencing system for commitment to the hospital, representativeness in the sample cannot be assumed, and the hospital population differs from other convicted rapist populations (e.g., at prisons) on characteristics such as racial composition, socio-economic status, etc.

The Atascadero population did provide several advantages. Some of the men had been exposed to research at the hospital before, and they seemed eager to contribute to what they saw as an academic and potentially therapeutic project. Because of participation in therapy groups at the hospital, they were open about their rape experiences, although their therapy exposure may have introduced a degree of treatment bias into their responses (e.g., in the usage of psychiatric and psychological terms and explanations for past behavior). Hospital records were made available for verification of interview information, as well as for the collection of additional data. Finally, the population's accessibility and the interest and support of the hospital staff were valuable to the entire data collection process.

The seven program directors who had rapists under their supervision assisted with selection of the subjects. The project goals and the need for a specific type of participant (i.e., excessively violent rapists) as well as the criteria for identifying this particular type of rapist were explained to the program directors. The rape and attempted rape offenses committed by prospective participants were discussed with ward staff, and Queen's Bench Foundation staff reviewed the hospital medical charts of the rapists to determine eligibility for the study.

The initial sample pool included 83 excessively violent rapists. The research was discussed with all the men in this pool, and 82 signed up for interviews.

Seven (7) of the original 82 offenders did not show up for the interview, in most cases because of medical or disciplinary restriction or because they were no longer interested in participating. A total of 75 interviews were conducted, however two homosexual rape cases were excluded from data analysis because of unique features of their crimes.

Overall, the participants were overwhelmingly young, white, high school graduates, primarily skilled or service workers, with varied criminal backgrounds.

76.8% were 29 years old or under.

75.3% were white.

68.5% were single.

50.7% were high school graduates.

68.5% had previously held skilled jobs (furniture maker, construction, automechanic, welder, truck driver, etc.) or service jobs (cook, maintenance workers, gardener, laborer, etc.); 24.7% (18) had held semi-professional jobs (optical technician, psychiatric technician, police cadet, etc.).

78.1% had incurred previous charges for non-sexual offenses (burglary, attempted murder, assault with a deadly weapon, larceny, drunk driving, etc.).

57.5% had been charged previously with attempted rape, 76.2% (32) were charged with one previous offense, and 23.8% (10) with two such offenses.

69.9% had at least one prior rape charge.

45.2% had prior charges for sexual assault other than rape or attempted rape (oral copulation, kidnapping, sodomy, child molesting, etc.).

DATA ANALYSIS

The small sample size exerted considerable constraint on the data, limiting the type and number of statistical tests that could be used for analysis. Testing[2] and analyses were limited to 73 interviews, and proceeded in the following sequence:

1. Frequency distribution for a descriptive summary of all the responses.
2. Pearson's correlational analysis for the identification of relationships between parts of variables in the study.
3. Two sets of factor analysis to allow consolidation of the numerous items measuring victim resistance and offender violence, and an additional correlational analysis using

the new variables generated by the factor analysis.
4. A multiple regression analysis using rape deterrence and completion of rape as dependent variables. This was based on several relationships established by Pearson's correlation.

RESEARCH FINDINGS

DEMOGRAPHIC CHARACTERISTICS

The frequency of various characteristics of victims and offenders in this research shows striking similarity to characteristics derived from other studies discussed in the literature on rape; in addition, demographic characteristics which emerged from this research were consistent with demographic characteristics found in the Queen's Bench Foundation victim research.

Age. Offenders and their victims were between 16 and 35 years at the time of the sexual assault. Most were 23 years and under. The offender study found the following age groupings:

69.9% (51) of the offenders compared to 63% (49) of the victims were 25 and under *at the time of the offense.* Within this group, 13% (10) of the victims were between 10 and 15 years old at the time of the offense.

20.5% (15) offenders compared to 9.3% (5) victims were between 26 and 30 years in age.

4.1% (3) offenders compared to 2.7% (2) victims were between 31 and 35 years old at the time of the offense.

5.3% (4) offenders compared to 13.3% (10) victims were 36 years and above.

These figures are not large enough to draw strong conclusions, but they indicate that rape is not entirely a peer phenomenon. There were several instances where offenders attacked women several years older or younger than themselves: there were 10 victims under 15 years in age, and 3 who were 50 and over.

---

[2] Very briefly, the frequency distribution stage of data analysis provides the basic *distributional characteristics,* degree of variability, etc. of each of the variables to be used in subsequent statistical analysis. Pearson's correlation measures the *strength of relationship* between two variables. Factor analysis enables *data reduction* by providing new factors/variables for subsequent statistical analysis. One function of multiple regression is to allow an analysis of the relationship between a criterion (dependent) variable and a set of predictor variables. Among other uses it indicates the extent to which certain variables predict another. (For a full description, see: Hubert Blalock, *Social Statistics,* New York: McGraw-Hill Book Company, 1960.)

Ethnicity. Typically offenders were of the same race and ethnic group as their victims.

75.3% (55) of the offenders compared to 74% (54) of the victims were white.

Marital Status

93.2% (67) of the offenders were single (includes divorced or separated) compared to 60.3% (44) victims who were single.

6.8% (5) of the offenders and 12.3% (9) of the victims were married.

Number of Assailants. The vast majority of instances (94.5%) involved a solitary assailant and a solitary victim. Three cases involved two assailants, and one involved four. There were four cases with two victims.

Victim/Offender Relationship. The majority of rape attacks (78%) in this study involved strangers.

78% (57) of the offenders were strangers to the victims; although 20.5% (15) of these men had seen their victims before, acquaintance was extremely superficial.

21.9% of the cases involved victims and offenders who were friends of some sort.

In two instances, victim and offender were related.

TIMES AND DATES OF OFFENSE

62.9% (46) of the offenses were committed between Thursday and Sunday with frequencies peaking on Friday (20.5%) and Sunday (17.8%)

50.7% (37) occurred at night; 34.2% (25) were committed during the afternoon, and 15.1% (11) during the morning.

CHARACTERISTICS OF SEXUAL ASSAULT

The Setting of the Attack. Almost as many offenders first encountered their victims at home as outside.

39.7% (29) of the offenders first encountered the victim in her home or nearby, e.g., getting into her car.

27.4% (20) encountered the victim on the street.

27.4% (20) encountered the victim at some other public place, e.g., bar, restaurant, grocery store, parking lot, bowling alley, school campus, etc.

5.5% (4) met the victim at the assailant's or a mutual friend's home.

Assailant activity at the time of the first encounter with victims shows an important trend with respect to the assailant's motivations that day.[3]

52.1% (38) stated that they were out looking for a victim to rape.[4]

23.3% (17) said they were either just "hanging out," standing around looking for something to do, or sitting around drinking and talking at a public place, such as a bar, restaurant, or school campus.

21.9% (16) were driving their cars (10) or riding or walking casually on the street (6).

2.7% (2) said they were burglarizing the victim.

Rapist's Activity Prior to the Sexual Assault. The offenders generally mentioned a recent disappointment which caused a high degree of frustration, depression, or anger just prior to their rape attacks. Several acknowledged planning the rape, and many described the disappointing or depressing experiences as *causal* to the rape. A considerable number recalled consuming alcohol after their disap-

---

[3] Due to multiple responses to interview questions, percentages throughout this text will not necessarily add to 100%.

[4] Most of these men explicitly said "rape." Others said "sex" but when probed further, indicated they knew it had to be forcible sex. A small number said they were hoping to seduce their victims but anticipated opposition from the women and expected they would have to force compliance.

pointments but before their rapes. The following summarizes the events preceding the rapes.

76.7% (56) of the offenders said they were feeling frustrated, depressed, angry, or rejected before they planned and/or committed their attacks.

57.5% (42) felt very strongly so, and 19.2% (14) felt somewhat so.

There was some variation in the source of the disappointment, but typically, it resulted from an argument or fight with a wife or girlfriend.

47.9% (35) attributed their disappointments to an argument or fight with wives or girlfriends.

20.5% (15) said that it was not necessarily a recent experience but rather a welling up of previous disappointments that were intensified by a recent incident.

13.7% (10) experienced a disappointment over work or money, with parents or siblings, or with other friends.

The extent of alcohol and drug use among the offenders immediately before their rape attacks was high. However, it should be noted that a correlational analysis of the data (discussed later) did not show any significant relationship between alcohol or drug use and intent to rape or actual rape.

61.6% (45) had been drinking before their assaults; 41.1% (30) drank liquor such as rum, whiskey, or wine, while the remainder drank beer.

35.6% (26) said they had been drinking heavily, 15.1% (11) moderately, and the rest only had a little to drink that day.

38.4% (28) had used drugs of some sort, mostly marijuana (32.6%); 61.6% (45) reported no drug use.

Planning of the Rape. The assailant's activity during his assessment and planning of the rape suggests some important trends. For ex-

ample, 79.5% (58) said *that they were watching their victims before they approached them.* Significantly too, 20.5% (15) reported they had seen their victims twice on the day of the rape incident; they committed their attacks the second time. Although this number is relatively small, its implications should be considered: in *certain instances* the rapist may assess and plan a rape attack after locating a potential victim, returning later to execute the rape. *A considerable amount of forethought about rape* was indicated by the offenders' responses to a question about what they were thinking of when they approached their victims that day.

68.5% (50)—over two-thirds—of the men said they were thinking of rape.[5]

26% (19) stated they were thinking of something casual, such as ordinary conversation, companionship, helping the victim by giving her a ride someplace, etc., or of nothing in particular.

4.1% (3) were thinking of robbing the victim.

One offender claimed that it was the victim who approached him.

The offenders were next asked what they were hoping would happen when they approached their victims.

71.2% (52) said they were hoping the victim would comply with their expectations.

21.9% (16) said they were not hoping for anything in particular.

2.7% (2) stated they were hoping to acquire money.

The next series of questions probed deeper into the nature of the offender's planning of the assault. The men were asked, for example, about intent to have sexual contact that day, intent to use violence, possession of weapon,

---

[5] Here again, many of these men explicitly said "rape." The others said "sex" but with further questioning, indicated they knew the sex had to be forcible as they did not expect the victims to comply.

type of weapon, regularity of possession of weapon, and familiarity of victim.

67.1% (49) said they intended to have sexual contact that day.

67.1% (49) said they had not intended to use violence that day, *but 32.9% said that they anticipated having to use violence that day.*

69.9% (51), however, *in spite of the sizable proportion who reported no intent to use violence, had a weapon that day in their possession.* About half of the armed attackers, 35.6% (26) stated that they usually carried a weapon.

47.9% (35) were armed with knives including butcher knives, paring knives, or switchblades; 15.1% (15) were carrying guns; and 6.8% (5) had other kinds of weapons—often meat forks. One offender had a club which he had made himself; another had a screwdriver; another had handcuffs; and one had a rock. Some of the rapists used rope and clothing found at the victims' house to tie or gag the women.

78% (57) of the offenders defined their victims as strangers, but *38.4% (28) indicated*

they had a particular woman in mind before the rape, and 34.2% (25) identified that woman as the eventual victim.

The response patterns in this set of items suggests a clear trend in the phenomenon of rape in this study: it is quite evident from the distributions noted above, that in the planning stages of the attack, the majority of the offenders were thinking of *forcible* sex.

Victim Selection. The participants' were asked what factors influenced their selection of a particular victim. Close to two-thirds (61.7%) of the offenders stated they chose a particular victim because she was available ("she was there") and/or defenseless. Selection factors were further delineated as follows (see Figure 1):

82.2% (60) of the offenders said they chose a particular victim because she was available.

71.2% (52) said because she was defenseless.

46.6% (34) said because they saw her as sexy (for example, she may have been dressed in clothes they found sexually arousing; several

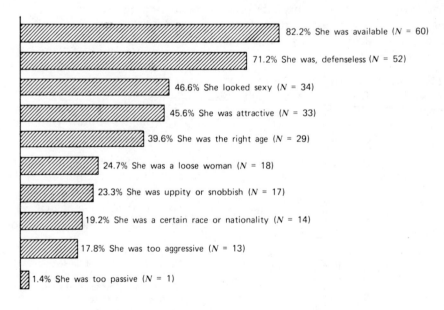

FIGURE 1. Factors in selection of rape victim.

commented that they felt other men might not perceive her to be "sexy")

42.5% (33) said because they found her physical appearance attractive. (There was little consistency in their criteria for attractiveness.)

39.7% (29) stated they chose their victims because they were the "right age" (which ranged from young girls 15 and under to women their own age, to 50 and over).

24.7% (18) claimed they selected their victims because they saw them as "loose" women (waitresses, hitchhikers who looked like hippies, and women who were said to have had sexual relationships with more than one man, for example, were described as "loose women.")

For other offenders, the selection of the victim was based on entirely different grounds: 23.3% (17) cited victim aggressiveness, and 17.8% (13) cited victim snobbishness as well as aggressiveness.

Initiation of the Sexual Assault. The research explored in detail the sequence of the events constituting the sexual assault, beginning with the assailant's first interaction with the victim, victim behavior and rapists' perceptions of her during the interim period before onset of the attack, the initiation of the attack, victim response at this point, and finally, assailant reaction to the victim's response.

When asked about their first interaction with their victims,

39.7% (29) of the offenders stated that they had spoken *casually* to their victims on the street or in another public place, such as a bar, restaurant, bowling alley, grocery store, or parking lot.

35.6% (26) accomplished their first interaction by *immediately grabbing* the victim and attacking her.

13.7% (10) awakened their victims from sleep.

12.3% (9) said they had knocked on the victim's door to gain entry.

Of particular importance are the cases in which the offender's first interaction occurred after *breaking into* the victim's house: 20.5% (15) of the offenders checked around the victim's house and entered through an unlocked door or window, cut holes through window screens, or knocked on the victim's door and forcibly pushed their way into her house when she opened the door. Two offenders said they were in the process of burglarizing the victim's house when they first interacted with their victims. Two other men were managers of apartment buildings where their victims lived and has easy access to the victims. One had given up his managing job when he committed the rape, but he knew the building very well and came by to visit other people quite often. When he came back to rape, he effortlessly entered the victim's apartment by climbing through a friend's bathroom into an airshaft and down some pipes to the victim's bathroom window. The other offender simply took his keys and entered his victim's apartment.

Of particular importance also are the cases in which the attack was preceded by an interim period of casual conversation: 50.7% (37) offenders indicated that they spoke to the victim casually before becoming openly aggressive in the attack. Duration of this interim period varied but was usually less than an hour.

20.5% (15) of the offenders spent 15 minutes or less in conversation.

21.9% (16) spent between 16 minutes and an hour.

The rest (6) spent two hours or more in conversation.

Usually, offender-victim activity during this interim period included walking, "sitting around" outdoors, or travelling (for example, to the victim's destination or a secluded area). The responses for these two items grouped as follows:

17.8% (13) were walking or "sitting around" outdoors with the victim.

12.3% (9) of the offenders were driving.

9.6% (7) of the offenders were talking with the victims while they (the victim) were at home relaxing (lying on bed, watching television, reading, etc.) or doing household chores.

24.7% (18) said they took their victims some place during this time: 13.7% (10) took her to some private place (victim's bedroom, other part of victim's house, a secluded area off a main street, etc.); 6.8% (5) took her to their house or car; 4.1% (3) took her to the victim's destination.

The offenders' description of their victims' behavior during this interim period showed some similarity. About two-thirds of the men who reported casual conversation described their victims' behavior as friendly.[6]

32.9% (24) of the offenders in the study felt that the victim was friendly.

15.1% (11) described her as scared.

9.6% (7) thought she was calm.

8.2% (6) found her sympathetic.

8.2% (6) described her as snobbish.

In four cases, a period of conversation occurred after the offender had executed an immediate attack on the victim. These four men said they had grabbed their victims, and after successfully intimidating them, tried to calm them through "casual" talk.

It was usually the offender who signalled the beginning of the attack, most often through physical force, the use of a weapon, or physical restraint of the victim: (See Figure 2.)

61.6% (45) of the men used physical force.

57.5% (42) used a weapon and a verbal threat.

43.8% (32) physically restrained the victim; e.g., choking.

Only 13.7% (10) said that they used an oral

threat only; oral threats were otherwise accompanied by another signal.

A few of the offenders, 15.1% (11), cited the expression of anger on the part of the victim as signalling the beginning of the attack, and a smaller percentage cited victim nervousness, 6.8% (5), or the victim's attempt to leave, 6.8% (5).

Despite the initiating role offenders played in signalling the beginning of their rape attacks, *45.2% (33) of the offenders claimed that their victims had "provoked" the attack.* A slightly larger percentage, 52.1% (38), stated that their victims did not influence the attack. Of the 33 men who felt that their victims had contributed to the rape.

24.7% (18) explained that provocation was in the form of victim resistance (physical, oral, or verbal, including insulting the assailant).

17.8% (13) claimed that the victim's attractiveness or friendliness and cooperativeness provoked the attack.

One of the remaining two offenders said he was angered by his victim's passiveness, while the other claimed that he became angry and raped the woman because she confused his attempt to rob her with an attempt to rape.[7]

Victim Resistance and Assailant Reaction. The offender frequently reported that their victims were taken by complete surprise when they were attacked. Yet despite this fact and the frequency with which the offenders used weapons (usually to intimidate victims at the beginning of the attack), *a sizable proportion, 68.5% (50) of the women resisted in some way.* (See Figure 2.)

64.4% (47) questioned their attackers asking, for example, "What are you doing?" "Why are you doing this?" "Leave me alone!" "Don't hurt me." "Stop" or "Get out of here!"

---

[6] There is an overlap in these percentages because the victims were placed in more than one category quite often; e.g., a victim was sometimes described as friendly and scared, or friendly and calm, etc.

[7] This offender stated that he saw the woman's confusion, and although he never robs and rapes during the same attack, he raped this victim after robbing her because "she offered it."

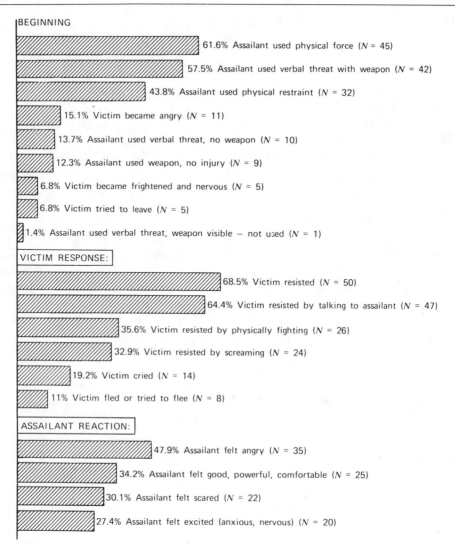

BEGINNING

61.6% Assailant used physical force (*N* = 45)

57.5% Assailant used verbal threat with weapon (*N* = 42)

43.8% Assailant used physical restraint (*N* = 32)

15.1% Victim became angry (*N* = 11)

13.7% Assailant used verbal threat, no weapon (*N* = 10)

12.3% Assailant used weapon, no injury (*N* = 9)

6.8% Victim became frightened and nervous (*N* = 5)

6.8% Victim tried to leave (*N* = 5)

1.4% Assailant used verbal threat, weapon visible — not used (*N* = 1)

VICTIM RESPONSE:

68.5% Victim resisted (*N* = 50)

64.4% Victim resisted by talking to assailant (*N* = 47)

35.6% Victim resisted by physically fighting (*N* = 26)

32.9% Victim resisted by screaming (*N* = 24)

19.2% Victim cried (*N* = 14)

11% Victim fled or tried to flee (*N* = 8)

ASSAILANT REACTION:

47.9% Assailant felt angry (*N* = 35)

34.2% Assailant felt good, powerful, comfortable (*N* = 25)

30.1% Assailant felt scared (*N* = 22)

27.4% Assailant felt excited (anxious, nervous) (*N* = 20)

FIGURE 2. Signals at beginning of attack, victim response, and assailant reaction.

35.6% (26) physically fought with their assailants.

32.9% (24) screamed.

19.2% (14) started crying.

11% (8) fled or attempted to flee

The offenders, on the other hand, reported a variety of emotional reactions to the victim's behavior at this point.

47.9% (35) said they felt very angry.

34.2% (25) said they felt powerful, good, dominant, or comfortable.

27.4% (20) said they felt excited (i.e., nervous or anxious).

30.1% (22) said that they felt scared.

It was at this stage, when victims resisted, that many of the men intensified their violence.

54.8% (40) offenders became *angrier* during the attack, and 32 of these attributed this change to victim resistance at the beginning of the attack.

Injury was caused in 61.6% (45) of the rape attacks, 46.5% of which ranged from moderate to extensive injury (such as cuts, severe choking which caused the victim a great deal of discomfort, and injuries from being repeatedly kicked, dragged, beaten, bruised). Very severe injury occurred in 22.7% (17) incidents, and included stabs, bruises, lacerations, etc., which produced a great deal of bleeding or swelling, or which resulted in unconsciousness.

75.3% (55) of the men had a weapon with them during the assault,[8] *although only a relatively small proportion, 16% (12), actually used their weapons to inflict injury. Physical strength caused most of the injury, 45.2% (33), usually in the form of bruises, cuts, lacerations, and scratches.*

54.8% (40) of the men said that the injuries were intentional, not necessarily because they wanted to hurt, but because their expectations were not being met.

Despite the extent and degree of assailant violence, in 32.9% (24) of the attacks, the woman successfully resisted the sexual assault. The men committed the following acts:

65.8% (48) of the men successfully consummated their rapes through coitus.

38.4% (28) had fellatio performed on them.

20.5% (15) performed cunnilingus on their victims.

8.2% (6) sodomized their victims.

Violence in Offenders.

Since the role of violence was a focus in this study, several questions addressed the events which intensified the violence. A large majority, 89% (65), said

---

8 This percentage is greater than that for possession of weapons prior to the attack because some offenders went into the victim's kitchen and got knives when she began to resist.

there was a particular point at which they decided to ''scare'' (i.e., intimidate) or hurt their victims.

53.4% (39) explained that they had decided to *scare* their victims at the beginning of the attack to force submission; 30.1% (22) decided to scare the victim when she resisted; and four offenders said they decided to scare their victims when they felt that the victim might ''blow it'' and they would get caught.

24.7% (18) of the men stated that they decided to *hurt* the victim when she started to resist either at the beginning of the attack or during the attack; 8.2% (6) decided to hurt the victim initially to intimidate her into submission; and three said they decided to hurt the victim either when they could not achieve an erection to consummate the rape, or after completing the rape when they thought about the possibility of getting caught. Some men who injured victims stated they did not intentionally hurt them.

Assailant's Expectations.

To further explore what women could have done to mitigate chances of injury, the offenders were asked if there was anything the victim did to cause his intensified violence and how he would have preferred her to respond. They were also asked what she could have done to *stop* him from escalating the violence.

24% (18) stated they were satisfied with the way their rape attacks had progressed.

45.2% (33) said they would have like their victims to have complied with them, fulfilling their expectations (usually surrender).

12.3% (9) said their expectations would have been met by victim support, sympathy, or ''concern (for them) as a person.''

11% (8) wanted their victims to struggle more vigorously, or to act scared so that their feelings of power could have been enhanced.

Over half, 56.2% (41), of the men stated that the victim could have inhibited them from further intimidating or harming her.

27.4% (20) explained that victims could have accomplished this by struggling more vigorously, screaming, or being more assertive (verbally and through body movement); 20% (15) claimed that victims could have accomplished this by simply complying and "enjoying" the experience; and *only 8.2% (6) felt that the expression of "concern as a person" for them by the victim would have been effective.*

Deterrence of Sexual Assault. Half the offenders, *50.7% (37), believed they could have been deterred.* Quite a few said that if their victims had put up a big struggle they would have "freaked" and run away.

37.1% (27) explained that their victims should have resisted more vigorously orally, physically, and verbally.

6 said that the victim's "concern for the offender as a person" would have deterred them.

5 stated that they would not have proceeded to have intercourse if their victims had complied outright.

Causes of Rape. When questioned about what they felt influenced them to commit rape, the offenders mentioned a number of factors: poor social relations with women, general inability to develop interpersonal relations, lack of self-confidence, negative self-concept, etc. (See Figure 3.) Developmental psycho-social dynamics of rapists were not a focus of the study and was not explored further.

*

CORRELATED DATA AND REGRESSION ANALYSIS

As noted previously, data analysis after the frequency distribution included the following methods:

1. Pearson's correlation between the items where relationships were anticipated.

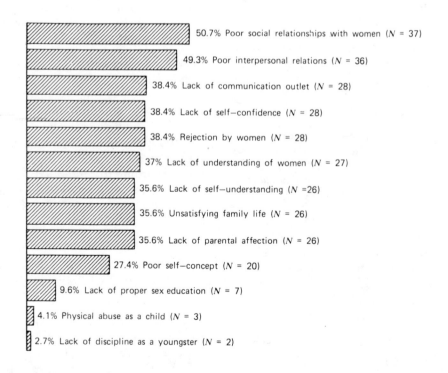

FIGURE 3. Causes of rape or attempted rape: offenders' opinions.

2. Scale construction of the variables resistance and violence preceded by a factor analysis of the respective item sets, and followed by Pearson's correlation between the new scaled variables resistance and violence, and deterrence.

3. A multiple regression analysis to determine the extent of predictability of each of six independent variables with respect to deterrence.

Significant findings revealed by these procedures are presented in the format of the questions stated in the research purposes.

1. What is a man looking for when he rapes?

According to most of the respondents in this study, 50.7% (37), *power* or *dominance* over their victims was their primary goal: "to overpower and control" them. This theme was expressed in a variety of forms:

A 24 year old who had raped a 28 year old woman recounted a story characteristic of others related in the course of the study:

> I walked off from a County farm; I had rape on my mind. I intended to rape off this chick I know . . . but some people came . . I went over to this lady's house . . . I was talking to her, stalling time, really planning how to rip her off . . . By "rape", I don't just mean intercourse. I mean to go through all the changes—me getting what I wanted. If she had agreed to give me a head job, I would have said, "No" and not raped her. If she had said, "yeah, let's go to bed," *I would have said, "No," as she would have been in control.*

A 34 year old offender defined rape as *misdirected violence* aimed at the achievement of dominance and power, which he believed most people achieve through communication and love. A 33 year old man who raped a 19 year old hitchhiker explained his rape as a means of expressing a *power-fantasy:*

> 'My fantasy was—before I stopped—that she was teasing me. So I had an attitude of "I'll show you". . . . *I wanted power over her . . . power to overcome my fear of women.*

Another 20 year old who raped a 40 year old woman explained:

> She was cooperating. It was fulfilling my fantasy (from before I woke her up). She was doing it just like it was nothing. My fantasy was she would give me what I wanted because I had the knife and she was scared. *I wanted her to be scared to keep me in control.*

For many of the offenders, exertion of dominance and power included elements of revenge and humiliation. Often it was not sufficient to control the victim, but the offender wished to "put her down" as well. For example, a 21 year old who raped a 42 year old woman said that initially he was seeking sex, but his account suggests more:

> I asked her to go out; she said "another time". . . I was interested in sex . . . I continued to tell her I wanted to take her out. She got even more upset . . . She slapped me and called me a punk . . . I got upset, so I knocked the shit out of her. "I'll show you; you just don't do that to me." I degraded the shit out of her. I was just getting even dealing with myself. . .

When the offenders were questioned specifically regarding their intentions as they approached their victim, the vast majority—91.8% (67)—spontaneously identified "rape" as their aim; few came close to implying "innocent" intentions though many said sex was on their mind—65.8% (48). Probing of their expectations regarding this intended sex revealed that they anticipated it would be forcible sex, and often their fantasies included strong elements of dominance and violence.

8.2% (6) said their initial aim was merely a casual visit.

8.2% (6) said their initial aim was to rob the victim.

Offender's Aims of Dominance, Humiliation and Revenge significantly correlated with Casual Conversation Prior to the Rape.

Several of the men explained that they usually spoke to their victims for a short while

(52.4% between 2 to 30 minutes) before executing the assault. Apparently this period was used to elicit certain kinds of behavior in their victims (e.g., sometimes resistance, sometimes fright, etc.) and to set the process of dominance in motion.

2. Does the rapist plan the attack?

According to the majority of the participants in this study, the answer is "Yes." The majority (65.8%) indicated they had planned to have sex that day, while 91.8% described rape as their intention. Of the latter, 9.3% specified that they were considering rape if the victim did not cooperate. None of the offenders anticipated compliance initially although they contemplated and desired it. In this context data, analysis revealed that:

1. Intent to Have Sex correlated significantly with:
   Aim to Rape
   Having a Particular Woman in Mind
   Knowing the Victim
2. Assailant's thoughts as he approached the woman correlated very highly with what he was hoping would happen when he encountered her
3. Assailant's Tendency to Watch and closely observe the victim (79.5%) correlated significantly with Victim being a Stranger (78%)
4. Assailant's Possession of a Weapon (69.9%) correlated highly with his use of Weapon to intimidate the victim (though most had stated they had no previous intentions to use the weapon)

In addition, it was clear in at least seven cases (Peeping Toms) that some rapists make a comprehensive assessment of a prospective victim and her environment, returning later to execute the rape.

> One 24 year old related that he had been out walking one night, after leaving a party because he didn't know many of the people. He saw a woman get out of a Volkswagen van and go to her apartment. He saw the light go on in her house, knocked on her door, and asked if she knew where——lived. When she said she didn't, he asked her if her husband was home. She said, "I'm not married." He went home for a knife and returned to the apartment to rape her."

Another 24 year old described one of his many rape attacks as follows:

> One evening he drove around for about an hour checking apartments for a victim, because single women often live in complexes. He found a woman's name on a mailbox and rang her bell, but no one answered. He entered the house through an open back window, unlocked the back door and left. After watching for about 15 minutes, the victim returned and he watched through the window 2–3 minutes. She puttered about the kitchen, then went to the bedroom and took off some clothes. "I was outside, building up my nerve. Then I went into the house, looked at her a few seconds, went to the bedroom door and showed her my gun . . .

3. Is a victim selected beforehand, and why is a particular woman selected?

Although victims were predominantly strangers (78%), assailants did engage in a selection process, often eliminating certain women until they found a suitable victim.[9] For example, 38.4% reported having a particular woman in mind; 34.2% said that this woman did become the victim. Often, they were looking for a *particular kind of victim* rather than a certain preselected woman. Further probing revealed that in addition to availability and defenselessness, perceived promiscuity or "looseness"[10] of women, apparent naivete, and ambivalent behavior were cited as decisive influences in the selection of victims. However, race, physical appearance (e.g., heavily built women), or assertive body language were

[9] . . . 82.2% chose a victim who was "available" and 71.2% chose a woman they perceived as defenseless and vulnerable.

[10] A perception of the rapist; often these men had never seen the woman before.

factors which led to elimination of prospective victims. Several men said that the prsence of males (i.e., if a man was in the victim's house or if the victim was married) would have made them change their minds immediately.

4. Does the assailant perceive the woman he attacks as having influenced his commission of the crime?

The participants were almost equally divided in their responses to this question: 52.1% said that they had already decided to rape when they selected the victim, but another 45.2% felt that their victims had precipitated the assault. When those who responded that the victim had "precipitated" the offense (33) were asked about the manner in which the victim incited the attack, 18 cited victim resistance and 13 cited victim attractiveness. However, both of these explanations are disputable.

In the instances involving victim resistance, the victim was resisting an attack already in progress. Victim attractiveness might contribute to rape in a passive sense, as the victim is not necessarily consciously participating in the fantasy which spurs the rapist to attack. Moreover, the criteria for attractiveness among these men varied considerably: some preferred older women, finding them more attractive and "sexy," others preferred females much younger than themselves. Others were attracted to women clothed a particular way; for example, one man considered tight pants an "invitation" while another was "turned on" by bare feet.

5. To what extent does the decision to rape include violence?

No clear answer to this question emerges from the data. Despite the extensive use of violence in the sample (see "Victim Resistance and Assailant Reaction"), the frequency of weapon possession (69.9%) and the degree of victim injury, the participants generally claimed that they had not intended to use violence (67.1%). Although only 32.9% acknowledged

their intent to use violence, 91.8% stated they had the intention to rape (i.e., intended to use force to win compliance), and 50.7% claimed they sought dominance, humiliation and/or revenge and 61.6% actually caused injury to their victims. On the basis of these data, it appears that *the decision to rape did include violence.* However, it is not possible to ascertain the exact extent to which violence was anticipated during the decision-making stage.

6. In the assailant's perception, is the amount of violence used influenced by the victim? If so, to what exent? What are the contributing factors?

The answer to the first part of the question is "Yes, sometimes," but a range of elements contributed. The assailants frequently became frightened during their rape attacks: *30.1% acknowledged getting scared after they had initiated the assault,* particularly when victims attempted to resist and especially when the victims screamed. Typically, they were afraid of getting caught.

Sometimes assailants instigated passive victims to resist by threatening to kill the victim even though she was complying. When the victim began to cry or plead for her life, the assailant then reacted violently. Often these men indicated their sense of accomplishment during the attack depended on their dominance of the victim, so they needed some form of resistance. Others saw ready compliance on the part of their victims as usurpation of the rapists' control of the situation—a control they needed before they could consummate the act of rape. For example, 27.4% reported becoming excited when the victim resisted their attacks. One participant stated:

> I hit her because I wanted to hit her—to let her know I was in command . . . Her responses weren't making me feel as good as I wanted to, so I decided to scare her to create this.

The data produced several correlations of varying degrees of significance among the items comprising victim response and the amount of violence used by the assailant.

Assailant Anger correlated with:

Victim influence of the offense (i.e., the assailant's perception that she had "provoked" him).

The victims' subsequent resistance.

Assailant's Use of Physical Force correlated with Victim Resistance.

Intensification of Assailant Anger correlated with:

Victim Resistance during coitus or attempted coitus.

Victim Anger.

Injury to the Victim.

Extreme Violence significantly correlated with Victim Uncooperativeness[11] (low or passive resistance) as interpreted by the assailant during the assault.

The most extreme violence was apparently elicited by resistance during coitus: 40% of the victims resisted during coitus and suffered increased violence as the assailant forced compliance.

7. What factors cause intensification of the degree and type of violence inflicted upon the victim?

This study indicates a great deal of violence, however, the sample bias must be noted: The subject population included only excessively violent rapists, approximately one-half the Atascadero MDSO population. If the excluded population of rapists who were not excessively violent were included, the incidence and degree of violence would have been significantly reduced.

Correlations in the previous sections show that victim resistance (especially screaming, but also physical resistance), feelings of fright on the part of some assailants after they had initiated their assaults, fears of being caught if their victims "blew it" either during the as-

sault or afterwards, victim anger, victim calmness or appearance of control during the attack instead of fright, and sometimes victim passiveness tended to precede an increase and/or an intensification of assailants' violence, ranging from wielding a weapon to actual infliction of injury. In approximately 7% of the cases studied, offenders recalled becoming extremely angry and sometimes more violent when they could not get an erection to consummate the rape.

The study also indicated that the rapes which were motivated by the *desire for revenge* upon certain individual women were often more violent than the others. In what was clearly the most excessively violent of all the sexual assaults described in the study, a 24 year old participant recalled the following experience:

> "I asked her to go to the party . . . she started calling me a son-of-a bitch, etc., and accused me of robbing her house . . . This was five days after I had gotten out of the County Jail . . . I was getting really paranoid as she said she was going to call the police . . . (Later that night around 11:30 p.m.) I saw her standing there in a negligee drinking a beer . . . Then I thought, "This nasty bitch is no good for anything but to be used. I'm going to fix her now so she doesn't screw anybody else."

Armed with a butcher knife, this offender entered this woman's house, and beat her continuously until daylight, dragging her all over the house, kicking her repeatedly, cutting her (she sustained several lacerations in her vagina), and eventually stabbing her through one hand to the floor. He left her thinking he had killed her.

Typically, participants said they increased their violence when their expectations for the rape were not being met by the victim; 68.5% wanted their victims to comply with their expectations.

8. How does the assailant respond to victim resistance?

---

[11] Extreme Violence and Uncooperativeness (low resistance) were both new variables generated by factor analysis.

The responses of assailants to victim resistance in this study showed some variation (see Figure 2). A large percentage (54.8%) reported getting more violent, sometimes losing control. Often the response was anger (47.9%). On the other hand, 34.2% felt powerful, dominant or good; 30.1% felt scared; and 27.4% felt excited.[12]

The data analysis with respect to the variables constituting this question were:

Victim Resistance during coitus or attempted coitus correlated with Assailant Getting Scared.

Victim Screaming correlated with Assailant Getting Scared;

Victim's Physical Resistance (Fought) correlated with Assailant Getting Angry;

Victim Anger correlated with Assailant Getting Angry;

Victim's Resistance correlated with Assailant getting *Angrier*.

The data analysis at this stage also revealed a very important correlation: *Extreme Violence correlated significantly with Deterrence*. Victim resistance was also related to intensification of violence. What the correlation suggests is that despite the precipitation of anger and increased violence manifested by some rapists during an assault, rape can still be deterred in some instances.

In three particular rape incidents where the men were armed (two with guns, one with a knife), the victims succeeded in deterring the rape without incurring any injury. In each case they remained quite calm, persistently resisting the attack by verbal objection and simultaneously attempting to persuade the assailant to put the weapon away. The offenders reported that they became extremely scared when they realized that they had not succeeded in intimidating their victims. In one of the incidents, the woman over-powered the rapist and grabbed the gun, then made him

leave her house. In the second, the woman struggled physically while verbally questioning her attacker about what he was trying to do, until she eventually wrested the knife from him. In the third case, the woman complied with her assailant's demands while she persuaded him to put his shotgun away. When the gun was safely out of sight, she grabbed her clothing and fled. It is important to note, however, that two of these attacks involved people who knew each other before the incident although there had been no sexual relationship between them.

9. How does the assailant account for his rape and other sexual assaults?

The respondents provided a wide variety of answers to this question, many of which sounded rather "cliche," probably due to the offenders' exposure to psychiatric and psychological theories about sexual assault. One offender who wanted his victim to "enjoy the sexual intercourse more" complained about the "John Waynism" in men in this society and the over-emphasis upon competition that characterized the male role in American society. He added that he turned to sexual crimes after his return from Vietnam: his experience in Vietnam left him with an emptiness which he felt motivated his commission of rape.

A number of other respondents attributed their crimes to their lack of trust and social relationships which, they claimed, would have provided them with a "sounding board" for articulation of fantasies and social and psychological problems. A few mentioned their emotional make-up and personal needs (e.g., the need to feel powerful) as contributing influence to their commission of rape.

Overall, however, the offenders profiled themselves as losers. Underlying almost all the factors they cited as motivating their crimes was a general feeling of inadequacy which they attributed to a number of sources: rejection by women, lack of self-confidence, poor self-concept, lack of affection from anyone, lack of control over their lives, etc. *Not one participant in*

---

[12] Percentages overlap because of multiple answers—many offenders had mixed reactions.

the study referred to the lack of a sexual outlet as a reason for the crime. This supports the hypothesis that sexual intercourse is only a secondary concern of the rapists.

*

PEEPING TOM RAPISTS

Peeping Toms are generally considered harmless men who achieve sexual gratification by surreptitiously watching women (frequently scantily dressed or undressing) in their homes. In short, Peeping is seen as an end in itself. Our data, although very limited with respect to Peeping Tom cases, suggested otherwise. Seven rapists in the research sample reported "doing some Peeping Tom stuff" prior to their rapes. In the particular incidents discussed in the interviews, peeping preceeded the sexual assault, and in all cases the rape was completed.

Five of the seven Peeping Toms were single, one was married, and one was separated. They ranged in age from 19 to 30 years. Six were 24 years old or under. Some of the more outstanding characteristics of their assaults are as follows:

6 had rape as their aim; 1 said he had sex in mind, later stating he knew it had to be forcible.

6 were armed with weapons (one had a gun; the others had knives, meat forks, etc.) The 7th—a 20 year old—raped an 86 year old woman using considerable physical force as she put up a vigorous struggle.

5 of the 6 who were armed said they did not usually carry weapons. Only 1 said he usually carried a weapon.

6 said they did not have a particular victim in mind that day, but that they selected their victims after watching them through their windows and assessing the victim's vulnerability as well as the "safety" of the attack (i.e., from discovery). The 7th offender said he had raped his victim before and was passing her house on this particular day watching. He saw the woman naked through her window, and soon after, he entered her house by cutting a hole through a bathroom window screen.

All 7 claimed they did not intend to use violence that day, but 6 of them were armed, and the weapons were used in every case to intimidate victims. The victims in three of the incidents received serious injury as a result of physical force on the part of the assailant: two were choked with considerable force, one was choked and knocked unconscious, and another was gagged with a towel.

6 broke into the victim's house by climbing through unlocked windows or entering through unlocked doors. Only one offender said that he entered the victom's house by first knocking and speaking to his victim. He pushed his way through the partially opened door after he discovered that the woman was unmarried and alone.

3 of these offenders said that they returned to their victim's house after their rapes to rape her again, but only one was successful. One changed his mind after he heard "shuffling" when he partially opened an unlocked window; he thought there was a man this time in the victim's apartment. The other did not get an answer when he knocked on the victim's door and her lights were off, so he thought she was not at home.

While the offenders in these rape incidents were watching their victims prior to the attack, the victims seemed to have been totally unaware of the potential attacker until the first interaction. And according to the offenders, the women were terrified when they were attacked. Faced with weapons at their throats or backs, none of them resisted physically. Four attempted to resist verbally, e.g., shouting, "Get out! Who are you?," "What are you doing here?," etc. Two victims screamed loudly. In one of these cases the assailant stuffed a towel into the victim's mouth gagging her, then knocked her unconscious—"because she was taking away my control of the situation." In the other case—that with the 86 year old woman—the offender stated that the victim hollered throughout the attack. This did not deter him (he completed the rape in about five minutes), but when he was leaving he saw several neighbors arriving at the house, responding to the victim's cries.

Unlike the majority of the other rape attacks, the Peeping Tom rapes were completed in 30 minutes or less, frequently in less than 15 minutes. All the victims were strangers to these offenders. It is important to note too that these rape attacks were extremely violent. For example, despite victim's entreaties and lack of vigorous physical resistance, the offenders showed no pity or consideration. One offender bluntly stated: "The first 30 seconds was the payoff. *I had the power to make her do anything.*" Another stated that although his victim was crying, "I didn't have any feelings at the time. We were just two pieces of meat." He knocked her unconscious before he left her apartment.

Significant in the Peeping Tom rapes is the *planning of the attack*, which in turn, seems to increase the probability that the rape attack will be completed. Typically, the Peeping Tom rapists watched their victims for a while (between 5 to 30 minutes). One of the men said that he was feeling very destructive that night, so he took a butcher knife and proceeded to slash cars. After this, he thought "about doing some Peeping Tom stuff," went to a nearby apartment building "to look for women," and caught sight of a woman through an open window. He observed her for a while, decided to rape her, and entered her house through an unlocked front door. The woman yelled when she saw him, but he showed her his knife and ordered her to follow him as he held the knife at her back. He added

> She was scared and quiet. She walked ahead, and I got sexually excited watching her. I felt her

bottom. She gave me a scathing look and said, "Is that all you want?" That made me feel small and angry with her. I cowered at first, but then put on my tough act. Suddenly, a car came by. I ran to hide, leaving her behind. I yelled for her to follow me, and she did. From then on, things changed. I felt she liked me . . . I also had the power back. She obeyed me.

This offender raped the woman soon after, and returned the next day to take her out. He also said that he planned another rape after this one. He was surprised to learn from the police that the victim in the previous rape incident had reported him.

In many ways, these seven offenders did not differ greatly from the other offenders. Nonetheless, there was a certain consistency in their mode of attack which usually began with peeping. These characteristics suggest that we should begin to re-examine the Peeping Tom phenomenon more critically. It might be, as was clearly the case in our sample, that sexual offenders who "peep" might not be as harmless and humorous as is often assumed. Rather, peeping might be the initial stage in a chain of events that lead to a rape attack. Their possession of weapons coupled with their expressed desire to dominate and control their victims (although not necessarily to inflict injury) was indicative of more than simple visual enjoyment.

A similar connection between exhibitionism and rape has been observed by the research staff at the Rape Crisis Center in Pueblo, Colorado. They are finding, at least tentatively, that a few of the rapists in their sample exposed themselves (exhibitionism), then proceeded to make contact with women immediately, or hid and attacked them shortly thereafter. We must note that these possibilities are being suggested only as tentative relationships. Further investigation is necessary.

29

RAPISTS TALK*

LYNDA LYTLE HOLMSTROM AND ANN WOLBERT BURGESS

Game theory has traditionally been used for analyzing zero-sum conflict situations. More recently game-theoretic frameworks have been generalized to analyze social situations "in which two or more persons or groups are in communication with one another and are engaged in goal-directed action" (Lyman and Scott, 1970:29). One can apply Lyman and Scott's categories of games to rape and see that several games are occurring simultaneously. The primary one is an "exploitation game." Secondarily, there may be a "face game," an "information game" or a "relationship game."

"Exploitation games occur on the brink of power relationships; that is, one actor hopes to obtain "imperative control" over another but it not absolutely sure he can do so" (Lyman and Scott, 1970:54). Lyman and Scott, as well as the authors of the present paper, utilize the Weberian definition of power; that is, "the probability that one actor within a social relationship will be in a position to carry out his own will despite resistance, regardless of the basis on which this probability rests" (Weber, 1947:152).

Source: "Rapists' Talk: Linguistic Strategies to Control the Victim," *Deviant Behavior* (October–December 1979) 1(1): 101–125. Copyright © 1979 by Hemisphere Publishing Corporation. Reprinted with permission.

* Revised version of a paper presented at the 9th World Congress of Sociology, Socio-linguistics Research Committee Program, Uppsala, Sweden, August, 1978.

The stereotype of the rapist's attack is that he attains power and control over his victim through strategies based on physical force. The present study shows that not only do rapists use physically based strategies, but they use a second set of strategies based on language. These linguistic strategies are the focus in the present paper. An analysis of the victim's linguistic coping strategies has been presented in a prior paper (Burgess and Holmstrom, 1976).

METHOD

This paper reports a subpart of a larger study investigating issues such as what occurs during the rape event, what problems victims experience in the aftermath of rape, and how institutions (police, hospital, court) react to rape victims.

SAMPLE

The sample for this paper consists of the 115 adult, adolescent, and child rape victims that arrived during one year at the emergency wards of a large municipal hospital. The sample is very heterogeneous and crosses the lines of class, race, religion, marital status, employment, and age. This variety is due to police protocol in crime victim cases (the police select which hospital to use) and to the hospital's location. The facility is situated near some of the poorer communities of the city, but colleges and universities also are located in its catchment area for crime-related emergencies.

DATA COLLECTION

The study in its entirety relied most heavily on in-depth interviews and participant observation, supplemented by other methods. Hospital staff telephoned us each time a sexual assault victim was admitted. Upon notification, we immediately went to the hospital to gather data—many times late at night or the early morning hours. Our typical practice was to have both authors present at the initial interview. Frequently one interviewed, while the other took notes that were as verbatim as possible. We did weekly follow-up interviews during the early postrape period and we gathered participant-observation data at the courthouse in cases that went to court.

A detailed report of the methods used has already been published (Holmstrom and Burgess, 1978a:5–29). Perhaps most important for this paper is to note that in interviewing we used flexible, open-ended interview guides and that the same list of general questions was asked of each victim. Early in the interview the victim often gave her own account of what happened. In telling this, the victim often included information on what the rapist said and what she said. In addition, we specifically asked what conversation occurred.

METHOD: ADVANTAGES AND DISADVANTAGES

A major methodological advantage is that the sample provides data primarily on *non*convicted rapists—a group seldom subjected to study. Of the 115 cases in the present study, only nine cases resulted in a conviction for rape (adult victim) or for abuse of a female child (victim under 16). The existing research literature on rapists, in contrast, is based primarily on data obtained from institutionalized rapists.

The main methodological drawback is that the data on what rapists say come from victims. The material is secondhand. There does not seem to be any way to get completely out of this difficulty. Rape is not something that researchers can witness firsthand. And only a small percentage of rapists are convicted and thus accessible to researchers. There are some partial ways out of the dilemma. One is to ask victims if the words they are reporting are their own or the same words the rapist used, and then to specifically request that they report the latter. Another is to compare the data on rapists' talk obtained from victims with that obtained from convicted rapists (Chappell and James, 1976). Undoubtedly, the data from victims are more accurate regarding themes of talk (which is what is analyzed in this paper) than they are regarding more technical aspects of language such as precise choice of words or intonation patterns.

FINDINGS

THE OCCURRENCE OF RAPISTS' TALK

Rapists' talk is a salient feature of the attack. In analyzing what victims reported that rapists said, 11 major themes emerged (see Table 1). What these themes have in common is that they each constitute a strategy for exercising power over the victim, either before, during, or after the rape.

Rapists' talk is a frequent component at the attack. In 115 reported rape cases, 102 victims stated that the rapist said something to them. In only five cases did the victim report an absence of talk by the rapist. In two of these five the victim was unconscious during the attack—one because she was immediately strangled from behind, the other from intoxication. (In the remaining eight cases, there was no data on the issue.)

GAINING ACCESS: INITIAL CONTROL OF THE VICTIM

The rapist's first goal is a pragmatic one. He must obtain a victim and get her sufficiently under his control so that he can then rape her. Among reported rapes, are two main styles of attack that we have called "blitz" and "confidence" (Burgess and Holmstrom, 1974b:4–11).

TABLE 1 Rapists' Talk: Linguistic Strategies to Control the Victim Before, During and After Rape

Threats	75
Orders	68
Confidence line	39
Personal inquiries of victim	28
Personal revelations by rapist	21
Obscene names and racial epithets	20
Victim's sexual "enjoyment"	19
Soft-sell departure (apologies, safe-return, socializing)	19
Sexual put-downs	9
Possession of women	6
Taking property from another male	5

The blitz rape is a sudden attack in which the rapist confronts the victim out of the blue. There is no preliminary interaction or warning. The emphasis is on physically based strategies. For example, the rapist may grab a woman walking on the street and shove her into a car. His physical action may be reinforced by verbal means. In the confidence rape, the emphasis is on linguistically based strategies. The rapist gains access by winning the confidence of the victim and then betraying it. His "line" may be supplemented by physically maneuvering the victim into a position or place from which it is difficult to escape.

Two main styles of linguistic strategies occur at the point in time when the rapist is trying to obtain a victim. One is that of threats and orders, the other the confidence line.

Threats and Orders. The linguistic strategies of threats and orders can occur in either blitz or confidence styles of attack. In the blitz, they support the rapist's quick physical action and may appear very early in the interaction. In the confidence style they do not surface until after the victim's confidence has been attained and betrayed. The switch to threats and orders may happen quickly or it may occur after extensive conversation.

The threats and orders, in either style of attack, typically tell the victim to cooperate or be hurt or killed. Victims reported being told, "If you resist, you're a dead woman," "I'll kill you

if you don't do it," "Do what I say or your kids will get it," "If you don't do what I say I'll kill you and lay you next to my [dead] mother," and "Fuck me good or I'll kill you." A 23-year-old virgin who became the victim of a blitz rape reported receiving these threats at the beginning and throughout the event:

> I've raped three other women and killed them and that's what's going to happen to you. (waving knife at her) Undress. If you don't hurry, I'll kill you. If you're not quiet I'll kill you. (poking knife at her nose and eyes) Maybe I'll take off your nose too. I'll cut them out. . . . (after raping her and seeing blood on her thighs) Don't worry, When I get through with you you'll be bloody all over. . . . (later) I have a gun. I'll shoot you or anyone who tries to help you. . . . (later) Suck it, suck it. If you don't get it up, I'll kill you.

A 17-year old victim of a confidence rape reported receiving the following threats after she and her date had been lured to an apartment by a confidence line:

> You're going to have to do me a favor. We're doing you a favor giving you a place to stay. (rapist was cleaning his toes with a knife) Look out the window. (victim looked and saw at least 10 males) They're all junkies. All I'd have to do is call them and they'd rape you and rob you and kill you.

Some threats focus on embarrassing the victim. One was told, "What would your mother say if you came home with no clothes?" Another reported, "They said they would tell my family and spread a rumor that I had a bad reputation unless I did it for them. They said, 'Do you want a bad reputation?'" Threats to harm or embarrass help to gain the submission of the victim. They also set the mood of the encounter—that of it being a frightening experience for most victims (Burgess and Holmstrom, 1974a:983).

The Confidence Line. The confidence-line strategy can be used with victims known to the rapist or with strangers. If he already knows the victim, his conversation builds on this existing relationship. If the victim is a stranger, he uses a conversation to gain trust. This talk creates an image of normalcy and everyday experience that belies what is to follow.

The confidence rapist has the task of maneuvering the victim to where he wants her or maneuvering himself to where she is (e.g., in the front door of her home). To accomplish these maneuvers, rapists trade on social conventions and everyday activities and expectations. Rapists *offer assistance* ("Do you want a ride [home]?" and "I'll go with you to [find your husband]—I know where he hangs out"); *request assistance* ("Honey, can we use your phone?" and "I need a ride home"); *promise social activities* ("Want to come to my place and talk and listen to the stereo?" "Let's go over [to the building]—we can play pool"); *promise information* ("I want to tell you something," "I have some information about your TV sets [that were stolen yesterday]"); *promise material items such as alcohol or drugs* ("We'll go to the house to get the papers [to roll the marijuana]"); *promise the possibility of employment and discuss business transactions* ("I need someone to do some line drawings"); *request her company while completing a task* ("Why don't you come on up while I put the groceries away?" "Come with me while I get my coat"); *refer to someone she knows or who might be there* ("I want to talk to you . . . about your "brother's situation," " "Is your old man home?"); and *trade on social pleasantries and niceties* ("I'm leaving town, I want to say good-by"). Sometimes the rapist's accomplice provides the con line. For example, one victim was persuaded to go to a house by two girls who said, "We know a good place to go—there'll be a party."

A small minority of con lines were elaborate. One victim who knew her assailant reported the following elaborate set-up.

Jessica was an art student and had met the rapist two weeks earlier at school. He told her he was a commercial artist and that he needed someone to do some line drawings for a job that he was working on. They arranged to meet and go to a studio, but when they arrived there it was closed. There was a note left about a package having been sent to his apartment. They went to the apartment to get the package. He opened it, revealing a pair of pink panties, a white lace robe, and two blue blouses. He said he wanted to show her the work to be done and that the light was better in the bedroom. They went into the bedroom and she sat on the floor and looked at several pictures of fireplaces which is what she would be drawing if she took the job. He then asked her if she had ever done any modeling and she said no. He said that the clothes that he had gotten in the package that morning were things that he was using for a job and if she would model them for him he wouldn't have to go out and hire someone. She refused, but after some further talk she finally agreed to model the clothes. He took several pictures of her in various combinations of the clothes and then left the room. She started to get dressed. He suddenly came back in the room and raped her.

Another victim whose assailants were strangers reported the following lengthy set-up:

It was about 8:00 p.m. Molly and David, her date, were on the Common. Two men who looked to be in their twenties approached them and asked if they wished to buy some pot. Molly and David said no. The men asked if they wished to smoke some and they again refused. The men, however, continued to talk with them. It was a pleasant and enjoyable conversation. Then one of the men asked what they were doing on the Common. Molly explained that they were waiting for a ride to go to a hotel to sleep. One of the men said they could sleep at his sister's—she had a spare room. Molly thought that was strange of them to say, but David didn't think it was, so they decided to go with the men. All four left to go to "the sister's place." Once in the apartment, the men locked the door. They talked about various things. The men, for example, asked Molly and David if they were a common-law couple. Molly and David decided to go along with that idea and said that they were. One of the men said he wanted to talk with David in another room. He asked David if he minded if he had sex with Molly.

At this point the conversation shifted to the need to repay favors and to the threats, quoted earlier, about junkies being outside the window. The men, joined by a third assailant, raped Molly and forced David to watch (Holmstrom and Burgess, 1978b:6). These assailants, incidentally, had a practice of also bringing neighborhood girls to the apartment and raping them (Burgess and Holmstrom, 1978:64–66).

The con lines of the rapists almost always sounded very ordinary. Their everyday quality is what makes them so effective. They sound credible at the time and do not arouse the victims' suspicions. Even the small percentage of lines that with hindsight look a bit far-fetched seem credible in the context in which they occur. This everyday quality is confirmed by data collected from convicted rapists committed to a maximum security mental institution (Chappell and James, 1976:16, 19). Rapists reported that, to get a victim to open a door, they said they were looking for a friend, needed to use the telephone, were undertaking a survey, making repairs, making a delivery, or making an inspection. To get a victim to go elsewhere the most common ruse was offering her a ride. Other gambit reported were "offers of amusement, assistance, money, food, alcohol, and drugs."

RAPING: SEXUAL CONTROL OF THE VICTIM

Contemporary researchers stress the violent nature of rape and see it as expressing power, conquest, aggression, anger, degradation, hatred, and contempt (Bart, 1975; Brownmiller, 1975; Burgess and Holmstrom, 1974a, 1974b; Cohen, Garofalo, Boucher, and Seghorn, 1971; Davis, 1968; Gelles, 1977; Griffin, 1971; Hilberman, 1976; Metzger, 1976; Russell, 1975; Schwendinger and Schwendinger, 1974). Rapists' goals on the social-psychological, motivational level are to demonstrate their power over the victim and to vent their anger at the victim. Sexuality is a component, but not the dominant factor (Groth, Burgess, and Holmstrom, 1977). The rapist's power and anger may be directed at the individual victim, at the male perceived to own her, or at the group she is perceived to represent. Rapists' goals in pair

and group rape may also include impressing their fellow rapists. Linguistic strategies are one type of means used to achieve these goals.

Threats. Threats may continue throughout the rape. The threats may escalate from those than seem designed primarily to gain the physical control of the victim to threats primarily to torment and terrify the victim. Following is a case in which the setting, the language, and the actions of the rapist, including the use of props, combined to maximize terror:

> Beth was walking back to her college dorm when a man grabbed her, threatened her with a knife, and forced her into a car. He went out on the highway which scared her. She thought, "This is the end." He took her to the woods and raped her there, holding a knife to her all the time. She was convinced as they went into the woods, that he was going to kill her. She kept thinking, "Well, good-by, this was nice being [in this world], but good-by now." Beth also reported, "He kept passing the knife back and forth and saying open your legs. He said he might take the knife and put it up me and cut me up inside. He said he might cut off my tits."

Orders. Orders may occur not only before but during the rape. They serve various functions. On the pragmatic level, orders often get the victim to do what the rapist wants. On the symbolic level, orders show both victim and rapist who has the power, who is in control. The rapist tells her to stop the behavior she is engaged in and do instead what he wants her to do.

The two most common types of orders are telling the victim to be quiet or unseen and telling the victim what to do sexually. Rapists tell victims "Shut up," "Be quiet," and "Keep your mouth shut." A quiet victim makes it easier to escape detection, as well as demonstrating who is in charge. Sometimes orders are given to avoid being seen ("Turn the light off," "Have your son go to bed. [victim protests] I *said*, have your son go to bed!" and "Put down the shades"). Sometimes an especially insulting twist is given to the order. A victim for example reported, "He told me not to scream. He said I wasn't justified in screaming."

Rapists order the victim about sexually. Victims reported being told "Blow me," "Fuck me good," "Open your legs," "Rub my dick," "Give us some head," and "Kiss me like you kiss your husband."

Also common are orders to remove clothing ("Well, what are you waiting for—take off your clothes") and to go somewhere ("Sit on the bed. [victim sits on chair] No, I said on the bed").

In a few cases victims were told to go to the bathroom and clean themselves ("Go wash yourself out"). In one unusual case the victim was given orders, after the last assailant had finished, to clean up the room and remake the bed. Thus as a final act of humiliation, she was ordered to pick up the mess made by her assailants.

The Victim's Sexual "Enjoyment." Whether rapists really believe that their victims enjoy the sex act with them is a controversial issue. Research suggests that one type of rapist acts under the illusion that his sexual prowess is so great that he greatly satisfies an initially protesting victim. Cohen et al. (1971:318) describe this type of rapist, noting that the rapist first repeatedly lives through the scene in fantasy:

> In the fantasy, the woman he attacks first protests and then submits, more resignedly than willingly. During the sexual act, he performs with great skill, and she receives such intense pleasure that she falls in love with him and pleads with him to return.

One difference from common adolescent fantasies is that the rapist acts out the fantasy again and again. Geis (1977:29) is more skeptical about the rapist's perception of the victim's enjoyment:

> Perhaps, as reports almost uniformly suggest, offenders believe that their victims like being forcibly raped. The fact that some rapists request testaments of their sexual skills from their victims

and that others attempt to make future appointments with them supports this idea. But we believe that for many, perhaps most, rapists there is a clear appreciation that their victims hate what is happening to them and that this is an important element of the behavior.

These two statements are not contradictory if one believes that not all rapists rape for the same reason—that the victim's "enjoyment" is important for some, but not for others.

Inquiries and statements by rapists about the victim's "enjoyment" occurred in our sample. Our interpretation is that at least some of these rapists do believe that the victim wants and enjoys the attack. The rape of a 17-year-old virgin by the man she dated over the summer is a case in point. She reported:

> I think he thought he was doing right. He sounded as though he thought I wanted it. It wasn't that way at all. . . . He even had the nerve to say to me after he did it that I should be glad he did it. . . . Something else that bothered me— when he was all through, I guess he was all through because the pain was gone and he was laying there but still on top of me he said, "It feels good to you doesn't it?" I just could not stand it and I told him to please just get off of me.

Other victims reported, "He wanted me to say I was enjoying it, I was supposed to moan for him" and, "He said, 'Don't you want me to come in you?' " In another case the rapist inquired repeatedly whether it felt the way it felt when she was with her husband. A few victims reported that the rapist wanted to see them another time. One victim said, "He kept wanting to know if it felt good and I had to say yes to keep him happy. . . . He also wanted to know if he could come and do it again."

Some cases are more difficult to interpret. It is not clear if the rapist is actually inquiring about the victim's enjoyment or whether the rapist knows the victim hates the experience and he is taunting her with comments about enjoyment. In one case, for example, the two rapists kept saying "Now this isn't really bad for you, is it? Aren't you enjoying it?" In context, this question seemed to be a taunt rather than a serious inquiry.

For victims who reply there is the added dimension that they were forced to talk against their will. One victim explained her reaction as follows:

> They asked if I liked it. I had to keep saying I liked it. I went along with it. I hope I didn't give them the idea that women would actually like such a thing, but I had to think of myself. I just wanted to get out of there so I pretended I liked it.

Victims, if they reply, answer in the affirmative. Thus they are coerced into saying they enjoyed what was one of the worst experiences of their lives.

Obscene Names, Dirty Sex, and Racial Epithets. Rape is seen as an act of humiliation (Hilberman, 1976:ix). One strategy to humiliate is to hurl insulting names and terms at a person. In the case of rape, these seem to consist primarily of sexual and racial epithets.

The cultural view of females divides them into madonnas and whores (Holmstrom and Burgess, 1978a:177), dutiful housewife-mothers and erotic lovers (Bullough, 1974:49), Virgin Marys and tempting Eves (Chafetz, 1974:39). Russell (1975:25) states, "[A female's] loss of virginity, particularly at a young age, can evoke in males a 'no holds barred' approach. The girls becomes a whore, and only a sucker would treat a whore well. Because a whore is seen as 'bad,' conscience can be suspended." Groth and Cohen (1976:233) note that the dichotomized view of women is especially pronounced among convicted rapists they have studied. In some gang rapes, the fact that the woman submits sexually to all the males (albeit under duress) confirms the offenders' view of her as a whore (Groth, 1978). There is also a cultural ambivalence about sex, with themes that include both its desirability and its dirtiness. With this cultural background, it is not surprising to find that rapists' talk often includes calling victims dirty sexual names.

The assailant came to the apartment of a family he had known for years. They were friends and the family had helped him at times—gotten him jobs, loaned him a car. The husband was away, but the wife and a teenage son were home. He came in and they chatted a while. He then beat and raped the wife. He said, "I'll treat you like a whore."

Other victims reported being called "bitch," "white pussy," "white tramp," "mother fucker," "half white nigger bitch," "fucking bitch," "black bitch," and "slut." As some of these quotes illustrate, the cultural ambivalence over women and sex becomes intertwined with the cultural ambivalence over race.

Sexual Put-Downs. Rapists' talk contributes to the humiliation of the victim by sexual put-downs, as well as by orders and dirty names. The rapist may blame the victim for his lack of sexual satisfaction or taunt the victim with accusations of sexual inadequacy. One victim reported, "He said I wasn't worth it, that he didn't get any pleasure from it." Others reported sexual put-downs and taunts such as "You're very cold," "It won't hurt you" (showing his "dick" to the victim), "Are you a prude?" and "You're gay, you're ruining the country."

Nonsexual put-downs were used in two additional cases. One victim was told, "You're kind of dumb, aren't you?" In a homosexual rape, the male victim was ordered to roll a reefer and the rapist taunted him for his inability to do it properly ("Don't you know how to do anything right?").

Rapists laughed at victims in four cases. At least three of these seem to be put-downs (rather than, for example, laughing for some other reason such as nervousness).

Taking Property. Rape is a violent act against the victim. But it can also be perceived as an act against another man's property. The target here is not so much the female victim but the other male to who she is perceived to belong—traditionally her father or her husband. Clark and Lewis (1977:11b), in their discussion of rape laws, state, "From the beginning, rape was perceived as an offence against property, not as an offence against the person on whom the act was perpetrated." A well-known legal analysis states that one "reason for the man's condemnation of rape may be found in the threat to his status from a decrease in the 'value' of his sexual 'possession which would result from forcible violation" (Yale Law Journal, 1952:73). Research both in the United States and abroad shows that men often have negative reactions to girlfriends or wives that are raped. Some American men are sympathetic to their raped wife or girlfriend; others, however, feel that they, not the woman, was the true victim (Holmstrom and Burgess, 1974). Ibo men often feel ambivalent since another male has shared their "property" (Mere, 1974).

Talk about taking another man's woman or female child occurred in five cases in our sample. There is no reason to assume that taking property as a theme would be restricted to group rape or to interracial rape, although the theme does seem especially prominent in accounts of rape *across group boundaries* (Cleaver, 1968:14–15; Fanon, 1968:254–59; Mere, 1974). In our sample, there were four cases where taking property was a particularly salient theme. These four were all multiple-assailant cases and three were interracial rapes. In two, the rape was carried out in the view of the date or boyfriend of the victim. In the case of Molly, the blacks taunted her white date (who had been presented to them as a partner in a common-law couple):

> The black men started joking and said, "I'm in love with Molly. She belongs to me now. David has lost her." They sang soul songs.

In the other case, the four assailants were white and the victim and her boyfriend were Canadian-Indian. The rapists said to the boyfriend:

> We're going to get some of her. (Holding up her underpants and bra) Know what these are? We're going to fuck your girl.

Cleaver (1968:14–15) talks of the black rape of white victims as an insurrectionary act.

> I became a rapist. To refine my technique and *modus operandi*, I started out by practicing on black girls in the ghetto—in the black ghetto where dark and vicious deeds appear not as aberrations or deviations from the norm, but as part of the sufficiency of the Evil of a day—and when I considered myself smooth enough, I crossed the tracks and sought out white prey. . . .
>
> Rape was an insurrectionary act. It delighted me that I was defying and trampling upon the white man's law, upon his system of values, and that I was defiling his women—and this point, I believe, was the most satisfying to me because I was very resentful over the historical fact of how the white man has used the black woman.

The cases in our sample of explicitly "taking property" suggest that many of the dynamics of insulting a male of another race are similar whether the assailants are black or white. Perhaps one can generalize and interpret many interracial rapes and other rapes that cross group boundaries as statements being made against a class or group of people that the rapists define as adversaries (Holmstrom and Burgess, 1978:249). The power and anger issues are directed not merely at the victim but at the group that is perceived as owning the victim.

Possession as Lover, Wife, or Prostitute. Possession of women, as discussed above, is an important issue for many men. In the previous section, the emphasis was on rape as a way to hurt other males by taking their property. The emphasis here is on rape as a way of gaining women for oneself—for one's own use. Having women for themselves was the explicit focus of conversation in six cases. One thing these six cases have in common is that they were all interracial rapes. In each instance, the victim was white and the assailant(s) black. The rapists talked of keeping the victim as lover, wife, or prostitute. The rapist thus would become the lover, husband, or pimp who would control her and control access to her. He would use her for sex and/or money. In one case, the rapist repeatedly referred to the victim as "my woman." In a group rape, one of the four rapists said he wanted to marry the victim and take her back to Africa. In the following case the focus is on prostitution:

> The rape continued through much of the night and it was early morning when the assailants led Molly from the locked apartment. An old black man was walking his dog and one of the assailants said, "Want her for $2?" The man said he was too old for that. One rapist, Clyde, said to Molly, "There could be a lot of money involved here if you would turn tricks for us." Hearing that they were trying to sell her scared her and she managed to start running and duck down an alley and hail a cab.

In contrast, the following case combines lover and prostitute themes.

> He said he wanted me to be his woman. He talked about that over and over. He wanted me to hustle for him on the streets because he was broke. He wanted me to like him. He thought if I stayed there long enough I would. . . . He said he would tie me up and keep me there and that I'd like it. He led me to believe he was going to keep me there. He asked me if I had ever done a trick. I didn't know what he meant and he told me it meant to hustle, to be a prostitute.

In still another case, the victim reported, "[The rapist] said if he ever saw me with another man he would kill me and the man. . . . He kept telling me I'd be all his, no one else's. It would just be me and him." Talk of possession conveys to victims the idea of the rapists' control continuing into the future. For victims, a crucial issue is how long will the control last.

The Information Game: Personal Inquiries.
"Information games arise whenever one actor wishes to uncover information from another who wishes to conceal it. In one sense information games overlap all others because knowledge of others is a prerequisite to social life, and individuals rarely convey openly the kind or amount of knowledge "required' by their fellows" (Lyman and Scott, 1970:58).

Rapists engage in information games. Their strategy of asking personal questions increases the victim's vulnerability. They seek details about the victim's biography, living arrangements, habits, and property. The victim does not necessarily provide the information. But even to be asked is upsetting. Furthermore, rapists sometimes do get victims to reveal information they would rather not.

Rapists ask questions that make the victim more accessible to future attack. Rapists, for example, often ask victims for identifying information—their name, telephone number, address. This is information victims do not wish to reveal since they fear the rapist might return. One victim, however, was so distraught that she revealed identifying information:

> He wanted my address. I felt that if I would convince him that I was being honest he would let me go. [What address did you give?] I told him where I lived, but not the right apartment number.

The revelation she made contributed to her sense of still feeling scared after the rape.

Rapists asked victims also about the "goods" that might be taken: sex and money. These inquiries often asked for very private information, that if provided would contribute to a sense of exposure. Inquiries included "How many guys have you had?" "Are you a virgin?" "Have you ever been touched before?" "Have you ever been eaten before?" and "How much money do you have?" One 13-year old victim was asked the following combination of personal data questions:

> Is this the first time you've ever fucked? . . . What's your name? What's your phone number? . . . Do you have any money?

Rapists also ask about the personal habits of the victim in regard to sex, money, and drugs. The information they obtain may later be used to discredit the victim. They asked, for example, "How much money do you make a night [from prostitution]?" and "Do you smoke grass?" In one case the victim admitted to the rapist that she used mescaline.

Presentation of the Self: Personal Revelations.

As Goffman (1959:4) states, "When an individual appears in the presence of others, there will usually be some reason for him to mobilize his activity so that it will convey an impression to others which it is in his interests to convey." Impressions, he notes, can be created either through verbal or non-verbal communication.

Rapists' talk includes biographical information about themselves. This strategy of biographical revelation helps them gain and maintain control over the victim. Whether the information is "true" is irrelevant. In Goffman's terms, the rapist gives a performance and biographical revelation is one aspect of this performance. From the possible identities rapists could present to be in control they typically present images of "the tough guy," the "dangerous guy," or the "guy deserving of sympathy." The first two impressions play on the victim's fears, the third impression plays on her sympathies.

The "tough" and/or "dangerous" modes included such statements as "He said he was out of jail just a week," "They said they had taken other girls to this place and done it," and "They said they had been in prison, that they were just out." The "sympathy" mode included such statements as "I'm out of work" or "I'm lonely." Some presented multiple identities—for example, a dangerous and a sympathetic (even pathetic) figure. In one case, for example, the 62-year-old victim talked to the rapist in an effort to calm him down and in the course of this lengthy conversation he revealed the following:

> I've stabbed women before, but I don't know if they died . . . . (swabbing her 3/4 inch wound that he had made with a surgeon's scalpel) I stole the scalpel from a hospital where I worked. . . . I worked once at [Central] Hospital and once at [Memorial] Hospital. . . . I know the neigh-

borhood, . . . I was just fired, . . . I don't have many friends because they don't like me doing this.

Another rapist said, "My mother died when I was 11 and I haven't been right since then,"— thus presenting a sympathetic image plus an implication of possible dangerousness.

"Tough" and the "soft-sell" approaches to maintaining power also appear at later stages in the rape event. Either approach may be used to cool the victim out. Either may be used by rapists to influence victims as they decide whether to pursue prosecution of the case.

Whether rapists present "true" information is not the main issue. Nevertheless, it is of interest that in presenting identities some rapists also presented identifying information. Some gave names, and some said where they were from ("I asked them where they went to school and they said [Central] High School," and "He said he was from South Carolina"). In one case, after the rape the rapist walked the girl home, gave her a present, and told her his telephone number and first name. The number and name were sufficient to lead to his identification and arrest; however, the trial verdict was not guilty (Holmstrom and Burgess, 1978a:198). In another case the assailants' strategy also backfired. They bragged to the victim about their prior exploits and the police were able to identify them using that information. One of the assailants was tried and the verdict was guilty of rape.

RAPING WITH OTHERS: MALE CAMARADERIE AND THE MALE AUDIENCE

Researchers have stressed that in multiple-assailant rape it is important to look not only at the rapists as individuals but at the group. They have emphasized the group process, especially how the leader is stimulated by the group (Blanchard, 1959:266), that group rape is not merely a series of single rapes (Lucas, undated), that roles and principles of collective behavior are involved (Geis, 1971:101, 113), and that male camaraderie is a focus of the interaction in group rape (Holmstrom and Burgess, 1978b:10–11).

Impression management in pair and group rape is more complicated because of the multiple audiences. In multiple-assailant rape the rapists talk not only to the victim but to each other. The main audience is the other males, the secondary audience is the victim.

The most common theme of conversation among these rapists concerns taking turns. The taking of turns is not just a pragmatic matter, but a focal point for impression management. Rapists tell each other to hurry up because they want their chance to do it. ("The others stood around and watched and yelled that they wanted their turn"). They urged each other to take a turn ("Get some of it too," and "This is good, you should try it").

Comments about what to do to the victim also were made. One can interpret these several ways. A real debate about what to do may be occurring among the assailants. Or the aim may be to impress the other males with how much one can frighten the victim. In one case the victim reported the assailant beat her date with a belt. Then, she said, "He came in with a belt and said he wanted to beat me. One of the others said, 'She'll be so beat you won't be able to knock her.' " In another case, the victim reported one rapist saying to the others, "Should we keep her all day? Let's do to her what we did to Jackie." In still another case, at least one assailant was taking drugs with a needle. One assailant wanted to inject dope into the victim, but the other assailant said no. They did not do it. In an atypical case, the discussion was whether to rape. One of the robbers said to the robber-rapist, "Why are you bothering with that?"

Identifying names were another component in some conversations. Rapists who were strangers to the victim would sometimes use each other's first names or nicknames. One can interpret such practice as due to carelessness, to a desire to get caught, or, most likely, to a belief that they will not get caught, that one can rape with impunity.

In a few cases, the themes reported were security precautions ("Get her away from here so she can't see the car") and orders to each other ("Take the TV").

DEPARTURE: CONTROL OVER THE VICTIM SQUAWKING

After rape, the rapist must return to the pragmatic goal of departing safely. Having obtained a victim, and raped her, he must now part ways and preferably in a manner that will prevent his arrest. To increase his chances of safe departure, the rapist often engages in what Goffman (1952:455, 462) calls cooling the mark out. He tries to continue to maintain control so that the victim will not raise a squawk. As Goffman notes, there are many procedures for "cooling," including the use or threat of force.

In the present study, rapists' conversation for dealing with the victim after the rape fell into two general types. There was the tough approach and the soft-sell. By definition, the present sample consists of those cases where the rapist's attempt to control disclosure and complaint by the victim was at best only partially successful. All the victims in the study had reported the rape to at least one authority—the hospital—and in some cases also to the police. Threats and soft-sell sympathy appeals did, however, deter some victims in the sample from pursuing prosecution (Holmstrom and Burgess, 1978a:122–23, 152). Many rapes, not located by such a sample, do not get reported at all.

Tough Approach: *Threats and Orders.* Rape is a frightening event for many victims. The terror is reinforced by rapists, orders saying not to tell, not to go the police. Threats frequently are made to injure or kill the victim if the rape is disclosed to others or reported to authorities. Victims reported that rapists said to them "Don't tell anyone or I'll kill you," and "If you go to the police . . . we'll get you when we get out of prison." Some rapists gave orders to increase the time they would have to leave undetected. ("Lie with your head covered for two minutes.")

Soft-Sell: Apologizing, Safe Return, and Socializing.

Rapists sometimes depart discussing themes that may appeal more to victims' sympathies. Some rapists apologize. One victim reported:

> I got up and put my clothes on. He asked if I was hungry, if I wanted to eat. He kept apologizing. . . . He said he was sorry I was so upset.

Another rapist combined the tough and soft-sell departures. The woman was asleep in her bed. He stabbed her in the stomach, then put a blanket over her head and kept it there while raping her. He later said:

> You might have to have a stitch in that [wound]. Do you have any bandaids? . . . I feel bad after I do these things. I feel ashamed. I hate to use the knife, but I just have to do it. . . . Keep the blanket over your head for twenty minutes. I'm leaving quietly. If you take off the blanket I'll finish you.

Another rapist, after the rape, showed the victim literature about Jesus.

Rapists, when departing, may focus on the victim's safe return home. They may offer to give her a ride or walk her back. They may point her in the correct direction. One said afterward, as if nothing had happened, "I'll see you—you know where [the Avenue] is." A black rapist said to a white victim as he left her, "You'll be all right [walking] on the street—both blacks and whites live here." Some rapists not only talk about a safe return, but take action to repair damage they have inflicted; one swabbed a knife wound, another put ice on the victim's bruises.

Conversation after the rape may also serve to normalize the interaction. Socializing makes it seem like nothing out of the ordinary has happened. In one case, after beating and raping a girlfriend on a Saturday afternoon, the rapist talked and played cards with her. He threatened her and told her if she went to the police he would kill her. He also wanted her to go with him to a party that Saturday night. Such conversation and actions may not normalize the interaction for the victim, but it makes the victim's allegation of rape less credible to outsiders. The account she gives sounds to others more like a social occasion and less like a rape. The case just described went to court. The assailant was found guilty of assault and battery and of unnatural acts, but on the rape charge the court found no probable cause. He received a one-year suspended sentence.

CONCLUSION

Rape is a crime of violence and force. By definition it cannot occur unless the rapist actively plays an exploitation game. For that reason, we have been primarily concerned in this paper with the linguistic strategies of the rapist as related to the power aspect of the interaction. The 11 themes discussed each constitute a linguistic strategy to control the victim either before, during, or after the rape. All interactions, however, contain within them a multiplicity of games. The themes in rapists' talk suggest that many rapists simultaneously exploit and attempt to "normalize" or "conventionalize" their exploitation. Rapists, for example, may seek and reveal personal information, request feedback on the adequacy of their sexual behavior, attempt to increase intimacy with the victim, suggest the desirability of a long-term relationship, or socialize with the victim after the rape. These themes of conversation increase the rapists' power over the victim. But they can also be seen as attempts to normalize what (at least from the victim's point of view) is essentially a nonnormal situation. They can be seen as efforts by the rapist to convince the victim, and perhaps himself as well, that what is happening is not so bad. Thus they constitute attempts by the rapist to transform an illegitimate act into a legitimate one.

REFERENCES

Bart, Pauline B. (1975). "Rape Doesn't End with a Kiss." Unpublished manuscript, Dept. of Psychiatry, Abraham Lincoln School of Medicine, Univ. of Illinois, Chicago. Published in abridged version in *Viva*, June 1975.

Blanchard, W. H. (1959). "The Group Process in Gang Rape." *Journal of Social Psychology* **49**:259–66.

Brownmiller, Susan (1975). *Against Our Will: Men, Women and Rape*. New York: Simon and Schuster.

Bullough, Vern L. (1974). *The Subordinate Sex: A History of Attitudes Toward Women*. Baltimore: Penguin Books. (First published 1973, University of Illinois Press.)

Burgess, Ann Wolbert, and Lynda Lytle Holmstrom (1974a). "Rape Trauma Syndrome." *American Journal of Psychiatry* **131** (September):981–86.

——— (1974b). *Rape: Victims of Crisis*. Bowie: Robert J. Brady.

——— (1976.) Coping Behavior of the Rape Victim," *American Journal of Psychiatry* **133** (April):413–18.

——— (1978). "Complicating Factors in Rape: Adolescent Case Illustrations." In Ann Wolbert Burgess, A. Nicholas Groth, Lynda Lytle Holmstrom, and Suzanne M. Sgroi, *Sexual Assault of Children and Adolescents*. Lexington, Mass.: D. C. Heath.

Chafetz, Janet Saltzman (1974). *Masculine/Feminine or Human: An Overview of the Sociology of Sex Roles*. Itasca, Ill.: F. E. Peacock.

Chappel, Duncan, and Jennifer James (1976). "Victim Selection and Apprehension from the Rapist's Perspective: a Preliminary Investigation." Paper presented at the 2nd International Symposium on Victimology. Boston.

Clark, Lorenne M. G., and Debra J. Lewis (1977). *Rape: The Price of Coercive Sexuality*. Toronto: Women's Press.

Cleaver, Eldridge (1968). *Soul on Ice*. New York: Dell, First published by McGraw-Hill.

Cohen, Murray L., Ralph Garofalo, Richard Boucher, and Theoharis Seghorn (1971). "The Psychology of Rapists." *Seminars in Psychiatry* **3**(August):307–27.

Davis, Alan J. (1968). "Sexual Assaults in the Philadelphia Prison System and Sheriff's Vans. *Trans-Action*, (Dec.):8–16.

Fanon, Frantz (1968). *The Wretched of the Earth*. New York: Grove. First published in 1961: Paris, Las damnès de la terre, François Maspero èditeur.

Geis, Gilbert (1971). "Group Sexual Assaults." *Medical Aspects of Human Sexuality* **5** (May):101–113.

———(1977). "Forcible Rape: An Introduction." In Duncan Chappell, Robley Geis, and Gilbert Geis (eds.), *Forcible Rape: The Crime, the Victim, and the Offender*. New York: Columbia University Press.

Gelles, Richard J. (1977). "Power, Sex, and Violence: the Case of Marital Rape," *The Family Coordinator* **26** (Oct.):339–47.

Goffman, Erving (1952). "On Cooling the Mark Out: Some Aspects of Adaptation to Failure." *Psychiatry* **15** (Nov.):451–63.

———(1959). *The Presentation of Self in Everyday Life*. Garden City, N.Y.: Doubleday Anchor.

Griffin, Susan (1971). "Rape: The All-American Crime." *Ramparts* **10** (Sept.):26–35.

Groth, A. Nicholas (1978). Private Communication.

Groth, A. Nicholas, Ann Wolbert Burgess, and Lynda Lytle Holmstrom (1977). "Rape: Power, Anger, and Sexuality." *American Journal of Psychiatry* **134** (Nov.):1239–43.

Groth, A. Nicholas, and Murray L. Cohen (1976). "Aggressive Sexual Offenders: Diagnosis and Treatment." In Ann Wolbert Burgess and Aaron Lazare (eds.), *Community Mental Health: Target Populations*. Englewood Cliffs, N.J.: Prentice-Hall.

Hilberman, Elaine (1976). *The Rape Victim*. Washington, D.C.: American Psychiatric Association.

Holmstrom, Lynda Lytle, and Ann Wolbert Burgess (1974). "Rape: An Indicator of Woman's Family Role." Paper presented at the 8th World Congress of Sociology, Toronto. Revised version, "Rape: the Husband's and Boyfriend's Initial Reactions," to appear in *The Family Coordinator*.

——— (1978a). *The Victim of Rape: Institutional Reactions*. New York: Wiley.

——— (1978b). "Sexual Behavior of Assailant and Victim During Rape." Paper to be presented at the American Sociological Association annual meeting. San Francisco.

Lucas, W. E. (undated). Unpublished communication cited in Gilbert Geis, "Group Sexual Assaults," *Medical Aspects of Human Sexuality* **5** (May): 101–113.

Lyman, Stanford M., and Marvin B. Scott, (1970). *A Sociology of the Absurd*, New York: Appleton-Century-Crofts, Meredith.

Mere, Ada A. (1974). Private communication. Unpublished research, Dept. of Sociology, University of Nigeria, Nsukka, E.C.S., Nigeria.

Metzger, Deena, (1976). "It is always the Woman Who Is Raped." *American Journal of Psychiatry*, **133** (April):405–08.

Russell, Diana E. H. (1975). *The Politics of Rape: The Victim's Perspective*. New York: Stein and Day.

Schwendinger, Julia R., and Herman Schwendinger (1974). "Rape Myths: in Legal, Theoretical, and Everyday Practice." *Crime and Social Justice* **1** (Spring-Summer):18–26.

Weber, Max (1947). *The Theory of Social and Economic Organization*, A. M. Henderson and Talcott Parsons trans. Glencoe: Free Press. Published previously as Wirtschaft und Gessellschaft.

Yale Law Journal, (1952). "Forcible and Statutory Rape: An Exploration of the Operation and Objectives of the Consent Standard." *Yale Law Journal* **62** (Dec.):55–83.

30

GAMES IN PROSTITUTION

MAXINE ATKINSON AND JACQUELINE BOLES

Most research on prostitution has dealt with it either as a form of deviant behavior or as one of the more extreme examples of occupational professionalization. In the first instance, studies typically examine the social causes of prostitution or the personality characteristics of the participants (Barclay and Gallemore, 1972; Chwast, 1971). In the second instance, the focus is on the patterns of recruitment, the socialization process, and the maintenance of occupational norms (Gray, 1973; Winick and Kinsie, 1973; Bryan, 1965). There has been only one major study of the relationship between prostitution and the law (Roby, 1972), and it stressed the relation of arrests for prostitution to changes in the legal code.

Virtually no attention has been directed toward the examination of the complex social relations that exist between prostitutes and the police. This paper is based upon the assumption that the prostitutes and vice officers each relate to their own elite publics, and the relationship between the prostitute and the vice officer is, in part, explained by the differential expectation these publics have of the incumbents of these two occupations. Specifically, this paper is directed toward an examination

of the scripted behavior of prostitutes and vice officers toward their differentiated publics as these two occupational groups cooperate to achieve their differing but interrelated goals.

PROSTITUTION AS AN ECOLOGY OF CONFIDENCE GAMES

Blumberg (1966) has analyzed the scripted activities of defense counselors toward their clients as a confidence game. He discusses the props and backstage behaviors by which the lawyer and court officials connive to produce a courtroom drama that impresses the defendant sufficiently to guarantee fee payment.

Fortune-tellers (Tatro, 1974; Tatro and Boles, 1975) also put on a performance to impress their clients with their ability to both predict the future and manipulate it to their client's benefit. The fortune-teller's monetary success is dependent upon her ability to sell the "mark" her "con."

Prostitutes, like criminal lawyers and fortune-tellers, can be viewed as participating in a confidence game with their customers to further their own monetary purposes. What happens, however, when the game is complicated by the fact that at least one other set of actors, i.e., the police, is engaged in a separate but interrelated confidence game of their own? How do the two games mesh and affect the performances of the respective actors?

Source: Maxine Atkinson and Jacqueline Boles, "Prostitution as an Ecology of Confidence Games: The Scripted Behavior of Prostitutes and Vice Officers." In Clifton D. Bryant (ed.), *Sexual Deviancy in Social Context*. London: New Viewpoints. A Division of Franklin Watts, 1977. Pp. 219–231. Reprinted by permission.

Long (1961:401) point out that communities consist of a multiplicity of institutions whose activities "consist of undirected cooperation . . . each seeking particular goals and in doing so, meshing with others." He uses the analogy of baseball to illustrate the importance of knowledge of the game being played and the social roles of the players to predict behavior in social institutions.

> For certain purposes the individual is a useful way of looking at people; for many others the role-playing member of a particular group is more helpful. Here we deal with the essense of predictability in social affairs. If we know the game being played is baseball and that X is a third baseman, by knowing his position and the game being played we can tell more about X's activities on the field than we could if we examined X as a psychologist or a psychiatrist . . . The behavior of X is not some disembodied rationality but, rather, behavior within an organized group activity that has goals, norms, strategies, and roles that give the field and ground for rationality. Baseball structures the situation. [Long 1961:401–2]

Long contends that the structured activities that he calls games provide a set of strategies and tactics by which the players achieve their ends relative to their general and elite publics who may or may not "know the score." Most importantly, the patterns of cooperation and conflict that characterize the relationships between actors in the community are, in part, determined by the articulation of the different games and the overlap of the relevant publics.

The vice officer, like the prostitute, is engaged in a sophisticated confidence game to convince his superiors and various portions of the general public of the effectiveness of his job performance. The behavior of the prostitute as she pursues her game, however, can discredit the performance of the vice officer in the eyes of his relevant publics.

RESEARCH METHODS

The data for this paper were gathered on the basis of an ongoing research project during an eight-month period, April to December 1975.

We began the initial research by conducting structured interviews with arrested prostitutes in the police station of a large metropolitan city located in the South. During that time, we observed the interactions between prostitutes and vice officers. We also observed vice officers at work in and out of the police station. The officers discussed with us the stragegies that they use to arrest prostitutes, their general attitudes toward prostitutes, and their feeling about the efficacy of their (and the courts') efforts to control prostitution.

Vice officers were observed both in the squadroom and in the hustling bar which they frequented. We have observed and interviewed prostitutes in the police station, strip clubs, massage parlors, and hustling bars,[1] and we have conducted fifteen in-depth interviews with "bar and bath" prostitutes on location.

We gained access to strip clubs through contacts made during a previous study (Boles and Garbin, 1974); however, access to the massage parlors was more difficult. The senior author met the owners of a massage parlor in a public restaurant after being introduced to them by an informant. Later, both authors were allowed unlimited access to the massage parlors and their female employees. The hustling bars were identified by the vice officers who initially accompanied the authors during their off-duty hours. The authors were introduced to the managers of the bars who cooperated by providing their protection and introductions to the prostitutes working out of their bars.

PLAYERS, PUBLICS, AND SCRIPTS

The purposes of vice officers are threefold: to make arrests to fulfill their quotas,[2] to minimize citizen complaints, and to avoid personal danger. Prostitutes wish to make sufficient money to satisfy themselves or their pimps, and to avoid hassles, arrest and personal harm. These various purposes are by no means mutually exclusive; they can be accomplished by the players adhering to the script. Gagnon and Simon (1973:20) define a script as "an organization of mutually shared conventions that allows two or more actors to participate in a complex act involving mutual dependence." Further, they define the three elements of a script as: "to define the situation and the actors and to plot the behavior" (Gagnon and Simon, 1973:19). Thus, the players must be cognizant of the game and the script as it relates to both generalized and elite publics.

Figure 1 represents a schematic diagram of relationships between prostitutes and vice officers and the general public and their elite public. The vice officers in this game have one vital elite public: their superior officers. In order to achieve their two major goals (fulfilling their quotas and minimizing citizen complaints) vice officers must accommodate themselves first to the goals of their superior officers and then to the expectations of the general public. In the process, they must cooperate with and gain the cooperation of prostitutes. Prostitutes, on the other hand, have two primary elite publics: vice officers and johns. In order to fulfill their goals (making money and avoiding hassles and arrests) prostitutes must accommodate themselves to these two elite publics.

The prostitution game is just a small part of the many games being played in this or any other territorial system.

> . . . the players in the one game make use of the players in another and are in turn, made use of by them. Thus, the banker makes use of the newspaper man, the politician, the contractor, the ecclesiastic, the labor leader, the civic leader— all to further his success in the banking game, but reciprocally, he is used to further the others' success in the newspaper, political, contracting, ecclesiastical, labor and civic games. Each is a piece of the chess game. [Long, 1961:403]

We recognize the myriad of games that are played simultaneously in the prostitution game; however, the focus of this paper will be an examination of: 1) the perspective of the prostitute as she adheres to her script in interacting with her two elite publics; and (2) the perspective of the vice officers as they interact

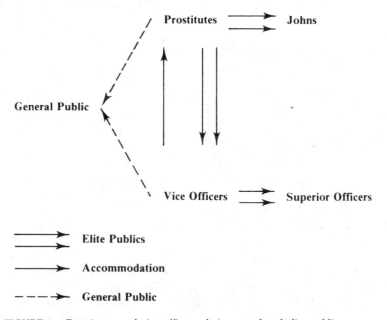

FIGURE 1. Prostitutes and vice officers: their general and elite publics.

with prostitutes to fulfill their goals in relation to their elite public and the general public.

THE PROSTITUTE'S GAME WITH THE JOHN

The costume of the prostitute varies according to her potential client, work place, and the image of herself she wishes to portray. Costumes of bar prostitutes vary from styled jeans to office attire to long gowns. It is important to look both attractive and respectable; a good bar prostitute should not look obvious (in contrast to a streetwalker). Costumes of female employees of massage parlors are more apt to be long seductive gowns chosen to accentuate aspects of their personalities perceived as attractive to customers. For example, three employees of one massage parlor chose black, red, and pink gowns to exemplify respectively seductiveness, passion, and innocence.

The experienced hooker realizes that prostitution is a "head game," and her job is to con the johns. As one prostitute said:

> I make most of my money with what's up here [points to head]. You've got to be able to find out what the trick wants and make him believe that you can and will do whatever he wants. But [she indicates younger and more attractive prostitute] she makes most of her money off her looks. That won't last.

Even a beginner realizes the importance of the con. A young prostitute, her third night on the job, said, "The main thing I've got to learn is street talk. You've got to be able to talk to them and make them think they're worth a hundred dollars. I know I can do it, but I gotta learn what those people want."

The stages of "roping" a trick are: (1) soliciting the customer, (2) establishing his identity, (3) determining his sexual preferences, (4) negotiating the price, and (5) making arrangements for consummation of the act. Bar prostitutes are more subtle than street prostitutes who solicit aggressively and hence raise public outcry which causes both the police and themselves trouble. Certain bars, cocktail lounges, and strip clubs have reputations for being hangouts for prostitutes, so that the customer feels confident that the unescorted girls sitting around the bar are hookers. If he is in doubt, he can always ask the bartender. The girls usually sit demurely at the bar, nursing their drinks. Occasionally, they may smile at a potential customer or give him "the look."

> I catch his eye and hold it for a few seconds. Then I slowly drop my gaze to his zipper. I hold my eyes there for a few seconds and then I slowly raise my gaze again until I meet his eyes again. He usually gets the message.

The customer will then sit down next to the girl; the prostitute must then establish the customer's credentials. Prostitutes know most of the vice officers, but occasionally a new recruit with false identification and a convention badge will enter the club. If any employee sees a known or suspected officer enter the club, he flashes a signal. One strip club, for example, turns on a red light under the bar. If the prostitute is suspicious, she asks the potential john for identification. She questions him: "Where are you staying?" "What convention are you attending?" If she is satisfied, she is then ready to discuss the customer's sexual preferences.

Working in a massage parlor simplifies the roping process.[3] The customer comes into the massage parlor and chooses a date. At one parlor, the girls are required to "decorate" a large window to attract passersby so that the customer's choice may be made prior to entering the establishment. These girls must also establish the identity of the customer. One girl "gooses" her customers around the waist as she says, "Ooh, come on honey, that's a sharp-ass suit." She simultaneously entices the customer and establishes if he is armed.

Learning to identify (smell out) a police officer is a basic part of the socialization of any prostitute. Though each girl may have particular strategies for identifying officers, all prostitutes know that vice officers try too quickly to push her into "naming a price."

Prostitutes are called upon to perform a wide variety of sex acts; bar and massage parlor prostitutes are probably asked to perform fewer marginal sex acts than street hookers; yet all prostitutes must find out what the customer requires because the fee she sets is largely determined by the type of sex act required. Straight sex (genital to genital) and masturbation are the cheapest; every variation increases the cost. The kinkier the act, the more it costs. Prostitutes usually have a bottom line below which they will not go. The experienced prostitute is skilled at negotiating her price upward so that the trick ends up paying more than he intended. As with the fortune-teller and the criminal lawyer, the prostitute must convince the client that she is worth the money he is going to pay. Considering the prices charged, that seemingly would not be an easy task. Girls employed in massage parlors charge a minimum of $25 (not including the cover charge paid to the establishment); whereas, most of the bar prostitutes ask a minimum of $50. Fees of over $100 are not uncommon. Street prices are highly variable.

Once the financial arrangement has been made, the prostitute and the trick conclude the deal; most bar prostitutes operate in and out of cooperating hotels. One strip club not located near a hotel provided bedrooms on the second floor for the convenience of prostitutes and inhouse strippers who turned tricks occasionally. Rooms are chosen for convenience and safety; most prostitutes prefer to use their own rooms for the safety feature. Those girls working in massage parlors have the advantage because the rooms are located on the premises.

The prostitute, like the lawyer and fortune-teller, must put on a performance that will convince the client he has gotten his money's worth. A satisfied customer will not cause trouble, i.e., demand his money back, act violently, complain to the police, or otherwise create a disturbance. Therefore, the prostitute uses her acting skills to conclude the transaction as quickly and satisfactorily as possible. All pros-

titutes develop tricks of the trade which they use to satisfy their customers; the more educated and sophisticated the prostitute, the more reliance on "psychology" and dramatics she places. Perhaps the most common ploy is to flatter the john in regard to his sexual prowess. One hooker reports she habitually uses the line, "Ooh, you're built like a football player." She said, "I've made more money with that line than fifty other prostitutes with one-hundred-pound boob jobs." A black prostitute said she frequently used the line, "Boy, you've got a big dick," because ". . . I'm black and they think that's more of a come on cause they think that all black dudes got dicks this long [indicating a couple of feet in length]" Occasionally, two prostitutes cooperate in conning the trick.

> If the trick is straight [genital sex] and he says he can't come until I do, then I moan and come. If a john wants to see two girls together, then the one with the longer hair goes down on the other one and pretends to come.

THE PROSTITUTE'S GAME WITH THE VICE OFFICER

Prostitutes, in order to accommodate vice officers, provide services that are both extrinsically and intrinsically rewarding to them, thus meeting their own goals of avoiding harrassment and arrest. The prostitute must structure her game so as to convince vice officers that she can provide services that, in turn, help them satisfy their superiors.

Prostitutes counsel and instruct wayward hookers, i.e., those who misbehave by causing trouble which brings them to the attention of the public. Hookers who solicit too aggressively, become offensively drunk, or otherwise cause a disturbance will be counseled by the usually older, wiser, "good" hooker on proper decorum. Often vice officers will ask their hooker friends to counsel with these troublesome young women who are causing citizen complaints.

The prostitute acts as informant. She knows about new girls coming to town, their troublesome habits and, more importantly, their troublesome friends.[4] Prostitutes feel no need to be loyal to others who endanger their precarious positions. As one said, "Some girls deserve to be arrested every night." Another respondent explained that some hookers steal from johns, keep up pimps, neglect their children, fight with other girls, and are too obvious in the way they dress and act. "They'll [the police] treat you right if you watch yourself."

Prostitutes are invaluable sources of information concerning drug traffic and gambling operations. Many lounges, bars, and strip clubs serve as distribution points for drugs. Also prostitutes are part of the night people (Boles and Garbin, 1974), and they meet with their friends at after-hours restaurants and clubs where they hear the latest gossip about the opening of new gambling establishments. Often they will be recruited as sticks (shills) for gambling houses and thus are in position to know the owners of these places. Arson is another crime that prostitutes often have inside information on as clubs and lounges frequently burn.

Prostitutes also offer police officers certain intrinsic rewards. There are only two possible alternate ways of relating to vice officers. Keeping out of their way is one method; it is, however, more satisfactory to be their friend. As was previously mentioned, there are a few hustling bars where prostitutes and vice officers meet as friends. A typical bar scene includes officers and prostitutes sitting around the bar engaging in friendly conversation on topics ranging from a recent football game to the officer's impending divorce. The officers pay no cover charge and are not charged for their drinks. Occasionally, these bars host more elaborate affairs. A group of hookers gave a farewell party for a sergeant on the vice squad who had been transferred to an outlying post.

The friendly prostitute helps the vice officer rationalize his role behavior. Many of the street prostitutes whom the officer arrests attack the officer's motivation. behavior, character, and integrity. The legitimacy of the laws he seeks to enforce are questioned. The morality of hiding in men's toilets, pretending to be johns, or spying on people carrying on their private affairs is discussed in vivid terms. The vice officer must legitimate his behavior to those he arrests as well as to himself, his superiors, and his friends and colleagues. The friendly prostitute supports his rationalizations: "You're just doing your job" or "You don't make these laws; you just enforce them."

This type of conversation leads quite naturally to discussion of the prostitute's role. She will often move the conversation into a discussion of the difficulties of her life which led her into prostitution. Add to that the touching story of her two-year-old whom she "tries to raise right," and the prostitute who is already friendly with the officer protects herself with an age-old con.[5]

Prostitutes provide sexual services for police officers; it is difficult for them to refuse. They are also recruited by vice officers and others to service judges, journalists, and politicians. As one hooker said, "I didn't charge for the [having sex with a state legislator]; that was public relations." Two female broadcasters were fired from a local talk show for quoting a lobbyist to the state legislature as saying, "You can get anything you want out of the state legislature by providing booze, broads, or porno." Attractive stripper-prostitutes are most often recruited to service influential politicians and their friends.

In sum, prostitutes are able to attain one of their primary goals by helping vice officers attain theirs. The good prostitute avoids arrest by providing services for officers: information, friendship, emotional support, and sex.

THE VICE OFFICERS' GAME WITH THE PROSTITUTE

Vice officers, like prostitutes, use costumes: leisure suits, blue jeans, overalls, and mod shirts. Many officers' costumes are highly idiosyncratic; one habitually wore a white fur hat, and another had an earring in one ear. Hairstyles and length, beards, and mustaches are part of the costume. Like prostitutes, officers try to adopt clothing and hairstyles that reflect their personalities. On special assignments officers may be dressed as conventioneers with badges, taxi-cab drivers, or street cleaners. Since officers may dress in whatever fashion will enhance their role performance,[6] they have become more difficult for prostitutes to identify. As one prostitute explained, "You just have to learn to pick them out; it's instinct I guess, It's harder now 'cause they're sneaky," Another said, "It definitely is easier to get arrested, like with the black guys [officers], they look like average dudes."

The strategy most often used by vice officers to apprehend prostitutes is called encouragement.[7] The vice officer poses as a potential john and invites the prostitute to make him an offer. Officers act their roles in bars, lounges, on the street, and in rooming houses and hotel rooms. Hotel rooms are rented by officers, and clothing and personal toiletries are planted so as to make the room look lived in. One conversation we recorded involved two vice officers planning to pose as street cleaners complete with uniforms and truck.

Officers also hide and listen. Two officers spent over three hours hidden under a stoop of a rooming house used by prostitutes. They were able to overhear a prostitute make an offer and thus effect an arrest. There are a variety of laws that can be used to arrest prostitutes other than solicitation. In the city where this research was conducted, there are twenty-two municipal ordinances alone that may be used to arrest prostitutes. Often the officer will arrest one prostitute on as many as three or four separate charges so that he can make several cases out of one arrest. Further, the quality of arrests is also important: the more serious the charge, the better the arrest. It is preferred to make an arrest for committing an illicit sex act than for just solicitation. In order to make an arrest for such an act, the officer must take

the hooker to a room (often his), get undressed, and go through the preliminaries of a sex act just prior to penetration. The male must have an erection for it to be considered a sex act, but if he penetrates, he is participating in the act himself and a case cannot be made.

Vice officers not only arrest prostitutes, they help them. Vice officers drop or reduce changes in exchange for information, help prostitutes' friends in court, provide inside information on the disposition of charges, and help prostitutes solve their personal problems. As Rubenstein (1973:207) reports: "His [the vice officer's] steadiest source of information is what he collects as rent for allowing people to operate without arresting them." A vice officer can be a good friend to a prostitute, in and out of court. In exchange for their friendship and help, vice officers expect cooperation in regulating prostitution and other consensual offenses in the community.

SUMMARY AND CONCLUSIONS

In this paper we have detailed some of the strategies used by prostitutes and vice officers to accommodate and cooperate with each other to maintain prostitution while achieving their own ends. Ideally, an ecological balance is maintained, so that each occupational group can achieve its own goals while only minimally interfering with goal attainment of the other. This system breaks down occasionally; unsocialized prostitutes come into town, raids are called for by the police administrators for their own purposes, a murder occurs which draws the public's attention to prostitution, a crusading reporter does a story on prostitution. However, the ecological balance is soon restored and prostitution flourishes.

The scripted relations between prostitutes and vice officers are part of the myriad of relations between groups that are involved, either directly or tangentially, in prostitution, itself just a small segment of what is called vice. Pimps, procurers, club and lounge owners, bartenders, and drug pushers are only a few of the occupational groups, many of whose members are engaged in prostitution-related activities. Gambling, narcotics, and pornography and other consensual crimes (Kaplan, 1973) operate similarly to prostitution in that members of diverse occupational groups accommodate and cooperate with each other to accomplish their goals while maintaining a smoothly operating system.

Consensual crimes, because of the nature of their organizational structure, are particularly sensitive to changes in the external environment, i.e., new laws, police commissioners, or police practices. These changes in the external environment cause readjustment throughout the system as it seeks to accommodate itself to the new situation. Newman and others have argued that police practices in relation to consensual crimes appear highly unpredictable, erratic, and idiosyncratic because they are sensitive to "pressures from both within and without the police department" (Newman, 1975:160).

We know very little about the relationships between "external pressures," and police practices and the responses of prostitutes, gamblers, pornographers, or other players whose scripts must be altered to meet these new conditions.

> It is difficult to identify these pressures and to measure their significance in relation to current police practices. The police seldom explain why they concentrate their detection efforts in one direction rather than another. As a consequence, this aspect of current criminal justice administration is little understood. [Newman, 1975:160]

Research on the linkages between changes in the external environment, police practices, and consensual crimes would further our understandings of a variety of problems including changes in arrest rates for consensual crimes, the social organization of various forms of vice, and the decision-making processes among vice officers.

NOTES

1. A hustling bar is a cocktail lounge that operates almost exclusively for the purposes of providing a meeting place for bar prostitutes and potential customers.

2. The establishment of production norms (or quotas) by work groups is well documented by studies of police officers as well as other occupational groups (Petersen, 1971; Rubenstein, 1973). The vice officers we observed operated with an informal quota system based upon a variety of factors: quality of cases versus quantity, informal work norms established by officers within the squad, and pressures for arrests from superiors outside the squad.

3. There are at least four types of massage parlors (Byrant and Palmer, 1975) characterized by differing modes of payment and services rendered. In the parlors we observed, the owners collected a fee from clients for the use of the premises; this fee included shower, sauna, and massage. Any other sexual services were contracted between the client and the female attendant.

4. The association of prostitutes with other criminals, often either gamblers or thieves, has been often documented (Chambliss, 1972; Jackson, 1972).

5. Hirschi (1962) points out how the prostitutes used "atrocity" stories or hard-luck stores in conning customers.

6. Vice officers have been allowed complete freedom of dress only since August, 1974.

7. "Encouragement is a word used to describe the activity of the policeman or police agent (a) who acts as a victim, (b) who intends by his action to encourage a suspect to commit a crime, (c) who actually communicates this encouragement to the suspect, and (d) who has thereby some influence upon the commission of the crime (Newman 1975:161)."

REFERENCES

Barclary, Kathryn, and Gallemore, Johnny L. (1972). "The Family of the Prostitute." *Corrective Psychiqtry and the Journal of Social Therapy,* **18** (4):10–16.

Blumberg, Abraham (1966). "The Practice of Law as a Confidence Game." *Law and Society Review* **11** (2):1–25.

Boles, Jacqueline, and Garbin, Albeno P. (1974). "The Strip Club and Stripper—Customer Patterns of Interaction," *Sociology and Social Research* **58** (2):136–44.

Bryant, Clifton, and Palmer, C. Eddie (1975). "Massage Parlors and 'Hand Whores,' Some Sociological Observations," *Journal of Sex Research* **2** (3):227–41.

Chambliss, Bill (1972). *Box Man: A Thief's Journey.* New York: Harper and Row.

Chwast, Jacob (1971). "Socio-psychological Aspects." *International Journal of Offender Therapy* **15** (1):24–27.

Ganon, John, and Simon, William (1973). *Sexual Conduct: The Social Sources of Human Sexuality.* Chicago: Aldine Publishing Co.

Gray, Diana (1973). "Turning Out: A Study of Teenage Prostitution." *Urban Life and Culture* **1** (4):401–25.

Hirschi, Travis (1962). "The Professional Prostitute," *Berkeley Journal of Sociology,* **7** (1):33–49.

Jackson, Bruce (1972) *Outside the Law: A Thief's Primer.* New Brunswick, N. J.: Transaction Books.

Kaplan, John (1973). *Criminal Justice: Introductory Case and Materials.* Mineola, N. Y.: Foundation Press.

Long, Norton (1961). "The Local Community as an Ecology of Games." In *Urban Government: A Reader in Administration and Politics,* edited by Edward Banfield. Glencoe, Ill.: The Free Press, 400–413.

Newman, Donald J. (1975). *Introduction to Criminal Justice.* New York: J. B.Lippincott Co.

Petersen, David (1971). "Informal Norms and Police Practice: The Traffic Ticket Quota System." *Sociology and Social Research* **55** (3):19.

Roby, Pamela (1972). "Politics and Prostitution: A Case Study of the Revision, Enforcement, and Administration of the New York State Penal Laws on Prostitution." *Criminology* **9** (February) 425–47.

Rubenstein, Jonathan (1973). *City Police.* New York: Farrar, Strauss and Giroux.

Smith, Alexander, and Pollack, Harriet (1975). *Some Sins Are Not Crimes: A Plea for Reform of the Criminal Law.* New York: New Viewpoints.

Tatro, Charlotte (1974). "Cross My Palms with Silver: Fortune-telling as an Occupational Way of Life." In *Deviant Behavior: Occupational and Organization Bases,* edited by Clifton Bryant. Chicago: Rand McNally.

Tatro, Charlotte, and Boles, Jacqueline (1975). "Fortune-telling: The Con and How It Works." A paper presented at the national meetings of the popular culture association in St. Louis, Mo.

Winick, Charles, and Kinsie, Paul M. (1973). *The Lively Commerce: Prostitution in the United States.* Chicago: Quadrangle.

SECTION VII

"RESPECTABLE" CRIMES

The flow of current political affairs has directed public attention to crimes of politicians, illegal political contributions by major corporations, and the other kinds of offenses committed by upper class and powerful segments of American society.

The first selection is taken from a staff report for a congressional investigation of corporate crime in America. Two portions of that report are included here: a description of Ford Pintos with fuel tanks that were alleged to explode in rear-end collisions; and PBB, an industrial compound that accidentally was mixed with dairy cow feed and necessitated the destruction of a large number of dairy herds in one part of the country.

One contemporary form of criminal behavior by middle and upper class individuals involves the manipulation and abuse of one of the minor dieties of our time: the computer. Parker reveals how the computer has been used in bank embezzlements and other criminal acts involving, government, consumers, and business operations. The selection describes instances of physical attacks on computers, software and data, along with the theft of computer hardware, software, and computer services.

The ever-popular crime of shoplifting seems to offer almost insuperable methodological problems for researchers, including differentiating employee thefts from those by customers and outsiders. In Cobb's study, the actions of talented shoplifters are detailed: concealment, identification of the store security staff, and a range of skillful and ingenious techniques.

The final selection is a short, almost surrealistic account of credit card madness. A young couple obtain an "avalanche" of credit cards and go on an irresistible, if highly illegal, orgy of spending and traveling.

31

EXPLOSIVE CARS AND SICK COWS

LIBRARY OF CONGRESS

CONGRESSIONAL RESEARCH SERVICE

[Editors' Note: The following two cases were among a series of background summaries prepared by the Congressional Research Service of the Library of Congress at the request of the Subcommittee on Crime of the House Committee on the Judiciary in their consideration of H. R. 7040, a bill requiring disclosure of certain information by business entities.

These were intended as "generally chronological summaries based on public documents and committee materials available at the time of writing. For this reason, factual coverage may be incomplete and legitimate defenses and justifications of those involved may not be reflected. The reports . . . were prepared by Geraldine Carr, Robert Civiak, James Mielke, and F. Angelyn Wells of the Science Policy Research Division," according to the introductory portion of this report.]

FORD PINTO

BACKGROUND

The Ford Pinto two-door sedan was introduced on September 11, 1970, as a 1971 model year vehicle. A three-door runabout version was introduced in February 1971 and the Pinto station wagon model was brought out on March 17, 1972. The design and location of the fuel

Source: Subcommittee on Crime, Committee of the Judiciary, U.S. House of Representatives, 96th Congress, 2nd Session. *Corporate Crime.* Committee Print No. 10 (1980), pp. 1, 8–11, 25–31.

tank in the Ford Pinto, and identically designed Mercury Bobcat, were unchanged until the 1977 model year when revision was required to meet new Federal safety standards for rear impact collisions. By that time over 1.5 million two- and three-door Pinto sedans and nearly 35,000 Bobcat sedans had been sold. Because of the different configuration of the station wagon model, the fuel tank was mounted differently and, consequently, was less susceptible to damage from rear end collisions. Production statistics for the pre-1977 Pinto and Bobcat by model year are given in Tables 1 and 2.

The 1971–1976 Pinto fuel tank is constructed of sheet metal and is attached to the undercarriage of the vehicle by two metal straps with

TABLE 1 Production Statistics for the Pre-1977 Ford Pinto

	2-door sedan	3-door sedan	Station wagon	Totals
Model year:				
1971	267,694	59,173	0	326,867
1972	171,616	187,657	96,221	455,494
1973	109,080	141,440	204,514	455,034
1974	120,911	159,999	217,351	498,261
1975	58,697	63,129	83,137	204,963
1976	86,842	87,101	99,138	273,081
Total	814,840	698,499	700,361	2,213,700

TABLE 2 Production Statistics for the Pre-1977 Mercury Bobcat

	3-door runabout	Station wagon	Totals
Model year:			
1975	14,605	17,851	32,456
1976	20,212	21,207	41,419
Total	34,817	39,058	73,875

mounting brackets. The tank is located behind the rear axle. Crash tests at moderate speeds have shown that, on rear-impact collisions, the fuel tank is displaced forward until it impacts the differential housing on the rear axle and/or its mounting bolts or some other underbody structure.

THE CAUSE FOR CONCERN

Public awareness and concern over the Pinto gas tank design grew rapidly following the 1977 publication of an article by Mark Dowie in Mother Jones, a West Coast magazine. This article was widely publicized in the press and reprinted in full in Business and Society Review. The article, based on interviews with a former Ford engineer, alleged that Ford Motor Company had rushed the Pinto into production in much less than the usual time in order to gain a competitive edge. According to the article, this meant that tooling began while the car was still in the product design stage. When early Ford crash tests allegedly revealed a serious design problem in the gas tank, the tooling was well under way.[1] Rather than disrupt this process, at a loss of time and money, to incorporate more crashworthy designs which Ford allegedly had tested, the article stated that the decision was made to market the car as it was then designed.

The Dowie article further included calculations reportedly contained within an internal company memorandum showing that the costs of making the fuel tank safety improvement

($11 per car) were not equal to the savings in lives and injuries from the estimated proportion of crashes that would otherwise be expected to result in fires. These "benefits" were converted into dollar figures based on a value of cost of $200,000 per death and $67,000 per injury, figures which were obtained from NHTSA. In addition the article stated that Ford had lobbied for eight years to delay the Federal standard for fuel tank safety that came into force with the 1977 model year. The article alleged that Ford's opposition to Federal Motor Vehicle Safety Standard 301 was stimulated by the costly retooling that would have been required when the Pinto was first scheduled for production. In response, a Ford official characterized the allegations made in the Dowie article as distorted and containing half-truths.[2]

THE NHTSA INVESTIGATION

Based on allegations that the design and location of the fuel tank in the Ford Pinto made it highly susceptible to damage on rear impact at low to moderate closing speeds, the National Highway Traffic Safety Administration (NHTSA) initiated a formal defect investigation on September 13, 1977. In response to the NHTSA's requests, Ford provided information concerning the number and nature of known incidents in which rear impact of a Pinto reportedly caused fuel tank damage, fuel system leakage or fire. Based on this information and its own data sources, in May 1978 NHTSA reported that, in total, it was aware of 38 cases in which rear-end collisions of Pinto vehicles had resulted in fuel tank damage, fuel system leakage, and/or ensuing fire. These cases had resulted in a total of 27 fatalities sustained by Pinto occupants, of which one is reported to have resulted from impact injuries. In addition, 24 occupants of these Pinto vehicles had sustained non-fatal burn injuries.[3]

[1] Dowie, Mark. How Ford Put Two Million Firetraps on Wheels. Business and Society Review, No. 23, Fall 1977, pp. 46–55.

[2] New York Times, Aug. 11, 1977, p. A–15.

[3] National Highway Traffic Safety Administration. Office of Defects and Investigation Enforcement. Investigation Report, Phase I. Alleged Fuel Tank and Filler Neck Damage in Rear-End Collisions of Subcompact Passenger Cars. 1971–1976 Ford Pinto, 1975–1976 Mercury Bobcat. May 1978. p. 4.

In addition the NHTSA Investigation Report stated that prior to initial introduction of the Pinto for sale Ford had performed four rear impact barrier crash tests. However as Ford reported, "none of the tested vehicles employed structure or fuel system designs representative of structures and fuel systems incorporated in the Pinto as introduced in September 1970."[4] These tests were conducted from May through November 1969.

Following initial introduction of the Pinto for sale, Ford continued a program of rear impact tests on Pintos which included assessment of post impact conditions of the fuel tank and/or filler pipe. Reports of 55 such tests were provided to NHTSA, including tests of Mercury Bobcats. Three items developed a history of consistent results of concern at impact speeds as low as 21.5 miles per hour with a fixed barrier: (1) the fuel tank was punctured by contact with the differential housing or some other underbody structure; (2) the fuel filler neck was pulled out of the tank; and (3) structural and/or sheet metal damage was sufficient to jam one, or both, of the passenger doors closed.[5] Review of the test reports in question suggested to the NHTSA investigators that Ford had studied several alternative solutions to the numerous instances in which fuel tank deformation, damage or leakage occurred during or after impact.[6]

The NHTSA investigation concluded that the fuel tank and filler pipe assembly installed in the 1971–1976 Ford Pinto is subject to damage which results in fuel spillage and fire potential in rear impact collisions by other vehicles at moderate closing speeds. Further, examination by NHTSA of the product liability actions filed against Ford and other codefendants involving rear impact of Pintos with fuel tank damage/fuel leakage/fire occurrences, showed that at that time nine cases had been completed. Of these, the plaintiffs had been compensated in 8 cases, either by jury awards or out-of-court settlements.

Following this initial determination that a defect existed and less than a week before a scheduled NHTSA public hearing on the Pinto fuel tank problem, Ford agreed to a voluntary recall.

CRIMINAL CHARGES

On September 12, 1978, following an accident involving the burning and death of three young women in a Pinto, a county grand jury in Indiana indicted Ford Motor Company on three counts of reckless homicide and one count of criminal recklessness. The charge of reckless homicide was brought under a 1977 revision of the Indiana Penal Code that allows a corporation to be treated as a person for the purposes of bringing criminal charges. On March 13, 1980, more than two months after the trial began, the jury found Ford not guilty.[7]

POLYBROMINATED BIPHENYLS

BACKGROUND

Polybrominated biphenyl is a general name referring to a class of industrial compounds; commercial products are mixtures of many forms of PBBs. PBBs are most commonly used in plastics and textiles as a flame retardant. The material has also been incorporated into auto upholstery, polyurethane foam, wire coatings and paints. The chemistry and stability of PBBs have not been well documented in the literature. Not enough is known to critically assess the extent of possible chemical conversion of PBBs in the environment. PBBs are thought to be less stable in the environment when compared to polychlorinated biphenyls (PCB's) because bromine atoms are more reactive.

[7] The staff of the Subcommittee on Crime wishes to note at this point that in the Indiana Pinto trial, the question of whether or not Ford Motor Co. officials knowingly or recklessly concealed knowledge of hidden serious dangers was not permitted by the trial judge to be placed in issue. Evidence along these lines was not permitted to go to the jury. Thus, no court or jury has yet ruled as to whether or not any corporate coverup occurred in the Pinto case.

[4] Ibid., p. 7.
[5] Ibid.
[6] Ibid.

PBSs are solid and have extremely low vapor pressure. Production, distribution, and usage of PBBs have not been as widespread as that of PCB's. The PBBs used in products have very little tendency to migrate from the products. PBBs are persistent and can be passed on for generations. PBBs are stored in the body fat, where they can remain indefinitely: during pregnancy they can cross the placenta to the developing fetus. They also appear in human breast milk. Scientists at Harvard University and the National Cancer Institute have found that PBB's contain two suspected carcinogens, napthlene and furan.

Michigan Chemical Corporation manufactured the polybrominated biphenyls, FireMaster BP-6 and hexabrominated biphenyl, for use as flame retardants in thermoplastics. Hexabrominated biphenyl is a mixture of brominated biphenyls with an average of six bromine atoms per biphenyl molecule. FireMaster BP-6 is a mixture of five brominated biphenyls.

Representatives of the Michigan Chemical Corporation, now owned by Velsicol Chemical Corporation, have stated that, to their knowledge, FireMaster PB-6 is the only polybrominated biphenyl produced in commercial quantity in the United States.[8] Production estimates for FireMaster PB-6 were: 1970, 20,000 lbs.; 1971, 200,000 lbs.; 1972, 2,300,000 lbs.; 1973, 3,900,000 lbs.; and 1974, 4,800,000 lbs. The company stopped PBB production in 1975.

FireMaster PB-6 has been used as a flame retardant in the manufacture of typewriter, calculator, and microfilm reader housings, radio and TV parts, miscellaneous small automotive parts and small parts for electrical applications. The use of FireMaster PB-6 has been retricted to those applications where the end-use product is not exposed to either animal or human food and there is no known use of the product in flame retarding fabrics where human exposures would occur.

[8] Michigan Chemical Co. Review of Polybrominated Biphenyls. Presented to the Michigan Environmental Review Board, September 1974.

The ultimate disposition of FireMaster PB-6 upon burial is uncertain. The Michigan Chemical Corporation claims that the material will eventually undergo oxidative/biological degradation, forming carbon dioxide, water, and bromine ions.

EPISODE

In October 1973, adverse health effects were observed in cattle in several dairy herds in the State of Michigan. At the time, the cattle refused to eat manufactured feed; milk production decreased; there was a loss in body weight and the cattle developed abnormal hoof growth with lameness; cattle and swine aborted; and farmers reported the inability to breed heifers after they consumed feed manufactured by Farm Bureau Services. A herd of some 100 head of cattle sent to slaughter during this time period exhibited enlarged livers.

Until April 1974, no one could identify the substance causing these adverse effects. Analysis of samples of the suspected feed by laboratories of the United States Department of Agriculture at Beltsville, Maryland revealed that the feed was contaminated with a flame retardant chemical, hexabrominated biphenyl. Dr. George Fries of USDA identified the PBB in specimens from contaminated cows only because he had worked with PBB and knew the rather complex gas chromatography technique needed to analyze for it.

Subsequent investigation revealed that the Michigan Chemical Corporation manufactured magnesium oxide, a dairy feed supplement sold under the tradename, Nutrimaster, and they also manufactured a flame retardant, hexabrominated biphenyl, sold under the tradename, FireMaster BP-6, at their St. Louis, Michigan plant. Although there are many hypotheses as to how these two products were mixed up, the following story seems to be the most commonly cited.

Sometime during the summer of 1973, at the Michigan Chemical Corporation's St. Louis Michigan plant, ten to twenty 50-pound bags of "FireMaster," the fire-retardant PBB, somehow were included in a truck load of "Nutrimaster," or magnesium oxide, a compound used to sweeten acidic feed.[9] The truck was headed for the Farm Bureau Services, Inc. (a subsidiary of Michigan Farm Bureau) feed mill at Battle Creek.

From 1971 to 1973, the Michigan Chemical Corporation produced several experimental batches of PBB's which had been pulverized to a fine white powder.[10] The appearance of the PBB's was not precisely identical to that of the magnesium oxide, but to an unpracticed eye, the two were very similar. Normally, the FireMaster would have been packaged in bags lettered in red and the Nutrimaster in bags with blue trim. But, because of a shortage of bags with pre-printed labeling, the FireMaster, as well as the Nutrimaster, were packaged in plain brown bags on which the trade names were stenciled in black. When the top of a bag was torn off and discarded, identification was essentially lost. How the FireMaster and Nutrimaster bags became mixed at the plant is still a mystery.

Roger Clark, an attorney for Michigan Chemical has stated that the building in which FireMaster was manufactured and stored was several hundred yards from those where Nutrimaster was produced and stored.[11] Also, it was common practice to load these products directly from the storage buildings onto trucks for shipment, with no need to move them to some common loading area where a mixup could have occurred. But, during the investigation of the incident, a partially filled FireMaster bag was found at Farm Bureau Services.

As a result of the mixup, the Farm Services Bureau mixed 500 to 1,000 pounds of FireMaster BP-6 with animal feed, in place of the Nutrimaster, apparently in the same proportion of use for the Nutrimaster.[12] It appears that three kinds of feed were initially involved in this episode with PBB levels as follows: Feed No. 405, 2.4. ppm PBB; Feed No. 410, 1790 ppm BPBB; and Feed No. 407, 4300 ppm PBB.

The feed was widely sold and distributed to Michigan farmers. Besides the heavy primary contamination caused by the initial mixing of PBB into feeds, there was secondary contamination resulting from traces of PBB remaining at the Battle Creek feed mill and at a number of other mills and grain elevators around the State. Originally, the contamination was thought to be limited to about 30 quarantined farms (where contamination exceeded 0.3 ppm in serum of animals) but further examination found PBB in swine, chickens, dairy products and eggs. The contaminant became widespread through a complex series of feed reprocessings, interfarm, feed trades, and use of protein supplement derived from contaminated animals before the PBB contamination was discovered. One egg farm is known to have sold 63,000 hens to a processor for the nation's largest manufacturer of canned soups. The chickens were sold because their egg production had dropped sharply; they had apparently been poisoned with PBB. Some of the eggs contained up to 4,000 parts per million PBB.[13]

It has been estimated that between the onset of contamination in the fall of 1973 and the establishment of the quarantine of affected herds and flocks in the spring of 1974, over 10,000 Michigan residents were exposed to PBB through consumption of milk, meat and dairy products. There was probably considerable variation in both duration of exposure and levels of exposure. As a group, the farm family members have been at greatest risk, followed by those individuals who purchased

[9] Carter, Luther J. Michigan's PBB incident: Chemical Mix-up Leads to Disaster, Science, vol. 192, Apr. 16, 1976, p. 240.

[10] Hecht, Annabel. PBBs: One State's Tragedy. FDA Consumer, February 1977, p. 22.

[11] Carter, Luther J., Science, p. 240.

[12] Cordle, F. et al. Human Exposure to Polychlorinated Biphenyls and Polybrominated Byphenyls. Environmental Health Perspectives, vol. 24, June 1978, p. 170.

[13] Brody, Jane E. Farmers Exposed to a Pollutant Face Medical Study in Michigan. The New York Times, Aug. 12, 1976, p. C20.

dairy products from contaminated farms on a regular basis.

Since the discovery in April 1974, 538 of the most heavily contaminated farms have been quarantined. More than 29,000 cattle, 5,900 hogs, 1,400 sheep and about 1.5 million chickens have been destroyed. In addition, at least 865 tons of feed, 17,990 pounds of cheese, 2,630 pounds of butter, 34,000 pounds of dry milk products, and nearly 5 million eggs have been destroyed.

The human health effects of PBB contamination are not clear. Although no specific effects have been ascribed to the contaminant, some families have reported psychological, neurological, skin, and joint symptoms; others have not reported these symptoms. Loss of sensation, persistent tiredness, loss of memory and deterioration of intelligence have also been reported. But no pattern of symptoms has been correlated, in a statistically significant way, with the concentration of PBB found in the human blood. Some with low blood levels have symptoms, others with high blood levels do not.

When the PBB contamination was first discovered in 1974, most Federal and State health officials contended that the substances would decompose. However, they have been found to persist in the environment, and now appear to be entering the food chain, soil, streams and swamps. According to Dr. Harold Humphrey, director of the Michigan Department of Public Health PBB study, investigations conducted since 1974 have found PBB in human breast milk in 96 percent of a statistical sample of breast feeding mothers in lower Michigan and in 40 percent of a similar group of mothers in the upper peninsula.[14] This indicates that persons living in Michigan during the 1973–1974 period, prior to the discovery and removal of contaminated food products from the market, had received some exposure to PBB through their normal food chain.

The concerns of Michigan residents continued into 1977. Results of tests for PBB in mother's milk as part of a larger study done by the Michigan Department of Health, found PBB in 22 of 26 samples tested.[15] These results were downplayed because the sample was reported to be too small, uncontrolled and not scientifically defensible. Another broader-based study completed in October 1976 revealed that 96 percent of mothers in lower Michigan had at least "trace" levels of PBB in their milk.[16] This finding did not persuade a panel of experts from the National Cancer Institute, the Food and Drug Administration, and the Center for Disease Control to change its original position in favor of continuing breast-feeding.

Chronic effects associated with exposure to PBB are unknown. Its potential for toxicity is five times greater than that of its relative, PCB. Animal experiments have shown that PBB is a potent microsomal enzyme inducer with teratogenic effects (i.e., capable of producing physical defects in offspring *in utero*) but, in general, its effects are largely unknown.

LITIGATION

Due to their economic loss, hundreds of farmers filed suit against Michigan Chemical Corporation and Farm Bureau Services for damages incurred as a result of destruction of their contaminated animals. Over 355 of the cases have been settled out of court for a total of $50 million. In 1977, Roy and Marilyn Tacoma, a Michigan farmer and his wife, filed suit against Michigan Chemical and Farm Services for $250,000 actual damages and up to $1 million for punitive damages for the loss of more than 100 cattle.[17] The Tacomas claimed that their cattle had to be destroyed after they ate feed contaminated with PBBs. After almost two years in court, they lost their case for "com-

[14] Michigan Screens Blood for PBB Contamination. Journal of Environmental Health, vol. 39. No. 6, p. 436.

[15] William K. Stevens, Events in Michigan Revive Concern Over Effect of PBB in Mother's Milk. The New York Times, Jan. 2, 1977, p. 28.

[16] Ibid., p. 28.

[17] *Tacoma* v. *Michigan Chemical Company and Michigan Farm Bureau Services*, Wexford County Circuit Court, State of Michigan, case 2933, filed 1977.

pensatory and exemplary damages'' for injuries their dairy herd had suffered. Michigan Circuit Court Judge William R. Peterson commented:

> The health of their (the Tacomas') animals was not impaired, nor was their performance in milk production affected by PBB. Most of the animals were never tested for PBB and the majority of those that were showed no sign of PBB. Plaintiffs have not shown any single incident of death that could be attributed to PBB.[18]

Judge Peterson also added that the preponderance of evidence indicated that low levels of PBBs were ''relatively non-toxic'' to cattle.

On November 28, 1977, the United States District Court for the Western District of Michigan filed criminal charges against Velsicol Chemical Corporation (formerly Michigan Chemical) and Farm Bureau Services for allegedly violating the provisions of the Federal Food, Drug, and Cosmetic Act by causing the adulteration of animal feeds with polybrominated biphenyls.[19] Velsicol was charged with commingling, (on or about May 2, 1973) one or more bags of Nutrimaster (magnesium oxide) with FireMaster (PBB) in plain brown 50 pound bags with only the trade names listed.[20]

Neither the Nutrimaster or the FireMaster bags listed the usual names of the product, the charges alleged, noting that the bags also failed to bear the name and place of business of the manufacturer, packer, or distributor. The counts, all listed as misdemeanors, indicated that magnesium oxide and PBB shipped by Michigan Chemical were fine powders similar in appearance.

Farm Bureau Services was alleged to have mixed the bags on four different dates with other animal feed ingredients, causing the food to be contaminated because: (1) it bore and contained an added poisonous and deleterious substance, PBB, which was unsafe; (2) it was unfit for food by reasons of the presence therein of PBB; and (3) it was prepared under unsanitary conditions whereby it may have been rendered injurious to health.[21] The charges carry a maximum penalty of $1,000 each.[22]

On December 19, 1977, Velsicol (Michigan Chemical) and Farm Bureau Services entered not guilty pleas before the U.S. Magistrate, Stephen W. Karr.[23]

On May 19, 1978, Velsicol and Farm Bureau Services, Inc. pleaded no contest to charges that they willfully contaminated cattle feed with PBBs and were fined $4000 each by Magistrate Karr.[24] The U.S. Attorney had sought a trial contending that the companies had knowingly endangered public health. But, Magistrate Karr ruled that the ''two companies have shown good faith in their efforts to deal with the situation and had already paid $40 million in claims to farmers whose cattle were destroyed due to PBB contamination''.[25]

The State of Michigan has also filed a suit against Michigan Chemical and Farm Services Bureau for damages resulting from the contamination of animals feed with PBB.[26] The State suit asks that the Farm Bureau and its subsidiaries and Michigan Chemical and its parent and related corporations be made to pay:

1. $59.2 million to cover expenditures Michi-

---

[18] Judge Throws Out PBB Damage Suit. Chemical and Engineering News, Nov. 6, 1978, p. 8.

[19] Criminal Charges Filed in PBB Tainting of Feed. The Washington Post, Nov. 29, 1977, p. C7.

[20] 1973 PBB Contamination of Feed Brings 4-Count Criminal Charges. Food and Chemical News. Dec. 5, 1977, p. 24.

[21] Ibid., p. 24.

[22] At the same time, James Brady, the U.S. Attorney for Western Michigan, set up a four-man task force composed of two members of the U.S. Attorney's office and two F.B.I. agents, to investigate allegations that contaminated cattle were sold illegally for food and that attempts had been made to cover up the incident. (U.S. Files PBB Charges. Chemical Week, Dec. 7, 1977, p. 14.)

[23] Two PBB Makers Plead Not Guilty in Feed Case. The New York Times, Dec. 30, 1977, p. C20.

[24] U.S. District Court, Western District of Michigan. *United States* v. *Velsicol Chemical Corp. and Michigan Farm Bureau Services, Inc.* Case G 77–178. Disposition on May 19, 1978.

[25] Ibid., p. 144.

[26] *State of Michigan* v. *Michigan Chemical Company and State of Michigan* v. *Michigan Farm Bureau Services, Inc.* Circuit Court of the State of Michigan, 78-21345, February 1978.

gan will make by 1982 because of PBB contamination;

2. $60 million in additional damages for their "gross negligence";
3. all additional expenses incurred by the State for research and other purposes to protect the health of its citizens.[27]

The State's suit charges both with 10 counts each of civil liability ranging from gross negligence to violations of implied and expressed product warranties and creating a nuisance.

Most recently, Velsicol Chemical Corporation and two of its employees, Charles L. Touzeau and William Thorne, have been indicted in Michigan for concealing data and conspiring to defraud the Federal Government during FDA's investigation of the PBB contaminated animal feed. The two count Federal Grand Jury indictment charges Velsicol, Touzeau and Thorne with lying to FDA inspectors about the processes involved in the production and storage of PBBs. The second count charges that the company and its employees conspired to keep FDA from the performance of its investigative and enforcement duties.

According to a General Accounting Office report, FDA had found deficiencies in the production practices of Michigan Chemical Corporation as far back as 1969, but most of these had been corrected after being called to the attention of the company's management.[28] Similarly, manufacturing deficiencies detected by FDA at the Farm Bureau Services feed manufacturing facility at Battle Creek had been corrected after FDA inspection.

The Federal indictment arose from information gathered in a grand jury investigation. It had been reported, in a suit brought by Roy and Marilyn Tacoma, that Michigan Chemical Corporation's St. Louis, Missouri plant oper-

ations manager, William Thorne admitted that he knew, in June 1973, that some bags of ground PBB were missing, but he failed to report it to anyone until after learning of the livestock feed problems nearly one year later.[29]

The grand jury indictment charged that beginning on or about April 19, 1974 and continuing thereafter through December 1976, the Velsicol Corporation, Omaha Properties, Inc., Charles L. Touzeau and William Thorne, plant manager and operational manager respectively, of Velsicol's St. Louis, Michigan plant "wilfully and knowingly, falsified, concealed, and covered up by trick, scheme and device, material facts relating to the potential and actual contamination and adulteration of food and drug products".[30] On April 26, 1974, the defendants told Charles S. Carns, an inspector for the Food and Drug Administration, that they had no knowledge of a possible contamination of cattle feed by PBB.[31] The indictment charged that prior to April 26, 1974, the defendants had knowledge of the possibility of magnesium oxide being contamined with PBB. The indictment states that "in truth and fact, . . . PBB (hexabrominated biphenyl) had been granulated and ground; that at times prior to April 26, 1974, PBB did resemble in physical properties and packaging Michigan Chemical Corporation's bagged magnesium oxide; and that hexabrominated biphenyl had been manufactured and processed in a system which was not entirely closed and which could cross-contaminate magnesium oxide".[32] The indictment also charged that the PBB (also referred to as FF–1 and BP–6) was stored with other company products which could have resulted in contamination and adulteration of food and drug products.[33]

---

[27] Michigan Files $100 Million Suite Over PBB Feed Mixture Incident. Chemical Regulation Reporter, May 3, 1978, p. 1856.
[28] U.S. Congress. General Accounting Office. PBB Contamination: FDA and USDA Monitoring Practices. June 1977, HRD 77–96.

[29] Toxic Materials News, Apr. 6, 1977, p. 69.
[30] United States v. Velsicol Chemical Corporation, Omaha Properties, Inc., Charles L. Touzeau, and William Thorne. U.S. District Court, Eastern District of Michigan, case 79-80270. Grand jury indictment, Apr. 26, 1979.
[31] Ibid., p. 2.
[32] Ibid., pp. 5–6.
[33] Ibid., p. 6.

The grand jury also indicted the defendants on charges of conspiracy to defraud the Food and Drug Administration in violation of Section 371, Title 18, U.S. Code by representing that they had no knowledge of possible contamination of animal feed by PBB.[34] As of April 1980, the Court was hearing pre-trial motions.

[34] Ibid., pp. 6–7.

32

COMPUTER ABUSE

DONN B. PARKER, SUSAN NYCUM, S. STEPHEN OURA

FOUR STUDIES OF COMPUTER ABUSE

Four studies have been made at Stanford Research Institute of specific types of computer abuse. The study on bank embezzlement[1] was done for the American Bankers Association, Operations and Automation Division; this study was particularly valuable because it was possible to statistically compare the computer-related cases with general bank embezzlement cases, whereas a direct comparison of all recorded cases to general white-collar crime is not possible because of the lack of data on the latter. Another study was done for the Lawrence Livermore Laboratory on reported cases involving multi-access or time-sharing computer systems.[2] The third study was on computer abuse in civil government; its results were presented[3] to the California State Assembly Committee on Efficiency and Cost Control, which was investigating the security problems that might be encountered in centralizing the State's computing facilities. The fourth study on consumer and business computer abuse covers primarily retail sales and services and is drawn from several sources.

All four studies are briefly summarized below.

Source: Computer Abuse: Final Report Prepared for the National Science Foundation (November 1973). Menlo Park, California: Stanford Research Institute. Pp. 35–46, 55–61, 91–101, 104–108, 110–111. (Editorial adaptations.)

BANK EMBEZZLEMENT

Out of 140 recorded cases of all types of computer misuse in the SRI data bank when this study was carried out, 18 involved banking, and 12 of these—most of which occurred since 1970—constituted embezzlement. These recorded cases appear to represent only a small fraction of the actual incidents of unauthorized acts in banking. In comparison, the Comptroller of the Currency reported 272 defalcations of all types of $10,000 or more in 1971.

The study of computer-related case histories supports the past findings of embezzlement research by criminologists. The definition of embezzlement varies among legal jurisdictions but is best defined here as criminal violation of trust. Donald Cressey, one of the foremost criminologists on white-collar crime, states his well-tested hypothesis as follows:

> Trusted persons become trust violators when they conceive of themselves as having a financial problem which is non-shareable, are aware that this problem can be secretly resolved by violation of the position of financial trust, and are able to apply to their own conduct in that situation verbalizations which enable them to adjust their conceptions of themselves as trusted persons with their conceptions of themselves as users of the entrusted funds or property.[4]

Computer technology has introduced new factors concerning the types of perpetrators, the forms of assets threatened, and embezzlement methods.

Programmers, system analysts, and computer and keypunch operators, either alone or in collusion with bank employees traditionally associated with embezzlement, represent new occupations in positions of trust and temptation. Asset data electronically and magnetically stored within computer systems are becoming popular targets, along with the negotiable instrument forms of assets.

Computer-related embezzlement methods include old elements of kiting, lapping, creating fictitious float, and manipulating checks, cash, and inactive accounts; but they now are perpetrated in EDP environments requiring modification or at least detailed knowledge of the computer programs and data file structures. Computer programs represent more exact and predetermined processes compared with the work procedures assigned to people in the previous manual systems, presenting a different environment for the embezzler.

The characteristics of the average bank embezzler have not changed much in the past 35 years. According to the FBI he is about 32 to 36 years old, he is married, and he has two children. However, one significant embezzlement feature has changed: the average bank embezzlement now continues for more than three years before discovery, a year longer than the period shown in 1935 statistics. According to the FBI, most embezzlers are not motivated by living beyond their means.

Of the cases examined in one study, 41 percent involved the unauthorized extension of credit to a customer and resulted in no personal benefit to the embezzler. In 22 percent of the cases, the perpetrator used stolen funds to engage in other business. Only 19 percent of the perpetrators were living beyond their means or were gambling.

Two kinds of simple embezzlement (without collusion) are associated with computer systems. External embezzlement is performed outside the computer system but requires the manipulation of input and output based on a knowledge of the computer application. Internal embezzlement originates from within the computer system staff. It requires the following:

1. Access to a computer.
2. Access to data files.
3. Access to computer programs.
4. System knowledge.
5. Means of converting fraudulent activity to personal gain.

Embezzlement can consist of both internal and external fraud when perpetrated by several people in collusion.

*

As indicated in Table I, one-third of the cases involved collusion—which was apparently needed to acquire all the necessary skills and access not possessed by any single party to the collusion. In 111 cases of general embezzlement involving losses over $10,000 reported in 1971, the position of the embezzler was known; only 13 of the 111 cases involved collusion. Table I compares the positions of embezzlers in computer-related and general cases.

Methods used by the computer-related bank embezzlers included four instances of unauthorized program changes to delete items in exception reports, one of changing credit limits, and one of accumulating into a favored account the round-down remainders from arithmetic calculations (this case is not verified). One theft of a computer program is recorded. The rest of the methods required input/output data manipulation using detailed knowledge of the computer programs. Two of these cases involved inactive account manipulations; one involved control total balancing; another took advantage of falsely created float by inputting checks as cash deposits; another involved check processing and Magnetic Ink Character Recognition (MICR) code defacing; and one took advantage of parallel operation of manual and computerized systems during the transition to a computer. Only one case of inactive account manipulation and the false

TABLE I Positions Held by Bank Embezzlers

Position	Number of embezzlers
Computer-related cases (11 total)[a]	
Vice president, EDP	4
EDP clerk	3
Programmer	3
Computer operator	2
Chief teller	1
Systems analyst	1
Vice president	1
General cases (111 total)[b]	
Operations vice president, manager, clerk	32
Loan officer, manager	29
Teller	22
President	14
Cashier	8
Director, stockholder, officer	5
Bookkeeper	3
Trust officer	3
Auditor	1
Computer operator	1
Proof department supervisor	1
Systems analyst	1

Source: Stanford Research Institute and Treasury Department.

[a] Collusion in four cases; the perpetrators in one case were not identified.

[b] Collusion in 13 cases.

float case were external embezzlements. All the others involved only EDP personnel or were cases of collusion involving both internal and external employees.

It is possible that embezzlement, fraud, forgery, and business-related thefts will decrease as the prevention and detection potential of computers is developed. The potential for cost-effective protection of business, financial and informational activity and data is far greater in EDP environments than in the manual environments they replace. The computer is an ideal tool to detect embezzlement activity, but how to use it effectively requires further development. The growing speciality of EDP audit in banks offers hope that audit control techniques will catch up with the advancing state of the art of computer usage.

The separation of responsibility in the new types of staff now in positions of trust appears to be the single most effective deterrent to internal embezzlement, from an operations point of view. External embezzlement control is a matter of building appropriate detection methods into the production application programs to alert EDP audit personnel about anomalous activity.

MULTI/ACCESS COMPUTER ABUSE

Of a total of 129 cases on file at the time this study was done, 19 involved multi-access computer systems. Two of the cases were thefts of entire operating systems and occurred in 1971. The remaining 17, all occurring since 1969, were limited to input/output manipulation of applications. Seven cases involved penetration of the operating systems. Four of the seven were unauthorized use of services; one was industrial espionage; another was vandalism; and the purpose of the last is undetermined. Five of the 19 cases occurred in university environments, the rest in businesses.

These 19 cases represent only 15 percent of the total recorded cases, probably because of the small number of multi-access systems, compared with on-site batch systems, that were in operation in the 1969–72 period. The small proportion may also be explained by the known time lag in discovering incidents, and it is suspected that more multi-access system penetrations are not detected compared with the more obvious physical access usually associated with other types of systems.

The total number of cases and the number of multi-access cases would almost certainly be far higher if a methodical search were conducted among academic institutions. Although more unique and sophisticated methods would probably be discovered, there is usually less serious damage, loss, or injuries in the university facilities than in business and government environments. However, there is a sinister potential for proliferation of acts in an academic environment. Students rationalizing these acts as games and legitimate challenges with relatively benign results could become a generation of computer users in business and government with different, ethical standards and great expertise in subverting computer systems. A study of cases in academic environments and a study of the attitudes and social values of students gaining such expertise would be valuable in predicting the trends and nature of computer-related crime.

A significant increase in multi-access cases can be predicted on the basis of the proliferation of such systems that contain, control, and process valuable assets. The historic laissez-faire philosophy of computer users toward proprietariness of data, programs, and computer services—and sometimes the user's image of the computer as an attractive subject of attack but not possessing personal attributes—are factors that support this expected increase.

Discussions with managers and systems programmers from computer time-sharing service companies, including four perpetrators of unauthorized acts, indicate that it is common practice to gain legitimate or unauthorized access to competitors' systems. Once access is gained, the perpetrators test the system's performance and features, take copies of programs and data files, test the security access control, and—on penetration into a privileged mode—take private information and subvert the operating system to make subsequent attacks simple. As a final act, they usually "crash" the system. In one example, the perpetrator was discovered by the victimized company and hired by the company to plug the hole he had found in the system. This young, skilled systems programmer performed the penetration by adapting his knowledge of his own company's system to the subject system. He later rationalized that this type of activity is not unethical or illegal, and challenged anybody to prove that it is in the absence of legal precedence, contractual agreements limiting activity, or visible protective signs or warnings.

A trend of increasing incidence of multi-access systems abuse could be reversed by (1) increasing the security of the systems to a point where only the most knowledgeable systems programmers associated with a system could penetrate it, (2) establishing norms of professional conduct inhibiting such activities, and (3) providing detection and warning features to confront an individual with the nature of his act and as a basis for legal action.

GOVERNMENT COMPUTER ABUSE

A total of 24 cases of computer abuse are recorded as having occurred since 1967 in local, state, and federal government facilities. Most of the cases occurred at the city and county levels. Table II indicates the breakdown of the cases by type, position of the main perpetrators or suspects, and number of perpetrators in collusion.

TABLE II Government Computer Abuse Cases

	Number
Case type	
Theft of address lists	5
Vandalism	4
Manipulation of checks	4
Confidentiality violation	4
Manipulation of payroll files and checks	3
Unauthorized sale of EDP services	2
Vote-counting fraud	2
Position of main perpetrator or suspect	
EDP employee	16
Elected official	2
Citizen	2
Private businessman	1
Manager of claims	1
Welfare employee	1
Policeman	1
People in collusion (10 cases)	
6834	
7034	30
7226	11
6741	5
7245	5
7241	5
7121	2
7044	2
7322	2
7227	?

Source: Stanford Research Institute.

None of these cases involved manipulation of computer programs, in contrast to other, nongovernment environments. This fact might be coincidence, or it might possibly be because a lack of controls in programs in government installations made unauthorized acts easy simply by manipulating input and output data. Another possibility is that unauthorized acts perpetrated within computers are so difficult to discover that no cases are known even though they may be numerous. Collusion has a high frequency of occurrence, and the number of perpetrators is surprisingly large per case. The reason may be the need for different skills, knowledge, and access to carry out an act within the compartmentalized and highly technical computer environment of government.

CONSUMER AND BUSINESS COMPUTER ABUSE

It might be assumed that if retail and other businesses were abusing people before computers were in use, they are still doing it in the same ways and to the same degree today with computers. Westin and Baker indicate that this might be true in their study of privacy and data banks.[5] Some factors may alter this position and are presented below in a conjectural fashion for the purpose of choosing the more fruitful areas for further investigation.

The Association for Computing Machinery, one of the major professional societies in the computer field (27,000 members), has 46 members serving as volunteer ombudsmen throughout the United States to aid people having difficulties in transactions involving the use of computers. A letter sent to these ombudsmen requested that they report on consumer problems they have encountered. Eight ombudsmen replied, but in only two incidents was ombudsman activity reported: one involved investigation of vote counting system failures in Detroit, the other involved assisting the State of Illinois Attorney General in prosecuting a fraudulent computer dating service that was not, in fact, using a computer.

Annual reports for 1970, 1971 and 1972 of the State of New York Attorney General's Bureau of Consumer Fraud and Detection[6] indicated 20,400 to 22,700 investigations of consumer fraud per year completed. Five examples

connected with computer use were cited, but there were no records indicating the total number of such cases. The examples given included computer dating bureaus that bilked customers, a computer programming school that failed to refund tuitions when it terminated classes, and public utility companies' failure to provide sufficient help to consumers in handling billing errors. Barnett Levy, Assistant Attorney General in Charge, stated that most consumer frauds involve computers in some form simply because of the pervasive use throughout retail business.

Levy is looking for opportunities to attack excesses in personalized computer letter and advertising. He claims that making letters look as though they are individually typed, with personal information about each addressee imbedded in the text and signed by a fictitious person, is a fraudulent practice.

The New York State Attorney General has been successful in preparing legislation to control excesses in computer dating services, trade schools and billing practices. However, little of this legislation directly relates to the roles played by computers.

The SRI case history file includes 13 cases, all perpetrated since 1970, of alleged abusive acts by businesses against consumers that resulted in law enforcement actions or litigation. (Many abuses identified only in newspaper accounts do not reach the formal complaint stage and are not included in the SRI file.) The 13 cases include computer processing of insurance policies, fraudulent use of mailing lists, unfair and fraudulent billing practices, incomplete criminal records retention, and dating services and trade schools engaging in false advertising.

Business fraud against consumers is normally one-to-many, one perpetrator with many victims. Computer abuse acts by consumers against retail businesses or government agencies may be just as frequent as abuses against consumers, but on a one-for-one, victim-perpetrator basis. The SRI case file contains 20 such cases against businesses. These cases include consumer vandalism against computers, computer input manipulation, counterfeiting to perpetrate fraud and unauthorized use of computer time-sharing services.

The American Federation of Information Processing Societies and Time magazine conducted 1,001 telephone interviews with a statistically drawn probability sample of the population of the United States in July and August, 1971.[7] The pertinent results are summarized below:

- Computer Problems—34 percent of those surveyed reported that they have had a problem "because of a computer." Billing problems were most frequent, accounting for almost half of the difficulties reported. Others included problems with banks, paychecks, schools, computers at work, credit cards (only 2 percent) and, to a minor extent, with magazine subscriptions purchase orders, credit, and taxes (1 percent each). About 75 percent of those surveyed reported they received an incorrect computerized bill. Of the 24 percent who reported difficulties, 71 percent placed the blame on the personnel of the billing company while 12 percent felt the computer itself was at fault.
- Computers and the Consumer—the public view of the use of computers in providing consumer benefits is generally positive. Approximately 89 percent felt computers will provide many kinds of information and services to us in our homes; 65 percent felt computers are helping to raise the standard of living; and 68 percent believe computers have helped increase the quality of products and services. However, on some topics, attitudes were less positive: 48 percent felt computers make it easier to get credit versus 31 percent who disagreed. Again, 48 percent felt the use of computers in teaching children in school should be increased, versus 25 percent who felt such use should be decreased.

Stories about the perverse nature of computer abuse, such as the well-circulated ones of persistent computer-produced dunning of consumers to pay $0.00 for a service or product is a popular topic in newspapers. It is easy to see how these incidents can occur and just as easy to see how they will disappear with improved design of computer applications, growing business experience in using computers, and public tolerance of these types of problems. However, intentional, premediated abuse by both sides—business and consumers—must be documented and investigated if it is to be finally controlled. The excesses of credit reporting services have already attracted controls in the form of the federal Fair Credit Reporting Act.

The following scenario depicts circumstances often lending to consumer problems. A business will go about automating a customer billing function by assigning a team of systems analysts and programmers, and may even include an accountant from the accounts receivable department familiar with the function but unfamiliar with computers. A budget and schedule are established. The specifications for the computer system are written according to what is thought the manual procedures accomplish. These, in turn, are interpreted by the EDP staff who write the computer programs. In the end, the specifications are not complete or not correct, the programmers do not interpret them correctly, the programs are not complete and do not work correctly, and the budget and schedule have run out.

At this point anguish sets in. All of the niceties, controls, and features to handle extraordinary and infrequent billing situations are dropped, and the programs are forced into production before the business is prepared to cope with a new and radical way of functioning. Most of the people who handled the unusual cases and complaints are given other assignments because it was assumed they would not be needed—that was one of the purposes of automating. The new billing system starts operation in a highly limited and rigid state. Customers are bombarded with wildly incorrect billings. Since the correction facilities of the programs were never fully completed, attempts at correction produce even more seriously incorrect results.

By this time the viability of the business is affected and management becomes seriously concerned for the first time. The EDP staff is put on probation, consultants are called in, more money is now being spent than ever before on billing, but gradually the system is corrected and enhanced to full operational capability. Not as much money is being saved as hoped, but some is. Billing becomes more efficient, and customers grudgingly admit they now have few problems and are getting better service than before. The people previously responsible for handling errors and complaints have been retrained in the new system and fulfill this function. New and improved features are added to the system to handle unusual cases, to control fraud, and to produce improved performance reports. When everything is finally running smoothly, volume increases, and then, for several reasons, the system becomes overloaded and obsolete and a new, different computer is needed. This causes the whole conversion process to start all over again.

This sad story is common throughout business and is often the cause of consumer problems. Fortunately the art of putting applications on computers is improving; it is leaving the "cottage craft" stage and becoming an engineering-type discipline. Thus problems in automation are gradually being overcome. A similar history can be related in other applications such as vote counting by computer.

A technical problem in the automation process can often force rethinking of acceptable ethical business practices. This is best illustrated by an example that occurred in Washington D.C. A bank there normally posted deposits and withdrawals in demand deposit accounts manually and in the order in which transactions occurred. A customer could make a deposit, then a withdrawal, and be assured they were posted in that order, thus avoiding overdraft situations. The process was then placed in the computer in a batch mode of op-

eration. Each night all withdrawals were batched and posted to all accounts and when overdraft conditions were found, penalties were automatically debited. Then deposits were batched and posted to all accounts. One of the bank's customers, a computer expert by chance, deposited a sum of money and then wrote a check the same day on part of the deposited sum. He was charged with an overdraft and complained to a bank officer who explained the way the computer system worked—the deposits and withdrawals are handled separately and not time-stamped, and there was nothing that could be done. Obviously unsatisfied with that, the customer finally found the manager of the computer operation and was shown exactly what the program directed the computer to do. The customer suggested this be changed and was told that it could be changed but it was standard banking procedure. He finally was able to convince the bank to send a notice to all customers explaining how the system functions and advising customers how to avoid overdrafts. Does this solve the problem?

*

LEGAL ASPECTS OF COMPUTER RELATED CRIME

For the purposes of this discussion, the incidents in the SRI data base have been classified into two categories. In the first, the question is what crimes, if any, have been committed. The second category contains those incidents in which the crimes are easily identifiable but in which the computer has had a direct impact in terms of mode of perpetration and form of detection. There is some overlap, of course.

In the first category are attacks on and theft, misappropriation, or misuse of hardware, software, and services. The second category of cases is analyzed in terms of the computer operation, i.e., input, processing, output, and control. Implicit in both types of incident are acts of conspiracy and obstruction of justice on the part of offenders, and procedural and constitutional considerations regarding their rights and the rights of others.

ATTACKS, THEFTS, MISAPPROPRIATION, AND MISUSE

Physical Attack on Computers. Physical attack on computer components was particularly prevalent during the recent period of campus unrest. Students and others, seeing the computer as a tool of warmongers or the establishment, sought to destroy it or capture it and hold it for ransom until various demands had been met by college administrations. In some cases the computer was attacked after the building or room which it occupied was broken into. Then it was bludgeoned, set on fire or flooded, or its cables severed. Fire bombing took place, and in the case of the University of Wisconsin (7012), the explosion took the life of a researcher.

Though dramatic, these acts for the most part constitute traditional elements of crimes to the person and property—malicious mischief, arson, burglary, bombing, murder, riot. Where the computer facility was occupied and shut down but not otherwise damaged, we may find extortion and criminal trespass. When perpetrators took away tapes or other materials in the course of their activities, we can find larceny and in some instances robbery.

Attack on Software and Data. Another type of vandalism occurred which left the hardware unharmed but attacked the software and data in the machine. Perpetrators in these instances did not necessarily enter the machine room physically but "broke into" the computer via card reader or on-line terminals, which were hardwired or connected to the system via phone lines. The legal questions here include: do these acts constitute malicious mischief, can we find a burglary, and what violation has occurred through such misuse of telephone services?

Perkins defines malicious mischief as the malicious destruction of or damage to the property of another.[8] Immediately we have a definitional problem—are software and data inside the machine property? The Model Penal Code 220.3 includes as criminal mischief "purposely or recklessly causing another to suffer pecuniary loss by deception or threat," thus broadening the base of liability. Nevertheless, the question of software as property has not been before many courts, and where it has, the issue has been treated in matters of theft of software, discussed later.

Should the act of damage to software or data constitute a felony, is a breaking and entering of an appropriate subject area burglary? In a jurisdiction which recognizes the breaking into a vending machine as burglary[9], could we find the nonphysical entrance to a computational machine a breaking? Further, not every initial penetration is unauthorized. A valid user may utilize what can be equated to his "key" to gain access to one part of the computer system and then, once inside, penetrate further into privileged areas in order to effect the damage.

At present, the use of the phone services to assist in perpetration of this type of activity falls only within the legal sanctions against obscene or harassing telephone calls.[10]. It may be appropriate to consider legislation more specific to the particular issue.

Theft of Hardware. The unlawful taking of hardware is another set of incidents. Inasmuch as this hardware is tangible personal property, the issues are traditional and the crimes include larceny, embezzlement, obtaining money under false pretenses, and associated offenses.

Theft of Computer Services. Theft of computer services presents some interesting questions. These incidents occur in one form when the perpetrator gains unauthorized access to all or a privileged part of a system, e.g., via telephone connection or onsite card reader. The name, account number, and passwords of others may be entered via terminal, punched card, or credit card. Thereafter, the perpetrator uses computer resources without paying. Can services such as computer time legally be the subject of a theft? The Model Penal Code 223.7 is helpful.

A person is guilty of theft if he obtains services which he knows are available only for compensation, by deception or threat or by false token or other means to avoid payment for the service. "Services" includes labor, professional service, telephone or other public service, accommodation in hotels, restaurants, or elsewhere, admission to exhibitions, use of vehicles or other moveable property . . . .

One of the recorded incidents (7042) involved a terminal in one state (Ohio) accessing the computer in another state (Kentucky). Here the court found a violation of 18 USC 1343 ". . . devise or intending to devise any scheme or artifice to defraud or obtain money or property by means of false or fraudulent pretenses, transmits or causes to transmit by wire. . . . in interstate commerce any . . . signals to execute such scheme." Then the court went on to say that if the law of Kentucky considered what was taken (computer services) as property, a theft of property could also be found.

Where the specific identification of another person, organization, or account is utilized in perpetration, the elements of forgery may also be present. Perkins enumerates the requirements of the offense as (1) a writing of such nature that it is a possible subject of forgery (has some value or purpose other than its own existence), (2) which writing is false, and (3) was made false with intent to defraud. The modern trend toward credit card-like access to the machinery may bring this mode of entry within the meaning of the credit card fraud sanctions.

The other prevalent form of theft of computer services is the misappropriation of services by employees authorized to use the computer services who convert them to their own use, e.g., set up a private service bureau or do work for outsiders on an overhead account. Here, an additional question may merit consideration—is it relevant that the machine was "idle" at the time of the misuse, in which case there would technically be no pecuniary loss?

Theft of Software. In at least one jurisdiction, software has been considered property within the meaning of the criminal code. *Hancock* v. *State*, Court of Criminal Appeals of Tesas, 1966 402 S.W. 2d 906 (6421), held that computer programs were property within the meaning of the state statutes defining offenses of theft. Subsequently, the perpetrator appealed from a denial of a writ for habeas corpus in which he contended he was unlawfully convicted of a felony theft (*Hancock* v. *Decher*, U.S. Court of Appeals, 5th Circuit 1967, 379 F 2d 552). The U.S. Court of Appeals affirmed the denial of habeas corpus, saying that the Court of Criminal Appeals construction of state theft law to include computer programs within the definition of property for theft purposes—which definition in turn included "all writings of every description, provided such property possesses any ascertainable value"—was not so unreasonable nor arbitrary as to be violative of due process. Further, the court found that the evidence amply supported the finding that the defendant committed the offense of stealing property worth more than $50, and that the trial court properly did not accept defendant's argument that the programs had ascertainable value only as paper, but considered them as writings under the property definition of the applicable provisions of the theft sections of the penal code.

The theft of software or data from within a computer raises the thorny problem of finding a taking, since the program is not removed from its owner's possession but at most copied. It is suggested that the focus be not on the property aspect of the act but on the dilution of value and loss of control. Similarly, where the elements of embezzlement are otherwise present, the focus should be on the breach of duty to the employer[11].

Should the software qualify as a trade secret—and here it must be assumed that state trade secret protection is viable[12]—there are a number of statutes available. In the Ward case (7121), the Superior Court of California,[13] affirmed by the Court of Appeals, found probable cause that the defendant had stolen, taken, or carried away an article representing a trade secret, which trade secret consisted of a computer program, the article being a copy of the program Ward caused to have printed out by his employer's computer, which he thereafter carried to his office in violation of California Penal Code 499c(b)(1). Further, the court found probable cause that having unlawfully obtained access to the program, without authority the defendant made a copy consisting of two printouts of an article representing that trade secret, and was thus in violation of 499c(b)(3).

The court, however, clearly pointed out that "article," as defined in 499c(a), must be tangible, although the trade secret it represents need not. Therefore, the mere transmission of electronic impulses over telephone lines from the trade secret owner's computer to the computer of the defendant's employer would not constitute an article. Thus, the question remains unresolved as to the liability of one who transmits impulses from one computer to another and simply uses the program in some way without causing a printout or other tangible article to be made.

Unauthorized Alteration of Software or Data.
Where data are not copied but altered within the host machine, the existing statutes prohibiting altering of records[14] appear applicable—assuming there is found no difficulty in identifying a computer record as a record within the meaning of the section.

Unauthorized Surveillance.
Unauthorized surveillance poses questions of invasion of privacy, whether accomplished by access from a terminal to the files or by interception of impulses from the computer by electronic or mechanical devices. The latter may come within the perview of federal or state wiretapping statutes, e.g., California Penal Code Section 634.

Word has come, as yet unconfirmed, of a recent Texas decision which held that installations monitoring transactions for internal security purposes must utilize the equivalent of a "beeper" on a phone line to let the user know his activity has been monitored.

CRIMES INVOLVING COMPUTER OPERATION

The second category of computer abuse incidents may be addressed from an operational viewpoint. The speed of the computer, its capability to manipulate large amounts of data, and the differences between the man-machine interface and the man-paper interface in manual systems have tended to alter both the mode of perpetration of certain business crimes and the method of their detection. Operationally, these matters can be classified as input, processing, output, and control.

Input. Incidents concerning input—data capture and entry into the system—include the instance of the keypunch operator who in the course of her duties as an employee of city government created the master file of parking meter offenses (7226); as a kindness to fellow employees, she ignored the manual record of their violations when punching the master list. This classification also includes the creation of entirely false records and the altering of amounts, names, etc., on otherwise authentic documents. A Canadian incident, for example, concerned the employee who altered the account number of deceased pensioners to his own and thereby collected their pension payments (71312).

Processing. Processing refers to the manipulation of information within the machine. Included here are transfers between accounts and masking of information. For example, one of the earliest reported cases involved a programmer who put in a patch to the system to cause it to ignore overdrafts on his account (6631). He was convicted of, and given a suspended sentence for, alteration of bank records.

Output.   Output incidents include the case of the employee who hit the repeat button on the printer and caused multiple copies of his legitimately prepared paycheck to be made (71314). A French incident involved an employee who was authorized to round salary figures to two decimal places instead of three (7133); he apparently added the remaining money to his own check.

Control.   Control is defined here as the ability to affect the total computer system. Many perpetrators have had to have that capability to carry off their schemes. Included here are the Union Dime Savings embezzlement of $1.5 million (7331) and the Equity Funding incident (7332). Where an individual has been able to accomplish his goal unaided by others, it is frequently due to his higher level of supervisory responsibility. One perpetrator became a vice president of his organization before he was caught. Other opportunities for unassisted activity come from lack of separation of functions or lack of controls over access to separated functions. Certain perpetrators have conspired with other insiders or with an outsider to carry off their plans. In New Jersey, bank employees and outsiders worked in concert (7033). The outsiders opened accounts. The insiders transferred funds from little used accounts to the accomplices' accounts. The insiders intended to alter the bank records (an additional crime) so as to conceal the transfer, but a fortuitous computer conversion by the bank occurred before this could be accomplished and the transfers were uncovered.

Large-scale activity can indicate great agility and technical expertise on the part of a single perpetrator, conspiracy among several, or reliance on a high degree of credulity and lack of imagination on the part of keypunchers, operators, and programmers who do not see or question the implications of what they are directed to do.

Control can also be defined as an affirmative activity by management, auditors and, where applicable, government officials. The computer has made the audit and reporting function both easier and more difficult. One could argue that a different standard of performance in terms of procedures employed to carry out one's responsibility has been thrust upon these groups by virtue of the computer. A computer-prepared report may be the best source of information to raise suspicions of untoward acts, yet at least in one case that record was not scrutinized by management until after the perpetrator had been exposed for other reasons (6631).

At the same time, undue reliance on a computer report and failure to look behind it to the truth or existence of the data it purports to reflect may subject the overly credulous to liabilities under federal and state securities, banking, insurance, and corporation acts. Yet, on the other hand, too close monitoring may raise privacy issues.

Possible New Legal Approaches   In summary, a host of legal issues has evolved in the recorded case histories, Many of these present unique questions of interpretation if addressed under existing law. It has been suggested by Professor Kaplan, consultant to this study, that a reasonable means of avoiding dissimilarity in approach to these issues is to draft a uniform computer abuse act that would identify in particular these special activities.

On the other hand, the current low level of agreement among computer specialists as to what constitutes ethical or legal activities in their field is a counter-indication that a modification is appropriate at this time.

It may be prudent to concentrate current efforts on extending the research which this initial study has begun into more detailed identification of problem elements, thus helping to ensure that future legislative recommendations will be relevant and practicable.

SUMMARIES OF SELECTED CASES

HANCOCK vs TEXAS, TEXAS—PROGRAM THEFT

A programmer stole $5 million worth of programs he was maintaining for his employer and attempted to sell them to a customer of his employer. He was convicted of grand theft and lost two appeals based on programs not being property as defined by theft laws. He served five years in prison.

*

MICR DEPOSIT SLIPS FRAUD, NEW YORK CITY— FRAUD

A depositor put a large sum of money in his account and asked for 1000 MICR-coded deposit slips. He placed them on counters in the bank and accumulated money in his account from other depositors.

*

WASHINGTON MICR DEPOSIT SLIPS FRAUD, WASHINGTON D.C.—FRAUD

A depositor exchanged blank deposit slips on the counter in the bank with his own MICR-coded slips. He accumulated $250,000 in four days from other people's deposits. He then withdrew $100,000, disappeared and has never been caught.

*

BENNET vs U.S.A., MINNEAPOLIS—ALTERING BANK RECORDS

A programmer altered his demand-deposit accounting program to ignore overdrafts in his checking account for about six months. He accumulated overdrafts of $1357 before he was caught by manual accounting when the computer failed. He made restitution and received a suspended sentence.

*

YOUTH CORPS PAYROLL FRAUD, NEW YORK— EMBEZZLEMENT

A data center employee printed Youth Corps payroll checks for nine months at 100 checks per month for a total loss of $2,750,000.

*

PROGRAMMED BIGOTRY, NEW YORK

A programmer was accused of bigotry because he programmed a computer to eliminate black

people in screening and selecting new employees.

*

NEW YORK UNIVERSITY VANDALISM, NEW YORK

Students held the Atomic Energy Commission computer for $100,000 ransom. Incendiary devices were defused before damage was caused. Two people were indicted on bomb conspiracy charges.

*

PHARMACEUTICAL COMPANY VANDALISM, NEW JERSEY

An employee destroyed on-line data files after being given notice of termination.

*

PUBLISHERS MAILING LIST THEFT, CHICAGO

Three million customer addresses were stolen by three night shift computer operators.

*

NEW JERSEY BANK EMBEZZLEMENT, NEW JERSEY

The computer systems vice president, senior computer operator, and three nonemployees of a bank were charged with transferring money from infrequently used savings accounts to newly opened accounts. They were detected when conversion to a new computer disrupted work.

*

LOS ANGELES WELFARE EMBEZZLEMENT THEFT, LOS ANGELES

Eleven County Department of Social Service employees used terminated state welfare numbers, changing names and addresses, to issue checks to themselves.

*

NEW YORK TWO-BANK FLOAT EMBEZZLEMENT, NEW YORK-JAMAICA, QUEENS

A bank vice president and four others deposited checks designated as cash deposits, which are recorded for immediate credit. Checks drawn on the account were good until the deposit checks were found not to be covered by another bank. The act was discovered when a bank messenger failed to deliver $440,000 worth of checks to the clearing house. The scheme worked for four years, with a total theft of $900,000.

*

IRS TAX CREDIT EMBEZZLEMENT, WASHINGTON, D.C.

An IRS adjustment clerk transferred unclaimed tax credits from one account through a chain of other accounts and finally to a relative's account. The act was discovered when auditors traced a complaint of no refund of a $1,500 tax credit.

*

MINNESOTA DATING BUREAU FRAUD, MINNEAPOLIS

A dating bureau was accused by the State Attorney General of falsely advertising that clients would be matched with compatible dates by computer.

*

COMPUTER SERVICE THEFT, DETROIT

Two engineers accidentally used a password one digit different than theirs. It belonged to the president of the time-sharing firm and allowed access to privileged customer and accounting data. Thus it allowed the engineers to use unlimited amounts of computer time and obtain customer information and proprietary program listing. Discovery was made by computer operators who noticed use of the password at unusual times. The engineers were fired, no other action was taken.

*

LIFE INSURANCE COMPANY, PAPER TAPE FAILURE VANDALISM, NEW YORK

Three on-strike computer maintenance technicians activated a field office data collection

system by prerecorded computer messages via telephone. The instructions were not to rewind paper tape, causing the next read command to read blank tape endlessly. Perpetrators were discharged and indicted under an obscene telephone call law.

*

RAILROAD THEFT, NEW YORK

A suspected organized crime attempt to manipulate input to a computerized inventory system to steal rolling stock.

*

PROGRAM EXTORTION, THEFT, LOS ANGELES

A programmer is alleged to have taken all his employer's programs to hold for extortion. The case was dropped for lack of evidence.

*

REGISTERED VOTERS LIST CIVIL SUIT, LOS ANGELES

A computer service used a registered voters address list for commercial purposes. A suit was filed by the state. It was settled out of court when the defendent paid $22,000.

*

NCIC INFORMATION THEFT, CHICAGO

A policeman is alleged to have obtained from the FBI National Crime Information Center (NCIC) the dossier of a man involved in transaction with the policeman's brother-in-law.

*

DOCTOR'S CLAIM, FRAUD, CANADA

A manager of claims of a government medical aid service introduced false doctor's claims into a computer system and directed payments to a fictitious doctor's office.

*

COLLECTION AGENCY FRAUD, TEXAS

A computerized collection agency sent new bills to people who had paid the bills the previous year. They relied on the discouragement of people fighting computerized systems.

*

TAPES AND DISKS, CALIFORNIA—VANDALISM

Employee of a Berkeley or San Francisco messenger service carrying tapes and disks between computer sites claims he used a magnet to destroy information. Presumed to be a case of malicious mischief.

*

INSURANCE COMPANY—VANDALISM

A tape librarian, disgruntled because she was fired, replaced all of the magnetic tapes in the vault with new, blank tapes during her 30-day notice period. The loss was estimated at $10 million.

*

TELEPHONE COMPANY ORDER SYSTEMS, LOS ANGELES—THEFT

The president of a telephone equipment distributor used a phone to enter orders for equipment, then picked the equipment up in a truck disguised as a telephone company truck. His company sold the equipment for several years before he was caught and convicted. He served two months in jail and now operates a computer security consulting firm.

*

DATA PREPARATION FRAUD, LANSING, MICHIGAN—UNATHORIZED ACT

According to Computerworld, five keypunch operators were discarding traffic tickets issued to their own and fellow workers' cars. A metermaid became suspicious after ticketing one car several days in a row. A three-part ticket with one copy to the supervisor as a control has been instituted.

*

MICR, RENO—COUNTERFEITING FRAUD

Phony airline payroll checks with counterfeited MICR codes passed successfully through a check reader, but were noticed in manual handling. No suspects have been identified.

*

COMPUTER SERVICE, TEXAS—THEFT

A high school student found a privileged password of the services analyst on a listing in a waste basket. He also obtained detailed specifications of the system. He used large amounts of computer time, played computer games, and obtained others customers' data. He was discovered when a computer operator noticed scratch tapes being read before being written. Restitution was made.

*

STATE OF ILLINOIS—THEFT

A computer operator was bribed for $10,000 to steal a tape reel of river registration addresses normally sold by the Driver Registration for $70,000.

*

HOMES IN CHICAGO—BURGLARY

$1 million in negotiable securities was stolen from burglarized homes. A raid on the suspects' residence produced a computer output listing of affluent supermarket owners.

*

EQUITY FUNDING LIFE INSURANCE, LOS ANGELES—ALLEGED FRAUD

Equity created 56,000 fake insurance policies and sold them to re-insurers. Insurance Commissioners in at least three states are investigating. The estimated loss is $2,000 million.

*

DIVIDEND PAYMENTS—EMBEZZLEMENT

A clerk caused the computer to issue dividend checks to former shareholders, but addressed to an accomplice, and then to erase records of the checks. The clerk was convicted for embezzling $33,000.

*

NOTES

1. D. B. Parker, Embezzlement by Computer, Proc. American Bankers Association, Operations and Automation Division. 1973.

2. D. B. Parker. Threats to Computer Systems, Final Report for U.S. Atomic Energy Commission, University of California, Lawrence Livermore Laboratory, California, March 14, 1973.

3. D. B. Parker. Testimony Before the State of California Assembly Committee on Efficiency and Cost Control. June 14, 1973.

4. D. Cressey. Other People's Money (Wadsworth, Belmont, California) 1971.

5. A. Westin, M. Baker. Databanks in a Free Society (Quadrangle Books, New York) 1972.

6. Louis J. Lefkowitz. Annual Reports, State of New York Attorney General's Bureau of Consumer Fraud and Detection, 1970, 71, 72.

7. AFIPS, Time Magazine National Survey of Public Attitudes Toward Computers. Time, Inc. 1971.

8. R. Perkins. The Criminal Law at 337 (2nd ed.). 1969.

9. See e.g., Chapter 38 Ill. Rev. Stats. Sec. 16–5.

10. See e.g., California Penal Code Section 653m (West 1969).

11. Note Theft of Trade Secrets: The Need for a Statutory Solution 120 Columbia Law Review 378. 1971.

12. J. Gambrell. Problems of Software Protection, Preceedings of the AFIPS, Stanford Law School, Joint Conference on Law, Computers, Society, June, 1973.

13. Ward. V. Superior Courts of the State of California, County of Alameda, Superior Court of the State of California. March 22, 1972. 3CLSR206. (Robert Bigelow. Computer Law Service (Chicago: Calahan Cc.) 1972.)

14. See e.g., California Penal Code Section 471.1

33

SHOPLIFTING

WILLIAM E. COBB

Shoplifting, along with employee theft, is unique among those crimes of theft which were investigated in that there is little consensus about the magnitude of the problem. The literature on these two crimes contains radically different estimates of their frequency of occurrence. The source of this estimation problem is the inability of retailers to accurately measure flows of inventory and, hence, inventory shortages.

Shortages (shrinkage in inventory not accounted for by sales records) can be segregated into two primary types. There are *apparent shortages* which are the direct result of errors (especially errors of omission) which appear on the accountant's ledger. There is no actual physical shrinkage but, on a dollar basis, the inventory will appear to have been reduced by more than total sales. The second type of shrinkage can be labeled *real shortage*. This real shortage of inventory stock is the result of losses to shoplifters and employee thieves.

APPARENT SHORTAGES: BOOKKEEPING ERROR

There are two basic methods of retail inventory measurement: cost accounting and retail accounting. Under the *cost method*, the book inventory control is used to accumulate cost figures, adding such information as purchases and transportation costs to the initial inventory amounts. At each physical inventory date, each inventory item is referenced to vendor's invoices in order to obtain cost information. Since this is both expensive and time consuming, the cost method is used frequently. Most stores have adopted the *retail inventory method*. Physical inventory values are compiled at marked retail prices. That is, inventory stock is recorded according to selling price, not cost.[1]

The major source of bookkeeping error in both methods of inventory accounting would seem to be the up and down gyration of prices in a store. If the price of an item is raised (marked up) and the accountant fails to record the increase, an apparent surplus will exist at the time that the physical inventory is taken. Conversely, if the price of an item is lowered (marked down), failure to record the markdown will result in an apparent shortage.

The general trend in retail stores is to "overprice" a product when it is initially placed in stock. The price is then reduced and the retailer advertises a "sale" in honor of some birthday, holiday, anniversary, or other "special" occasion. Since price changes of this nature far outnumber price increases, the random occur-

Source: The Economics of Shoplifting. Ph.D. Dissertation, Virginia Polytechnic Institute and State University, 1973. Pp. 2–6, 36–51 (Editorial adaptations.) Reprinted by permission of William E. Cobb, West Virginia of Graduate Studies.

[1] For a good description of the retail method, see *Retail Inventory Made Practical* (New York: National Retail Merchants Association, 1971).

rence of a failure to record will probably be a failure to record a price reduction. Hence, normal store policy accompanied by less than perfect bookkeeping should lead to apparent shortages.

In addition to the pseudo-sales which merchants often advertise, there are often legitimate temporary reduction in the prices of certain items in order to attract customers. If the number of items purchased at the "sale" price is not accurately kept, apparent shortages will once again appear on the accountant's ledger. According to one retailer, Walter E. Reitz of the Hecht Company in Washington, D.C., "In these domestic departments where they mark the whole stock down for a sale, purchase at the new price, and mark so much of it back after the sale, we have found some departments making gross errors—$15,000 or $18,-000, in some cases."[2]

Apparent shortages, in and of themselves, are of little concern to the retailer. His major interest is minimizing real shrinkage (theft). It is difficult to separate the shortage, which his books reveal, into apparent and real shortages. As Reitz has said:

> The whole shortage situation resolves itself around the fact that there is a difference between a physical and a book inventory. Part of these errors are, of course, in the control division, in the accounting. Some of them are made by the people that initiate paper, in the receiving and marking and so forth. The difficulty is, we have never been able, I guess—any of us—to know to what degree we have errors.
>
> The most important thing you can do is try to keep the errors at a minimum. We make a lot of errors because [sic] although the percentage is small, the numbers are so high.[3]

A great number of security experts argue that bookkeeping error accounts for only 5 percent of the total reported shrinkage. On the other hand, the following passage points up the difference of opinion which exists on this subject.

> Some of the panel members agreed, however, that in general at least half and probably a much greater proportion, of all shortages can be rightfully attributed to errors in record-keeping and to system breakdowns, aside from any question of theft, either internal or external. Those who would attribute as much as 75% of total shortages to record keeping, etc., pointed out the tremendous number of instances occurring daily where opportunities exist for errors and omissions which contribute to the shortage picture. They felt that the cumulative total of such daily incidents greatly outweighed occasions of theft by either employees or the general public and that this fact must be taken into consideration in any attempt to allocate responsibility.[4]

REAL SHORTAGES: SHOPLIFTING AND EMPLOYEE THEFT

If, in fact, bookkeeping error accounts for over 50 percent of reported shortages, quite obviously shoplifting and employee theft account for less than 50 percent. Many security experts vehemently disagree with this. They argue that 25 to 40 percent of shrinkage is the result of shoplifting, 60 to 75 percent is the result of employee theft, and the residual is relegated to bookkeeping error.[5]

One author, Joseph G. Metz, a former member of the National Commission on the Causes and Prevention of Violence, argues that, ". . . all businesses lose five times as much money to their own employees as they do to the outside shoplifter."[6] On the other hand, a study reported by the Virginia Retail Merchants Association indicated that, of the amount lost through theft, both shoplifting and inter-

---

[2] This statement was made at a panel discussion of retailers and then published as, *Stock Shortages: Their Causes and Prevention* (New York: National Retail Merchants Association, 1959), p. 37.

[3] *Ibid.*, p. 34.

[4] *Ibid.*, p. 62.

[5] C. H. Almer, *The Fight Against Shoplifting in Sweden and West Germany: A Comparative Study* (Boras, Sweden: AB Boras Tryckservice, 1971).

[6] Joseph G. Metz, *The Economics of Crime*, Economic Topic Series (New York: Joint Council on Economic Education, 1971), p. 4.

nal pilferage, 78 percent was stolen by shop-lifters and 22 percent by pilfering employees.[7] One of the problems to be dealt with in the text is the estimation of the relative weights of shortages as between shoplifting and employee theft.

*

APPREHENSION OF SHOPLIFTERS: TECHNOLOGICAL CONSTRAINTS

To summarize, merchandise in retail stores is positioned so that customers—and thieves—can handle it. Merchants wish neither to offend shoppers with store policy nor to arrest them falsely. In this section, the effect of these two factors on shoplifting techniques is discussed. Emphasis is placed on the physical impossibility of apprehending most shoplifters.

As with the previous two costs, both the cost (loss) of stolen merchandise and the cost of detecting shoplifters are related to apprehension effort. The four costs are summed to provide a relationship between apprehension effort and the total loss of dollars which results from shoplifting.

*

SUCCESSFUL SHOPLIFTING: AN OVERVIEW

Successful shoplifting requires only that the thief be briefly shielded from the view of the clerk or store detectives; this can be accomplished by the use of display racks or counters, the position of the body or clothing of the thief, or the position of the body of a confederate or innocent shopper. No action will be taken against the thief unless store personnel *observe the concealment* or theft and *observe all activity of the thief from that moment until apprehension.* Exceptions to this rule occur only when electronic detection apparatus is in use.[8]

[7] Virginia Retail Merchants Association, *The Retail Review*, September, 1970.

[8] The professional thief who suspects possible television surveillance will conceal an item in an obvious manner, discreetly replace it on the counter or rack, the move to a quiet corner of the floor to observe any on-rushing detec-

A theft is either successful or unsuccessful in the split second required to conceal the merchandise. *The place and method of concealment are important only because of the time constraint involved.* Since the crucial factor is insurance that no one witnesses the theft, concealment must be a quick maneuver.

Once certain of freedom from electronic surveillance, the thief must also insure that no clerk or detective witnesses the theft. The method used is a function of the ingenuity of the shoplifter. Any action which distracts from the movement of the hands contributes to the success of the theft. It is difficult to steal any item without the use of the hands. Since both clerks and detectives are aware of this fact, they watch the hands of shoppers relatively carefully.

Clerks are generally unconcerned about theft and seldom watch shoppers at all. It is easy to neutralize clerks either by sending them away for some type of merchandise or by spending enough time in their area so that they lose interest in making a sale. Disposing of the store detective is only slightly more difficult.

IDENTIFYING THE STORE DETECTIVE

If the thief is able to identify the store detective, shoplifting is made more simple.[9] In order to show that such identification requires only a minimum of effort, it is necessary to examine the magnitude of the job facing the store detective. Because of the proof-positive doctrine, the store detective must observe any theft for which he makes an arrest. Clearly the large number of shoppers which enter a store precludes observation of each one of them. The detective must make some conscious selection of whom he ought to keep under surveillance.

tives. If there is a closed circuit television hook-up in use, detectives will come running to the "scene of the crime." Since customers seldom run through a store, the thief can presume that the area is being scanned by cameras. This is a proven method for discovering "dummy" television cameras.

[9] Store detectives are normally incognito so that the potential shoplifter must consider all shoppers as potential detectives.

TABLE I. Male/Female Shoplifting Frequency Comparison

City	Males Followed	Male Shoplifters	%	Females followed	Female shoplifters	%
New York store #1	156	10	6.5	344	32	9.2
New York store #2	135	7	5.7	226	12	5.3
Boston	149	4	2.6	255	14	5.4
Philadelphia	132	8	6.0	250	22	8.8
Totals	572	29	5.0	1,075	80	7.4

Source: Saul D. Astor, "Shoplifting Survey," *Security World*, VIII (March, 1971), 34.

How can the detective choose when to follow whom? General consensus among security experts is that there is little, if any, correlation between an individual's physical characteristics (sex, age, race, or general appearance) and his proclivity to shoplift. These same experts give only general impressions about the hours, days, and months in which shoplifting is greatest.

The small amount of data which is available can be misleading. For instance, it is generally true that more females than males are arrested for shoplifting. A report published by Management Safeguards, Inc., of New York revealed that from a random sample of 1,647 shoppers followed in four general merchandise stores, 80 females shoplifted while only 29 males stole.[10] These two facts seem to indicate that females are more likely than males to shoplift. Security personnel, confronted with these statistics are quick to argue that more shoplifters are female simply because more shoppers are female. When the Management Safeguard statistics were adjusted to account for the fact that only 34.7 percent of their sample was male, the resultant data still showed that 5 percent of male shoppers stole while 7.4 percent of female shoppers were shoplifters (see Table I). The test for the significance of the difference between two proportions reveals that this difference is significant—once more indicating that women, in fact, are more likely than men to shoplift.

Security experts counter this statistic with the argument that women steal "more" because women spend more time in the store per shopping trip than do men. A study . . . indicated that males do spend less time than females per shopping trip to a store—16 percent of the average. Using this figure, the Management Safeguard results can be adjusted, showing that the number of female shoplifters per female customer-minute spent in the store is 1.23 times the number of male shoplifters per male customer-minute. Once more the different is significant.

The data do seem to indicate that the detective should spend relatively more time watching females.[11] However, I have found no security expert who agrees with this policy. Detectives are explicitly trained to make no selection on the basis of physical characteristics.

The detective is not left without a method of selecting suspects, however. The detective realizes that the thief will wish to be aware of any potential witnesses to the crime. He knows that the thief will be watching clerks and customers, alertly awaiting the opportunity to steal. Experience proves that the honest customer seldom takes his eyes off the merchandise. In fact, it is the objective of the store manager to set up his displays to encourage this behavior. He wants the customer to look at his merchandise, to handle it, and to buy it.

[10] Saul D. Astor, "Shoplifting Survey," *Security World*, VIII (March, 1971), pp. 34–5. As will be discussed in Chapter VI, there were some apparent weaknesses in Astor's study.

[11] It is worth noting that every male arrested while I was doing "field work" for this study wore a hat of some kind. This should pose an interesting research project for psychologists which could aid the store detective in creation of a "profile" for the average shoplifter.

Thus, while the honest customer looks at *merchandise*, the shoplifter looks at *people* around him. The detective is aware of this difference and watches the eyes of shoppers for a clue as to their intentions. Quick eye movements reveal many, if not most, potential shoplifters.

The detective, then, *is* able to narrow the number of suspects. But the system he uses can also be used by the potential shoplifter to identify the detective. Just as the eye movements of the thief reveal him to the detective, the eye movements of the detective reveal him to the thief. The detective who pretends to be a shopper spends more time watching people around him—in order to watch eye movements and catch thieves—than he spends looking at merchandise. To a third party, the detective and the shoplifter behave in an almost identical manner.[12]

COMMON TECHNIQUES OF SHOPLIFTING (WITHOUT BOOSTER DEVICES)

The *large shopping bag* is a most effective tool of the shoplifter. It is not uncommon for a legitimate shopper to place a shopping bag at his feet while he examines merchandise on a display counter or rack. These shopping bags normally gape open at top unless secured in some manner. The careful shopper, fearful of the pickpocket and sneak thief, will often place the bag on the floor between his legs in order to protect merchandise already purchased. This habit is a boon to the shoplifter who mimics this behavior. The shoplifter will stand very close to the display containing the desired merchandise, placing a large shopping bag on the floor between his legs. He will "handle" the merchandise until certain that he is unobserved and, at that moment, quickly drop the object into the open bag. Unless store personnel are alert during the split second the merchandise is dropped, the theft has been successfully accomplished as soon as the thief

picks up the bag. No one can demand to look into the bag unless the customer-thief is first arrested; and, because of the danger of a false arrest suit, arrest is unlikely unless the thief carelessly lets someone see him drop the item into his bag.

Larger purses are also effective places of concealment for stolen items. Once restricted to use by women, the introduction of male purses has generalized the technique somewhat. There is a myriad of legitimate reasons for a purse to be opened in a retail establishment so that an open purse attracts no undue attention. The thief simply waits until he is free from observation and quickly inserts the merchandise into the purse.

All manner of clothing can be used for *concealment* or *psuedo-concealment* of stolen merchandise. A sweater or coat carried over the arm provides adequate concealment for items hastily placed under it. Loose or bulky clothing, especially an overcoat, conceals merchandise worn or quickly inserted under it.

"Pseudo-concealment" is a rather audacious and clever method of shoplifting. The price tags are removed from clothing, jewelry, gloves, scarves, billfolds, pocketbooks, or other items which are normally worn or carried by shoppers. The thief then wears or carries the merchandise as if it were his own. Under many shoplifting laws, even if the thief is seen removing the tags, he breaks no law until he attempts to leave the store with the unpurchased items. If the thief suspects that he was seen removing tags, he simply walks around the store, determining if he is being followed. If not followed, the thief quickly exits with the merchandise. If he is being followed, he returns the items and can move on to a new department or store.

In one retail establishment a young lady was seen entering a fitting room with four pairs of stockings. An alert employee saw her exit the fitting room carrying no stockings. The store manager detained the female and called the police. Upon their arrival, officers observed that the suspect was wearing *all four* pairs of

---

[12] I personally tested this method of pinpointing undercover store detectives. Unannounced, I visited a large department store and, within ten minutes, had identified all security personnel with 100 percent accuracy.

the stockings—one over the other. The suspect, however, had violated no law. She had not left the store with unpurchased items. Neither had she concealed any items—the stocking were clearly visible even though she was wearing them. The suspect returned the merchandise and was allowed to leave the store.

Ticket and cap switching is another relatively safe method of shoplifting. Cap switching is made feasible because of the desire of manufacturers to make one size cap or lid for varying sizes of a product. Alert sales clerks may sometimes notice that an item has the wrong price on it. Incorrect prices on merchandise are often the fault of stock personnel. For this reason, if a clerk does notice a mistake, he normally apologizes to the customer and reveals the true price. The shoplifter can pretend to be irritated and return the item to its shelf or rack. Ticket and cap switching is most effective in a discount or grocery store where all items are purchased at the exits. Cashiers in these stores seldom pay attention to the prices of most items.

Two methods of shoplifting involve *the use of sales receipts*. In one instance, the thief either saves a receipt from a previous purchase at the store, or picks up a loose one from the floor or a trash bin of the store. This procedure allows the thief to steal an item priced the same as that on the receipt. However, most receipts are numbered so that an alert employee or detective can determine on which day the receipt was issued.

The experienced thief can avoid the embarrassment of this discovery, if he uses a confederate. The confederate buys an item, gets a legitimate receipt, leaves the stores, and gives the receipt to the actual shoplifter. The shoplifter will then enter the store to steal an item identical to the one purchased. Even if apprehended, he will possess a correct receipt. Store personnel might suspect something "shady," but they will be forced to apologize for the inconvenience of detaining the thief. Not only

has a successful theft been carried out, but also a false-arrest suit may be possible.[13]

Team stealing of any type is, by far, the most difficult to detect. Some members of the team can draw attention to themselves while others rob the store. Phony arguments, fights, or fainting spells are a few methods of distraction. With a large team, no distraction is necessary. Since only a few seconds are required for successful concealment, store personnel cannot adequately observe several potential thieves at once. During research which was undertaken for this dissertation, a team theft was observed. Nine male juveniles entered the clothing department of a store. Several were identified by store personnel as previous shoplifters. Additional detectives were called and eventually seven members of the security force were watching the youths. Even with an almost one-to-one ratio of detectives to the potential thieves, the boys were able to cluster around a display counter in such a way as to make accurate observation impossible. The detectives could only make their presence known in the hope of scaring off the boys. This failed and the detectives became suspicious, and rightly so. On another floor another group of youths were apparently helping themselves to merchandise secure in their belief that their nine confederates were keeping the store detectives busy. Not one of the fifteen youths involved was apprehended.

One unsophisticated, but effective, method of shoplifting is *to grab merchandise and run* from the store with it. If no store detective is nearby, this is a safe technique. Few sales personnel

---

[13] When an arrest is made, detectives immediately go to the department from which the stolen merchandise was taken and note the number on the store receipt register. (These numbers, ordered consecutively, coincide with the customers' receipt numbers.) If the detective did not follow this procedure, it would be possible for the arrested thief, out on bond, to purchase an item identical to the one which he was arrested for stealing. When he comes to trial, he could present a legitimate sales receipt as proof that he purchased the item.

are willing or able to give chase. Most detectives are willing, but few are able to catch a fast running shoplifter. If the sneak thief is pursued, he need only "ditch" the merchandise in some obscure place. No crime can be proven if the merchandise is not recovered.

A risky, but often used, technique is the *hiding of an item* or items inside large merchandise to be purchased. This is an unsafe method since, if the clerk decides to inspect the larger item, it is difficult for the thief to deny intent to steal.

There is one situation in which this procedure is relatively safe. In most grocery stores the customer is provided with large brown bags which may be used in the produce department. It is easy to place expensive steaks in the bottom of these bags and cover them with potatoes. Few grocery store cashiers are going to inspect a bag of potatoes. The thief gets steak for about 30 per pound.

A most amazing technique of shoplifting is commonly referred to as *"crotch-walking."* An item is placed between the legs of the thief and gripped with the upper thighs. A long dress or coat conceals the merchandise. With a little practice, the shoplifter is able to appear to be walking normally while moving only the legs from the knee down. Large females have been known to walk out of a store carrying large watermelons or portable television sets in this manner. There is one report of a "female professional who escaped with a fifteen pound ham between her thighs by climbing an eight foot fence and outrunning two male detectives, all without dropping the booty."[14]

The final category of shoplifting techniques to be discussed in this section is perhaps the most widespread of the methods employed. A general name for this classification is "the fitting room theft." For many years customers were permitted to carry bundles of clothing

into fitting rooms with no questions asked. If a large number of items were taken into the fitting room, even an alert clerk found it difficult to ascertain that all were returned to the display racks. Store personnel are more careful today. They do not allow many items to be taken into a fitting room at one time. This is not an effective measure, though, since it is difficult for a clerk to keep track of even a few items, especially when his department is busy.

One unique fitting room theft involves men's pants or jeans. The thief examines several pairs of pants. After examining one pair, he holds it into a very small bundle and lays this bundle on the display counter beside other pants which he is "looking over." When he feels that no one is alert, he slides the folded pair of pants into the waistband of another pair. He then carefully picks up several pairs of pants—including the pair which now conceals the folded pants—and requests a fitting room. Even if the clerk keeps track of the number of pairs of pants carried into the fitting room, he will not be aware of the hidden pair. Once in the fitting room, the thief can loosen his belt and place the folden pants in the back of his own pants. An overcoat completely conceals the stolen item.

If the shoplifter wishes to get a sports coat to go with the pants, he may wear a topcoat with a zip-out lining. He will unzip the lining and removes his topcoat, leaving the lining on as a vest-sweater. He then will "try on" the sports coat which he desires. If unobserved, he will quickly put on his topcoat over the sports coat, which now is worn *between* the lining and his overcoat. Once he zips up the lining, the sports coat is concealed even if he opens the overcoat.

Another fitting room theft is called the "packaging technique." An item is carried into a fitting room. Hidden wrapping paper and ribbons are then used to gift wrap the merchandise. Nothing is less suspicious to store personnel than a wrapped package.

[14] McCabe, "Shoplifting in Iowa," p. 12.

COMMON TECHNIQUES OF SHOPLIFTING (WITH BOOSTER DEVICES)

Some shoplifters plan the crime far enough in advance so that they are able to prepare special clothing and containers to be used in commission of the theft. Such devices are called "boosters." Although the theft may prove to be easier with such paraphernalia, the shoplifter must balance this benefit against the stiffer penalty that can be expected if he is apprehended while using these aids. Judges tend to be less lenient when there is evidence of premeditation. For this reason, the use of boosters appears to be the exception rather than the rule.[15]

One aid in shoplifting is known as a *"booster box."* A large box is wrapped and actually tied with string. This usually puts the sales clerk at ease since a thief cannot discreetly untie a box and place merchandise inside. However, the string is a ruse. One end of the box is constructed so that merchandise can be inserted. This is normally accomplished with a hinged end which flips open inwardly.

A purse can be an effective booster box. A false bottom will allow merchandise to be placed in the purse without the obvious action of opening it.

Another common device is *the "drop bag."* Cloth bags—pillow cases, or their equivalent— are pinned or sewn into coat linings. Merchandise can easily be slipped inside the coat and into the bag.

For the shoplifter who does not like the drop bag, a variety of hooks and fasteners can be designed which may be placed inside a garment or on a belt. Heavy items are more cumbersome with these aids than with the drop bag.

Coats with "slashed pockets" are appropriate with drop bags or hooks and fasteners. The pockets of the coat are removed so that the hands are loose under the coat, while appearing to be resting in the pockets. The sales clerk can be distracted by one hand while the "pocketed" hand reaches out of the coat, seizes the desired merchandise, and inserts it into the drop bag or places it on the fasteners.

Double elastic waist bands which form hidden pockets inside skirts and trousers can be substituted for the drop bag or the hooks and fasteners. All of these boosters require that some type of coat be worn to conceal the merchandise. They are appropriate only in cool or damp weather.

The simple *umbrella* is a very effective booster device, although, again, the thief must be certain that the weather is appropriate for carrying one. Fasteners are placed inside the umbrella to hold the ribs open. The umbrella is then carried over the arm so that it hangs below the counter level. It is then an easy task to discreetly remove an object from the counter and drop it into the umbrella.

Before leaving the discussion of who shoplifts and how they do it, one interesting point comes to mind. Two categories of shoppers are provided unlimited license to steal—using whatever techniques they choose. Security personnel have an unwritten policy of releasing all elderly or pregnant persons who are caught shoplifting. (At least one large chain department store has put this policy in writing. "It is the general policy of ——— to prosecute shoplifters and pilferers, except when obvious (a) mental cases, (b) seniles, or (c) pregnant women are involved.") It has been learned through bitter experience that courts seldom convict these persons. The courts sympathize with the condition, age or pregnancy, of the accused. If one considers the "five-finger discount" awarded to the elderly—all ethical considerations set aside—their potential level of income rises dramatically. The policy of releasing these individuals is a type of income redistribution to them.

The methods which were described above are not the only ones used by shoplifters, but do represent a large percentage of thefts which occur.

---

[15] To some extent, this fact seems to offer credence to the view that severity of punishment *is* taken into account by shoplifters.

34

FUN AND GAMES WITH CREDIT CARDS

PETER S. GREENBERG

The story you're about to read is true. Only the names have been changed—36 times to be exact. It all began in San Diego in December 1972. John Weimar, 27-year-old door-to-door encyclopedia salesman, was making the rounds when he saw a credit card lying face up on the sidewalk. He checked the expiration date and pocketed the card. After all, Christmas was coming.

When Weimar returned home that evening, he surprised his wife with several hundred dollars worth of gifts. Was Natalie Weimar shocked or outraged when she learned where they'd come from? Not exactly. John earned barely $10,000 a year and, as she later told authorities, she "felt so good having things."

Within a few days, John was again going door to door, only this time he went to every conceivable San Diego retail outlet and applied for credit cards in the fictitious name "James F. Grynde." When he started using this name, Weimar had no birth certificate, no back-up credit and no reliable references. He resorted to outright lying. On the applications, Grynde made himself a captain in the Marine Corps; his wife became an Avon lady. He also awarded himself a B.A. in political science from Colum-

Source: Peter S. Greenberg, "Fun With John and Natalie," *New Times* (August 7, 1978), **11**(3): 12–13. Reprinted by permission.

bia University. For references, he listed his parents, who supposedly resided in Philadelphia.

An avalanche of plastic soon arrived at the Gryndes' post office box: Bank-Americard, Master Charge, American Airlines, Pan Am, TWA, National, Hertz, Avis, Saks Fifth Avenue, J.C. Penney and seven oil company credit cards. Within three short months, at least 56 cards were sent to the couple. As each new one arrived, the account number was used as a credit reference to apply for yet another card.

The scam was nearly infallible. The couple ate free, drove free and dressed free. When they needed to generate capital, they would charge merchandise at a local department store and then drive across town and sell it for cash.

By mid-1973, they had changed their names again. Grynde became Vernon Becker, then a series of Johns: Wilson, Warner, Davis, Taner. For a brief time, he became Edward Squirrel, then eight more Johns: Wiener, Winer, Winar, Wener, Weiner, Browning, D'Azur, Taner-West. And Natalie herself tried ten name variations.

Each time, they received more credit cards, and each card was issued on the basis of totally bogus information. (Weimar had never been in the Marine Corps, nor had he ever attended Columbia. The parents' Philadelphia "address" was a vacant lot.) Although their daily take from the credit cards was often in the hundreds, none of the companies seemed able—or willing—to stop them.

Then, after two years of scamming with dozens of low-limit "revolving credit" cards, the couple hit the jackpot: Not one, but two American Express cards arrived. Weimar took their advertising to heart—he never left home without them. He packed up his wife and off they flew for a whirlwind European spending spree.

Once there, Weimar used his TWA "Getaway" card to fly his mother-in-law over to join them. For the next five months, it was Europe on no dollars a day, renting the best cars, staying at $100-a-night hotels, and eating at the most expensive restaurants. They racked up more than $81,000 in European purchases.

Before their return to San Diego in 1976, the Weimars had changed their names again—to William and Doreen Bennett. This time John promoted himself to a major in the Marine Corps. Natalie (Doreen) claimed a degree from Fordham University in Queens, New York. (Fordham is in the Bronx.) And once again, the cards kept coming in.

Then, surprise of surprises—Grynde/Bennett received his first turn-down. After a three-and-a-half-year perfect record, Diners Club said no. Their refusal was based not on bad credit but rather on the number of inquiries on Grynde/Bennett's quickly expanding credit file.

Weimar was insulted. His pride was hurt. Two weeks later, he reapplied. On the second attempt, his income had miraculously increased from $12,000 to $18,000. He was rejected again. And again. The company began to get curious *only* after the seventh application and routinely turned the case over to the post office.

San Diego postal inspector Bill Burgess first saw the Diners Club report in the summer of 1976. He checked with a dozen major credit card companies, and although none of them had previously contacted authorities, they all claimed to be looking for the mysterious Grynde/Bennett.

"We tried to follow them through their credit card purchases," Burgess reported, "but we were always three weeks behind."

Not surprisingly, no one knew where the couple was. On a hunch Burgess ran a motor vehicle check and came up with drivers' licenses for the couple. He took his case to Assistant U.S. Attorney Michael Lipman.

"You'll never find them," Lipman argued. "By the time we get our information, these jokers are always eight months ahead of us."

Six months later, during a slight drop in his work load, Lipman was able to take the case to a grand jury. They returned an 11-count indictment *in absentia*. The *San Diego Union* printed the story, along with the license photos.

At this point the Weimars were still in San Diego, but they had changed their names again—this time to D'Azur. And, since their return from Europe, Natalie had given birth to a baby girl. (Needless to say, the hospital delivery costs were charged—and the child's name had already been changed.)

The D'Azur's landlord recognized them from the story in the *Union* and called the San Diego police. When the officers arrived at the residence, neighbors told them that the couple had hurriedly packed their 14-month-old baby into their 1964 tan Chrysler.

The Weimars were headed south down State Highway 163, and they were apprehended a few miles north of the Mexican border. A preliminary search revealed a stack of blank credit card applications and a blue plastic folder containing false identification papers for yet another alias—Michael Phillips. In another folder, incredibly enough, were pages of detailed listings of all their credit card purchases, ripoffs and cash profits.

The lists, written by John Weimar, seemed to include every phony credit charge over a five-year period, ranging from a $6 camera lens hood bought in Berlin to a $36 owl key ring purchased in Innsbruck to $3,500 worth of furniture charged at the Broadway department store in San Diego.

Weimar couldn't resist making some additional margin notes. On his hotel entries (30 in Europe alone) Weimar recorded that the Bristol Hotel in Naples was not a favorite ("in and out in an hour"), and he labeled the Penta Airport Motel in London "small" and "dirty."

"So far," said Lipman, "we can document better than $100,000 in fake charges." (Investigators at the Weimar house later found and seized 10 diamond rings, dozens of watches, more than 60 camera lenses, 25 leather coats, boxed suits, gold coins, rings, pendants and pearls.) Using Weimar's own calculations, the total is well above $200,000. Yet, none of the credit card companies has applied for restitution.

"This was one of the most outrageous frauds in San Diego history," Lipman claims. "But the significance of the case lies not in the fraud but in the attitude of the credit card companies. One would have to logically conclude that they have decided they're better off taking the losses than checking out the applications. Clearly in this case, no one did their homework."

At his sentencing hearing John Weimar seemed to agree. "It all started out as a joke." Weimar pleaded before U.S. District Court Judge Gordon Thompson, Jr. "Identities were fabricated and credit applications were sent to various companies to see if they would send credit cards.

"When the first companies sent credit cards, we thought of ending the joke right then and paying for the charges we'd made, but it seemed so easy. We continued because nobody ever said 'Stop.' "

Judge Thompson wasn't laughing. Both Weimars were sentenced to five-year prison terms. For her role in the crime, the mother-in-law, who was not indicted, was given the chore of babysitting for the child. But the beauty of the crime, if indeed there is one, is that the Weimars may not be forced to repay any of the companies. And, under current statutes, in 20 months the couple will be eligible to apply for parole—and, conceivably, some new credit cards.